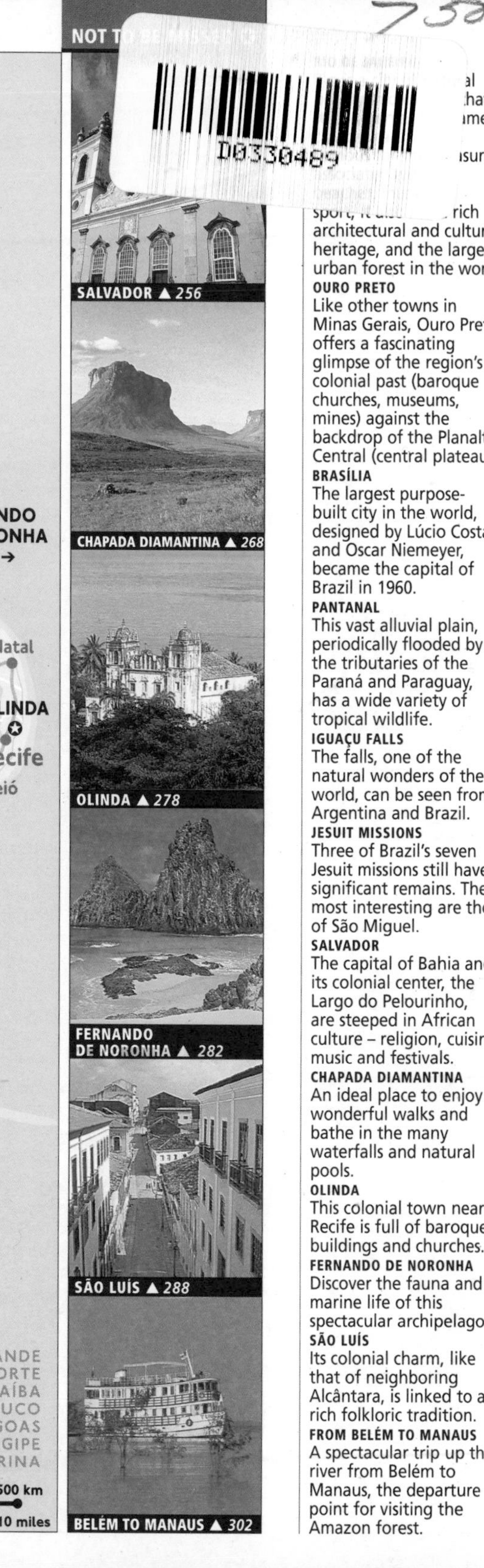

SALVADOR ▲ 256

CHAPADA DIAMANTINA ▲ 268

OLINDA ▲ 278

FERNANDO DE NORONHA ▲ 282

SÃO LUÍS ▲ 288

BELÉM TO MANAUS ▲ 302

...al ...that ...ame ...isures ... sport, it also ... rich architectural and cultural heritage, and the largest urban forest in the world.

OURO PRETO
Like other towns in Minas Gerais, Ouro Preto offers a fascinating glimpse of the region's colonial past (baroque churches, museums, mines) against the backdrop of the Planalto Central (central plateau).

BRASÍLIA
The largest purpose-built city in the world, designed by Lúcio Costa and Oscar Niemeyer, became the capital of Brazil in 1960.

PANTANAL
This vast alluvial plain, periodically flooded by the tributaries of the Paraná and Paraguay, has a wide variety of tropical wildlife.

IGUAÇU FALLS
The falls, one of the natural wonders of the world, can be seen from Argentina and Brazil.

JESUIT MISSIONS
Three of Brazil's seven Jesuit missions still have significant remains. The most interesting are those of São Miguel.

SALVADOR
The capital of Bahia and its colonial center, the Largo do Pelourinho, are steeped in African culture – religion, cuisine, music and festivals.

CHAPADA DIAMANTINA
An ideal place to enjoy wonderful walks and bathe in the many waterfalls and natural pools.

OLINDA
This colonial town near Recife is full of baroque buildings and churches.

FERNANDO DE NORONHA
Discover the fauna and marine life of this spectacular archipelago.

SÃO LUÍS
Its colonial charm, like that of neighboring Alcântara, is linked to a rich folkloric tradition.

FROM BELÉM TO MANAUS
A spectacular trip up the river from Belém to Manaus, the departure point for visiting the Amazon forest.

RIO DE JANEIRO
BRAZIL

KNOPF GUIDES

● Encyclopedia section

NATURE The geomorphology, biogeography and climate of Brazil (the flora and fauna of the region's habitats are covered in insets within the itineraries).
HISTORY The history of Brazil from 1500 to modern times, with more in-depth treatment of the major events that have marked the country's history. Key dates appear in a timeline alongside the text.
ARTS AND TRADITIONS The traditions and customs of Brazil and their expression within a modern context.
ARCHITECTURE The country's architectural heritage: a look at rural and urban buildings as well as major civil, religious and military monuments, with the focus on style and typology.
AS SEEN BY PAINTERS These pages present a chronological or thematic selection of paintings from all periods of Brazilian history.
AS SEEN BY WRITERS An anthology of texts, taken from works of writers past and present, from Brazil and around the world, arranged thematically.

▲ Itineraries

Each itinerary begins with a map of the area to be explored.
✪ **NOT TO BE MISSED** These sites should be seen at all costs. They are highlighted in gray boxes in the margins. The focus is on the practical aspects of visiting these sites.
★ **EDITOR'S CHOICE** Sites singled out by the editor for special attention.
INSETS On richly illustrated double pages, these insets turn the spotlight on subjects deserving more in-depth treatment.

◆ Practical information

All the travel information you will need before you go and when you get there.
HOTELS AND RESTAURANTS A selection of useful addresses.
PLACES TO VISIT A handy table of addresses and opening times.
APPENDICES Bibliography, list of illustrations and index.
MAP SECTION Maps of Rio de Janeiro City, preceded by a street index; grid references allow the reader to pinpoint a site.

Each map in the map section is designated by a letter. In the Itineraries, all the sites of interest are given a grid reference (for example: ◆ **A** B2).

The mini-map pinpoints the itinerary within the wider area covered by the guide.

The itinerary map shows the main sites.

● ▲ ◆ The above symbols within the text provide cross-references to a place or theme discussed elsewhere in the guide.

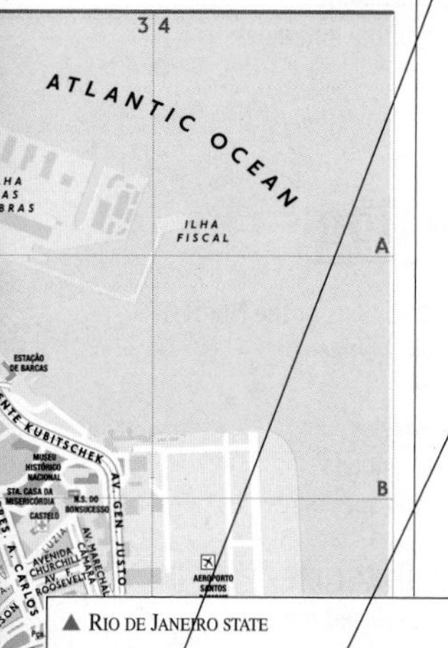

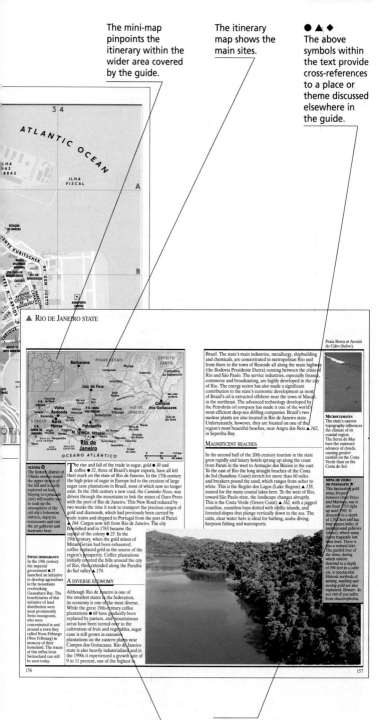

▲ RIO DE JANEIRO STATE

Praia Brava at Arraial do Cabo (*below*).

OLINDA ✪
The historic district of Olinda centers round the upper streets of the hill and is easily explored on foot. Staying in a *pousada* (inn) will enable you to soak up the atmosphere of the old city's bohemian districts, enjoy its restaurants and visit the art galleries and museums here.

The rise and fall of the trade in sugar, gold ● *30* and coffee ● *32*, three of Brazil's major exports, have all left their mark on the state of Rio de Janeiro. In the 17th century the high price of sugar in Europe led to the creation of large sugar cane plantations in Brazil, most of which now no longer exist. In the 18th century a new road, the *Caminho Novo*, was driven through the mountains to link the mines of Ouro Preto with the port of Rio de Janeiro. This New Road reduced by two weeks the time it took to transport the precious cargos of gold and diamonds, which had previously been carried by mule trains and shipped to Portugal from the port of Parati ▲ *164*. Cargos now left from Rio de Janeiro. The city flourished and in 1763 became the capital of the colony ● *23*. In the 19th century, when the gold mines of Minas Gerais had been exhausted, coffee replaced gold as the source of the region's prosperity. Coffee plantations initially covered the hills around the city of Rio, then extended along the Paraíba do Sul valley ▲ *174*.

SWISS IMMIGRANTS
In the 19th century the imperial government ● *25* launched an initiative to develop agriculture in the mountains overlooking Guanabara Bay. The beneficiaries of this initiative of land distribution were most prominently Swiss immigrants, who were concentrated in and around a town they called Nova Friburgo (New Fribourg) in memory of their homeland. The traces of this influx from Switzerland can still be seen today.

A DIVERSE ECONOMY

Although Rio de Janeiro is one of the smallest states in the federation, its economy is one of the most diverse. While the great 19th-century coffee plantations ● *68* have gradually been replaced by pasture, and mountainous areas have been turned over to the cultivation of fruit and vegetables, sugar cane is still grown in extensive plantations on the eastern plains near Campos dos Goitacazes. Rio de Janeiro state is also heavily industrialized and in the 1990s it experienced a growth rate of 9 to 11 percent, one of the highest in Brazil. The state's main industries, metallurgy, shipbuilding and chemicals, are concentrated in metropolitan Rio and from there to the town of Resende all along the main highway (the Rodovia Presidente Dutra) running between the cities of Rio and São Paulo. The service industries, especially finance, commerce and broadcasting, are highly developed in the city of Rio. The energy sector has also made a significant contribution to the state's economic development as most of Brazil's oil is extracted offshore near the town of Macaé, in the northeast. The advanced technology developed by the Petrobrás oil company has made it one of the world's most efficient deep-sea drilling companies. Brazil's two nuclear plants are also located in Rio de Janeiro state. Unfortunately, however, they are located on one of the region's most beautiful beaches, near Angra dos Reis ▲ *162*, in Sepetiba Bay.

MAGNIFICENT BEACHES

In the second half of the 20th century tourism in the state grew rapidly and luxury hotels sprang up along the coast from Parati in the west to Armação dos Búzios in the east. To the east of Rio the long straight beaches of the Costa do Sol (Sunshine Coast) stretch for more than 60 miles and breakers pound the sand, which ranges from ocher to white. This is the Região dos Lagos (Lake Region) ▲ *158*, named for the many coastal lakes here. To the west of Rio, toward São Paulo state, the landscape changes abruptly. This is the Costa Verde (Green Coast) ▲ *162*, with a jagged coastline, countless bays dotted with idyllic islands, and forested slopes that plunge vertically down to the sea. The calm, clear water here is ideal for bathing, scuba diving, harpoon fishing and watersports.

MICROCLIMATES
The state's uneven topography influences the climate of its coastal region. The Serra do Mar bars the eastward advance of clouds, causing greater rainfall on the Costa Verde than on the Costa do Sol.

MINA DE OURO DE PASSAGEM ★
This fascinating gold mine, located between Ouro Preto and Mariana, was in use from 1719 right up until 1985. It descends to a depth of 1,312 feet and has four square miles of underground galleries (*above*), where many slaves tragically lost their lives. There is also a natural lake. The guided tour of the mine, during which visitors descend to a depth of 394 feet in a cable car, is spectacular. Historic methods of mining, washing and sieving gold are also explained. Beware: do not visit if you suffer from claustrophobia.

156 157

✪ This symbol indicates a place that is not to be missed.

★ The star symbol indicates sites singled out by the editor for special attention.

● Encyclopedia section

▲ Itineraries in Rio de Janeiro and Brazil

◆ Practical information

RIO DE JANEIRO ▲ 113
The *cidade maravilhosa* occupies a spectacular site between ocean, mountains and forest. Rio is a city of many faces – colonial, imperial, modernist, popular, sports-loving, frivolous and festive. It is a noisy, exuberant, colorful city suffused by the warmth and hospitality of the *carioca* population.

RIO DE JANEIRO STATE ▲ 155
This small state (17,000 square miles) offers a wide range of itineraries. Choose from the coastal beaches, islands, bays and lagoons of the Região dos Lagos and Costa Verde, the imperial city of Petropólis, the Atlantic forest of the Serra dos Órgãos and Itatiaia national parks, and the 'coffee route'.

MINAS GERAIS ▲ 179
Take an amazing trip back in time to the age of gold and diamond mining. Discover old colonial towns (Sabará, Ouro Preto, Mariana, Congonhas, São João del Rei, Tiradentes, Mariana, Serro) with their baroque churches and architecture, museums and former mines, as well as caves and spectacular landscapes – mountain ranges, plateaus, waterfalls...

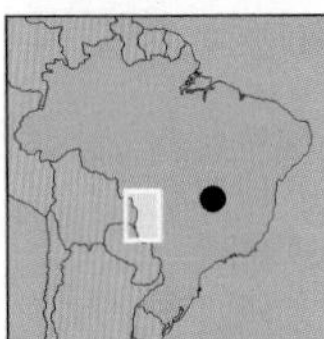

WEST-CENTRAL ▲ 199
Urban itinerary: Brasília, the largest purpose-built city in the world, designed by urban planner Lúcio Costa and architect Oscar Niemeyer, and capital of Brazil since 1960.
Natural itinerary: the Pantanal, a vast alluvial plain of some 54,000 square miles where a great wealth of animal and bird life exists alongside a major cattle-farming region.

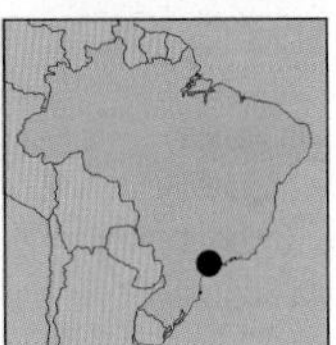

SÃO PAULO ▲ 217
São Paulo, the economic heart of Brazil, is also the country's most 'vertical' and cosmopolitan city, a megalopolis with some 20 million inhabitants. The *paulista* coast (the coast of São Paulo state), a natural extension of the Costa Verde, is renowned for its beautiful beaches and remaining areas of *mata atlântica*.

THE SOUTH ▲ 231
To the many natural attractions of this region of extremes – the Iguaçu falls, Serra do Mar and Ilha do Mel, the beaches and coast of Santa Catarina, the canyons of Rio Grande do Sul – add the reminders of its unique history and settlement (Guaranî Jesuit missions, gauchos) and the innovative urban development of Curitiba.

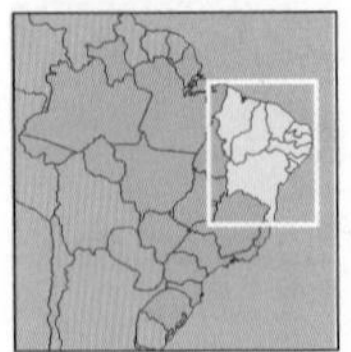

THE NORDESTE ▲ 251
The states of Bahia, Pernambuco and Maranhão, with their capitals Salvador, Recife and São Luís, have a rich colonial past and a culture inherited from Africa. The region's attractions include a coast bordered by long palm-fringed beaches, the fauna and marine depths of the Fernando de Noronha archipelago, the colonial towns of Olinda and Alcântara, and the Parque Nacional da Chapada Diamantina.

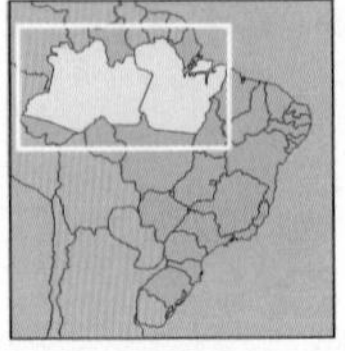

THE NORTH ▲ 293
Brazil's most 'Amerindian' region invites you to visit the cities of Belém and Manaus, explore the Ilha de Marajó on the Amazon river estuary, sail up the Amazon river from Belém to Manaus, stay in the Amazon forest and discover the region's flora and fauna.

ALL INFORMATION CONTAINED IN THIS GUIDE HAS BEEN APPROVED BY THE MANY SPECIALISTS WHO HAVE CONTRIBUTED TO ITS PRODUCTION.

ARTUR HENRIQUE BARCELOS
Historian, archeologist and photographer. Author of 'Guaraní Jesuit missions' (Itinerary).

RODRIGO BENTES MONTEIRO
Historian and lecturer at the Catholic University of Rio de Janeiro. Author of 'Petrópolis' and 'Teresópolis and the Parque Nacional'.

NICOLAS BOURLON
Doctor of environmental sciences. Author of 'Atlantic coastal forest' and 'Atlantic forest'.

VINCENT BROCHIER
Author of 'Getting there', 'Getting around', 'Staying in Brazil from A to Z' and co-author of the 'Hotels and restaurants' section.

NIREU CAVALCANTI
Historian, writer and lecturer at the Universidade Federal do Rio de Janeiro. Author of 'From colonial to imperial Rio', 'In the Haussmann style', 'Avenida Presidente Vargas', 'São Cristóvão' and 'Toward Zona Norte'.

JEAN-FRANÇOIS CHOUGNET
Historian working in the cultural field. Author of 'Toward modernity: the first skyscrapers', 'Brazilian modernism', 'Brazil as seen by painters' and 'Brasília'.

MANUÈLE COLAS
Author of 'Bairro da Luz', 'Centro' and 'Liberdade, Bela Vista and Bixiga'.

MARIA CELESTE CORRÊA
Journalist. Author of 'Porto Alegre and the Serra Gaúcha' and 'Gauchos'.

BEATRIZ HELENA DA COSTA NUNES
Guide and tour organizer. Author of 'The *fazendas*, from Vassouras to Valença', 'Parque Nacional do Itatiaia' and 'Penedo and Visconde de Mauá'.

JEAN-PHILIPPE DELORME
Coordinator for the Pantanal nature reserve. Author of 'The Pantanal'.

DIDIER DRUMMOND
Architect and lecturer at the ALBA (Lebanese School of Decorative Arts). Author of 'The development of *favelas* on the *morros* of Rio' and 'Types of *favelas*'.

ARMELLE ENDERS
Historian and assistant professor at the University of Paris-IV (Sorbonne). Author of 'Chronology', 'The meeting of two worlds and the fate of the American Indians', 'The great age of gold and diamonds', 'The coffee empire', 'Slavery, abolition and immigration', 'Getúlio Vargas', 'Sugar and the *engenho*' and 'Rise and fall of the rubber trade'.

ALAIN FONTAN
Journalist and writer, Brazilian correspondent for the French magazines *L'Équipe* and *France Football*. Author of 'Soccer' and 'Sport in the city'.

CÉDRIC GOTTESMANN
Co-author of the 'Hotels and restaurants' section

EVELYNE HEUFFEL
Guide and tour organizer. Author of 'From Lapa to Santa Teresa', 'From Glória to Sugar Loaf mountain', 'Cosme Velho, Laranjeiras and Catete', 'From Botafogo to Gávea', 'The Botanical Gardens', 'The city and the sea', 'Sepetiba and Ilha Grande' and 'Parati'.

ARNO ALVAREZ KERN
Historian and archeologist, lecturer at the Catholic University of Porto Alegre. Author of 'Guaraní Jesuit missions' (Architecture).

ARMELLE LE BARS
Lecturer at the University of Paris-III (new Sorbonne). Author of 'Language: Brazilian Portuguese', 'Along the coast of São Paulo state' and 'Useful words and expressions'.

MARCELO MACCA
Journalist. Author of 'The South', 'Curitiba and the Campos Gerais', 'From Curitiba to the coast via the Serra do Mar', 'The Iguaçu falls', 'São Luís', 'Parque Nacional dos Lençóis Maranhenses', 'Alcântara', 'Belém' and 'Ilha de Marajó'.

RENATA MELLO
Photographer and reporter. Author of 'Bonito'.

IDELETTE MUZART FONSECA DOS SANTOS
Lecturer at the University of Paris-X (Nanterre). Author of 'Folk traditions of the Nordeste'.

ANGELO OSWALDO DE ARAÚJO SANTOS
Mayor of Ouro Preto. Ex-Secretary of State for Culture in Minas Gerais. Author of 'Minas Gerais', 'Belo Horizonte and surroundings', 'Ouro Preto, a baroque gem', 'Museu da Inconfidência', 'From Ouro Preto to Mariana', 'Congonhas', 'From São João del Rei to Tiradentes' and 'Diamantina and Serro, on the diamond trail'.

EDUARDO PETTA
Journalist. Author of 'Florianópolis' and 'Santa Catarina Island and the coast'.

RAFAEL PIC
Assistant editor of *Muséart* magazine. Author of 'Baroque church architecture', 'The baroque in Minas Gerais' and 'Urban baroque: stylistic evolution'.

JEAN-MARC PONS
Ornithologist and assistant professor at the MNHN (French National Museum of Natural History) in Paris. Author of 'The Pantanal' and 'The Amazon'.

FRANCK RIBARD
Anthropologist and lecturer at the Universidade Federal do Ceará. Author of 'An ethnically diverse nation', 'Fortaleza and its beaches' and 'The coastal region'.

BERTRAND RIGOT-MULLER
Economist and cultural affairs representative at the French Consulate in Rio. Author of 'Food: *feijoada*', 'Rio de Janeiro city', 'Modernist Rio', 'The city and the forest', 'Rio, a fortified city', 'Around the bay', 'Rio de Janeiro state', 'From Maricá to Arraial do Cabo' and 'From Arraial do Cabo to Búzios'.

PATRICK RIGOT-MULLER
Aka 'Helicóptero', teacher of *capoeira*. Author of 'The *capoeira*'.

MUNIZ SODRÉ
Professor in the Department of Communications at the Universidade Federal do Rio de Janeiro (UFRJ), writer and author of '*Telenovelas*'.

HEIDI STRECKER GOMES
Journalist and arts lecturer. Author of 'By boat from Belém to Manaus, via Santarém' and 'Manaus'.

KADYA TALL
Anthropologist and lecturer at the EHESS (French School for Advanced Social Studies). Author of 'Religion and popular cults'.

HERVÉ THÉRY
Geographer and lecturer at the École Normale Supérieure (teachers' training college) in Paris. Author of 'Geomorphology', 'Biogeography', 'Climate', 'The Nordeste' and 'The *sertão*'.

NICOLAS TIPHAGNE
Ph.D. in ethnology at the University of Paris-VII (Jussieu), associate member of the EREA (Amerindian ethnology research team). Author of 'Life on the river', 'Salvador', 'Ilha de Itiparica Island and the Recôncavo region', 'The north coast', 'The south coast', 'Chapada Diamantina ', 'The North' and 'People of the Amazon Forest'.

RAFAËLA VERISSIMO JACCOUD
Translator and specialist in Portuguese literature. Author of 'São Paulo: the western districts' and 'São Paulo: a magnet for immigrants'.

SUZANA VERISSIMO
Journalist. Wrote 'Recife', 'Olinda and surroundings', 'Exploring the interior and the south coast', 'Parque Nacional Marinho de Fernando de Noronha'.

AGUEDA VILHENA VIALOU
Ph.D. in prehistory and researcher at the MNHN (French National Museum of Natural History) in Paris. Author of 'Caves and prehistoric people'.

VERA LÚCIA VILHENA DE TOLEDO
Historian, children's author. Author of '*Fazendas*'.

ARIANE WITKOWSKI
Assistant professor at the University of Paris-IV (Sorbonne). Author of 'Rio Carnival', 'Music' and 'Music and carnivals in the Nordeste'.

MAGALI ROUX
Additional writing.

ADVISOR: BERTRAND RIGOT-MULLER
Economist and demographer, and working in cultural diffusion at the Rio French consulate.

KNOPF GUIDES

This is a Borzoi Book
published by Alfred A. Knopf

Completely revised
and updated in 2005

Published in the United States by Alfred A. Knopf, a division of Random House, Inc., New York, and simultaneously in Canada by Random House of Canada Limited, Toronto. Distributed by Random House, Inc, New York.

Knopf, Borzoi Books, and the colophon are registered trademarks of Random House, Inc

www.aaknopf.com

ISBN-10: 0-375-71117-1
ISBN-13: 978-0-375-71117-6

Originally published in France by Nouveaux-Loisirs, a subsidiary of Editions Gallimard, Paris, 2000 © 2000 Editions Nouveaux-Loisirs.

Series editors
Shelley Wanger and Clémence Jacquinet

Translated by
Wendy Allatson and Sue Rose

Edited and typeset by
Book Creation Services, London

Printed in Italy by
Editoriale Lloyd

BRAZIL

Original French-language edition

EDITION
Alexandre Tiphagne, assisted by Virginia Rigot-Muller; Sophie Bezançon

GRAPHICS
Brigitte Célérier, assisted by Ana Carolina Dias

LAYOUT
Isabelle Roller

ILLUSTRATIONS
Cover: Henri Galeron;
Nature
François Desbordes, Franck Stéphan;
Architecture
Philippe Candé, Jean-Marie Guillou, Bruno Lenormand, Jean-François Peneau, Maurice Pommier, Claude Quiec, Christian Rivière, Jean-Sylvain Roveri;
Maps
Vincent Brunot, Stéphane Girel (Rio City) and Anne Bodin (color)

MAPS:
Édigraphie,
Patrick Mérienne (Nature and Pantanal)

Encyclopedia section

ugusto Malta (1908)

Nature

● Geomorphology

Pico da Neblina

The Pico da Neblina (9,892 ft), Brazil's highest point, rises in the extreme north of the country. To climb it, one needs special authorization and the logistical support from the Brazilian army.

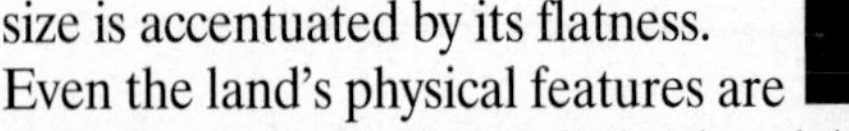

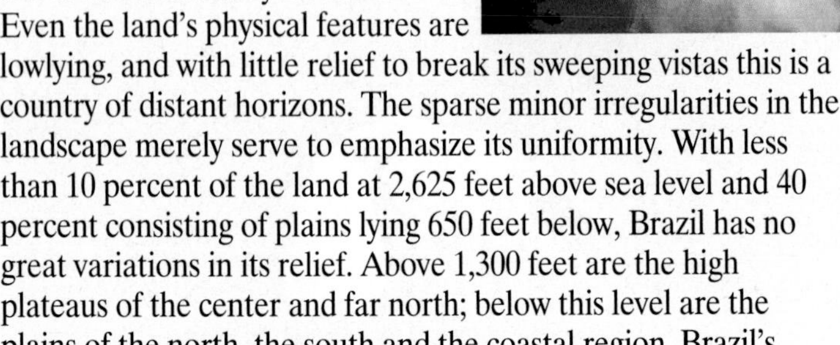

Brazil is a vast landmass whose great size is accentuated by its flatness. Even the land's physical features are lowlying, and with little relief to break its sweeping vistas this is a country of distant horizons. The sparse minor irregularities in the landscape merely serve to emphasize its uniformity. With less than 10 percent of the land at 2,625 feet above sea level and 40 percent consisting of plains lying 650 feet below, Brazil has no great variations in its relief. Above 1,300 feet are the high plateaus of the center and far north; below this level are the plains of the north, the south and the coastal region. Brazil's topography broadly reflects its geology.

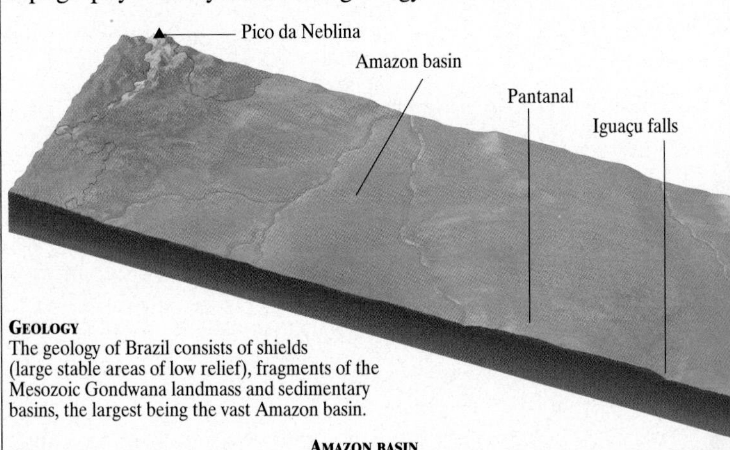

Geology

The geology of Brazil consists of shields (large stable areas of low relief), fragments of the Mesozoic Gondwana landmass and sedimentary basins, the largest being the vast Amazon basin.

Amazon basin

The Amazon ▲ *294* flows at a rate of more than 52,834,400 gallons per second and carries more than one billion tons of suspended sediment a year. The river's formidable force has resulted in the formation of a great alluvial plain on which inlets and lakes form a maze of waterways stretching for hundreds of thousands of square miles ▲ *304*.

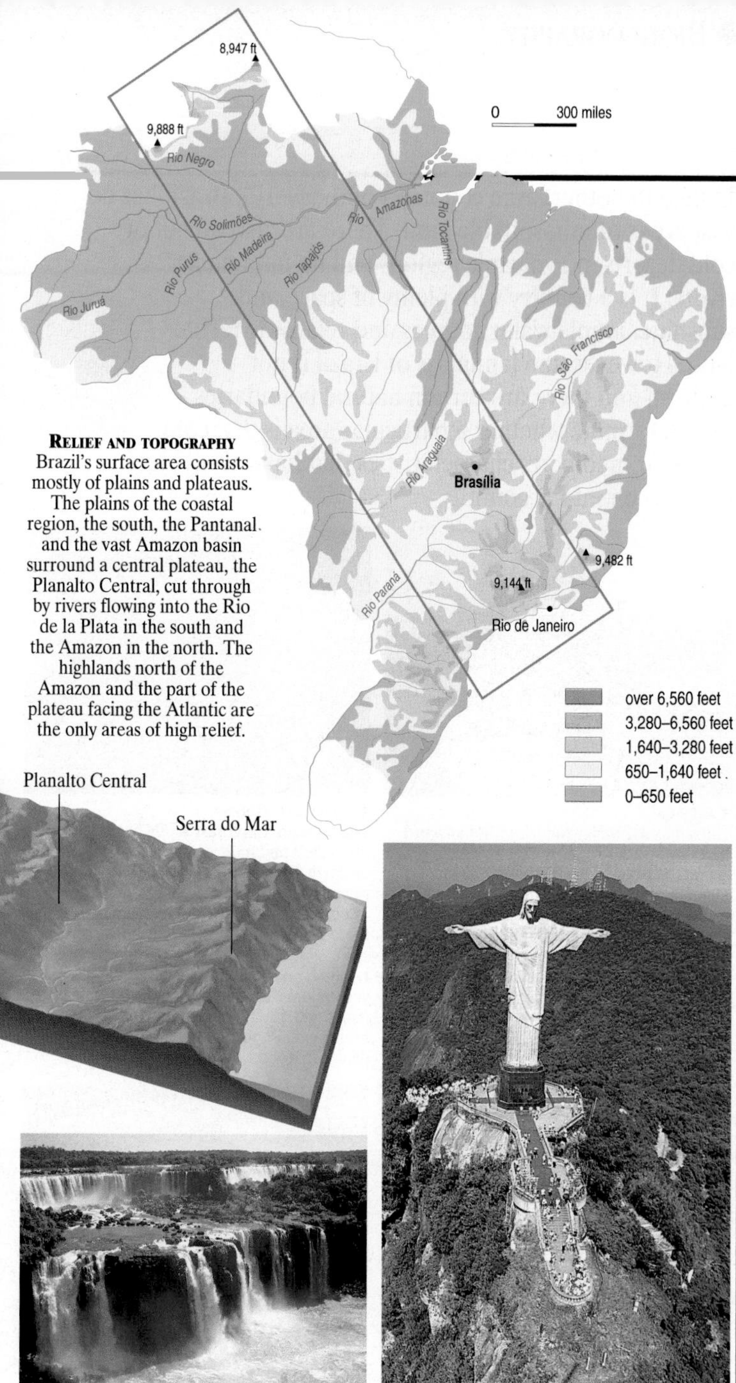

RELIEF AND TOPOGRAPHY
Brazil's surface area consists mostly of plains and plateaus. The plains of the coastal region, the south, the Pantanal and the vast Amazon basin surround a central plateau, the Planalto Central, cut through by rivers flowing into the Rio de la Plata in the south and the Amazon in the north. The highlands north of the Amazon and the part of the plateau facing the Atlantic are the only areas of high relief.

IGUAÇU FALLS
As it flows over the edge of the basalt plateau to join the Paraná below, the Iguaçu creates spectacular waterfalls. The Iguaçu falls ▲ *238* consist of 275 falls cascading over a precipice 1¾ miles wide. A few miles upstream is one of the largest hydroelectric power stations in the world ▲ *239*. It generates enough electricity to supply both southern Brazil and the whole of Paraguay.

SERRA DO MAR
The steep, densely forested slopes of the Serra do Mar form part of the natural setting that gives Rio de Janeiro, the *cidade maravilhosa* (city of marvels), its appeal but they present a challenge to town planners and architects. Parque Nacional da Tijuca, the world's largest urban national park, offers *cariocas* (Rio's inhabitants) a welcome respite from the oppressive heat of summer ▲ *150*.

Rio
Rio Juruá

Unlike the other large countries of the world, Brazil has no vast areas of inhospitable land. There are also no hot or cold deserts, no volcanic regions and no untamable rivers. It is a country with plenty of space and sunshine, ample water sources and relatively fertile land. However, the landmass of Brazil is not uniform and there are certain natural boundaries that determine whether a particular area is dry, cold, fertile or mediocre, characteristics that have always had to be taken into account.

'CAATINGA'
The *sertão* ▲ 254, an American Indian word meaning 'white forest', is Brazil's dryest region. Its poor, stony soil has a patchy covering of low, thorny scrub, known as *caatinga*, where cactus thrives. This vegetation is so well adapted to long periods of drought and periodic rainfall that a shower is enough to bring it into bloom. While the *sertão* supports extensive cattle farming, crops are concentrated in valleys watered by seasonal rivers, along watercourses or on the wetter, higher slopes known as *brejos*.

AMAZON RAINFOREST
The Amazon rainforest ▲ 304 has one of the richest and most complex ecosystems on earth. Thousands of species of plants (many of which are still unrecorded), insects, birds, reptiles and mammals live there in a complex and closely related symbiosis. The structure of the Amazon rainforest itself consists of several levels of vegetation, with trees heavily covered in lianas and other plants that either use their branches as support or live as parasites on decaying wood.

'CERRADO'
Much of the Planalto Central is covered by grassland. It is dotted with stunted trees that have become adapted both to the alternately dry and wet seasons of the tropical climate and to the acid soil, which causes their twisted growth. The Planalto Central supports a complex range of vegetation, from low scrub on the plateaus to gallery forests bordering the rivers, as well as forested slopes and slopes covered in the denser scrub known as *cerrado*.

PANTANAL
The Pantanal ▲ 210 is a large swampland covering an area of some 89,000 square miles. This extensive alluvial plain is periodically flooded by tributaries of the rivers Paraná and Paraguay. The Pantanal lies in Bolivia, Paraguay and the Brazilian states of Mato Grosso and Mato Grosso do Sul. The vast open spaces of this swampland make it an ideal environment in which to view wildlife ▲ 214, which includes a large population of waterfowl, fish and caimans.

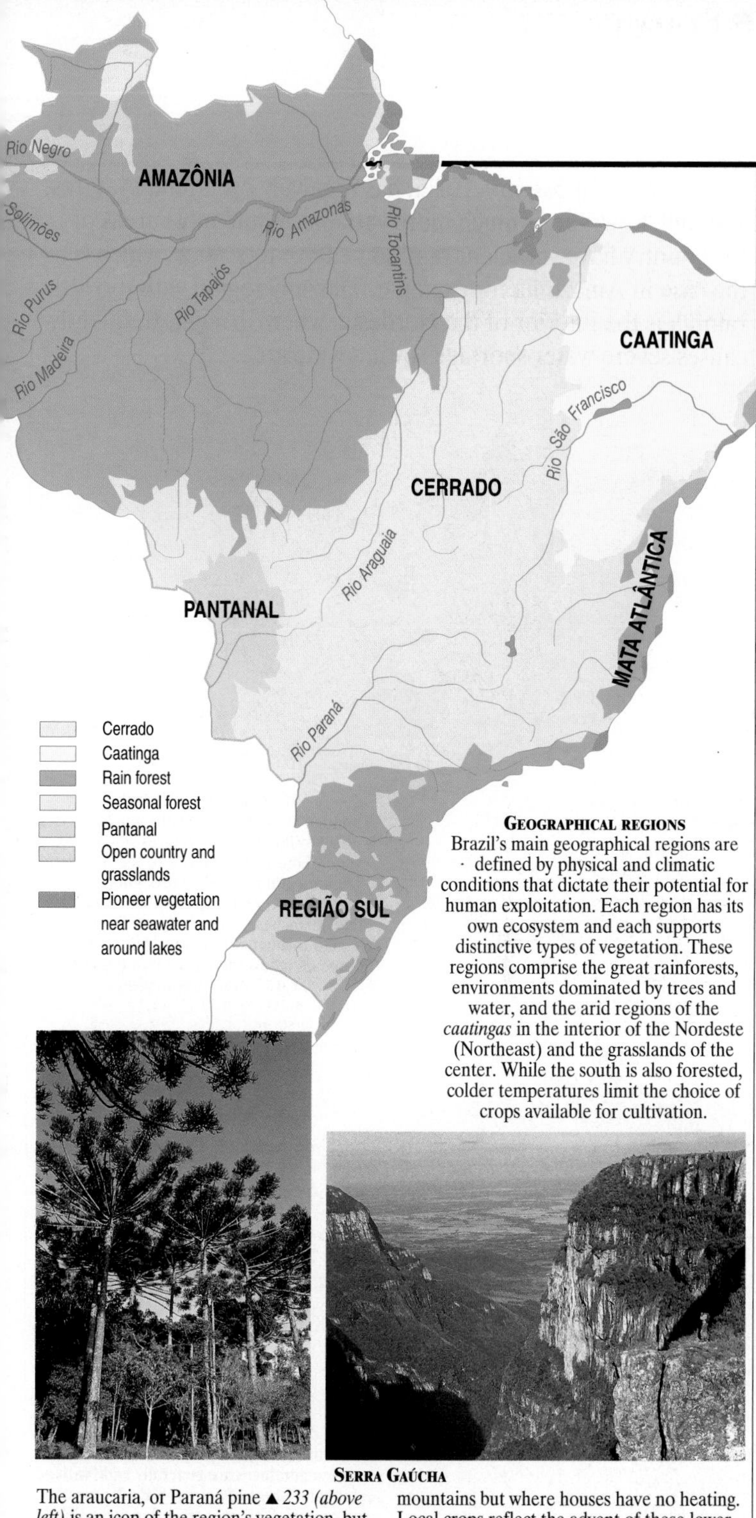

Geographical regions

Brazil's main geographical regions are defined by physical and climatic conditions that dictate their potential for human exploitation. Each region has its own ecosystem and each supports distinctive types of vegetation. These regions comprise the great rainforests, environments dominated by trees and water, and the arid regions of the *caatingas* in the interior of the Nordeste (Northeast) and the grasslands of the center. While the south is also forested, colder temperatures limit the choice of crops available for cultivation.

Serra Gaúcha

The araucaria, or Paraná pine ▲ *233 (above left)* is an icon of the region's vegetation, but has in fact almost died out there. The climate can be very cold in the Rio Grande do Sul ▲ *245*, where snow sometimes falls in the mountains but where houses have no heating. Local crops reflect the advent of these lower temperatures. Coffee, which is no longer grown in regions susceptible to frost, is gradually being replaced by wheat and vines.

Being a tropical country, Brazil has relatively even temperatures. Rainfall, however, is much more variable. While most areas of the country have sufficient rain, some have too much, which is the case in Amazonia for example. The only region with too little rainfall is the interior of the Nordeste, where drought frequently causes severe water shortages over a wide area.

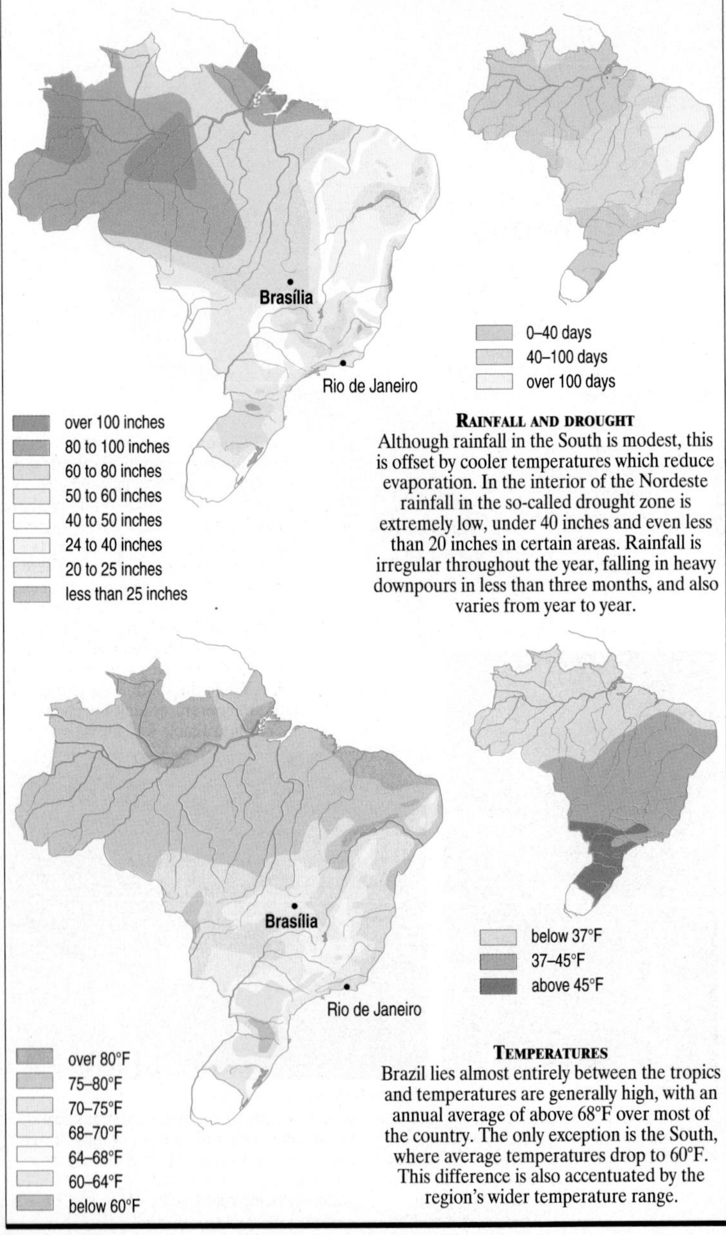

RAINFALL AND DROUGHT
Although rainfall in the South is modest, this is offset by cooler temperatures which reduce evaporation. In the interior of the Nordeste rainfall in the so-called drought zone is extremely low, under 40 inches and even less than 20 inches in certain areas. Rainfall is irregular throughout the year, falling in heavy downpours in less than three months, and also varies from year to year.

TEMPERATURES
Brazil lies almost entirely between the tropics and temperatures are generally high, with an annual average of above 68°F over most of the country. The only exception is the South, where average temperatures drop to 60°F. This difference is also accentuated by the region's wider temperature range.

History

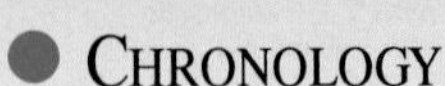

CHRONOLOGY

–?12,000 BC The first humans reach the South American continent.

AD 1200 **12th–16th centuries** South coast settled by Tupí-Guaraní peoples.

1450

1492 Christopher Columbus discovers America.

1494 Treaty of Tordesilhas.

1498 Vasco da Gama reaches India by sailing round the Horn of Africa.

1500 Cabral discovers 'Terra de Santa Cruz'.

1549 Foundation of São Salvador da Bahia de Todos os Santos and arrival of the Jesuits.

1550

1555–60 Colony of France Antarctique established in Guanabara Bay.

1560

THE COAST, WHERE TWO WORLDS MET

Human occupation of the coast of Brazil began some 12,000 years ago when it was settled by peoples who subsisted on fishing and gathering. Evidence of their presence and activities takes the form of sometimes substantial piles of shells and bones known as *sambaquis*, from the Tupí words *tamba* (shell) and *ki* (deposit), left on the shores of southern Brazil. In the 12th century these fisher-gatherers were driven out or subjugated by the Tupí-Guaraní peoples, who migrated from a region that is now Paraguay. It was mainly the Tupí who were encountered by the Portuguese and other Europeans when they began to visit the coast of Brazil in the early 16th century. While the Spanish aimed to reach the Indies by sailing west, landing in America in 1492, the Portuguese favored an eastern maritime route. This is why, under the terms of the Treaty of Tordesilhas, signed by Spain and Portugal in 1494, lands discovered to the east of a meridian running 370 leagues west of the Cape Verde Islands were granted to Portugal: these lands included part of what was to become Brazil. In 1498 Vasco da Gama reached India via the eastern route by sailing round the Horn of Africa.

STAGES OF COLONIZATION

'TERRA DE SANTA CRUZ', LAND OF THE HOLY CROSS

In 1500 a second fleet, under the command of Pedro Álvares Cabral, set out for the Orient by sailing southwest across the Atlantic. In the South Atlantic Cabral discovered a land that he named Terra de Santa Cruz (Land of the Holy Cross), taking possession of it for Manuel I of Portugal (*above*). Over the next few decades the only attraction of this coastal territory was its *pau-brasil* (brazilwood) – for which Terra do Brasil was later named – whose bark yielded a scarlet dye that was highly prized in Europe. Portugal's trade with Asia was, however, much more profitable. In 1530 'Brazil' was divided into fifteen captaincies (*capitanias*) which were given to Portuguese nobles. With the exception of Pernambuco ▲ *274* the system failed to ensure the prosperity and security of a land whose coastline was frequented by British, French and Dutch ships. In 1549 a central administration under the control of a governor-general was set up in the capital, São Salvador ▲ *256*. The northeastern coast of Brazil, which was closer to Portugal and more strictly administered, developed more rapidly than the south, which had a smaller Portuguese population and was vulnerable to foreign attack. In 1555 the French, who did not acknowledge the Treaty of Tordesilhas, established France Antarctique, a small colony in Guanabara Bay, where Rio de Janeiro ▲ *114*, *152* was later founded, and placed it under the command of Nicolas Durand de Villegagnon, a Knight of Malta. In 1560 they were driven out by Governor Mem de Sá. The French attempted to establish a second colony, France Équinoxiale, in northern Brazil. In the early 17th century they founded the town of São Luís do Maranhão ▲ *288*, but under pressure from the Portuguese abandoned it in 1615.

1580 Philip II of Spain becomes king of Portugal.

1640 Portugal regains independence with the accession of Dom João IV.

1695 Gold discovered in Minas Gerais.

1750 Treaty of Madrid: Spain recognizes Portuguese sovereignty in Brazil.

1580 | **1610** | **1640** | **1700** | **1730** | **1770**

1565 Estácio de Sá founds the town of São Sebastião do Rio de Janeiro.

1612–15 Colony of France Équinoxiale established in São Luís do Maranhão.

1630–54 The Dutch capture Pernambuco, allowing them to gain control of northern Brazil.

1729 Diamonds discovered in Minas Gerais.

1763 Rio de Janeiro becomes the capital of the viceroyalty.

A SUGAR ECONOMY

The economy of the colonies was based on sugar cane and sugar mills (*engenhos*) ▲ *270* and on the 'importation' of African slaves ● *34*. In the early 17th century Bahia and Pernambuco were the first sugar producers in the world. They were the pride of the Portuguese empire, but their prosperity led the Dutch West Indies Company to launch attacks on them. The Dutch took Bahia in 1624, although they subsequently lost it, and seized Pernambuco in 1630. However an uprising in Pernambuco and conflicts with earlier settlers (*right*) forced the Dutch to leave Brazil in 1654.

COLONIAL BRAZIL'S GOLDEN AGE (18TH CENTURY)

Until the late 17th century the Portuguese – which Friar Vicente do Salvador, writing in 1627, described as 'crabs clinging to the shore'– did not venture into the interior. However, the discovery of gold on the Planalto Central ● *30* in 1659 led to the settlement of the region, which in 1720 became the administrative center of Minas Gerais ▲ *180*. Towns such as Ribeirao do Carmo (in Mariana province), Vila Rica (in Ouro Preto) and São João del Rei sprang up, their prosperity marked by the building of lavish baroque churches ● *72* and the development of a sophisticated cultural life. Gold and precious stones destined for Portugal's royal treasury were transported to Parati ▲ *164* and shipped out of Rio de Janeiro, which began to prosper as a result. During the War of the Spanish Succession, in which France fought England and Portugal, French pirates launched raids on Brazil's riches. Although Duclerc's attempt to capture Rio de Janeiro in 1710 failed, Duguay-Trouin succeeded the following year, plundering the city and exacting a substantial ransom for its release. In 1763 Rio's growing importance prompted the viceroy to leave Salvador, in Bahia, and take up residence there, making it the capital of Brazil.

1808 Portugal's royal court moves to Rio de Janeiro.

1816 The French artistic mission arrives in Rio.

1835–45 *Farrapos* war in the South and secession of Rio Grande do Sul.

1780 **1810** **1820** **1830** **1840** **1850**

1789 The conspiracy of Minas Gerais (*Inconfidência Mineira*) is denounced.

1822 Prince Dom Pedro declares Brazilian independence.

1831 Dom Pedro I abdicates.

1840 Dom Pedro II comes of age.

1850 End of the slave trade.

TIRADENTES AND THE 'INCONFIDÊNCIA MINEIRA'

In 1750 the quantity of gold yielded by the mines of Minas Gerais began to decline, causing the Portuguese crown to levy even more onerous taxes ● *31*. Heavily indebted, and inspired by the American Civil War, in February 1789 a group of former government officials plotted to assassinate the governor, also intending to stir up a popular rebellion against the tyranny of the king of Portugal in the name of the 'freedom of Minas Gerais'. The conspirators finally abandoned their plot and one of them, Joaquim Silvério dos Reis, denounced this disloyalty to the Portuguese crown. The incident became known as the *Inconfidência Mineira*. Reis' eleven coconspirators were condemned to death, but only Joaquim José da Silva Xavier, nicknamed Tiradentes ('tooth-puller'), was hanged (*left*), on April 21, 1792. Tiradentes, a sub-lieutenant in the dragoons, was of lower social status than the other *inconfidentes*. His exemplary courage during his trial and execution fired popular imagination and made him a martyr. He was hanged in Rio and parts of his dismembered body were displayed at road junctions to encourage his compatriots to remain loyal to the Portuguese crown. In the late 19th century the Republicans made Tiradentes a national hero, the precursor of Independence, and since 1890 the anniversary of his execution has been marked by a public holiday in Brazil. Tiradentes the martyr is still widely invoked as a figurehead in Brazilian political debates. He stands as the symbol of freedom and patriotic resistance in the face of treachery, of which Silvério dos Reis is seen as the embodiment.

BRAZIL AS A MONARCHY AND AS AN EMPIRE

A CROWNED HEAD IN AMERICA (1808–22)

At the end of 1807 the Portuguese royal court, under threat of invasion by the troops of Napoleon I, sought refuge in Brazil. As a result Rio de Janeiro became the capital of the Portuguese empire and acquired a number of institutions befitting its new role. Brazil itself ceased to be a colony and was elevated to the status of kingdom. Its ports were opened up to trade with friendly nations (in particular England), printing presses were set up and university faculties created. A contingent of French artists, including painter Jean-Baptiste Debret and architect Grandjean de Montigny ▲ *119*, was invited to introduce the Brazilians to European fine arts. In 1821 Dom João VI was recalled to Portugal by a revolution aiming to impose a constitution that would reverse the concessions granted to Brazil. He named his son Pedro (*right*) Prince Regent and governor of Brazil. Dom Pedro refused to comply with Lisbon's orders. On the advice of statesman José Bonifácio de Andrada e Silva, he proclaimed Brazilian independence on the banks of the River Ipiranga (São Paulo) on September 7, 1822 and was crowned emperor in December.

1864–70 War with Paraguay.	1886 All slaves over the age of 60 are declared free.	1893–4 Civil war in the South.	1917 Brazil enters World War One on the side of the Allies.	1924 The Prestes column sets out.

1860 — 1880 — 1890 — 1910 — 1920 — 1925

1871 All children born to slaves are declared free.	1888 Abolition of slavery.	1889 The monarchy is overthrown and the Brazilian Republic proclaimed.	1896–7 Canudos War, in the state of Bahia.	1922 Week of Modern Art in São Paulo. The *tenentes* rebellion in Rio de Janeiro.

From Dom Pedro I to Dom Pedro II

Dom Pedro I, the legitimate heir to the Portuguese throne, was suspected of wanting to re-establish ties between the two monarchies. He abdicated on April 7, 1831 and returned to Portugal, leaving behind his five year-old son Dom Pedro de Alcântara. His abdication was followed by a succession of regencies during which Brazilian unity was threatened on a number of occasions. Between January 1835 and October 1836 the state of Pará was ravaged by the violent Cabanagem Rebellion ▲ *298* and, between 1835 and 1845, Rio Grande do Sul was swept by the *farrapos* war (the 'war of the ragged ones') ▲ *247*. The government, backed by the imperial majority in 1840, succeeded in restoring order and bringing the country under centralized control. Under Dom Pedro II (1840–89) Brazil conducted an active diplomatic policy in the La Plata basin and joined Argentina and Uruguay in a bloody war against the Paraguay of Francisco Solano López. In 1870 the regime was challenged by the Republicans who had gained significant support in the state of São Paulo and the city of Rio de Janeiro. Abolitionists campaigned for the end of slavery and, on May 13, 1888, the Portuguese Princesa Isabel signed the *lei áurea* (golden law) that abolished slavery ● *35*. With abolition the empire lost the support of the slave-owning nobility in the province of Rio. On November 15, 1889 a handful of Republican conspirators, who were supported by elements from the army, overthrew the monarchy and established the Brazilian Republic.

A philosopher king
Dom Pedro II (1825–91) was an emperor with a broad interest in science and philosophy. He was a member of the French Académie des Sciences, learnt Hebrew and Russian and was interested in photography, astronomy and geography. He corresponded with Louis Pasteur and other famous scientists of the time, and traveled widely in the United States, Europe and Egypt Thanks to his tireless efforts, Brazil was allowed to take part in the World's Fair.

Brazil's unstable Republican regimes

The First Republic (1889–1930)

After playing a key role in promoting Republican propaganda, the Positivists, who were versed in the ideas of French philosopher Auguste Comte, were soon removed from positions of power, except in Rio Grande do Sul. The First Republic's early years were troubled by serious unrest and in 1895–7 the federal army was hard pressed to quell the Canudos War, a popular rebellion led by Antonio Conselheiro in Canudos, in the *sertão* of Bahia ▲ *254*. The Federal Republic of Brazil invested its member states (which the former provinces had now become) with a high degree of autonomy. The constitution of 1891 was Brazil's longest-lived basic Republican law. However, while politics remained the preserve of a small elite, the system of direct election, which excluded the illiterate (constituting the majority of the population), was systematically flouted by electoral fraud. In the 1920s the social changes that the country was experiencing, and the increasing inflexibility of the First Republic, merely served to highlight the discrepancy between the regime and the aspirations of developing public opinion. Army officers (*tenentes*) who wanted to revive the Republic stirred up rebellions such as those of the Forte de Copacabana in Rio (1922) and in São Paulo (1924). Between 1924 and 1927 the most famous of these *tenentes*, Luís Carlos Prestes (1898–1990), traveled 16,775 miles through the interior of Brazil leading a phalanx of revolutionaries who flouted the authorities. Feted for this prestigious exploit, Prestes later became one of the leaders of the Brazilian Communist Party.

1932 The state of São Paulo rebels against the federal government.

1942 Brazil declares war on the Axis powers.

1951 Getúlio Vargas is elected president.

1958 Brazil wins its first soccer World Cup.

1930 — 1935 — 1940 — 1950 — 1955 — 1958

1930 End of the 'Old Republic' as Getúlio Vargas comes to power.

1937 Getúlio Vargas proclaims the Estado Novo (New State).

1945 Vargas is deposed and the country returns to democracy.

1954 Vargas commits suicide.

1956 Juscelino Kubitschek (JK) is elected president.

THE REVOLUTION OF 1930 AND THE VARGAS ERA (1930–54)

In March 1930 Getúlio Vargas (1882–1954) ● *36* was beaten in a parody of an election, but in October he and his supporters launched the revolutionary movement that brought down the 'Old Republic'. There followed a provisional government, during which the 'Constitutionalist Revolution' took place in the state of São Paulo in 1932, and in 1934 Vargas was elected president by Congress. However, in 1935, on the pretext of a communist rebellion, Vargas established a police state. In 1937 he suspended the old constitution and imposed a dictatorship under the name Estado Novo (New State). Although Brazil had initially been sympathetic toward the Third Reich, in February 1942 the country entered World War Two on the side of the United States. In 1944–5 a Brazilian Expeditionary Force (FEB) took part in the liberation of Italy. The end of the war weakened the Estado Novo, whose authoritarian regime seemed incompatible with the defeat of fascism. Vargas was forced to stand down and withdrew to his residence in Rio Grande do Sul. He was reelected president in 1951 but committed suicide in August 1954.

'BOSSA NOVA' BRAZIL (1956–60)

Juscelino Kubitschek (1902–76, *above*), who was elected president in 1956, aimed to reconcile a respect for democracy with the economic growth of the Vargas era. According to his election slogan – 'Fifty years in five!' – he wanted to speed Brazil toward development and industrialization. The icons of this euphoric period were *bossa nova* music ● *52* and the Volkswagen Beetle, which was produced by the Brazilian automobile industry and which was an object of desire for a fast-developing middle class. The period was also marked by Brazil's first soccer World Cup victory in 1958 (winning team, *below*). Kubitschek, nicknamed the 'bossa nova President' or JK, launched an ambitious program of national integration, central to which was the construction of an extensive road network and a new purpose-built capital, Brasília ▲ *200*. Built in record time in the middle of the *cerrado* ● *18*, it was intended to open up the country's interior. It also signaled Brazil's ambition to be a pioneering nation in the modern world.

1960 Brasília becomes capital of Brazil.

1964 Military coup.

1969–74 Presidency of General Médici.

1974–85 Opening-up of military regime.

1992 President Collor de Mello impeached.

1995 Fernando Henrique Cardoso elected president.

1960 | 1970 | 1980 | 1990 | 1995 | 2005

1961 Investiture and resignation of President Jânio Quadros, who is replaced by Vice-President João Goulart.

1979 Revocation of Institutional Act No. 5 (AI 5) and political amnesty.

1989 Collor de Mello wins the first direct presidential election since 1960.

1994 The Plano Real brings hyperinflation under control.

2003 Lula da Silva elected president.

MILITARY RULE (1964–85)

Heavy debts were the downside of the Kubitschek era. Denouncing political mismanagement and populist policies, the opponents of Vargas and Kubitschek feared the political instability brought by the chaotic presidency of right-wing populist Jânio Quadros and the excesses of his successor João Goulart, who was close to Vargas. In 1964 strikes multiplied and economic problems worsened. While an element of the Left advocated a radical approach, the Right wanted to remove populism from the Brazilian political stage and return the country to order. To do this, the Right enlisted the support of the army, which saw as a threat the spread of subversive ideas in its ranks. On March 31 there began what the military labeled the Revolution of 1964. By April that year democracy in Brazil was dead, although it was not until 1968 that the regime hardened its resolve. Institutional Act No. 5 (AI 5) removed those civil liberties that still remained and instituted systematic repression. Between 1968 and 1976 the army and police justfied torture and imprisonment as a means of dealing with underground movements' terrorism and guerrilla warfare. This period of dictatorship, during which hundreds of people unaccountably disappeared and left-wing intellectuals were forced into exile, coincided with Brazil's 'economic miracle', when the economy grew at an annual rate of some 10 percent. Although it would incur further debt, Brazil began to export industrial products. In the late 1970s the regime gradually became more liberal. There was a political amnesty, exiles were allowed to return and, in 1982, Brazilians were once again allowed to vote for their government. In 1984, during the *diretas-já* (Elections Now) campaign, millions took to the streets to demand the direct election of their president (*below*). However, it was the electoral college appointed by the dictatorship that elected a civilian president, Tancredo Neves, in 1985. Neves died before taking office, and his place in the Planalto, the presidential palace in Brasilía ▲ *205*, was taken by Vice-President José Sarney, the former chairman of the party that had supported the military regime.

THE 'NEW REPUBLIC'

The return to democracy, with such tangible signs as the direct election of President Fernando Collor de Mello in 1989, met with enthusiastic support. In June 1992 Brazil, which was seeking a permanent seat on the UN Security Council, hosted the Earth Summit (the United Nations Conference on Environment and Development) in Rio de Janeiro. Along with neighboring Argentina, Uruguay and Paraguay, Brazil also joined Mercosul, a regional trade organization formed in January 1995. In 1992, the resignation of Collor de Mello (who was impeached for corruption), plunged the 'New Republic' into political crisis. It also faced serious social, financial and economic problems. The implementation of the Plano Real in 1994 curbed inflation (which had reached 5,130 percent that year). However the economic growth and monetary stability the country gained during the presidency of FH Cardoso were not enough to reduce social inequalities or the public debt. In 2003, Lula da Silva, a former metal worker who belonged to a post-dictatorship union movement, was elected president with a socially ambitious program.

Around 1500 the land later known as Brazil was populated by an estimated five million American Indians of four main linguistic and cultural groups: the Tupí, Gê, Arawak and Carib. From then until the second half of the 17th century, the country was peopled mostly by American Indians and *mamelucas* (of American Indian and Portuguese descent). But the exploits of the *bandeirantes* (adventurers), the arrival of African slaves and of European immigrants changed the makeup of this colonial society. Disease, slavery, cultural melding and interbreeding dispersed the native population so that, by the end of the 20th century, it was reduced to just 350,000.

THE FIRST JESUIT MISSION IN AMERICA

The first Jesuits, or Fathers of the Society of Jesus, landed in Brazil in 1549 (*below*) and were to play a key role in converting the native peoples to Christianity. The Jesuits learned American Indian languages and studied native cultures, and to spread their teaching they developed a *lingua geral* (general language). Based on the Tupí vocabulary, it enabled speakers of the various Tupí-Guaraní dialects to communicate. The Jesuits also founded colleges, including that of São Paulo in 1554 ▲ *220*, and established villages known as missions (*missão* or *redução*), where they encouraged the native peoples to settle. The largest missions, which were inhabited by the Guaraní, were located in the Jesuit province of Paraguay, on the edge of the Spanish and Portuguese empires ▲ *248*. However this created conflict with Portuguese settlers and the Jesuits were expelled from both Portugal and Brazil in 1759.

THE FIRST TRADE LINKS

In the 16th century the meager wealth of the Brazilian coast was a disappointment to the Portuguese. There was no gold or silver, but only a tropical redwood (*pau-brasil*) whose bark yielded a scarlet dye, exotic animals and 'American savages'. The Portuguese and French who came to collect cargos of redwood, or 'brazilwood', needed the labor of the American Indians (*above*). During this period many seafarers settled in Brazil and adopted native customs, sleeping in hammocks and eating the cassava flour that took the place of bread flour.

CLAIMING TERRITORY
Portuguese navigators in the great Age of Discovery adopted the custom of placing a large stone (*padrão*) incised with the Portuguese coat of arms on the shores of lands that they claimed for their country. *Padrões* thus marked the routes of the navigators as they made their way along the coasts of Africa, Asia and Brazil. The *padrão* in Porto Seguro ▲ *267* marks Cabral's landing there on April 22, 1500.

THE SPIRIT OF THE 'BANDEIRANTES'
The *bandeirantes* were explorers and hunters of American Indians who contributed to the discovery of the country's interior and its rich natural resources. Antônio Tavares Raposo exemplified these brave and violent men. In 1629 he ravaged the Jesuit missions set up in Guaraní territory and in 1648 led an expedition from São Paulo to Paraguay and the Chaco desert. Having reached the foothills of the Andes, he then followed the Amazon downstream, arriving at Belém do Pará ▲ *298* in 1651. Today the *bandeirantes* are held up as heroes of the conquest of Brazilian territory and of the enterprising spirit of the state of São Paulo.

AMERICAN INDIAN SLAVERY
In theory it was legal to enslave American Indians only if they were prisoners of war. In the south of the colony, however, they were enslaved indiscriminately. Adventurers (*bandeirantes*) from São Paulo, who were often American Indians or mixed race themselves, went on raids into the interior to capture slaves (*right*). In the 17th century they even carried out a number of attacks on Jesuit missions in the south ▲ *248*.

AMERICAN INDIANS OF BRAZIL IN THE 16TH CENTURY
In about 1500 Brazil's coastal area was populated by the Tupí, while the central plateau was occupied by the Gê and the Amazon basin by Arawak, Carib and Tupí peoples. The Tupí were subdivided into various, often antagonistic, groups. Tupí-Guaraní societies were semi-nomadic, with a culture centered on war, and a tradition of vendettas and ritual cannibalism. The French and Portuguese became embroiled in these intertribal conflicts, the French forming alliances with the Tupinambá and the Portuguese with their enemies, the Tupinikin.

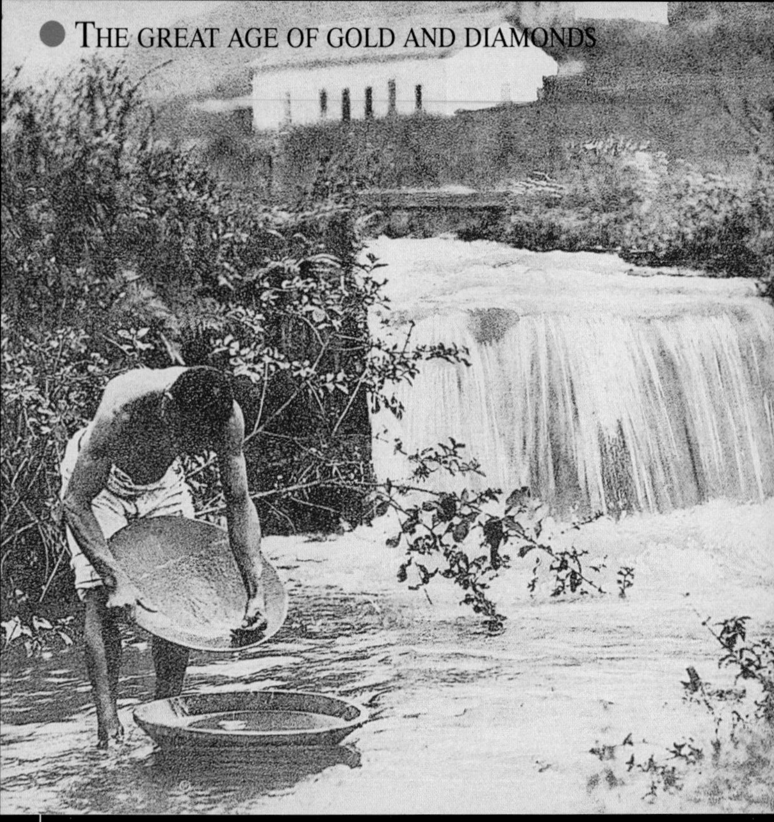

Two hundred years after they first settled in Brazil, the Portuguese discovered the country's huge resources of gold and precious stones. In Minas Gerais *bandeirantes* from São Paulo found abundant quantities of gold in the alluvial deposits of the Rio das Velhas in 1695 and diamonds at Serro Frio in 1729. Gold was also discovered in the Mato Grosso and in the Goiás but it was in the newly created captaincy of Minas Gerais (General Mines) that a brilliant culture developed between 1733 and 1755, when gold mining was at its peak. For the first time in the country's history, populations left the coast to settle in the interior. As a result, in 1763 the capital was transferred from the viceroyalty of Salvador to Rio de Janeiro. However, gradual decline set in during the second half of the 18th century.

THE 'CAMINHO NOVO'

Throughout the 18th century gold from Minas Gerais was transported down the mountains to the port of Parati ▲ *164* and from there was carried by boat to Rio de Janeiro. The booming mining economy led to the development of agriculture and stock farming, which was needed to feed the mining population. This in turn meant that a new road, the *Caminho Novo*, was needed for the mule trains that brought in supplies and merchandise. The road ran from Minas Gerais via Vale do Paraíba to Rio de Janeiro, which became the capital of Brazil in 1763.

FROM CAMPS TO HISTORIC CITIES

Some of the prospectors' camps in Minas Gerais grew into prosperous boom towns, among which were Sabará, Vila Rica and São João del Rei. Their inhabitants were drawn from a wide cross-section of society. As well as the middle classes, who were involved in the mining industry, there were rich *fazendeiros* (planters), as well as magistrates and government officials, craftsmen of all kinds, including carpenters and goldsmiths, and of course slaves. The mass of the free population, even when local gold and diamond extraction was at its height, lived in poverty.

Gold-panning slaves
In about 1775 slaves made up one half of Minas Gerais' 300,000 inhabitants. When the region's alluvial deposits had given up all their gold, the precious metal had to be extracted by far more arduous methods from underground galleries. The 'useful' life of a mining slave was rarely longer than ten years. Slaves were strictly supervised (*below*) to prevent them stealing gold.

The gold rush
The discovery of gold caused the first great wave of Portuguese emigration to Brazil. During the 18th century Brazil's population rose from 340,000 to 3.5 million. The lure of gold in Minas Gerais also led to migrations within Brazil itself; these internal migrants were mainly *Paulistas* (from Sao Paolo) and Bahians. Portugal used Brazilian gold to purchase imported British goods and to finance such extravagant projects as the construction of the National Palace in Mafra, in west-central Portugal. Brazilian gold was thus in circulation in Britain and elsewhere in Europe.

Church of the Rosary
The banning of official religious orders in Minas Gerais led to the rapid evolution of Third Orders and lay brotherhoods. During the colonial period some brotherhoods embraced slaves and the poor. Black people worshipped at Nossa Senhora do Rosário (Our Lady of the Rosary) (*below*) or Santo Antônio Preto. The Third Orders were popular with the aristocracy.

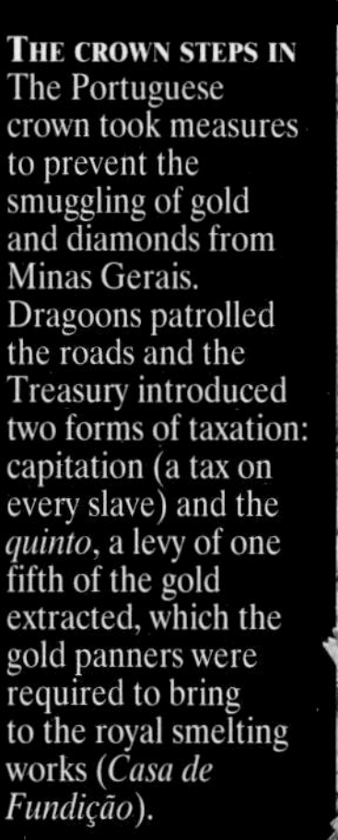

The crown steps in
The Portuguese crown took measures to prevent the smuggling of gold and diamonds from Minas Gerais. Dragoons patrolled the roads and the Treasury introduced two forms of taxation: capitation (a tax on every slave) and the *quinto*, a levy of one fifth of the gold extracted, which the gold panners were required to bring to the royal smelting works (*Casa de Fundição*).

LES CAFÉS DU BRÉSIL

Coffee seeds were first planted in Brazil, in the province of Pará, in 1727, but it was the establishment of coffee plantations on the outskirts of Rio de Janeiro in the early 19th century that proved to be a stroke of genius. A green swathe spread along the Paraíba do Sul valley toward the provinces (now states) of São Paulo, Minas Gerais and Paraná. In 1860 the province of Rio de Janeiro was producing 78 percent of all the coffee grown in Brazil. By about 1900 São Paulo produced two thirds of the national yield. As sugar and gold had been, coffee was the key to the profitable exploitation of entire regions. The country's largest export, it triggered the industrial development that has made São Paulo what it is today.

NEW PIONEER FRONTS

Following the introduction of coffee new regions stretching from Rio de Janeiro to São Paulo and Minas Gerais were put under cultivation, and new settlements grew up. Meanwhile, soil exhaustion was causing the earliest plantations to decline. Because it scorched the land and surged onward to new conquests, Brazilian writer Monteiro Lobato compared coffee to Attila the Hun. As land became exhausted the country's economic hub shifted to the province of São Paulo whose vast tracts of *terra roxa* (purple land) were ideal for coffee-growing.

THE RISE OF SÃO PAULO

Profits from the coffee trade led to the rapid development of cotton mills, textile factories, breweries and flour mills on the outskirts of the city of São Paulo. Coffee growers and industrialists had elegant mansions (*palacetes*) built on the Avenida Paulista ▲ *223*, an elegant thoroughfare in a city embellished and enhanced by prestigious buildings. In 1920 São Paulo's industrial production exceeded that of Rio de Janeiro. Sao Paulo, the *bandeirante* capital, had become the capital of the most powerful state in the federation of Brazilian states.

Overproduction

By the early 20th century Brazil was producing too much coffee. Taking action against falling prices, the coffee growers of São Paulo stockpiled part of the national production. This was close to 75 percent of the annual global coffee yield. Despite the negotiation of a fair world price for coffee and a major publicity campaign, serious coffee crises continued. Between 1933 and 1944 Brazil destroyed the equivalent of three times the world's annual coffee consumption. By 1996 coffee constituted 11 percent of Brazil's exports.

The age of the 'coffee barons'

During the reign of Dom Pedro II ● *25* the planters (*fazendeiros*) in the province of Rio de Janeiro were the first to make their fortune from coffee. Many of these 'coffee barons' were ennobled by the emperor. Their plantations covered thousands of acres and they owned hundreds of slaves.

Coffee exports

After the coffee harvest, which takes place between June and November, the beans are soaked, hulled, dried and graded. They are then despatched to the port of Santos ▲ *228*, the country's import-export center, where they are loaded onto ships and transported to Europe and the United States.

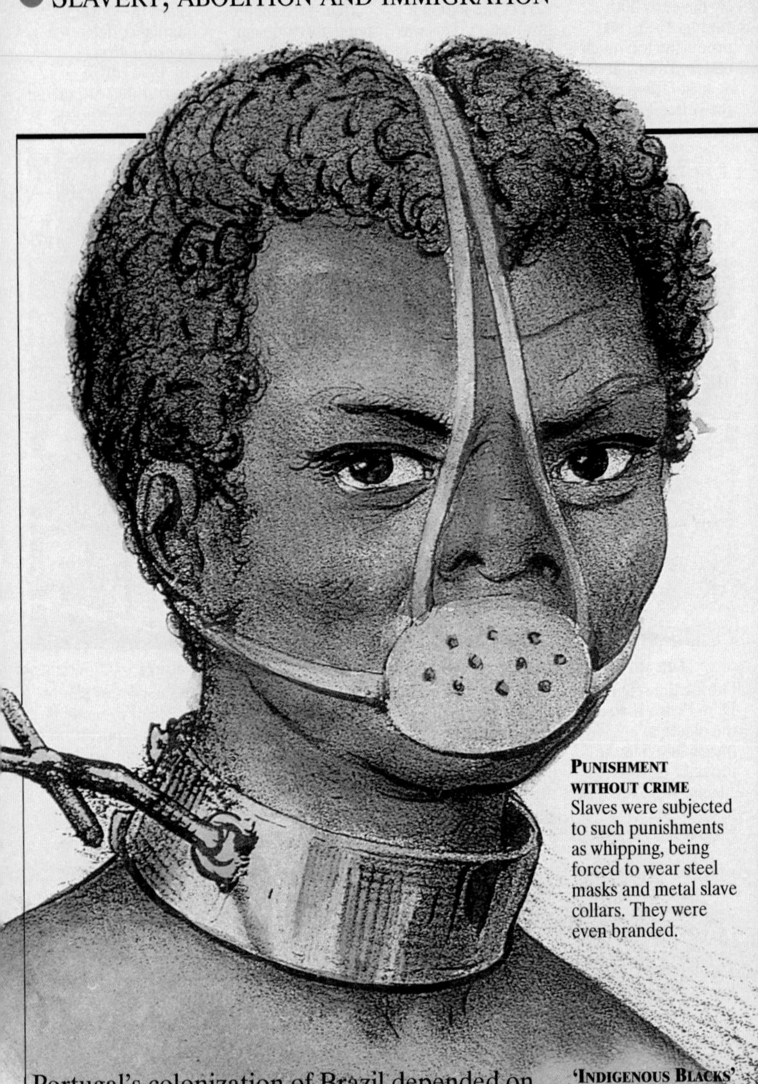

PUNISHMENT WITHOUT CRIME
Slaves were subjected to such punishments as whipping, being forced to wear steel masks and metal slave collars. They were even branded.

Portugal's colonization of Brazil depended on the use of slaves, who were drawn initially from the indigenous population and later from Africa. During the slave trade between Africa and the New World, Brazil took 3.5 million of the twelve million African slaves brought to the American continent. The trade continued until 1850 and slavery was not abolished until 1888. Between 1888 and 1930 almost four million immigrants, mostly from southern Europe and Asia, settled in Brazil, especially in the state of São Paulo. The descendants of this immigrant workforce have found it easier to integrate into elite Brazilian society than have the children and grandchildren of slaves.

'INDIGENOUS BLACKS' AND 'GUINEA PIECES'
African slaves, or 'Guinea pieces', were considered more resilient than the American Indians, or 'indigenous Blacks'. The slave system divided African slaves into two main groups, Sudanese or Bantu, depending on their African port of embarkation. The Sudanese were shipped from ports on the Bight of Benin (Gulf of Guinea) to northeastern Brazil, while the southeast 'imported' Bantus from the Congo and Angola.

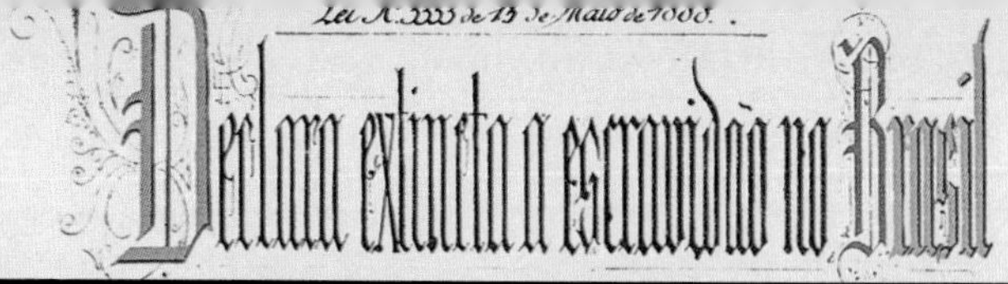

Lei N.3353 de 13 de Maio de 1888.

Declara extincta a escravidão no Brasil

CONFLICT AND RESISTANCE
In both urban and rural areas slaves lived in *senzalas* (slave houses) ● *69* in a specially designated slave district. Their history is punctuated by resistance which was expressed as rebellion or flight. To escape from their white masters, slaves fled and formed refugee communities of varying sizes known as *mocambos* or *quilombos*. The best known, the Palmares *quilombo* in Alagoas, remained independent for almost a century (1604–94). It was destroyed in spite of the determination of its chief, Zumbi, one of the most popular historic figures among Afro-Brazilians. In the years preceding the abolition of slavery, the number of *quilombos* increased, especially in the cities, where slaves merged into the free population. Brazil's slave-dependent society lived in perpetual fear of slave rebellions.

SLAVE LABOR
The first African slaves to reach Brazil landed in São Vicente in 1538. African slaves worked on the plantations ● *68*, but also in the cities as vendors, servants, manual workers and porters. In 1848 slaves made up 25 percent of the 300-strong workforce in the smelting works of Barão de Mauá, pioneer of Brazilian industrialization.

ABOLITION
On May 13, 1888 Princesa Isabel, daughter of Dom Pedro II, signed the *lei áurea* or 'golden law' (*above*) proclaiming the abolition of slavery. This concluded a lengthy process initiated by British and Brazilian abolitionists in 1807. However, the belated anti-slavery law made no provision for the newly freed slaves.

BRAZIL, LAND OF PROMISE
The coffee growers of São Paulo attempted to replace slaves with a paid workforce by hiring immigrants, most of whom were Italian. However, because the coffee growers imposed draconian conditions that shattered any hopes of prosperity and condemned the immigrants to vegetate like poor agricultural workers on the *fazendas* ● *68*, they left to seek work in the city ▲ *226*. By contrast small and medium-sized land-ownership developed in the German and Italian 'colonies' that took root in the states of Rio Grande do Sul and Santa Catarina.

JAPANESE IMMIGRANTS
In 1908 the first Japanese immigrants arrived aboard the *Kasato Maru*. They were brought (*below*) to work on the coffee plantations of São Paulo. The *fazendeiros* considered them less demanding and more amenable than Italian agricultural workers.

Brought to power by the Revolution of 1930, Getúlio Vargas governed Brazil almost continuously from then until 1954, though under very different regimes. He was head of the provisional government (1930–4), constitutional president (1934–7), president through a *coup d'état* (1937–45) and president by direct election (1950–4). Both in the form of state intervention in the Brazilian economy and in the social policy that 'Getúlio, Father of the Poor' devised, his legacy has dominated Brazilian political life to the present day. It was also under Vargas that industrialization became a major national aim. His suicide completed his elevation to the status of hero.

A gaucho politician

Getúlio Dornelles Vargas (1882–1954) was born into an influential family of ranchers from São Borja in the state of Rio Grande do Sul, on the Argentinian border. After a short time in the army he decided to study law and subsequently went into politics.

The Revolution of 1930

On October 3, 1930 Getúlio Vargas led a revolutionary movement heading out of Rio Grande do Sul. This band of gauchos reached Rio de Janeiro, where they managed to depose Washington Luiz, president of the corrupt and unpopular Old Republic.

From the Old Republic to dictatorship

Vargas opposed the constitution adopted in 1934 and proclaimed the Estado Novo (New State) in 1937. Under this authoritarian regime all political parties were outlawed, state autonomy was replaced by a strong centralized government and the police hunted down communists and opponents of the regime. Until 1942 Brazil openly supported the Third Reich. The regime's propaganda department (DIP) orchestrated the Vargas personality cult and promoted popular culture and interbreeding as national values.

The industrialization of Brazil

Among the aims of the Estado Novo was to secure Brazil's economic independence and develop heavy industry. In exchange for military bases in the Nordeste and for Brazil's support in World War Two, the United States lent assistance in the building of steel works in Volta Redonda. Steel production began in 1964, marking a major step forward in the establishment of the country's industrial production.

Vargas, the popular Premier

Social legislation such as the minimum wage, which was introduced in 1940, was presented to the 'workers of Brazil' as a gift from the state. The unions, controlled by the Department of Labor, organized and mobilized the working population in support of the government. May 1 (Labor Day) was a national holiday celebrated with official backing, as well as a pretext for well-ordered parades before the head of state. On May 1, 1943 a labor code – the Consolidação das Leis do Trabalho (CLT) – was issued. This made particular provision for paid holidays and also outlined a social welfare scheme. These measures contributed to Vargas' indisputable popularity.

'Returning on the arm of the people'
The image of the old dictator 'returning on the arm of the people' was the leitmotif of Vargas' presidential campaign of 1950. Although he was democratically elected, he soon faced social, economic and political problems. Comparing Vargas to an incorrigible dictator who was capable of hurling Brazil into chaos, the opposition relentlessly attacked the government and its labor minister, João Goulart ● *27*.

The death of Vargas
In August 1954 Vargas was called upon to resign. This came in response to an assassination attempt organized by Vargas' supporters on journalist Carlos Lacerda, one of the president's most virulent opponents. To forestall a *coup d'état* Vargas shot himself through the heart in his bedroom in the Palácio de Catete ▲ *139*, at dawn on August 24, 1954. In a suicide note to the people of Brazil Vargas described his death as a sacrifice for the nation's freedom. His suicide provoked an intensely emotional reaction. As huge crowds gathered along the route of his funeral cortege, protesters stoned the newspaper offices and headquarters of the opposition, whom they held responsible for Vargas' death.

Today Portuguese is spoken by 10 million people in Portugal and 160 million in Brazil. Although Brazilians and Portuguese speak basically the same language, in Brazil it has been enriched with variations introduced over the centuries. This variant of Portuguese is the official language of Brazil's vast territory.

Brazilian Portuguese

In terms of accent and pronunciation, Portuguese as it is spoken in Portugal, its country of origin, and in Brazil has evolved in different directions according to widely disparate contexts and influences. Differences in Brazilian Portuguese, which are particularly apparent in the spoken language and in regional expressions, are mainly the result of the influx of slaves and immigrants ● *34*.

Tupi influence

The evolution of the Brazilian variant of the language began when Portuguese colonists came into close contact with the native people. Tupí words are applied to certain plants and animals, such as *ipê*: (green ebony), jacaranda, *maracujá* (passion fruit), *abacaxi* (pineapple), *tatu*: (armadillo) and *jacaré* (caiman). Also of Tupí origin is the prefix *ita* (stone), as in Itatiaia and Itacolomi, and the suffixes *açu* (big) and *mirim* (small), as in Iguaçu and Parati-mirim. Some first names (such as Iracema and Iara) and names of towns (Ubatuba and Caraguatatuba) are also of Tupí origin.

Recent developments

In Brazilian Portuguese new words and new meanings for existing words are constantly developing to express the great diversity of regional customs, such as carnivals, dances, street theater and religious festivals, and key events in the country's social, political and economic life. Spread by the press and television, new expressions, many of them humorous, become common currency throughout the country. Active in this diffusion are the *telenovelas* ● *60*, which tend to set a nationwide standard for the Portuguese spoken in Brazil today.

African influence

Of the many African languages spoken by slaves brought to Brazil, two influenced Brazilian Portuguese particularly strongly. Yoruba, spoken by the African tribes from around the Bight of Benin, has contributed terms associated with religion, lending such words as *candomblé* (a traditional African religious ceremony), *orixás* (the gods of this religion), Iemanjá (a sea goddess), Xangô (god of fire and thunder) and Exu (the devil). Yoruba also suffuses the terminology of Bahian African cuisine, providing such words as *acarajés* (black bean fritters) and *azeite de dendé* (palm oil). The second African language that influenced Brazilian Portuguese is Kimbundu, spoken by the Bantu peoples of Angola and the Congo. From Kimbundu come words associated with life on the *fazenda* ● *68* – *senzala* (slave house) and *engenho de bangüê* (sugar-cane mill) – and terms that have entered the everyday vocabulary: *moleque* (kid), *caçula* (youngest member of a family), *cochilar* (to doze) and samba ● *51*.

Arts and traditions

Immigrant family in Rio Grande do Sul.

Through a long process of interbreeding, the population of Brazil has evolved from its Native American, European and African roots into an ethnically diverse nation. Scattered across a vast area, the ethnic and cultural mix of Brazil's population also has a wide geographical span, its great diversity accentuated by distinct regional environments. Against this background the country's ethnic diversity has been officially recognized and appreciated. This is especially the case since the 1930s, when Brazil had emerged as an independent nation seeking to establish its own national identity. The federal and idealist concept of racial democracy that resulted from this situation is reflected in the fact that such popular cultural elements and events as the samba ● *51*, the Rio Carnival ● *46*, soccer ● *58* and the dish known as *feijoada* ● *62* have been elevated to the status of national symbols.

INTERBREEDING

The program of national integration initiated by Getúlio Vargas ● *36* in the 1930s aimed to make the most of racial interbreeding, the country's greatest and most positive characteristic. This led to Brazil being held up as the 'country of racial democracy'. The half-caste as a central figure of Brazilian society had already been extolled in romantic literature. No member of Brazilian society was held in higher esteem or inspired greater flights of fancy than the *mulata*, the half-caste woman. Embodying the physical appearance, the qualities and the dynamism of her diverse ancestry, the *mulata* epitomized the sensuality and strength of character of the archetypal Brazilian woman.

LAND OF A THOUSAND FACES

Pardo, *moreno*, *caboclo*, *sarará* and *mulato* are just some of the numerous terms that are used to describe the great variety of shades in the multicolored Brazilian nation. These terms reflect the extent and depth of the ethnic mix that has taken place between peoples originating from all over the world. In various forms this racial diversity is found throughout Brazil's extensive territory.

European immigration

In the late 19th century waves of emigrants left Europe, those heading for Brazil becoming much more numerous after the abolition of slavery ● *34*. The impulse for this emigration had two main causes: while manpower was needed for the economic exploitation of Brazil's vast territory, land shortages, hardship and famine had struck certain European countries. Influenced by the ideas of French ethnologist and diplomat Joseph-Arthur Gobineau and the theories of 'biological racism' inherited from Europe, successive Brazilian regimes and governments hoped to implant a white Catholic population by integrating European immigrants into Brazilian society. During the industrial boom of the early 20th century, these immigrants were lured to the great industrial centers of the south with promises of work and regular pay.

Black culture is recognized

In the 20th century black people and American Indians were still confined to the lower social strata and continued to live on the margins of society. Although race remained a key social issue in Brazil it became increasingly clear that the theories of biological racism, which saw Brazil as a country with a dominant population of cultured whites, were completely at odds with reality. Culturally, spiritually and socially, the Brazilian people as a whole have a vivacity and strength of character that has its roots in the long struggle that black people have had to preserve their cultural identity. Brazil's various religions, as well as its food and its music, all bear the marks of the country's African heritage. However, they have now acquired a distinct Brazilian identity in which the various constituents of this ethnically diverse nation can be discerned.

Religion in Brazil is the product of cultural intermingling. While the theory advanced by Pernambucan sociologist Gilberto Freyre (1900–87) – that the modern Brazilian is a hybrid of American Indian, African and Portuguese descent – may not stand up to observation, just such a process of hybridization applies to religion. In Brazil popular religion involves a rare kind of creativity involving borrowing, syncretism and the addition of new elements. Despite advances made by the Pentecostal churches, the dominant religion in Brazil is still Roman Catholicism. Yet being a Catholic does not preclude the practice of other religions. The cult of saints exists alongside spiritualism, American Indian shamanism and possession cults introduced by African slaves, central to which are spiritual mediums.

THE 'ROMARIA'
The pilgrimage, or *romaria*, is a traditional aspect of religion in Brazil, especially in the Nordeste. A *romaria* usually brings together rural workers, independent farmers and women seeking the intervention of a patron saint in personal and family misfortunes.

CATHOLIC RITUALS
Brazilian Catholicism involves a variety of rituals, particularly the *lavagem* – the ritual washing of church steps (*left*) – and charismatic masses. The *lavagem*, carried out in fulfillment of a promise, was widespread in Portugal. In the church of Nosso Senhor do Bonfim ▲ *261*, in the Bahian city of Salvador, this act of penitence has assumed its own particular character since it includes pagan rituals. The charismatic movement was born of a reaction to the Pentecostal churches and can also include elements from other religious traditions.

PENTECOSTAL CHURCHES
The portrayal of non-Christian religions as demonic is one of the central tenets of the new Pentecostal churches which, in recent decades, have weakened the power of the Roman Catholic church. The IURD (Universal Church of the Reign of God), founded in Rio de Janeiro by Bishop Macedo in 1977, is a leader in this field. The mission of the IURD is to uncover the pagan gods that possess the souls of the faithful. Drawing as it does on the symbolism of Afro-Brazilian cults, its aims are paradoxical: many of its adherents espouse the spiritual world that it decries.

IEMANJÁ, GODDESS OF THE SEA
The sea goddess Iemanjá, mother of the *orixás* (African gods), is also the 'mother' of all Brazilians. She is honored as a patron saint on December 31 in Rio de Janeiro ▲ *144* and on February 2 in Salvador ▲ *258,* when offerings of flowers, perfume and bars of soap are placed on the seashore or in small boats (*above*). It is possible to gain the goddess's favor without being a member of an Afro-Brazilian cult.

'CANDOMBLÉ'
This possession cult, which orignated in the former Slave Coast of Africa, involves an initiation rite. In a sacred area (*terreiro*), where public and private rituals are held, the 'mother' (*left*) or 'father of a saint' directs the ritual activities of her or his 'son' and 'clients'. The possessed are taken over by their god during festive commemorations conducted by the master or mistress of the house.

The *capoeira* is the legacy of the African slave trade. In Brazil more than anywhere else in the world, the African diaspora was subject to an extensive interbreeding with people of other races. This was actively encouraged by the whites, who wanted to reduce the risk of slave rebellions. As a result, this section of the population had no ties other than their African origins. It was not long before they formed centers of resistance to fight against their physical and cultural oppression. This only served to strengthen deep-rooted African traditions. From this melting pot emerged the *capoeira*, an amalgam of African tribal combat, music, songs and dance. As a popular art form the *capoeira* is today one of the greatest symbols of Brazil's national identity.

SONGS

How to perform the *capoeira,* together with other knowledge linked to this ritual combat, is passed on by oral tradition. Songs (*ladainhas* or *corridos*) play an important part in this. Their subject matter is wide-ranging but often refers to former slave masters or to the age of slavery. The singer must be able to use the words of his song to increase or slow down the tempo of a combat as required. He must also ensure that those taking part in the *roda* (rondo) join in with the refrain at the appropriate moments.

MUSICAL INSTRUMENTS

In the rondo a band of percussion instruments (*below*) beats out the rhythm of the *capoeira*. During the combat the *capoeira* dancers must listen to the rhythm that is being played and perform the corresponding movements. The main instrument is the *berimbau*, consisting of a wooden bow braced with a wire string, and a calabash (gourd) that functions as a sound box. The *berimbau* is accompanied by the *pandeiro* (a sort of tambourine), the *atabaque* (a variation on the conga drum) and the *agogô* (a double metal bell).

FROM ILLEGAL PRACTICE TO NATIONAL ASSET

Precisely how the *capoeira* came into being is unknown. Originally a form of African tribal combat, it was practiced by black slaves in Brazil but was regarded as an expression of rebellion by their masters. Although performing the *capoeira* was forbidden, over the centuries it was taken up by other lower-class sections of Brazilian society, losing none of its combative elements. By the 19th century, it had become so widespread that it was officially banned. The *capoeira* was not officially reinstated until 1932, during the Vargas regime ● *36*, when it was proclaimed a national sport.

'CAPOEIRA ANGOLA' AND 'REGIONAL CAPOEIRA'
'Regional *capoeira*' was developed in Salvador (*right*), in the early 20th century, by the famous master Bimba (1899–1974). It was a new, more martial and acrobatic form of *capoeira* and had no associations with banditry. Bimba's 'academy' was the first to be officially recognized by the state and came to embody the rehabilitation of *capoeira* during the 1930s. However, seeing regional *capoeira* as a departure from the original form, traditionalists worked to keep alive their own style, which became known as '*capoeira* Angola'. Pastinha (1889–1981), a master of this art, was acknowledged as its greatest exponent.

THE 'CAPOEIRA' FOR ALL AGES
The *capoeira* seems to have crossed the social divide between the lower classes and Brazil's social elites. It is practiced by all age groups, from nursery school infants to university students, in dance schools and most especially in the street. You can watch *rodas* (rondos) performed in the streets of Rio and Salvador (*above*) and may even come across the famous master of *capoeira* Leopoldina, one of the oldest exponents of *capoeira carioca*.

'CAPOEIRA' IN THE WORLD TODAY
Capoeira is now practiced as a sport by thousands of men and women not only in Asia and America, but also in Europe, the Pacific islands and of course in Africa, where it originated.

From humble origins to national festival

In the late 19th century the Portuguese *entrudo* was displaced by a carnival exclusively for the social elite. While the rich enjoyed themselves in clubs and paraded in *corsos* of expensive cars, poorer people organized their own processions, the informal *ranchos* and *blocos carnavalescos*, which were to lead to the establishment of samba schools. Founded in Rio in the 1930s, these schools gradually became more ambitious. Their annual parade, officially recognized in 1935, reached such a size that a special venue, the Sambódromo, was built in 1984. Preparations for carnival last for nealy a year and are the work of professionals. When an *enredo* (theme) has been chosen, a *samba-enredo* contest is held and work is started on the costumes and floats.

The 'entrudo', a European legacy
The *entrudo*, a popular but unsophisticated street carnival, was imported to Brazil from Portugal in the 17th century and was banned by the authorities in the 20th century. The *entrudo* did not involve music and dance nor Venetian-style masks but was simply an excuse to shower passers-by with eggs, flour, whitewash, urine or, if they were lucky, scented water and *limões de cheiro* (fragrant lemons). This graphic scene from an *entrudo* taking place in the slave district of Rio (*below*) was painted by Jean-Baptiste Debret ● *84* in the 19th century.

The 'corso'
In 1907 a car taking the daughters of President Alfonso Pena to a carnival ball on the Avenida Central ▲ *122* started a new fashion, the *corso*. This parade of convertibles is accompanied by the throwing of streamers and confetti. Until the 1930s the *corso* was a middle-class feature of carnival.

Street carnival
Since the creation of the Banda de Ipanema in 1965, the *blocos de rua* have multiplied, and up to thousands of sympathizers gather behind a *bateria*. These informal parades – *sympatia e quasa amor* in Ipanema, *Carmelitas* in Santa Teresa – are organized as early as the second weekend before the carnival. For the schools of the second and third ranks, the authorities organize less elaborate parades outside the Sambódromo ▲ *126*, on Avenida Rio Branco ▲ *122* in the city center, and on Avenida Intendante Magalhães in the northern district of Campinho.

'La cidade do Samba'
In 2005 the city of Rio has put some buildings in the harbor district at the disposal of the 14 schools of the *grupo especial.* Each school is free to set up its own workshops there, and to create and produce shows all year round.

Financing carnival
Although Rio city council subsidizes the parades and the samba schools receive royalties from broadcasting and sales of the *sambas-enredo* CDs, most of the finance for carnival is drawn from funds generated by the *jogo do bicho*, an all-powerful albeit unofficial lottery that is usually tolerated by the authorities. The *bicheiro* (one who runs the lottery) is often president of a samba school and may also be the manager of a soccer team. However, since the mid 1990s, the various schools have been trying to get financial support from a wide range of sources, including patronage from large corporations.

The earliest samba schools
In 1928 musicians from the *bloco* Deixa Falar (Let Them Talk) gathered in the Estácio district, in the center of Rio, to celebrate carnival to the sound of a new rhythm, the samba. With a touch of irony, either by analogy with the teacher-training school nearby or out of desire for respectability, they called their *bloco* a samba school. Other schools were founded in the suburbs: Mangueira (1929), Portela (1935), Vila Isabel and Viradouro (1946), Império Serrano (1947), Beija-Flor (1948), Salgueiro (1953), Padre Miguel (1955) and Imperatriz Leopoldinense in 1959. The most recent are Tradição (1984) and Grande Rio (1988).

Preparations
Since the 1960s preparations for carnival are handled by *carnavalescos* from cultured or artistic backgrounds. They choose the *enredo* (parade theme) and submit it to the samba school composers. The winning *samba-enredo* that will be sung by thousands of participants in the parade (*left*) is chosen through a contest at the *quadra* (schools' headquarters). The rehearsals in the *quadras* (music) and in the *sambōdromo* (parades) become more intensive from December. Floats, costumes and decorations (*above* and *below*) are made in carpentry and sewing workshops in the *barracões*, often located in the city center near the parade route.

Rio's samba schools took off when the city council organized a contest to encourage competition. Parades take place from Carnival Friday through Mardi Gras, with those of the *grupo especial*, from the most prestigious schools, performed on the intervening Sunday and Monday nights. The judging is broadcast on television and a winners' parade is held on the next Saturday. Each school must incorporate certain elements in its performance: *comissão de frente* (parade leaders), *carro abre-alas* (opening wing), *mestre-sala e porta-bandeira* (dance master and flag bearer), *bateria* (percussion), *carro de som* (music float), *carros alegóricos* (floats), *alas* (wings) and *destaques* (celebrities). Marks are awarded for *bateria*, *samba-enredo*, harmony, presentation, *enredo*, allegories and decorations, costumes, *comissão de frente*, *mestre-sala e porta-bandeira* and *conjunto*.

'DESTAQUES'

The *destaques* are celebrities who, perched on the floats, are there simply to be admired. Selected for their glamor and their fame, the *destaques* include public figures, television stars and top models as well as famous people from the world of the arts, sport and showbusiness, and members of the jet set.

'COMISSÃO DE FRENTE'

This group, the 'board of directors', originally comprised ten to fifteen VIPs including founder members or veterans of the school who belong to the *Velha Guarda* (old guard). They are sometimes dressed in the *maneira tradicional*, wearing dinner jackets and top hats, or alternatively dressed in the *maneira adequada*, wearing costumes in keeping with the *enredo*, or carnival theme. The *comissão*, who leads the parade, must win the approval of the crowd, greeting the onlookers 'in a pleasant, polite and friendly manner'. Today the *comissão de frente* is usually replaced by a dance routine commissioned from a renowned choreographer.

FLOATS IN THE PARADE

Like everything else at the Rio Carnival since the 1970s, the floats seem to get larger every year. They consist of polystyrene or fiberglass structures mounted on truck chassis, which are completely invisible. Each float has a specific function. The *carroabre-alas* (leading float) displays the title of the *enredo* (theme) in giant letters, while the *carros alegoricos* illustrate the carnival theme. On the *carro de som* (music float) the *puxadores*, accompanied by musicians (and relayed by loudspeakers), perform the *samba-enredo*, so that those in the different *alas* (parts of the procession) can maintain the correct pitch and rhythm of the music.

'MESTRE-SALA' AND 'PORTA-BANDEIRA'
The *mestre-sala*, a male dance master, and the *porta-bandeira*, a female flag bearer *(left)* are essential elements of the parade. The couple carry the colors of their samba school and must dance with 'grace, agility and dignity'.

'ALA DAS BAIANAS'
The number and nature of the various *alas* depends on the size of each school and the theme of its parade. Each school must, however, feature a children's *ala (ala dos meninos* or *ala mirim*) and an *ala das Baianas* (*left*), honoring the elderly women of Bahia who developed the genre of the samba in Rio in the early years of the 20th century ● *51*. The simplicity of their traditional costume and the elegance of their slow, almost priestly movements are in keeping with the respect they inspire.

'ALA DA BATERIA'
In the event of a tie between two contestants, it is the *ala da bateria* (percussionists' wing) that determines which school is the eventual winner. Conducted by a *diretor de bateria*, this wing may comprise as many as three hundred skilled percussionists. At the rear the *surdos* (*surdo de marcação* and *surdo de repique*) mark time with *taróis*. At the front are the musicians playing smaller instruments such as the *tamborim*, *chocalho*, *pandeiro*, *reco-reco*, *agogô* and *cuíca*, *ganzá* (*left*).

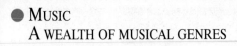

'Pagode'
Since the mid-1980s informal Sunday meetings of *sambistas* (samba performers) in the suburbs of Rio have become increasingly popular. At its best, the *pagode* is a development of the traditional *partido alto,* based on a strong percussion part and a series of improvizations. At its worst it is an unsophisticated yet commercially successful type of samba, like the *sambão* of the 1970s. Either way the *pagode* is an undeniable source of enjoyment among certain sections of the urban lower classes and a source of profit for record companies. The main innovation brought by the *pagode* is the introduction of the easily transportable banjo and tom-tom (*left*). The *pagode* market is overcrowded, but Almir Guineto, the irreverent Zeca Pagodinho and the late Jovelina Pérola Negra are noteworthy exponents of the genre.

Of all forms of artistic expression current in Brazil, it is music that has the widest audience. People from all walks of life are able to sing hundreds of refrains in chorus and in tune. These refrains are living archives of the collective memory, treasures of lyric poetry and political satire, chronicles of daily life and election songs, sporting anthems and recipes. Famous singers and musicians past and present are part of the national pantheon and the object of national pride. Formed in the crucible of ethnic cross-fertilization and metaphorical cannibalism, the popular music of Brazil is for ever evolving and always at the cutting edge. It is widely seen as one of the most important musical cultures in the world. Unfortunately much of the music broadcast by local radio stations is of a lesser quality.

'AXÉ MUSIC'
In the late 1980s the term *axé music* or *música de axé* was applied to the commercial pop music of Bahia, played by more or less sophisticated artistes and groups (*right*), and to which people danced during Carnival ▲ *272*. With her pleasing voice and engaging repertoire, Daniela Mercury is recognized as the most accomplished exponent of *axé-music*.

'FORRÓ'
At dances in the Nordeste ▲ *252* and in regions with a high percentage of *Nordestino* immigrants ▲ *227*, the *forró* is danced to the sound of the *sanfona* (accordion). In the 1940s, singer, composer and accordionist Luiz Gonzaga (1912–89) (*below*) popularized the basic syncopated rhythm of the *forró* (the *baião*) and established it as a musical genre. His famous *Asa Branca*, about a migratory bird from the Nordeste, is not only a beautiful metaphor but also a classic Brazilian song.

SAMBA
The origins of the samba (an African word) lie in the secular and religious gatherings that were held, often clandestinely, by Bahian women living in the poor districts of Rio in the early decades of the 20th century. One such was the famous Tia Ciata. With Noel Rosa (1910–37, *below*), born into a middle-class family in Vila Isabel, the genre took a decisive turn: Rosa was an inspired writer of lyrical, satirical and philosophical sambas. The 1940s and 1950s saw the development of the *samba-canção*, a slow, melancholy variant that existed alongside the *samba de carnaval*, which is associated with dancing. Today's great *sambistas* include Paulinho da Viola, Martinho da Vila and Nelson Sargento (*bottom*).

'CHORO'
Originating in Rio in the late 19th century, the *choro* or *chorinho*, which grew out of the appropriation and reinterpretation of the waltzes, polkas and mazurkas that black slaves heard in their masters' drawing rooms. The *choro*, which is still popular with amateur and professional musicians in Brazil today, is played by a basic trio of flute, guitar and *cavaquinho* (an instrument similar to a ukulele), to which can be added a *pandeiro* (tambourine), clarinet, saxophone, trumpet and vocals. Pixinguinha (1897–1973), a flautist, saxophonist, arranger and band leader (*drawing, far left*), wrote some great *choro* classics. His *Carinhoso* is taken up as a refrain at all *rodas de choro*.

Marisa Monte, Milton Nascimento and Chico Buarque (*opposite*).

Like the *choro* and the samba, *bossa nova* developed in Rio but, unlike its prestigious forerunners, it originated in the city's smart Zona Sul district. Emerging in the late 1950s, it was the result of a melding of jazz and *samba* brought about by the classically trained pianist and composer Antônio Carlos Jobim, the lyricist Vinícius de Moraes and an exceptional musician, João Gilberto. From a dissident element of *bossa nova* developed the more committed *canção de protesto* (protest song). Song festivals organized by national television in the 1960s brought into the limelight such artistes as Chico Buarque de Holanda, Milton Nascimento, Jorge Ben Jor and *tropicalismo*. This generation of gifted composers, whose music appealed particularly to students, was dubbed MPB (*música popular brasileira*) by purists.

CHICO BUARQUE DE HOLANDA

Born in 1944 into a cultured family, Chico Buarque de Holanda came to fame at the 1966 MPB festival with *A Banda* (The Band), which was placed equal first with *Disparada*, a *canção de protesto* by Geraldo Vandré. A sensitive and accomplished songwriter, Chico Buarque de Holanda is a musician in the mainstream of the best Brazilian tradition. He is also committed to just causes, and songs such as *Construção*, (Construction), *Apesar de você* (In Spite of You) and *O que será* (What Will Be) ensure his universal popularity.

'BOSSA NOVA'

The lyrics of *bossa nova*, on such themes as a girl from Ipanema, the Corcovado ▲ *151*, a lover's tiff over the words of a song and the delicious pain of heartache, reflect the carefree life enjoyed by wealthy Brazilians during the Kubitschek era ● *26*. Many lyrics were written by the poet Vinícius de Moraes.

MILTON NASCIMENTO

A native of Minas Gerais, Milton Nascimento is one of the most highly rated Brazilian artistes both at home and abroad. He has an exceptionally fine voice and his music – with elements of jazz, Beatles influence, Brazilian rhythms, the folklore of Minas Gerais and classical and religious music – has a universal appeal.

Three of the great names in *bossa nova* hold an admiring audience in thrall. *From left to right*: Luís Bonfá who, with Tom Jobim, produced the soundtrack of *Orfeu Negro*; João Gilberto, a singer and guitarist renowned for his whispering and innovative *batida* (off-beat rhythm); and Tom Jobim, creator of outstandingly sophisticated harmonies.

Female singers
From Carmen Miranda to Elizete Cardoso, Nana Caymmi, Elza Soares and Marisa Monte, Brazil has had no shortage of great female vocalists. Elis Regina (1945–82), from Rio Grande do Sul, began her career in Rio in the era of *bossa nova*, and her eclectic range, incorporating many other genres,

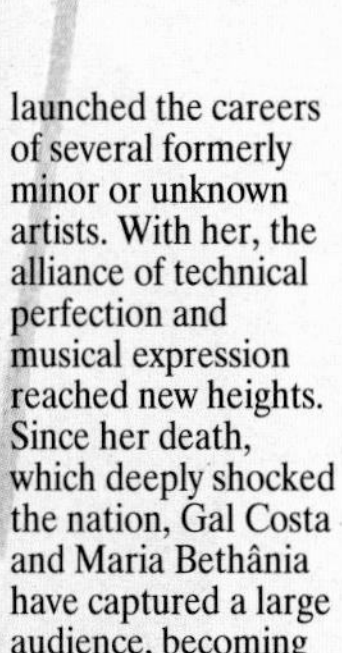

launched the careers of several formerly minor or unknown artists. With her, the alliance of technical perfection and musical expression reached new heights. Since her death, which deeply shocked the nation, Gal Costa and Maria Bethânia have captured a large audience, becoming two of Brazil's most popular female singers.

'Tropicalismo'
The second MPB festival held by TV Record in 1967 brought to fame Caetano Veloso and Gilberto Gil, two *baianos* based in São Paulo and both born in 1942. Their style is a skillful combination of international pop and traditional Brazilian rhythms. With a group of poets, musicians, movie directors and sculptors, they launched *tropicalismo,* a style that created a few shockwaves. The movement's flagship album *Tropicália* (1968) with its 'family photo' sleeve (*right*) acquired cult status. Featured are (*left to right, standing)* Sérgio and Arnaldo Batista on either side of Rita Lee (members of rock group Os Mutantes), and composer Tom Zé; (*seated*) arranger Rogério Duprat, Caetano Veloso (holding the portrait of Nara Leão), Gal Costa and the poet Torquato Neto; (*seated front*) Gilberto Gil with the photo of lyricist Capinam.

The new generation
Over the last twenty years Brazilian music has been devoid of the dynamism and originality of earlier times. The future, however, looks promising. While rock, with such bands as Paralamas do Sucesso, Titãs and Legião Urbana, has developed mainly in Rio, São Paulo and Brasília, new talent is currently emerging from the Nordeste with Chico Science, Lenine, Chico César and Zeca Baleiro. Carlinhos Brown, whose musical background is steeped in *baiano* rhythms and who is leader of the band Timbalada, has produced a striking fusion of Brazilian, African and Caribbean music.

Folk traditions of the Nordeste

The popular culture of the Nordeste region is delightfully original and diverse. It is found in markets and souvenir stores, in the booklets known as *folhetos de feira* and in the woodcuts decorating their front covers, as well as in bars and at festivals, where improvised contests between two *cantadores* (singers) accompanied by their *viola* (guitars) take place. Iberian and Mediterranean heritage is very much in evidence, as in the so-called 'dramatic dances', but there are also elements of African and American Indian culture. The major festivals of the year are Christmas, with *reisados* and other *bumba-meu-boi*, Carnival, celebrated in Salvador and Olinda, and Midsummer's Day, feted especially in the interior.

Festa Junina
The feasts of Saint John, Saint Anthony and Saint Peter, held in June, are the Nordeste region's major festivals. Originating in European rural tradition, these festivals (*left*) are the major celebrations held in the *sertão* ▲ *254*, especially in years when rainfall had been abundant and there is plenty of maize to make the traditional dishes, *canjica*, *pamonha* and *cuscus*. Square dancing is accompanied by small country bands consisting of an accordion, triangle and drum.

'Literatura de cordel'

Literatura de cordel is the collective term for chapbooks (*folhetos de feira*). These are small-format booklets of 8 to 16 pages *(above)*, printed on poor-quality paper and sold in thoroughfares and in public places, such as streets, markets and bus stations. Their name derives from the fact that they were originally sold by chapmen or pedlars. The rhymes that they contain (they are always in verse) are reminiscent of *cantoria* and their themes include tragic or comic events of the present day or traditional tales of fantasy, chivalry and heroism.

Woodcuts The woodcuts that once graced the covers of *folhetos* are no longer restricted to this medium. Now seen in art galleries, many are today produced not by folk craftsmen but by an educated class of artists using a variety of styles. The images are clearly depicted and thickly drawn, with subtle effects created by the skillful use of various materials. Pernambuco and Ceará have several talented popular engravers, including J. Borges, José Costa Leite and Dila.

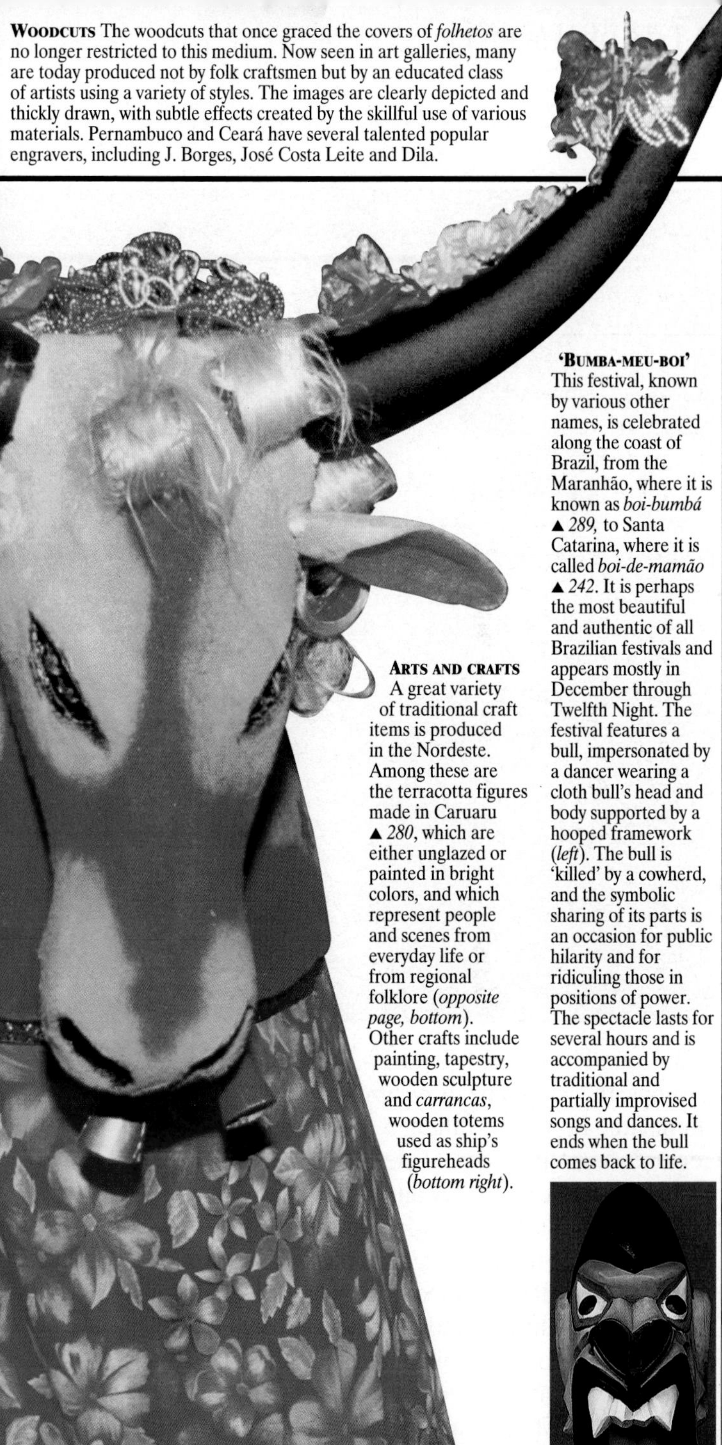

'Bumba-meu-boi'
This festival, known by various other names, is celebrated along the coast of Brazil, from the Maranhão, where it is known as *boi-bumbá* ▲ *289,* to Santa Catarina, where it is called *boi-de-mamão* ▲ *242*. It is perhaps the most beautiful and authentic of all Brazilian festivals and appears mostly in December through Twelfth Night. The festival features a bull, impersonated by a dancer wearing a cloth bull's head and body supported by a hooped framework (*left*). The bull is 'killed' by a cowherd, and the symbolic sharing of its parts is an occasion for public hilarity and for ridiculing those in positions of power. The spectacle lasts for several hours and is accompanied by traditional and partially improvised songs and dances. It ends when the bull comes back to life.

Arts and crafts
A great variety of traditional craft items is produced in the Nordeste. Among these are the terracotta figures made in Caruaru ▲ *280*, which are either unglazed or painted in bright colors, and which represent people and scenes from everyday life or from regional folklore (*opposite page, bottom*). Other crafts include painting, tapestry, wooden sculpture and *carrancas*, wooden totems used as ship's figureheads (*bottom right*).

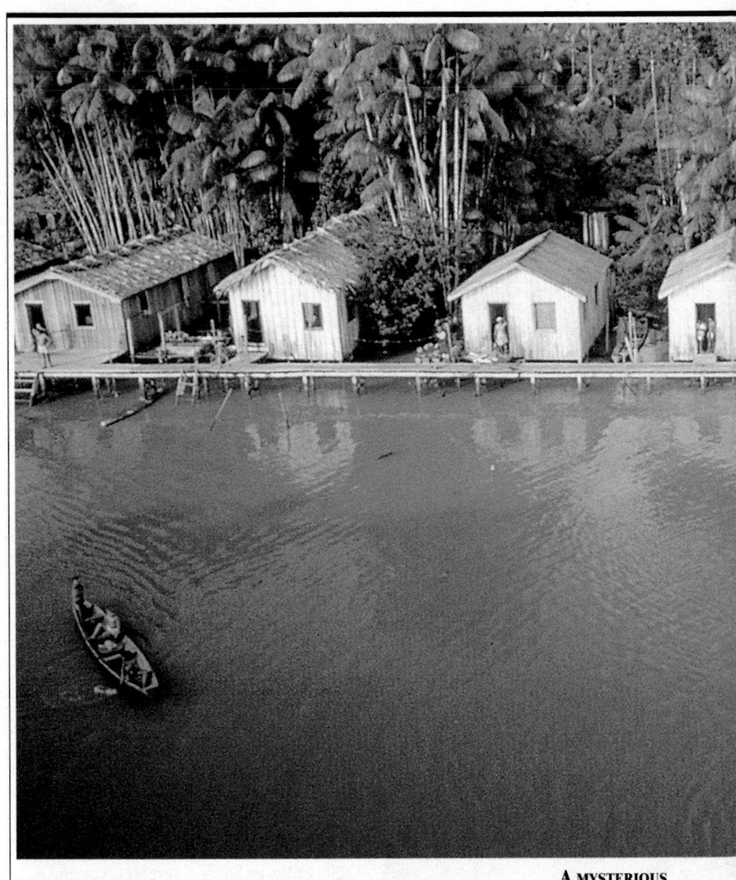

With countless rivers, tributaries, lakes and swamps, the landscape of Amazonia is dominated by water. Although the water in this region is sometimes crystal-clear, it is more often black and acidic or muddy and rich in nutrients. The Amazon starts below Manaus, where the black waters of the Rio Negro join those of the muddy, yellow Rio Solimões. The slow-moving waters of the Amazon and its tributaries are populated by hundreds of animal species, some still undocumented. These watercourses also provide those who live along their banks with a means of transport, trade and therefore survival. The *caboclos*, people of mixed white and American Indian descent, have adapted their lifestyles to the river in all its seasonal guises, living by the riches it has to offer.

A MYSTERIOUS WATERY WORLD
When water levels rise, the *caboclos* living on the banks of the Amazon are cut off. Their only source of food at these times is fishing but this is a perilous occupation as many dangerous aquatic or amphibious animals lurk in the waters. The *caboclos* also have to beware of the *cobra grande* (giant cobra), the *cavalo marinho* (sea horse) and *botos encantados* ▲ 303 (pink dolphins), those real or imaginary denizens of the deep that snatch men and women and carry them off into their enchanted watery world.

RIVERBANK 'CABOCLA' HOUSES
Annual periods of high water affect the *caboclos* living along the riverbanks. They occur in the summer months of both the northern and the southern hemispheres: November–April in the south and May–October in the north. Because of this the *caboclos* build their houses on piles made of rot-proof wood, with palm fronds or corrugated iron for the roofs. These building techniques have been introduced into towns and cities by *caboclos* who settle in low-lying urban areas (*baixadas* in Belém) or in areas near rivers (*beiradões* in Manaus).

FISHING ON THE AMAZON
Nets, hoop nets and various other traps are used to catch small species of fish such as *tambaquis* and *pacus*. The American Indians also catch fish with a bow and arrow and by a method known as *timbó*. This involves blocking off an inlet of the river and beating the water with the stems of lianas that are poisonous to fish. The sap thus released asphyxiates the fish, which are then taken from the water and threaded onto sticks by the gills. Turtles, caimans and manatees or *peixe-boi* ▲ *307* are also hunted. Larger animals such as the manatee and *piraruc*u are killed with a harpoon (*left*). Fishing is the main source of protein for the inhabitants of towns and cities along the Amazon, but as it becomes more intensive it is threatening many species of turtle as well as populations of manatee and fish such as the *pirarucu*.

SHIPPING ON THE AMAZON
For large-tonnage cargo ships the Amazon ▲ *294* is navigable from its mouth as far upriver as Iquitos, in Peru, a distance of 2,485 miles. As well as ocean-going cargo ships, all kinds of vessels ply this extensive river network. Craft on the Amazon and its tributaries include the lateen-sail dugouts of the *caboclos*, the boats of the American Indians – canoes propelled by paddles – motorized boats with palm houses (*right*), coasters with rounded prows carrying people and cargos of goods, and the barges that the *garimpeiros* (gold diggers) use to work the riverbed. When they are moored together in the ports of Belém ▲ *298*, Manaus ▲ *310* and other towns and cities along the Amazon, these boats form floating villages.

IN THE STREET AND ON THE BEACH
In Brazil soccer is played in the street, on 'sand lots' and on wasteland rather than on grass pitches. It is played everywhere by teams of all ages. For the younger generation, for whom Romário is a role model, it also offers a chance to escape the poverty of the *favelas*.

Soccer, the national sport, occupies a central place in Brazilian society. Like the country's language, it is also a multifaceted phenomenon. The game was introduced to Brazil in the early 20th century by sailors of Britain's Royal Navy when they put in at such ports as Rio de Janeiro, Santos (the future 'coffee port') and Rio Grande in the south. However it was not until twenty years later that Brazil's youth took an interest in this new sport from the English-speaking world. Its popularity increased with the involvement of the descendants of slaves and of the growing Italian, Polish and German communities that had settled in São Paulo, Curitiba and Porto Alegre respectively. The first soccer championship in Brazil was held in São Paulo on the eve of World War One. The country did not win its first South American championship until 1919 and its first World Cup until 1958. Today Brazil is the only country to have won the World Cup five times.

GARRINCHA (1933–83), THE LITTLE SPARROW
Pelé, who was named 'Athlete of the Century' in 1980, is the most famous Brazilian soccer player ever. But for the *carioca* supporters lucky enough to see him play in the 1960s Garrincha was in a class of his own. Although one of his legs was deformed and shorter than the other, this unrivaled dribbler broke through all defenses. With his shortened stride, he would encourage the opposing defenders to attack him, sell them a dummy by passing (usually to the right) and then aim with surgical precision for the foot or head of his center-forward. Manuel dos Santos, popularly known as Garrincha (tropical sparrow), was a natural genius, with a style that was simple but deadly. He won Brazil the 1962 World Cup virtually singlehanded.

TITLES
Brazil has won more world soccer titles than any other country. The Brazilian team, the *Seleção,* is the only team to have competed in each World Cup since it began in 1930 and to have won it five times. Brazil won in Sweden (1958) and Chile (1962) with Garrincha, Pelé (*left*), Didi, Zagallo and Nilton Santos. With Tostão, Rivelino, Carlos Alberto, Gerson and Pelé, Brazil won again in 1970 and was permanently awarded the Jules Rimet Trophy (awarded 1930–70). Romário led them to their fourth trophy win (now the World Cup) in the USA, in 1994. Ronaldo (*top*) was the indisputed star of their fifth World Cup title win, in Japan in 2002.

MARACANÃ – ESTÁDIO MÁRIO FILHO ▲ *131*

When Brazil was chosen to host the first postwar World Cup the authorities threw themselves wholeheartedly into preparations. President Dutra decided that the largest stadium in the world should be built. Covering 46 acres and built with the labor of 10,000 people, this magnificent concrete complex can hold 180,000 spectators. Filled with a crowd of characteristically vocal supporters, the stadium becomes like an active volcano as shouts erupt from a craterlike bowl filled with brightly colored shirts, banners and flags. For soccer fans, Macaranã, named for the beautiful tropical bird prized by the American Indians, is a magical, Dantesque, heavenly and devilish place. Without Macaranã Brazilian soccer would not be what it is today.

SOCCER SUPPORTERS

Having the status of an art, soccer is part of Brazil's social fabric. It has a massive following and the two top teams, Flamengo ▲ *141* in Rio and Corinthians in São Paulo, draw crowds of fanatical supporters. Each group of supporters, or *torcida*, has its own chairman and directors. Some *torcidas* – such as Jovem Fla (Young Flamengo) and Gaviões da Fiel (Sparrowhawks of the Faithful), who support Corinthians – make long coach journeys to see their teams. Their club helps with transport and contributes to the cost of buying banners, smoke bombs and percussion instruments that the *torcidas* use to create the magic and atmosphere of Carnival among the enthusiastic crowd.

The *telenovela*, or 'televised novel', broadcast on television and watched by millions every day, is the most popular narrative genre in Brazil. Taking a novelistic form, it combines the melodrama of soap opera with such ageless themes as love and loss, and incorporates elements from literature and aspects of current events. In the *telenovela* fact and fiction are closely intertwined so that urban and rural life are chronicled in a new way. Whereas the movies generally take extraordinary stories as their theme, the *telenovela* portrays reality in fictional form by dramatizing everyday events or by making the minutiae of ordinary life part of the drama. Since the demise of TV Manchete (1998), TV Globo, is the only channel to produce *telenovelas* on a regular basis. SBT and Record prefer to broadcast Mexican dramas.

JANETE CLAIR
This television scriptwriter, who had her first success in 1970–1, is regarded as Brazil's leading writer of *telenovelas*. Janete Clair skillfully gave the melodramatic aspect of the genre (a trait particularly associated with Cuban and Mexican *telenovelas*) a Brazilian flavor. For many years and until her death, Clair and her husband, Dias Gomes, were the most highly regarded couple in the world of television drama.

'PANTANAL'
In *Pantanal*, one of the most successful soap operas broadcast on TV Manchete (a channel now no longer in existence), family dramas were set against the backdrop of large estates and the beautiful landscapes of this eponymous region in west-central Brazil, with its lush vegetation, rivers and waterfalls, cattle and wild animals ▲ *210*. It was *Pantanal* that made Marcos Palmeira *(right)* a star of the Brazilian *telenovela*.

V GLOBO: FACTS ND FIGURES

TV Globo was created in 965 by the Roberto Marinho media group. Today it has 13 subsidiaries, has a 65 percent share of the market and accounts for 75 percent of Brazilian television's advertising revenue. With 8,000 employees, TV Globo broadcasts 4,420 hours of its own productions per year (2002) and its programs are shown in 130 countries worldwide. The Projac studios, opened in 1997, occupy an area of 320 acres in the Jacarepaguá district of Rio de Janeiro.

A Brazilian technique

Shooting the episodes of a *telenovela* a few days before they are due to be broadcast means they can reflect current events. TV soaps provide a forum for debate that influences various aspects of everyday life by launching new fashions, including new words and expressions, discussing current events and promoting public information campaigns. TV Globo broadcasts four *telenovelas* a day, including (*from top to bottom*): *Esperança*, *Sabor da Paixão* and *Mulheres Apaixonadas*.

Fiction and fact

On February 25, 2003 Brazilian television launched a major first. Rio had just experienced an exceptional day of violence – an unprecedented trial of strength in which drug dealers put store keepers out of business and set fire to buses in order to paralyze the city. At 6pm the author of *Mulheres Apaixonadas* (Passionate Women) decided to adapt a scene in that evening's episode to incorporate the information broadcast on radio. Viewers who saw the day's events reported on the 8 o'clock news were surprised to hear them discussed in the episode of *Mulheres Apaixonadas* broadcast just one hour later.

'CAIPIRINHA'
A *caipirinha* is a cocktail made with *cachaça* ● *64*, lime, sugar and crushed ice.

The dish known as *feijoada* is thought to have originated in the kitchens of *senzalas* (slave houses) during Brazil's colonial period, when it consisted of *feijões pretos* (black beans) and scraps of meat left over from slave masters' meals. With a few regional variations, *feijoada* is today Brazil's national dish. In Rio it is served as a traditional Saturday lunch, a social event which has its own particular ritual. As music plays in the background, *caipirinhas* (*cachaça* cocktails) and ice-cold beers (*cervejas estupidamente geladas*) are served with *pestiscos* (appetizers), so as to create a convivial atmosphere until everyone has arrived. Guests need not be too punctual, however, as on such occasions *feijoada* is usually not served until mid-afternoon.

INGREDIENTS (SERVES 10–12)
5 cups black beans
2¼ lb dried beef
½ lb pig's ears and tails (optional)
2 pig's trotters (optional)
1 lb pork sausages
2–3 smoked sausages
1¼ lb pork chops or smoked shoulder
1 lb salted pork (fillet or neck)
½ lb bacon
5 cups rice
10 *couve* leaves (greens)
7 cups cassava flour
8 oranges
3 limes
1 bunch of coriander (cilantro)
1 red chili pepper
1 cup of olive oil
a few bay leaves
parsley
4 cloves of garlic
4 onions
salt
butter or margarine

1. Prepare a day in advance by soaking the black beans and the salted and dried meats in separate containers. Change the water several times so as to draw out the salt.

2. The next day, drain the meat and cut it into chunks, removing any fat. Put all the chunks into a pan of water and boil until cooked.

3. Simmer the beans in a large pot of water for 1 hour. Add the dried meats, offal, bacon and pork. Cook for a further 45 minutes. Add the sausages, two cloves of crushed garlic, two chopped onions, the bay leaves and coriander. Simmer for 1 hour.

4. Wash the *couve* and cut them into strips by rolling them up and slicing them (*above*). Put them in a sieve and rinse them with boiling water, then drain.

5. Heat some of the olive oil in a pan and brown the *couve*, together with two cloves of crushed garlic. Stir for a few minutes. Cover and simmer for 5 minutes.

6. Cook the rice.

7. Prepare the *farofa*. Brown the cassava flour for a few minutes in butter or margarine, stirring to prevent it from burning. Add the chopped parsley (and raisins and black olives if required). Mix well.

8. Prepare the sauce. Mix the juice of three limes with two chopped onions, a generous handful of parsley, some of the crushed chili (the amount varying according to its piquancy), olive oil and 2–3 cups of meat and bean stock. Season to taste.

9. Serve the *feijoada* accompanied, in separate dishes, by the *farofa*, the rice, the chopped *couve*, the sauce and six oranges cut into pieces. The *feijoada* will be lighter if you add the juice of two oranges before serving it.

'LANCHONETES' AND 'BARRACAS'
These little stalls, where you can enjoy a *suco* or a snack, are found everywhere on the streets of Brazil.

'GOIABADA'
This fruit jelly (*doce*), made with guava (*goiaba*), is often eaten with cheeses from Minas Gerais ▲ *197*. There is also a *cocada* (sweetened coconut) flavor and a *bananada* (banana) flavor.

GUARANÁ
The powder extracted from the berries of this Amazonian shrub is believed to have energizing properties.

DRINKS
Brazilians love *sucos* (fruit juices), *refrigerantes* (sodas), especially Guaraná, and *cervejas* (beers) served *bem geladas* (well chilled) in 600ml bottles or *chopp* (draught).

'DOCE DE LEITE'
This preserve made with milk is very popular in Minas Gerais. It is also eaten with cheese.

'CACHAÇA'
Cachaça, also known as *pinga* or *aguardente*, is a spirit made from cane sugar. There are many different brands, each varying quality and different taste. *Cachaça*, drunk throughout Brazil, is also used to make *caipirinhas* ● *62* and *batidas* (fruit-based cocktails).

'MATE'
Mate ▲ *233,* a hot drink, is an institution in Rio Grande do Sul.

COFFEE
Brazilians like their coffee (*cafezinho*) very hot and sweet.

FOOD
Cassava flour (*farinha*), black beans (*feijão*) and rice (*arroz*) are staples of the Brazilian diet. Coconut milk is used in the cuisine of coastal in the Nordeste.

Architecture

DÉCOR. Wood carvings were a dominant feature of the elaborate architectural and artistic decoration of Jesuit churches.

During the 17th and 18th centuries, in the extensive border territories between Portuguese and Spanish colonial territory, the Jesuits established villages where they encouraged Guaraní American Indians to settle. These villages, known as *aldeias* or *pueblos*, soon grew into towns, each of around 7,000 inhabitants. The style of these missions was similar to that of the settlements established on border areas where the 'civilized and Christian' territory held by Europeans ended and the 'barbaric and pagan' world of the native peoples began. The way in which these villages were planned and built is a fusion of European and indigenous cultural traditions.

FIRST PHASE: BEFORE 1680

The earliest missions to be set up by the Jesuits were laid out in a precise and well-ordered manner. Their general arrangement was much less complex than that of later missions. Based on a central square and a church around which the American Indian houses were arranged, the layout was somewhat similar to that of the indigenous villages of Amazonia, the area from which the Guaraní originated. Each dwelling was separate from the other and each housed an extended family consisting of several nuclear families.

SECOND PHASE: AFTER 1680

Missions were organized around a **central square (1)** and along an axis that ran through the square, linking the entrance to the village with the **church (2)**. This arrangement can be seen in the 18th-century plans of the villages of São João Batista and São Miguel Arcanjo ▲ *248* (*below* and *opposite*). Both the layout and the buildings were designed in the manner of a stage set, the emphasis being on façades and external appearances. The **cloister (3)**, an area reserved exclusively for the Jesuits and which contained their living quarters, was out of bounds for American Indian women. The cloister usually consisted of a square area made into a garden and surrounded by a gallery. A veranda with a tiled roof gave protection from sun and rain. The Jesuits' living quarters always contained the *armeria* (armory), a highly secure room with a loophole window and a door opening onto the cloister courtyard. Originally the king of Spain decreed that the firearms kept in the armory were to be

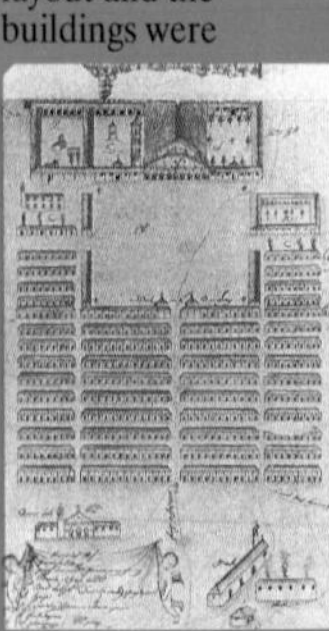

Detail of a capital (*above*).

The church (2): reconstruction of the façade of São Miguel Arcanjo ▲ *249*. On account of its size, its architecture and its position the church was the mission's focal point. The design of mission churches, rectangular basilicas with a central nave flanked by aisles, was based on that of the Jesuit church of Il Gesú, in Rome. The earliest mission churches were built of wood and brick and later of stone, with a terracotta-tile floor. The roof projected beyond the side and front walls, protecting the Guaraní faithful from sun and rain.

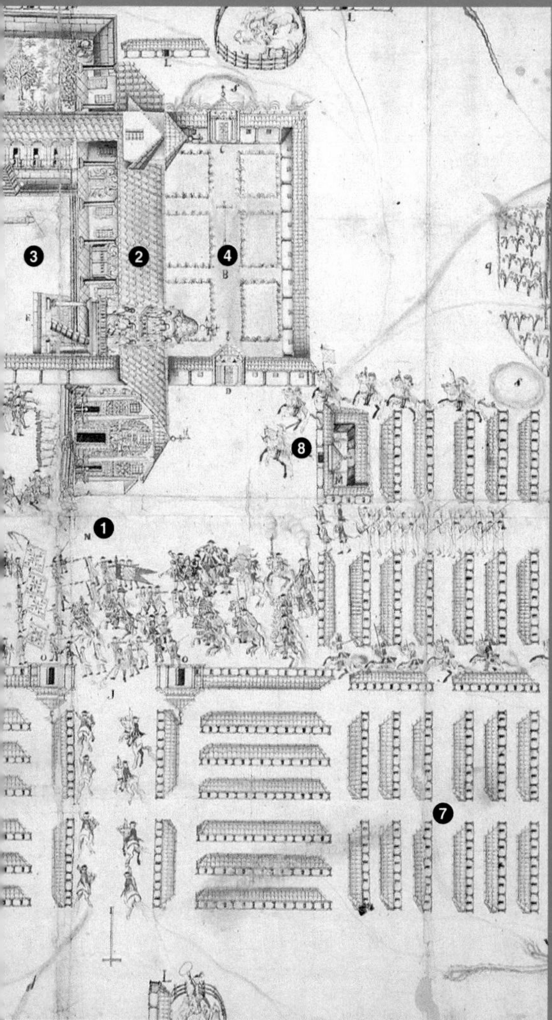

used to defend the frontier against the Portuguese. However, under attack by the Spanish and Portuguese ▲ *248*, the Guaraní joined forces with the Jesuits, using these weapons to defend the mission. The cloister of São Lourenço Mártir ▲ *249* still has its *armeria.* As in medieval monasteries the cloister adjoined the church, which in turn adjoined the **cemetery (4)**. Close to the cloister were farm buildings and **workshops (5)**. Here, wood and stone were carved, metal cast, leather tanned and fabric woven by the Guaraní, who became carpenters, weavers, armorers, sculptors, painters, potters, tanners and bakers. A central element of Jesuit missions was the **farm (6)**, which consisted of a fruit orchard, a kitchen garden and a physic garden with medicinal plants and herbs. The central square was surrounded by ***okas*** **(7)**, the rectangular houses of the Guaraní. The only house with a patio was the **cotiguaçu (8)** which accommodated widows and orphans.

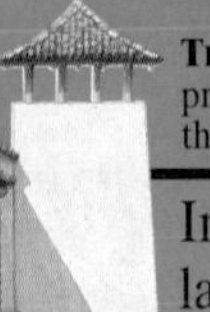

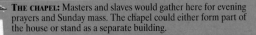

THE CHAPEL: Masters and slaves would gather here for evening prayers and Sunday mass. The chapel could either form part of the house or stand as a separate building.

In Brazil the agricultural exploitation of land on a commercial scale led to the development of *fazendas*. These large country estates comprised not only plantations but also living accommodation and agricultural buildings. *Fazendas* where sugar cane was grown were known as *engenhos*. Both sugar cane and coffee underpinned an economic system that depended on the labor of slaves working on large agricultural estates to produce a single export crop. Between about 250 and 1,000 people lived and worked on a *fazenda*.

MATERIALS

The outer walls of estate houses were originally made of a mud- or dung-based material known as *taipa* or *pau-a-pique*. Walls and foundations could also be built in stone and in the late 19th century with bricks produced on the *fazendas*. The walls were coated with *tabatinga* (a kind of clay) and were later painted yellow, blue, red or white. The upper storys were floored with boards made from Brazilian wood or with imported pitch pine.

ARCHITECTURAL STYLES OF THE 'CASA-GRANDE'

The *casa-grande* (main house) was the planter's residence and the headquarters of the *fazenda*. It was a large, thick-walled building, usually with an upper story, like the **Fazenda São Gonçalo (1)** in São Paulo. While the first floor served as a storehouse, the second contained living quarters. Some *casas-grandes*, like the **Fazenda Bocaina (2)**, in Rio, were built in the Portuguese style, sometimes with a veranda in the center of the façade, pierced by windows and reached by one or two flights of stone steps. As the *fazendas* formed closer ties with the Portuguese court in Rio, the neoclassical style was applied to the *casa-grande,* as in the **Fazenda Pau Grande (3)** in Rio. Part of the neoclassical decorative repertoire were tiles, columns, pilasters, statues and pediments.

'Fazenda' Pau d'Alho ▲ *175*

The 'casa-grande' (1)
The *casa-grande* always occupied a dominant position, usually along one side of a large rectangular area known as the *terreiro*. The gardens **(2)**, often with a ceramic pool in the center, lay in front or to the side of the *casa-grande*, while the kitchen gardens and orchards **(3)** lay at the back. Buildings set around the *casa-grande* included the chapel **(4)**, kitchens and outbuildings **(5)**, storehouses and stables **(6)**, workshops for carpentry and metalworking **(7)** and the overseer's house **(8)**.

The 'terreiro' (9)
When the coffee harvest was brought in, the coffee beans were washed and spread out to dry on the *terreiro*, a rectangular paved area similar to a large stone-flagged or tiled terrace. At the end of the day the beans were piled up into heaps and covered over to protect them from the damp night air.

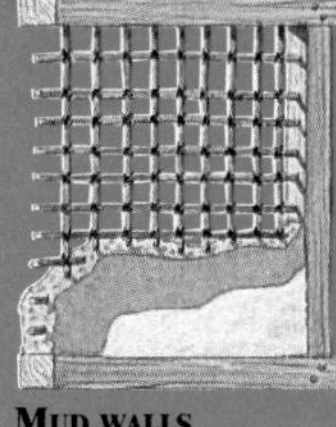

Mud walls
The walls were made from *taipa*, earth mixed with pebbles, or *pau-a-pique*, soft earth or cattle dung reinforced with lengths of bamboo.

The 'senzala' (10)
The slave house, known as the *senzala* (*above*), was built in *pau-a-pique* or brick and was often divided into rooms, with one room for each family. Pieces of wood set into the walls served as clothes hooks, the beds were made of wooden planks and there were clay pitchers for storing water. The *senzala* for unmarried male slaves was located at a distance from the main slave house and was locked at night.

Machines (11) and granary (12)
After the coffee beans had been dried, they were stored in the granary until they were hulled in hydraulic machines by means of a sieve and crusher. Slaves then gathered up the beans. From about 1880 the beans were hulled by steam-driven machines.

Décor
Some *casas-grandes* had opulent, richly furnished drawing rooms with glass chandeliers, paintings, tapestries and a piano, all imported from Europe.

Water mills (13)
Flour, the staple food on the *fazenda,* was obtained by grinding cassava and maize in water mills. The mills were often located outside the *fazenda* walls.

Baroque church architecture

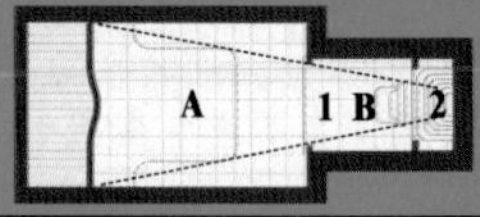

Ground plan.

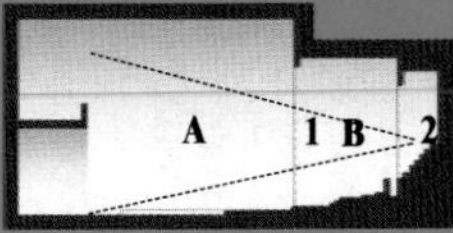

Section of elevation.

The term 'baroque' usually brings to mind an abundance of lines and outrageous proportions. However, like that of the Portuguese churches on which many of them are based, the design of baroque Brazilian churches is restrained and compact. Most have a unified interior consisting of a nave without side aisles, and have a pitched roof and no dome. The transept is barely perceptible and there is only a minimal use of scrolls on the façade. The focal point of the interior, which has a richly painted ceiling, is a large chapel (*capela-mor*) at the east end. Created with deliberate panache, this rich effect seems designed to contrast with the sober exterior. Most baroque chapels are richly decorated with *talha*, polychrome and gilt woodcarving.

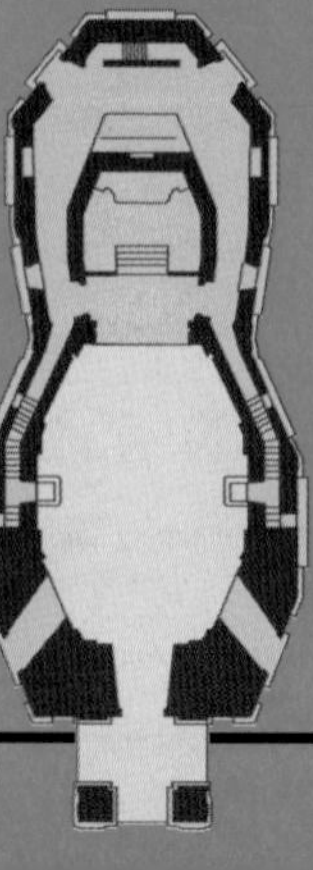

The interior
The typically Brazilian church interior is simple but dramatic in its effect. All lines converge on the high altar. The congregation look down a broad nave (A), toward the chapel, the *capela-mor* (B), at the east end. The *capela-mor* contains the presbytery (1) and high altar (2), with a table and a statue of the Madonna and Child or the patron saint.

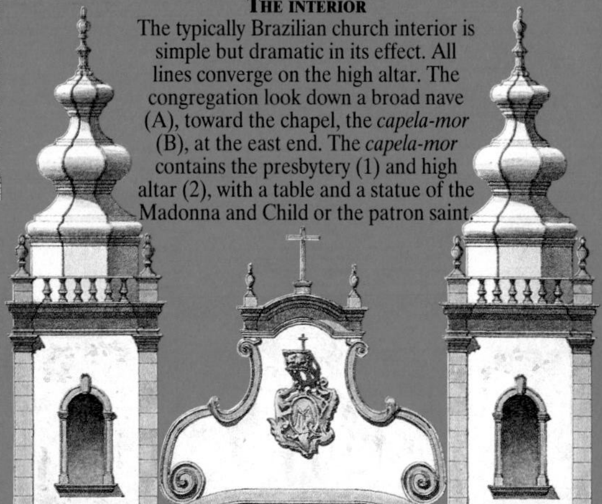

Centralized plan
The delightful Nossa Senhora da Glória do Outeiro ▲ *134*, in Rio, based on an unusual figure-of-eight plan, was Brazil's first polygonal church. Completed in 1739, its curved walls introduced Rio to the baroque style developed by Francesco Borromini in Italy and Johann Blasius Santini Aichel in Bohemia. The church has single tower at its west end and a flat roof.

The façade: N.S. dos Prazeres, Monte dos Guararapes, Recife
The presence of Franciscan friars in the Nordeste led to the development of a particular type of church (*above*). The arcaded portico emphasizes the order's tradition of welcome. The circular window has been lowered so as to give free reign to the pediment's curves and counter-curves. The towers are crowned by onion domes.

SCULPTURE
The façade of the Ordem Terceira de São Francisco in Salvador ▲ *257* exemplifies the typically baroque avoidance of undecorated space (*left*). This façade, unique in Brazil, is reminiscent of the exuberant ornamentation seen elsewhere in Latin America, particularly Mexico. The pilasters rising from the lower tier of the façade are faced by atlantes in the upper tier, where they merge with a mass of carved foliage. Under the unblinking gaze of the saints in the niches, consoles and grotesque figures carved in relief add to the exuberance. The central cross and corner finials lightly offset the overall density of the scheme.

'AZULEJOS'
The most sumptuous way of decorating churches was to hang their walls with Flemish tapestries. However the high cost of tapestries, and wars with the Dutch ● *23,* restricted their availability. An alternative took the form of panels of *azulejos*, the blue and white tiles widely used in Portugal. Tilework in the Franciscan monastery in Salvador ▲ *257* (*above* and *below*) depicts moralizing subjects published as prints in Antwerp.

'TALHA' (SÃO BENTO, RIO)
The decoration of Brazil's baroque churches owes much to the use of *talha*, or ornamental carving. The monastery church of São Bento ▲ *119* (*above*) gives an overview of the repertoire. Canopies, cabled columns, flames and acanthus leaves are juxtaposed in joyful profusion. Stylistic differences are due to the fact that a century separates the earliest *talhas* from those of the rococo high altar.

Joel, one of the twelve prophets sculpted by Aleijadinho and his studio between 1800 and 1805, is an example of the baroque sculptural style of Congonhas ▲ *192*.

The 18th century can be regarded as Brazil's golden age ● *23*, and it is in Minas Gerais that the manifestations of that age reached their greatest heights. Colonized by *bandeirantes* (adventurers), the region enjoyed great and sudden prosperity when alluvial gold was discovered there in 1695. The authorities in Lisbon, anxious to control the supply of gold, banned religious orders from the province. Although taxes were levied by the Portuguese crown, part of this wealth was invested in local projects. While lay brotherhoods of private individuals financed the construction of many churches, the municipal authorities built mints and town halls.

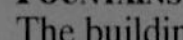

CASA DE CÂMARA E CADEIA, MARIANA ▲ *190*
The ban on the construction of monasteries and private mansions meant that public buildings, especially town halls and prisons (*above*), both of which were located next to churches, are the most typical buildings of the period. Decorative features on secular buildings consisted mostly of dressed stone steps, window arches and wrought-iron grilles.

FOUNTAINS
The building frenzy that swept Minas Gerais affected even smaller architectural features. Fountains took the form of miniature church pediments and often incorporated a saint's statue, as in the Chafariz de São José in Tiradentes ▲ *195* (*below*).

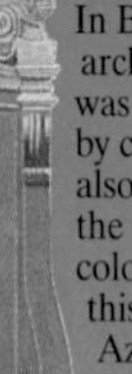

DOORS
In Brazilian baroque architecture, relief was not only created by carvings but was also brought out by the use of contrasting colors. Doors, such as this one in the Casa Azul in Sabará ▲ *183*, were often painted in bright tones, such as green, deep red and blue, which gave private residences their own distinctive character.

'MERCADO MUNICIPAL', DIAMANTINA ▲ *19*
Although the only building materials available wood, pisé and sun-dried brick, this did not pr the creation of elegant churches and other buil Diamantina market (*below*) inspired Niemey presidential palace in Brasília ▲ *208*.

NOSSA SENHORA DO ROSÁRIO DOS PRETOS, OURO PRETO ▲ *188*

This church (*right*), built by the Brotherhood of the Rosary ● *31* and based on an oval plan, is one of the most distinctive in Brazil. Behind the convex façade is a **galilee (1)** or columned portico serving as an antechamber to the **nave (2)**. This culminates in the **chapel (3)** (*capela-mor*), in which stands a fine carved altarpiece.

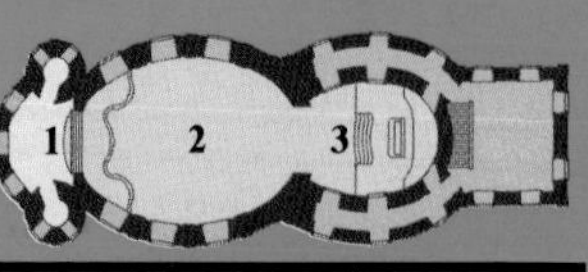

SÃO FRANCISCO DE ASSIS, OURO PRETO ▲ *188*

In the design of this church in Ouro Preto (*below*) architect Aleijadinho ▲ *181* incorporated elements of the style of Borromini. Two circular towers with obelisk finials frame the façade, emphasizing its rounded elements, which are further accentuated by the scrolls in the pediment. Between the Ionic columns on pedestals, in place of what would normally be a central circular window is a carved soapstone relief ▲ *191* of St Francis in ecstasy. The oval windows are a novel element originating in Bohemian architecture.

The house known as the Casa do Padre Inácio in Cotia, São Paulo state.

Apart from a few isolated examples, such as Salvador's *cidade baixa* (lower city) ▲ *260*, Brazilian towns and cities were not methodically laid out to an idealized plan, as were those in Spanish America. City planning in Brazil was in fact closer to the model of medieval towns. During the 17th and 18th centuries, the great baroque era, religious buildings were raised on high ground. Each church proudly stood on its own parvis, an often irregularly shaped square and a space onto which municipal buildings did not encroach. But the governor's palace and town hall also stood on their own square and housing grew up between these three major urban landmarks.

ROW HOUSES

The elegant colonial houses in the town of Ouro Preto ▲ *184* (*right*) reflect the former prosperity of Minas Gerais ● *30*. In this hilly state, where many medieval-style towns were established, early wattle-and-daub construction was soon superceded by stone and whitewash. Colonial houses were built on stone foundations, and because there was no courtyard, the first story opened straight onto the street. The main story, on the second level, was pierced by large windows and doors and was faced with a wrought-iron balcony. The pitched roof was clad in roman tiles.

Sobrados, or two-story colonial houses, in Cachoeira ▲ *263* (*left*), Olinda ▲ *278* (*far left*) and Salvador ▲ *256* (*below*).

'SOBRADOS'

Like those in northern Portugal, Brazilian *sobrados* had pitched roofs covered with roman tiles and broad gutters that prevented rain from running down the walls. While the first story served as a storehouse, the second, which was sometimes faced with balconies, was where official business took place.

THE DEVELOPMENT OF WINDOWS
The earliest houses of the *bandeirantes*, of which the Casa do Padre Inácio (*opposite page*) is an example, had very few windows in their mud walls. Later, wooden shutters were sometimes decorated with *moucharabieh*, Moorish pierced wooden panels, a device introduced via Portuguese architecture. With the sash windows characteristic of many 18th-century monasteries came a range of sophisticated variations and elegant semicircular transoms.

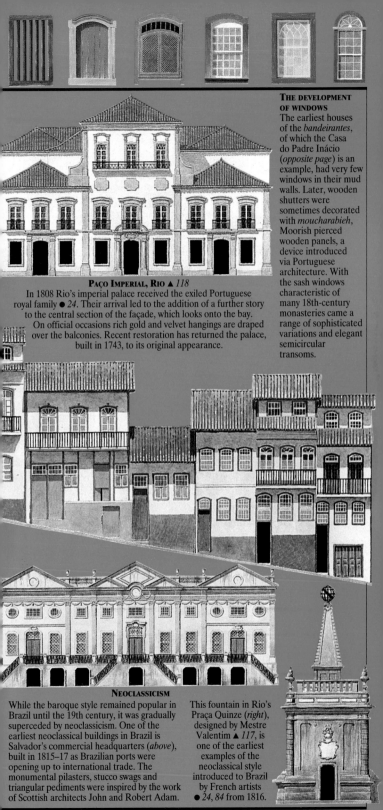

PAÇO IMPERIAL, RIO ▲ *118*
In 1808 Rio's imperial palace received the exiled Portuguese royal family ● *24*. Their arrival led to the addition of a further story to the central section of the façade, which looks onto the bay. On official occasions rich gold and velvet hangings are draped over the balconies. Recent restoration has returned the palace, built in 1743, to its original appearance.

NEOCLASSICISM
While the baroque style remained popular in Brazil until the 19th century, it was gradually superceded by neoclassicism. One of the earliest neoclassical buildings in Brazil is Salvador's commercial headquarters (*above*), built in 1815–17 as Brazilian ports were opening up to international trade. The monumental pilasters, stucco swags and triangular pediments were inspired by the work of Scottish architects John and Robert Adam.

This fountain in Rio's Praça Quinze (*right*), designed by Mestre Valentim ▲ *117*, is one of the earliest examples of the neoclassical style introduced to Brazil by French artists ● *24*, *84* from 1816.

Poster for the Congresso Pan-Americano de Architectos, a conference on architecture held in Rio de Janeiro in 1930.

Ever since Brazil was colonized, building and urban planning there have been regarded as nothing less than heroic. Many urban building projects have thus been extremely bold. Two such examples are the great Avenida Central, opened in Rio de Janeiro in 1905, and the leveling of *morros* (hills) there in preparation for the 1922 Exposição Internacional (World Fair). Equally ambitious is the Viaduto do Chá, in central São Paulo, and the creation of two new capital cities: Belo Horizonte, completed in 1897 and Brasília in 1960.

TEATRO MUNICIPAL, RIO DE JANEIRO

In 1903–6, under the direction of Pereira Passos, Rio's 'architect-mayor', the Avenida Central ▲ *122* was driven through the city center. This was part of an urban development project inspired by Baron Haussmann's transformation of Paris in the 19th century. The fascination with Paris peaked with a contest for the design of façades to line the new avenue. Only a few still stand: they include the Clube Naval and the Teatro Municipal, opened on July 14, 1909 and very evidently of French inspiration. Designed by Francisco Pereira Passos (the mayor's nephew), it makes reference to the Paris Opera, which also inspired the Teatro Municipal in São Paulo ▲ *221*.

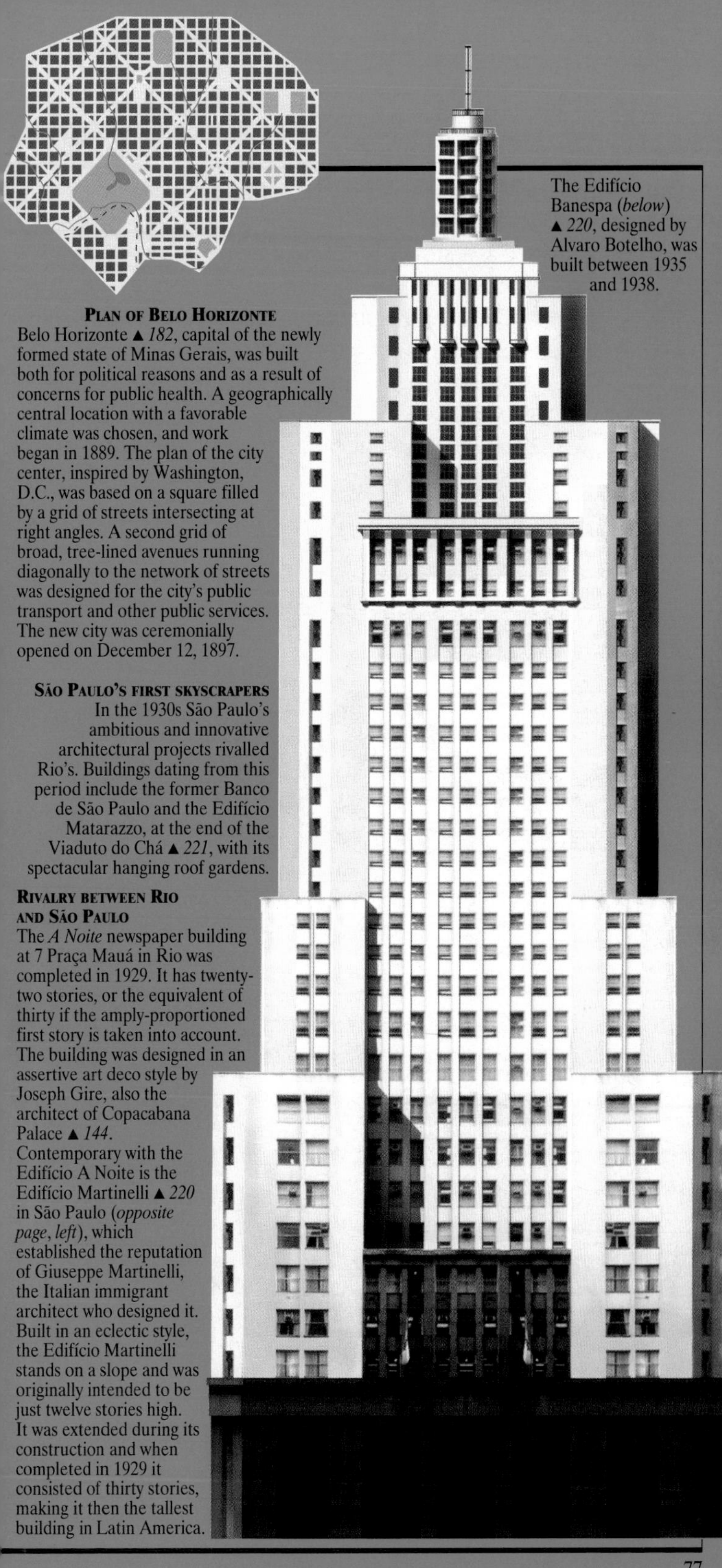

The Edifício Banespa (*below*) ▲ *220*, designed by Alvaro Botelho, was built between 1935 and 1938.

Plan of Belo Horizonte

Belo Horizonte ▲ *182*, capital of the newly formed state of Minas Gerais, was built both for political reasons and as a result of concerns for public health. A geographically central location with a favorable climate was chosen, and work began in 1889. The plan of the city center, inspired by Washington, D.C., was based on a square filled by a grid of streets intersecting at right angles. A second grid of broad, tree-lined avenues running diagonally to the network of streets was designed for the city's public transport and other public services. The new city was ceremonially opened on December 12, 1897.

São Paulo's first skyscrapers

In the 1930s São Paulo's ambitious and innovative architectural projects rivalled Rio's. Buildings dating from this period include the former Banco de São Paulo and the Edifício Matarazzo, at the end of the Viaduto do Chá ▲ *221*, with its spectacular hanging roof gardens.

Rivalry between Rio and São Paulo

The *A Noite* newspaper building at 7 Praça Mauá in Rio was completed in 1929. It has twenty-two stories, or the equivalent of thirty if the amply-proportioned first story is taken into account. The building was designed in an assertive art deco style by Joseph Gire, also the architect of Copacabana Palace ▲ *144*.
Contemporary with the Edifício A Noite is the Edifício Martinelli ▲ *220* in São Paulo (*opposite page, left*), which established the reputation of Giuseppe Martinelli, the Italian immigrant architect who designed it. Built in an eclectic style, the Edifício Martinelli stands on a slope and was originally intended to be just twelve stories high. It was extended during its construction and when completed in 1929 it consisted of thirty stories, making it then the tallest building in Latin America.

Le Corbusier's 'pilotis' design rejected by Niemeyer.

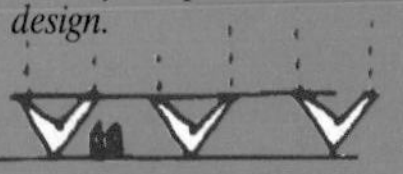

Niemeyer's 'pilotis' design.

Modernist architecture, launched by Le Corbusier and Walter Gropius in Europe, reached North America in the 1920s, where it developed into the International style. In Brazil, where European influence was more direct and earlier to take root, modernism led to the development of the very specific architectural style known as Brazilian modernism, or *modernidade*. Its pioneer was the Russian immigrant Gregori Warchavchik (1896–1972) and it developed further during the Vargas era of the 1930s to 1950s ● *26*, when architects such as Lúcio Costa, Afonso Reidy and Oscar Niemeyer took up public commissions.

NIEMEYER'S 'PILOTI' ARCHITECTURE
Modern Brazilian architecture is based on the use of concrete pillars, known as *pilotis,* and suspended elements. Oscar Niemeyer, who was preoccupied by the invention of novel shapes in architecture, produced many variations on this theme, especially in Brasília ▲ *200*. In Niemeyer's hands, the *piloti* is a free-standing element, a kind of column around which a building develops and on which it rests. This concept has offered many possibilities for later architects, including Lina Bo Bardi and Paulo Mendes da Rocha, who are fascinated by suspended and precariously balanced forms.

'AZULEJOS' IN 'MODERNIDADE'
Azulejos ● *71* have been brought back into fashion by the modernist trend that has also made efforts to preserve Brazil's heritage. The modernists' love of this style of tilework continues, as seen in many modern buildings, such as Rio's Palácio Capanema and in Pampulha and Brasília.

OSCAR NIEMEYER AND FLUIDITY OF FORM
The parabolic arches of the triple-aisled Igreja de São Francisco de Assis (1943, *above*) in Pampulha ▲ *182* were inspired by the shape of airplane hangars, although here they blend into a series of sensual curves. Niemeyer was fascinated by the fluidity of curves, a property that finds its ultimate expression in his design for the domes of the Congresso Nacional in Brasília (*below*).

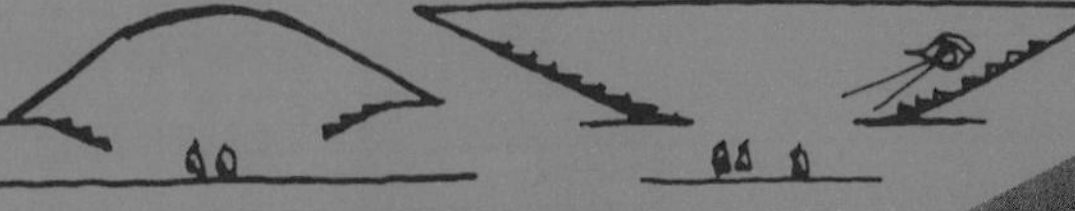

THE 'PILOTI' AS A STRUCTURE (MUSEU DE ARTE MODERNA, RIO ▲ *125*)
Rio's Museum of Modern Art (1953–9) (*below*) is Afonso Reidy's most outstanding achievement. Reidy (1909–64) designed the building as a huge glass case suspended from an obtuse-angled portico, creating a flexible space whose transparent walls are open to the surrounding environment. The concept is very similar to that of the Museu de Arte in São Paulo ▲ *224*, designed by Lina Bo Bardi (1914–92) and completed in 1968.

Sketch by Niemeyer for the Supremo Tribunal Federal (Supreme Court) in Brasília ▲ 205.

Le Corbusier and Brazil

Modern Brazilian architecture has an identity closely associated with Le Corbusier (1887–1965). Invited to lecture in Rio in 1929 the French architect was enthusiastic about the city and especially what he sensed to be the very flexible nature of its urban development. He returned in 1936 to work on various projects, including the Palácio Capanema Ministry of Education building, and the university campus. However the completed *palácio* differed significantly from Le Corbusier's plans, leaving him somewhat embittered.

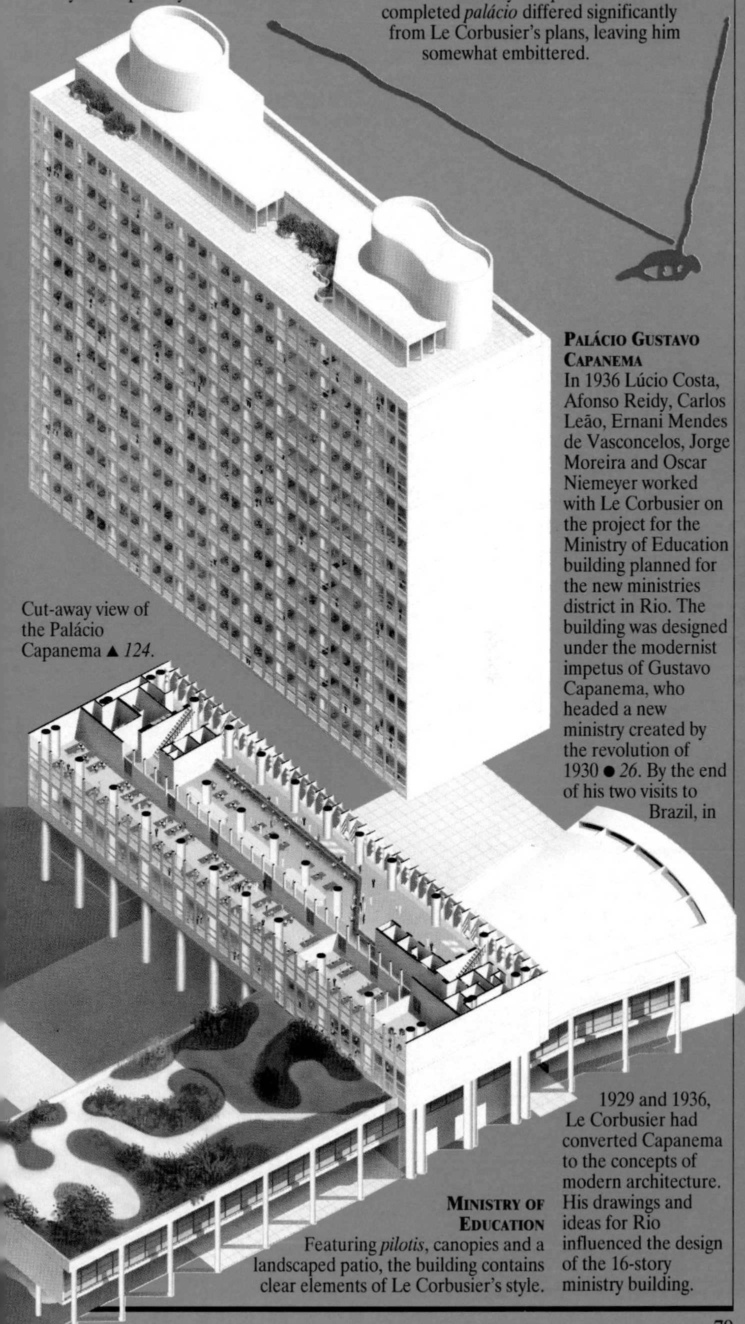

Palácio Gustavo Capanema

In 1936 Lúcio Costa, Afonso Reidy, Carlos Leão, Ernani Mendes de Vasconcelos, Jorge Moreira and Oscar Niemeyer worked with Le Corbusier on the project for the Ministry of Education building planned for the new ministries district in Rio. The building was designed under the modernist impetus of Gustavo Capanema, who headed a new ministry created by the revolution of 1930 ● *26*. By the end of his two visits to Brazil, in 1929 and 1936, Le Corbusier had converted Capanema to the concepts of modern architecture. His drawings and ideas for Rio influenced the design of the 16-story ministry building.

Cut-away view of the Palácio Capanema ▲ *124*.

Ministry of Education

Featuring *pilotis*, canopies and a landscaped patio, the building contains clear elements of Le Corbusier's style.

THE DEVELOPMENT OF 'FAVELAS' ON THE 'MORROS' OF RIO

The earliest *favelas* grew up at the beginning of the 20th century. Their inhabitants, the *favelados*, could not have foreseen that, decades later, their great-grandchildren would be living in the same conditions of insecurity and poverty, and that *favelas* would inexorably grow in size and number. At the dawn of the new millennium these shanty towns are home to almost 20 percent of the population of Rio de Janeiro, São Paulo and other cities in southern Brazil. With the authorities overwhelmed by the extent of the problem and despite vigorous initiatives and relocation programs, the *favelas* have become self-contained towns in the concrete jungles of modern Brazil.

FIRST STAGE
In 1897 soldiers returning from Canudos ▲ *255* set up a camp for their families on Rio's Morro da Providência while they were waiting to be relocated. They named the camp *favela* (the name of a shrub) for the *morro* (hill) on which their camp in Canudos had been located. The term was soon applied to all makeshift dwellings built illegally on Rio's *morros*. These rustic shanties were constructed of planks collected from building sites and fixed to a framework of wooden posts. Roofs were made from woven palm fronds, corrugated iron or flattened jerrycans. The shanty's one room had an earth floor and food was cooked outside on a wood fire.

SECOND STAGE
With a shortage of housing, the *favelas* expanded and the rustic shanties evolved into more permanent dwellings. The *favelados* replaced loose planks, re-covered their roofs, added doors and windows and created a cooking area inside.

RURAL EXODUS
From 1940 rural poverty together with the economic boom in the cities of southern Brazil caused a massive rural exodus to Rio and São Paulo. Over the course of sixty years more than 40 million Brazilians left the interior for the coastal cities.

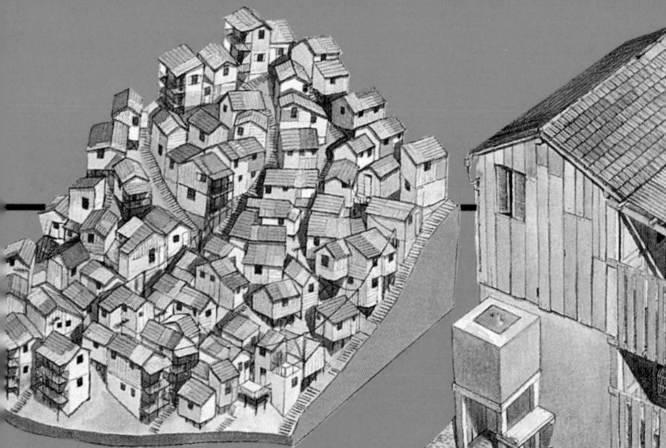

Third stage

The number of *favelas* grew, so that in Rio in 1980 there were 300 *favelas* housing about 25 percent of the urban population. The *favelas* also grew in size, becoming self-contained towns within the city – Rocinha ▲ *146*, for example, with 150,000 inhabitants. *Favelas* also became more densely packed as shacks were extended and every inch of space was used. Some *favelados* added an upper story, a 'kitchen' with a sink, and a bedroom separate from the living area. They demonstrated an amazing ability to adapt and proved to be ingenious builders, adapting their dwellings to sloping sites, and collecting or appropriating all kinds of materials. They also began to organize water and power supplies, create narrow streets, build flights of steps and install sewers. *Favelas* were becoming real towns with their own building regulations and neighborhood rules, as well as their own residents' associations.

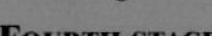

Fourth stage

In time the shacks became sturdy houses as the use of concrete slabs, breeze-blocks and brick walls made it possible to build several stories. To recuperate their outlay *favelados* began to sell their concrete roof space to other families, who moved in above. Property speculation has changed the face of the *favelas*. The houses now have kitchens and bathrooms, while the richer *favelados* install grilles and reinforced doors just as their neighbors in the city do.

Social organization

Like the city the *favelas* have their own bakers, craftsmen, traders and café owners. Some inhabitants grow rich by selling water and electricity, or building houses to rent out. At night the samba school ▲ *130* and *gafieira* (dance hall) ▲ *121* come to life. Associations organize schools, community buildings and churches. But these maze-like *favelas* also attract drug dealers who trade protection and a place to hide against financial aid for the very poor.

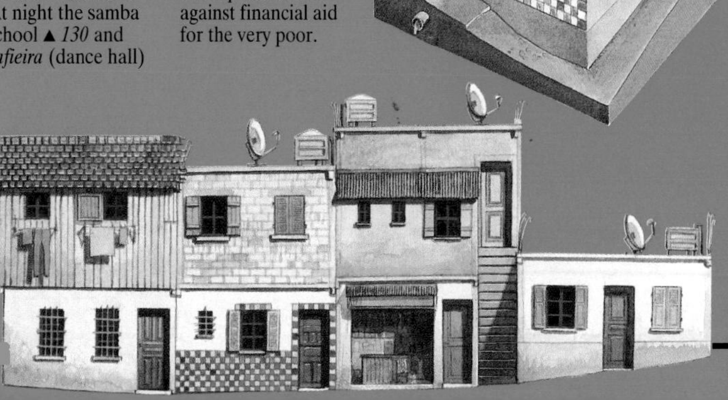

Types of 'favelas'

A social reality
Brazil's *favelas* illustrate the extent of the social problem created by the exodus of the rural population toward the cities, the growing divide between rich and poor and the authorities' inability to integrate the very poorest people into the community. The first *favelas* were built on green spaces around the edges of city districts, on the steep hillsides or *morros* of Rio (**3, 4**) and Salvador (**1**). In Manaus *favelados* living on the riverbank have built riverside towns on piles (**2**). The suburban relocation programs of the 1960s and 1970s failed because low incomes made it impossible for *favelados* to live far from the city center. Today efforts to tackle this social problem are focusing on the redevelopment of the *favelas* and the recognition of property rights (pioneered by the Favela-bairro project). The Favela da Maré (**5**), between the freeway and the head of Guanabara Bay near Rio's international airport, was based on Amazonian riverside villages. It was demolished and its inhabitants relocated in small houses.

Rehabilitation
The Favela-Bairro Project (**6**) was launched by Rio city council in 1996. Its aim is to integrate the *favelas* into the city by taking responsibility for their streets and sewers, and providing garbage collection and power and water supplies, while also encouraging residents to support the project.

Brazil as seen by painters

In 1816 French scholar and art critic Joachim Lebreton gathered together a group of disgraced Bonapartists, artists Nicolas Taunay and Jean-Baptiste Debret and architect Grandjean de Montigny ▲ *119*, to help found the Academia Imperial de Belas Artes in Rio de Janeiro. They played a key role in introducing the academic style of painting to Brazil. Instrumental in this process was NICOLAS TAUNAY (1755–1830) who painted views of Rio, including *Largo da Carioca* (1) ▲ *120*. THOMAS ENDER (1739–1875) traveled to Brazil in 1817–18, during which time he produced 652 watercolors and drawings, including this view (2) looking from Corcovado ▲ *151* toward the Serra dos Órgãos. In 1636 the young Dutch artist FRANS POST (1612–80) accompanied Mauricio de Nassau ▲ *275* to the Nordeste where he stayed until his return to Europe in 1648. His technique (that of the Haarlem school, in which landscape is depicted as a series of planes) resulted in scenes that are enhanced by the strangeness of the Brazilian environment. This new method of portraying the tropical landscapes of the New World would be echoed by Gobelin tapestries depicting scenes of the Indies. Frans Post's work consists of paintings executed both in Brazil and those done from memory on his return to Europe. Examples can be seen in several American museums, in the Louvre in Paris (including the *Village of Serinhaem in Brazil* (3) and in Ham House in London.

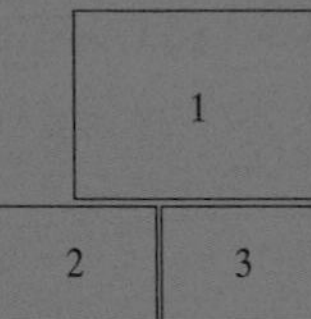

'My painting is peasant painting. If you like my peasants, well and good, if not, find another painter.'

Cândido Portinari

CÂNDIDO PORTINARI (1903–62) is a major figure in Brazilian art. His often very moving pictures depict the work and suffering of Brazilian laborers. In 1928 this gifted student of the Escuela de Belas Artes (School of Fine Arts) won an award that enabled him to travel in Europe. Portinari was particularly fascinated by Italian Renaissance painting, which influenced his early years. He won recognition at the Pittsburgh Exhibition in 1935 with his prize-winning canvas *Café*. The portrait *Mestiço* ('half-caste', *left*) dates from 1937. In 1944 he returned to the themes of his childhood in Brodósqui, in the state of São Paulo. Portinari is also known for the many murals that adorn buildings in Brazil and other countries. In Brazil the government commissioned from him the *azulejo* ● *71* panels and frescos (1936–44) in the function rooms of the Rio's Palácio Capanema ● *79* ▲ *124,* and in 1944 he painted the frescos in the Igreja de São Francisco de Assis in Pampulha ● *78* ▲ *182*. Portinari's work in other countries includes *War and Peace* (1957), a fresco in the UN Building in New York, and *Discovery and Colonization*, a painting in the Library of Congress in Washington, D.C. His work has been shown in major national and international exhibitions.

ISMAEL NERY (1900–34) is a painter whose style is not easily categorized. During his lifetime he exhibited his work only twice, in his home town of Belém (1928) and in Rio (1929), and sold only one painting. Nery's travels in Europe brought him into contact with Cubism and Surrealism. In *Namorados* (1927, *above*), for example, the geometric elements of Cubism give way to heartfelt emotion, and the painting betrays Nery's greater interest in the individual than in society in general. He was not recognized as a painter until long after his death.

JOSÉ PANCETTI (1904–58), who was a sailor before he took up painting, was a sensitive and captivating landscapist. His paintings depict imaginary scenes which, although somewhat disembodied, also very accurately record Brazil's coastal landscapes, with their soothing, mysterious blue tones. This is clearly seen in *Praia da Gávea* (*right*). Alfredo Volpi (1896–1988), who was born in Italy and brought up in Brazil, is noted for his urban landscapes. He was a self-taught artist who developed a distinctive style based on his observation of everyday life. His progressively dematerialized façades and his manipulation of color, which he used to depict suburban landscapes and the towns of the interior, earned him a distinctive place in the history of painting in Brazil. In *Arcos e Bandeiras* (Arches and Flags, *right*), painted in the late 1950s, Volpi used the leitmotif of the flag, with which he was obsessed throughout his career (he became known as the 'flag painter'). For Volpi flags and architectural elements had no narrative function, even though they conveyed typically Brazilian visual impressions. Rather, they were motifs that served as mediums for his experiments with shapes and colors.

The work of TARSILA DO AMARAL (1886–1973) is an example of the modernist trend highlighted by Modern Art Week, held in São Paulo in 1922 ▲ *218,* and by Oswald de Andrade's *Manifesto Anthropofágico*. Her *faux-naif* style and urban landscapes influenced by Fernand Léger, such as *Estrada de Ferro*, *Centro do Brasil* (1924, *right*), make her a leading artist. Her later work focuses on more social themes.

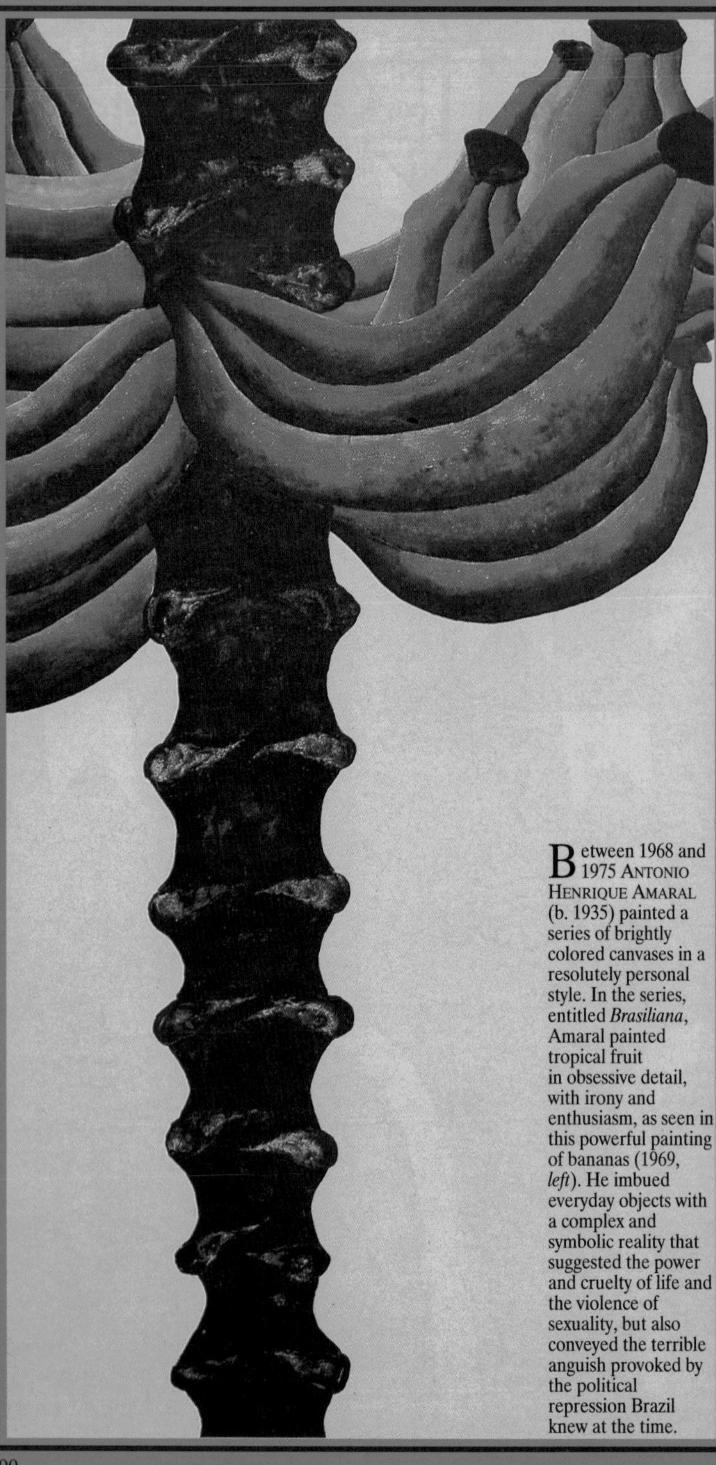

Between 1968 and 1975 ANTONIO HENRIQUE AMARAL (b. 1935) painted a series of brightly colored canvases in a resolutely personal style. In the series, entitled *Brasiliana*, Amaral painted tropical fruit in obsessive detail, with irony and enthusiasm, as seen in this powerful painting of bananas (1969, *left*). He imbued everyday objects with a complex and symbolic reality that suggested the power and cruelty of life and the violence of sexuality, but also conveyed the terrible anguish provoked by the political repression Brazil knew at the time.

Brazil as seen by writers

In 1500, Pedro Álvares Cabral (1467–1520) led the Portuguese expedition that first discovered Brazil. Scholars still debate whether the land was found by chance during an attempt to find a route to India, or whether there was a deliberate intention to stake a claim to lands of which there was at least some previous knowledge. Whichever is true, a letter sent back to the Portuguese King Manuel by Pedro Vaz de Caminha d.1500) is regarded to be the birth certificate of Brazil.

"We made sail and steered straight to the land, with the small ships going out in front…until half a league from the shore, we cast anchor in front of the mouth of a river…The captain sent Nicolao Coelho on shore in a boat to see that river. As soon as he began to go thither men assembled on the shore, by twos and threes, so that when the boat reached the mouth of the river 18 or 20 men were already there. They were dark and entirely naked without anything to cover their shame. They carried in their hands bows with their arrows. All came boldly towards the boat and Nicolao Coelho made a sign that they should lay down their bows, and they laid them down. He could not have any speech with them there, nor understanding which might be profitable because of the breaking of the sea on the shore. He gave them only a red cap (barrete) and a cap of linen (carapuça) which he was wearing on his head, and a black hat. And one of them gave him a hat of long bird feathers with a little tuft of red and grey feathers like those of a small parrot. Another gave him a large string of very small white beads; these articles I believe the captain is sending to your highness. And with this he returned to the ships because it was late and he could have no further speech with them on account of the sea."

PEDRO VAZ DE CAMINHA, *LETTER TO KING MANUEL, 1ST MAY 1500*,
TRANS. WILLIAM BROOKS GREENLEE,
LONDON HAKLUYT SOCIETY, 1938

Pedro de Magalhães Gandavo (d.1576) is considered to have written the first official history of Brazil, approximately 70 years after its discovery. His Histories of Brazil give a unique insight into the naming of the land.

"The news [of the discovery]…was received with much pleasure and satisfaction: and from that time on he began to send more ships to those regions; and so, little by little, the country was explored, and [ever] more was learned about it, until finally the country was entirely divided into Captaincies and settled in the way it is today. ...After spending some days there, taking on water and waiting for suitable weather before departing, he [Pedro Álvares] wished to give a name to the Province he had so recently discovered; so he ordered a Cross to be raised on the highest branch of a tree, whither it was lifted with great solemnity...and the name of Sancta Cruz was given to the land; for the Holy Mother Church was celebrating the feast of the Holy Cross that very day...[the land] was destined to be possessed by the Portuguese... it does not seem reasonable that this name should be withdrawn from it, nor that we should forget it so universally for another which an ill-advised public gave it after the dye-wood began to be exported to the Kingdom [of Portugal]. We call it *brazil* because the wood is red and resembles hot coals, and thus the land got the name of Brazil."

PEDRO DE MAGALHÃES GANDAVO,
THE HISTORIES OF BRAZIL BY PEDRO DE MAGALHÃES GANDAVO WITH A FACSIMILIE OF THE PORTUGUESE ORIGINAL,
TRANS. JOHN B. STETSON, JR., NEW YORK, 1922

From as early as the middle of the 16th century both the English and Irish were interested in the possibility of exploring the fabled resources of the great river of the Amazons. The following extract, from a history of such settlers, describes the colonial rivalry that ensued.

"During the first half of the seventeenth century, English and Irish projectors made ... considerable profits from tobacco, dyes and hardwoods. Indeed, the profitability of their holdings was such that, when reprisals by the Portuguese made the river too risky for foreign interlopers after 1630, former English and Irish planters sought to be allowed to return to the river under the licence of first the Spanish and then the Portuguese crown.

...

The Irish ventures in the Amazon, although begun in partnership with the English, can now be seen to have developed into a quite distinct initiative. Some twelve years before the transport of indentured servants to the Leeward Islands began, Irish merchants and gentlemen had established small colonies of their compatriots on the Amazon. By the early 1620s their experience of the river and their expertise in the Indian languages was well known. They were eagerly sought after by the English and Dutch to direct their enterprises... The Amazon...was the focus of fierce colonial rivalry. The failure of the English and the Irish to hold on to it reflects more about European international relations than it does about the suitability of the environment of Amazonia for northern Europeans."

JOYCE LORIMER, *ENGLISH AND IRISH SETTLEMENT ON THE RIVER AMAZON 1550–1646*, LONDON HAKLUYT SOCIETY, 1938.

William R Shepherd's 19th-century American history of 'our southern neighbours' provides a detailed and fascinating insight into the development of Brazil.

"...the first impulse toward independence was given by the Portuguese royal family. Terrified by the prospective invasion of the country by a French army, late in 1807 the Prince Regent, the royal family, and a host of Portuguese nobles and commoners took passage on British vessels and sailed to Rio de Janeiro. Brazil thereupon became the seat of royal government and immediately assumed an importance which it could never have attained as a mere dependency.... The colonial subjects could not fail to contrast autocracy in Brazil with the liberal ideas that had made headway elsewhere in Spanish America. As a consequence a spirit of unrest arose which boded ill for the maintenance of Portuguese rule.

Of all the Hispanic nations, however, Brazil was easily the most stable. Here the leaders, while clinging to independence, strove to avoid dangerous innovations in government. Rather than create a political system for which the country was not prepared, they established a constitutional monarchy. But Brazil itself was too vast and its interior too difficult of access to allow it to become all at once a unit, either in organization or in spirit. The idea of national solidarity had as yet made scant progress. The old rivalry which existed between the provinces of the north, dominated by Bahia or Pernambuco, and those of the south, controlled by Rio de Janeiro or Sao Paulo, still made itself felt. What the Empire amounted to, therefore, was an agglomeration of provinces, held together by the personal prestige of a young monarch.

Thanks to the political discretion and unusual personal qualities of 'Dom Pedro', his popularity became more and more marked as the years went on. A patron of science and literature, a scholar rather than a ruler, a placid and somewhat eccentric philosopher, careless of the trappings of state, he devoted himself without stint to the public welfare. Shrewdly divining that the monarchical system might not survive much longer, he kept his realm pacified by a policy of conciliation. Pedro II even went so far as to call himself the best republican in the Empire. He might have said, with justice perhaps, that he was the best republican in the whole of Hispanic America. What he really accomplished was the successful exercise of a paternal autocracy of kindness and liberality over his subjects."

WILLIAM R SHEPHERD, *THE HISPANIC NATIONS OF THE NEW WORLD, A CHRONICLE OF OUR SOUTHERN NEIGHBOURS,* YALE UNIVERSITY PRESS, 1919

In the introduction to his account of travels in Brazil in the 1850s, Alfred Russel Wallace (1823–1913) describes 'An earnest desire to visit a tropical country, to behold the luxuriance of animal and vegetable life said to exist there, and to see with my own eyes all those wonders which I had so much delighted to read of in the narratives of travellers...some far land where endless summer reigns.' What follows are his first perceptions of Brazil.

"About a fortnight after our arrival at Para there were several holidays or festa as they are called. Those of the 'Espirito Santo' and the 'Trinidade' lasted each nine days. The former was held at the cathedral, the latter at one of the smaller churches in the suburbs. The general character of these festas is the same, some being more celebrated and more attractive than others. They consist of fireworks every night before the church;... processions of saints and crucifixes; the church open, with regular services; kissing of images and relics; and a miscellaneous crowd of Indians, all dressed in white, thoroughly enjoying the fun, and the women in all the glory of their marine gold chains and earrings. Besides these, a number of the higher classes and foreign residents grace the scene with their presence; showy processions are got up at the commencement and termination, and on the last evening a grand display of fireworks takes place...provided by 'Juiz da festa' or the governor of the feast – a rather expensive honour among people who, not content with an unlimited supply of rockets at night, amuse themselves with great quantities during the day for the sake of the whiz and the bang that accompany them...Music, noise and fireworks are the three essentials to please a Brazilian population; and for a fortnight we had enough of them, for besides the above mentioned amusements, they fire off guns, pistols and cannon from morning to night."

ALFRED RUSSEL WALLACE, *A NARRATIVE OF TRAVELS ON THE AMAZON AND RIO NEGRO, WITH AN ACCOUNT OF THE NATIVE TRIBES, AND OBSERVATIONS ON THE CLIMATE, GEOLOGY, AND NATURAL HISTORY OF THE AMAZON VALLEY,* REEVE AND CO, LONDON, 1853

Joshua Slocum (1844–1909), one of the best known sailors in North American history, wrote about many of his adventures on the high seas. This excerpt comes from his chronicle about the delivery of a warship The Destroyer *to Brazil in 1894.*

"Frankly it was with a thrill of delight that I joined the service of Brazil to lend a hand to the legal government of a people in whose country I had spent happy days; and where moreover I found lasting friends who will join me now in a grin over peacock sailors playing man-o-war. To these friends let me tell now, who have come from the war, the story of the voyage of the famous Destroyer: the first ship of the strong right arm of future Brazil.

February 9th, 1894, the Destroyer sailed for Bahia, accompanied by the Moxoto, the handy torpedo boat. On the 13th she arrived at the destination, Everything was funeral quietness at Bahia. The occasional pop of a champagne cork, at the 'Paris' on the hill, might have been heard, but that was all, except again the sunset gun. The rising sun had to take care of itself. The average Brazilian Naval man is an amphibious being, spending his time about equally between hotel and harbor, and is never dangerous. I was astonished at the quietness of Bahia, there was not even target practice. Indeed the further we got away from stirring New York, the less it looked like war in Brazil."

JOSHUA SLOCUM, *VOYAGE OF THE DESTROYER FROM NEW YORK TO BRAZIL,* PRESS OF THE ROBINSON PRINTING COMPANY, BOSTON, 1894

The Austrian biographer, essayist and short story writer Stefan Zweig (1881–1942) provides a more contemporary view of Brazil, this time with anthropological perspective.

"For four hundred years now the masses have been boiling and fermenting in the enormous retort of this country – new material constantly being added, and the mixture being constantly shaken up. Is this process now definitely finished? Have these millions already taken form and shape of their own? Is there in existence today something one could call the Brazilian race, the Brazilian man, the Brazilian soul? On the question of race, Euclydes da Cunha, the gifted expert on Brazilian national character, long ago gave a definite denial when he explained simply: '*Nao ha um typo anthropopologico Brasileiro*' – 'There is no Brazilian race.' Race, if one must use this doubtful and today most over-rated term at all, means a thousand-year-old combination of blood and history. With a real Brazilian, on the other hand, all memories of prehistoric times slumbering in his unconscious must hark back to the genealogy of three continents at once: of the European coasts, the kraals of Africa, and the American jungle. The process of becoming a Brazilian is not only one of becoming acclimatized to Nature, to the spiritual and material conditions of a country, but above all a problem of transfusion; because the majority of the Brazilian population – with the exception of a few late immigrants – represents a mixed breed of the most complicated and diverse kind. Besides, each member or part of this threefold home country – the European, the African, and the American – has layers within itself. The first European arrival in Brazil, the Portuguese of the sixteenth century, is anything but of pure race. He represents, in fact, a mixture of his Iberian, Roman, Gothic, Phœnician, Jewish and Moorish ancestors. Actually, the original population of Brazil is divided into two separate groups – the Tupis and the Tamoyos."

STEFAN ZWEIG, *BRAZIL, LAND OF THE FUTURE*,
TRANS. ANDREW SAINT JAMES,
CASSELL AND CO. LONDON, 1942

Brazilian literature of the 20th century became enthused with the plight of people in Brazil who had fought for their rights in the previous century. Canaan, by José Pereira da Graça Aranha (1868–1931) and subtitled 'a pessimistic novel of ideas', was one of the first books to tackle the struggle between old Brazil and European immigrants. Set in a small town, this scene follows two of the main characters as they offer a critique of Brazilian life.

"'A country without justice is not a country to live in; it is nothing but a conglomeration of barbarians...' affirmed Maciel, following his bent of talking in general terms.

'In Brazil there is no law,' he continued, 'and no one can feel safe. The trial is conducted in such a way that the accused has no chance. Listen, if a man tries to seize another man's property, he finds in our judicial system, in the way of conducting trials, all possible help to carry out his nefarious intention. And if that man be a magnate, nobody can bother him. No; no even I.'

'Justice is but an illusion the world over,' said Milkau.

'But in Brazil conditions are much worse than elsewhere, because it is not a case of rare eclipses of justice.'

Milkau listened thoughtfully to the magistrate, who went on impelled by a desire to confess the faults of his country.

'This that we call a nation is nothing, I say. We did have here once a semblance of liberty and justice, but to-day all that has ended. This poor Brazil is but a corpse that is rapidly decomposing...The *urubus* are coming...'

'Where from?'

'From everywhere; from Europe, from the United States... It is a conquest...'

'I don't believe that,' asserted Milkau.

'They will come. How could we live on in our present condition? Where is the moral foundation that shall support us abroad when here, at home, we are struggling in the greatest disorder and despair? What is happening to the country is that it is undergoing a character crisis. It hasn't one single fundamental virtue...'

'That is the character of the race,' explained Milkau.

'Yes, my friend. Here the race is not distinguished by any prominent conservative virtue; there does not exist a common moral fund. I may add that there are no two Brazilians alike, and that, therefore, it would be futile to attempt to form an idea of

the collective virtues and defects by judging merely by one of us. Which is our social virtue? Not even courage, the most rudimentary and instinctive of them all, is with us cultivated sanely and constantly, in a superior way. In this country, bravery is nothing more than a nervous impulse. Look at our wars! What cowardice is written in their history!...There was a time when our piety and our kindness were loudly proclaimed. Collectively, as a nation, we are bad, hysterically, uselessly bad...!'

...'See what happens to patriotism here,' continued Macial after a brief interval. 'In Brazil the great mass of the people has no such feeling. Here there is a cosmopolitanism which is not the expression of a comprehensive and generous philosophy but is merely a symptom of moral inertia, an indication of the untimely loss of a feeling – patriotism – which would very well harmonize with the backward state of our culture. You must notice that our patriots are all men of hatred and of blood, that is to say, they are savages.'

'There is no doubt,' assented Milkau, deeply interested in Maciel's frank analysis, 'that there is a vast disparity between the different strata of the population. This lack of homogeneity is probably the cause of that instability...'

The judge reflected awhile, then leaning over table, he looked at Milkau and spoke to him in a more decisive and vibrant tone.

'You are right. The Brazilian people, as a whole offer an aspect at once of decrepitude and childishness. The decadence of our people presents a deplorable mixture of the savagery of the new-born races with the degeneracy of the races that are becoming exhausted. There is general confusion. The currents of immorality flow through our people without meeting obstacles in any of our institutions. Such a nation as ours is ready to receive the worst evil that can befall in the world: arbitrary and despotic governments. If society is a creation of suggestion, what can you expect of the feelings, the ideals of the uncultured masses when their imagination is being bewildered by the spectacle of the most brazen degradation in the governing classes? What reaction will not be caused in dull intellects by the scorn of those leaders for an ideal, for superior things, and their love for position and graft? And it isn't the government only. It is all of them: the subservient judiciary, ready to plunder private property, the public servants, the military, the clergy, all of them are sliding down a dangerous incline...'"

JOSÉ PEREIRA DA GRAÇA ARANHA, *CANAAN, A PESSIMISTIC NOVEL OF IDEAS (1902)*
TRANS. MARIANO JOAQUIN LORENTE, GEORGE ALLEN AND UNWIN LTD, 1921

Another distinct strand of Brazilian literature can be seen with the considerable influence of the Modern Art movement, originally influenced by French symbolists. Macuanaíma *(1928) by Mário de Andrade (1893–1945) is considered to be exemplary of such work, and the author himself was hailed as the 'Pope of Modernism'. In the story, the titular character passes through many weird and fantastic situations, mirrors of Brazilian culture, which are told through legend, myth and satire. Below is an example of the latter.*

"São Paulo is endowed with many burly and pugnacious policeman, who live in expensive splendid white palaces. These cops strive to balance the excess of public wealth so as not to devalue the uncountable gold of the Nation; they apply such diligence in this effort that at every opportunity they squander the Nation's money, be it for parades at glittering and uniforms…be it finally in hounding those incautious townsfolk leaving the movie or theater, or taking a spin in their automobile... When the payroll of these Police becomes too great, the men are sent to remote and less fertile parts of the country where they are devoured by the tribes of anthropophagous giants that infest the geographical extent of our native health, in the inglorious task of bringing to the ground honest governments; this with the approval and consent of the population in general, which is absolved from blame by the operations of the ballot box and governmental divertissement. These troublemakers capture the policeman, roast them and eat them in the German style; and their bones falling onto the barren soil, become excellent fertilizers for the coffee groves of the future."

MÁRIO DE ANDRADE, *MACUANAÍMA: THE HERO WITHOUT ANY CHARACTER* (1928), TRANS. E.A. GOODLAND, QUARTET, LONDON 1984

Euclides da Cunha's (1866–1909) epic novel, Rebellion in the Backlands *is an account of a rebellion against the Brazilian government led by a religious fanatic. Embellished with lengthy descriptions of the Brazilian landscape the book is a pessimistic view of Brazilian life and conditions at the end of the 19th century.*

"The jagunco, pillager of cities, thereupon took the place of the *garimpeiro*, who pillaged the earth for diamonds. And the political chieftain replaced the *capangueiro*, or gang leader of old. This transition affords a fine example of environmental reaction...

We have seen how amid the whirlwind movement of the bandeiras... they grew up here that race of brave and diligent mamelucos which so opportunely made its appearance in our colonial history as a conservative element, constituting the case of our nationality in process of birth and creating a state of equilibrium between the madness of the gold rushes and the romantic Utopias of the apostolate... [The country] underwent a transformation in contact with the gain-lusting sertanistas... from the east, frightening the savage with fire and sword, and founding settlements which, unlike those already in existence, did not possess a cattle ranch as a nucleus but, instead, the ruins of the *malocas*, or native villages. They rode roughshod over the region... when the exhausted mines called for such equipment as would make possible an intensive exploitation, they then began eyeing the virgin and opulent land which lay ahead of them, in the heart of the country..."

EUCLIDES DA CUNHA, *REBELLION IN THE BACKLANDS* (1902)
TRANS. S PUTNAM, UNIVERSITY OF CHICAGO PRESS, 1995

Brazil is a land rich in poetry. From the lyrics that accompany dance to the everyday nature of life in the country, Brazil has inspired poets from around the world. This selection presents two of the most famous Brazilian poets and looks at the writing of a famous non-Brazilian, Rudyard Kipling, who was inspired to write verse about the country and its people.

Carlos de Drummond de Andrade(1902–87), one of the most famous of all Brazilian poets, was influenced by modernism and by a growing sense of Brazilian national identity which later became more political. A civil servant, he also added translations from French and Spanish poetry to his literary work and became friends with the English-language translator of Brazilian poetry, Elizabeth Bishop.

Itabiran Confession

For many years I lived in Itabira.
Basically I come from Itabira.
That's why I'm sad, proud – ironclad.
Ninety percent iron in the sidewalks.
Eighty percent iron in the soul.
And this detachment from whatever in life is porous and
communicative.

The aching for love that frustrates my work
also comes from Itabira; from its white nights without women
or horizon.
And that habit of suffering which so humors me
is a pure Itabiran legacy.

Have a look at my mementos, collected at Itabira.
This Saint Benedict, carved by old Alfredo Duval.
And my tapir hide draped over the parlor sofa.
Not to mention this pride, this lowered head…

I used to have gold, cattle, ranches.
Today I'm a civil servant.
Itabira's nothing more than the photograph on the wall.
But how it lingers!

CARLOS DRUMMOND DE ANDRADE, (TRANS. THOMAS COLCHIE) FROM *TRAVELLING IN THE FAMILY, SELECTED POEMS OF CARLOS DRUMMOND DE ANDRADE*, ED. THOMAS COLCHIE AND MARK STRAND, ECCO PRESS, HOPEWELL, NEW JERSEY, 1986.

The poetry of Joao Cabral de Meloneto (1920–) contains many images of social conditions of the northeastern region of Brazil where he was born and raised. He is considered one of the most important poets of the post-war generation.

The Man from Up-country Talking

The man from up-country disguises his talk:
the words come out of him like wrapped-up candy
(candy words, pills) in the icing
of a smooth intonation, sweetened.
While under the talk the core of stone
keeps hardening, the stone almond
from the rocky tree back where he comes from:
it can express itself only in stone.

That's why the man from up-country says little:
the stone words ulcerate the mouth
and it hurts to speak in a stone language;
those to whom it's native speak by main force.
Furthermore, that's why he speaks slowly:
he has to take up the words carefully,
he has to sweeten them with his tongue, candy them;
well, all this work takes time.

JOAO CABRAL DE MELO NETO, (TRANS WS MERWIN)
AN ANTHOLOGY OF TWENTIETH CENTURY BRAZILIAN POETRY (1972),
ELIZABETH BISHOP AND EMANUEL BRASIL (EDS.)
WESLEYAN UNIVERSITY PRESS

Acting on doctors advice, following an illness, the British author, Rudyard Kipling (1894–1956) embarked upon a voyage to Brazil in March 1927. The trip yielded many fascinating insights and collected thoughts about Brazil, not least an expression of admiration for the Brazilian people, as seen in the following verses from one of his poems.

Have you no Bananas, simple townsmen all?
'Nay, but we have them certainly
We buy them off the barrows, with the vegetable-marrows,
And the cabbage of our own country.
(From the costers of our own country.)'

Those are not Bananas, simple townsmen all.
(Plantains from Canaryward maybe!)
For the true are red and gold, and they fill no steamer's hold,
But they flourish in a rare country.
(That men go far to see.)
...

But you must go to business, simply townsmen all,
By 'bus and train and tram and tube must flee'.
For your Pharphars and Abanas do not include Bananas
(and Jordan is a distant stream to drink of, simple townsmen),
Which leaves the more for me."

RUDYARD KIPLING, *BRAZILIAN SKETCHES*,
PE WATERS AND ASSOCIATES, 1989

Rudyard Kipling's observations of Brazil included much about the city of Rio de Janeiro. His descriptions of carnival time in the city begin this look at different views of the cosmopolitan city as compared to the beauty and overwhelming vastness of the countryside, including the Amazon rainforest.

"...at Carnival time...the city of Rio went stark crazy. They dressed themselves in every sort of fancy-kit; they crowded into motors; they bought unlimited paper serpentines, which, properly thrown, unroll five fathoms at a flick; and for three days and three nights did nothing except circulate and congregate and bombard their neighbours with these papers and squirts of direful scent.

...

The Brazilian takes his play, as he takes his life, in his stride, and his quick speech and gestures do not reach back to his mind. He has studied samples of every nationality established under his skies these many, many years. He has been used to the English trader for generations, and there are many English-stock families, who long ago attached themselves to the national fortunes – bilingual folks with two sides to their heads, who act as unofficial interpreters and ambassadors at a financial or commercial pinch. The old experienced mercantile firms also sent out the type of Englishman most likely to be acceptable. For the Brazilian has not yet reached the impersonality of ideal 'business'. If he likes you as an individual, he will do more than anything for you. If he doesn't, he will do less than nothing. If he knows little about you, but perceives that you have manner and a few trifles of that sort, he will wait and see. And he has heaps of leisure."

RUDYARD KIPLING, *BRAZILIAN SKETCHES*,
PE WATERS AND ASSOCIATES, 1989

Like Kipling, the Reverend TB Ray also produced his own sketches of Brazil in the late 19th century. As he states, 'I have confined myself to sketches about Brazil because I did not desire to write a book of travel, but to show how the gospel succeeds in a Catholic field...'. His notes encompass further observations of Rio de Janeiro.

"The city, in the most beautiful and picturesque way, avails itself of all possible space, even in many places climbing high on the mountain sides and pressing itself deep into the coves. Perhaps no city in the world has a more picturesque combination of mountain and water with which to make a beautiful location.

There are several places from which splendid views of the city can be had, but none of them is comparable to the panorama which stretches out before one when he stands on the top of Mt. Corcovado. The scene which greets one from this mountain is indescribable. The Bay of Rio de Janeiro, with its eighty islands, Sugar Loaf Mountain, a bare rock standing at the entrance, the city winding its tortuous way in and out between the mountains and spreading itself over many hills, the open sea in the distance and the wild mountain scenery to the back of us, constitute a panorama unsurpassingly beautiful.

There is a street which is dear to the Brazilian...the Rua d'Ouvidor. Down here flows a human tide such as is found nowhere else in Brazil. No one attempts to keep on the pavement. The street is given over entirely to pedestrians. No vehicle ever passes down it until after midnight. In this narrow street, with its attractive shops filled with the highest-priced goods in the world, you can soon find anyone you wish to meet, because before long everyone who can reach it will pass through. In this street the happy, jesting, jostling crowd is in one continuous 'festa'."

REVEREND TB RAY,
BRAZILIAN SKETCHES, 1882

Magalhães Gandavo, the first historian of Brazil, had much to praise in this new land.

"[the Province] is very delectable and refreshing to a great degree: the whole of it is covered with lofty thick woods, and is watered with many delightful streams, with which all the land is abundantly supplied; it is always green with the same temperature of spring that April and May offer us here [in Portugal]. For this reason they do not have the colds or frosts of winter to injure the plants as they injure our plants. In a word, Nature has so acted in respect to all things in the Province, and has so moderated the air, that one is never aware of excessive cold or heat."

PEDRO DE MAGALHÃES GANDAVO, *THE HISTORIES OF BRAZIL BY PEDRO DE MAGALHÃES GANDAVO WITH A FACSIMILIE OF THE PORTUGUESE ORIGINAL*, TRANS. JOHN B. STETSON, JR, NEW YORK, 1922

Likewise, Alfred Russel Wallace's view of the country's vastness during his travels in the 19th century brings an interesting description of Brazil nut harvesting.

"Perhaps no country in the world contains such an amount of vegetable matter on its surface as the valley of the Amazon. Its entire extent, with the exception of some very small portions, is covered with one dense and lofty primeval forest, the most extensive and unbroken which exists upon the earth.

...[The Brazil nut tree] takes more than a whole year to produce and ripen its fruits. In the month of January I observed the trees loaded at the same time with flowers and ripe fruits, both of which were falling from the tree; from these flowers would be formed the nuts of the following year; requiring eighteen months for their complete development from the bud. The fruits which are nearly as hard and heavy as cannonballs, fall with tremendous force from the height of a hundred feet, crashing through the branches and snapping off large boughs... Persons are sometimes killed by them, and accidents are not infrequent among the Indians engaged in gathering them".

ALFRED RUSSEL WALLACE, *A NARRATIVE OF TRAVELS ON THE AMAZON AND RIO NEGRO, WITH AN ACCOUNT OF THE NATIVE TRIBES, AND OBSERVATIONS ON THE CLIMATE, GEOLOGY, AND NATURAL HISTORY OF THE AMAZON VALLEY*, REEVE AND CO, LONDON, 1853

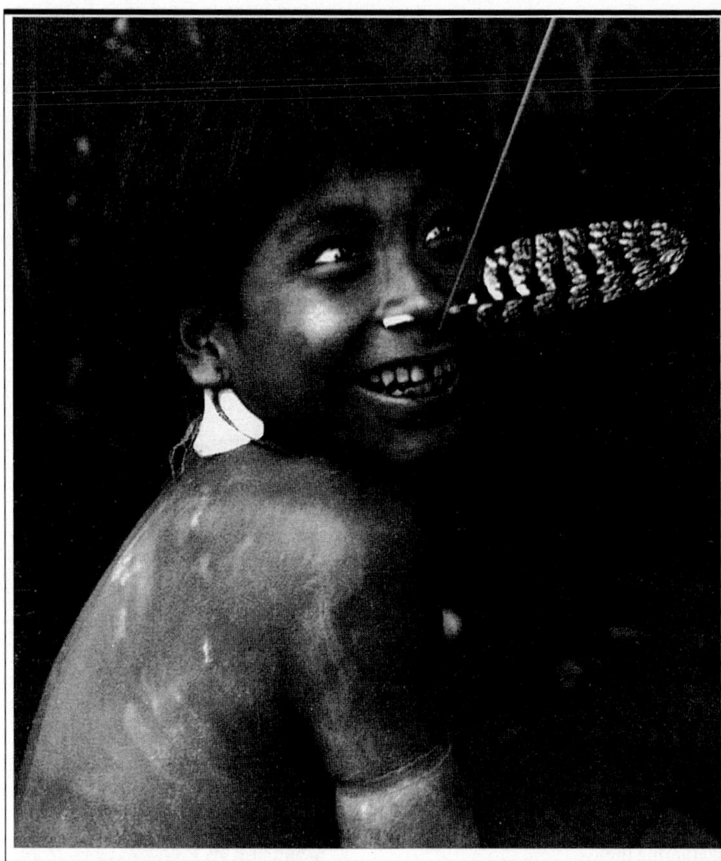

From the very first descriptions of the Brazilian aboriginal peoples in the letter sent back to Portugal in 1500 by Pedro Vaz de Caminha, travellers, historians and authors alike have held a fascination with their rituals and way of life.

"These Indians live in villages: each village has seven or eight houses which are very long like a rope walk or warehouse, constructed of wood almost entirely, and covered with palm leaves or other similar forest plants: they are filled with people from one end to the other, each person having his allotted place with a location for the hammock in which he sleeps...In every house all live together in harmony, without any dissension amongst them: on the contrary, they are so friendly with one another that what belongs to one belongs to all, and when one of them has something to eat, no matter how small, all his neighbors share in it.

...

The language spoken along the whole coast is the same...[it] is very soft and easily learned by any of the tribes. There are some words of it which are employed only by females, and others serve only for the males. It lacks three letters... namely *F*, nor *L*, nor *R*, a very wonderful thing, for they have neither *F*aith, *L*aw, nor *R*uler: and thus they live without order, [having besides no idea] of counting, weights or measures. They adore nothing, nor do they believe that after death there is glory for the good and punishment for the wicked. Their belief in the immortality of the soul is only this, that their dead will go through a future life wounded or cut in pieces or in the condition in which he left this life. And when one of them dies, their custom is to bury him in a hole seated on his feet with the hammock beside him that served him for a bed in life. Then for the first few days his relatives place food on the grave, and some of them are even accustomed to put the food in the grave at the time of burial; and they absolutely believe that they eat the food and sleep in the hammock which is with them in the grave. These people have no king or any one to administer justice, except a chief in each village which is like a captain, whom they obey voluntarily and not through constraint."

PEDRO DE MAGALHÃES GANDAVO, *THE HISTORIES OF BRAZIL BY PEDRO DE MAGALHÃES GANDAVO WITH A FACSIMILIE OF THE PORTUGUESE ORIGINAL*, TRANS. JOHN B. STETSON, JR, NEW YORK, 1922

Alfred Russel Wallace also made copious notes about the Indians who he had met and who had helped him during his exploration of the natural history of the Amazon Valley.

"The Indians of the Amazon and its tributaries, are of a countless variety of tribes and nations; all of whom have peculiar languages and customs, and many of whom have some distinct physical characteristics. Those now found in the city of Para and all about the lower Amazon have long been civilised, have lost their own language and speak the Portuguese, and are known by the general names of Tapúyais [they] are short, stout and well made. They learn all trades quickly and well, and are a quiet, good-natured inoffensive people."

ALFRED RUSSEL WALLACE, *A NARRATIVE OF TRAVELS ON THE AMAZON AND RIO NEGRO, WITH AN ACCOUNT OF THE NATIVE TRIBES, AND OBSERVATIONS ON THE CLIMATE, GEOLOGY, AND NATURAL HISTORY OF THE AMAZON VALLEY*, REEVE AND CO, LONDON, 1853.

In 1913 Theodore Roosevelt (1858–1919) led a scientific expedition that culminated in the exploration of an unmapped river deep in the Brazilian jungle. The aim of the trip was to escape the pressures of political life in the United States and find new challenges for his restless energy. The ravages of disease and illness took their toll on the former president during the exploration but he was undaunted in his travels, considering it his 'last chance to be a boy'. He begins by likening the first immigrants to the country to a similar process that occurred in the development of the United States.

"In short, these men, and those like them everywhere on the frontier between civilization and savagery in Brazil, are now playing the part played by our back-woodsmen when over a century and a quarter ago they began the conquest of the great basin of the Mississippi; the part played by the Boer farmers for over a century in South Africa, and by the Canadians when less than half a century ago they began to take possession of their Northwest. Every now and then some one says that the 'last frontier' is now to be found in Canada or Africa, and that it has almost vanished. On a far larger scale this frontier is to be found in Brazil – a country as big as Europe or the United States – and decades will pass before it vanishes. The first settlers came to Brazil a century before the first settlers came to the United States and Canada. For three hundred years progress was very slow – Portuguese colonial government at that time was almost as bad as Spanish. For the last half-century and over there has been a steady increase in the rapidity of the rate of development; and this increase bids fair to be constantly more rapid in the future.

The Paulistas, hunting for lands, slaves, and mines, were the first native Brazilians who, a hundred years ago, played a great part in opening to settlement vast stretches of wilderness. The rubber hunters have played a similar part during the last few decades. Rubber dazzled them, as gold and diamonds have dazzled other men and driven them forth to wander through the wide waste spaces of the world. Searching for rubber they made highways of rivers the very existence of which was unknown to the governmental authorities, or to any map-makers. Whether they succeeded or failed, they everywhere left behind them settlers, who toiled, married, and brought up children. Settlement began; the conquest of the wilderness entered on its first stage.'

THEODORE ROOSEVELT, *THROUGH THE BRAZILIAN WILDERNESS*, JOHN MURRAY, LONDON, 1914

Theodore Roosevelt's travels in the Amazon led at times to great hardships and illness. The following extract shows his determination to succeed in putting a new geographical feature on the map.

"We had been two months in the canoes; from the 27th of February to the 26th of April. We had gone over 750 kilometres. The river from its source, near the thirteenth degree, to where it became navigable and we entered it, had a course of some 200 kilometres – probably more, perhaps 300 kilometres. Therefore we had now put on the map a river nearly 1,000 kilometres in length of which the existence was not merely unknown but impossible if the standard maps were correct.

We spent a last night under canvas, at Pyrineús' encampment. It rained heavily. Next morning we all gathered at the monument which Colonel Rondon had erected, and he read the orders of the day. These recited just what had been accomplished: set forth the fact that we had now by actual exploration and investigation discovered that the river whose upper portion had been called the Dúvida on the maps of the Telegraphic Commission and the unknown major part of which we had just traversed, and the river known to a few rubbermen, but to no one else, as the Castanho, and the lower part of the river known to the rubbermen as the Aripuanan (which did not appear on the maps save as its mouth was sometimes indicated, with no hint of its size) were all parts of one and the same river; and that by order of the Brazilian Government this river, the largest affluent of the Madeira, with its source near the 13th degree and its mouth a little south of the 5th degree, hitherto utterly unknown to cartographers and in large part utterly unknown to any save the local tribes of Indians, had been named the Rio Roosevelt.

We put upon the map a river some fifteen hundred kilometres in length, of which the upper course was not merely utterly unknown to, but unguessed at by, anybody; while the lower course, although known for years to a few rubbermen, was utterly unknown to cartographers."

THEODORE ROOSEVELT,
THROUGH THE BRAZILIAN WILDERNESS,
JOHN MURRAY, LONDON, 1914

Perhaps the last word should go to the Reverend T.B. Ray who comments on the fondness for coffee in Brazil

"One cannot help being impressed also by the prevalence of coffee-drinking stands and stores – especially if he meets many friends. These friends will insist upon taking him into a coffee stand and engaging him in conversation while they sip coffee. On many corners are little round or octagonal pagoda-like structures... The coffee drinking places are everywhere and most of them are usually filled. The practice of taking coffee with one's friends must lessen materially the amount of strong drink consumed by the Brazilian. Nevertheless, that amount of strong drink is, alas, altogether too great."

REVEREND TB RAY,
BRAZILIAN SKETCHES,
1882

Itineraries

▲ Dunes in the Parque Nacional dos Lençóis Maranhenses.

▼ A meandering river in Amazonia

Peak near Teresópolis ▲

▲ Flamengo supporters at Maracanã Stadium

Tyrolean interior in southern Brazil ▼

Man wearing the strip of the national soccer team with a *mãe de santo* ▼

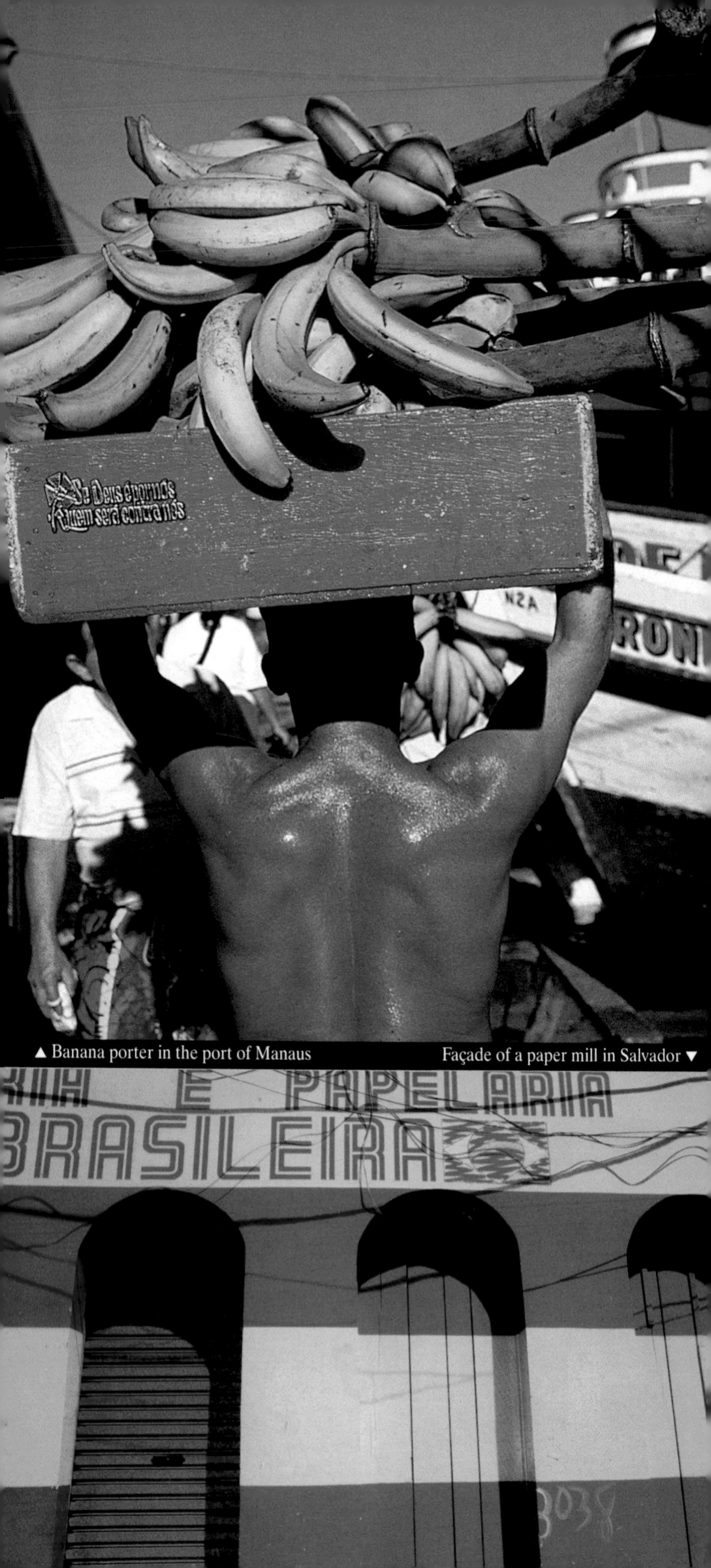

▲ Banana porter in the port of Manaus

Façade of a paper mill in Salvador ▼

Rio de Janeiro

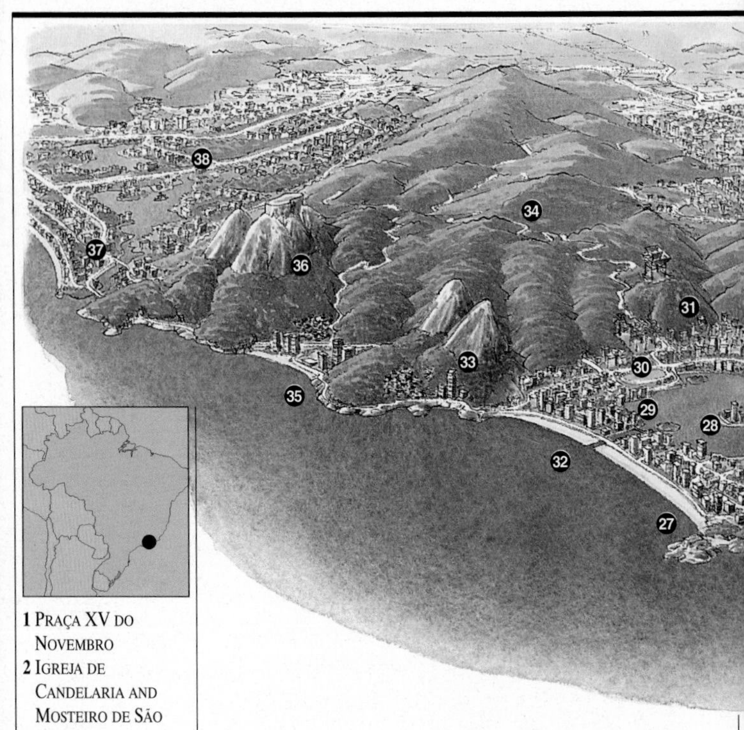

1 PRAÇA XV DO NOVEMBRO
2 IGREJA DE CANDELARIA AND MOSTEIRO DE SÃO BENTO
3 ILHA FISCAL
4 PONTE RIO-NITEROI
5 ESTAÇÃO CENTRAL DO BRASIL
6 PALACIO DO ITAMARATY
7 CATEDRAL METROPOLITANA
8 ARCOS DA LAPA
9 TEATRO MUNICIPAL
10 MUSEU DE ARTE MODERNA
11 AEROPORTO SANTOS-DUMONT
12 MONUMENTO AOS PRACINHAS, PARQUE DO FLAMENGO AND MARINA DA GLÓRIA
13 PRAIA DO FLAMENGO
14 IGREJA DA GLORIA
15 SAMBODROMO
16 CAMPO DE SÃO CRISTOVÃO
17 QUINTA DA BOA VISTA (MUSEUM AND ZOO)
18 AEROPORTO INTERNACIONAL DO GALEÃO

After driving out the French from the colony established by Villegagnon ● *22* in 1555, the Portuguese went about settling the region around Guanabara Bay. The town of Rio was officially founded in 1565 by Estácio de Sá, who named it São Sebastião de Rio de Janeiro. The Portuguese drove the American Indians back into the interior and, having founded a settlement near Pão de Açucar, they established the town on Morro do Castelo (Castle Hill). The Jesuits ▲ *116* also built a monastery there. Other religious orders settled on the hills, which were healthier than the swampland occupied by the outlying districts of Rio. The Franciscans settled on Morro Santo Antônio ▲ *120*, the Benedictines on Morro São Bento ▲ *119* and the Carmelites on a site now occupied by Praça XV de Novembro ▲ *117*. Rio flourished during the second half of the 18th century, when gold from Minas Gerais bound for Portugal was shipped from its port, and in 1763 it became the capital of Brazil. Most of the city's many baroque churches date from this period, as do the fortifications that the Portuguese built around the bay ▲ *152* to defend Rio against attacks from the French and Dutch. However, it was the arrival of the Portuguese royal family (1808–21), who fled Lisbon to escape Napoleon's advancing troops, that radically transformed the city. Various restrictions, including embargos on manufactured goods, salt mining and university education, made the colony entirely dependent on the capital. Under the auspices of the Prince Regent, the future Dom João VI, and his court the colonial city soon evolved into a European-style metropolis. The opening of Brazil's ports to international trade in 1808 was the first major step in the

THE CARIOCA. Rio's inhabitants (*cariocas*) are named for the Carioca, a stream that rises in the Paineiras ▲ *150* and that provided Rio with drinking water until the 19th century. It was diverted at Dois Irmãos ('two brothers'), from where it flowed through the *bairro* of Santa Teresa and back to the city center via the Lapa aqueduct ▲ *132*. Its water fed public fountains, including those on Largo da Carioca ▲ *120* and Praça XV de Novembro ▲ *117*. Today the Carioca runs beneath Rua Cosme Velho and Rua das Laranjeiras ▲ *138* but can still be seen on Largo do Boticário ▲ *138* and at its mouth on Praia do Flamengo ▲ *135*.

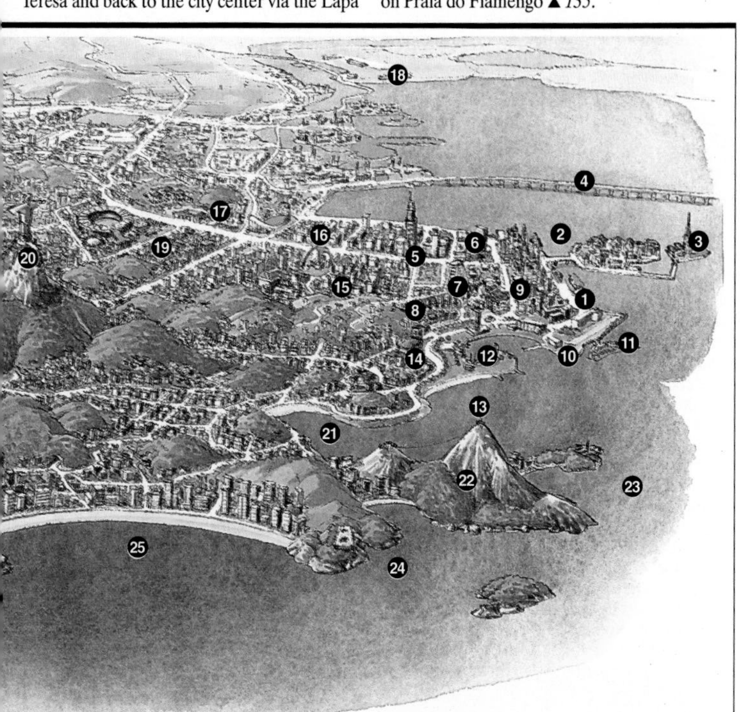

expansion of the economy. With the impetus given by the French artistic mission ● *84*, a group of French painters whom he invited to Rio in 1816, the Prince Regent was able to re-create the splendors of court life that he had known in Portugal and to nurture the arts and sciences. French influence continued to make its mark on Rio throughout the 19th century, and from 1870 until the 1920s the city underwent explosive expansion as immigration was encouraged. Housing began to be built on the drained swampland north of Rio, and in the 1920s the fashion for ocean bathing attracted wealthy residents to the Atlantic beaches on the southern side of the city. The historic parts of the old city were gradually abandoned as its inhabitants moved into other districts: Flamengo and Botafogo during the 19th century ▲ *140*, Copacabana in the 1920s ▲ *144*, Ipanema and Leblon in the 1950s ▲ *145*, and São Conrado and Barra from the 1970s ▲ *147*. Today some ten million people live in the *bairros* (districts) lining the bays, while Centro (the city center) is virtually uninhabited. Now Rio's commercial district, Centro is busy during the day but deserted at weekends. Wealthy residential districts have developed in Zona Sul, located along the beaches to the south of the city. Meanwhile, Zona Norte, the northernmost part of Rio, which includes the *bairros* of Nova Iguaçú, São João de Meriti and Duque de Caxias, consists of industrial areas and a working-class suburb cut through for more than thirty miles by Avenida Brazil. Zona Sul and Zona Norte are separated by a mountain range covered with lush vegetation and incorporating the Parque Nacional de Tijuca ▲ *150*.

19 MARACANÃ
20 CORCOVADO AND CRISTO REDENTOR
21 PRAIA DE BOTAFOGO
22 PÃO DE AÇUCAR
23 FORTALEZA DE SÃO JOÃO
24 FORTE DUQUE DE CAXIAS
25 PRAIA DE COPACABANA
26 FORTE DE COPACABANA
27 PRAIA DE IPANEMA
28 LAGOA RODRIGO DE FREITAS
29 JOQUEI CLUBE
30 JARDIM BOTÂNICO
31 VISTA CHINESA
32 PRAIA DO LEBLON
33 MORRO DOIS IRMÃOS
34 FLORESTA E PARQUE DA TIJUCA
35 PRAIA DE SÃO CONRADO
36 PEDRA DA GÁVEA
37 BARRA DA TIJUCA
38 JACAREPAGUÁ

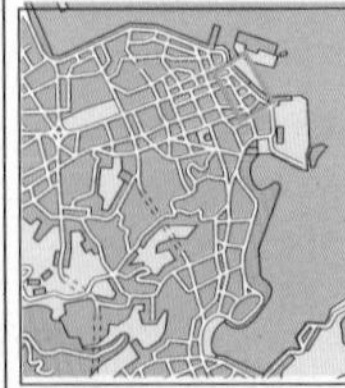

MUSEU DA IMAGEM E DO SOM
The Museum of Image and Sound occupies a building at Praça Rui Barbosa 190 (*below*) that was constructed for the 1922 World Fair ▲ *125*. The museum's audiovisual and photographic archive, in particular, amply illustrate the history of MPB (Brazilian popular music) ● *52* and the development of Rio (documented by photographs taken by Augusto Malta ● *10*).

LARGO DA MISERICÓRDIA ◆ A B3-C3

Toward the end of the 16th century Rio began to spread out around the hill known as Morro do Castelo. The center of this expansion was Largo da Misericórdia, the square fronting the Igreja de Nossa Senhora do Bonsucesso. The chapel of Nossa Senhora da Misericórdia that was built at the foot of Morro do Castelo was later renamed Nossa Senhora do Bonsucesso for the Madonna that graces one of its altars. In 1582 the Jesuit priest José de Anchieta ▲ *220* organized the building of the city's first hospital, the Santa Casa da Misericórdia, next to the chapel.

LADEIRA DA MISERICÓRDIA. In the late 16th century a steep path was created to link the upper and lower parts of the city. The only surviving section of this path, which was paved with rounded cobbles known as *pé-de-moleque* (urchin's feet), is to the right of the main entrance of Nossa Senhora do Bonsucesso. It has great historic importance since this is all that remains of Rio's origins, as Morro do Castelo itself was leveled in 1920.

IGREJA DE NOSSA SENHORA DO BONSUCESSO. The original church was extended and renovated several times until 1780. Three altarpieces in the nave, originating from the Jesuit church of Santo Inácio that once crowned Morro do Castelo, are fine examples of Jesuit mannerist art. The church also houses Bandeiras da Misericórdia, flags used during parades and in processions of condemned prisoners, painted by the freed slave Manoel da Cunha e Silva, as well as a number of 17th- and 18th-century paintings including the *Vision of the Virgin*, *Nossa Senhora da Misericórdia* (Our Lady of Mercy) and *Nossa Senhora da Penha* (Our Lady of Sorrows).

MUSEU HISTÓRICO NACIONAL. The museum was founded in 1922 to preserve the institutional memory of Brazilian society. It has a rich and varied collection of more than 30,000 pieces, including works of art and furniture dating from the colonial and imperial periods, a collection of more than 100,000 coins and medals, and archives comprising some 40,000 documents. As well as a valuable collection of Oriental ivory, the museum also has permanent exhibitions on daily life in Brazil and the major periods of the country's history.

MUSEU HISTÓRICO NACIONAL
The Museum of Brazilian History was built over the remains of several military buildings, including the Forte de Santiago ▲ *152*. The cannons (*above*) on the patio still point toward the sea and the arsenal.

TOWARD PRAÇA QUINZE DE NOVEMBRO ◆ A B3-C3

From Rua da Misericórdia there are two ways of walking to Praça XV de Novembro.

PRAÇA MARECHAL ÂNCORA. On Saturday mornings the best route is via Praça Marechal Âncora, as on that day the square is filled with two picturesque markets, the *feira do troco* (flea market) beneath the viaduct, and the *feira de antiguidades* (antiques market) beneath the Alba Mar restaurant. The Alba Mar, which specializes in seafood, occupies the tower of

Peregrinations of Rio's cathedral
In the 18th century the original cathedral, on Morro do Castelo, had to be moved nearer the center of the expanding city. From 1738 to 1808, while the new cathedral was being built, the see was transferred to the Igreja de Nossa Senhora do Rosário ▲ *121*. When the Portuguese court ● *24* arrived in Rio, the unfinished cathedral, on Largo de São Francisco, was used for military purposes and the see was again transferred, to the Igreja de Nossa Senhora do Carmo. Rio's new cathedral ▲ *124* opened in 1976.

a former market. This was a metal building dating from 1908 and demolished when the viaduct was built in the 1950s.
Rua Dom Manoel. At no. 15 a building in an eclectic style houses the Museu Naval (Maritime Museum) and the naval records office. The museum, founded in 1686, has a major collection of old charts, model boats and documents relating to the history of the Portuguese and Brazilian navies.
Rua Santa Luzia. Turn off Rua da Misericórdia into Rua Santa Luzia and you will come to the Santa Casa da Misericórdia. This neoclassical building was built in the mid-19th century on the site of the original hospital. The entrance hall and first-floor corridors house an impressive collection of portraits of the hospital's benefactors. Continue past the Igreja Santa Luzia and along Avenida Presidente Antônio Carlos, which is continued by Rua 1 de Março beyond Praça XV de Novembro. On the left you will see the 42-story Faculdade Cândido Mendes, a university building that stands in the courtyard of the Convento do Carmo.

Praça Quinze de Novembro ◆ A B3

During the colonial period this square was the gateway to the city and the hub of its social and political life. Some of the old wharves at the foot of the fountain carved in 1738 by Mestre Valentim ● *75* have been demolished. Today the fountain stands in the center of the square and the modern quays lie further back. The narrow streets in this district are vestiges of the colonial period. Among them is the typically colonial Beco dos Barbeiros ('barbers' cul-de-sac'), with a central runnel that once channeled rainwater and sewage.
Igreja de Nossa Senhora do Carmo. The church, built in 1752, served as Rio's cathedral from 1808 to 1976. The beautiful wood sculptures and altarpieces that decorate it are the work of the two greatest artists of Brazil's colonial period, Inácio Ferreira Pinto and Mestre Valentim. There is also a painting of the twelve apostles by José Leandro de Carvalho, and a very fine depiction of Nossa Senhora da Cabeça.

Igreja Santa Luzia
When this tiny church at Rua Santa Luzia 490 was built in 1752 it had a single tower. The church acquired its present form during its renovation in 1884. Bounded by sea and mountains until the early 20th century it is today surrounded by apartment buildings (*above*).

Mestre Valentim (1737–1813)
The son of a Portuguese nobleman and a slave woman, Valentim da Fonseca e Silva was born in Minas Gerais and came to Rio in 1764. He was a friend of Viceroy Dom Luiz de Vasconselos, and contributed to the viceroy's scheme to embellish the city, creating several monuments. Valentim is regarded as the greatest Brazilian sculptor of the late 18th century. His finest work is the Capela do Noviciado in the Igreja de Nossa Senhora do Carmo in Rio.

IGREJA DA ORDEM TERCEIRA DE NOSSA SENHORA DO MONTE DO CARMO. This impressive church was built to complete the religious complex of the Convento do Carmo. Work on its construction began in 1755, but its present appearance dates from 1810. The church's most important works of art are in the CAPELA DO NOVICIADO, near the sacristy. They include a small and still perfectly preserved wooden altar carved by Mestre Valentim.

PAÇO IMPERIAL. In 1743 the warehouses of the royal mint, extended by José Fernandes Pinto Alpoim, became the residence of the governor of the captaincy of Rio de Janeiro. In spite of its modest dimensions the residence was was converted into a royal palace for Dom João, the exiled prince regent, in 1808. It became the Paço Imperial (Imperial Palace) ● *75* in 1822.

ARCO DO TELES AND TRAVESSA DO COMÉRCIO. Among the buildings surrounding the square were three impressive *sobrados* (houses with several stories) ● *74* designed by José Fernandes Pinto Alpoim. Through the first *sobrado* ran a passage linking the square with the Travessa do Comércio. Today the passage leads to a maze of pedestrianized streets hung with old street lamps and lined with houses with colorful façades (*above*). Altered in the 19th century, this is a perfectly preserved part of Rio, and it comes to life in the evenings when the working day is over. A few ship's chandlers, harking back to the district's former port activity, still survive among the restaurants and art galleries. On the corner of Rua do Ouvidor ▲ *121* is one of the city's most picturesque churches, the tiny NOSSA SENHORA DA LAPA DOS MERCADORES. Its beautiful baroque decoration has recently been restored.

CORREDOR CULTURAL DO CENTRO
This 'corridor' defines a conservation area in the Centro, between the Museu de Arte Moderna ▲ *125* and Praça Mauá. The area contains many historic buildings and the façades of the *sobrados* here have been authentically restored.

ILHA FISCAL
This turquoise palace (*above*) was designed by the Italian architect Del Vecchio in the neo-Gothic style and built in the 1880s. The last ball given by the Portuguese royal court, on November 11, 1889, was held here. Surrounded by water, it is reached from the quay of the Espaço Cultural da Marinha.

CANDELÁRIA AND SURROUNDINGS ◆ A B2-A2

A stroll through this historic enclave reveals the presence of several cultural centers, which are concentrated in the Corredor Cultural, and leads to Praça Pio X, with the impressive church of Nossa Senhora da Candelária.

IGREJA DE NOSSA SENHORA DA CANDELÁRIA. The church, one of the largest and most lavish in the city, was begun in 1775,

The Paço Imperial (*right*) now houses a cultural center, stores and the Atrium restaurant.

but it was altered several times until it was consecrated in 1898. The neoclassical dome, completed in 1877, is framed by eight large white marble statues. The richly decorated interior is clad in polychrome marble and features murals by João Zeferino da Costa. The cross on the square in front of the church commemorates street children who were massacred by a death squad in July 1993.

CASA FRANÇA-BRASIL. In 1820 the Portuguese civil administration hastily commissioned this customs house in response to merchants' pressing demands. The architect was Grandjean de Montigny, and work was completed in ten months, a record for the time. This is why the building, in the neoclassical style, has a simple exterior, with a roof in the Portuguese colonial style. However, its proportions and interior decoration mark the break away from colonial architecture and the adoption of French neoclassicism, a style that Grandjean de Montigny introduced to Brazil. Having fulfilled its intended role for over half a century, the building has since 1900 served as a center for the promotion of cultural exchange between France and Brazil.

CENTRO CULTURAL BANCO DO BRASIL. Occupying the former headquarters of the Banco do Brasil, this cultural center is the largest in Brazil, containing exhibition halls, theaters and a movie theater, a library and bookstore. With the nearby Casa França-Brasil, the CENTRO CULTURAL DOS CORREIOS (Post Office Cultural Center) and the surrounding art galleries, it forms a major cultural hub in the heart of the city.

IGREJA E MOSTEIRO DE SÃO BENTO. Follow Rua 1 de Março to Rua Dom Gerardo, where you will come to the bottom of the Ladeira de São Bento. This sloping alley leads up to summit of a hill on which the Benedictines who settled in Brazil at the end of the 16th century built a church and monastery. Work on the monastery began in 1587 and continued for two hundred years. Its present appearance dates from the 18th century. The church's sober façade is in stark contrast to the exuberant decoration of its interior ● *71*. The huge nave is covered with *talha* ● *70*, and painted wooden sculptures covered with gold leaf decorate the walls, the high altar and the two side altars. Chandeliers, silver torchiers and ceiling paintings of the Madonna complete the decoration of this unique baroque interior.

GRANDJEAN DE MONTIGNY (1776–1850)

This architect was a member of the French artistic mission ● *84* invited to Brazil in 1816 by Dom João. He helped found the Academia Imperial de Belas Artes (later the Escola de Belas Artes) in Rio, and introduced the neoclassical style ● *75* to Brazil. Of the buildings that he designed in Rio, only the Casa França-Brasil and the Solar (villa) Grandjean de Montigny ▲ *141* still stand today.

IGREJA E MOSTEIRO DE SÃO BENTO ✪

This religious ensemble at Rua Dom Gerardo 68 is a masterpiece of colonial baroque architecture. It is open daily, 8am–noon and 2–5.30pm. Women are not allowed inside the monastery. Visitors may come here to hear Gregorian chants sung on Saturdays at 7.15am and Sundays at 10am.

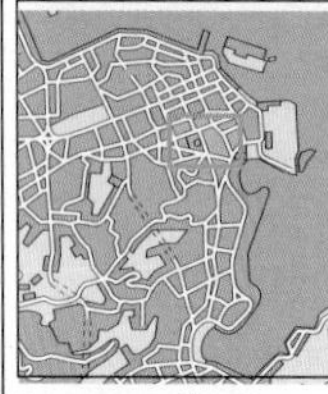

IGREJA DA ORDEM TERCEIRA
The exquisite baroque decoration of the Church of the Third Order was executed between 1732 and 1740. The wood carvings and the altar are by Manuel de Brito, and the eight paintings, as well as the decoration of the ceiling over the nave, are by Caetano da Costa Coelho. These two Portuguese artists inspired others in Rio and elsewhere in colonial Brazil. Above the high altar is a remarkable figure of a seraphic (six-winged) Christ.

CONVENTO DE SANTO ANTÔNIO ★
The religious complex of Santo Antônio at Largo da Carioca 5 is easily accessible from the Carioca metro. It is open Monday–Friday, 8am–5pm.

LARGO DA CARIOCA ◆ A C2

In 1723 the first public fountain in Rio was built on the site of what is now Largo da Carioca (Carioca Square). It was fed by water from the Carioca ▲ *115*, a stream which rises in the Paineiras ▲ *150*. While nothing remains of the fountain today, the square (*above*) has become one of the busiest in Rio, with street vendors, traveling performers and evangelical preachers.

★ CONVENTO DE SANTO ANTÔNIO. This architectural complex, built on a hill by the Franciscans, comprises a convent (1608) and two churches. The Igreja da Ordem Terceira de São Francisco da Penitência, which is one of the city's earliest and finest examples of baroque architecture, has been completely restored. It contains fine wood paneling, torchiers and paintings.

RUA DA CARIOCA. This street is lined with *sobrados* ● *74* and a variety of stores, especially stores selling musical instruments. Bar Luiz, at no. 39, is a traditional German-style *bierkeller* (brewery) founded in 1887. The *chopp* (draft beer) served here is reputed to be the best in Rio. The Iris movie theater at no. 49 has a striking Art Nouveau interior and a magnificent metal staircase (1912). At weekends the Iris is the venue for events hosted by Rio's top DJs. On this street there are also a number of *sebos* (secondhand booksellers), including Aimée Gilbert (at no. 38) and Aniqualhas Brasileiras (at no. 10), specializing in rare Brazilian and foreign books.

PRAÇA TIRADENTES AND SURROUNDINGS ◆ A B2-C2

Rua da Carioca leads to Praça Tiradentes, where there is an impressive equestrian statue of Dom Pedro I ● *25*. In the early years of the 20th century the square, which was filled with theaters and cabarets, was the center of *carioca* nightlife. Today it is busy during the day but almost deserted at night.

THEATERS AND 'GAFIEIRAS'. The first theater to be built on Praça Tiradentes opened in 1813 but was rebuilt several times. The present building, named for the 19th-century Brazilian actor João Caetano, was completely rebuilt in the

Convento de Santo Antônio (*right*).

1970s. On the far side of the square is the TEATRO CARLOS GOMES, which opened in 1872, was rebuilt in 1905 and subsequently restored in the Art Deco style. It was named for the famous Brazilian composer Antônio Carlos Gomes, who wrote the opera *O Guaraní*. Dance enthusiasts will like the famous Gafiera Estudantina dance hall (*right*), at Praça Tiradentes 79, where they can dance the samba, rumba, tango etc., and the Centro Cultural Carioca, at the *sobrado* of Rua do Teatro 37, for samba and chorinho.

RUA REGENTE FEIJÓ AND RUA LUÍS DE CAMÕES. Some fine examples of the *sobrados* that are typical of historic Rio can be seen on Rua Regente Feijó, which leads off Praça Tiradentes. On Rua Luís de Camões, which cuts across Rua Regente Feijó, is the CENTRO DE ARTES HÉLIO OITICICA.

IGREJA DE NOSSA SENHORA DA LAMPADOSA. This delightful little church is wedged between two buildings on Avenida Passos, near the intersection of this avenue and Praça Tiradentes. It was built by a black brotherhood in 1748 and rebuilt in the neo-colonial style in 1934. On April 21, 1792 Tiradentes ● *24* prayed in front of this church on his way to the gallows on the square that now bears his name.

LARGO AND IGREJA DE SÃO FRANCISCO DE PAULA. Continue along Rua Luís de Camões, past the REAL GABINETE PORTUGUÊS DE LEITURA (Royal Library of Portuguese Literature), and you will come to Largo de São Francisco, a square dominated by the impressive Igreja São Francisco de Paula. The church contains fine wood carvings by Mestre Valentim and Antônio de Pádua e Castro, and frescos by Manoel da Cunha e Silva. During the Empire ● *25* various official ceremonies took place in this church.

IGREJA DE NOSSA SENHORA DO ROSÁRIO E SÃO BENEDITO. A narrow street leads from Largo de São Francisco to Praça Monte Castelo, a popular meeting place, with bar and restaurant terraces. At Rua Uruguaiana 77 stands the church of Nossa Senhora do Rosário e São Benedito, erected in 1708 by brotherhoods of slaves and freed slaves ● *31*. Gutted by fire in 1967, the church was rebuilt to a plan by the architect Lúcio Costa ▲ *201*, who also devised its restrained decoration.

RUA DO OUVIDOR. From the Igreja Nossa Senhora do Rosário e São Benedito turn right along Rua Uruguaiana and you will come to Rua do Ouvidor, the center of fashion and society life in 19th-century Rio. At its height during the early years of the 20th century the street became a kind of catwalk as men and women paraded up and down it sporting their smart Parisian outfits. A few vestiges of this district's fashionable past still survive: one is the CONFEITARIA COLOMBO at Rua Gonçalves Dias 30, a street adjacent to Rua do Ouvidor. This glamorous Art Deco tearoom, which opened in 1894, still has its original large jacaranda-framed mirrors, colored skylight and marble tables, and mouthwatering pastries are still served there.

REAL GABINETE PORTUGUÊS DE LEITURA
The library, opened in 1887, is a fine example of the Portuguese neo-Manueline style. The delightfully old-fashioned interior (*above*) houses a major collection of Portuguese literature.

CENTRO DE ARTES HÉLIO OITICICA
This arts center is housed in a fine pink neoclassical building dating from 1872. The center hosts exhibitions of modern art, especially of work by the conceptual artist Hélio Oiticica (1937–80).

THE FRENCH IN RUA DO OUVIDOR
Several French milliners opened shops in this street, which is also lined by stores with such names as Tour Eiffel and Notre Dame. Rua do Ouvidor was also the haunt of intellectuals who frequented the editorial offices of the *Jornal do Comércio*, founded by a Frenchman named Plancher, and the bookstores Garnier, Laemmert and Mougre.

In 1843 the French engineer Henri de Beaurepaire Rohan presented to the city authorities his plan for the redevelopment of colonial Rio. He suggested leveling the hills of Castelo and Senado, widening the streets and opening up broad avenues to make the city more attractive, more functional and healthier. While very little of the work was actually carried out, the idea of creating a modern city captured the imagination of the urban planners and engineers, who approved Beaurepaire Rohan's proposals. Plans for the radical reform of Rio in the style of Haussmann's Paris ● *76* were put forward in the early 20th century and a number of projects were undertaken under the aegis of Rio's mayor Francisco Pereira Passos. One of these involved creating the symbolic Avenida Central, which was built in 1904–5 and renamed Avenida Rio Branco in 1912.

Museu Nacional de Belas Artes
The building that has housed the National Museum of Fine Arts (*bottom*) since 1937 dates from 1906–8 and originally accommodated the Escuela de Belas Artes. The main façade features a frieze of medallions, painted by Henrique Bernardelli, depicting the members of the French artistic mission ● *24*, *84* and Brazilian artists. The impressive Carrara marble staircase in the lobby leads to the museum's galleries. On the third floor is a major collection of works by 19th-century artists including Vitor Meireles, Pedro Américo, Bernardelli, Debret and Taunay ● *84*. The museum also has a valuable collection of Italian paintings, a few 'must sees' by Frans Post ● *84* and a gallery devoted to Eugène Boudin. The 20th-century gallery includes works by Lasar Segall, Anita Malfatti, Cândido Portinari ● *86*, Alfredo Volpi ● *88* and Tarsila do Amaral ● *89*.

Aerial view of the Teatro Municipal (*left*).

Francisco Pereira Passos
An engineer by profession, Pereira Passos was mayor of Rio from 1902 to 1906. He modernized the city and made it a cleaner place to live so as to prevent outbreaks of plague. He widened streets and opened up broad avenues, such as Avenida Mem de Sá, Avenida Beira Mar and Avenida Central. Despite his brief tenure as mayor, his vision made him the Haussmann of Brazil.

Biblioteca Nacional
The National Library (*left*), in a building dating from 1905–10, grew from the royal Portuguese collection that was brought to Rio from Lisbon in 1808. With more than three million volumes, Brazil's National Library is now one of the largest libraries in Latin America. Two bronze statues, *Intelligence* and *Learning*, by Corrêa Lima and Rodolfo Bernardelli stand at the entrance.

The creation of Avenida Central
Almost 100 feet wide and over one mile long, Avenida Central (*below*) was created to improve access to Rio's port area. The Parisian-style avenue came to symbolize Rio's *belle époque*. The original major buildings on the avenue were the Biblioteca Nacional, Teatro Municipal (*below, center picture*) and Museu de Belas Artes.

Central is renamed Rio Branco
Property speculators homed in on the once-beautiful Avenida Central and, in less than a hundred years, it had become the bland Avenida Rio Branco that it is today. Some of the buildings along the avenue still recall its original splendor, for example the Justiça Federal (at no. 241), the Clube Naval (at no. 180) and the Da Travessa bookstore (at no. 44).

Cinelândia
The creation of Praça Floriano (*left*) in the 1920s was closely connected to the plan for opening up Avenida Central. Popularly known as Cinelândia because of the many movie theaters there, the square was also lined with various theaters, tearooms and restaurants, and it was the focus of Rio's nightlife. Today Praça Floriano is busy at lunchtime and at the end of the working day when a colorful clientele fills the bars and restaurants there.

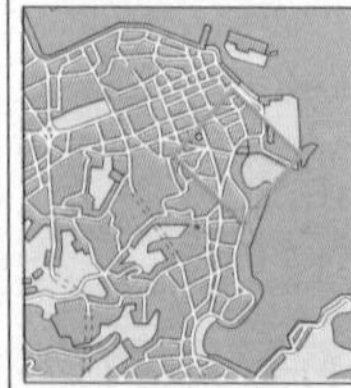

In 1926, four years after the World Fair ▲ *125* and Modern Art Week ▲ *218*, the mayor of Rio, Antônio Prado Júnior, set about radically modernizing the city. He invited a team of foreign engineers to submit a master plan under the direction of the French urban planner Alfred Agache. Although it was never fully completed, the Agache Plan changed the face of the city center. It was this initiative that created such features as the broad avenues of the Castelo district, apartment buildings with parking lots in their interior courtyards, alleyways passing through buildings and linking one street with another, and gallery-sidewalks beneath buildings on *pilotis*. This modernist initiative thus opened Brazilian architecture to the innovative influence of Le Corbusier ● *78*.

FROM AVENIDA CHILE TO PALÁCIO CAPANEMA ◆ A C2-C3

Some major examples of Le Corbusier's modernist idiom are very much in evidence on the route from Avenida República do Chile to the Palácio Gustavo Capanema. The avenue was built on the site of Morro Santo Antônio, a hill that was leveled in 1958–60.

CATEDRAL METROPOLITANA. Among the impressive buildings separated on Avenida Chile is the cathedral (*left*), which was completed in 1976. It is also known as the Nova Catedral or Catedral São Sebastião. The great conical nave, over 340 feet in diameter at the base, is pierced by four 200-foot-high windows and can hold up to two thousand people.

EDIFÍCIO DA PETROBRÁS. Another impressive building on Avenida Chile are the offices of the Brazilian oil company Petrobrás. The hollowed-out façades of the cube-shaped building, completed in 1968, offer glimpses of hanging gardens.

PALÁCIO GUSTAVO CAPANEMA. Continue along Avenida Chile and, after crossing Avenida Rio Branco, follow Avenida Almirante Barroso. From there turn right into Avenida Graça Aranha. The Palácio Gustavo Capanema ● *79* is at Rua da Imprensa 16, just behind the church of Santa Luzia ▲ *117*. The design of the palace (*left*) is based on a drawing by Le Corbusier elaborated by a group of young architects working under the direction of Lúcio Costa ▲ *201*. Begun in 1937 and completed in 1943, it became the symbol of modern architecture in Rio. It is named for the minister who sponsored its construction. The remarkable *azulejo*

ALBERTO SANTOS-DUMONT (1873–1932) ▲ *169*
This pioneer of aviation (*below*) was educated in France, where he made his first balloon ascent in 1897. In 1901 Santos-Dumont won the Deutsch Prize for a return flight in an airship between Saint Cloud and the Eiffel Tower. In 1906 he made the first powered flight at Bagatelle, traveling 196 feet in the biplane 14-bis. Later he perfected the design of his airplanes and created the famous Demoiselle monoplane.

tilework panels and frescos in the state rooms are by Cândido Portinari ● *87*. Nearby, in Rua Araújo Porto Alegre, which intersects Rua da Imprensa, stands the building of the Associação Brasileira de Imprensa (Brazilian Press Association). Designed by the Roberto brothers, it dates from 1936–8 and is notable for the modernity of its design and the extensive use of awnings, an architectural innovation at the time.

PARQUE DO FLAMENGO ◆ **A** C3-C4–D3

From Rua Araújo Porto Alegre walk up the right-hand side of Avenida Presidente Antônio Carlos, to the Parque do Flamengo ▲ *135*. Some of the earth and rubble from Morro Santo Antônio, the hill leveled in 1958–60, was used to extend the land beside the Aeroporto Santos-Dumont out into the sea and create the Parque do Flamengo. On this huge expanse of artificial land are the Museu de Arte Moderna and the Monumento aos Pracinhas.

MUSEU DE ARTE MODERNA. The Museum of Modern Art (MAM) is one of the finest and most original examples of modern architecture in Rio. Its two levels, 425 feet long and 80 feet wide, are supported by a series of reinforced concrete arches, with no interior pillars. It was designed by Afonso Eduardo Reidy, one of the team of architects who designed the Palácio Capanema. Work began in 1954 and the project was completed in 1967. The gardens, designed by Roberto Burle Marx ▲ *147*, show great creativity. Housing the Gilberto Chateaubriand Collection, the museum contains the world's finest assemblage of modern and contemporary Brazilian art. It also has a library and a film archive.

AEROPORTO SANTOS-DUMONT. A walk through the extensive and pleasant gardens surrounding the MAM brings you to the Santos-Dumont airport, another fine example of modernist architecture, designed by the Roberto brothers in 1937 and opened in 1944. The garden opposite the airport is one of the first designed by Roberto Burle Marx.

MONUMENTO AOS PRACINHAS. Continue through the Parque do Flamengo, to the right of the MAM, and you will come to the war memorial (*below*) commemorating those who died in World War Two. The monument, designed by Marcos Konder Neto and Hélio Ribas Marinho and unveiled in 1960, pays tribute to the members of the Brazilian Expeditionary Force (FEB) who died alongside the Allies, particularly at the Battle of Monte Cassino in Italy.

THE CHATEAUBRIANDS OF BRAZIL
Assis Chateaubriand, whose father named his children for the French writer Chateaubriand, whom he admired, was a Brazilian press baron. A great patron of the arts, he founded the MASP in São Paulo ▲ *224*. His son Gilberto assembled a major collection of contemporary Brazilian art which he bequeathed to the MAM in Rio.

1922 WORLD FAIR
The World Fair held to mark the centenary of Brazil's independence opened in Rio on September 7, 1922. The location was the esplanade that was created when Morro do Castelo was leveled and beaches were banked up. Only two of the pavilions survive. The French pavilion, a replica of the Petit Trianon at Versailles, is now the Academia Brasileira de Letras (at Avenida Presidente Wilson 203), founded in 1896 by Machado de Assis. The pavilion of the Distrito Federal houses the Museu da Imagem e do Som ▲ *116*.

▲ Avenida Presidente Vargas

The destruction of colonial Rio
When it was first opened the avenue was the largest urban thoroughfare in Brazil, and hundreds of buildings were destroyed to make way for it. They included some of Rio's major colonial churches, notably the baroque São Pedro dos Clérigos, Senhor Bom Jesus, São Domingos de Gusmão, Nossa Senhora da Conceição. The city hall was also razed and some of the wooded parkland in the Campo de Santana was lost.

Sambódromo ● *46*
During Carnival the Special Group, made up of Rio's fourteen top samba schools, parades in the Passarela do Samba, better known as the Sambódromo, designed by Oscar Niemeyer ▲ *203*. Located in Avenida Marquês de Sapucaí, it is easily reached from Praça Onze subway station on Avenida Presidente Vargas.

Under the dictatorship of Getúlio Vargas ● *36*, Dosdworth, mayor of Rio from 1930 to 1945, continued the development of the city proposed by the Agache Plan ▲ *124*. Under his aegis an avenue three miles long and over 260 feet wide was cut through the historic center of Rio from the Igreja de Candelária to Praça da Bandeira. The new thoroughfare was named Avenida Presidente Vargas for the president-dictator. It was not, however, completed according to the original plans and from the Igreja de Candelária ran only to Rua Uruguaiana, which had the gallery-sidewalks proposed by Agache. With the opening of Rio's two main avenues, Avenida Central in 1905 and Avenida Presidente Vargas in 1946, the city's old urban fabric, dating from the colonial period, was obliterated.

The Saara district ◆ **A** B2. A few examples of colonial architecture and of the eclectic style of the 19th century can still be seen in this mainly pedestrianized district between Avenida Central and Avenida Presidente Vargas. Turn off Avenida Presidente Vargas near the subway station and follow Rua Uruguaiana, which leads to some typically 19th-century streets: Rua da Alfândega, Rua do Senhor dos Passos and Rua Buenos Aires, and Rua da Conceição, Avenida dos Passos, Rua do Regente Feijó and Rua Tomé de Souza, which intersect them. These streets form the working-class district of Saara, named for the association of Arab traders who settled in what was effectively an open-air shopping mall. Today there are also Chinese, Japanese and Korean merchants and all kinds of stores, including several specialist shops. Saara's main attractions include the Arab restaurants and grocery stores selling exotic-looking produce.

Campo de Santana ◆ **A** B1. Rua da Alfândega, Rua do Senhor dos Passos and Rua Buenos Aires, which run parallel to Avenida Presidente Vargas, all lead to this magnificent park designed in the style of an English romantic garden. It was laid out in 1873 by the French landscape designer Auguste Glaziou ▲ *128* and officially opened in 1880 in the presence of Dom Pedro II ● *25*. The park is dotted with fountains, pools, grottos and bridges, and its winding pathways are shaded by trees – indigenous *jequitibá*, *abricó-de-macaco*, *figeira* and exotic jackfruit. The air is filled with birdsong and echoes to the cries of tamarins, while groups of agoutis roam free on the grass.

Stores in the Saara district
You will find hardware and stationers' stores on Rua Buenos Aires, stores selling leather goods, jewelry and specializing in festival items on Rua Senhor dos Passos, fabrics and perfumery on Rua da Alfândega, and carnival paraphernalia on Avenida Passos.

Praça da República ◆ **A** B1-C2. The square, which surrounds Campo de Santana, is dominated by some impressive historic buildings. These include the former Arquivo Nacional building (at no. 26); the central fire station (at no. 45); the former palace of the Conde dos Arcos, now the Senate; the law faculty of the Universidade Federal do Rio de Janeiro; the former Casa da Moeda (the mint), now occupied by the Arquivo Nacional (which has just been completely restored); and the Museu Deodoro (at no. 197). The latter was originally the residence of Marshal Deodoro da Fonseca, leader of the movement that overthrew the monarchy in 1889 and the first president of the new republic.

Estação Dom Pedro II and Palácio Duque de Caxias ◆ **A** B1. Opposite Campo de Santana, on the far side of Avenida Presidente Vargas, are two examples of the monumental and authoritarian Art Deco architecture of the Vargas era. The central railroad station, Estação Central do Brasil, designed in 1937 and opened in 1943, is famous for its tower and clock. The Palácio Duque de Caxias, dating from 1941 and formerly the war ministry building, stands opposite the mausoleum of Deodoro da Fonseca, a hero of the war against Paraguay ● *25* and commander-in-chief of the Brazilian army, for whom the palace is named. The building houses the archives of the Brazilian army and an important collection of maps.

★ **Palácio do Itamaraty** ◆ **A** B1. As you walk along Avenida Marechal Floriano, which runs parallel to Avenida Presidente Vargas, you will come to the Palácio do Itamaraty, with palm trees in its grounds. The palace houses the Museu Histórico e Diplomático, run by the Brazilian Foreign Office. This beautiful residence, built between 1851 and 1854, belonged to Francisco José da Rocha, Baron of Itamaraty, who made his fortune from coffee plantations. The reception rooms give some idea of the luxurious lifestyle of a nobility made wealthy by the coffee trade ● *32* in the Empire period. In 1889 the palace became the base of the new republic, before the latter was transferred to the Palácio do Catete ▲ *139* in 1897. Until 1960, when the Brazilian capital was transferred from Rio to Brasília ▲ *200,* the Palácio do Itamaraty housed the Foreign Office. In 1970 it was converted into a museum, which has the finest collection of historical maps of Brazil and holds archives of the Brazilian diplomatic service.

Palácio do Itamaraty ★
The palace is situated at Avenida Marechal Floriano 196, very near Presidente Vargas subway station. With an interior courtyard, palm trees and swans, it is a haven of peace and quiet in the heart of a bustling district. It is open to visitors Monday, Wednesday and Friday, 1.15–4.15pm. There are free guided tours.

Centro Cultural da Light
The cultural center, next to the Palácio do Itamaraty, occupies the premises of Light, Rio's former electricity company, which was founded in 1911. The displays here trace the history of the city's electrification. The center also houses a large collection of maps and photographs of Rio, and also organizes concerts or modern art exhibitions.

AUGUSTE GLAZIOU
French landscape designer Auguste Glaziou was invited to Brazil by Dom Pedro II to redesign the gardens of Quinta da Boa Vista. Glaziou also laid out Rio's Passeio Público, the Campo de Santana and Praça XV do Novembro, and founded the city's parks and gardens department, which he headed from 1869 to 1897.

THE SKELETON OF THE MUSEU NACIONAL
An 11,500-year-old human skeleton discovered in Minas Gerais and recently reconstructed at the University of Manchester, in Britain, is the oldest so far discovered on the American continent. The head belongs to a woman, nicknamed Luzia, whose negroid features call into question existing theories that the people who arrived via the Bering Strait during the Ice Age were America's first human inhabitants.

After the expulsion of the Jesuits from Portugal and its colonies in 1759 ● *28* what is now the district of São Cristóvão, which belonged to the order, returned to the Portuguese crown. The land was auctioned and as a result, the city of Rio, whose boundaries had formerly stopped at the edge of this private estate, was able to expand. Magnificent *fazendas* (plantations) and imposing residences then sprang up.

PRAÇA MÁRIO NAZARETH ◆ **E** B3. The former country house of the Jesuit order stands on this square off Rua São Cristóvão. In 1764 it became a leper-house, a groundbreaking institution run by the brotherhood of the Santíssimo Sacramento da Candelária, which still exists today. Although this large complex has been altered and extended several times over the centuries, its original Jesuit architecture, most notably the church, survives.

SOLAR DA MARQUESA DE SANTOS ◆ **E** B2-B3. The fine neoclassical building at Avenida Dom Pedro II 28 that houses the MUSEU DO PRIMEIRO REINADO was commissioned by Dom Pedro II for his mistress Domitila de Castro Canto e Melo, better known as the Marquise de Santos. Completed in about 1825, this beautiful little palace has paintings and bas-reliefs by Francisco Pedro do Amaral and the French brothers Marc and Zéferin Ferrez, and furniture and works of art dating from Brazil's imperial period.

★ **QUINTA DA BOA VISTA** ◆ **E** C2. A little further on is the former residence (*below*) of the Brazilian royal family. The original *quinta*, a farmhouse with several verandas and 300 windows, was the country residence of Elias Antônio Lopes, a rich merchant from Rio who presented it to the Prince Regent, Dom João ● *24*, when he arrived in Brazil. Dom João is said to have been touched by this priceless gift and described it as 'a royal veranda', the like of which he had never owned in Portugal. Altered and extended several times, the building became the official residence of the emperors of Brazil. Dom Pedro I commissioned Pierre Joseph Pézerat to carry out the conversion, as the result of which the original house was transformed into an impressive neoclassical palace. The style of the new building, together with its parkland setting, the layout of the pathways and its formal gardens earned it the name 'tropical Versailles'. Later Dom Pedro II ● *25* commissioned the French landscape designer Auguste Glaziou to redesign the park, which was then officially opened in 1876. From 1808 Quinta da Boa Vista was closely linked to the Portuguese royal family until their exile in 1889.

MUSEU NACIONAL. In 1892 the Museu Nacional was transferred to the former imperial palace, which had been totally stripped of all icons of the monarchy. This major scientific institution contains fine collections of Brazilian natural history, and many artefacts relating to its archeology and anthropology, as well as an important collection of meteorites and a section devoted to Egyptology.

JARDIM ZOOLÓGICO. In 1945 a project was launched to convert part of Quinta da Boa Vista into a zoo. Since 1888 the

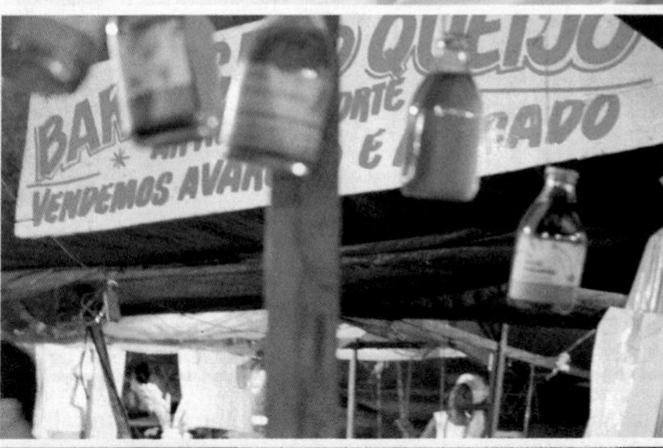

existing zoo had been located in the Vila Isabel district. Today the zoo houses one of the country's largest collections of animals, which number some two thousand and includes more than 350 Brazilian and foreign species.

★ **Feira de São Cristóvão ◆ E** B2. This spectacular *nordestino* market (*top*) is held daily in the São Cristóvão district. It is laid out in the Pavilhão de São Cristóvão. During the day the market is filled with stalls selling all kinds of produce, including meat, *cachaça* ● *64* and medicinal herbs, and a wide range of other items, such as clothes, hammocks and souvenirs. After 9pm the *barracas* (refreshment stalls) open to serve food and drink, while dancing to the sound of *forró* ● *51* groups goes on until dawn.

Estádio São Januário ◆ E A1. The stadium of the Vasco da Gama soccer club is also located in the São Cristóvão district. The club was founded by the Portuguese inhabitants of Rio and was the first to admit black and half-caste players. The stadium, built in 1927 with a seating capacity for 80,000 spectators, was the largest in Rio until the Maracanã ● *59* was built after World War Two. Under the government of Getúlio Vargas, Estádio São Januário was used for such major political occasions as international Labor Day, celebrated on May 1.

FEIRA DE SÃO CRISTÓVÃO ★
The market is open every day, but to make the most of this great open-air festival it is best to go on a Saturday night, preferably quite late. The most convenient way of getting there is by taxi.

'CARIOCA' SOCCER CLUBS
Rio's first soccer club, the Fluminense Futebol Clube ▲ *138*, was founded in 1902. Its team was made up of young middle-class players from the city's Zona Sul. In 1912 a rift led to the formation of a new team, Flamengo ▲ *141*, which has become the most popular club in Rio. The Vasco da Gama club (hat seller, *left*) was founded in 1898 to mark the fourth centenary of the discovery of the New World ● *22*. Initially a boating club, in 1916 it turned to soccer and became the club of the Portuguese community. For several years now, the Vasco da Gama club, like the Botafogo club, has been at the top of the league of Brazilian soccer clubs ● *58*.

QUINTA DA BOA VISTA AND JARDIM ZOOLÓGICO ★
The São Cristóvão metro is within easy reach of the former imperial residence and gardens (open daily, 8am–7pm) where you can see the fine collections of the Museu Nacional and the many different species of animals in the Jardim Zoológico.

Many of the neoclassical houses and warehouses built in the second half of the 19th century still stand in Zona Norte.

MANGUEIRA, VILA ISABEL AND SALGUEIRO ◆ E C1 F B2

The parade of the samba schools during the Rio Carnival ● *46*, *48* is the largest and most elaborate of Brazil's traditional events. In the 1960s the Rio Carnival was so widely publicized that it attracted tourists from all over the world. The event costs millions of dollars and involves thousands of professional craftsmen and artists who design and work on it throughout the year. Three of the best-known samba schools are Mangueira, the oldest and certainly the most popular, Salgueiro, whose innovative ideas transformed the esthetics of the samba school parade during the 1970s, and Vila Isabel, the first to have a female president. It is certainly worth watching some of the schools' 'rehearsals', which are held every weekend from August onward in certain working-class districts of Rio's extensive Zona Norte. These 'rehearsals' become increasingly colorful and animated as Carnival approaches.

ESCOLA DE SAMBA DA MANGUEIRA. This school, whose colors are pink and green, was founded in 1928. Its *quadra* is at Rua Visconde de Niterói 1072, behind the Maracanã stadium and at the foot of the *favela* for which it is named. The school has produced a number of famous composers, including Cartola, Carlos Cachaça, Padeirinho and Pelado. However, the Escola de Samba da Mangueira is not only famous for promoting the tradition of authentic samba. It is also playing an increasingly important role in the care and education of the children of the nearby *favela*. The establishment of the Vila Olímpica de Mangueira, a sports training center, is a leading example of the school's role within the community.

ESCOLA DE SAMBA UNIDOS DE VILA ISABEL. The school was founded on April 4, 1946 and its colors are blue and white. It has only recently found a *quadra* worthy of its status. Its headquarters are on Avenida 28 Setembro, in the Vila Isabel district.

'FALSE FRIENDS' OF CARNIVAL VOCABULARY
An *escola de samba* (samba school) is not in fact a school but a society whose members meet to organize a carnival parade. The city's first samba society settled in Rio next to the École Normale, and retained the prestigious term 'école' (school) in its title. Other societies followed suit. Nor do the schools actually rehearse for the carnival parade. Events held in the *quadra* (the school's 'rehearsal' venue) are used to try out the sambas written by the school's composers and, in October, to select the samba that will be played at the official parade. These 'rehearsals' are also an opportunity to present the school's *enredo* (theme) and costumes to the public and the press.

Escola de Samba Unidos do Salgueiro. On April 3, 1953 the *sambistas* of three *blocos* (full samba schools), Unidos do Salgueiro, Depois eu digo and Azul e Branco, merged to become the Salgueiro school. Its red-and-white banner (*right*) bears the motto *Nem pior, nem melhor, apenas uma escola diferente* (Neither worse, nor better, just a different school). Its *quadra* is located at Rua Silva Teles 104, in the Andaraí district.

Maracanã ◆ E C1

Brazil's favorite sport, soccer ● *58* only really became popular when factory workers began to form their own teams. An example is Bangu Atlético Clube, which was founded in a textile factory. As soccer attracted more supporters the various clubs began to build their own stadiums. The first to do so was Fluminense, which built a stadium in Laranjeiras ▲ *138*, in 1919, followed by Vasco da Gama, in São Cristóvão ▲ *129*, in 1927. Vasco da Gama was the largest, with a seating capacity for 80,000. After World War Two Brazil hosted the World Cup, for which a stadium, the largest in the world, was built in Rio. The Estádio Mário Filho, popularly known as the Maracanã ● *59* (*below*), was opened on June 16, 1950. It was designed for 180,000 spectators but new safety regulations now limit its capacity to 100,000. The matches that are played here are unforgettable, especially if the top teams are playing. Fla x Flu (Flamengo v. Fluminense), for example, is a classic.

Maracanã ✪
The chance to watch a match in this legendary stadium is an opportunity that should not be missed. The stadium is easily reached by metro (alight at Maracanã). With passionate spectators chanting songs, brandishing colors and letting off fireworks, these matches are a truly electrifying experience. The Museu de Esportes Mané Garrincha at Rua Professor Eurico Rabelo, Portão 18, is also worth a visit. The museum was founded in 1947 and documents Brazil's sporting heritage, with Brazilian soccer and great Brazilian players in pride of place.

UERJ campus ◆ E C1

The Universidade do Estado do Rio de Janeiro, or UERJ, was founded in 1950. In the 1970s it was transferred to its present campus near the Maracanã. Today the UERJ has some 18,000 students, 2,000 lecturers and 5,000 clerical staff. It is one of Rio's two public universities, the larger being the Universidade Federal do Rio De Janeiro (UFRJ), which was created when several faculties merged in 1937. Since 1960 the UFRJ's main campus has been on the Ilha do Fundão, near the international airport, although a number of its departments are based at various locations in the city center.

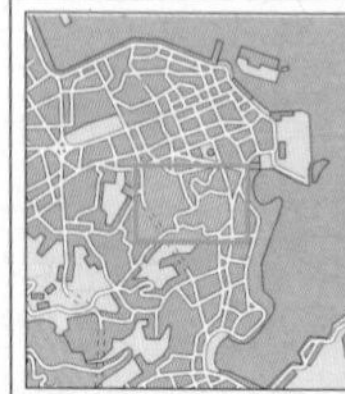

AN INTENSE NIGHTLIFE
The new life brought recently to some streets of Lapa led to the opening of numerous restaurants, bars and *gafieras*, to the delight of nightowls. They meet there for a drink or a dance to the rhythms of sambas, *chorinhos* or *forros*.

The itinerary from Lapa to Santa Teresa follows in the footsteps of artists, poets and musicians from all periods of Rio's history.

LAPA: A DISTRICT WITH A RICH HISTORY ◆ A C2-D2

PASSEIO PÚBLICO. The Passeio Público, the city's first public garden, lies between Cinelândia ▲ *123* and Largo da Lapa. Its prominent fountain, featuring two caimans spewing out a jet of water, is one of the many works by Mestre Valentim ▲ *117*. However, the present park was designed in the 19th century by the French landscape gardener Auguste Glaziou. It is an ideal place for romantic walks, and its quiet, shady corners inspired poets, artists and musicians, among them Olavo Bilac, Vitor Meireles ▲ *122* and Chiquinha Gonzalga, whose busts line the pathways.

LARGO DA LAPA. The IGREJA NOSSA SENHORA DA LAPA was built in 1751 on swampland bordering the beach. In the 18th century the church's convent housed a seminary. It then become a refuge for Carmelite nuns evicted from Praça XV de Novembro ▲ *117* in 1810, when the Portuguese royal family arrived from Lisbon. In the 1920s Lapa acquired a more sulphurous reputation courtesy of the French (or more often Polish) women who moved into the district's hotels and turned many of the unrefined planters into 'gentlemen'. Its proximity to Avenida Central ▲ *123* and to the splendors of this avenue made Lapa a district renowned for its nightlife, its bohemian lifestyle and all kinds of excesses. Today Lapa is known for the bars located at the foot of the aqueduct, on Rua Mem de Sá, Rua Joaquim Silva and Ladeira de Santa Teresa, the open-air performances on the esplanade, the performances of the Circo Voador and the Fundição Progresso. This cultural center at Rua dos Arcos 28–42 is housed in a former foundry (dating from 1881) where many of the city's wrought-iron grilles were made. The large wall painting next to the cultural center, depicting the façade of the music school, extends the cityscape and evokes an earlier age.

ARCOS DA LAPA. The forty two arches of the Arcos da Lapa form an impressive backdrop to the Lapa district. In 1723 this aqueduct began carrying the fresh water of the Carioca ▲ *115*

ARCOS DA LAPA
Streetcars run between Lapa and Santa Teresa (*below*) along the Arcos de Lapa. Depicted in a mural *(above)*, this aqueduct is as much a part of Lapa and Santa Teresa as the music and nightlife of these districts.

to the public fountain at the foot of the Convento de Santo Antônio on Largo da Carioca. It was completed in 1750 but fell into disuse a hundred years later. It was, however, sufficiently sturdy to be used as a viaduct, and from 1896 streetcars ran along it as far as the hill of Santa Teresa.

★ THE 'LADEIRAS' OF SANTA TERESA ◆ A D1-D2

Originally a place of refuge for runaway slaves, the hills of Santa Teresa, with *ladeiras* (steep streets) and flights of steps, were urbanized in the 18th century when a water supply was provided by tapping the Carioca. The district is named for the Convento de Santa Teresa. To reach the convent leave Lapa via Rua Teotônio Regadas, past the Cecília Meirelles concert hall, and climb a flight of colored steps (*right*). From the convent the steps lead on to Rua Hermenegildo de Barros, Rua Dias de Barros and Rua Murtinho Nobre.

A STREETCAR NAMED 'BONDINHO'. The *bonde* (tram), which was originally drawn by mules, became the most popular form of transport when the Light company ▲ *127* electrified the city's tramlines in the early 20th century. The sole survivors of these memorable times still jolt their way along the aqueduct (*below left*), through the district of Santa Teresa and to the top of the hill. Street children like to ride on the running boards of these ancient streetcars, which are now classified as historic monuments.

EXPLORING RIO'S 'MONTMARTRE'. To explore this fascinating district, the best place to start is the PARQUE DAS RUÍNAS at Rua Murtinho Nobre 169. This was the home of Laurinda Santos Lobo, an elegant society lady who in the 1940s surrounded herself with the city's artistic and intellectual elite. The MUSEU CHACÁRA DO CÉU, at Rua Murtinho Nobre 93 nearby, is one of the city's most interesting museums. In a house in typically 1950s style and set in a garden designed by Burle Marx ▲ *147*, it displays the private collections of Raymundo de Castro Maia (1894–1968), an industrialist and patron of the arts. Works on display include paintings by great 20th-century masters and many watercolors by Jean-Baptiste Debret ● *84*.

VISITING THE STUDIOS AND BARS. Once a year, during a weekend in September, some fifty artists open their studios to the public. However, they will also make you welcome if you knock on their door at any other time of the year. All you have to do is ask at the bars on and around LARGO DO GUIMARÃES where they are well known and where you will find them drinking in the evening with *chorinho* and pop musicians, especially in the Arnaudo, Simplesmente and Sobrenatural bars. The nearby MUSEU DO BONDE, housed in the tram maintenance workshop on Rua Carlos Brant, traces the history of Rio's tramway. The Centro Cultural Laurinda Santos Lobo, at Rua Monte Alegre 306, is housed in one of the district's most beautiful residences.

CONVENTO DE SANTA TERESA
The Convento de Santa Teresa, at Ladeira de Santa Teresa 52, dates from 1750. It is fronted by impressive grilles through which the plaintive chanting of the nuns within can be heard at certain times of day.

CENTRO CULTURAL PARQUE DAS RUÍNAS
Having exhibition galleries and a café terrace, this cultural center also offers a unique view of the bay. All that remains of the house, built in the 1950s, is the shell, which now serves as a viewpoint.

SANTA TERESA BY STREETCAR ★
The *bondinho* (streetcar) runs from 7am to 10pm every day. Departures are every 15 minutes from the small station at Rua Hélio Garna 65, in front of the Petrobrás building ▲ *124*. The first stop is at the Curvelo station but you can ride as far as the small square of Largo das Neves.

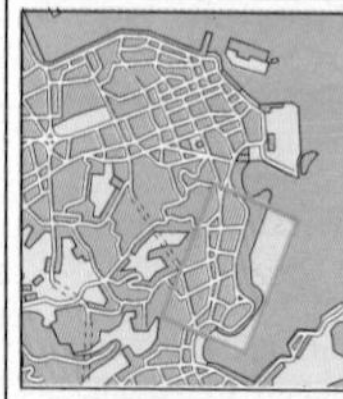

The districts of Glória, Flamengo and Botafogo are the city's natural extension along the beaches. In the 19th century the nobility began to build their residences here to escape the overpopulated city center.

GLÓRIA AND ITS CROWNING GLORY ◆ B A2-A3

Rua Santa Cristina leads down from Santa Teresa and into Rua Benjamin Constant. At no. 74 is the Templo da Humanidade, where the positivist religion of the 19th-century French philosopher Auguste Comte is practiced. On Sunday mornings you can attend a service in the temple where intellectuals and scientists act as saints, under the watchful eye of a bust of Clotilde de Vaux, Comte's muse. At the end of the street, on the left, is Praça Paris, a square with a formal garden surrounded by grilles. It was designed in the 1920s by the French urban planner Alfred Agache ▲ *124*.

IGREJA NOSSA SENHORA DA GLÓRIA DO OUTEIRO ★
The church, with the Marina da Glória in the foreground (*above*), is one of Rio's picture postcard images and was often painted by European artists. It is located at Ladeira Nossa Senhora da Glória 26. The museum of religious art is open Monday through Friday 8am–noon and 1–5pm (8am–noon at weekends).

★ **NOSSA SENHORA DA GLÓRIA DO OUTEIRO.** The tiny baroque church of Nossa Senhora da Glória do Outeiro (Our Lady of the Glory of the Knoll) ● *70* is a masterpiece of colonial architecture. This delightful building (*left*), designed by José Cardoso Ramalho and taking the form of a double octagon, was completed in 1739, and is the district's crowning glory. The interior and the sacristy have 18th-century *azulejos* ● *71* depicting scenes from the Old Testament. In the early 20th century, before the Aterro (embankment) was built, the waves still lapped at the foot of the rock on which it perches like a sentinel. From this vantage point the church appears to be looking down on the statue of Pedro Álvares Cabral ● *22* below, who discovered Brazil in 1500.

MUSEU DA IMPERIAL IRMANDADE DE NOSSA SENHORA DA GLÓRIA DO OUTEIRO. Behind the church stands the Museum of the Imperial Brotherhood, which contains a collection of religious objects and other items, including silverware, jewelry and furniture, that once belonged to the imperial nobility. There are three ways of reaching the church and museum: by flights of steps, by the Ladeira da Glória that rises past the Turístico hotel or alternatively by a small funicular, the *plano inclinado* on Rua do Russel, a fine example of the few 'inclined planes' and funiculars that still allow easy access up and down the hills of Rio.

FLAMENGO ◆ B B2-C3

Beyond the Praia do Russel, the Glória hotel and the statue of São Sebastião (the city's patron saint), lies the PRAIA DO FLAMENGO. This street, meaning Flamengo Beach, is so named because it bordered the beach until it was covered by

Positivism
Positivist ideas were disseminated in Brazil in the 1850s by intellectuals such as Benjamin Constant Botelho de Magalhães and Miguel Lemos, who founded the positivist church in Brazil in 1881. Positivist philosophy reinforced criticism of the monarchy and contributed to the spread of republicanism. Order and Progress, the motto on the Brazilian flag, reflects this influence.

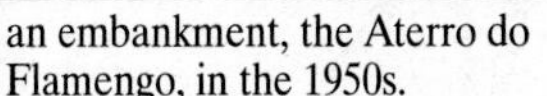

an embankment, the Aterro do Flamengo, in the 1950s.

Praia do Flamengo. This avenue, once lined with embassies and chancelleries, is still an upper-class part of Rio. While the impressive residential block at no. 88 is in the style of a Florentine palazzo, that at no. 116 is reminiscent of Baron Haussmann's Paris. The Castelinho ('little castle') at no. 158, one of the last remaining early 20th-century seafront villas, is dizzyingly eclectic, while Art Deco rules at no. 224 and no. 268 (the Edificio Biarritz). At Rua Dois de Dezembro 63 is the Museu do Telefone. Occupying the former telephone exchange, built in 1918, the museum takes you on an interesting journey back in time. Running parallel to Praia do Flamengo is Rua Marquês de Abrantes, where at no. 66 is an old house now occupied by the Armazém do Chope bar. Live *chorinho* music ● *51* can be heard here on Thursday nights.

Aterro do Flamengo. This embankment can be explored on foot or by bicycle. It begins near a distinctively modern complex consisting of the Aeroporto Santos-Dumont, the Museu de Arte Moderna and the Monumento aos Pracinhas ▲ *125*. Designed by Burle Marx ▲ *147* in the 1960s, in response to the need to open up new access routes to the districts bordering the Atlantic, the Aterro is a long embankment covering an area of some fifty acres. It is a vast urban green space, divided by numerous pathways and planted with a great variety of Brazilian and exotic plants. It is open to everyone and is one of the city's busiest parks, especially on Sundays when the seafront roads are closed to traffic. A range of sporting activities is available, with soccer pitches, tennis and volleyball courts and adventure playgrounds. Other facilities include the Marina da Glória, the departure point for trips round the bay ▲ *154*; the Museu Carmen Miranda with its collection of costumes, shoes and hats belonging to the famous singer; and Porcão Rio, a *churrascaria* (barbecue restaurant) with large bay windows.

Art Deco
The Glória (*above*) was built as a hotel for the delegates who came to the World Fair held in Rio in 1922 ▲ *125*. The elegant stairway decorated with bronze allegories and fronting the building once led to the seafront, which has since been pushed back by the Aterro do Flamengo.

Carmen Miranda
Carmen Miranda (*below*) reached the pinnacle of stardom on the North American showbiz scene in the 1940s and 1950s with her wild and exotic sambas. This diminutive goddess returned to Brazil proclaiming: *'Yes, nós temos bananas!'* ('Yes, we have bananas!').

△ From Glória to Sugar Loaf mountain
Urca and Sugar Loaf mountain

PÃO DE AÇÚCAR ✪
To make the ascent to the summit of Sugar Loaf mountain, take the cable car (*above*) from Avenida Pasteur 520. The service runs from 8am to 10pm, with departures every thirty minutes and continuously in peak times. The 4,590-foot climb takes six minutes. From Zona Sul you can reach the cable car station on buses 500, 511 or 512, and from the city center or Flamengo on bus 107.

Beyond Aterro do Flamengo lies Praia de Botafogo, a small bay within Guanabara Bay. In the 16th century the French ● *22* christened it *le lac* (the lake) because of its calm waters encircled by mountains. Beyond Praia de Botafogo lies the Urca district, nestling at the foot of Sugar Loaf mountain.

Urca and the quiet life ◆ **B** D2-D3

Avenida Pasteur. The neoclassical buildings at nos. 250 and 280, on the right-hand side of the avenue, are those of the old Universidade Federal. During the reign of Dom Pedro II they were occupied by the country's first lunatic asylum, and today still house some of the university faculties. The tranquillity typical of old universities pervades the building's long corridors, which overlook flower-filled patios. The chapel and lecture halls, at the top of a flight of steps, are open only on special occasions. Two impressive buildings stand opposite the select Iate Clube (Yacht Club). They are the Companhia de Pesquisa e Recursos Minerais (a center for mineralogical research) and the pink building of the Instituto Benjamin Constant (an institute for the blind).

Praia Vermelha. In the military zone of the Red Beach, so named because of the bloody battles fought between the Portuguese and the French in the 16th century ▲ *154*, two monuments stand out. One pays tribute to the courage of those who defended Brazil in the war with Paraguay ● *25*, while the other commemorates the Communist military coup of 1935 ● *26*. From the beach it takes twenty to thirty minutes to walk through the quiet Urca district, which was built on an embankment at the foot of Sugar Loaf mountain in the early 20th century. Along the seafront promenade, which leads to the small Praia da Urca and its old casino, fishermen cast their lines against the backdrop of Enseada de Botafogo and the sunset behind Corcovado ▲ *151*.

Estacio de Sá
Situated in the Aterro do Flamengo (Flamengo Park), a monument in the form of a pyramid designed by Lúcio Costa ▲ *201* pays tribute to Estácio de Sá, the army officer who was killed while attempting to drive the French out of Guanabara Bay in 1567. Estácio de Sá was also the founder of Rio de Janeiro.

The thirty-minute walk round MORRO DA URCA starts on the coast path at the northern end of Praia Vermelha. Overlooking the Atlantic, the path offers a magnificent view of the ocean and of the *morros* at the entrance to the bay. About half way along the path, a narrow trail to the left climbs steeply through woodland and up to a pass from where there is a panoramic view of the bay. The path on the right leads to the foot of the sheer rockface of Sugar Loaf mountain. Following the path on the left for thirty to forty minutes leads to the MORRO DA URCA cable-car station.

A ROMANTIC WALK
A path planted with bamboo starts, curiously enough, from the bottom of the steps leading to the toilets on the platform of Sugar Loaf mountain. It runs high above the narrows at the entrance to Guanabara Bay, which is guarded by two early 17th-century fortresses, the Fortaleza de São João and Fortaleza de Santa Cruz ▲ *153*.

SUGAR LOAF MOUNTAIN ◆ B D3-D4

The Portuguese name PÃO DE AÇUCAR (*above right*) may refer to the conical clay molds used to refine sugar (the basis of Brazil's economy in the 16th century) into a conical lump called a sugar loaf. Equally possible, however, is that it may be a corruption of *pau-nh-açuquá*, the Tamoyan American Indian word for a high, pointed or isolated hill.

THE CABLE CAR. In the first stage (1,886 feet) as you ascend to the Morro da Urca (735 feet), with a panoramic restaurant, the landscape unfolds to reveal views of the blue-green Atlantic on one side and the gray waters of the bay on the other. The second stage (2,625 feet) is a vertiginous journey (*top*) to the summit (1,300 feet) rising vertically above the bay. From here check out the legend of Guanabara Bay which tells how God, on a reconnaissance flight on the second day of the Creation, accidentally dropped a collection of natural beauty spots that He had intended to scatter throughout the world. The beaches and districts you've already explored stretch out in miniature far below and, at end of the bay, the bridge and town of Niterói are like figments of the imagination. In the distance is the statue of Christ the Redeemer on the Corcovado.

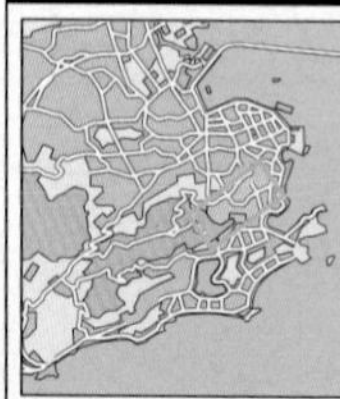

Many *chácaras* (estates) flourished in the Carioca valley during the 19th century. Today the stream that flowed through them is covered by Rua Cosme Velho and Rua Laranjeiras. A walk down these streets reveals the vestiges of these great estates and the wealth of a bygone age.

COSME VELHO ◆ F C3

MUSEU DE ARTE NAÏF
The Museum of Naive Art contains thousands of paintings, including works by Heitor dos Prazeres, a *sambista* who took up painting late in life, and Lia Mittarakis (*above*). Paintings are on sale in the museum store.

SUNDAY OUTINGS IN COSME VELHO. In 1882, Emperor Dom Pedro II ● *25*, who had a liking for walking, nature and trains, commissioned the Estrada de Ferro do Corcovado (Corcovado Railroad). The train winds up the Corcovado (Hunchback), which commands a view over Rio on one side of the Floresta da Tijuca ▲ *150* and of the Atlantic on the other. On Sundays the hill is invaded by day-trippers who climb to the panoramic viewpoint and picnic high above the city. Although the small cog railway that snakes up from the station at Rua Cosme Velho 513 to the foot of the statue of Christ the Redeemer has been modernized ▲ *151*, the train still crawls along at a snail's pace. However this gives passengers the opportunity to admire the vegetation and the view of the city. Very near the station are the MUSEU INTERNACIONAL DE ARTE NAÏF, at Rua Cosme Velho 561, and LARGO DO BOTICÁRIO.

★ **LARGO DO BOTICÁRIO.** In the 1940s a whole section of historic Rio was demolished to make way for Avenida Presidente Vargas ▲ *126*. Dona Silvinha Bittencourt, a society lady, witnessed the destruction with a heavy heart. She managed to salvage stones, tiles, street lamps and other materials, and commissioned Lucio Costa ▲ *201* to use them to decorate Largo do Boticário (Apothecary's Square), accessible via an alleyway at Rua Cosme Velho 857. Here the Carioca still flows peacefully. The name of this stream embodies one of the very few pieces of American Indian culture to have been passed on to Rio's inhabitants: in Tupí *carai* means 'white man' and *oca* 'hut'. Walking back down the street you will come to a baroque fountain at Rua Cosme Velho 109. The fountain is fed by the iron-rich waters of the Bica da Rainha (Queen's Spring) which were enjoyed by the shrewish Carlota Joaquina, wife of Dom João ● *24*, and by the Portuguese royal family.

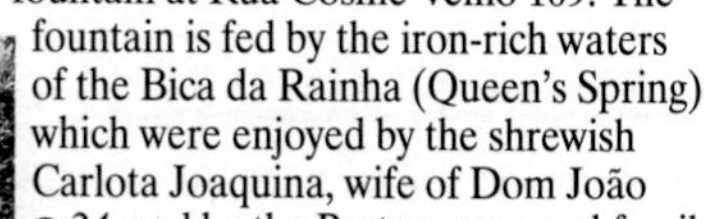

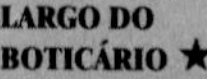

LARGO DO BOTICÁRIO ★
The most impressive example of recreated colonial architecture (*above*), with its *azulejos* and colored windows, stands at the end of Beco do Boticário, the alleyway linking Largo do Boticário with Rua Cosme Velho.

LARANJEIRAS ◆ B B1-B2

RUA DAS LARANJEIRAS. The presence of various schools and colleges here enhances the pleasant atmosphere of this district which, in spite of intensive urban development, still has a bucolic feel. In the evening the relaxed friendly bars of the old São José market, on the corner of Rua Laranjeiras and Rua Gago Coutinho, are filled with a regular clientele.

PALÁCIO DAS LARANJEIRAS. The palace, at Rua Gago Coutinho 106, was built by the Guinle family in 1914 and is the official residence of the governor of Rio state. It is surrounded by the PARQUE GUINLE, a haven of peace and a popular children's playground. There is also an interesting residential development here designed by Lúcio Costa. Nearby, at Rua Alvaro Chaves 41, are the fine headquarters of Fluminense Futebol Clube.

Largo do Machado. This square, which is filled with flower and plant sellers, is the heart of the district. In the afternoon older residents come here to play cards or dominoes beneath the trees. At weekends, it is the meeting place of the district's *nordestino* community. It is also a major stop on the metro and bus routes serving Centro and Zona Sul. At the far end of the square (*below*) stands the impressive Igreja Matriz Nossa Senhora da Glória (1872), the district's parish church.

Catete ◆ B A2

Rua do Catete. The street, a focal point for the aristocracy and wealthy merchants during the Empire ● *24*, became the showcase for the old republic and then for the society women who visited the presidential palace in the 1920s and 1930s. The smart fashion boutiques of that period have given way to small retailers, seedy hotels and restaurants. This busy, colorful working-class district has a slightly old-fashioned atmosphere and is a pleasant place to stroll.

★ **Museu do Folclore Edison Carneiro.** This small museum at Rua do Catete 181 contains a collection of automata of musicians and circus performers. The secondhand bookstore at no. 164 has some finely bound antiquarian books and antique prints.

Museu da República. Brazil was declared a republic in 1889 but it was only later that this pink palace, built in 1866, became the residence of the next eighteen presidents of Brazil. It was owned by Barão de Nova Friburgo, an extremely wealthy coffee planter, and was named the Palácio das Águias (Palace of the Eagles) for the bronze eagles, defenders of republican institutions, crowning pediment. Juscelino Kubitschek ● *26*, the last president to occupy the palace, left it in 1960 for Brasília, the newly founded capital. The palace, at Rua do Catete 153, is now open to visitors. It contains a large cultural center, with a theater, movie theaters and exhibition galleries, and a series of rooms devoted to the history of the Brazilian republic, in which its founding father, Getúlio Vargas ● *36*, has pride of place. You can visit the room where the great statesman committed suicide in 1954 by shooting himself through the heart: the pyjamas he was wearing are on display. You can also read the suicide note that he left for the people of Brazil, in which he described his death as a sacrifice for the nation's liberty.

Palácio Guanabara
The Palácio Guanabara, in Rua Pinheiro Machado, stands opposite the line of palm trees on Rua Paissandu. It was begun in 1853 and, from 1865, was the residence of the Conde d'Eu and Princesa Isabel ● *35*, ▲ *169*. Since 1960 it has been the seat of the government of Rio state.

Craft stores
Pé de Boi, a store at Rua Ipiranga 55, in Laranjeiras, offers an extensive range of craft items from all over Brazil, with some particularly splendid pieces from Minas Gerais and Pernambuco.
Brumado, at Rua das Laranjerias 486, offers an interesting range of American Indian jewelry and ceramics.

Museu do Folclore ★
The popular cultures of various regions of Brazil are the subjects of the museum's displays. It is open Tuesday through Friday, 11am–6pm (3–6pm at weekends).

Gardens of the Palácio do Catete
A wide range of cultural activities, including plays and concerts, take place in the gardens of the presidential palace. In a corner of the park is an Italian bistro serving excellent tropical salads.

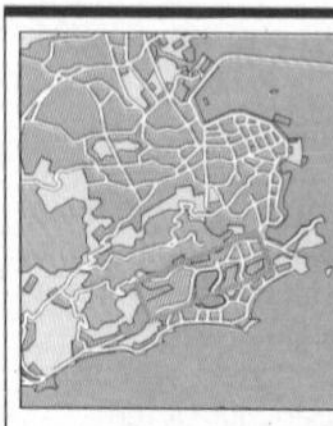

Rui Barbosa
The writer and politician Rui Barbosa (1849–1923) championed the great causes of Brazilian public life. An abolitionist and democrat, he held several positions in public office and played a key role in the consolidation of the country's republican institutions.

Heitor Villa-Lobos (1887–1959)
Regarded as the father of modern Brazilian music, Villa-Lobos gave classical music an authentically Brazilian feel. He traveled throughout Brazil collecting traditional melodies, which he then incorporated into his compositions. The pieces written by this prolific composer, including his famous *Bachianas Brasileiras*, are performed throughout the world, and especially in the Museu Villa-Lobos (*below*).

From the beach, the oldest road that led back to the sugar cane plantations of the Lagoa (Lagoon) passed through what are now the districts of Botafogo, Humaitá and the Jardim Botânico.

Botafogo and Humaitá ◆ B D1 D A4

Rua São Clemente. During the late 19th century Botafogo was a district in which *cortiços* (cheap boarding houses) stood alongside *palacetes* (small palaces). With poorer housing along the *vilas* (narrow streets) and in the cul-de-sacs, and fine residences on Rua São Clemente, this pattern continues today. At no. 134 is the Casa de Rui Barbosa (*below*), built in 1850 and the former residence of the famous Brazilian politician. The living rooms of the house are open to the public and a fine collection of antique law books is on display. At no. 117 is the former Colégio Jacobina, which still has its original façade. It is now a municipal cultural center devoted to architecture. The Palácio da Cidade, at no. 360, once the British Embassy, is now the city hall.
Intersecting streets. The narrow streets set perpendicular to Rua São Clemente are still stylish. Although it is somewhat unassuming, the Museu do Índio, at Rua das Palmeiras 55, is worth a visit for the large Xingu hut that forms part of the displays, and for its American Indian craft store. The Museu Villa-Lobos, at Rua Sorocaba 200, is devoted to the memory of this great Brazilian composer. A varied program of concerts is also given there.
Humaitá. Rua Visconde de Caravelas is renowned for its small restaurants, which occupy former residences. In the evening the gay community meets in the bars of Rua do Conde de Irajá and Rua do Visconde da Silva, while the young smart set meets in the Ballroom, a fashionable nightclub on Rua Humaitá. The older generation prefer the Sunday evening *chorinho* ● 51 concerts on the bistro terraces in the covered market of Cobal.

Rua Jardim Botânico ◆ D B2-B3

Walking up Rua Jardim Botânico, you will pass Rua J.J. Seabra and Rua Maria Angélica on the left. These streets are full of young people and small lively restaurants, among which is the Caroline Café, a popular venue for singles.
★ **Parque Lage.** This peaceful park is located at no. 414, on the right of Rua Jardim Botânico. In 1920 the Italian contralto Gabriela Bezanzoni, famous for her role in the opera *Carmen*, persuaded the Conde Lage, to build her the palace that now accommodates the school of visual arts.
Capela Nossa Senhora das Cabeças. At Rua Faró 80, toward the upper end of the street, is one of Rio's oldest chapels, built in

"According to his calculations, the land would be worth a fortune once the huge inn had been built, the enormous inn that would put an end to all the seedy little boarding houses in the cul-de-sacs of Botafogo."

Aluísio Azevedo

1625. It contains a statue of the Madonna, carved in Portugal, which is reputed to cure headaches.

★ **JARDIM BOTÂNICO.** Rejoin Rua Jardim Botânico and visit the fascinating Botanical Gardens at no. 920, ▲ *142*. Until 1808 the area covered by these gardens was a sugar cane plantation.

★ LAGOA RODRIGO DE FREITAS ◆ D B3-C3

A HEART-SHAPED LAGOON. Five of Rio's districts, delineated by the summit of the Morro Canta Galo, that of the Morro Dois Irmãos, the Tijuja forest and the beaches on the ocean front, surround the Lagoa Rodrigo de Freitas. The five-mile circumference of this heart-shaped lagoon is punctuated by sports grounds and private watersports clubs. *Kiosques* (open-air restaurants serving various kinds of food) attract families at weekends and young people and musicians on summer evenings. Near the Parque dos Patins is one of the heliports that operate flights across the city. A stiff half-hour climb along marked footpaths leads to the top of the seven-acre PARQUE DA CATACUMBA, at Avenida Epitácio Pessoa 3000. Originally a *favela* that was demolished in 1970, the hill commands a particularly fine view of the lagoon. Works by Brazilian artists are exhibited in the park, and on Sunday afternoons free concerts are held in the amphitheater there.

PARQUE LAGE AND JARDIM BOTÂNICO ★
The Parque Lage is not far from the Jardim Botânico and both are open daily, from 9am to 5pm. Buses with 'Via Jardim Botânico' on the windshield go past the gardens. These buses include nos. 594, 170 and 172, departing from the city center, and 571, 572 and 569, which run only in Zona Sul.

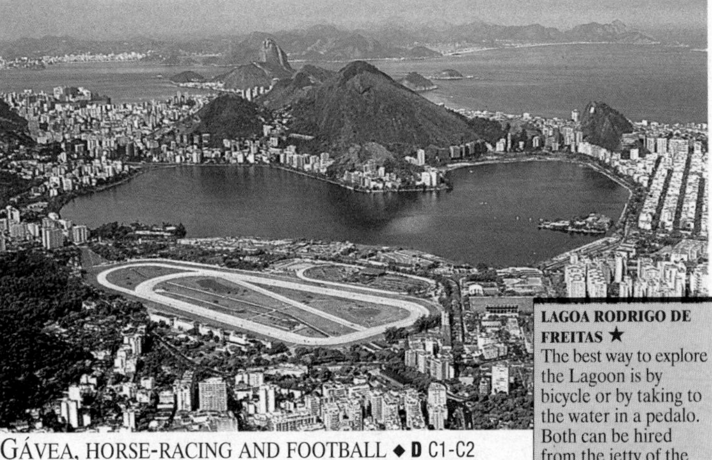

LAGOA RODRIGO DE FREITAS ★
The best way to explore the Lagoon is by bicycle or by taking to the water in a pedalo. Both can be hired from the jetty of the Parque Tom Jobim.

GÁVEA, HORSE-RACING AND FOOTBALL ◆ D C1-C2

Opposite PRAÇA SANTOS-DUMONT, where there is a bric-á-brac market on Sundays, stand the impressive white buildings of the racetrack known as the JÓQUEI CLUBE (Jockey Club). On race days the stands are open to everyone. As you walk back up Rua Marqués de São Vicente it is worth making a detour to the PLANETÁRIO, at Rua Padre Leonel Franca 240. On a large hemispherical screen beneath a dome, you can view the cosmos as it appears from south of the Equator. A little further is the SOLAR GRANDJEAN DE MONTIGNY ▲ *119*, set amid the delightful gardens of the Pontífica Universidade Católica (Catholic University). The *solar* is the former residence of Grandjean de Montigny, the architect who was a member of the 1816 French mission ● *24*, *84* and the founder of the Escuela de Belas Artes ▲ *122*.

FLAMENGO FUTEBOL CLUBE
Originally a rowing club, founded in 1895 in the Flamengo district, this became a soccer club in 1912. Known as Rubro-Negro (Red and Black) for the color of its strip, it has counted Zico and Romário among its players and is the most popular soccer club in Rio ● *59*.

The quest for exotic spices led Portuguese navigators to sail the seas and defend their cargoes against pirates. When he landed in Rio in 1808 the future king Dom João VI decided to build a powder factory on the site of a large sugar cane plantation located some way outside the city. Next to it he laid out a garden in which to plant precious seeds from the Orient. The avenue of clove trees that still stands today is a vestige of that garden. The garden expanded and became the Horto Real (Royal Garden). Pedro I opened it to the public and in 1824 gave Brother Leandro do Sacramento the task of transforming it into a botanical garden centered around a lake. Plants arrived from all over the world. Pedro II loved to walk along its shady avenues and laid on family picnics beneath the arbors. Today information boards set along the main avenues help visitors to find their way around.

Solar da Imperatriz
A thirty- to forty-minute walk walk up Rua Pacheco Leão, which runs along the boundary of the Botanical Gardens, leads to the Horto Real (Royal Garden) and the Solar da Imperatriz. The owners of this magnificent building, which has recently been restored, would receive the imperial family here when they walked in the Botanical Gardens.

One of the many orchids (*right*) in the Orquidário (Orchid House) and the lake (*below*).

Wildlife
If you walk quietly you will see *micos* (tamarins) ▲ *172*, birds of paradise, moorhens, squirrels, butterflies and, if you are especially lucky, toucans.

Thousands of plants
Just a stone's throw from the bustle of the city over 6,000 species of plants produce buds, open, unfurl, bloom and fade. The garden, a haven of peace and quiet on the edge of the forest, covers 350 acres, almost one third of which are open to the public.

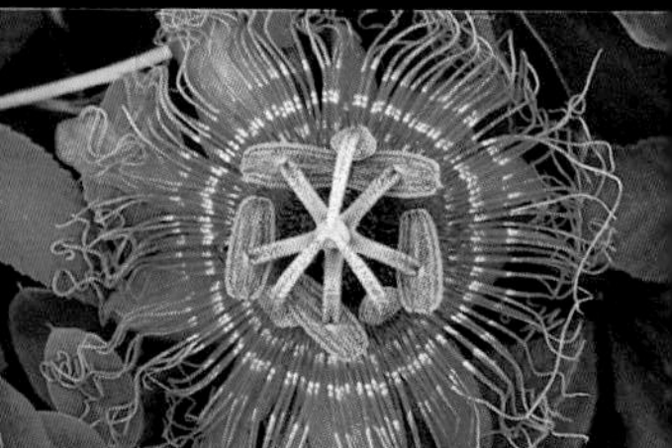

BUILDINGS IN THE BOTANICAL GARDEN
'he portico of the ormer Academia mperial de Belas Artes designed by Grandjean de Montigny ▲ *119* was ransferred to the Botanical Gardens when the academy was demolished. The portico and its bronze ountain (*above*) stand at the end of he central avenue. The powder factory, of which the walls and portico with the Portuguese coat of arms survive, was converted into a playground. The Casa os Pilões, built in 800, housed the water-driven millstones that crushed the coal used o make powder. The main building of the *engenho* ▲ *270* of Nossa Senhora da Conceição, dating from 1596 and the oldest in the region, houses the visitor center, a souvenir and bookstore and a cafeteria.

THE SEASONS
The lotuses and orchids come into flower in January and February, followed in March and April by the *Vitória régia* (*above*), the giant Vitoria Regis water lilies of Amazonia ▲ *304*. Winter days are brightened by clusters of the flowering *ipê roxo*.

THE AVENUE OF ROYAL PALMS
In the early 19th century a Portuguese navigator imprisoned by the French on the island of Mauritius brought back seeds of the royal palm, which became known in Rio as the imperial palm. Only the estates visited by the emperor were allowed to plant these palms, which were laid out along avenues. Such avenues of palms can still be seen in the Brazilian countryside today.

▲ The city and the sea from Copacabana to Leblon

Iemanjá
On New Year's Eve Rio's *umbanda* centers celebrate the festival of Iemanjá on Copacabana beach. In the 1970s, the influx of tourists, firework displays and open-air concerts turned this event into a festival attended by two to three million people, all dressed in white in honor of Iemanjá, goddess of the sea ● *43*.

'Postos'
The various *postos*, (lifeguard stations) double as rallying points for different groups of people. At *Posto* 6 fishing boats come in and a fish market is held; *Posto* 8 is a gathering point for surfers; *Posto* 9 is for hippies; *Posto* 10, opposite the Country Club, is a rendezvous for preppies; and *Posto* 11 is for mothers and babies.

Separated from the city center by a range of *morros* (hills), the beaches along Rio's Atlantic coast stretch for more than eighteen miles. This is where anything and everything can happen. Expect the unexpected and enjoy the atmosphere, the ocean and the sight of brightly colored *cangas* (long wraparound skirts). Don't forget to sample a glass of coconut milk and some delicious grilled prawn kebabs.

Copacabana, 'Princesinha do Mar' ◆ C A3 B1-B2 C1

In the early 20th century Rio met the fashion (new in Brazil) for sea bathing by building two tunnels, the first in 1892 and the second in 1906, creating a tramway link to a coastal spot called Copacabana. The dunes there were soon dotted with villas, followed by Copacabana Palace, built by the French architect Joseph Guire in 1923. This established the district's renown, which reached its peak in the 1940s and 1950s. Copacabana was then known as the *Princesinha do Mar* (Little Princess of the Sea). Apartment blocks quickly replaced the villas. In the 1970s, Avenida Atlântica was widened, a Portuguese stone *calçadão* (sidewalk) was built and the beach extended.

Praia do Leme. Beyond the Méridien hotel 'Copa' is known as Praia do Leme, and the beach here is quieter. From the fishermen's path along the rocks, the northern end of the beach offers a sweeping view across to the Forte de Copacabana ▲ *153*, at the southern end. A paved road from the barracks at the northern end of the beach leads to the top of the Morro do Leme and the Forte Duque de Caxias (1913–19). This viewpoint commands a panoramic view of the beaches of Copacabana and Niterói and the entrance to the bay.

Avenida Atlântica. This avenue and the adjacent streets are lined with buildings whose façades illustrate the evolution of 20th-century architectural styles. The buildings at Rua Duvivier 43 and Rua Viveiros de Castro 116 and 123 are fine examples of the Art Deco style. But the 'princess' now has a few wrinkles, and 'Copa' has become the preserve of the golden youth of yesterday. Aging beaus while away the day playing cards and former beauties walk their poodles by the ocean. At night Copacabana is taken over by prostitutes and transvestites.

Avenida Nossa Senhora de Copacabana. The avenue, running parallel to Avenida Atlántica, is the district's main shopping street and thoroughfare. It is therefore very congested and heavily polluted. Although it offers everything you need, Ipanema is a much more pleasant place to shop.

Ipanema, preserve of the 'garotas' ◆ C D1 D D3-D4

Arpoador. Some Sundays, in summer, open-air concerts are held in the Parque Garota de Ipanema, which lies between Copacabana and Ipanema. From the park you can reach the Arpoador ▲ *148*, the rock overlooking the little Praia do Diabo, a beach from which whales were harpooned in the early 20th century. With the sun setting behind the Morro Dois Irmãos, this viewpoint is popular with courting couples.

Ipanema. The beach is the preserve of wealthy young Brazilians and pretty girls (*garotas*) who, around 4–5pm in summer, perform a ritual striptease in reverse, putting their clothes back on for the journey home. The young men show off their muscles playing *futevolley* ▲ *149* or at the horizontal bar. Ipanema is the birthplace of *bossa nova* ● *52* and one of the district's best-known streets is named for one of its creators, Vinícius de Moraes. According to local legend the lyric-writer Moraes and the composer-musician Tom Jobim wrote their famous hit *Girl from Ipanema* in the bar that was then renamed Garota de Ipanema. Rua Visconde de Pirajá is a street for shopping, visiting art galleries or simply window shopping. The café-bookstores here, such as Letras e Expressões at no. 276 and Livraria da Travessa at no. 572, stay open late into the night. A visit to the museum of precious stones and stone-cutting workshop of jewelers Amsterdam-Sauer and their rivals H. Stern will reveal the wide variety of Brazilian stones. The Feira Hippie, a craft market selling jewelry, leather goods and objets d'art, is held on Sundays on Praça General Osório.

BEACHES OF ZONA SUL ✪
The ocean here can be dangerous, with large breakers and strong currents. Lifeguard stations (*postos*) are dotted along the shore at 900-yard intervals. *Postos* also have toilets and showers for the use of the public (a small charge is made). When in Rio do like the *cariocas* and take as little as possible to the beach.

'Kiosques'
Leaving Rio without drinking a coconut milk at one of the *kiosques* (refreshment stalls, *above*) on the beach, is tantamount to treason.

The 'calçadão'
This seafront sidewalk is decorated with mosaics in a pattern of wavy motifs emblematic of Rio. On Sundays, one side of the avenue is closed to traffic and given over to sports enthusiasts.

LEBLON AND THE INTELLECTUALS ◆ D D1-D2

A FAMILY BEACH. Beyond the canal bordering the JARDIM DE ALÁH, the beach becomes the Praia do Leblon, named for Charles Leblon, who owned property here in the 19th century. The far end of Praia do Leblon is marked by the Mirante do Leblon, a rock that is permanently pounded by waves. Until the abolition of slavery there was a famous *quilombo* ● *35* here.

'FINAL DO LEBLON'. The streets at the Leblon end of the beach, including Rua Ataulfo de Paiva and Rua Dias Ferreira, are a favorite meeting place for intellectuals, who can be seen sitting together discussing politics or literature. The bookstores, secondhand booksellers, grocery stores and bistros here stay open until early morning (*madrugada*).

SÃO CONRADO: LUXURY AND 'FAVELAS' ◆ F D1-D2

AVENIDA NIEMEYER. This coast road, a former racetrack, zigzags for three miles high above the Atlantic. It was opened in the early 20th century to link Praia do Leblon and Praia São Conrado, to the west. The Favela da Rocinha on the MORRO DO VIDIGAL is a world away from the luxury of the Sheraton hotel, with tennis courts and swimming pools. Pope John Paul II gave a ring to the *favela's* reception committee before going on to visit it when he came to Brazil in 1980.

LIMITED HORIZONS
Shut away in *condomínios* (highrise apartment blocks) the young people of Barra, sociable yet timorous and given to free spending, effectively live in a ghetto. When they go out it is always by car, and either to get to school or go out to a club. They also enjoy spending sprees in Barra's shopping centers, such as Barrashopping, Via Parque or Fashion Mall, or visiting one of the theme parks, such as Rio Water Planet or Terra Encantada, on the other side of Avenida das Américas.

ROCINHA
With between 60,000 and 150,000 inhabitants (estimates vary) the Favela da Rocinha (*right*) is a self-contained town within the city ● *81*. At night its twinkling lights shine as brightly as those of the international luxury hotels located on the seafront a stone's throw from the Gávea Golf Club. Favela Tour organizes official tours of Rocinha (tel. 3322 2727; 9989 0074).

São Conrado. This modern district developed in the early 1970s after the the Zuzu Angel tunnel was built. It lies between the mountains and the huge Favela da Rocinha ● *81*. The end of the beach, Praia do Pepino, is used as a landing strip by hang gliders and paragliders who launch themselves from the top of Pedra Bonita ▲ *149*, which can be reached on foot from the top of the Estrada da Canoa.

Barra's American way of life ◆ G C1-C2 D1

Avenida Lúcio Costa. This 11-mile avenue runs beside the rough, green waters of the Atlantic, and there is a touch of Florida about it. Throughout the district of Barra da Tijuca, more than 250,000 *emergentes* (nouveaux riches) live in the mainly highrise blocks of the *condomínios*, secure and well-guarded private residential estates. Blighted by development in the space of twenty years, the district is a property developer's paradise. There is a faint urban plan, with blocks of houses, tower blocks and small apartment blocks stopping at the Parque Ecológico Chico Mendes (Avenida das Américas, Km 17.5) and becoming more widely spaced at the Recreios dos Bandeirantes, the last mile of Avenida Lúcio Costa. On the right of Avenida das Américas is the enormous Riocentro exhibition center, at Avenida Salvador Allende 6555, and the Nelson Piquet racetrack, on Avenida Embaixador Abelardo Bueno.

Museu Casa do Pontal. Lying beyond the Recreios dos Bandeirantes, at Estrada do Pontal 3295, this private museum has a fine collection of popular art amassed over forty years by the French collector Jacques Van de Beuque. Amusing automata act out scenes from everyday town and country life. The great popular artists, including Mestre Vitalino, GTO and Antônio Poteiro, are well represented.

★ The farther beaches

From the Recreios dos Bandeirantes follow the coast to Prainha, a small and unspoiled natural beach. Prainha and the neighboring Grumari beach, cradled by a hill commanding a spectacular view, are a surfer's paradise. At the far end of the beach the road climbs to a low pass where you can stop at the restaurant Point de Guaratiba, whose terrace has a panoramic view of the Restinga de Marambaia. On the way down, bear left to the delightful port of Barra de Guaratiba, where there are small restaurants, notably Tia Palmira at Caminho de Souza 18.

★ Sítio Burle Marx. The house and gardens of the famous landscape designer Roberto Burle Marx are open to the public, offering visitors peace and tranquillity.

Aerial view of Barra (*top*) and the Lagoa de Marapendi, the lagoon. The elevated monorail shuttle to the Barrashopping center (*above*).

Sítio Burle Marx and the farther beaches ★

The Sítio Burle Marx, at Estrada da Barra de Guaratiba 2019, is located 28 miles from Rio and is open to the public by appointment (tel. 2410 14 12). The beaches of Prainha and Grumari (the latter is a listed natural heritage site) are about eighteen miles from Rio. As public transport to the Sítio Burle Marx as well as to the beaches is poor, it is best to go there by car.

Burle Marx's country estate

Landscape designer Roberto Burle Marx (1909–94) acquired his estate in 1949. It is delightfully bucolic, and the greenhouses there contain plants that inspired his designs. Burle Marx, who came from Lyon, in southern France, created landscape designs in Rio, São Paulo and Brasília. Also a painter, he designed gardens as if they were abstract paintings.

In Rio de Janeiro sport is a part of daily life. While soccer remains Brazil's most ubiquitous and popular sport, beach and water sports also have a large following of keen enthusiasts. Rio's most popular soccer clubs, which include Flamengo and Vasco da Gama, have the words *Futebol e Regatas* attached to their name, indicating their multidisciplinary nature. Television, the movies and advertising have also helped to promote these new sports, which increasingly appeal to those seeking active vacations. Thus surfing, *futevolley*, beach volleyball (which is now an Olympic sport) and mountaineering have become hugely popular, enhanced by Rio's luxuriant natural setting and favorable climate as well as by its extensive beaches.

BEACH FOOTBALL

The main problem with playing beach football is the condition of the 'pitch'. The players' feet sink into the soft sand and the ball tends to rebound unpredictably. Brazilian footballers tackle these disadvantages by lifting the ball with one foot and kicking it with the other, and prevent it touching the sand when they receive it. This fascinating interplay of deft passes involves a series of perfectly executed moves. As a result Brazil has so far been undefeated in international tournaments both in Europe and South America.

SURFING

The first surfboard, weighing 176 pounds, was made in Brazil by Osmar Gonçalves just before World War Two. It was in the 1960s that Arpoador ▲ *145*, a fashionable beach in Ipanema, became the birthplace of surfing. At the time young enthusiasts planed their mother's ironing boards to surf the breakers. Inspired by Maraca, the first Brazilian to ride the 'pipelines' and surf the 20-foot breakers of Sunset Beach in Hawaii, young *càriocas* practice at Barra da Tijuca. These youngsters are now being placed in major international competitions. Gustavo Kuerten, winner of the Roland Garros tennis championship, is also a keen surfer.

Paragliding and hang gliding

Pedra Bonita ▲ *147*, a flat *mesa* (table) overlooking the Praia do São Conrado, is a perfect 'runway' for paragliders and hang gliders. A following wind enables gliders to make fabulously scenic flights over tropical forest to the beaches.

Beach athletes

Brazil's multiracial melting pot has produced the *carioca*, the biotype of the bronzed athlete. People like this are seen all along the coast. Their elegant bearing, supple movements and natural aptitude for sport makes the beaches of Rio one large tropical sports venue. At dawn the *calçadões* ▲ *145* are full of walkers, joggers and cyclists.

'Futevolley'

Soccer and volleyball, sports associated both with relaxation and skill, have combined to create a new sport in which the players' acrobatic movements are almost balletic. As world champions in both disciplines, the Brazilians have very easily taken to *futevolley*. The only element taken from volleyball is the net, and the ball is fielded with feet, head and chest rather than with the hands. With two, or more usually, four, players on each side, this is a sport in which a cool head, a good eye for the ball and physical fitness are essential. The international striker Romário, the most technical of all players, is the undisputed master of *futevolley*. This sometimes devilish game has given rise to betting and is an attraction in its own right for purists and tourists alike.

A 'GREEN' EMPEROR
During the colonial period the slopes of the *serra* were gradually deforested as trees were felled to provide fuel for the brick kilns and sugar factories and to clear the land needed by the expanding *fazendas* ● *68*. By about 1850 the *serra* was completely bare. Streams, including the Carioca ▲ *115*, dried up and the city was threatened by a shortage of drinking water. Dom Pedro II expropriated the *fazendas* and launched a program of reafforestation. In 1861 he created two parks, the Tijuca and Paineiras forests. From 1861 to 1874 Major Gomes Archer planted 60,000 trees over 40,000 acres with the help of six slaves.

TIJUCA PARK AND FOREST ★
Because the park covers uneven ground you are advised not to leave the network of signposted paths and forest roads without a guide.
A pleasant way to enjoy the park is to walk along the Paineiras road at weekends or on public holidays, when it is closed to traffic.

★ PARQUE NACIONAL DA TIJUCA ◆ F C1-C2

The history of the Parque Nacional da Tijuca is closely linked to that of Rio itself. The reafforestation policy launched by Dom Pedro II ● *25* in the late 19th century was continued into the 20th, so that almost all the park's *mata atlântica* ▲ *172* is secondary forest. It is Rio's green lung and, covering over 8,000 acres, it is the largest urban forest in the world. In 1991 Unesco declared it a biosphere reserve.

ESTRADA DA VISTA CHINESA. Leaving the Horto district via Rua Pacheco Leão, you will come to the small Oriental-style pavilion of VISTA CHINESA, from where there is a panoramic view of the Corcovado, Sugar Loaf Mountain, the Lagoon and the jagged ranges of Niterói in the distance. A little further on is the Mesa do Imperador (Emperor's Table), which offers another view of Zona Sul and was one of Dom Pedro II's favorite family picnic spots.

PAINEIRAS. To enter the forest from the Cosme Velho district take the Ladeira Guararapes. The Paineiras road, which climbs to the summit of the Corcovado, leads into the Estrada do Redentor. About three miles of the road are closed to traffic at weekends and on public holidays, when walkers, joggers and cyclists come to enjoy the pure air and the freshness of the waterfalls along the way.

★ FLORESTA DA TIJUCA ◆ D A1-A2

Tijuca, meaning 'muddy land' in Tupí-Guaraní, originally referred to the district surrounding the mountain range. By extension the name was applied to the range itself and then to the Barra da Tijuca district. The Floresta da Tijuca, reached via Praça Afonso Vizeu in the Alto da Boa Vista district and the most frequented part of the park, was formerly a coffee *fazenda* (estate) owned by the Taunay family. The forest was laid out by the French landscape designer Auguste Glaziou ▲ *128* in 1874.

ESTRADA DA CASCATINHA. At the entrance into the forest the road passes the foot of the Cascatinha Taunay, the 98-foot waterfall painted by 19th-century European artists. From there it winds through the trees: these include the majestic *jequitibás*, *ipês* (green ebony) with yellow or purple flowers, *embaúbas* with distinctive silvery foliage, and exotic species such as eucalyptus, mangoes and jackfruit trees. The impatiens growing at the edge of the road is known locally as *maria sem-vergonha* (Shameless Mary). It is not unusual to come across groups of *micos* (tamarins) or the slightly larger *macacos pregos* (macaques). There are also over 150 species of birds, among which humming birds (*above*), known as 'flower-kissers' (*beija-flores)* in Portuguese, *sabiás*, *bem-te-vis* ▲ *230* and even large-billed toucans are relatively common.

CAPELA MAYRINK. The road leads on to this chapel, built in 1860 and restored from 1943 at the instigation of the park's administrator and patron of the arts, Castro Maya, who commissioned Cândido Portinari ● *86* to paint the three panels depicting the Madonna, Saint Simon and Saint John of the Cross. Continuing along the forest road you can take a break at one of two restaurants, Os Esquilos (The Squirrels), in the former residence of a French aristocrat, Baron d'Escragnolle, the park's administrator from 1874, or at the Floresta higher up.

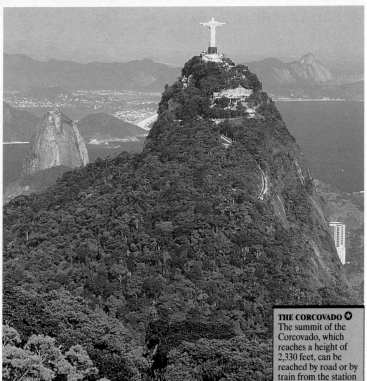

THE CORCOVADO ✪
The summit of the Corcovado, which reaches a height of 2,330 feet, can be reached by road or by train from the station at Rua Cosme Velho 513. Access to the belvedere is now easy thanks to the escalator that was installed in January 2003.

THE CORCOVADO ◆ D A3

ESTRADA DE FERRO CORCOVADO. During the colonial period the forest paths leading to the summit of the Corcovado were replaced by a road and then by a cog railroad, which was opened in 1884. The railroad enters the forest over a 250-foot-long iron bridge that is visible from the Ladeira do Ascurra in Cosme Velho. Initially a steam railway, it was electrified in 1912, becoming Brazil's first electric railroad.

CRISTO REDENTOR (CHRIST THE REDEEMER). The idea of erecting a gigantic statue of Christ to protect Rio originated in the 19th century. It was to be unveiled in 1922 to mark the centenary of Brazil's independence ● *25* but due to lack of funds the statue was not completed in time. The platform at its foot offers an all-round panorama of Rio in its spectacular setting: Zona Norte with the Maracanã stadium in the foreground, the concrete jungle of Centro, the Ponte Rio-Niterói, and the beaches of Guanabara Bay and Zona Sul where concrete buildings alternate with the *morros* whose forested slopes the *favelas* are eroding. In the background the jagged outline of the Serra do Mar running from Sugar Loaf mountain to the Serra dos Orgãos completes this breathtaking landscape.

CHRIST THE REDEEMER
The statue, unveiled in 1931, consists of reinforced concrete clad in soapstone chips. It is 98 feet high and 92 feet across at its widest point and is set on a 26-foot-high plinth. The project of a Christ with outstretched arms watching over the city was conceived by the engineer Heitor da Silva Costa who commissioned the French sculptor Paul Landowski to create the head and hands of the statue.

Its geographical setting and the effective system of defenses built around it made Rio de Janeiro a securely fortified city from colonial times. Several attempts at invasion by the French and the Dutch, and from the 18th century onward the need to protect consignments of gold arriving from Minas Gerais, led to the construction of a complex system of coastal fortresses. These fortifications occupied the city's most commanding, and most beautiful, vantage points. Although they were rarely called upon to fend off foreign invaders, Rio's defenses played an important role in keeping their locations free of urban sprawl.

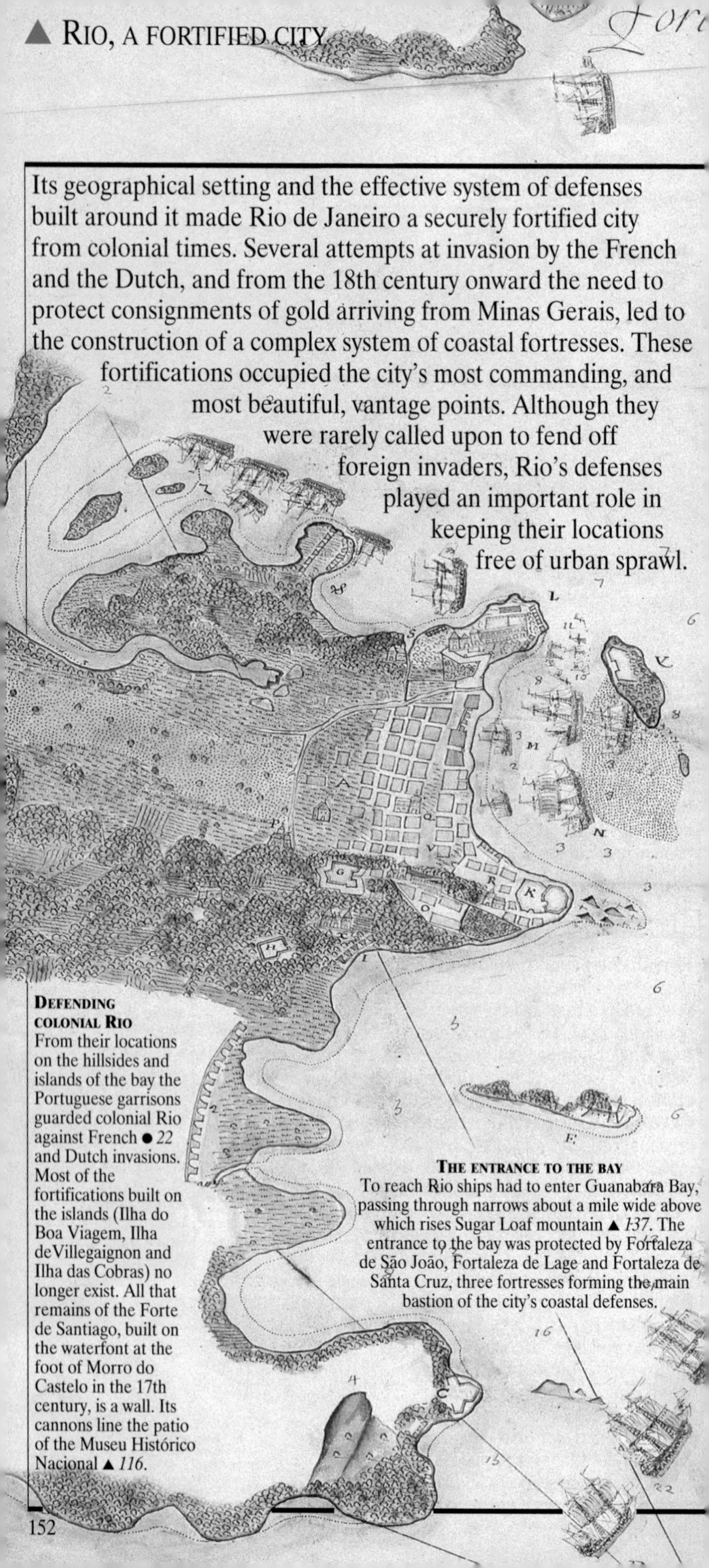

DEFENDING COLONIAL RIO
From their locations on the hillsides and islands of the bay the Portuguese garrisons guarded colonial Rio against French ● *22* and Dutch invasions. Most of the fortifications built on the islands (Ilha do Boa Viagem, Ilha deVillegaignon and Ilha das Cobras) no longer exist. All that remains of the Forte de Santiago, built on the waterfont at the foot of Morro do Castelo in the 17th century, is a wall. Its cannons line the patio of the Museu Histórico Nacional ▲ *116*.

THE ENTRANCE TO THE BAY
To reach Rio ships had to enter Guanabara Bay, passing through narrows about a mile wide above which rises Sugar Loaf mountain ▲ *137*. The entrance to the bay was protected by Fortaleza de São João, Fortaleza de Lage and Fortaleza de Santa Cruz, three fortresses forming the main bastion of the city's coastal defenses.

Fortaleza de São João

In the early 17th century four batteries were installed on Morro Cara de Cão, on the side of the hill facing Rio. The present fortress was built during the reign of Dom Pedro II ● *25* and was opened in 1872 to mark the fiftieth anniversary of Brazil's independence (*below center*). Access is via Fortaleza Urca on Avenida João Alves. A vaulted porchway dating from the 17th century leads to a double tier of galleries, some with cannons still pointing toward the ocean. The terrace offers a spectacular view of the sea.

Fortaleza da Lage

The Ilha de Lage, a virtually inaccessible rocky island pounded by waves and located at the center of the entrance to the bay, was chosen as the site of the third fortress. This completed the city's maritime defenses. In the 18th century two enormous chains, one almost 2,000 feet long and the other almost 3,000 feet long, were hung between this fort and the Fortaleza de São João and Fortaleza da Santa Cruz. At night they were stretched across the entrance to the bay to guard against invasion. The fort also housed prominent political prisoners, including José Bonifácio de Andrade, in 1832, and the poet Olavo Bilac, in 1892. The present casemate dates from 1907 and is not open to the public.

Fortaleza de Santa Cruz

In 1555 Villegagnon ● *22* installed a battery on the imposing rocky outcrop that marks the entrance to the bay on the side nearest to Niterói. Twelve years later Estácio de Sá ● *136* built the first Portuguese fort there. The present fort dates from 1863 (*left*). The walls overlooking the sea contain three tiers of batteries and enclose an interior courtyard and chapel, the Capela Santa Bárbara (patron saint of artillerymen). The fort was used as a political prison and still has the cells, execution wall, torture chamber and *cova da Onça* (jaguar's pit) from where victims were thrown into a pit that was open to the sea.

Forte de Copacabana

The army still occupies the rocky promontory between Copacabana beach ▲ *144* and Ipanema beach ▲ *145*. You can reach this fortress from *Posto* 6 on Copacabana beach or via the *ciclovia* (cycle track) on the Ipanema side of the promontory. Forte Copacabana was built between 1908 and 1914 on the site of a chapel, the Capela Nossa Senhora de Copacabana. Inside the fort (*left*), which is camouflaged by a concrete shell up to 40 feet thick, is a reconstruction of the living conditions of a garrison under siege. There is also a museum documenting glorious moments in Brazilian military history.

PONTE RIO-NITERÓI
The Ponte Presidente Costa e Silva, opened in 1974, is a feat of technical engineering. Spanning Guanabara Bay, it links Zona Norte and Niterói. It is about eight miles long and its central arch, about 2,600 feet long and 260 feet high, is designed to allow cargo ships to pass beneath it.

AMERICAN INDIANS OF THE BAY
French navigators who came to Brazil to collect cargoes of *pau-brasil* (tropical redwood) ● *28*, for which they enlisted the help of the Tamoios, prepared the way for the foundation of the colony of France Antarctique ● *22* in 1555. To drive out the French the Portuguese formed an alliance with the Termiminós, enemies of the Tamoios. When the French were expelled, Arariboia, chief of the Termiminós, was rewarded with the lands of Niterói.

The haphazard way in which Rio's suburbs developed and the lack of any coherent policy for the preservation of sites of historic importance or natural beauty have adversely affected Guanabara Bay and the surrounding areas. However, it is still worth taking one of the boat trips that leave from the Marina da Glória ▲ *135*. A short tour lasting about two hours takes in the Ilha Fiscal ▲ *118*, Ilha de Boa Viagem and the forts at the entrance to the bay ▲ *152*. Longer trips to Paquetá and the islands outside the bay are also possible.

NITERÓI

To reach the town of Niterói from Rio either cross the toll bridge or catch a ferry from Praça XV de Novembro ▲ *117*. The ferry crossing takes between seven and twenty minutes, depending on the boat.

BOA VIAGEM. Walk south along the bay and you will come to the Ilha de Boa Viagem, which can be reached via a footbridge. On the island are the remains of a fort and the Igreja Boa Viagem, which both date from the 17th century. The very plain church is the most popular in Niterói.

MUSEU DE ARTE CONTEMPORÂNEA. A little further on is the Museum of Contemporary Art, built in 1996 on a promontory overlooking the bay. This museum, designed by Niemeyer ▲ *203* in the form of a flying saucer, houses Dr João Satamini's collection of contemporary Brazilian art.

BEACHES OF THE ATLANTIC. On the far side of the rocky promontory occupied by the Fortaleza de Santa Cruz ▲ *153* lies a very different landscape, that of the beautiful beaches of Piratininga and Itaipu, reachable by road from Icaraí.

PAQUETÁ

This little island can be reached by boat from Praça XV de Novembro, and the crossing takes between twenty minutes and one hour, depending on the boat. There are no cars on the island but you can hire bicycles or a horse-drawn carriage to tour the island. Features of interest are the island's 19th-century *solares* (middle-class residences), the Igreja do BOM JESUS DO MONTE (1769), the CAPELA SÃO ROQUE (16th century) and a beach, the Praia da Moreninha.

PARQUE DARKE DE MATOS. This park, at the southern tip of the island, offers a beautiful view of Paquetá and the island of Brocoió, where there is an unusual early 20th-century villa, now serving as the summer residence of the governor of Rio. Check the return times of the boats before you set out. In fine weather aim to make the return journey at sunset, when you will be treated to some unforgettably beautiful sights.

Rio de Janeiro state

The rise and fall of the trade in sugar, gold ● *30* and coffee ● *32*, three of Brazil's major exports, have all left their mark on the state of Rio de Janeiro. In the 17th century the high price of sugar in Europe led to the creation of large sugar cane plantations in Brazil, most of which now no longer exist. In the 18th century a new road, the *Caminho Novo*, was driven through the mountains to link the mines of Ouro Preto with the port of Rio de Janeiro. This New Road reduced by two weeks the time it took to transport the precious cargos of gold and diamonds, which had previously been carried by mule trains and shipped to Portugal from the port of Parati ▲ *164.* Cargos now left from Rio de Janeiro. The city flourished and in 1763 became the capital of the colony ● *23*. In the 19th century, when the gold mines of Minas Gerais had been exhausted, coffee replaced gold as the source of the region's prosperity. Coffee plantations initially covered the hills around the city of Rio, then extended along the Paraíba do Sul valley ▲ *174*.

A DIVERSE ECONOMY

Although Rio de Janeiro is one of the smallest states in the federation, its economy is one of the most diverse. While the great 19th-century coffee plantations ● *68* have gradually been replaced by pasture, and mountainous areas have been turned over to the cultivation of fruit and vegetables, sugar cane is still grown in extensive plantations on the eastern plains near Campos dos Goitacazes. Rio de Janeiro state is also heavily industrialized and in the 1990s it experienced a growth rate of 9 to 11 percent, one of the highest in

SWISS IMMIGRANTS
In the 19th century the imperial government ● *25* launched an initiative to develop agriculture in the mountains overlooking Guanabara Bay. The beneficiaries of this initiative of land distribution were most prominently Swiss immigrants, who were concentrated in and around a town they called Nova Friburgo (New Fribourg) in memory of their homeland. The traces of this influx from Switzerland can still be seen today. Many of the buildings here are in the style of chalets, many of the farmers have Swiss surnames and there are people with rosy complexions that mark them out as being unmistakeably of European origin.

Brazil. The state's main industries, metallurgy, shipbuilding and chemicals, are concentrated in metropolitan Rio and from there to the town of Resende all along the main highway (the Rodovia Presidente Dutra) running between the cities of Rio and São Paulo. The service industries, especially finance, commerce and broadcasting, are highly developed in the city of Rio. The energy sector has also made a significant contribution to the state's economic development as most of Brazil's oil is extracted offshore near the town of Macaé, in the northeast. The advanced technology developed by the Petrobrás oil company has made it one of the world's most efficient deep-sea drilling companies. Brazil's two nuclear plants are also located in Rio de Janeiro state. Unfortunately, however, they are located on one of the region's most beautiful beaches, near Angra dos Reis ▲ *162*, in Sepetiba Bay.

MAGNIFICENT BEACHES

In the second half of the 20th century tourism in the state grew rapidly and luxury hotels sprang up along the coast from Parati in the west to Armação dos Búzios in the east. To the east of Rio the long straight beaches of the Costa do Sol (Sunshine Coast) stretch for more than 60 miles and breakers pound the sand, which ranges from ocher to white. This is the Região dos Lagos (Lake Region) ▲ *158*, named for the many coastal lakes here. To the west of Rio, toward São Paulo state, the landscape changes abruptly. This is the Costa Verde (Green Coast) ▲ *162*, with a jagged coastline, countless bays dotted with idyllic islands, and forested slopes that plunge vertically down to the sea. The calm, clear water here is ideal for bathing, scuba diving, harpoon fishing and watersports.

Praia Brava at Arraial do Cabo (*below*).

MICROCLIMATES
The state's uneven topography influences the climate of its coastal region. The Serra do Mar bars the eastward advance of clouds, causing greater rainfall on the Costa Verde than on the Costa do Sol. The Cabo Frio-Búzios peninsula is known for its mild climate, low rainfall and sea breezes that prevent summer temperatures from becoming uncomfortably high.

Mata atlântica ▲ *166*, ▲ *172* around the Riberão das Lajes reservoir (*below*).

The Região dos Lagos: from Maricá to Arraial do Cabo

Igreja Nossa Senhora de Nazaré at Saquarema
The church was built on the rock (*above*) where a wooden statue of the Madonna is said to have been found after a storm, in 1630. The church, which was rebuilt in 1837, still contains the statue, which the local people believe is capable of working miracles. Every year, on September 8, thousands of pilgrims travel great distances to come to this church to honor the Madonna of Nazaré, who is the patron saint of Saquarema. The town is the second most important place of pilgrimage after Belém ▲ *299*, where the annual ten-day festival of Nazaré takes place.

Beyond Niterói the beaches ★ of the Costa do Sol stretch for more than sixty miles. This is the Região dos Lagos, where the landscape is punctuated by beautiful coastal lakes, or lagoons.

From Maricá to Araruama

Despite its proximity to metropolitan Rio, the countryside around Maricá (meaning 'scrub' in Tupí) is relatively unspoiled, especially along the coast and around the lagoons.

Maricá. For a drive along Maricá's great 12-mile beach, take the RJ102, a minor road that runs between the lagoons and the sea (*above*). To reach this road take either one of two turnings off the Rodovia Amaral Peixoto (RJ106): at Km 21 turn right onto the RJ110 at São José de Imbassaí, where there is a small 17th-century chapel. From here, as it runs toward the sea, the road offers a beautiful view of the lagoon and the Atlantic. Alternatively you can turn off the RJ106 at Km 31, passing through the town of Maricá, where there is a fine late colonial church dating from 1802. From there you can join the RJ102 via a road leading down to the sea, with the lagoons of Maricá on the right and of Barra on the left.

Ponta Negra. At the far end of Maricá's long beach is Ponta Negra, a village dominated by a rocky spur jutting out into the ocean. The road beyond the canal climbs to a small lighthouse commanding spectacular vistas in which the blues and golds of the sea, the beaches and the lagoons stretch away to infinity.

Saquarema. Beyond Ponta Negra the RJ102 runs on between the lagoons and the ocean. At the far end of the 13-mile Jaconé-Saquarema beach is the little church of Nossa Senhora de Nazaré, proudly set on a rock. The town, whose name in Tupí means 'lake without shells' (as opposed to the shell-rich Araruama lagoon), is a popular resort where

FROM RIO TO THE REGIÃO DOS LAGOS ★
The beaches of the lake region can be reached via the Rodovia Amaral Peixoto (RJ106) or, for those that lie beyond Araruama, via the BR101 and the Rio Bonito-Araruama freeways. The region is well served by a number of buses that leave from the Rodoviária (bus station) in Rio. The three resorts on Cabo Frio (Cold Cape) are easily reached from Rio via the freeway that traverses the hinterland: the Niterói–Rio Bonito road (BR101) and then the Rio Bonito–Araruama toll expressway.

cariocas have built second homes on the streets parallel to the beach. Saquarema can also be reached from the RJ106 by turning off to the right at Km 64, at the village of Bacaxá.
ARARUAMA. About six miles beyond Bacaxá you come to Araruama, the last and largest lagoon on the Costa do Sol. Its shallow waters cover more than 115 square miles and are particularly well exposed to the sun. This makes them well suited to salt panning, so that salt marshes and lakeshore mills form part of this picturesque landscape. Araruama means 'lake of macaws' and, although the macaws that gave it its name no longer frequent the lagoon, there is still a wealth of plant and animal life there. Children play happily in the warm, shallow waters of the beaches of Araruama, Iguaba Pequena and Iguaba Grande. Like the other beaches along this stretch of coastline, access to the strip of sand that separates the lagoon from the Atlantic is along bumpy tracks, but being amidst the exhuberant beauty of this natural environment is worth the uncomfortable journey.
PRAIA SECA. At Km 80.5 on the RJ106 turn off onto the RJ132 and, eight miles further on, you will come to this delightful little beach on the lagoon. The road continues through a wild and beautiful landscape. On the right are paths leading off over the dunes and down to the pounding rollers of the Atlantic. On the left paths lead to the lagoon, and its beaches and salt marshes. The road continues through this wild landscape and after 28 miles reaches Arraial do Cabo.

ARRAIAL DO CABO

This resort is renowned for having the clearest water on the coast of southern Brazil. Set on the tip of a promontory, surrounded by beautiful sheltered beaches and nestling in a natural harbor with limpid, fish-filled waters, Arraial do Cabo is very popular with scuba divers.

SAQUAREMA
The Praia de Itaúna, beyond the church, is a favorite beach with sports enthusiasts. The breakers here are particularly suitable for surfing championships.

THE FISHING INDUSTRY
The ruins of a whale processing plant and the bones of a killer whale in Arraial do Cabo's maritime museum are vestiges of the region's former economy. Since whaling was banned in the region the only economic activities in Arraial do Cabo are fishing by traditional methods and the production of soda ash (a raw material used in glassmaking), obtained from shells gathered in the Araruama lagoon. The Companhia Nacional Alcalis, whose factory is at Arraial do Cabo, is a major producer of this substance.

The Região dos Lagos: from Arraial do Cabo to Búzios

The first settlers in Brazil
Sent by the king of Portugal to take possession of the 'discovered' territories ● *22*, Amerigo Vespucci, landed on the shores of this small paradise in 1503. He laid a stone marker ● *29*, which can still be seen at Praia dos Anjos (below the church of Nossa Senhora dos Remédios), and left twenty four men, who formed the first Portuguese community in Brazil. The story is said to have inspired Sir Thomas More's *Utopia* (1516).

Coastal resorts
The neighboring towns of Cabo Frio and Búzios are well provided with hotels. During the summer they also have a vibrant nightlife, which centers around the Portinho district in Cabo Frio and Rua das Pedras in Búzios. Around Búzios, and less noticeably around Cabo Frio, the developers who built *condomínios* (private residential estates) in the hinterland took care to design buildings in keeping with the local rustic style.

Beaches. While Praia Grande, a beach where there are powerful breakers, attracts surfers, the waters of Prainha and Praia dos Anjos are much calmer. A small paved road winds to the top of the Pontal do Atalaia, at the tip of the cape, access to which is via the Condomínio Pontal do Atalaia. The wide view of the sea, the beaches and the Ilha de Cabo Frio opposite is probably almost exactly as it was when the first European navigators set eyes on it.

Boat trips. For an unforgettable experience take a boat trip from Praia dos Anjos. You will glide over crystal-clear waters, swim at the small beach on the Ilha de Cabo Frio and visit the sea cave known as the Gruta do Búfalo.

Dunes. Constant winds have blown the fine sand here into huge dunes around Arraial do Cabo and the most beautiful of them lie along the road to Cabo Frio. They include the Dama Branca (White Lady), whose summit offers a magnificent view of the salt marshes and the great Praia do Cabo Frio.

Cabo Frio

The history of Cabo Frio is closely linked to that of the neighboring town of Arraial do Cabo. Although the Portuguese had attempted to colonize the region, the French controlled it for over a century, extracting the finest *pau-brasil* (brazilwood) ● *28* on the coast. It was not until 1615, when the first fort was built, that Portuguese settlers colonized the region. Today Cabo Frio is essentially a tourist town, and it underwent rapid development in the 1950s and 1960s.

A colonial town. Several vestiges of Cabo Frio's colonial past survive. They include the church of Nossa Senhora da Assunção (1615), the former convent of Nossa Senhora dos Anjos, built in the late 17th century and converted into a museum of religious art, and the church of São Benedito (1761). The fort of São Mateus, built on the ruins of a French fort known as the Casa da Pedra, stands at the entrance to the channel linking the Araruama lagoon to the ocean (*below*).

Praia do Forte. Cabo Frio is very popular during the high season (December–February). Its main attractions are centered around the beautiful Praia do Forte, which stretches for over four miles to Arraial do Cabo. A constant stream of bare-footed vendors ply the beach selling shrimp kebabs, donuts, fried fish, oysters, tropical fruits, sorbets and all kinds of cold drinks. Just outside the town, on the far side of the channel, are two more beaches, Conchas and Peró.

★ Armação de Búzios

Despite the heavy traffic that inevitably slows road travel at certain weekends during the summer, Armação de Búzios is easily accessible from Rio (112 miles to the west) via the Rio Bonito–Araruama freeway. Just before São Pedro d'Aldeia, turn off toward Campos on the RJ106 and ten miles further on fork right to Armação de Búzios. As it approaches this small town, the road runs alongside Praia Rasa, one of sixteen beaches on the peninsula.

Manguinhos and Geribá. These two beaches, on either side of the isthmus, attract different sorts of people. The calm waters and constant winds at Manguinhos, a narrow strip of sand bordered by middle-class villas, draw swimmers and windsurfers. Geribá, by contrast, is a trendy beach where *cariocas* wanting to see and be seen rub shoulders with actors from TV Globo's *telenovelas* ● *60*. A path at the end of the beach leads to the little creek of Ferradurinha.

Ferradura. Back on the main road, just before Armação, a double track on the right leads to the perfectly semicircular beach of Ferradura (meaning 'horseshoe'). The fact that it is protected from the Atlantic breakers by a narrow bottleneck makes it ideal for watersports. While older people sit in the shade of straw huts and enjoy the local fried fish, the younger generation makes the most of the facilities on offer, which include jet skiing and, for the very young, rides on a *banana* (an enormous floating banana pulled by a motorboat).

Armação. Most of the bars, stores and *pousadas* (taverns) in the area are concentrated in Armação. The main street, the famous Rua das Pedras, with rough-cut paving stones, is a top-quality shopping center with off-the-peg fashion and traditional crafts. In summer the atmosphere in the street reaches its peak between midnight and 2am, when young holidaymakers gather outside Chez Michou, a pancake house.

Praia dos Ossos. At the other end of Armação the street leads to the Praia dos Ossos (Bone Beach) district, named for the bones of the whales that were once butchered and processed nearby. From the small square you can get to the beach and port where *saveiros* will take you on a boat trip or taxi-rafts will ferry you to the neighboring beaches. On the left the beach is dominated by the tiny church of Sant'Ana, which offers a splendid view of the sea. On the right a path leads to the little beaches of Azeda and Azedinha, which are popular for their delightful setting. If you continue straight on from the square you will come to the beaches of João Fernandes, which is overlooked by a luxury hotel, and João Fernandinho. Both are very popular during the summer season.

A cosmopolitan town

The fishing village of Búzios rapidly developed as a coastal resort when the young *carioca* smart set came to its beaches in the 1970s. The Mediterranean-style peninsula also attracted many tourists from abroad, particularly Argentinians, who have opened stores and charming little *pousadas* (taverns), and French people, who have opened restaurants.

Beautiful beaches round Búzios ★

Apart from Manguinhos, Geribá and Ferradura, Búzios is surrounded by many more beaches, some of which are quite difficult to reach. Discover them on foot or by car as you explore the roads and tracks that cross the peninsula. Tartaruga, Forno, Brava and Olho de Boi are just four of them.

Búzios and Brigitte Bardot

In the early 1960s the French actress Brigitte Bardot spent a few weeks in a small villa on Praia Manguinhos. She was, however, probably more attracted by the charms of Brazilian playboy Bob Zagury than the beauty of the location. She never returned, not even to open Búzios' only movie theater, the Gran Cine Bardot. Even so her name is still used to promote the resort, which is often compared to Saint-Tropez.

FOLIA DOS REIS AT ANGRA DOS REIS
On Twelfth Night, or Folia dos Reis, small groups of people dressed up in folk costume go from house to house performing dances that, despite the occasion, are pagan rather than Christian. Angra dos Reis (Kings' Cove) is named for Twelfth Night, as the Portuguese landed there on January 6, 1502.

SCUBA DIVING
The waters off Angra dos Reis and around Ilha Grande are a paradise for scuba divers and harpoon fishermen. Divers are likely to encounter the green and blue fish known locally as *guarajuba*.

BY SCHOONER TO THE ISLANDS
Many boats make the trip from the port of Vilha do Abraão to the island's beaches. Departures are usually at 10.30am. You can arrange boat trips with local fishermen or take a water-taxi. Diving among shoals of colorful fish, eating crabs grilled on the beach and sunbathing are some of the pleasures on offer to holidaymakers here.

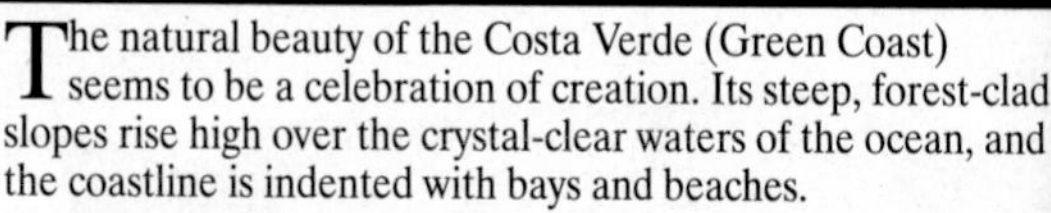

The natural beauty of the Costa Verde (Green Coast) seems to be a celebration of creation. Its steep, forest-clad slopes rise high over the crystal-clear waters of the ocean, and the coastline is indented with bays and beaches.

BAÍA DE SEPETIBA

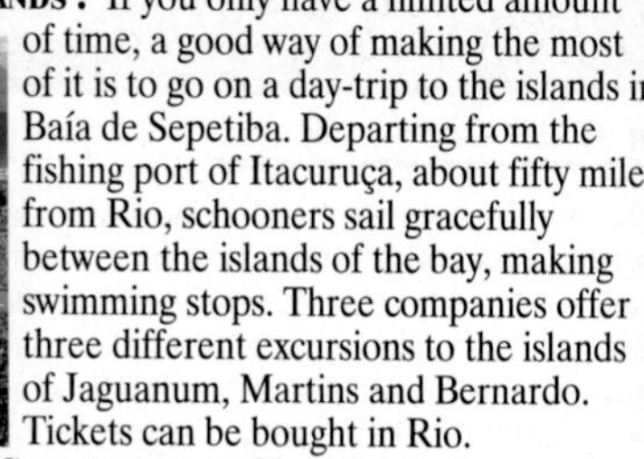

THE 'TROPICAL ISLANDS'. If you only have a limited amount of time, a good way of making the most of it is to go on a day-trip to the islands in Baía de Sepetiba. Departing from the fishing port of Itacuruça, about fifty miles from Rio, schooners sail gracefully between the islands of the bay, making swimming stops. Three companies offer three different excursions to the islands of Jaguanum, Martins and Bernardo. Tickets can be bought in Rio.

THE BR101 (RIO–SANTOS ROAD). The Rio–Santos road ▲ *228* winds for almost 155 miles along the Baía de Sepetiba before reaching Parati, and ample time is needed to take in all that this route has to offer. While the landscape is sparsely dotted with attractive *fazendas*, along the coastline an endless succession of beautiful beaches and scenic islands is revealed. Beyond the small resort of MURIQUI, it is worth making a detour to MANGARATIBA, which has a colonial church, the Igreja de Nossa Senhora da Guia, and a shady square. From Mangaratiba you can take a boat to Ilha Grande.

ANGRA DOS REIS. The sumptuous villas of wealthy people nestle in the creeks around Angra dos Reis (Kings' Cove), 96 miles from Rio. On New Year's Day the town is filled with tourists who come to celebrate the festival of Nossa Senhora dos Navegantes (Our Lady of the Navigators), when water tournaments are held, and at Folia dos Reis (Twelfth Night). Although the town center is crowded with a rather chaotic assemblage of buildings, colonial houses dating from the mid-18th century can still be seen at Rua Honório Lima 62, Rua Professor Lima 150, 154 and 156 and Rua Arcebispo Santos 125 and 135. The town's churches and convents are more widely scattered. The chapel of NOSSA SENHORA DA LAPA DA BOA MORTE (1752) is located near the quays of Lapa, the parish church of NOSSA SENHORA DA CONCEIÇÃO (1626–1750) is on Praça General Silvestre Travassos, and the soberly elegant chapel of SANTA LUZIA (1632) is at Rua do Comércio 194, Angra's busiest street. The convents of Nossa Senhora do Carmo, built by the Carmelites in the early 17th century, and of São Bernardinho de Sena, built by the Franciscans between 1758 and 1763, offer spectacular views of the bay. Angra's virtue is chiefly as the departure point for excursions through the *mata atlântica* ▲ *166, 172*, where there are waterfalls, natural beauty spots and spectacular view points, and for boat trips to the many beaches and islands, particularly to ILHA GRANDE, which lies off the end of the bay.

★ ILHA GRANDE

Covering 60 square miles, Ilha Grande is the largest island in Baía de Sepetiba, and it is now a protected site. The island was once the haunt of plunderers and buccaneers who lay in

wait in the creeks ready to intercept vessels loaded with gold that sailed from the port of Parati. In the late 19th century the island was the location of one of Brazil's harshest penal colonies, where bandits and prominent political prisoners, including the writer Graciliano Ramos, were held.

Vila do Abraão. This delightful little village should not be missed. The waterfront is lined with many charming *pousadas* (inns). There are no cars and no supermarkets, and the silence here is broken only by the lapping of waves, the shouts of fishermen and the clopping of mules.

Lopes Mendes. Following a path from Vila do Abraão that climbs through forest then runs along a succession of beaches, you will reach Lopes Mendes, a large deserted beach opening straight on to the Atlantic. As this walk takes two to three hours, make sure that you start back in time to reach Vila do Abraão before nightfall. If you prefer to make the return trip by boat from the beaches of Mangue or Palmas, make arrangements for this with one of the fishermen the day before.

Antigo Presídio. The walk along the mountain road from Vila do Abraão to the Antigo Presídio takes about three hours. Although the cell blocks of this former prison have been demolished, the main buildings on the beach of Dois Rios house an institute of marine research.

Freguesia de Santana. To give yourself enough time to visit the island's many creeks and stop in fishing villages like Saco do Céu allow a whole day for the return trip from Vila do Abraão. From Angra the Rio–Santos road continues toward Parati, passing one of Brazil's two nuclear power stations.

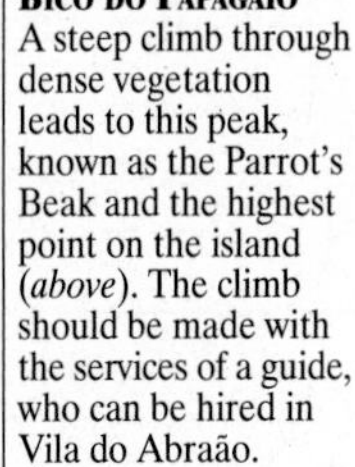

Bico do Papagaio
A steep climb through dense vegetation leads to this peak, known as the Parrot's Beak and the highest point on the island (*above*). The climb should be made with the services of a guide, who can be hired in Vila do Abraão.

"Between the soldiers' boots, I could see the outside world, the sun, water, islands, hills and a nearby landfall that was getting bigger." Graciliano Ramos

Antigo Aqueduto
From Vila do Abraão you can walk to the ruins of the Lazareto, a former leper house, and to an 19th-century aqueduct now overgrown with vegetation, and a waterfall where you can bathe.

Ilha Grande ★
This island, the largest in Baía de Sepetiba, can be reached by boat either from Angra dos Reis or from Mangaratiba. The 1½-hour crossing brings you to the village of Vila do Abraão. There is no motorized traffic on Ilha Grande, and its many attractions include walks through the *mata atlântica*, for which you will need a good pair of walking boots, as well as wild, unspoiled beaches and scenic boat trips. Among the island's most beautiful beaches are Praia de Lopes Mendes and Praia do Leste e do Sul. The latter (*left*) is also a biosphere reserve. It can be reached from the beach and village of Aventureiro.

PAVED AND FLOODED STREETS
The streets of Parati are paved with *pé-de-moleque* (urchin's feet), the name given to the rough stone paving on which urchins ran barefooted. The streets leading down to the ocean are low-set and slightly sloping so that they are flooded and washed clean at high tide.

THE PORT OF PARATI
Some 1000 tons of gold and 220 lb of precious stones were shipped from Parati before the *Caminho Novo* ● *30* opened in 1723. This road from Minas Gerais to Rio de Janeiro reduced journey times to the coast by two weeks.

In the 18th century Parati, which lies between two rivers some 150 miles from Rio, was a small town whose livelihood depended on its proximity to sugar cane mills and to the ocean. An American Indian trail led from the town through the mountains and on to Minas Gerais where gold and diamonds had just been discovered ● *30*. Parati therefore became an ideal port from which to ship the precious metal that would make the fortune of the Portuguese crown. However, these cargos were soon being transported not to Parati but along the *Caminho Novo* (New Road) to Rio. Parati was not to prosper again until the coffee boom of the 19th century and the rise of tourism in more recent times.

★ PARATI, A COLONIAL TOWN

With five streets running parallel to the ocean intersected by four streets cutting across them at right angles, the old center of Parati reflects the town's colonial past. Classified as a World Heritage Site by UNESCO in 1966, it has been used as the setting for several historical movies. It is indeed easy to imagine slaves paving the streets with *pé-de-moleque* (a type of rough-hewn stone) or being thrown into the Cadeia Pública, the prison, which is now the CASA DO ARTESÃO (Artisan's House). You can also visualize the town's wealthy inhabitants making their way along RUA DO COMÉRCIO, still lined with stores, to the Sobrado da Prefeitura (Town Hall) to join fellow members of the Masonic lodge, whose influence is reflected in the triangular motifs on the town's façades and cornerstones. You can almost hear the women chatting in secluded courtyards and see them crossing the shady gardens of PRAÇA DA MATRIZ on their way to mass in the parish church of NOSSA SENHORA DOS REMÉDIOS (the town's patron saint) on Praça Monsenhor Hélio Pires, or the older church of SANTA RITA (1722) near the market, most of whose treasures are now displayed in the Museu de Arte Sacra. During the colonial period, the blacks would gather in front of NOSSA SENHORA DO ROSÁRIO E SÃO BENEDITO, on Rua Samuel Costa, which they built in 1725. Parati is steeped

in colonial history and is pervaded by a colonial atmosphere. It has a number of delightful *pousadas* (inns), all decorated in rustic colonial style, and restaurants serving tasty seafood and regional dishes. In the countless craft stores such well-made items as model boats and masks are offered for sale.

FORTE DEFENSOR PERPÉTUO. Follow Rua Santa Rita, the continuation of the town's only bridge, which rises as it leads away from the port. Turn right along Rua do Comércio and continue for about 20 minutes, when you will come to the Morro da Vilha Velha (Old Town Hill). In 1703 a fort was built on the hill to defend the town against pirates. It was rebuilt in 1822 and named Forte Defensor Perpétuo (Fort of the Perpetual Defender) for Dom Pedro I ● *24*. From here there is a panoramic vista over Praia do Pontal (Point Beach) and a romantic view of the bay. The fort now houses the Centro de Artes e Tradições Populares de Parati, a small museum of folk art and regional traditions, with displays of canoes, nets and other traditional fishing equipment.

PRAIA DO JABAQUARA. Again follow Rua Santa Rita, the street that rises away from the port, but this time turn left along Rua do Comércio and follow it down to Praia do Jabaquara, a beach with clam fishermen and small waterfront cafés. At low tide it is possible to walk to the island opposite the beach.

CACHOEIRA DO TOBOGÃ. Take the road that heads inland toward Cunha. More energetic visitors can climb to the little church of La Penha, near a large waterfall with an *escorrega*, a kind of natural water chute where local children swim. The waterfall can be reached by bicycle, which can be hired by the hour or the day from the tourist office in Parati.

'FAZENDA' MURYCANA. The *fazenda* lies about 2½ miles down a dirt track branching off from the right of the road to Cunha. This 17th-century sugar plantation, or *engenho* ▲ *270,* still has the ancient stills that were used for making *cachaça* ● *64*. You can hire horses at the *fazenda*.

BOAT TRIPS
Schooners and fishing boats run trips from the quay in Parati around the little islands in the bay and to the more distant beaches of Barra Grande, Parati-Mirim and Sono.

PARATI ★
Parati, situated on highway BR101 about 150 miles west of Rio de Janeiro, is an historic town with paved streets and old churches. Bahia de Ilha Grande, the bay fronting Parati, is lined with 300 beaches and has 65 islands.

DELICIOUS 'CACHAÇA'
In August the Festival da Pinga, when the local *cachaça* is feted, brings the sleepy town of Parati to life. It is also an opportunity to sample one of Brazil's best-known liquors.

Because overland access to it was difficult, at least until the Rio–Santos road (BR101) was opened in the 1970s, the coastal forest around Baía da Ilha Grande was spared the deforestation that devastated other tracts of Brazil's Atlantic forest during the periods of gold mining, coffee and sugar cane plantations and latterly of steel production. The relative isolation of this coastal forest has meant that its *mata atlântica* is intact, from the high-altitude grasslands of the Parque Nacional da Serra da Bocaina to the coastal vegetation of the islands in the bay.

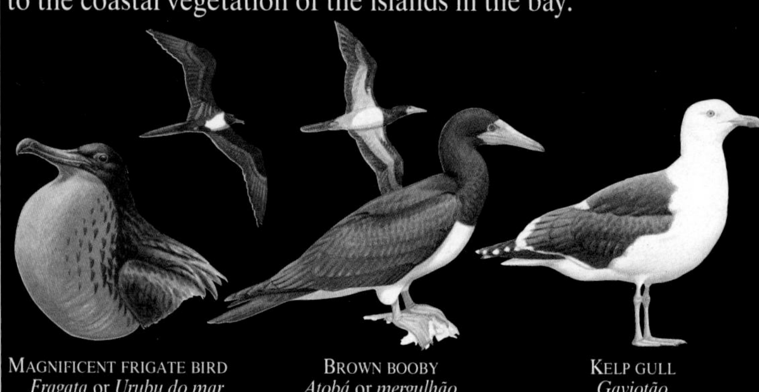

MAGNIFICENT FRIGATE BIRD *Fragata* or *Urubu do mar* (*Fregata magnificens*)

BROWN BOOBY *Atobá* or *mergulhão* (*Sula leucogaster*)

KELP GULL *Gaviotão* (*Larus dominicanus*)

BAÍA DA ILHA GRANDE
Ilha Grande, which covers 60 square miles and rises to an altitude of 3,146 feet at its highest point, has one of the last surviving ecosystems typical of the coastal area south of Rio. It features *restingas* (low vegetation that grows among dunes), mangroves, lagoons, forest (covering 97 percent of the island's area) and rocky coasts. A program of conservation has been launched to preserve these ecosystems but the lack of funds and the indifference of local population (Caiçaras, Guaraní) makes it slow. In the area around Parati the community of Caiçaras live by producing and selling handicrafts and by exploiting *palmito* (a type of palm) and *caixeta* wood.

Parque Marinho do Aventureiro
The southern shore of Ilha Grande is sparsely populated and still relatively unfrequented by tourists. The beaches (*right*), mangroves and ocean floor (*below*) are protected sites within the Parque Marinho do Aventureiro.

Dolphins
Three species frequent Baia da Ilha Grande: *Sotalia fluviatilis* ('Rio de Janeiro dolphin'), *Steno bredanensis* (rough-toothed dolphin) and *Delphinus delphis* (short-beaked common dolphin). They can be seen in the late afternoon as they leave Guanabara Bay with the tide.

Museu Imperial

THE ORIGINS OF PETRÓPOLIS
In 1822 Dom Pedro I ● *24* fell in love with the Serra dos Órgãos but was frustrated in his attempt to buy a *fazenda* from Padre Correia on the Caminho de Ouro (the Gold Path). In 1830 he acquired the nearby Fazenda do Córrego Seco. The house and chapel of Fazenda do Padre Correia are about four miles from Petrópolis on the road to Teresópolis.

LANDSCAPE DESIGNERS AND BOTANISTS
In 1870 Jean-Baptiste Binot, one of Don Pedro's landscape designers in Petrópolis, built an orchid house, the Orquidário Binot. Today the nursery, on Rua Fernandes Vieira in Retiro, exports orchids, bromeliads, ferns and plants. Auguste François Glaziou ▲ *128*, Dom Pedro II's other landscape designer, laid out the garden of the Solar Tavares Guerra, on Avenida Ipiranga, behind the cathedral. The garden has been preserved in its original state.

The Serra dos Órgãos, lying north of Guanabara Bay, is a mountain range named for its tubular rock formations, which have the appearance of organ pipes. This *região serrana*, or mountainous region, of Rio de Janeiro state contains a national park that is one of the most representative of Brazil, as it includes fine swathes of the country's endangered *mata atlântica* ▲ *172*. The *região serrana* also boasts several cities, which because of their historic interest and modern amenities are ideal for cultural and green tourism.

PETRÓPOLIS, AN IMPERIAL CITY

Petrópolis, 41 miles northwest of Rio on highway BR040, lies at an altitude of 2,654 feet and has a population of 300,000. The city is named for Dom Pedro II, emperor of Brazil from 1831 to 1899 ● *25*, and still bears the mark of his presence. Seeking refuge from the oppressive heat of Rio, the royal court made Petrópolis its summer residence. As such the city enshrines the most important legacy of Brazil's imperial age. Petrópolis is laid out to a plan based on three main principles: the course of rivers was not diverted, the mountainsides were kept free of development and plots of land were laid out along the courses of rivers and the foot of mountains.

✪ **MUSEU IMPERIAL.** To get a sense of the city in its imperial days start at the Museu Imperial (*top*). Originally the Palácio Imperial, the building was commissioned by Dom Pedro II in 1843 and work, to a design by the German architectural engineer Júlio Köeler, began in 1845. The palace, whose sober lines and pink and white façade reflect the personality of Dom Pedro II, was closely linked to the foundation of the city, and was the first residence in Brazil specifically designed for the monarch and his family. The garden, by the French landscape designer Jean-Baptiste Binot, is filled with luxuriant vegetation. When the republic ● *25* was proclaimed, the palace was converted into a school and became a museum in 1940.

CATEDRAL DE SÃO PEDRO DE ALCÂNTARA. Rua da Imperatriz leads to the cathedral, which is dedicated to Saint Peter, patron saint of the empire. Built between 1884 and 1925, it is in the French neo-Gothic style and contains the tombs of Dom Pedro II, the empress Dona Tereza Cristina, Princesa Isabel ● *35* and her husband Louis-Philippe Gaston d'Orléans, the Conde d'Eu and the grandson of the French king Louis-Philippe. You can climb to the top of the cathedral tower, which offers a panoramic view of the city.

Dom Pedro II's imperial crown, made of gold set with pearls and diamonds.

Avenida Köeler. This avenue, which runs between the cathedral and Praça Rui Barbosa, is divided lengthwise by a central canal spanned by the red bridges that are typical of Petrópolis. The avenue is a fine example of Köeler's skillful combination of urban planning and natural features. On the right, at the end of the avenue nearest the cathedral, stands the Palácio de Princesa Isabel (1853) and a little further on the Palácio Köeler (1872), now the city hall.

Casa de Santos-Dumont. At the far end of the avenue lies Praça Rui Barbosa. Across this square is Rua do Encanto, which slopes up to the Casa de Santos-Dumont. This small chalet-like house, built in 1918, has stairs with offset steps and an ingenious shower, and reflects its owner's inventive flair. It also contains photographs of Alberto Santos-Dumont ▲ *125* flying his famous biplane 14-bis *La Demoiselle* in 1906, and some of his personal possessions. Depressed by the use of his invention in World War One, Santos-Dumont withdrew to Petrópolis.

Palácio Rio Negro. Return to Avenida Köeler and, walking back along the opposite side of the avenue, you will pass this impressive palace, built in an eclectic style by the Barão de Rio Negro in 1889. From 1896 to 1903 it was the seat of the government of Rio de Janeiro state, then became the summer residence of the presidents of the republic. Continue along the avenue and you will find yourself back at the cathedral.

Palacete do Barão de Mauá. From the cathedral Rua 13 de Maio leads to a neoclassical baronial palace, the Palacete do Barão de Mauá, which is on the far side of the Piabanha river. Today the building houses the city's tourist office (Petrotur). In 1854 the Barão de Mauá ● *35* financed the construction of the first railroad linking Rio de Janeiro to the foothills of the Serra dos Órgãos.

Palácio de Cristal. On the far side of a bridge spanning the Piabanha river stands the palace given to Princesa Isabel by her husband the Count of Eu. It is a fine example of the steel-and-glass architecture typical of the second half of the 19th century. Its metal framework was a gift from the French government. The palace, completed in 1884, hosted botanical and ornithological exhibitions and is still a venue for concerts and exhibitions. With special lighting it is a particularly impressive sight at night. From Petrópolis take highway BR495 Teresópolis, a town with closer links to the Parque Nacional da Serra dos Órgãos.

MUSEU IMPERIAL ★
The museum's collections of jewelry, mahogany furniture, paintings and accessories trace the history of the Portuguese house of Braganza and of the Brazilian monarchy. Exhibits of particular interest include the imperial crown (*above*) and the imperial scepter (*below*), symbols of an empire founded in the tropics ● *24*.

Palácio Quitandinha
As you enter Petrópolis from the direction of Rio, along the Quitandinha highway, you will see the Palácio Quitandinha, a Romanesque-style building of monumental proportions that overlooks a lake shaped like a map of Brazil. The palace was built as a casino in 1944. When gambling was made illegal in 1946 it was converted into a hotel, and during the 1950s and 1960s it became a major venue of shows and events put on for Brazilian high society. It is now a conference center and is open to the public.

▲ Serra dos Órgãos Teresópolis and the Parque Nacional

Dedo de Deus
The Dedo de Deus, or Finger of God (*opposite page, top*), clearly visible from the Rio–Teresópolis road (highway BR116), is the most famous site in Rio de Janeiro state's *região serrana*, or mountainous region. According to popular tradition the Dedo de Deus created the mountains of Teresópolis, while the hand of man built the inviting hotels and and restaurants, set apart from the bustle of the city.

Low-growing vegetation
The park's luxuriant vegetation includes orchids, ferns, begonias, bromeliads (*below*) and xaxins, the fibrous trunks of certain kinds of ferns that are much sought after for making pots for houseplants.

Teresópolis

The town of Teresópolis, situated 33 miles from Petrópolis (via highway BR495) and 56 miles from Rio de Janeiro (via highway BR116), was founded in 1880 in honor of the empress Dona Tereza Cristina. Until the 18th century the region was ignored by the Portuguese colonists. The mountainous terrain and cool climate were not conducive to the establishment of new settlements, and the Portuguese were more interested in land on which they could cultivate the region's profitable tropical produce. In the 19th century it became a favorite destination for foreign naturalists traveling in Brazil. From 1850 it became popular with holidaymakers from Rio, who still come here to enjoy the coolness of what is Rio state's highest town. Its fine setting at an altitude of 2,985 feet in the center of the Serra dos Órgãos makes it an ideal place from which to visit the national park and enjoy such eco-friendly activities as climbing, walking and horse riding. The studs of Teresópolis produce the country's finest thoroughbreds. Because of its high altitude, Teresópolis is the Brazilian soccer team's favorite training ground. Its beautiful setting is still one of the town's major assets.

Colina dos Mirantes. When the sun shines, this hill (which is accessible via Avenida Feliciano Sodré) offers a spectacular view of the Serra dos Órgãos, a contrasting landscape of blue sky, lush vegetation and gray rocks. The town's elongated form is dictated by the mountainous topography surrounding it. In the words of the historian Sérgio Buarque de Holanda, who studied the origins of Brazil, 'the town's silhouette merges into the landscape'.

✪ Parque Nacional da Serra dos Órgãos

The Parque Nacional da Serra dos Órgãos, which lies between the municipalities of Teresópolis, Petrópolis and Magé, was created in 1939 to preserve the region's biodiversity. This mountainous park covers 27,000 acres, its topography bristling with gneiss and granite peaks and scored by deep valleys. Some of the peaks rise to great heights and have unusual names: Escalavrado (Flayed Man, 4,613 feet), Cabeça de Peixe (Fish Head, 5,512 feet), Dedo de Deus (Finger of God, 5,551 feet), Agulha do Diabo (Devil's Needle, 6,725 feet), Pedra do Sino (Bell Rock, 7,424 feet) and Pedra do Açu (Great Rock, 7,365 feet). You can walk along the pathways in the park and admire spectacular waterfalls and beautiful natural pools. For more serious walkers there is a 26-mile hike from Teresópolis to Petrópolis, which takes three days and must be made with a guide. The hike takes in the Pedra do Sino, which can also be reached from the entrance to the park, along a good pathway in five hours and without a guide. The park's flora ▲ *172* comprises lush vegetation and trees such as *jequitibá*, the jacaranda, cedar, cinnamon tree, cabbage palm and bamboo. Several rare species of birds, including the hyacinth macaw ▲ *210*, exist alongside *sabiás* (thrushes), goldfinches, partridges and quails. Among the park's small mammals are monkeys ▲ *172*, *preguiças* (sloths), armadillos, *pacas* and *cutias* (agoutis), and *porcos-do-mato*

(peccaries). Temperatures are low in winter and can fall as low as 23° F in the high mountains. Summers are warm, with heavy rainfall caused by the warming of the air along the Atlantic coast.

SEDE DO PARQUE. The main entrance to the park is about half a mile from Teresópolis along highway BR116 in the direction of Rio. From the entrance you can choose several footpaths or go climbing, but be aware that some climbs cannot be attempted without the services of a guide. Also within reach from here are large natural pools and the Paquequer river, where you can swim in summer. There are also picnic areas and gardens. For longer stays the park has camping sites as well as accommodation for groups. For the latter it is advisable to book in advance.

SUB-SEDE DO PARQUE. The secondary entrance to the park is 7½ miles further on, at Km 98 on highway BR116. From here relatively easy footpaths lead to some of the Soberbo river's finest natural pools, which include the Poço Verde (Green Well). Near this entrance is the MUSEU VON MARTIUS, named for the German naturalist Karl Freidrich von Martius, who traveled in Brazil between 1817 and 1820. He produced several studies of the flora, fauna and American Indian populations of Brazil. The museum was founded in 1967, and occupies the main house of a plantation, the Fazenda Barreira, on which Von Martius stayed while he was in Brazil.

THE SERRA'S VIPS
Among the famous travelers who ventured into the Serra dos Órgãos was the watercolorist Jean-Baptiste Debret ● *24, 84* and the naturalists Karl Freidrich von Martius and Johann Baptist von Spix. In 1822 Dom Pedro I ● *24* was so taken with the region that he wanted to build a palace here.

THE PARK ★
The park, for which there is an admission charge, is reached via Teresópolis on highway BR116. The best time of year for walking and climbing here is from May through October, while swimming in the rivers and natural pools is best from November through February.

BROWN HOWLER MONKEY
The Atlantic forest harbors more than 20,000 species of plants, 261 species of mammals, 620 species of birds and 260 species of amphibians.

The Brazilian *mata atlântica* is a dense, semideciduous tropical rainforest. In 1500 it covered an area of almost 2,500,000 square miles along the coast between the states of Rio Grande do Sul and Rio Grande do Norte. Its topography, together with heavy rainfall and a maritime influence have given the Atlantic forest exceptional biological diversity, and it was classified as a Unesco Biosphere Reserve in 1991. Although just 7 percent of the original forest remains, it still covers extensive tracts of Rio de Janeiro state, ranging from sea level to the Pico da Bandeira (9,482 feet), its highest point. These areas, whose remoteness ensured their survival, now form part of four national parks.

BRAZILIAN RUBY HUMMINGBIRD

BANDED COTINGA

GOLDEN LION TAMARIN
The population of *mico-leão-dourado* has been reduced to a few hundred individuals.

RED-CAPPED MANAKIN

RED-TAILED AMAZON PARROT

EPIPHYTES AND BROMELIADS
While some bromeliads, such as *Aechmea sp. (top)* have elongated leaves, others, like *Vriesea sp. (above),* have shorter, broader leaves.

TALL TREES UNDER THREAT
Certain trees that have been exploited since colonial times are now under threat of extinction. Among them are the *pau-brasil*, the *jequitibá* and the jacaranda.

LUSH VEGETATION
In summer the forest is dotted with blazes of color as certain trees come into flower (*top*). Among these flowering trees are the *ipês amarelo* and *roxo* (*Tabebuia chrysotricha and heptaphylla*) and the *quaresmeira* (*Tibouchina granulosa*). Other trees typical of the *mata atlântica* are the *embaúba* (*Cecropia glaziovii*), whose silver-gray leaves are a favorite food of sloths, *jatobá* (*Hymeneae courbatil*) and *pau ferro* (*Caesalpinea ferrea*). Tree ferns grow profusely on the banks of streams and rivers (*above* and *left*).

ALONG THE RIO PARAÍBA: THE 'FAZENDAS', FROM VASSOURAS TO VALENÇA

THE 'FAZENDA': A CENTER OF POWER AND WORK ● *68*
Fazendas were divided into clearly defined areas. The *casa-grande*, the residence of the owner of the plantation and of the slaves, was characterized by its sophisticated architecture and furnishings. The garden, often laid out by European landscape designers, was at the front of the *fazenda* and royal palms sometimes stood at its entrance. The *terreiro* was a rectangular paved area where coffee beans were dried before being stored in silos. The *senzala*, made from *pau-a-pique* ● *69* or brick, was the communal slave house. These buildings were surrounded by the plantations, which was created by clearing and burning the forest and planting coffee bushes on the hillsides. All this work was done by slaves.

PRAÇA BARÃO DE CAMPO BELO
In the center of this square (*right*) stands an imposing freestone fountain created by by Soto Garcia de la Vega in 1846. The parish church of Matriz de Nossa Senhora da Conceição was built in 1846 on the site of a chapel at one of the highest points in the town. The impressive houses surrounding the square were the residences of coffee barons. Among them is the neoclassical Palacete do Barão do Ribeirão, dating from 1860, on Rua Barão de Vassouras.

The Vale do Paraíba was the setting of one of the great chapters in the history of Brazil, a story that unfolds as you travel along the river and visit the rich coffee *fazendas* (plantations) established in the valley in the 19th century. The Vale do Paraíba, which had been a major communication route since the 18th century ● *30,* experienced its golden age in the 19th with the discovery of 'black gold' (coffee) ● *32.* Visiting the *fazendas* – which centralized the economic, social, political, administrative and religious activities of their inhabitants – offers an insight into this powerful and wealthy rural society. It was based on slave labor ● *34* and the progressive decline of slavery in Brazil from the second half of the 19th century, combined with an intensive agriculture that caused runoff and soil erosion, led to the region's decline. Even so its important cultural heritage survives and can still be seen in and around Vassouras, Valença and Barra do Piraí, the main departure points for visiting the *fazendas*.

VASSOURAS, TOWN OF THE COFFEE BARONS

The itinerary begins in Vassouras, the region's major financial center during the prosperous period of the coffee boom. The town, situated 72 miles from Rio de Janeiro at an altitude of 1,424 feet, has a population of about 30,000.

PRAÇA BARÃO DE CAMPO BELO. The square (*above*), with gardens and royal palms, dates from 1835. It is surrounded by some of the town's oldest buildings.

PRAÇA SEBASTIÃO DE LACERDA. This quiet and peaceful square, planted with Indian figtrees, lies behind the church. The fountain was a gift from Dom Pedro II in 1848.

MUSEU CASA DA HERA. The museum, at Rua Fernandes Junior 160, near the square, occupies the former residence of Joaquim José Teixeira Leite, a wealthy 19th-century coffee merchant, and later of his daughter Eufrásia, who lived in Paris in the late 19th century. Most of the furniture and ornaments in the richly decorated drawing rooms were imported from Europe. The museum's evocative atmosphere and décor embody the town's imperial age.

'FAZENDAS' AROUND VASSOURAS. Several *fazendas* are within easy reach of Vassouras. The Fazenda SÃO FERNANDO (*opposite page, top*) is located 13 miles from the town at Km 218 on highway BR393. It has been recently restored and still

has its *casa-grande*, whose main entrance has a flight of stone steps, and its chapel. The FAZENDA CACHOEIRA, three miles from the town via highway BR393 and then RJ127 (at Estrada Cachoeria Grande 1393), has also been restored and its *casa-grande* has a distinctive interior, with furniture and decorative objects. The FAZENDA SECRETÁRIO, twelve miles from Vassouras on the RJ115, is worth visiting for its grand gardens and architecture, including a tower with two clocks which show the time in Brazil and in France.

VALENÇA

Most of the coffee *fazendas* are located around Valença. The town is 100 miles from Rio de Janeiro and 35 miles from Vassouras, and lies at an altitude of 1,850 feet. It has a population of 62,000 and is the center of cultural tourism in the region.

FROM VASSOURAS TO VALENÇA. From Vassouras take highway BR393 and then the RJ145 toward Valença. About three miles outside the town, is the FAZENDA SANTO ANTONIO DO PAIOL, built in 1804. It once had an infirmary where slaves were treated. Also preserved here is original documentation on slavery, including a register indicating the name, place of origin, price and profession of each slave. Further along the RJ145, just before Valença, a track leads to the FAZENDA CAMPO ALEGRE, which has an open-air museum with *terreiros* (areas where coffee beans were dried), silos and old machinery and tools. Refreshments are served in the mill.

FROM VALENÇA TO RIO DAS FLORES. Another interesting *fazenda* is that of PAU D'ALHO ● *69*, 2½ miles from Valença. It has a beautiful natural setting, and visitors can also enjoy tea and regional dishes there. Just outside Rio das Flores is SÃO POLICARPO, one of the twenty three *fazendas* owned by the Visconde de Rio Preto. Now restored, it is a fine example of an urban colonial residence built in a rural setting. The gardens were designed by French landscape designer Auguste Glaziou ▲ *128*. To reach the FAZENDA SANTA ROSA, a former plantation that produces good-quality *cachaça* ● *64*, continue along the RJ145, turn onto the RJ151 beyond the town of Manoel Duarte and then bear to the right along a dirt track. On your return journey you may like to stay overnight in one of the region's old plantations, such as the Arvoredo or Ponte Alta *fazendas*, between the towns of BARRA DO PIRAÍ and PIRAÍ, beyond the bridge over the Paraíba river. The FAZENDA PONTE ALTA , built in 1815, lies off the main road about two miles beyond Santanésia. It has a perfectly preserved *senzala*, now a museum of slavery.

A DAY IN THE LIFE OF A SLAVE

The day began when a bell sounded at 4am. The slaves would wash, dress and line up with their work tools for the overseer's roll call. After eating cassava washed down with hot coffee they went to work on the plantation as dawn was breaking. They worked until 8am, when another signal announced breakfast and a half-hour break. At midday they drank coffee and were allowed to smoke during their ten-minute break. They continued working until late afternoon. If rain threatened, they would gather up the coffee laid out on the ground to dry and take it back to the silos. At the end of the working day, fires were lit in the *senzala* (slave house) and the slaves grilled a supper of bananas, potatoes, maize and cassava. They ate and smoked until 8pm, when the fires were put out and the slaves went to bed.

1 and 2. Manakins **3.** Golden lion tamarin **4.** Jararaca snake

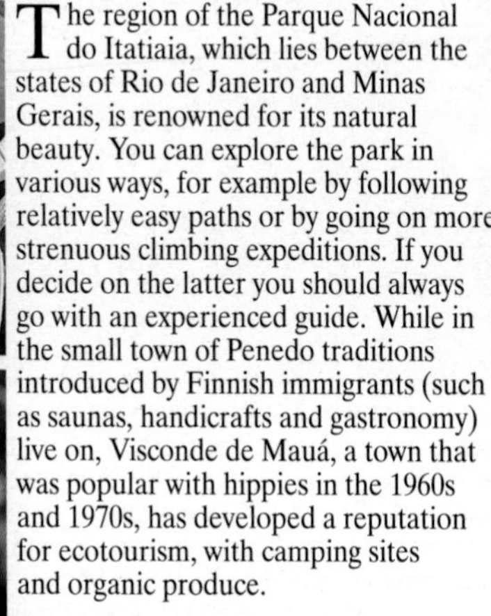

The region of the Parque Nacional do Itatiaia, which lies between the states of Rio de Janeiro and Minas Gerais, is renowned for its natural beauty. You can explore the park in various ways, for example by following relatively easy paths or by going on more strenuous climbing expeditions. If you decide on the latter you should always go with an experienced guide. While in the small town of Penedo traditions introduced by Finnish immigrants (such as saunas, handicrafts and gastronomy) live on, Visconde de Mauá, a town that was popular with hippies in the 1960s and 1970s, has developed a reputation for ecotourism, with camping sites and organic produce.

✪ Parque Nacional do Itatiaia

The Parque Nacional do Itatiaia (*itatiaia* means 'pointed rocks' in Tupí-Guaraní) is located 112 miles from Rio de Janeiro, from which it is reached via the Rodovia Presidente Dutra (BR116), and 3 miles from Penedo. The park lies in the Serra da Mantiqueira, a mountain range with rocky escarpments bordering the valley of the Paraíba river. The park owes its biodiversity to the different altitudes of these escarpments. Founded in 1937, Parque National was the first conservation area to be created in Brazil. Covering more than 74,000 acres, it includes a large area of *mata atlântica* ▲ *172*. With rivers, lakes, waterfalls and mountains, it has a rich ecosystem and a great diversity of plants and animals. As well as 400 species of birds and 50,000 species of insects, there are also such rare and endangered species as the *muriqui*, jaguar, *lobo-guará* (maned wolf) and harpy eagle. The park covers three main topographical levels. You enter on the lower level, lying at an altitude of 2,625 to 3,937 feet, where you can still drive and walk easily among the vegetation, the mountain streams and the waterfalls. The plantlife consists of huge trees (*paneiras*, *cedros*, *jequitibás* and jacarandas), giant ferns (*samambaias*) and luxuriant, low-growing vegetation, including begonias, bromeliads and orchids.

Pedra do Último Adeus. Several of the pathways through the park lead to some spectacular natural sites. Among

them is the Pedra do Último Adeus (Rock of the Final Farewell), which is about a mile from the park entrance, on the left of the road. The rock offers a panoramic view of the Campo Belo river, which eventually forms the Lago Azul (Blue Lake). Despite its evocative name, the lake's waters are in fact tinged with shades of green by the reflection of the vegetation that surrounds it.

MUSEU DA FLORA E DA FAUNA. The museum contains exhibits of the park's most representative species of plants and animals. On display are 2,300 species of plants and stuffed animals, including sloths, maned wolves and monkeys. The museum also has collections of spiders and insects, including a wide variety of butterflies, all mounted and labelled, as well as preserved reptiles and stuffed birds, such as toucans, hummingbirds, burrowing owls, harpy eagles and other birds of prey.

CAMINHO DAS CACHOEIRAS. This road, the 'Road of the Waterfalls', ascends past a succession of spectacular waterfalls draped in lush vegetation. They include Poronga (33 feet high), with a deep natural pool; Pitu; Maromba (16 feet high), with a small lake; Itaporani (three falls 33 to 39 feet high), where the air is filled with many species of beautifully colored butterflies; and Véu da Noiva (Bride's Veil), over 98 feet high.

TRILHA DOS TRÊS PICOS. The 'Trail of the Three Peaks' lies on the park's second level, which is at an altitude of 3,937 to 6,233 feet. Here the Atlantic forest becomes more diverse, with a predominance of araucarias (Paraná pines) ● *19* and mosses. The steep but not particularly difficult pathway here enables you to walk the three miles to the Bonito river waterfall and, a little further on, to a rock formation whose three peaks rise to a height of 5,250 feet.

PICO DAS PRATELEIRAS AND PICO DAS AGULHAS NEGRAS. The park's third level is characterized by dramatic volcanic rock formations (*above*), whose color ranges from copper to an intense black. The rocks rise to heights of over 8,200 feet. The best way to enter the park at the third level is via highway BR354, which passes the town of Engenheiro Passos. The highest peaks in the range are the Pico das Prateleiras (Peak of the Shelves), at 8,333 feet, and the Pico das Agulhas Negras (Peak of the Black Needles), at 9,144 feet. You can climb both peaks but you need to be fit and in good physical condition and it is essential to go with an experienced guide. There are mountain refuges along the way, at around 8,000 feet, where you can stay overnight.

PARQUE NACIONAL DO ITATIAIA ★
The best time to visit the park is in winter (June through August). At that time of year, however, temperatures can be quite low, sometimes falling to 23°F at 7,220 feet. If you want to see the waterfalls and swim in the natural pools, the best time to go is in summer (October through February). The hotels are located on the park's lower level.

SPRINGS
The park has some three hundred crystal-clear springs that rise in the mountains and form dozens of waterfalls, mountain streams and rivers, including the Paraíba river.

ORCHIDS
Orchid enthusiasts can visit the orchid room at the Simon hotel, at an altitude of 3,773 feet. The permanent exhibition, as well as regular events, attract orchid-lovers from all over Brazil.

ALONG THE RIO PARAÍBA: PENEDO AND VISCONDE DE MAUÁ

EUROPEAN HERITAGE
The reafforestation and cultivation of fruit trees in the Penedo region was carried out by Finnish immigrants. They also introduced the sauna to Brazil, substituting the northern European birch for tropical eucalyptus as heating fuel. In Penedo and Visconde de Mauá European influences, especially German, Swiss and Scandinavian, can be seen in handicrafts and tapestry, as well as in architecture (*above right*) and in gastronomy, including various types of bread, jams and preserves, and a taste for trout.

WATERFALLS IN VISCONDE DE MAUÁ
One of the region's main tourist attractions are its *cachoeiras*, or waterfalls (*top left*). While the Cachoeira da Santa Clara (130 feet deep) is the most beautiful, the Véu da Noiva (over 98 feet deep) has a natural pool surrounded by dense tropical vegetation. Maromba has an *escorrega*, a kind of natural water chute.

PENEDO, A FINNISH TROPICAL PARADISE

About four miles from the Parque Nacional do Itatiaia, highway BR116 (the Rodovia Presidente Dutra) crosses the road leading to Penedo. This small town is 105 miles from Rio and lies at the foot of the Serra da Mantiqueira at an altitude of 1,968 feet. It was founded in 1929 by a group of Finnish immigrants who were entranced by the beautiful surroundings and settled on the lands of the former Fazenda Penedo, a coffee plantation.

AVENIDA DAS PEDRAS. This avenue is Penedo's focal point. The Casa de Pedras (the first Finnish building), the house of Father Christmas, Praça Finlândia and the Museu Finlandês da Dona Eva, which has collections of photographs, documents and early 20th-century furniture. On Saturday nights the nearby Clube Finlandês holds Finnish dances accompanied by traditional folk groups.

FOREST AND WATERFALLS. A little higher up the mountains, but still easily accessible, are three waterfalls. From Praça Finlândia follow Avenida das Três Cachoeiras for 1½ miles. The Três Cachoeiras (Three Waterfalls) are surrounded by bamboo, palms and fruit trees that are the habitat of many species of birds and butterflies. From here several paths lead into the heart of the dense forest.

VISCONDE DE MAUÁ

Outside Penedo a partially metalled road on the left leads to the peaceful village of Mauá, situated at an altitude of 3,937 feet. After climbing for 15 miles you will be rewarded by breathtaking scenery. This area offers several possibilities for ecotourism and leisure activities in a spectacular setting where the hillsides are covered with araucarias ● *19* and where there are waterfalls and natural pools. You can swim and go canoeing on the Preto river, or follow footpaths bordered with flowers. The village and the surrounding land were once owned by Irineu Evangelista de Souza, Barão then Visconde de Mauá ● *35*. The region known as Visconde de Mauá includes the villages of Mauá, Maromba and Maringá which are all departure points for visiting its many waterfalls.

Minas Gerais

A brilliant culture Besides spectacular baroque architecture, the golden age of Minas Gerais also inspired poets, writers and musicians. Musical life in the province, in which brotherhoods played a prominent part, flourished particularly toward the end of the 18th century. Composers in Minais Gerais, including José Joaquim Emerico Lobo de Mesquita (1746–1805), Inácio Parreira Neves, Francisco Gomes da Rocha and Manual Dias de Oliveira, wrote mainly religious music. Their compositions are being studied, played and recorded today more than ever than in the past.

Minas Gerais, the 'province of mines', seems to have been predestined as a center of baroque culture. The jagged peaks of high mountains and a landscape bathed in golden light make it the perfect setting for a baroque world, rich in gilded rocaille. After the Portuguese set foot in Brazil at the beginning of the 16th century, another two hundred years were to elapse before the country's fabulous wealth of gold and diamonds, as well as abundant other minerals and precious stones, were located. Knowing nothing of gold and gems, Brazil's native inhabitants were unable to satisfy the Europeans' thirst for information as to the whereabouts of these riches. The extensive mountain chains standing like a barrier between the coast and the interior also prevented them from exploring the region's dense forests. In the late 17th century, however, inroads made by the famous *bandeirantes* (adventurers) ● *28*, opened up the gold-rich heart of Brazil. This led to a veritable invasion. Not only did the inhabitants of entire towns leave Portugal for Brazil but gold hunters from São Paulo, Bahia and Rio de Janeiro also migrated to the region, and thousands of Africans were brought over to work in the mines ● *31*. New towns sprang up throughout the region, and this urban culture, fuelled by the fortune buried in the alluvium, led to the flowering of baroque culture, characterized by flamboyant churches, sublime music and passionate poetry. In Minas Gerais, the wealth generated by the mines fired religious faith, and numerous churches were built to give thanks to God and in celebration of this easily won fortune. The European architects and painters who crossed the Atlantic to build and decorate these churches trained some outstanding pupils, including the architect and sculptor Antônio Francisco Lisboa, known as Aleijadinho ▲ *181*, and the painter Manuel da Costa Ataíde ▲ *192*.

The *Inconfidência Mineira*, a conspiracy of 1789 inspired partly by Enlightenment thinking and mounted with the aim of securing independence from Portugal ● *24*, symbolized the apogee of a culture that had developed in the tropics. This cultural turmoil resulted in the creation of a remarkable legacy: the towns of Ouro Preto ▲ *184* and Diamantina ▲ *196*, and the church at Congonhas ▲ *192,* all three of which are Unesco World Heritage Sites. The highly developed culture and learning resulting from the wealth generated by mining explains why Minas Gerais came to play a key role in the life of the country. In terms both of its population and of its economic activity, Minas Gerais is the second-largest state in the federal republic, after São Paulo. It also has excellent conditions for economic growth and offers an impressive range of tourist attractions. Besides its fine historic gold- and diamond-mining towns, Minas Gerais also has some superb landscapes and sites of natural beauty. Its wide rivers, national parks and mountains, its prehistoric painted caves and the picturesque traditions of the rural way of life that survives there complete the variety of attractions that make Minas Gerais a uniquely fascinating and distinctive world.

ALEIJADINHO, GENIUS OF THE MOUNTAINS
Antônio Francisco Lisboa (1738–1814), better known as Aleijadinho, was probably Brazil's greatest artist. The son of Portuguese architect Manual Francisco Lisboa and of an African slave, he was nicknamed Aleijadinho (little cripple) as the result of a disease that deformed his limbs in the latter part of his life. Aleijadinho gave Minas Gerais many great works of art ▲ *186*, *192* and has been referred to as the Michelangelo of the tropics.

The summit of Pico do Itacolomi ▲ *190* (*above*) seen from Ouro Preto (*left*).

PRECIOUS STONES
Minas Gerais is rich in precious stones, including aquamarines, citrines, diamonds, emeralds, rubellites, blue and imperial topazes, and tourmalines. The town of Diamantina ▲ *196* derives its name from the diamonds that gold diggers used as backgammon counters before they realized the true value of these precious gems.

OURO PRETO, A BAROQUE GEM

BLACK GOLD
The gold found in the vicinity of the town was called *ouro preto* (black gold) because it was covered with a black gangue, or mineral matter. It also stayed exceptionally shiny after it was melted. This type of gold gave its name to Ouro Preto, the capital of Minas Gerais from 1721 to 1897.

EXPLORING OURO PRETO ★
Allow two days to explore this colonial gem and get a taste of all that it offers both by day and by night. Sturdy shoes are essential for walking the steep cobbled *ladeiras*, which are slippery after rain. Staying an extra day means that you can also explore other attractions, such as the Minas de Passagem, Mariana and Congonhas, which can be reached by buses leaving from the Rodoviára at Rua Padre Rolim 661.

Ouro Preto, a town with several baroque churches, perches on hilltops at an altitude of 3,609 feet. The former capital of Minas Gerais, it was founded in 1698 and named Vila Rica de Ouro Preto (Rich Town of Black Gold) in 1711. It is remarkably well preserved and has a strikingly authentic atmosphere. Declared a national monument in 1933, it was listed as a World Heritage Site by Unesco in 1980, becoming the first location in Brazil to be accorded this status. Palaces, mansions, churches and small chapels line the town's *ladeiras* (steep streets, *above*), which are also graced by many bridges and fountains. With rich and unusual gilt wooden carvings, a wealth of rococo paintings and countless other decorative details, the churches here offer a mesmerizing visual experience. The town's many museums display something of the artistic and cultural riches of Minas Gerais, while the mines and the Casa dos Contos (Counting House) document the history of its mining industry. Precious stones, jewelry, handicrafts and works of art can be purchased here, and the town also offers excellent regional cuisine. The Parque do Itacolomi and picturesque colonial villages such as Lavras Ñovas, São Bartolomeu and Mata dos Palmitos, which are interspersed by waterfalls, are within easy reach.

PRAÇA TIRADENTES, A CENTRAL LANDMARK

On this square, in center of the town, stands a statue erected in honor of the national hero Tiradentes ● *24*.
PALÁCIO DOS GOVERNADORES. North of the square stands Governor's Palace, which resembles a fortified house. It was built from 1740 under the supervision of Aleijadinho's father, Manuel Francisco Lisboa, to plans by Brigadier José Fernandes Pinto Alpoim. When the state capital was transferred to Belo Horizonte, the palace became the home of the Escola de Minas (Mining School), founded in 1876 by

'In Ouro Preto, another town lies hidden behind this town. There is no point exploring the streets, bridges, slopes and sacristies, if you don't surrender entirely to it.'

Carlos Drummond de Andrade

the French engineer Claude Henri Gorceix. Most of its rooms are now filled by the MUSEU DE CIÊNCA E TÉCNICA (Museum of Science and Technology), which contains one of the world's largest collections of minerals, including a display of rocks so extraordinary that they could be mistaken for modern sculpture.

CASA DE CÂMARA E CADEIA. On the south side of the square stands the former city hall, which was also used as a prison. This imposing building houses the MUSEU DA INCONFIDÊNCIA ▲ *186*, which illustrates life in the colony in the 18th century, when gold extraction was at its height.

IGREJA DO CARMO. Next to the museum stands the elegant and imposing Igreja do Carmo. Begun in 1766 and completed in 1772, the church was designed by Manuel Francisco Lisboa, and altered by his son. The MUSEU DO ORATORIO, in a former Carmelite house in front of the church, has a superb collection of over two hundred Brazilian baroque oratories. Near the church stands the TEATRO MUNICIPAL, thought to be the oldest theater and opera house still in use in South America. Opened in 1770, it could seat an audience of over three hundred. The theater is open to the public, and visitors may also watch rehearsals.

PILAR ALTARPIECE BY XAVIER DE BRITO
Francisco Xavier de Brito came to Brazil from Lisbon with his uncle, who was also a sculptor. Active initially in Rio de Janeiro, Xavier de Brito came to Ouro Preto in 1741, where he worked on the altarpiece of the church of Nossa Senhora do Pilar (*detail above*) from 1746 to 1751. The exuberant profusion of plant motifs, carved by local sculptors and often overloaded with fruit and palmettes, is carefully controlled here. Incorporating carved canopies and twisted columns, this huge altarpiece is a genuine architectural creation.

EXPLORING THE 'LADEIRAS' IN THE PILAR DISTRICT

Off Praça Tiradentes, the steep Rua Direita (officially Rua Conde Bobadella) leads to the Pilar district.

CHAFARIZ DOS CONTOS AND CASA DOS CONTOS. The beautiful fountain known as the CHAFARIZ DOS CONTOS stands in the center of Praça Reinaldo Alves de Britolies, a small square at the foot of Rua Direita. It was built in 1760 near the CASA DOS CONTOS (Counting House), where gold was weighed and melted down. This house was also used to imprison the *inconfidentes*, including the poet Cláudio Manuel da Costa, who committed suicide here. It currently houses a library and a museum with former slave quarters and displays of coins and furniture.

RUA SÃO JOSÉ. This busy shopping street, reached by crossing the Ponte dos Contos, is always crowded on weekdays. It is lined with colonial houses, whose windows, colorful doors and balconies open straight onto the street, giving the impression of a medieval theater.

✪ **MATRIZ DE NOSSA SENHORA DO PILAR.** Turning left onto Largo da Alegria, you can take Rua des Escadinhas to the parish church (*matriz*) of Pilar. It was opened with great ceremony in 1733, when the baroque style was at its height, thus celebrating the importance of gold and the construction of the town. Some 900 lb of the precious metal cover the decorative woodwork in the church. The high altar, dating from the 1740s, was made by the Portuguese sculptor Francisco Xavier de Brito, and the paintings depicting scenes from the Gospels are by João Carvalhaes.

MATRIZ DO PILAR ★
This parish church, on Praça Monsenhor Castilho Barbosa, is open noon–5pm. An annex of the church houses the Museu de Arte Sacra (Museum of Religious Art).

▲ Museu da Inconfidência, A Palace Amid Churches

This torch-bearing angel (*below*) is another example of the work of sculptor Aleijadinho.

The legacy of Aleijadinho
The wooden statue of St George (*right*), commissioned by the city hall, was carried on horseback as part of the Corpus Christi processions. While this piece demonstrates Aleijadinho's dazzling virtuosity, his drawings and sketches (*opposite page*) show his talent as an architect.

The Museu da Inconfidência was established in tribute to the famous conspirators who in 1789 sought to wrest independence from Portugal. In their memory, objects relating to the history of the *Inconfidência Minera* ● *24* were collected. As well as secular and religious works of art, exhibits include documents and items associated with the history of Minas Gerais and relating to life in the colony during the 18th century. This fascinating collection is displayed in a large and elegant building fronted by a double stairway leading up to massive doors. Once the municipal hall, the building contained a prison on street level and law courts on the second story. Opened in 1944, this is one of the most interesting museums in Minas Gerais, with displays realistically evoking the great age of gold-mining in Brazil.

The first story
The displays on the first story consist of objects evoking daily life in the colony. These include wooden and stone sculpture, tools and implements, furniture, door locks, firearms and swords, oil lamps and lanterns, as well as various methods of transport including examples of the sedan chairs in which slaves would carry young ladies up and down the steep streets of the town. Also on display are pipes hewn in soapstone ▲ *191* and once used for the town's extensive system of running water.

The 'Inconfidentes'
Two rooms are devoted to the *inconfidentes*, the conspirators of 1789. One contains manuscripts and objects belonging to Tiradentes ● *24*, including a pocket watch (*right*) and a copy of the United States Constitution, legal documents and fragments of the gallows on which he was hung. The other room is a pantheon where the ashes of the *inconfidentes*, brought back from Africa where the rebels died in exile, are kept in stone tombs.

Moucharabieh
These wooden lattice windows ● *75*, an Arabic element incorporated into Portuguese buildings, allowed those within to look out onto the street while also protecting their privacy from the prying eyes of strangers without.

THE SECOND STORY
A magnificent staircase crowned by the Portuguese royal coat of arms leads up to the second story. This part of the museum is dedicated mainly to 18th-century artefacts. Particularly fine examples of furniture are those with trompe-l'oeil decoration. The collection also includes several paintings by Manuel da Costa Ataíde ▲ *192*, as well as a large number of niches and altars, period furniture and beds belonging to the bishops of Mariana ▲ *190*.

PRISON AND PUNISHMENT
The thick bars on the palace's large windows are a reminder that the building was once a prison. Various iron instruments used for torturing and punishing slaves are displayed in a cell looking onto the inner courtyard.

CONSTRUCTION OF THE PALACE
In 1784, when he arrived in Vila Rica de Ouro Preto, the young Portuguese governor Luís da Cunha Menezes decided to build a new town hall and prison. According to custom both were incorporated into one building, which was known as a *casa de câmara e cadeia* ● *72*. The governor himself designed this building, which is in the neoclassical style and which, wishing to create a grand impression, he probably based on the Campidoglio in Rome. To obtain the necessary, and unpaid, workforce for this huge project Luís da Cunha Menezes ordered that anyone who walked through the streets of Ouro Preto without showing due respect was to be imprisoned. Work started in 1784 and the building, constructed in locally quarried quartzite, was completed in 1854.

▲ Minas Gerais Ouro Preto, a Baroque gem

A small spiral staircase at the entrance to this beautiful parish church leads up to the organ loft, an excellent vantage point from which to admire the interior. The church has an excellent small museum, which is laid out in the sacristy, the crypt and the consistorial chamber. The chest of drawers in the sacristy is remarkable for the size of the jacaranda planks of which it is made. The silk vestments decorated with gold embroidery also bear witness to the opulence of this period. Behind the church stands the Centro de Convenções (conference center). The former station further on is a vestige of the railroad opened in 1889 by Dom Pedro II.

Igreja Nossa Senhora do Rosário dos Pretos. Continue along Rua Antônio de Albuquerque, past the Capela do Senhor do Bonfim (1776) and a fountain, the Chafariz da Glória (1752), to the Church of the Rosary ● *73*. Built by slaves in the first half of the 18th century and belonging to their brotherhood, this monumental church is notable for its oval plan. The window balustrades are made of soapstone ▲ *191* and the plain interior is offset by the fine paintings decorating the altars.

Antonio Dias, the Paulistas' district

From Praça Tiradentes you can reach the Antônio Dias district by walking along Rua Ouvidor (officially Rua Cláudio Manuel). The tourist office at Rua Ouvidor 61 was once the house of Tomás Antônio Gonzaga, one of the *inconfidentes*. To the right is Largo do Coimbra, a square where a crafts market is held and where stands the impressive church of São Francisco de Assis (*top*).

✪ **Igreja de São Francisco de Assis.** This church was designed in 1766 by Aleijadinho. The medallion on the west front, the two pulpits at the crossing and the soapstone basin

Two rival districts
While the Antônio Dias district was the home of the founding pioneers who came from the São Paulo region, the Pilar district housed a concentration of Portuguese immigrants. Conflict between these two districts inevitably broke out. To avoid tension it was mutually agreed that in alternate years each of the two parishes should take a turn to organize the Holy Week celebrations (*above*). This tradition, which originated in the early 18th century, has persisted to the present day.

An 18th-century painted wood statue of Santa Efigênia (*right*), in the church of Nossa Senhora do Rosário in Ouro Preto.

in the sacristy contrast strongly with the superbly carved cedarwood high altar, showing the Virgin Mary being crowned by the Holy Trinity. The magnificent painting decorating the wooden ceiling over the nave is by Manuel da Costa Ataíde ● *192*. It depicts the Virgin as a beautiful black woman surrounded by black saints and angels.

AROUND PRAÇA ANTONIO DIAS. After walking round Largo de Coimbra by turning right past the Casa de Cláudio Manuel da Costa, follow Rua Bernardo Vasconcelos to Praça Antônio Dias, a square on which stands Ouro Preto's second parish church, the MATRIZ DE NOSSA SENHORA DA CONCEIÇÃO. This church, designed by Manuel Francisco Lisboa and built between 1727 and 1746, nestles at the bottom of the valley in the Antônio Dias district. The side altars sparkle with decorations of gilded wood. The MUSEU ALEIJADINHO, which occupies the rooms of the sacristy, contains several masterpieces by this great sculptor and architect, particularly notable being four cedarwood lions on which coffins were laid at funerals, and the small painted soapstone sculpture of São Francisco de Paula. From the square, Rua Dom Silvério leads to the mine of Encardideira or the MINA DO CHICO REI. Abandoned in 1888, this once-prolific mine had over 4,265 feet of tunnels, as well as secret passages. Back in the square, you can glimpse the Igreja da Nossa Senhora das Mercês and Igreja Nossa Senhora das Dores in the distance.

IGREJA DE SANTA EFIGÊNIA. Follow Rua da Conceição across a bridge, the Ponte Antônio Dias, that leads to the Largo Marília de Dirceu, a square named for the muse of the poet Tomás Antônio Gonzaga, then walk up the *ladeira* Santa Efigênia to the church of the same name. The climb from the square is rewarded by a spectacular overview of the town. The church, designed by an anonymous architect, was built by freed slaves between 1733 and 1745, and its construction is said to be connected to the story of Chico Rei. It contains some impressive baroque wooden carvings and an altar by Francisco Xavier de Brito.

RUA PADRE FARIA. This street, which leads to the Igreja do Padre Faria, contains a fountain built by Aleijadinho in 1761. It is also the location of the MINA E FONTE DO BEM QUERER, a mine worked in the 18th century and which still has a running spring. The IGREJA DO PADRE FARIA, a little further on, is the oldest place of worship in the town. It was built between 1701 and 1704 and with its massive three-armed papal cross it is a typical example of the architectural style of Minas Gerais. Although it is plain and unadorned outside, the church has a striking interior, with gilt wooden carvings and lavish paintings. You can return to the town center by catching a minibus near the church.

CHICO REI, THE GOLD KING

Chico Rei was an African tribal king. After he and his family were bought at the slave market in Rio de Janeiro, he managed to buy his family's freedom in Ouro Preto first by smuggling gold dust from the mine under his fingernails and in his hair, and then by working his own gold mine, which he did from 1702 to 1730. The freed slaves staged huge festivals that gave rise to the folk tradition of the *congados*, a local manifestation of Afro-Christian religious syncretism. Every inch a king, Chico Rei walked at the head of these processions, wearing a cape and crown and carrying a scepter.

IGREJA DE SÃO FRANCISCO DE ASSIS ✪

This church, regarded as Aleijadinho's finest work, is one of the most important sights in Ouro Preto. It is open 8.20–11.45am and 1.30–4.45pm.

MINA DE OURO DE PASSAGEM ★
This fascinating gold mine, located between Ouro Preto and Mariana, was in use from 1719 right up until 1985. It descends to a depth of 1,312 feet and has four square miles of underground galleries *(above)*, where many slaves tragically lost their lives. There is also a natural lake. The guided tour of the mine, during which visitors descend to a depth of 394 feet in a cable car, is spectacular. Historic methods of mining, washing and sieving gold are also explained. Beware: do not visit if you suffer from claustrophobia

AROUND OURO PRETO

PARQUE ESTADUAL DO ITACOLOMI. You can enjoy some fine walks in this scenic park situated to the south of the town. Its paths take in views of waterfalls, interesting rock formations and the Pico do Itacolomi. This peak, eleven miles from Praça Tiradentes, soars to a height of 5,748 feet and climbing it takes three hours. It served as a landmark for the first *bandeirantes*, who discovered gold in its vicinity, and later for all those who were drawn here in the gold rush ● *30*.

ESTRADA REAL. Leading to Ouro Branco, nineteen miles away, the Estrada Real, or Royal Road, traverses beautiful mountain landscapes and passes small villages that seem to be frozen in time and where craftsmen can be seen carving soapstone. Among the most attractive are the villages of Lavras Novas and Chapada, where there is a chapel dedicated to St Anne.

CACHOEIRA DAS ANDORINHAS. Four miles north of Ouro Preto are the impressive cascades known as the Swallows' Waterfall, which feed into the Rio das Velhas. The site also offers breathtaking views of the mountains in the Parque Natural do Caraça ▲ *183*, where there is an 18th-century hermitage and a neo-Gothic chapel.

MARIANA

THE CARAÇA HERMITAGE
This hermitage, situated at an altitude of 4,265 feet in the Parque Natural do Caraça, was built in the late 18th century by the Portuguese friar Lourenço. The large neo-Gothic chapel there was built in 1883.

The town of Mariana, just over two miles from the Passagem gold mine, was founded in 1696 after a gold-rich river, the Ribeirão do Carmo, was discovered. It was named Mariana for Maria Ana of Austria, queen of Portugal, when it became a royal town on the appointment of the first bishop in 1745. The best way of exploring Mariana, which is laid out around three squares and which has interesting churches and colonial houses, is on foot.

PRAÇA MINAS GERAIS. On this square, which is reached via Rua Macedo and Rua Dom Silvério, stands the impressive CASA DE CÂMARA E CADEIA, built in 1784 and currently home to the town council. Opposite this building is the Pelourinho, a pillory where slaves and criminals were tortured. There are also two churches on the square. One is the IGREJA DE SÃO FRANCISCO DE ASSIS, built between 1763 and 1794 and fronted by a door with a beautiful carved pediment. The sacristy ceiling was decorated by Ataíde, who is buried in the church. The other church, the IGREJA NOSSA SENHORA DO CARMO, built in 1784, was ravaged by fire in 1999, just as renovation work on it had almost been completed.

IGREJA DE SÃO PEDRO DOS CLÉRIGOS. Following Rua Dom Silvério you pass the chamfered façade of the church of Nossa Rainha dos Anjos, built in 1784, then reach the church of São Pedro dos Clérigos. Begun in 1752 but never completed, this oval church has an ocher granite façade and an altar by the school of Aleijadinho. Walking back down this street and turning right into Rua das Mercês you will see the blue and white façade of the Igreja das Mercês, built in 1787. Walk a little further on then look back to the hilltop church of São Pedro dos Clérigos, which perches above slopes covered with dense vegetation, then turn left into Rua Dom Viçoso and head toward PRAÇA GOMES FREIRE. This pleasant tree-lined square is perfect for taking a break before visiting the MUSEU ARQUIDIOCESANO (archdiocesan museum), in Rua Frei Durão, leading off the square.

CATEDRAL BASÍLICA DA SÉ. Built between 1711 and 1760, this cathedral, on Praça Cláudio Manuel, is one of the most richly decorated churches in Brazil. It contains twelve elaborate altars, some of which are by Francisco Xavier de Brito, and a rare Arp-Schnitger organ with 964 pipes, made in Hamburg in 1701 and presented to the bishop of Mariana by José I in 1753. Recitals given on this instrument are the highlight of the town's major music festivals. An organ recital is also given every Sunday at 12.30pm.

RUA DIREITA. This picturesque street is lined with the studios of painters and wood carvers and with many colonial houses. Particularly noteworthy are the Casa do Barão de Pontal, at no. 54, and the Casa de Alphonsus de Guimarães, at no. 35, which contains a small museum devoted to this symbolist poet.

IGREJA NOSSA SENHORA DO ROSÁRIO DOS PRETOS. The hilltop church of Our Lady of the Rosary can be seen in the distance from Rua Macedo. It can be reached by crossing a small bridge and the railroad and then following Rua do Rosário. This church, built between 1752 and 1775, contains some fine, vivid paintings by Ataíde.

CACHOEIRA DO BRUMADO. Several small villages around Mariana are known for their imposing churches and their high-quality handicrafts. Among them is Cachoeira do Brumado, which lies seven miles from Mariana. The work of master sculptors based there attracts many visitors to the village.

SOAPSTONE OR 'PEDRA SABÃO'
Soapstone, or steatite, is a soft stone that is easy to carve. It held a strong appeal to sculptors who settled in Minas Gerais. Soapstone reliefs and sculptures can be seen everywhere, from façades and fountains to altarpieces and pulpits. Soapstone carvings are still produced by a large number of craftsmen working today.

MUSEU ARQUIDIOCESANO
The archdiocesan museum contains paintings by Ataíde and sculptures by Aleijadinho as well as fine silverware and religious objects. The wood carvings on the magnificent bishop's throne in the main reception room are by Aleijadinho.

The ceiling of the Catedral Basílica da Sé in Mariana.

St Peter (*below*)

At an altitude of 2,854 feet and overlooking a lush valley ringed by mountains lies Congonhas do Campo. This town, 55 miles from Belo Horizonte and 72 miles from Ouro Preto, is a religious and artistic shrine. In 1757 the Portuguese hermit Feliciano Mendes erected a cross here and the following year began to build a basilica that became a popular place of pilgrimage. The leading artists commissioned to decorate it included the woodcarver Francisco Vieira Servas and the painter João Nepomuceno Correia e Castro, and in the late 18th century Aleijadinho and Ataíde. The sculptures that Aleijadinho created here are a rare achievement in the history of art, and it is largely because of them that the religious complex was declared a World Heritage Site by Unesco.

AS CAPELAS DOS PASSOS
Six chapels front the Basílica do Bom Jesus de Matosinhos (*right*), which stands in the grand setting of an amphitheater of mountains. The chapels are filled with a total of sixty six life-sized painted cedarwood statues illustrating seven scenes from the Passion of Christ. The most impressive of these statues, carved by Aleijadinho ▲ *181*, is the figure of Christ (*right*). The poignancy of these outstanding works of art conveys the transcendent mood of the scenes from the Passion. The chapels line the slope leading up to the basilica and the narrative depicted by the statues begins in the lowest chapel. The best way to appreciate these works of art is to take the chapels in sequence, progressing in a zigzag up the slope, just as the pilgrims who came here would do as they retraced the Road to Calvary.

MANUEL DA COSTA ATAÍDE (1762–1830)
This baroque artist, who is without doubt Brazil's greatest painter, collaborated with Aleijadinho at Congonhas, with stunning results. Half the cedarwood statues that Aleijadinho carved here were painted by Ataíde, as were the panels of many altarpieces and the false wooden *azulejos* that were created as a substitute for this desirable tilework. Ataíde's grandiloquent style was, however, better suited to larger spaces, such as ceilings.

THE SIX CHAPELS
The first chapel, depicting the Last Supper, shows Christ surrounded by the Apostles. The next depicts Christ on the Mount of Olives as the angel holds the bitter chalice while Peter sleeps. The third shows Christ's arrest: the apostle Simon Peter has just cut off Malchus' ear and Christ is about to heal him. The fourth chapel shows the Flagellation and Christ crowned with thorns. The fifth depicts the journey to Calvary, with Christ carrying his cross amid a crowd of distraught onlookers. The subject of the sixth chapel is the Crucifixion.

THE ROMARIA
This huge circular building, located behind the basilica, houses the Hall of Miracles and a collection of votive offerings. From September 7 to 14, when the festival of Bom Jesus is held, the Romaria is filled with 20,000 pilgrims.

'A universal genius, this inspired mulatto carved heroic statues, like these soapstone prophets, whose stirring gestures are silhouetted against the sky in Congonhas do Campo.'

Germain Bazin

The origins of the Congonhas statues
While the layout of the religious complex at Congonhas was inspired by that of Bom Jesus in Braga, northern Portugal, the Congonhas statues reflect various different influences. Dressed in oriental clothing these biblical figures are reminiscent of those seen in 18th-century Flemish paintings. Also discernible in their style are vestiges of the Romanesque and Gothic styles evident of Portuguese art, as well as Renaissance and baroque traits.

The prophets
The four major prophets, Isaiah, Jeremiah, Ezekiel and Daniel, and eight minor prophets, including Obadiah, (*above*) and Joel (*right*), are grouped in dramatic fashion in front of the façade. Only one statue, that of Daniel, with his attribute, the lion, is carved from a single block. Created without the help of an assistant, this figure best exemplifies Aleijadinho's enduring skill. He was then over 70 years old.

The prophets' terrace
Between 1800 and 1805 Aleijadinho carved a group of twelve soapstone statues of Old Testament prophets. Effectively arranged on the small square in front of the basilica of Bom Jesus do Matosinhos, the group creates what historian Germain Bazin described as a 'soapstone ballet'. The overall effect is indeed very powerful. Inside the basilica, which is decorated in the rococo style, some unusual reliquaries rest on the altars.

PEWTER IN SÃO JOÃO DEL REI
Pewterwork is a specialty of the region. You can buy a wide range of pewter items in stores in the center of São João del Rei (on Avenidas 31 de Março and on Leite Costa). Visiting small towns in the area, such as Prados, Coronel Xavier Chaves and Resende Costa also provides the opportunity to appreciate other local crafts, which are extremely diverse and of a high quality.

MUSEU REGIONAL
The 18th-century colonial residence at Rua Marechal Deodoro 12 houses the museum of local history. It has an interesting collection of religious artefacts as well as furniture, farming implements and tools dating from the 18th and 19th centuries. Certain rare and valuable pieces provide an insight into everyday life and religious faith during the great age of gold mining ● *30*, when artistic activity in Minas Gerais was at its height.

Lying at the southern extremity of the Serra do Espinhaço, a large mountain chain running the length of Minas Gerais, is the Serra de São José. As it stretches between the towns of São João del Rei and Tiradentes this huge natural barrier stands like a gigantic rampart cutting through the magical landscape of lush valleys.

SÃO JOÃO DEL REI

The busy, flourishing town of São João del Rei lies at an altitude of 2,986 feet at the foot of the Serra do Lenheiro, 124 miles from Belo Horizonte. It still retains vestiges of the past, with some superb churches and large colonial dwellings. The town is bisected by the Lenheiro, a river spanned by two 18th-century stone bridges that enhance the townscape.

CATEDRAL DO PILAR. Built in 1721 and originally a church, this cathedral, on Rua Getúlo Vargas, is a jewel of baroque architecture. The high altar, in Dom João V style, is particularly illustrative of baroque artistic ideals. The presence of two churches at either end of the street, the Igreja de Nossa Senhora do Rosário and the Igreja de Nossa Senhora do Carmo, which has a façade by Aleijadinho, demonstrate the importance placed on religion.

MUSEU DE ARTE SACRA. Walking toward the Igreja de Nossa Senhora do Rosário, built in 1719, you will pass the museum of religious art (on Largo do Rosário). The impressive collection of 18th-century statues and gold and silver artefacts that it contains highlight the theatrical nature of religious life during the baroque era.

IGREJA DE SÃO FRANCISCO DE ASSIS. Having passed the Igreja de Nossa Senhora do Rosário and crossed the Ponte do Rosario, you will come to this charming rococo church (*below*), on Rua Padre José Maria Xavier. It was designed by Aleijadinho and built by Francisco de Lima Cerqueira in 1774, and its curvilinear design and carvings are similar to those of the Igreja São Francisco de Assis in Ouro Preto ▲ *189*. On Sundays the Ribeiro Bastos orchestra, founded in the 18th century, plays at the 10am mass.

MEMORIAL TANCREDO NEVES. Walk back along Rua Padre José Maria Xavier, past the attractive colonial houses at nos. 174 and 118, to this arts center. Dedicated to the memory of President Tancredo Neves ● *27*, it gives an overview of political life in Brazil between 1940 and 1985.

TEATRO MUNICIPAL AND MUSEU FERROVIÁRIO. The municipal theater and the railroad museum are reached by walking back up Avenida Eduardo Magalhães and Avenida Hermílio Alves. Although there has been a theater in the town since the heyday of gold mining, this neoclassical building dates from 1893. Nearby is the museum, housed in the former station. It documents the early days of the railroad, built by local landowners and opened in 1881 by Dom Pedro II ● *25*. After visiting the museum take a train ride on the Maria Fumaça train ★ to Tiradentes.

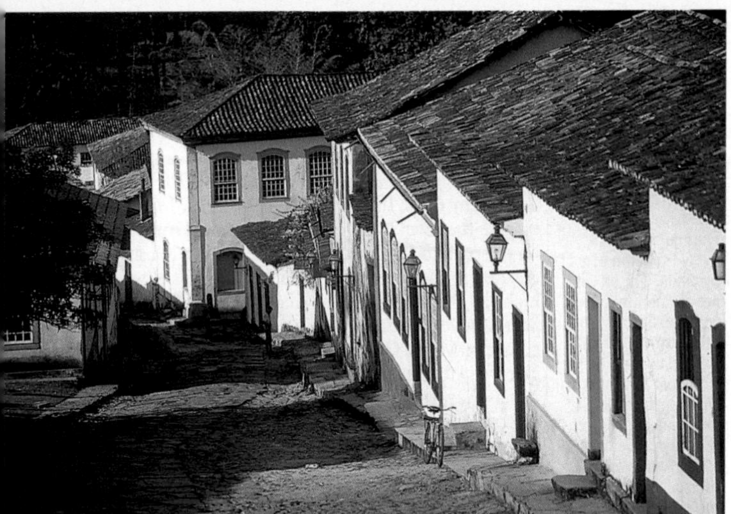

Tiradentes

Formerly a district of São João del Rei, the town was named Tiradentes (for the leader of the *Inconfidência Minera* ● *24)*, when the Republic was proclaimed. The rebel Tiradentes was born in the Fazenda do Pombal nearby, of which ruins survive. This well-preserved and historic town is attractive to visitors, who will enjoy strolling along its cobbled streets, which have a lively atmosphere and which are lined with chapels, workshops, galleries, restaurants and craft stores.

Matriz de Santo Antônio. The parish church of St Anthony (on Rua da Câmara) is one of the most dazzling baroque religious buildings in Brazil and the largest in the region of Rio das Mortes (meaning 'river of the dead' and named for victims of the wars waged between gold diggers in the early 18th century). The high altar glitters with magnificent gilt wooden carvings: according to a local saying, the angels sing and dance for joy in this church. It has a rococo organ made in Porto in 1790. On the small square in front of the church, a wooden cross and a soapstone sundial ▲ *191* stand against the outline of the great mountain that forms a backdrop to the town.

Chafariz de São José. Leaving the church square, follow Rua da Câmara, passing the Casa da Câmara, a verandaed house that has accommodated the town council since 1718, and the Solar do Ramalho, at no. 124, a residence built in 1702 and now home to an art gallery and an orchestra founded 100 years ago. Beyond is the Chafariz de São José. The fountain, dating from 1749, was built to give the town an attractive focal point.

Rua Direita. Walk back along Rua da Câmara and turn left into this street, where the Igreja do Rosário dos Pretos is located. The church was built by slaves in 1727 and its altar niches are filled with statues of African saints. Opposite the church is a former prison dating from 1730 and now housing an art gallery.

Museu do Padre Toledo. Further along Rua da Câmara, turn right toward Largo do Sol. Lining this square are the Capela de São João Evangelista and the Museu do Padre Toledo. The museum is laid out in a mansion that belonged to Padre Carlos Toledo, the parish priest who was another hero of the *Inconfidência Minera*. The mansion's wooden ceilings are painted with depictions of the five senses, and the museum displays colonial furniture and artefacts.

THE MARIA FUMAÇA TRAIN ★
This train has run without interruption and with the same Baldwin locomotives since 1881. Traveling at 15 mph, it makes the 9-mile journey from São João del Rei to Tiradentes in about half an hour. From the Estação Ferroviária, Avenida Hermílio Alves 366, departures are at 10am and 2.15pm, with return journeys at 1.20pm and 5pm Friday through Sunday.

Horse-riding
For visitors who prefer sightseeing on horseback, treks are organized in São João del Rei and Tiradentes. The itineraries take in various villages in the locality, including Arcângelo, Vitoriano Veloso and the lovely little town of Prados.

DIAMANTINA AND SERRO, ON THE DIAMOND TRAIL

FESTIVALS IN DIAMANTINA
The town of Diamantina has a lively tradition of festivals. The streets are frequently filled with music and are often thronged with folk festivals. The *vesperata* is a local custom: at dusk musicians come out onto balconies or sit at the windows of houses playing their instruments in the cool night air; others ply the sidewalks all through the night, singing serenades. During religious festivals, such as that of the Divino Espírito Santo at Whitsun, or of the Festival of the Rosary in October, large ceremonial processions take place. At the Festival of the Rosary, the streets of Diamantina, as well as its church, built in 1728, are filled with folk characters such as *marujos*, *catopês* and *caboclinhos*. These festivals keep alive Afro-Brazilian cultural traditions.

From Belo Horizonte take highway BR040 toward Brasília, turning off to the Gruta Rei do Mato ▲ *182, 198,* just outside the town of Sete Lagoas, and the Gruta do Maquiné, on the road to Cordisburgo. In Sete Lagoas is a small museum devoted to the great writer João Guimarães Rosa. Then take highway BR 259 to the colonial towns of Diamantina and Serro. Beyond Curvelo, a town marking the geographical center of Minas Gerais, the lush hilly landscape of the south gives way to the *sertão* ▲ *254*, the stark landscape of northern Minas Gerais, consisting mostly of rocky outcrops and of plateaus densely covered in scrub known as *cerrado* ● *18*. In the region of the diamond mines, the landscape, dominated by the Pico do Itambé, becomes mountainous again.

DIAMANTINA

The city of Diamantina (*below*) lies 180 miles north of Belo Horizonte. The untold riches discovered on the blue-tinged ridge of the Serra do Espinhaço became the subject of many legends. In the early 18th century, gold diggers established several small villages in the region. Quite by accident these prospectors made a startling discovery: the white stones that they found strewn about on the ground and that they used as backgammon counters were not pieces of worthless crystal but diamonds. The town then prospered and grew. The many baroque churches in the region were decorated by artists such as José Soares de Araújo, Silvestre de Almeida Lopes and Caetano Luís de Miranda.

CATEDRAL. The city's central landmark is its imposing neo-colonial cathedral, built in the 1930s. The cathedral square is a good departure point for exploring the city, which is filled with colonial buildings that have a simple charm.

MUSEU DO DIAMANTE. The diamond museum, located opposite the cathedral, occupies the house of Padre Rolim, a conspirator in the *Inconfidência Minera* ● *24* and the lover of one of Chica da Silva's daughters. Exhibits include tools and instruments used for mining diamonds, as well as furniture and artefacts, and documents relating to the period.

A street in Diamantina

Igreja do Carmo. With its gold altars and painted ceilings this church, on Rua do Carmo, is the most opulent in Diamantina. Unusually the bell tower is at the rear of the church. This was at the request of a former slave girl who did not wish to be woken by the bells. The girl was Chica da Silva, whose irresistible beauty helped her become the mistress of João Fernandes de Oliveira, the wealthy diamond contractor. The composer Lobo de Mesquita ▲ *180* used to play the church's late-18th-century organ.
Casa de Chica da Silva. The house of Chica da Silva, the woman who was regarded as the queen of Diamantina and who lived a life of luxury until João Fernandes returned to Portugal, stands at the end of the road, beyond the bishop's residence. It has a veranda with moucharabieh screens, a rear courtyard and rooms filled with period furniture.
Mercado Municipal. Next to the Igreja do Amparo stands the former cattle market to which *tropeiros* ▲ *233* would bring their animals. The market is still redolent of the atmosphere of the large livestock fairs that were held during the diamond era.
Museu Juscelino Kubitschek. Rua São Francisco leads to the modest house where Juscelino Kubitschek, former mayor of Belo Horizonte, governor of Minas Gerais and president of Brazil ● *26*, was born. It is now a museum devoted to the life of this remarkable man, grandson of poor Czech immigrants.

Caminho dos Escravos
The 'Slave Road' is an old paved road level with the former entrance into Diamantina. It leads to the Serra da Jacuba, the Gruta do Salitre (six miles away), the waterfalls and rock paintings ● *198* of Sentinela (six miles away), the market town of Biri-Biri (nine miles away) and the small villages of São Gonçalo do Rio das Pedras and Milho Verde. These villages on the road to Serro offer several possibilities for ecotourism and are not to be missed.

The Serro region

Serro. The colonial town of Serro, formerly called Vila do Príncipe, lies 56 miles south of Diamantina and is surrounded by granite peaks. Serro has a lively popular culture and also produces the famous *queijo serrano*, a local cheese. The town has several baroque churches and a small museum of local history, laid out in the Casa dos Ottoni. The 18th-century parish church, the Matriz da Conceição, is impressive for the height of its adobe walls. Also notable are the Igreja do Carmo, on Praça João Pinheiro, the central square, and the Capela de Santa Rita, which overlooks the town from a hilltop.
Pico do Itambé. North of Serro, the road leading from the village of Santo Antônio do Itambé to Pico do Itambé passes many waterfalls and natural pools, including those at Fumaça, Água Santa, Nenem and Rio Vermelho. To reach the summit, which rises to a height of 6,706 feet, you must follow an unmetalled road for six miles. The final six miles up to the peak are best covered on horseback and with the aid of a guide.
Parque Nacional da Serra do Cipó. South of Serro, following a track heading for the historic town of Conceição do Mato Dentro, then taking highway MG010 will bring you to the entrance to this national park. Covering 83,520 acres, the park consists of *cerrado*, grassland with very varied vegetation, including cactuses and orchids. With several spectacular waterfalls, this is a breathtakingly beautiful landscape. The wildlife here includes otters, woodpeckers, wildcats, capybaras, anteaters, stags and an endangered species of wolf. Although walking and climbing in the park, as well as crossing rivers and bathing, are easier in the dry season, which runs May through November, the waterfalls are more dramatic and many more plants are in bloom in the rainy season, from December through April.

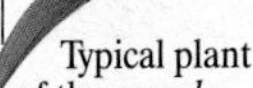
Typical plant of the *cerrado*

Cheeses of Minas Gerais
Minas Gerais is a cheesemaking region. When gold-mining ceased to be profitable, the region's inhabitants turned to agriculture and stockbreeding. Cheesemaking began in the 19th century. The best-known of all the *queijos de Minas* (Minas cheeses) is *queijo do Serro*, a round, white cheese produced in the Serro area. The *serra da Canastra* is another. The famous *pão de queijo* (cheese loaf) also forms part of the local heritage and is found in every house in Minas Gerais.

GRUTA DE CERCA GRANDE. Prehistoric artists used the uneven surface of cave walls to give life to the animals that they painted on them (*below*). Ranging from caimans and jaguars to deer, armadillos and fish, these animals, which prehistoric people either feared or hunted, are depicted in flat areas of red and yellow, and skillfully drawn either in profile or from above.

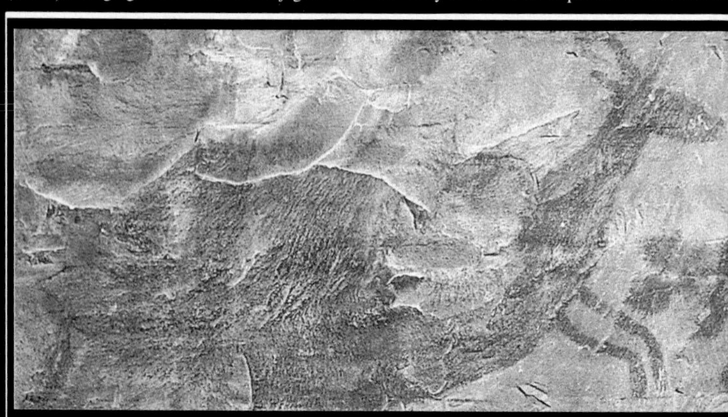

Lagoa Santa Man, who lived 12,000 years ago, became the first famous prehistoric man in the world when he was discovered in 1835. The fossilized bones were found by Danish archeologist P.W. Lund 25 miles from Belo Horizonte in one of the region's many caves and rock shelters. These prehistoric sites, which are not open to visitors, also contained the bones of extinct species, such as giant sloths, and beautiful paintings. In the 18th century, other small caves further to the north were used as dwellings by gold diggers and diamond miners. Slaves sheltering in these caves also left evidence of their enforced presence in the form of graffiti on the cave walls. Containing fantastic mineral formations, other large caves, such as Maquiné and Lapinha, are yet another aspect of Minas Gerais' great history.

GRUTA DO SUMIDOURO
Rocky outcrops have been used by prehistoric people all over the world. Caves provided shelter but because of their warm hues and the unevenness of the rock, cave walls also offered an ideal surface on which they could paint or engrave their mysterious signs. The limestone walls of Sumidouro cave, in the Lagoa Santa area, bear many geometric symbols and depictions of animals, which are arranged as if they were in an imaginary picture frame. The cave also offered the additional advantage of being near water.

PREHISTORIC BALLET
The symbolic manner in which human figures were depicted made possible great freedom of expression. A cave near Lagoa Santa contains about twenty strange human figures. Shrouded in semidarkness, they consist of silhouettes 16 to 20 inches high, arranged in two friezes. The figures seem to be dancing. The prehistoric artist depicted these human silhouettes in a highly schematic way, bringing them to life through their gestures. These paintings have an esthetic power that almost puts them on a par with modern Western art.

West-Central

The road linking the state of Acreto Brasília under construction in 1960, as two Native Americans pass by (*right*).

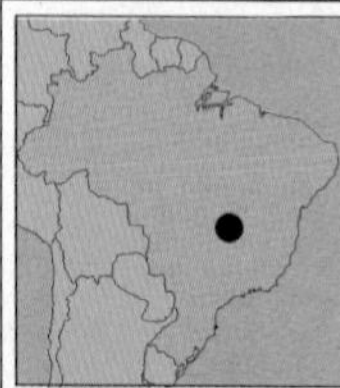

Brasília lies in the Planalto Central ● *17*, Brazil's geographical center. Located at the heart of Goiás state, it is 631 miles from São Paulo, 713 miles from Rio de Janeiro and 1,380 miles from Recife. Brasília and its immediate surroundings form the 2,245-square-mile Distrito Federal (Federal District), which has a special status in the Brazilian constitution.

The city's *trilhas fundamentais,* or insecting lines (*above*)

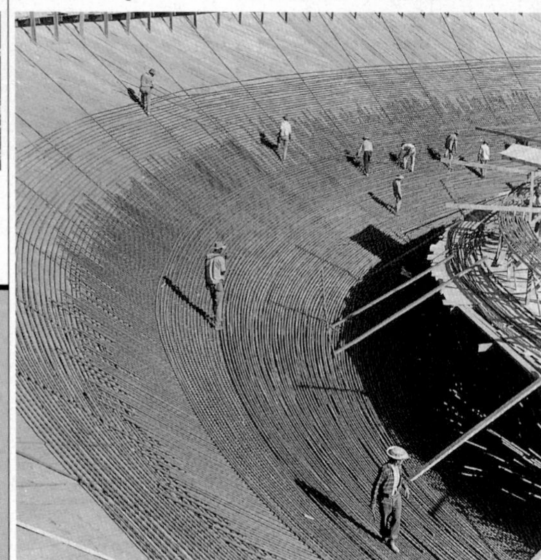

BRASÍLIA ✪
It takes at least a day to explore the main attractions of Brasília, the national capital and a city with a unique layout and architecture. Mostly because distances in this huge metropolis are so great, it is easier to get around by car than on foot.

HISTORY

In 1823, a year after Brazil was granted independence, José Bonifácio, a statesman during the imperial period ● *24*, mooted the idea of a new capital, named Brasília. The aim was to decentralize the country's economic activities, which were concentrated along the coast. In 1892 the government committee set up to explore the Planalto Central chose an area of 5,560 square miles for the future capital. However, the project was postponed indefinitely and left in abeyance for the first half of the 20th century. The initiative was relaunched in 1955 by Juscelino Kubitschek ● *26* during his electoral campaign. Once elected, the new president put before Congress the Bill of Anapolis, which proposed the creation of the New Capital Urbanization Agency (Companhia Urbanizadora da Nova Capital, or NOVACAP). This proposal was unanimously carried by Congress and an international Competition for Ideas was launched. The winner among the twenty six contestants was urban planner Lúcio Costa: his famous airplane-shaped city plan formed the basis of the Plano Piloto (Pilot Plan). His extensive proposal, which comprised twenty three points and various sketches, paid particular attention to the physical features of the chosen site. By the time it was approved, certain projects outside the city, such as the Palácio da Alvorada (the presidential residence) and the airport, had already been undertaken by Oscar Niemeyer ▲ *203*, whom president 'JK' had frequently

Scenes at the official opening of Brasília on April 20, 1960

'To return the land to pedestrians the flow of traffic has been planned with no junctions... The suggested solution is easy to carry out: two axes, two central divider strips, one platform, two wide thoroughfares.' Lúcio Costa

commissioned when he was mayor of Belo Horizonte ▲ *182*. Work on the new city began in 1956 and, as planned, it was officially opened on April 21 1960. At that time, eleven ministerial buildings, the three main buildings on Praça dos Três Poderes, the Palácio da Alvorada, the Brasília hotel (now demolished) and four residential districts (Superquadras Sul 105, 106, 107 and 108) had been built. Nine others were still under construction, as was the bus station, which was opened in the fall of that year. Building continued from 1961 to 1964 during the presidencies of Quadros and Goulart ● *27*, when the university was opened and many districts in the city's south wing were completed. The military coup of 1964 ● *27* slowed the project down and, because of his close links with the banned Communist Party, Oscar Niemeyer was no longer commissioned. Some of his projects, such as the new airport, were never taken beyond draft form. It was not until the 1980s that new buildings designed by Niemeyer were constructed.

To appreciate this unique city to the full, it is necessary to understand the basic principles of Lúcio Costa's plan. The Pilot Plan, or PP, is based on the fundamental idea of two lines intersecting at a right angle, a motif that stamps its identity on the site and that came to delineate Brasília's central districts. To mold the city's layout to the topography of the site, one of the axes was bent to form a curve that then became part of a triangle. While the straight axis was chosen as the location for the city's political, commercial, economic and military facilities, the curved axis, which gave the plan the appearance of an airplane, was to be the area of the residential districts. These were divided into *superquadras*, or blocks about 800 feet square. A large artificial lake, the Lago do Paranoá, formed the eastern boundary of the city.

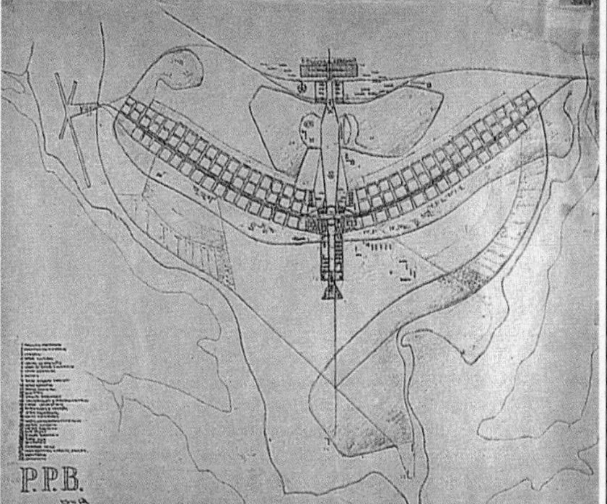

Lúcio Costa on the building of Brasília

'The plan to build Brasília in the empty savanna, 600 miles from the coast, was initially received with generally favorable reactions from

abroad, particularly because people were surprised at its spare, elegant, innovative, even unusual architecture. Then they started to turn their noses up at the city, criticizing it as a missed opportunity because, among other failings, the poor were not well housed here. As if, simply by moving the capital, urban planning could solve an age-old economic and social problem ... there is no point bothering to visit Brasília if you have prejudices and preconceived ideas about civilization. Stay at home.'

Three sketches by Lúcio Costa showing the genesis of the main plan for Brasília, which evolved from the initial shape (*above left*), and Costa's overall plan of the city (*left*).

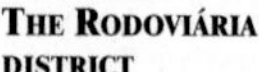

The Rodoviária district
This sector is one of the liveliest in the capital, but the density of its layout is ill-suited to its population, which has grown dramatically. An additional problem in this district concerns the metro: although work on the new metro system began in 1992, its opening has been continually postponed.

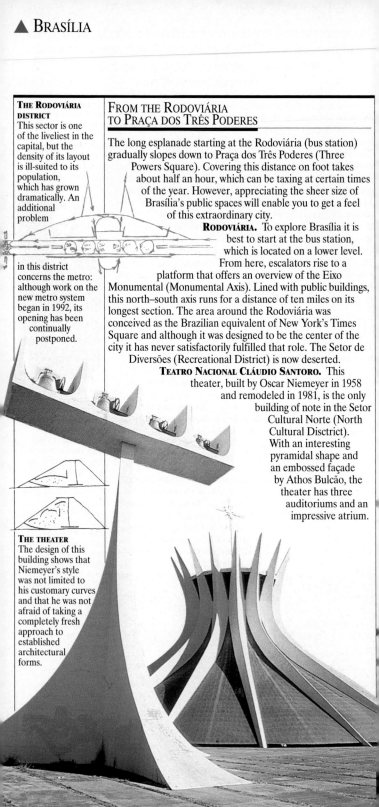

From the Rodoviária to Praça dos Três Poderes

The long esplanade starting at the Rodoviária (bus station) gradually slopes down to Praça dos Três Poderes (Three Powers Square). Covering this distance on foot takes about half an hour, which can be taxing at certain times of the year. However, appreciating the sheer size of Brasília's public spaces will enable you to get a feel of this extraordinary city.

Rodoviária. To explore Brasília it is best to start at the bus station, which is located on a lower level. From here, escalators rise to a platform that offers an overview of the Eixo Monumental (Monumental Axis). Lined with public buildings, this north–south axis runs for a distance of ten miles on its longest section. The area around the Rodoviária was conceived as the Brazilian equivalent of New York's Times Square and although it was designed to be the center of the city it has never satisfactorily fulfilled that role. The Setor de Diversões (Recreational District) is now deserted.

Teatro Nacional Cláudio Santoro. This theater, built by Oscar Niemeyer in 1958 and remodeled in 1981, is the only building of note in the Setor Cultural Norte (North Cultural Disctrict). With an interesting pyramidal shape and an embossed façade by Athos Bulcão, the theater has three auditoriums and an impressive atrium.

The theater
The design of this building shows that Niemeyer's style was not limited to his customary curves and that he was not afraid of taking a completely fresh approach to established architectural forms.

ESPLANADA DOS MINISTERIOS
The architectural ensemble of Brasília's ministry buildings is counterbalanced by the Congress building. The two outstanding buildings here are those of the Ministry of Justice and of the Ministry of Foreign Affairs.

CATEDRAL METROPOLITANA. Walking toward Praça dos Três Poderes, you will see the Catedral Metropolitana silhouetted on the south side of the square. Designed by Oscar Niemeyer, the cathedral has a striking circular nave supported by 16 concrete columns. It was still not completed when it was officially opened and its stained-glass windows were added later. Entry to the cathedral is via an underground passage that acts as a place of quiet reflection. Suspended from the ceiling above the nave are three angels by Alfredo Ceschiatti ▲ *182*, a sculptor whose work frequently appears in buildings designed by Oscar Niemeyer, and who also created the *Four Evangelists* that stand at the entrance.

ESPLANADA DOS MINISTÉRIOS. You will then come to the 'Ministries Esplanade', on which stand 16 identical buildings designed by Niemeyer, some of which have annexes. The layout of these government offices has changed slightly over the years. Brazil's major federal ministries, such as the Ministry of Defense (which occupies four buildings) and the Ministry of Finance, were originally located on the north side. The social ministries, such as the Ministry of Culture, which houses a small exhibition room and a movie theater, were located on the south side. Refreshment stalls that have spontaneously appeared near the ministries on the south side of the esplanade relieve the starkness of this somewhat austere environment.

OSCAR NIEMEYER
Born in Rio de Janeiro in 1907, Oscar Niemeyer came to prominence with several early works, such as the Obra do Berço in Rio and a hotel in Ouro Preto. In 1942 he designed buildings for Pampulha ● *78* and in 1956 became a consultant for NOVACAP, the agency that directed the construction of Brasília. Although many of Niemeyer's buildings predate the military coup of 1964 ● *27*, many of his later Brazilian projects were never completed. He then received major commissions from France, Italy and Algeria.

TWO FOUNDATIONS AND A MUSEUM
Besides the government buildings on Praça dos Três Poderes are three smaller buildings. One, in a circular building near the Palácio do Planalto, is the Fundação Niemeyer, which documents the construction of the buildings on the square. Another is the Espaço Lúcio Costa, which contains a model of the city. The third is the Museu da Cidade (**9**), which was built in 1958 and which since 1988 has had a commemorative function. A sentence by President Kubitschek ● *26* of October 2, 1956 is engraved on the marble: 'From this central plateau, from this lonely place that will soon become the nerve center of important national decisions, I look again to my country's future and I see a new dawn

and feel an unshakeable faith and boundless confidence in my country's destiny.' Within, sixteen engraved sentences tell of Brasília's origins and the decisions that resulted in the transfer of the capital.

PRAÇA DOS TRÊS PODERES

'Three Powers Square' is the emblem of Brasília, and its symbolic importance is marked by the national flag, which flutters from a 300-foot-tall flagpole.

PALÁCIO DOS ARCOS AND PALÁCIO DA JUSTIÇA. Beyond the 16 ministry buildings are two distinctive buildings housing government departments. On the south side is the Palácio dos Arcos, the building of the Ministry of Foreign Affairs (**1**), and better known as the Palácio Itamaraty for the premises once used by Brazilian diplomatic staff in Rio ▲ *127*. Completed in 1962, it is a variation on the peristyle plan, consisting of glass boxes surrounded by an elegant concrete portico. In the lake fronting it stands a work by Bruno Giorgi entitled *Meteoro*. Opposite is the Palácio da Justiça (**2**), housing the Ministry of Justice. Begun in 1962 and completed in 1970, the building is arranged around four waterfalls that seem to cascade from the façade (when, that is, they are in working order).

CONGRESSO NACIONAL (3). At the far end of the esplanade, a gentle slope leads down to the Congresso Nacional, where the Federal Parliament is based. The building's design

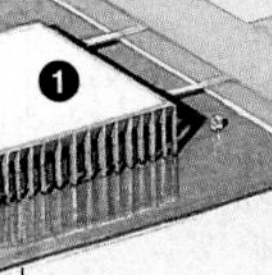

symbolizes Brazil's two-chamber system of government. The small dome is the roof of the meeting place of the Senate (which has eighty one elected members comprising three representatives for each of the twenty six states and three for the Federal District. Beneath the inverted dome is the Chamber of Deputies (with 513 directly elected members). The twin towers, initially designed to house the offices of members of parliament, now accommodate the offices of the parliamentary

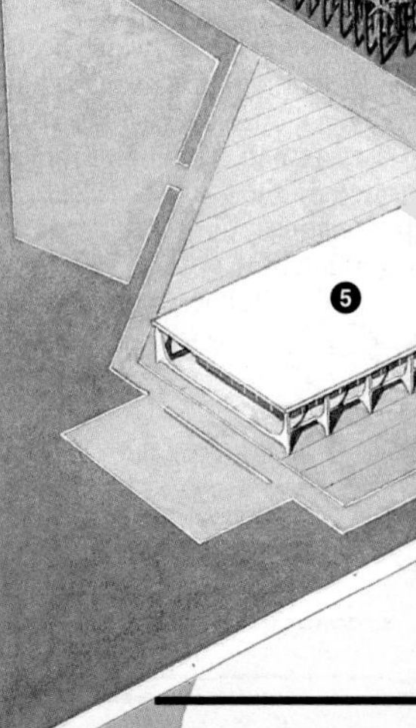

administration. The members of parliament have their offices in annexes on either side of the esplanade. It is odd that the entrance faces the Esplanada dos Ministérios rather than Praça dos Três Poderes, which would be more in keeping with this, the 'Three Powers Square'. Niemeyer had in fact devised a plan to remedy this situation, but it was never implemented.

PALÁCIO DO PLANALTO (4). Leaving the Congresso Nacional retrace your steps and cross the embankment leading to Praça dos Três Poderes. The Palácio do Planalto, which houses the president's office, is on the north side. Built in 1960, this glass palace was intended to symbolize transparency in the exercise of power.

SUPREMO TRIBUNAL FEDERAL (5). Counterbalancing the Palácio do Planalto at the other end of the square, and having the same architectural idiom, is the Supreme Court. This rectangular building, a modern interpretation of the classic Greek temple, seems to float or to be suspended in space. A statue of Justice by Alfredo Ceschiatti stands at the entrance.

PANTEÃO DA PÁTRIA TANCREDO NEVES (6). Closing the vista in the direction of the lake is the Panteão de Pátria Tancredo Neves. This flame-like building, a gift from the Bradesco Foundation (a bank and insurance company), was opened in September 1986. Within is a room containing a polyptych by João Camara depicting the life and execution of Tiradentes ● *24*. The signifance of this building is summed up by the words of former president José Sarney ● *27*: 'The passion for freedom never dies.'

THREE DECORATIVE SYMBOLS. There are three decorative elements on Praça dos Três Poderes. The first is the universally famous statue of

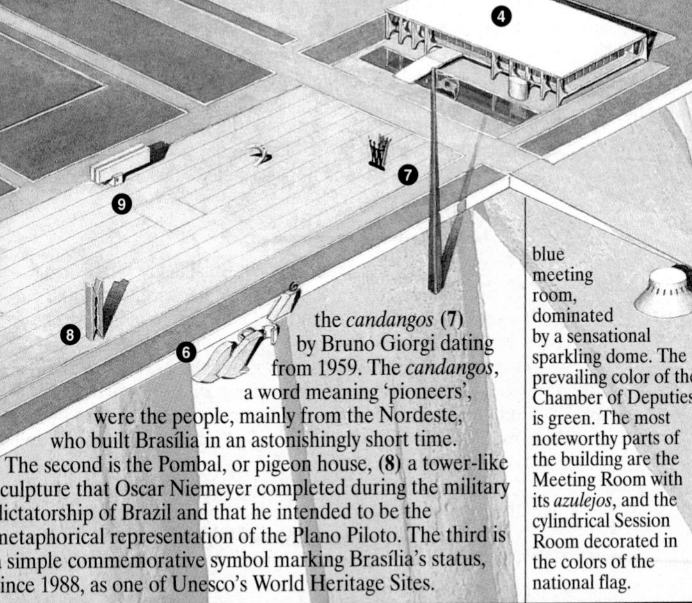

the *candangos* **(7)** by Bruno Giorgi dating from 1959. The *candangos*, a word meaning 'pioneers', were the people, mainly from the Nordeste, who built Brasília in an astonishingly short time. The second is the Pombal, or pigeon house, **(8)** a tower-like sculpture that Oscar Niemeyer completed during the military dictatorship of Brazil and that he intended to be the metaphorical representation of the Plano Piloto. The third is a simple commemorative symbol marking Brasília's status, since 1988, as one of Unesco's World Heritage Sites.

The sculpture *Meteor* and its reflection (*above*), and the statue of the *candangos* (*background*), works by Bruno Giorgi.

TOUR OF THE TWO CHAMBERS

The two chambers can be visited separately. Tours start from the entrance of Parliament's vast white reception hall. The length of the tour depends on whether parliament is in session or not. The Senate tour starts with a visit to the museum of the history of the Senate which exhibits various objects and souvenirs from the imperial and republican eras ● *25*. You will also be shown the Senate's blue meeting room, dominated by a sensational sparkling dome. The prevailing color of the Chamber of Deputies is green. The most noteworthy parts of the building are the Meeting Room with its *azulejos*, and the cylindrical Session Room decorated in the colors of the national flag.

MEMORIAL JK
The memorial to former president Juscelino Kubitschek ● *26* on Praça do Cruzeiro continues the Eixo Monumental in the west. Unveiled in 1981, the memorial contains Kubitschek's tomb and a statue of JK, as he was popularly known, looks down from a striking 92-foot-high pedestal. This caused controversy in Brazil, with some critics accusing Niemeyer of giving undue prominence to the hammer and the sickle, the motifs of Russian communism. The stark interior has an exhibition documenting the president's life.

WALKING UP THE EIXO MONUMENTAL

To explore the Eixo Monumental (Monumental Axis) take a bus or taxi and ride along it as far as the Torre de Televisão.

TORRE DE TELEVISÃO. The television tower, an elegant needle rising 1,043 feet into the air, was designed by Lúcio Costa and opened in 1967. Passing the cluster of stalls that mar its appearance at the base, enter the building and take the elevator up to the observation platform, which commands a vista of the city with a clear view of the Pilot Plan ▲ *201*. On the second floor is a museum of gems and a bar with a panoramic view. Behind the television tower, at the center of the axis, are various less attractive buildings, such as the Centro de Convenções (conference center), built by Sérgio Bernardes and the future home of the Museu do Índio (Museum of the American Indian).

PARQUE DA CIDADE. Contrary to first impressions, Brasília is not a city of unrelieved concrete and asphalt. Its green lung is the 988-acre City Park, with entrances at Q901 and Q912 South. The park was designed by Lúcio Costa, Oscar Niemeyer and Burle Marx and has all the regular leisure facilities as well as a cycle track and catering outlets. One of the park's most popular attractions is the swimming pool, with three-foot-high artificial waves.

SETOR MILITAR URBANO. If you have time and can hire a car, pay a visit to the Palanque Monumental. This huge concrete sail, built by Niemeyer and opened in 1973, stands in the Setor Militar Urbano (Urban Military Sector), in front of the army headquarters. Further along, before you get to the railroad station, is the pretty army church, also built by Niemeyer. Also on the Eixo Monumental, on the same side as the Setor Militar Urbano, is the long narrow Palácio Buruti, headquarters of the Federal District administration.

PARQUE NACIONAL DE BRASÍLIA. This 18,642-acre park lies beyond the Setor Militar Urbano, in the northeastern part of the Federal District (six miles from the center on the Via Epia). The park offers visitors the opportunity to see the flora and fauna of the *cerrado* ● *18*. Another of the park's attractions is the network of abundant springs created by the interplay of porous and impermeable rocks.

RESIDENTIAL DISTRICTS

Certain residential districts of Brasília are also worth a visit. These are laid out in two symmetrical north and south wings, Superquadra Sul and Superquadra Norte, on either side of the Eixo Rodoviário. On its eastern side, the *superquadras* and *quadras* (apartment blocks) are numbered 200, 400 and 600, and on its western side 100 and 300. The odd numbers 500, 700 and 900 complete this western side. An address in Brasília always specifies 'north' or 'south' and is generally abbreviated as SQS (Superquadra Sul) or SQN (Superquadra Norte) followed by the three-digit number of the *quadra*. Blocks of low-rise housing are located at the far end of both wings and are named QI for Quarto Individua (Individual District) or QL Quarto Lago (Lake District), indicating their proximity to the lake.

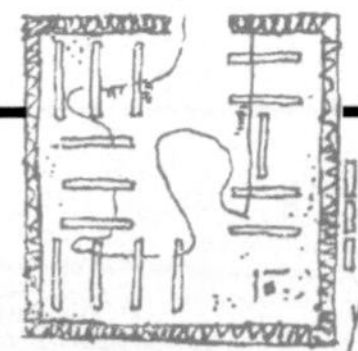

Superquadra Sul. To gain an insight into the thinking behind the layout of Brasília's residential districts, make for Quadra 107 and Quadra 108 in Superquadra Sul (SQS 107 and SQS 108), which were among the earliest to be built. On this side of the axis, these residential blocks are set on concrete pillars and rise to seven stories. (On the north side of the axis the blocks are only four stories high.) The buildings have a rectangular plan, and there are between eight and 11 in each *quadra*. Designed to suit a middle-class lifestyle, each apartment is typically divided into three areas: a reception area including the living room and the *copa*, a small room in Brazilian houses that is customarily connected to the kitchen; a living area; and an area reserved for domestic staff. Within each *quadra* is a green space that covers 60 percent of its area. The *quadra* itself was designed as a residential area with local facilities such as stores, schools and crèches. *Quadras* were arranged in groups of four, and local stores were concentrated along the two axes separating them (*entrequadras*). The Igreja de Nossa Senhora de Fátima, known as the *Igrejinha* (little church), is also located in Entrequadra 307–308. This beautifully proportioned church, designed by Oscar Niemeyer, was officially opened in 1958. Also on the eastern side of the Eixo Rodoviário stands the Santuário dom Bosco, at Via W3 Sul, Q702 (W3 indicates a smaller road running parallel to the Eixo Rodoviário). This spectacular church with blue stained-glass windows rests on 58-foot-tall pillars and a huge chandelier hangs from the center of the ceiling. The church is dedicated to Dom Bosco, the Italian priest, since canonized, who in 1883 had a vision that a new civilization would emerge on the 15th parallel.

Shopping
The locations for stores were carefully chosen, as were those of all the capital's essential services and activities. Two main areas were selected: one was a shopping thoroughfare that once stretched the entire length of Via W5 but which has since become very run down, and an area for various local stores. However, as the city developed, local stores gradually deteriorated, although bars and restaurants, particularly in Entrequadras 402–403, 404–405 and 408–409, in the south have flourished. Shopping malls have also appeared. The first of these was the Conjunto Nacional, near the Rodoviária. Two other large shopping malls have recently been built. These are Brasília Shopping in the north (SCN Quadra 05) and Pátio Brasil in the south (SCS Quadra 07).

Niemeyer's s ketches for the columns of the Palácio da Alvorada.

THE BANKS OF THE LAGO DO PARANOÁ

Opposite the city lies the Lago do Paranoá, a huge artificial lake covering nearly fifteen square miles and having a fifty-mile perimeter.

PALÁCIO DA ALVORADA. From Praça das Três Poderes walk south along Avenida das Nações (Nations Avenue) to the interesting Palácio da Alvorada (Palace of the Dawn), which President Lula decided to open to the public. This presidential residence, built on the lakeside in 1956–8, is one of the emblems of Brasília. With this building Niemeyer aimed to create a new esthetic consisting of a synthesis of European grandeur and Brazilian grace by constructing a truly palatial residence. The building takes the form of a rectangular box sandwiched between two projecting stories that, supported by columns, create a wide external gallery. These columns have been replicated all over the world and have been used in other contexts by Niemeyer. An attractive

PALÁCIO DA ALVORADA
Niemeyer designed this palace as if it were a sculpture: 'I remember the pleasure it gave me to draw the columns of the Palácio da Alvorada and the even greater pleasure I felt when I saw them imitated everywhere. It was an architectural surprise in contrast to the surrounding monotony.' This was Niemeyer's way of creating interaction between his architecture and his sculpture.

'... these suburbs some distance away from the Pilot Plan are called "satellite towns", as if the people who live there had come from the Moon or Mars.'

Bernard Mathieu

chapel that clearly shows the influence of the chapel of Notre Dame du Haut at Ronchamp, in France, by Le Corbusier, was built next to the palace at the same time.

MUSEU DE ARTE DE BRASÍLIA. Also near the palace, in the Setor de Hotéis e Turismo and standing next to the Concha Acústica open-air theater, is Brasília's art museum, which contains a collection of 20th-century Brazilian art. On the same road (L4 Norte) lies the earliest and still largely intact district of wood-built housing that accommodated the city's construction workers, and the small wooden church of Pampulha.

JARDIM BOTÂNICO. The botanical gardens, (whose entrance is near Q1 23, Sul, Setor de Mansões Dom Bosco, beside the lake), are an ecological reserve covering more than 11,164 acres. Parts of the reserve are open to visitors and there is a fascinating garden of medicinal plants and trees.

THE SATELLITE TOWNS

Brasília was designed to house 500,000 inhabitants. The city and its suburbs now contain two million inhabitants, 500,000 of whom live in the Pilot Plan zone. This has led to the often uncontrolled growth of satellite towns. The earliest were designed to be temporary towns that would be demolished when the new capital was completed but that have, however, remained and have spread due to a lack of proper planning. The largest satellite towns are situated to the west: Taguatinga, Sara Kubitschek, Vila Matias, Vila Dimas and, closer to the city, Cidade Livre (founded in 1956) and Núcleo Bandeirante (1961). Sobradinho, Vila Planalto, Vila Amaury and Plantaltina have sprung up in the east.

CATETINHO. Although visiting these towns is not a priority, if you are in the area it is worth seeing Catetinho, the temporary presidential palace built in 1956 and named for the ex-presidential Palacio do Catete in Rio ▲ *139*. This magnificent building by Niemeyer, 17 miles from the center, includes vestiges of the time of the *candangos* ▲ *205*.

MUSEU VIVO DA MEMÓRIA CANDANGA. Also worth a visit is the museum devoted to the *candangos* on Via Epia Sul Lt. D in Núcleo Bandeirante. Housed in the Juscelino Kubitschek de Oliveira hospital, Brasília's original wooden hospital, its collection consists of mementos and other material documenting the capital's construction.

A SPIRITUAL CITY
As can be seen on virtually every street corner and from the 'I love Jesus' car stickers in the back windows of so many cars, Brasília is a very spiritual city. Via W5 Sul (W is pronounced as in English, and five as *cinco*) is lined with places of worship for all denominations. The Templo de Boa Vontade (headquarters of the Legião de Boa Vontade, or 'Legion of Goodwill', founded by Alziro Zarur) is located on this axis (W5 Sul Q915). The pyramidal Templo de Boa Vontade (Temple of Goodwill), crowned by a crystal weighing 46 lbs, is open to followers of all faiths, 24 hours a day. Near Brasília, and lying six miles further along the DF15, is the community of the Vale de Amanhecer (Valley of the Dawn). Founded by Neiva Chaves Zelay (known as Tia Neiva), it is regarded as the most impressive syncretic religious center in the country (*below*).

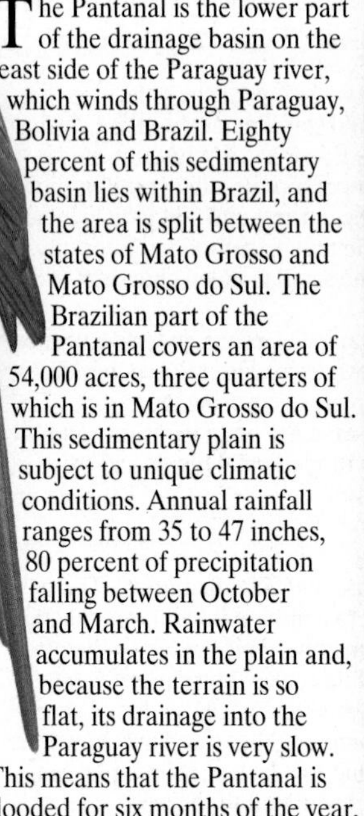

HYACINTH MACAW
This large parrot, known as *Arara preta* in Mato Grosso, is immediately recognizable by its magnificent deep violet-blue plumage and its long tail feathers. It has a huge bill for cracking open nuts and hard fruit, particularly the palm fruits on which it feeds. As they are endangered, trade in these birds is illegal.

The Pantanal is the lower part of the drainage basin on the east side of the Paraguay river, which winds through Paraguay, Bolivia and Brazil. Eighty percent of this sedimentary basin lies within Brazil, and the area is split between the states of Mato Grosso and Mato Grosso do Sul. The Brazilian part of the Pantanal covers an area of 54,000 acres, three quarters of which is in Mato Grosso do Sul. This sedimentary plain is subject to unique climatic conditions. Annual rainfall ranges from 35 to 47 inches, 80 percent of precipitation falling between October and March. Rainwater accumulates in the plain and, because the terrain is so flat, its drainage into the Paraguay river is very slow. This means that the Pantanal is flooded for six months of the year, when the depth of the water ranges from as little as 8 inches to as much as 8 feet. Only the most elevated areas of land in the plain are not submerged, becoming places of refuge for cattle and wildlife. These periods of flooding are interspersed by extremely dry periods. It is these alternating conditions that create the Pantanal's unique and varied habitat. Those same conditions, however, also severely limit the region's economic activity, which is based on extensive cattle-breeding. This traditional activity, introduced into the region two hundred years ago, has shaped the landscape and is largely responsible for the Pantanal's wealth today as well as for the preservation of its ecological balance. Over recent years, however, the Pantanal's traditional *fazendas* (plantations) have been abandoned, a gradual process that threatens to upset the region's delicate ecological balance. The three main arteries into the Pantanal are from the southeast via Campo Grande, the state capital of Mato Grosso do Sul, with 700,000 inhabitants; from the west via Corumbá, with 100,000 inhabitants; and from the north via Cuaibá (*above right*), the state capital of Mato Grosso, with 500,000 inhabitants. Each of these towns has an airport and travel agencies and are therefore good points of departure for a stay in the Pantanal. Besides the taxi planes that fly into the heart of the

THE 'JACARÉ', OR CAIMAN Widespread in South America, these caimans will happily live in rivers, lakes, pools, swamps or even cattle pools. They will also live in close proxmity to humans.

AN ISOLATED AREA ✪ With no roads or other means of access over much of its area, the Pantanal is further cut off from the outside world from October to March because of the floods. During these, airplanes and horses are virtually the only practical means of transport for the region's inhabitants. It is best therefore to visit the Pantanal between April and September. Fishing is a popular activity for visitors.

MAINTAINING A DELICATE BALANCE The delicate ecological balance maintained by cattle-breeding in the Pantanal is in the process of breaking down, posing a serious threat to this unique natural environment. Since 1998 the government of Mato Grosso do Sul, with financial support from the European Union, have been working to promote the Pantanal's economic development and preserve its unique ecosystem.

Pantanal and self-catering accommodation on *fazendas*, there are several ways of exploring this part of Brazil. Every day buses travel the 250 miles between Campo Grande and Corumbá, along BR262, which passes through the small towns of Aquidauana and Miranda. This metalled road crosses the Serra de Maracajú, a geographical boundary between the plateau and the Pantanal plain, and then runs alongside it for 185 miles. To reach Corumbá, take a ferry across the Paraguay river. Although the scenery is less spectacular than along the Transpantaneira, it still offers beautiful views of the southern Pantanal and also passes the *pousadas* on the banks of the Aquidauana river. The Transpantaneira is a raised road running for about 90 miles north to south across the Pantanal from Poconé to Porto Jofre.

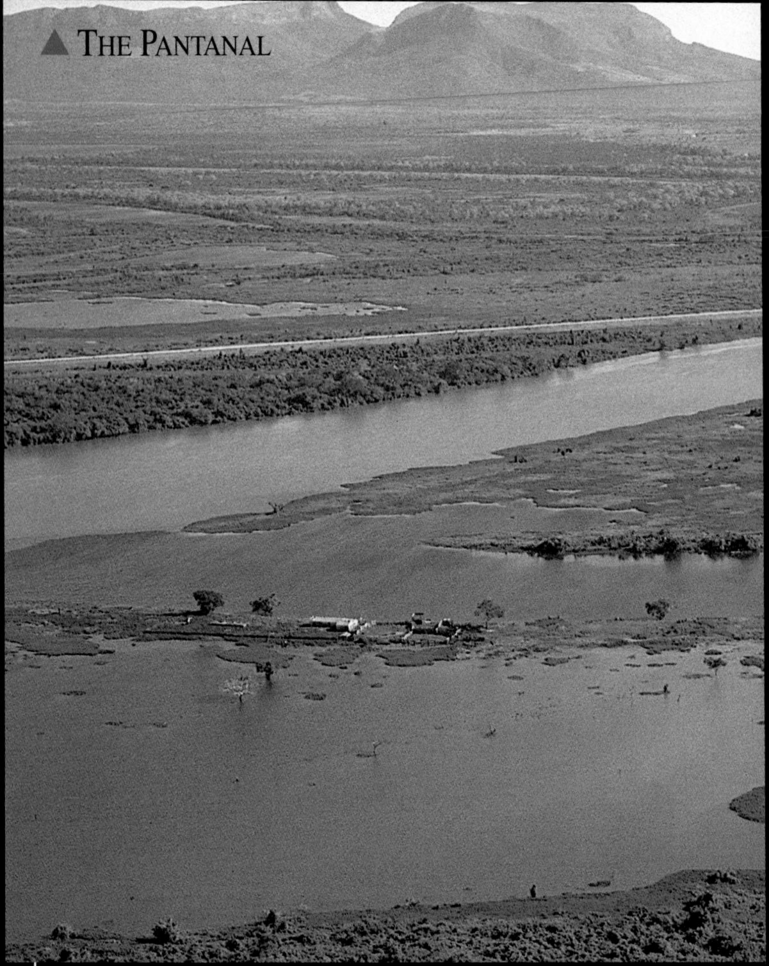

FLOODING IN THE PANTANAL
The long periods of flooding affecting this region gave the Pantanal its name. The word is derived from *pantano,* meaning 'swamp' in Portuguese. The sources of the rivers that flow across the Pantanal lie in the surrounding plateaus. The terrain of the Pantanal is very flat and the highest areas of land, which rise to about ten feet above the level of the plain, remain above the flood line throughout the year. Houses and farms are built on these elevated areas, which also support woodland and a varied vegetation, including green ebony and orchids, that provides shelter for wildlife and cattle.

Cattle-breeding In the Pantanal, cattle are bred extensively on ranches that may cover anything from 25,000 to 125,000 acres. The animals are reared in semi-freedom. When they are ready to be taken to market they are rounded up and split into herds by *peões* (cowherds). The herds, which may contain over 1,000 head of cattle each, are driven in large convoys (*comitivas*) to the cattle fairs. These cattle drives, which typify the economic activity of the Pantanal, can last as long as one month, the length of time it can take to make the journey from the *fazenda* to the market.

The Pantanal attracts many species of waterbirds. These birds include large numbers of great egrets, wood storks and jabirus, all of which gather in great flocks to rest or sleep in the trees. Flocks of southern screamers can also be seen resting in the treetops for long periods of time. The anhinga, or American darter, a diving bird related to the cormorant, perches in the trees so as to dry its feathers, which, strangely for a waterbird, are not impervious to water.

CAPYBARA OR CABIAI
Weighing between 77 lbs and 146 lbs, this is the world's largest rodent. It lives near water in family groups of up to six individuals. When alarmed it dives into the water.

MARSH DEER
Solitary during periods of flooding, these deer gather in groups during the dry season, converging around pools of standing water and using the marshy vegetation as cover.

GIANT OTTER
These otters, which usually live in small groups, are a joy to watch. Lively, friendly and inquisitive creatures, they are also expert at catching fish.

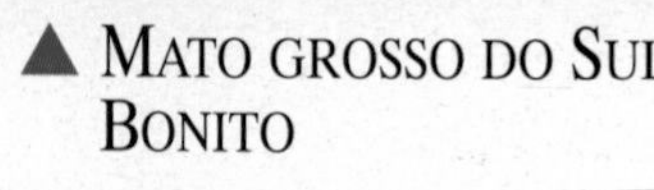

AQUARIO NATURAL
The source of the Formoso river, four miles from Bonito, is like a giant aquarium (*above*). Many kinds of aquatic plants and freshwater fish (*below*) can be seen in its limpid, tinted waters. You must wear a life jacket when you swim and time in the water is restricted so as to avoid stirring up the bottom of the lake and clouding the water.

Although the town of Bonito, lying near the Serra da Bodoquena, 154 miles from Campo Grande, borders the Pantanal, it shares none of the latter's characteristics. Even so, in this small paradise in southeastern Mato Grosso du Sul, water is again the main attraction. Most places of interest here can be visited with local guides. The abundant fossils of marine animals found in the Serra da Bodoquena indicate that this region was once covered by the sea. As the Andean cordillera was pushed up and the topography of Brazil changed, the sea retreated. Over thousands of years, the limestone-rich waters of the rivers that then began to flow through the area deposited sediment that has created a stunningly beautiful landscape.

CACHOEIRA DO RIO DO PEIXE. These waterfalls are the most spectacular in Bonito. Besides the beautiful falls, the two-hour walk here with the owner of the Água Viva *fazenda* takes in natural swimming pools created by accumulations of limestone and small underwater caves.

GRUTA DO LAGO AZUL. Blue Lake Cave is located 12 miles from Bonito. Having penetrated over 1,000 feet into the cave, you come to a dark blue lake 295 feet beneath the level of the entrance. In December and January the rays of the morning sun reach down into the cavity and are reflected in the lake, creating a sight of breathtaking beauty (*bottom left*). There is an entrance charge and children under five are not allowed.

RIO DA PRATA. Although it is 34 miles from Bonito, this is the best place to come for a swim. A three-hour walk down the river, during which you can see the fish and water plants, leads to a large watering place, called *vulcão* (volcano), that has crystal-clear waters.

São Paulo

SEMANA DE ARTE MODERNA
In 1922, the centenary of Brazilian independence ▲ *125* was marked in São Paulo by a singular event. This was Modern Art Week ● *89*, an avant-garde forum that brought together painters, writers and intellectuals keen to take Brazilian culture in a new direction.

With 18 million inhabitants, São Paulo is the most densely populated city in South America and the third-largest in the world after Mexico City and Tokyo. It is situated near the south coast, 267 miles from Rio, 364 miles from Belo Horizonte and 631 miles from Brasília. Often described as a tropical New York, it is the most modern and cosmopolitan city in Brazil, and its huge dimensions and striking contrasts are the legacy of its astonishingly rapid growth. Capital of the state of São Paulo and the driving force behind the Brazilian economy, the city handles 50 percent of the country's industry. Having become Brazil's industrial, financial and cultural capital in just fifty years, São Paulo is a multifaceted city that is ever changing and continuing to expand.

HISTORY

São Paulo was founded in 1554 by Jesuits who had come to Brazil to establish a mission dedicated to St Paul. Until the 17th century the village was also used by *bandeirantes* (adventurers) ● *29* as a base for their exploratory expeditions into Brazil's interior. São Paulo did not officially become a city until 1711 and, for two centuries, continued to be a small frontier town, used as a base by sugar merchants on their way to the port of Santos ▲ *228*. In the 19th century Dom Pedro's declaration of Brazilian independence ● *24* on the banks of the Ipiranga (1822) and the construction of a law school gave São Paulo a political and intellectual importance. The city then underwent a period of great economic and demographic growth. This was brought about by the booming coffee trade ● *32*, the construction of a railroad between Jundiaí and Santos and the abolition of slavery, all of which attracted a large influx of immigrants ● *35*. Additionally the fall in European imports to Brazil during World War One boosted industrial expansion.

São Paulo is not an easy city to explore on foot. It has developed, and continues to expand, with virtually no coherent program of urban planning, so that by its very nature it is a city for which it is difficult to devise a logical itinerary both in terms of time and of space. Focal points of interest to visitors tend to shift and new districts spring up. However, the oldest and most interesting parts of the city are the Luz and Centro districts, where a few rare buildings surviving from the colonial period stand alongside skyscrapers built in the early 20th century. Traveling east to west, you will pass through Luz, Centro Velho and Centro Novo, Liberdade (the Japanese district), Bela Vista and Bixiga (the Italian district), then Pacaembu, Higienópolis and Consolação. You will then come to São Paulo's financial district, located next to the *alamedas* (lanes) of Cerqueira César, the city's leading shopping area. Heading southwest, you will cross the pleasant garden districts of Jardim América, Jardim Paulista and Jardim Europa, and the Parque do Ibirapuera, then reach the lively Itaim district, followed by the Pinheiros district and, on the other side of the Pinheiros river, Butantã and leafy Morumbi.

MUSEU DE ARTE SACRA ✪
With some 14,000 pieces, the museum of religious art in São Paulo holds one of the greatest collections of Brazilian colonial art in the world. Exhibits include 18th-century religious sculptures; paintings by Brazilian and foreign masters depicting martyrs, the Madonna, clergymen and historical figures; church fittings, and furniture that once belonged to prominent people of the Empire period ● *25*.

BAIRRO DA LUZ

In this district, the District of Light, several features of interest are located around the chaotic Avenida Tiradentes.

MOSTEIRO DE NOSSA SENHORA DA LUZ. (Avenida Tiradentes, 676, Metro Tiradentes). Built in 1775, the Convent of Our Lady of Light is the oldest example of colonial architecture in the city. The convent houses a community of nuns belonging to a closed order, and the building's left wing contains the MUSEU DE ARTE SACRA ★.

PINACOTECA DO ESTADO. Walk down Avenida Tiradentes, turn right at Praça da Luz and you will come to the State Art Gallery, a neoclassical building (*above*) designed by Brazilian architect Ramos de Azevedo. Opened in 1905 and built to house the School of Applied Arts, the building was never fully completed: the exposed brick walls give an insight into the building techniques of the time. The art gallery, which has recently been restored, contains an important collection of paintings by 19th- and 20th-century Brazilian artists ● *86* including Di Cavalcanti, Cândido Portinari and Lasar Segall, as well as sculptures, drawings and engravings. The entrance to the art gallery is via the JARDIM DA LUZ, a garden that was popular for family outings in the early 20th century.

ESTAÇÃO DA LUZ. Opposite Praça da Luz is the Estacão da Luz, the railroad station. Listed as a historic monument, this is another of the city's landmarks and it recalls the heyday of the coffee trade ● *32*. It was directly inspired by Westminster Abbey and all the building materials were imported from England. Ravaged by a fire in 1946, it was then renovated and slightly altered. Next to it stands Júlio Prestes railroad station, now disused and converted into a concert hall, the Sala São Paulo, in 1999. The concert hall has a resident orchestra and seating for 1,600.

MUSEU DO IPIRANGA
The museum, in the Parque da Independência, at one end of Avenida Dom Pedro I in Ipiranga, was built to celebrate Brazil's independence. Its collection is based on a gift of jewelry, American Indian weapons and other objects, as well as insects, reptiles and other stuffed animals, made by Counselor Francisco de Paula Mayrink. The museum also has some 200,000 19th-century pieces. The Renaissance-style Palácio Ipiranga, which houses the museum, was designed by the Italian architect Tomasso Gaudenzio Biezzi, and work on it began in 1885.

SALA SÃO PAULO DE CONCERTOS
Housed in the concourse of the former Júlio Prestes railroad station (*below*), this concert hall was restored in 1999 to provide a home for the São Paulo State Symphony Orchestra.

From Avenida Paulista to Parque do Ibirapuera

Avenida Paulista. Opened in 1891, this avenue was the first metalled public highway in the city. At the height of the coffee era ● *32* magnificent villas set in private parkland were built along it. Avenida Paulista, popularly known as the Champs Elysées of São Paulo, remained largely residential until 1952, when the ban on the building of office blocks was lifted. Among the avenue's surviving villas is the Casa das Rosas, at no. 37, which is listed as a historic monument and houses exhibition rooms. Avenida Paulista is today lined with skyscrapers along three miles of its length. Notable modern office blocks include those of the FIESP, at no. 1313, of the Gazeta, at no. 900, and of the MASP, at no. 1578 ★.

Parque Trianon. The MASP building faces the Parque Trianon, behind which lies the elegant Jardim Paulista district. A wealthy clientele patronizes the restaurants, high-class confectioners and smart designer stores along Rua Haddock Lobo, Rua Pamplona, Rua Alameda Santos and Rua Oscar Freire.

The garden districts. The Jardim América, between Rua Estado Unidos, Rua Atlântica, Rua Groenlândia and Avenida 9 de Julho, and the Jardim Europa, between Rua Groenlândia, Rua Áustria, Rua Itália and Rua Rússia, are in striking contrast to the rest of São Paulo, because this part of the city is very flat and is planted with trees. The streets, named for countries in America and Europe, are lined with smart residences in various styles including French, English, Spanish and colonial. On Praça Nossa Senhora do Brasil, at the intersection between Rua Colômbia and Avenida Brasil, in Jardim América, stands the Igreja de Nossa Senhora do Brasil (*right*). It was built in 1942 in the 17th-century colonial style. The Igreja de São José on Rua Dinamarca in Jardim Europa was completed in 1930. Both churches are popular for wedding ceremonies.

Parque do Ibirapuera. Follow Rua Estados Unidos to Avenida Brigadeiro Luis Antônio, which leads to Parque do Ibirapuera, the only green space in the city center. At the entrance the Monumento às Bandeiras, a statue by Vitor Brecheret, commemorates the *bandeirantes* ● *28*. The park, covering 395 acres and designed by Oscar Niemeyer ▲ *203* and Burle Marx ▲ *147*, was a gift from the Matarazzo family. It was opened in 1954 to mark the 400th anniversary of the founding of São Paulo. At weekends thousands of *paulistas* come to enjoy its lakes, playing fields, race tracks, planetarium and museums, particularly the Biennial Pavilion and Museu de Arte Moderna (MAM). The latter contains an important collection of paintings, artefacts, engravings and sculptures by Brazilian artists working from 1920 to the present day. There are free concerts in the park on late Sunday monings.

Museu de Arte de São Paulo (MASP) ★
With works by Renoir, Van Gogh, Picasso, Degas, Rembrandt and other masters, the museum contains the most comprehensive collection of European paintings in Latin America. Its collection of works by Brasilian artists, including Portinari ● *86* and Di Cavalcanti, is equally fine. It was founded in 1947 by Assis Chateaubriand ▲ *125* and moved to its current premises in 1968. The building, by Lina Bo Bardi, rests on four pillars set 260 feet apart. The museum, at Avenida Paulista 1578, is open Tuesday through Sunday, 11am–6pm. On Sundays an antiques market is held on its esplanade.

From Itaim to Morumbi

Itaim. Bounded to the north by the gardens district, to the east by Vila Novo Conceição, to the south by Brooklin and to the west by Morumbi, the busy Itaim district is densely packed with office blocks (on Avenida Brigadeiro Faria Lima and Avenida Presidente Juscelino Kubitschek), luxury stores (in Shopping Iguatemi, Alameda Gabriel Monteiro da Silva, with interior design stores) and fashionable restaurants. Itaim is frequented by wealthy *paulistas* who until recently favored the area around the Jardim Paulista and the Cerqueira César. The Museu da Casa Brasileira, housed in a 1940s building at Avenida Brigadeiro Faria Lima 2705, documents the development of domestic furniture in Brazil since the 17th century.

Pinheiros. The Pinheiros district lies within the triangle formed by Avenida Rebouças, Avenida Doutour Arnaldo and the Pinheiros river. Rua Teodoro Sampaio, with many small stores selling musical instruments and furniture, is now the district's main shopping area. Bargain hunters flock to the friendly Saturday flea market on Praça Benedito Calixto. This is an excellent place to come to hear Brazilian music and sample dishes from the Nordeste and Minas Gerais. Although it is mainly a middle-class district with comfortable houses, the Pinheiros district also takes in the Vila Madalena quarter, a bohemian area popular with students. Busy restaurants and bars with live music stay open late, particularly around Rua Morato Coelho and Rua Fradique Coutinho. On the other side of the Pinheiros river is the campus of the University of São Paulo (USP), the grounds of the Butantã Institute, at Avenida Dr Vital Brasil 1500, and the Museu de Arte Contemporânea (MAC), whose collection includes works by Portinari ● *86*, Volpi ● *88*, Tarsila do Amaral ● *89*, Picasso, Miró and Braque.

Morumbi. The tree-lined Morumbi district underwent a real-estate boom more recently than did the gardens district, with the construction of impressive residences and luxury apartment blocks. The Fundação Maria Luísa e Oscar Americano at Avenida Morumbi 3700 contains a large collection of paintings, furniture, carpets, silverware and ceramics by Brazilian artists such as Portinari and Lasar Segall, and artists with connections to Brazil, such Frans Post ● *84*. The 18-acre park, which is equally fine as those laid by Alfredo Volpi and Burle Marx, is worth a visit in itself (*below*). A little further on is the Palácio dos Bandeirantes, headquarters of the state government, whose collections are open to visitors at weekends. The district's other principal attractions include the Estádio de Morumbi, home of São Paulo Futebol Clube and the world's largest private stadium. The Cemitério do Morumbi, at Rua Deputado Laércio Corte 468, is the final resting place of racing driver Ayrton Senna. Visitors from all over the world come here to lay flowers on his tomb.

Instituto Butantã
Renowned for the serums and vaccines it produces from the venom of snakes and scorpions, the Butantã Institute was founded in 1901 by Doctor Vital Brasil. This was at the request of the government and in order to combat an epidemic of plague that was ravaging the port of Santos ▲ *228*. The institute has over 1,000 species of snakes, scorpions and spiders.

Teatro Alfa
This modern theater is in the outlying district of Santo Amaro, just beyond Morumbi. Opened in 1998, it has become established as one of the best concert halls in São Paulo.

▲ São Paulo, a magnet for immigrants

Caution von 15000 Rubel.

Beförderung von Passagieren nach allen Welttheilen

Passage-Billet

für die Reise von Libau via Hull-Liverp

Between 1882 and 1978 2.5 million immigrants from over fifty different countries came to the state of São Paulo. Initially most of them settled in the countryside but as industrialization gained momentum the city of São Paulo acted as an increasingly powerful magnet, drawing in both foreigners and Brazilians, the latter mainly from the Nordeste. Unlike other cosmopolitan cities such as New York, whose inhabitants describe themselves as Italian-American or Afro-American, for example, São Paulo encourages cultural fusion. This wide-ranging immigration has left its mark on the city's architecture, fashions, food and festivals, as well as in labor relations and education. More recent immigrants include Koreans, Chinese and Taiwanese and people from elsewhere in Latin America.

The Portuguese and the Spanish

Before World War Two the Portuguese (*below*) were very active as storekeepers and owned most of the city's bakeries. The Spanish, by contrast, had a virtual monopoly on the scrap industry.

The Syro-Lebanese

Although the Syro-Lebanese contingent was not large, it drastically changed the face of retail trade in São Paulo, particularly in Rua 25 de Março ▲ *221*. Between 1905 and 1946 around 50,000 Syrians and Lebanese settled in São Paulo, mainly in the Santa Efigênia and Sé districts ▲ *220*.

THE ITALIANS
Arriving in large numbers from 1870, the Italians now number over 950,000 and constitute the largest community of non-Portuguese in São Paulo. Settling mainly the Brás and Bixiga districts ▲ *222*, they provided much of the labor force during the city's early industrialization and contributed to its urbanization (*main picture*). Their presence has profoundly influenced the *paulista* accent.

THE NORDESTINOS
The policy implemented by Getúlio Vargas ● *36* with the aim of discouraging European immigration to Brazil sparked a wave of internal migration. Attracted by the numerous work opportunities provided by a flourishing city, huge numbers of Nordestinos (from the Nordeste) arrived in São Paulo (*bottom*) in the 1930s and again in the 1960s. They constitute the lower classes in São Paulo and provide an unskilled labor force, being casually employed on building sites. Today six million Nordestinos live in the state of São Paulo. Living mainly in the eastern part of the capital, they have made São Paulo the largest Nordestino city in the country. The Nordestinos keep alive their festivals and customs, particularly the *forró* ● *51*, which has now been appropriated by the *paulistas*.

THE JAPANESE
In 1908, after a journey of 54 days aboard the *Kasato Maru*, the first Japanese immigrants landed in Santos ● *35*. They numbered 781; most of them settled in rural areas and would not move to the capital until the 1950s. While earlier generations of Japanese immigrants would cherish the hope of returning home one day, their descendants now regard Brazil as their homeland. São Paulo, and particularly the district of Liberdade ▲ *222*, is now home to the largest expatriate Japanese community. These Japanese work mainly in the food industry.

ILHA DE SÃO SEBASTIÃO
Before the arrival of the Europeans this island was known to the Tupinambá American Indians as Ciribaï, meaning 'tranquil place'. It was named St Sebastian Island by the Italian navigator Amerigo Vespucci when he landed there on January 20, St Sebastian's Day, in 1502. The island was used as a hideout by pirates, who concealed their treasure here. It became inhabited in 1608, and tobacco, cassava, banana and sugar cane brought it prosperity. It was also a base for illicit slave trading, which continued here even after abolition ● *35*.

Running south to north along São Paulo state's coastline ★, highway SP055 passes many beautiful beaches offering everything from family seaside resorts to fashionable hangouts for surfers. There are also more inaccessible beaches that can be reached only via paths through tropical forest or from the sea by boat.

FROM SANTOS TO BERTIOGA

SANTOS. Founded in 1535 on an island 45 miles from what is now the city of São Paulo, Santos has become the largest town on the coast of São Paulo state. Take time for a leisurely exploration of the town's historic center, taking in the faded splendor of its old buildings, particularly the residences of 19th-century coffee barons, and stroll along the quayside of Brazil's largest port.

SÃO VICENTE. The town is set on a promontory opposite Santos. Founded in 1532, São Vicente is one of the oldest towns in Brazil, yet only a small part of its historic heritage has survived. A notable vestige is the MATRIZ DE SÃO VICENTE on Praça do Mercado. This parish church, completed in 1542 and rebuilt in 1757, contains painted wooden statues dating from the colonial period. The town's extensive brown sandy beach is held to be the most popular in Brazil.

GUARUJÁ. Located on the island of Santo Amaro, 55 miles from São Paulo, this large, elegant seaside resort has luxury hotels and small *cabanas* right on the beach. Being conveniently near to São Paulo and having beautiful long beaches, this resort is very popular with the people of São Paulo. However, the Eden and Pernambuco beaches, six miles from the center of Guarujá, are less crowded.

BERTIOGA. This small town, lying 67 miles from São Paulo, has fallen victim to property developers, who use its beaches as a magnet to attract visitors. From here you can take boat trips to beaches on the Ilha de Santo Amaro. Bertioga is also the departure point for hikes in the Serra do Mar. The four-mile walk to Trilha da Água, for example, takes three hours.

THE PORT OF SANTOS
Santos has become Brazil's largest port. Its expansion is due to three main factors: coffee exports ● *32*, immigration ● *35* and its proximity to São Paulo.

TUPÍ PLACE NAMES
Certain places along the coastline of São Paulo state are still known by their Tupí names. Guarujá means 'island of the sun', Bertioga comes from the word *pirati-oca,* meaning 'refuge of the *tainha* fish' and Caraguatatuba is derived from *caraguata*, meaning 'large bromeliad'.

FROM SÃO SEBASTIÃO TO CARAGUATATUBA

SÃO SEBASTIÃO. This coastal town, 126 miles from São Paulo, lies opposite the Ilha de São Sebastião. Noteworthy buildings in its well-restored historic center include the 17th-century MATRIZ SÃO SEBASTIÃO on Praça Major João Fernandes, the former prison (now the military police headquarters), and some fine early 20th-century residences, such as the

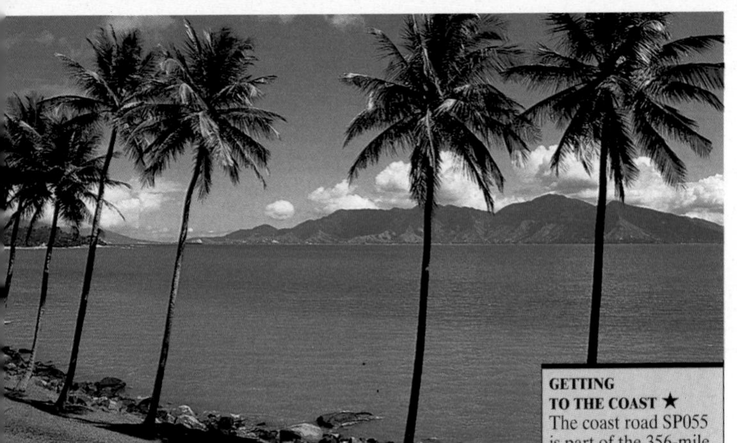

Casa Dória on Rua Antônio Cândido. It is pleasant to wander through these narrow streets, admiring their colonial houses, or visit the old *fazendas* ● *68*, where mills, sugar presses and other historic plantation machinery is displayed. The *fazenda* of Santana in Pontal da Cruz, for example, is two miles from the town center. For 60 miles on either side of São Sebastiáo the coastline consists of a succession of bays and white sandy beaches, with a scattering of islands. The most popular beaches are Maresias, 17 miles from São Sebastiáo on the Costa Sul, Boiçucanga, 22 miles away, and Camburi, 25 miles away.

Ilha de São Sebastião. This island, popularly known as Ilhabela (Beautiful Island), is a 15-minute ferry ride from São Sebastiáo. Covering 127 square miles and having 22 miles of beaches, it is the largest island along this stretch of coastline. The sugar cane grown here makes excellent *cachaça* ● *64*. The large market town of Vila Ilhabela has a rich colonial heritage; especially notable is its parish church, the Matriz Nossa Senhora d'Ajuda, on Praça Professor Alfredo Oliani, which was built by slaves in 1532. Narrow roads and dirt tracks allow the island to be explored by car, on horseback, by bicycle or on foot. By any of these means visitors may travel inland to admire the islands's 360 waterfalls and explore hills densely covered with the *mata atlântica (*Atlantic forest) ▲ *166*, *172*, or marvel at the sea views and breathtakingly beautiful beaches, which are more sheltered on the north and west coasts and wilder in the Baia de Castelhanos, on the east coast. Beyond São Sebastiáo, the Serra do Mar skirts the coast and steep roads wind through *mata atlântica* then drop down to join the coast road, which passes small inlets lined with golden sand, large bays and strings of islands, some very small, that can be reached by sailboat.

Caraguatatuba. Although this large seaside resort lying 109 miles from São Paulo has no great appeal, it offers many leisure activities. From the vantage point of the Tamoios highway (SP099, between Km 67 and Km 71) that cuts through the *mata atlântica* of the Serra do Mar, Caraguatatuba looks like a jewel in the setting of a magnificent bay. Either side of the resort are large beaches, such as Massaguaçu (6 miles away) and Tabatinga (11 miles away). However, off highway SP055, just outside Maranduba is a dirt track that is barely suitable for vehicles but that leads to Caçandoca Beach, which often hums with the sound of music. A small chapel nestles beneath the leaves of *chapéus de sol* ('sun hat trees') and a river flows down along the end of the beach. Cross this river and follow the steep path to the small beach of Caçandoquinha, where *caiçara* fishermen spread their nets out to dry.

GETTING TO THE COAST ★
The coast road SP055 is part of the 356-mile highway running from Rio de Janeiro to Santos and continued by the BR101. To make the most of the beaches is it best to come to the coast in summer (December through February). Other attractions, such as the Atlantic forest, hiking trips and historic buildings, can be enjoyed at any time.

Fishing
The *caiçara* fishermen live on the coast and fish for *robalos* (bass), *garoupas* (groupers) or *pargos* (sea bream). Cooked in a fresh coriander (cilantro) sauce, these fish are served with *pirão* (cassava meal cooked in court bouillon) and with cold beer brought in by motorboat.

Caçandoquinha to Saco das Bananas
Walking around the pink granite tip of Caçandoquinha Beach will reveal a splendid view of the islands. Just before Raposa Beach, a tiny cove, the granite is very jagged but by following the steep path through forest and brush you will come to the small harbor of Saco das Bananas. The fishing boats used here are canoes hollowed out of a single tree trunk in the American Indian fashion.

BIRDS
The tropical vegetation is home to *saíras*, small tanagers such as the *sete cores* or seven-colored tanager (*right*), and *tiê sangues* or blood-red tanagers ▲ *143*, as well as a population of screeching parrots and parakeets that feed on the ripe golden fruit of the palm trees. Added to this is the call of the *bem-te-vi* ('Yes, I've seen you'). Oblivious to this din, the tiny *beija-flores* (hummingbirds) ▲ *150* flit about like bumblebees as they suck the nectar of delicate flowers.

BEACHES NORTH OF UBATUBA
On the north side of Ubatuba are some less accessible beaches surrounded by steep inclines. They include Vermelho do Norte (six miles from Ubatuba), Itamambuca (nine miles away), Promirim (14 miles away) and Ubatumirim (21 miles away).

THE GUARANÍ
These Native Americans live in various reserves, the largest of which is Boa Vista, an *aldeia* (hamlet) on the road to the Promirim waterfalls. The chief of this tribe of Guaraní, who came here from Paraguay about sixty years ago, is *cacique* Marcos Tupí. With financial aid from FUNAI ▲ *297*, he opened a center selling handicrafts. This provides a vital source of income for these people, who speak only Guaraní and who live on the fringes of the modern world.

Make your way back to Caçandoca along the forest path and rejoin highway SP055, following it as it runs behind the beaches at Maranduba as far as the immense LAGOINHA BEACH. Walk along this beach until you come to a stream flowing into the sea. A path lined with lush tropical vegetation winds along the coast. The beaches here, the nearest of them tiny inlets with granite rocks and tall stands of green and gold bamboo, stretch to infinity. A few fishermen's houses perch on the cliffs. The path continues to BONETE BEACH, which is lined with palms and fig trees overgrown with stupendous bromeliad flowers. Follow the stream to the village of Bonete, which is inhabited by the families of *caiçara* fishermen.

FROM UBATUBA TO PICINGUABA

UBATUBA. This delightful seaside resort, 142 miles from São Paulo, is built around the historic site where the Jesuit Padre Anchieta ● *220* signed a peace treaty with the Tupinambá American Indians in 1563. The resort has no fewer than eighty beaches and around fifteen islands. The most scenic beaches to the south of Ubatuba, like Lázaro, Domingas Dias and Sununga, which is nine miles away, have good facilities and are surrounded by splendid villas with lush gardens densely planted with species of *mata atlântica* vegetation.
ILHA DE ANCHIETA. From December through February an *escuna* (small motor schooner) takes visitors from the port of Saco da Ribeira, eight miles from Ubatuba, to this island. Covering three square miles, the island is an ecological reserve, with a wide variety of plants, and a breeding ground for sea turtles. It also has some beautiful beaches, among the finest being Presídio and do Sul.
PICINGUABA. Make your way back along the coast to Picinguaba, 29 miles from Ubatuba, where the bay has many small deserted inlets. On the roadside here groups of American Indians offer basketry and other artefacts for sale. On the same side of the road, at the end of a path through a patch of forest, stands the CASA DA FARINHA, a cassava flour mill. This fine building still has the large wheel that brought water from the river, as well as grinding stones, graters and presses, and the vats in which the flour was washed and roasted. The final place of interest along the coast is Picinguaba, a small *caiçara* fishing village reached via a long, almost impassable, path. There you can see fishermen mending their nets, which they spread out on their brightly colored canoes. The villagers have no electricity and their lives are ruled by sun and wind rather than by *telenovelas* ● *60*.

The South

'YERBA MATE'
This indigenous plant, used by the Guaraní to make a bitter hot drink, was one of southern Brazil's highly prized natural resources. The main center of production was Paraná, but it was Rio Grande do Sul that turned *yerba mate* (meaning 'calabash herb'), in the form of *chimarrão* ▲ 247, into a symbol of the South. Following American Indian custom, *chimarrão* is drunk from a calabash passed from hand to hand, preferably among friends.

The South (*Região Sul*) comprises the states of Paraná, Santa Catarina and Rio Grande do Sul. Covering 7 percent of Brazil's landmass, it contains 24 million inhabitants, which comprise 15 percent of the country's population. This subtropical region supports a varied flora, including forests of araucaria or Paraná pine, *mata atlântica* ▲ *166, 172* and mangroves. The South also has many natural attractions, among the most spectacular of which are the Iguaçu falls ▲ *238*, the Ilha do Mel ▲ *237*, the beaches of Santa Catarina ▲ *240* and the canyons of the Rio Grande do Sul ▲ *245*. With the evocative ruins of Jesuit missions ▲ *248*, it is rich in historical interest. It is also distinctive for its great cultural diversity, a quality that sets it apart from other regions of Brazil and that has fostered a deep-rooted regionalist zeal among its inhabitants.

HISTORY

The southern provinces, initially held by Spain, were occupied in the 17th century by *bandeirantes* ● *28* from São Paulo. They remained part of Brazilian territory partly due to the Portuguese policy of colonization, Portugal having decided to extend its control as far as south as the Rio de la Plata, but mostly because the region's economy complemented the

'[auracarias are of] the opposite shape to that of our fir trees… their trunks are surrounded by tiers of branches forming hexagonal layers that become larger and larger, the top one spreading out like a giant umbrella.'

Claude Lévi-Strauss

gold-mining industry of Minas Gerais ● *30*. The process of imposing European civilization on the South was largely accomplished by the Spanish Jesuits, who set up *cristiano-guaraní* model republics ▲ *248* in the gaucho territory of what is now the state of Rio Grande do Sul. The prosperity of these missions, and the large numbers of culturally integrated Guaraní that they housed, proved irresistible to the *bandeirantes*, who destroyed the villages and enslaved the American Indians, selling them on to sugar mills in the Nordeste (northeast). Throughout the 18th century and into the mid-19th, the region underwent rapid growth thanks to the breeding of cattle, draft oxen, saddle horses and pack mules for sale to the states of São Paulo and Minas Gerais. The continuous movement of people and animals into the fields and Araucaria forests of the South was called *tropeirismo*. The *tropeiros* (mule-drivers, cowherds and cattle traders) founded several towns in the region and their lifestyle had a profound influence on its culture: *churrasco* (meat roasted in embers), *chimarrão* (a hot drink made from *mate*) ▲ *247* and leatherwork are just three examples. However, the cultural diversity of the South is due most particularly to the large number of immigrants who settled there from the 18th to the 20th centuries. In the 18th century, with the ultimate aim of gaining control of Spanish-held territory, the Portuguese government shipped whole communities from the Azores to Brazil. Most of these families settled along the coast of Santa Catarina state, adopting a lifestyle that was more indigenous than Azorean, planting and eating cassava, corn, beans and pumpkins. The second wave of immigrants arrived mainly in the final two decades of the 19th century. Germans, Italians, Poles, Ukrainians, Japanese and Lebanese formed large communities in the states of Paraná, Santa Catarina and Rio Grande do Sul, adding their speech, customs and traditions to an already rich regional culture.

Araucarias
This coniferous tree, with distinctive tiers of branches, is one of the two species of pine native to Brazil and is an emblem of the South. Araucaria forests once covered 66 percent of Paraná, Santa Catarina and Rio Grande do Sul, the three states of the South. But the auracaria is now almost extinct: only 12 percent of the protected reserves remain and of these a mere two percent is virgin forest.

Real Caminho do Viamão
This was the oldest and best-known *tropeiro* (mule-drivers') road in the South, walled sections of which remain in the state of Santa Catarina (*left*). The road left the town of Viamão, in the state of Rio Grande do Sul, and ran as far as Sorocaba, in the state of São Paulo, where large cattle fairs were held. Numerous towns grew up at spots where the *tropeiros* would stop to rest with their herds. Many of these, like Castro ▲ *235* and Lapa, both in Paraná, keep alive the memory of the *tropeiros* in their customs and festivals.

THE LIGEIRINHO
Unlike that of most Brazilian cities, Curitiba's public transport system serves both the city's affluent districts and poorer outlying districts. A key part of this system is the Ligeirinho, an express bus that operates like an overground metro. Tickets are bought at tubular stations, which are made of glass and have an interesting design. The city authorities have launched several initiatives to encourage *Curitibanos* to use public transport rather than their cars.

The city of Curitiba is a patchwork of different cultures. When it was founded, in 1693, its population was American Indian and Portuguese. In the 18th century, it became a stopping place for *tropeiros*, and in the 19th century many immigrants from Germany, Poland, Italy and Ukraine settled there. The city, capital of the state of Paraná, now has some 1.6 million inhabitants. It covers a plateau set at an altitude of 3,000 feet and its many green spaces are filled with araucaria, or Piraná pine. This tree gave the city its name: Nossa Senhora da Luz dos Pinhais de Curitaba (Our Lady of Light of the Pines of Curitiba). *Curitiba,* from *curii* (pine tree) and *itibo* (many), is an American Indian word meaning 'many pines'. In terms of its architecture and urban planning, Curitiba is highly regarded. It has received various United Nations awards, including the Habitat Scroll of Honor in 1992 for its Lixo que Não é Lixo (Trash That Isn't Trash) initiative. This efficient system of collecting and recycling garbage involves purchasing usable waste from disadvantaged sections of the community. The British architect Richard Rogers regards Curitiba as a remarkable example of far-sighted urban development, and the town has certainly found effective solutions to common urban problems, such as transport.

THE HISTORIC CENTER

The Setor Histórico, Curitiba's historic center, has been restored and pedestrianized. It contains many vestiges of the colonial town, as well as art galleries and cultural centers, and many bars and restaurants.

LARGO DA ORDEM. This picturesque cobblestoned square contains an old drinking trough where settlers and *tropeiros* brought their horses to drink. The buildings that line the square are either in the colonial style, like the Casa Romário Martins at no. 30, or neoclassical, dating mostly from the 18th and 19th centuries. The IGREJA DA ORDEM TERCEIRA DE SÃO FRANCISCO DAS CHAGAS, built in 1737 and restored in 1880 and 1978, is the focal point. The best day to come here is Sunday, when the square is filled with the colorful stalls of the Feirinha de Artesanato, a market selling antiques and local produce.

RUA DAS FLORES. To get to this road, also known as Avenida Luiz Xavier, from Largo da Ordem, walk through the pedestrianized area to Praça Tiradentes and the CATEDRAL BASÍLICA MENOR, built between 1876 and 1893 in the neo-Gothic style. From here follow Rua Garcez, which leads to Praça Generoso Marques and the MUSEU PARANAENSE, housed in an Art Nouveau building. The many documents and objects in the museum's collection relate to the archeology, ethnology and history of Paraná (Caingang and Guaraní Indians, *yerba mate*, the Portuguese presence). You will then come to the pedestrianized Rua das Flores, the main shopping street. Visit the Boca Maldita, a platform for political demonstrations, the reciting of poetry and a meeting place for debate, rumour, politics and soccer. Curitiba's merit lies in its unusual and effective urban planning rather than in its architecture. It also serves as a

POTY LAZZAROTO (1924–98)
Some of Curitiba's streets, such as the Travessa Nestor de Castro, near Largo da Ordem, are decorated with unusual paintings and frescos by Poty Lazzaroto, a book illustrator native to Paraná. His work was keenly sought by Brazilian publishers and he was particularly famous for illustrating the works of Jorge Amado, Guimarães Rosa, Gilberto Freyre and Graciliano Ramos.

point of departure for some sites of great natural beauty, such as the Campos Gerais and the Serra do Mar.

The Campos Gerais

This extensive plateau, lying at an altitude of over 3,000 feet, consists of fallow land and araucaria forest. It also has some fantastic rock formations.

Parque Estadual de Vila Velha. This state park, accessible on BR376 toward Ponta Grossa, lies 52 miles from Curitiba. It contains twenty two extraordinary rock formations dating from the Carboniferous period (300 million years ago). These

sandstone pillars, sculpted by rain and wind, are named for their suggestive shapes, such as Taça (cup), Camelo (camel), the Esfinge (sphinx) and Bota (boot). Allow two hours to walk round these formations, following the park's marked footpaths. The Furnas (caverns), also known as the Devil's Cauldrons, are another of the park's attractions. These three enormous chasms are about 330 feet deep and are half-filled with water. An elevator inside one of them takes visitors down to a point just above the lake.

Castro. This town, 42 miles from Vila Velha, was once a *tropeiro* stopping place. The parish church, the Matriz Santana do Iapó, built in 1750, contains a baroque altar and some superb stained-glass windows and ornaments. The Museu do Tropeiro, in an 18th-century building, exhibits old maps and saddles, clothes and other everyday items used by the *tropeiros*.

Cânion de Guartela
The Iapó river flows through this enormous fault, regarded as the sixth-largest canyon in the world. It is on highway PR340, 28 miles from Castro in the direction of Tibagi. The region has many waterfalls and caves with rock paintings. The largest waterfall is that of the Rio Lageado do Pedregulho, which is 656 feet high.

City of stone
In the mythology of the Caingang, American Indians who live in what is now the state of Paraná, along with the Guaraní, the eroded stones of Vila Velha are the remains of an ancient warrior city. To these American Indians Vila Velha is known as Itacueretaba, which literally means 'Vanished City of Stone'.

The tasty pine nut
The Caingang regarded the *pinhão* (pine nut) as the tastiest of all fruit. The taste for *pinhões* was acquired by the *Paranaenses* (inhabitants of Paraná), and *pinhões* on sale in Curitiba's markets or on stalls in the squares are a common sight. While the American Indians would roast them in embers (*sapecada*), the Paranaenses and the people of the South mostly prefer them boiled.

'BARREADO'
The origin of this *Paranaense* dish dates back to the period of the *entrudo*, the old Portuguese carnival ● *46*. It is prepared in a clay *barreado*, a casserole dish, and the lid is sealed with pastry made of cassava flour. In this way, the pieces of beef cook in their own juices for a long time and become very tender. The recipe includes tomatoes and spices and the dish is served with bananas, oranges, white rice and cassava flour.

THE SERRA DO MAR AND THE COAST

★ **THE CURITIBA-PARANGUÁ RAILROAD.** The best way to reach the coast from Curitiba is to take the Curitiba-Paranguá train. This railroad, a feat of engineering dating from 1880, runs through Brazil's dense Atlantic forest ▲ *172*. On its 70-mile journey the train passes through thirteen tunnels carved through solid rock and crosses forty one bridges spanning abysses and foaming rivers. The view from the carriage windows is breathtaking and you will see a variety of trees in the tropical forest, including *sapucaias*, green ebony, jacarandas and *guapiruvus*. Tiny brightly-colored flowers, like the *marias-sem-vergonha*, cover the damp surface of the rocks. The first stop, Marumbi, is the entrance to the Parque Estadual do Marumbi, a favorite destination for climbers and hikers in Paraná. For walking enthusiasts, the park has three marked paths leading to Monte Olimpo, whose peak, as 5,076 feet, commands a spectacular all-round view of the Serra do Mar. The second stop is the colonial town of Morretes, 37 miles further on, founded in 1721 and famous for its banana brandy and the regional dish, *barreado*. From Morretes, you can visit the small colonial village of Porto de Cima, where you can enjoy beautiful riverside walks along the Nhundiaquara and Antonina. Founded in 1721, this was once a trading port from which bananas and *yerba maté* ▲ *232* were exported. It is now in ruins.

PARANAGUÁ. This town, the last stop on the line, was founded in 1549 and is the oldest town in the South. Although it is now one of Brazil's busiest ports, Paranguá still has the tranquil atmosphere of a provincial town, the façade of old villas lazily reflected in the still waters of the Itiberé (*below*). The historic center, which is currently undergoing restoration, has some refreshingly plain churches, with none of the customary exuberance of Brazil's baroque churches. The cathedral of Nossa Senhora do Rosário, completed in 1578, is the oldest. The church of

TRAIN RIDE ★
The spectacularly scenic train ride through the Serra do Mar and the Atlantic forest departs from Curitiba at 8am and 9am from the railroad station, the Estação Rodoferroviária, at Avenida Presidente Alfonso Camargo 330. The trip from Curitiba to Paranguá takes four hours. Return journeys are by bus or by train departing at 3pm and 4pm.

São Benedito, built by a slave brotherhood in 1784, is another fine architectural ensemble. The former Colégio dos Jesuitas, completed in1752, is now the MUSEU DE ARQUEOLOGIA E ETNOLOGIA. The museum contains pieces collected from the region's *sambaquis* ● 22, examples of primitive and folk art as well as tools, implements and machinery for making flour and *cachaça*, as well as baskets and other everyday items. Various other traditional techniques, particularly those used in fishing, are also illustrated.

ILHA DO MEL AND GUARAQUEÇABA

✪ **ILHA DO MEL.** Boat trips to the Ilha do Mel depart from the quayside, in the center of Paranguá. This island, off Paranguá Bay, is a nature reserve with beautiful beaches and rustic *pousadas*. It also has historic buildings such as the Fortaleza de Nossa Senhora dos Prazeres, built between 1767 and 1779 by the Portuguese to protect the bay and the port from the Spanish. It was completely restored in 1995. Four miles from the fortress stands the Farol das Conchas. This lighthouse, opened in 1872, offers a breathtaking view of this beautiful island.

GUARAQUEÇABA. From Paranguá this attractive fishing village can be reached by boat in 1½ hours. Its beaches are almost deserted and it has relatively plain houses built in the Portuguese colonial style. Surrounded by the Atlantic forest, Guaraqueçaba is the guardian of one of Brazil's most important natural environments. The village is the base for visits to the PARQUE NACIONAL DE SUPERAGÜI, whose flora and fauna remain virtually intact. The national park is part of the Lagamar estuary, which is formed by the confluence of fourteen rivers flowing down from the Serra do Mar toward the Atlantic Ocean. The estuary continues as far as the south coast of São Paulo state, thus supporting one of the largest mangrove forests in Brazil. The 53,000-acre park comprises two islands, Superagüi and Peças. It is a sanctuary for many endangered species, including the *mico-leão-de cara-preta* (black-faced lion tamarin), and includes one of the best-preserved expanses of Atlantic forest. The park is also home to a wide variety of birds, and many plants such as bromeliads (plants of the pineapple family) and orchids grow there.

ILHA DO MEL, LAND OF HONEY ★
The Ilha do Mel, Honey Island, acquired its name in the 17th century, when swarms of bees built nests in the hollows of trees, particularly on the more sheltered southern side of the island. No vehicles or draft animals are allowed on this island. It can be reached from Paranguá and can be seen by boat or explored on foot, along paths running through the forest.

AZURE JAY
This colorful bird, the emblem of Paraná, is one of the most common species in araucaria forests. According to popular legend, the bird received its blue plumage from God because it had helped Him to sow pines by burying the kernels in the forest floor.

△ Paraná The Iguaçu falls

Iguaçu, 'Great Water'

In the far western side of Paraná, 390 miles from Curitiba, lies the remarkable PARQUE NACIONAL DO IGUAÇU. Comprising 460,000 acres of unspoiled rainforest, this national park forms part of the forest that less than fifty years ago covered almost the entire state of Paraná. The most impressive feature of this reserve is its famous waterfalls. There are 275, some as high as 260 feet, and they extend for a distance of 1½ miles. These are the cataracts of the Iguaçu, the river whose name in Caingang means Great Water, *ig* meaning 'water' and *açu* meaning 'great'. The source of the Iguaçu lies near Curitiba, at an altitude of 2,950 feet. Flowing right across the state of Paraná, the waters thunder over the cataracts, then join the Paraná. FOZ DO IGUAÇU, the town nearest the falls, lies at the geographical center of the La Plata basin, on the border between Argentina and Paraguay.

✪ **THE FALLS.** These falls straddle the border between Brazil and Argentina. Of the nineteen large falls, three (Floriano, Deodoro and Benjamin Constant) are on the Brazilian side and sixteen (including Santa María, Dos Hermanos, San Martin, Adán y Eva, Bosetti, Véu de Noiva and Garganta do Diabo) are on the Argentinian side. The best views of the falls are from the Brazilian side. The scenic riverside path leading to the cataracts cuts through stretches of forest and past basalt rocks. The highlight of this walk is the point at which you cross the walkways leading to the edge of the falls. With airborne water droplets creating colorful rainbows, the humidity here is such that it is impossible to stay dry. The Argentinian side offers views of the spectacular Garganta do Diabo (Devil's Throat), where the water thunders down from a height of 2,700 feet at a rate of some 390,000 cubic feet per second. You can reach the Garganta do Diabo by crossing walkways above the river in the national park on the

THE LEGEND OF IGUAÇU

The Guaraní explain the origin of the cataracts with a legend. Naipi was a woman of such radiant beauty that the waters of the Iguaçu stopped when she looked in them to admire herself. For this reason, she was given to M'Boi, the serpent-god. But the warrior Tarobá, who was in love with her, carried her off. In his wrath M'Boi ripped open the earth, creating the gorge that formed the cataracts. Naipi became a rock at the foot of the falls and Tarobá was turned into a palm tree. Although he can gaze upon his love, he cannot touch her.

Argentinian side. On the Brazilian side the Macuco Safári offers thrill-seekers the opportunity of a dramatic view of the cataracts from the river itself: an inflatable boat holding twenty five people is driven against the current up toward the Garganta do Diabo.

Parque Nacional do Iguaçu. The entrance to the park is at the end of the Rodovia das Cataratas. This reserve has a particularly rich fauna, with over three hundred species of birds, including green woodpeckers, birds of prey, toucans and egrets; forty four species of mammals, including tapirs, capybaras, otters and jaguars; and over 1,400 species of butterfly. However, only a few of the park's paths are open to the public. Hikers wishing to explore its flora and fauna more thoroughly should obtain permission from the Brazilian Institute of the Environment (Ibama), which is located in the park. For those interested in ornithology the Ilha do Sol agency organizes photographic and birdwatching safaris led by specialist guides. Although the best time to see the falls in Brazil is the summer, each season has a special advantage. In spring, from September through November, the tropical forest is filled with brightly colored flowers, particularly orchids, you can see a greater variety of birds, and it is the time when *piracema* (large schools of fish traveling upstream to spawn) can be observed in the rivers. Spring is also the season when the forest and its rivers seem to explode with life.

The Itaipu dam

The Itaipu dam lies 12 miles from Foz do Iguaçu. This artificial lake, 124 miles long and about 4 miles wide, is one of the largest in the world. Harnessing the power of the water, its hydroelectric installations are large enough to provide enough power for the whole of Paraguay and southern Brazil. The lake is also excellent for watersports and for rewarding fishing trips.

A bad ecological record

The park constitutes no more than one percent of the forest that once covered the state of Paraná. Of all Brazilian states, this one has suffered one of the fastest rates of deforestation. From 1963 to 1973, 60 percent of its forests were cleared for agriculture or timber.

The Iguaçu falls ✪

The best time to visit the Iguaçu falls is between December and February. During this period the rains are not so heavy and the cataracts are in full flow, the average rate of flow increases from 353,000 cubic feet a second to over 1,000,000 cubic feet. Although the best view of the falls is from the Brazilian rather the Argentinian side, the one-hour walk organized by Macuco Safári, as well as helicopter flights above the falls, are also highly recommended.

WITCHES
On nights when there is a full moon, old women of Azorean descent, who speak with a strong Portuguese accent, close their doors and windows earlier than usual and recite prayers while scattering cloves of garlic all over their houses. This is a precaution against the depradations of witches who on these nights, according to popular belief, go in search of small children for their macabre rituals. The witches of Santa Catarina island, and other legends, have been immortalized by the writer Franklin Cascaes.

HERCÍLIO LUZ BRIDGE
This 2,700-foot long suspension bridge, with its iron frame and two 245-foot high towers, was featured on the town's first postcard. It was opened in 1926 and for many years provided the main link between the island and the mainland. Now in a bad state of repair, it is open only to pedestrians.

Florianópolis, capital of the state of Santa Catarina, is located on the island of Santa Catarina, less than a mile from the mainland. As well as having 42 beaches, the city is surrounded by mountains, dunes and mangroves. While the northern part of the island is more modern and more geared to tourism, its southern and western parts have retained closer links with the past. The cattle farms, mills, stills and colonial residences conjure up the age of the settlers whom the Portuguese brought from the Azores in the 18th century to occupy land coveted by the Spanish crown. Santa Catarina, known locally as Magic Island because of an Azorean legend, is a Brazilian mecca for outdoor sports such as hang gliding, climbing, hiking and most particularly surfing.

HISTORY

When Brazil was discovered, the island of Santa Catarina was inhabited by the Carijó American Indians, who knew it as Meyembipe, meaning Coastal Island. Its development dates from the 16th century, when it was inhabited mainly by shipwrecked sailors and by smugglers of contraband timber. It was not until 1726, with the arrival of the *bandeirante* Francisco Dias Velho, that the town was officially founded, and named Nossa Senhora do Desterro. At this point the American Indians were either enslaved or exterminated. The island's distinctive culture took root with the arrival of over 5,000 Azoreans in 1748. Desterro, then still a small town, grew into the capital of Santa Catarina. It was renamed Florianópolis in 1895 in honor of the first Brazilian president, Floriano Peixoto. The city now has 300,000 inhabitants.

CENTRAL FLORIANÓPOLIS

With narrow streets and old buildings, central Florianópolis has great historical and architectural interest.
THE OLD QUAYS. The Mercado Público, a covered market built in 1898, stands on Avenida Paulo Fontes, which runs along the waterfront. Stroll through it and feast you eyes on the freshly caught fish, then stop at stall 32 for some delicious *bolinhos de bacalhau* (small cod fritters). Nearby is the former Alfândega (customs house), built in 1875.
PRAÇA 15 DE NOVEMBRO. This square, opposite the market, lies at the heart of the colonial town. The 100-year-old fig tree that grows in the square is a focal point for sellers of local handicrafts, who lay out there wares around it. The square is dominated by the CATEDRAL METROPOLITANA, built in 1773 and remodeled in the 20th century. It stands on the site of a chapel built by Dias Velho and dedicated to Nossa Senhora

do Desterro. Next to it is the magnificent PALÁCIO CRUZ E SOUZA, built in the 18th century and completely restored. This palace, once the governor's residence, is a blend of baroque and neoclassical styles, and it has some highly elaborate ceilings. It now houses the Museu Histórico de Santa Catarina, in which works of art and furniture acquired by various governors of Santa Catarina state are displayed.

PONTE HERCÍLIO LUZ. Boat trips to the Ilha de Anhatomirim leave from this bridge. On the island stands the Fortaleza de Santa Cruz, a fortress built between 1739 and 1744 to defend the town against the Spanish, then used as a prison in the 19th century. The island's other main attraction is the Baía dos Golfinhos (Dolphin Bay), a haven for over 500 dolphins.

THE ISLAND'S EAST COAST

LAGOA DA CONCEIÇÃO. This lagoon lies in the eastern part of the island, six miles from the center. The Estrada Geral da Lagoa, the road leading to it, climbs to a hilltop with a view of the lagoon, the dunes and the ocean. As it winds down the other side of the hill the road offers many opportunities to admire the spectacular landscape that spreads out below.

PRAIA DA JOAQUINA. There are several good restaurants and bars on AVENIDA DAS RENDEIRAS, which runs alongside the lagoon. The road leads to the fishing village of BARRA DA LAGOA, which has a huge sweeping beach, to the Praia da Joaquina. This beach, nine miles from the center and very crowded in summer, is famous because the national surfing championships are held here. The dunes at Joaquina are particularly good for sandboarding (dune surfing).

PRAIAS MOLE E GALHETA. Further north are two beautiful sandy beaches: the Praia Mole, two miles from the lagoon along the Estrada Geral da Barra (11 miles from the center); and its continuation, the unspoiled Praia de Galheta, which is popular with nudists.

THE ISLAND'S SOUTH COAST

The remoter beaches on the south side of the island are exceptionally beautiful.

MORRO DAS PEDRAS. Watch the waves lashing the rocks from the top of this hill, 12 miles from the center along the Antiga Estrada Velha. The beach and fishing village of ARMAÇÃO are two miles away. Take a boat tour to the ILHA DO CAMPECHE, whose rocky north coast has several American Indian rock carvings. Further inland, behind the Praia da Armação, extends the Lagoa do Peri, the only freshwater lagoon on the island and a haven for many plants.

FISHING
Having made improvements to the *pirogues* used by the Carijó American Indians, the Azoreans turned to the sea as their primary means of subsistence. In some fishing villages, such as Armação or Barra da Lagoa, the boats set out to sea before dawn every day. Other fishermen prefer river mouths, where they fish with the *tarrafa* (a type of trammel net). Between May and July you can watch fishermen trying to catch whole schools of mullet, often bringing in enough fish to last a whole year.

SURFING
Florianópolitanos love surfing. A soapstone statue ● *191* in honor of surfers has been erected on Mole Beach, a soft sand beach that is particularly suitable for the sport.

Pântano do Sul. The beach is 2½ miles from Armação, and a group of fishermen here supply the island with shrimps and fish such as mullet. From here, it is about an hour's walk along the footpath to Lagoinha do Leste, the island's wildest and most unspoiled beach.

The island's west coast

The western part of Santa Catarina island has a succession of tranquil bays and a population of Azorean descent.

Ribeirão da Ilha. This old colonial town in the southwest of the island lies 18 miles from the center and is reached by the Estrada Geral do Ribeirão da Ilha. The town has the highest concentration of Azoreans on the island, and colonial buildings survive here. A path from the Caieiras da Barra do Sul, nine miles from here, leads to the Praia dos Naufragados, an unspoiled beach near which are two rusting cannons.

Santo Antônio de Lisboa. The beaches of Santo Antônio de Lisboa and Sambaqui are in the northwest of the island, six miles from the center on the Caminho dos Açores. Although the sea here is calm it is unsuitable for bathing. Sambaqui has some pretty Azorean houses and various Azorean folk dances and traditions survive.

The island's north coast

Estrada Geral do Norte da Ilha. This road leads to the narrow, fairly crowded beaches of Jureré (15 miles from the center), Canavieiras (17 miles) and Ingleses (20 miles), which are particularly popular with Argentinians. The sea here is warm, clear and calm. The ruins of the Fortaleza de São José da Ponta Grossa are little more than a mile away. This hilltop fort was built in 1740 between the cliffs and the white sand of the Praia do Forte. The beaches of Brava, 22 miles from the center on the Estrada Geral da Ponta das Canas, and Santinho, 24 miles from the center on Estrada D. João Becker, are less crowded although the sea here is rough and bathing dangerous.

The state's southern coastline

With surfboards and teams of oxen, asphalt and mills the southern coastline of the state of Santa Catarina is both modern and traditional. It also has beautiful beaches, and this mixture of attractions draws thousands of tourists to the region every year. In September and October its southern coast is also a migratory route for right whales.

Beaches around Garopaba. The lovely beaches around this coastal town (60 miles from Florianópolis on highway BR101 then SC169) are a good place to watch fishermen at work. Particularly worth visiting are the unspoiled beaches of Silveira (2 miles from the center), Ferrugem (5 miles), Siriú (7 miles) and Rosa (10 miles). At Guarda do Embaú (22 miles northward along highway BR101) are a beach, a river, dunes, a stretch of *mata atlântica* ▲ *166, 172* and a hamlet.

Azorean architecture
Buildings in the Azorean style can still be seen in the narrow streets of certain parts of Santa Catarina. The closely packed houses have large windows and walls faced with clay. Ribeirão da Ilha has some fine examples of Azorean architecture, which is also seen in baroque churches. The mortar used is made of whale oil, sand and clay.

Folk traditions
The island and state of Santa Catarina were strongly marked by the arrival of immigrants from the Azores, Italy and Germany, each of whom brought their own distinctive cultures. This legacy lives on both in festivals and in everyday life. Azorean folk traditions include *boi-de-mamão*, a kind of bull worship still practiced by the islanders. Until the early 1980s this included a bullfight in which the crowd played the part of the bullfighter. Another popular tradition is the *pau-de-fita*, a ceremonial dance performed around a tall pole hung with colored ribbons that circling dancers weave into patterns.

Central São Francisco do Sul
There are many well-preserved colonial buildings in São Francisco do Sul's historic center, the Centro Histórico, particularly in Rua Babitonga, Rua Fernandes Dias, Rua Reinoldo Tavares, Rua Floriano Peixoto and Rua Lauro Müller. Built in 1699, the Matriz Nossa Senhora da Graça (*left*) on Praça Getúlio Vargas still has its original walls, which are faced with mortar made of whale oil, sand and shell lime.

Laguna. Further south, 77 miles from Florianópolis, is the small fishing town of Laguna, which is flanked by beaches. The town's historic center has several colonial buildings. The Casa Anita Garibaldi, on Praça República Juliana, is a museum in which the personal belongings of Garibaldi's Brazilian wife are displayed. From Laguna you can catch a ferry to the Farol de Santa Marta ★.

Farol de Santa Marta ★
A ten-minute ferry ride from Laguna takes you to the Farol de Santa Marta, a working lighthouse built by the French in 1891. It overlooks an expanse of dunes and deserted beaches. Here dolphins can often be seen frolicking among surfers and fishing boats.

The state's northern coastline

Costa Dourada. Santa Catarina's 'gold coast', marred only by the skyscrapers in the coastal resorts of Itapema and Camboriú (respectively 41 and 50 miles from Florianópolis on highway BR101) also has some deserted beaches. They are around Porto Belo (41 miles from Florianópolis on highway BR101, then four miles on SC412) and Bombinhas (four miles from Porto Belo). These sheltered beaches with calm waters can be reached by footpaths. Bombinhas is one of the best diving centers in southern Brazil. You can take a boat to the Reserva Biológica do Arvoredo, a marine park consisting of three islands that is a paradise of biodiversity.
São Francisco do Sul. This island (140 miles from Florianópolis on highways BR101 and BR280) was discovered by the French in 1504. The town, the oldest in the state, was not founded until the 17th century. The lives of its 30,000 inhabitants are ruled by the sea. Several boathouses line the natural harbor, including one housing the Museu Nacional do Mar. The island's coastline is also dotted with *sambaquis* ● *22*. The most popular tourist beaches are Itaguaçú (9 miles from the town), Ubatuba (10 miles) and Enseada (11 miles). Surfers prefer Prainha (12 miles away) and Praia Grande (13 miles). The latter is a huge deserted beach with dunes.

National museum of the Sea
The collection of boats in this museum is the only one of its kind in Brazil. A large number of boats from all regions of Brazil are displayed and the history of whalers from the Azores is documented. The star exhibit is *Paraty I*, the rowing boat in which Amyr Klink, a Brazilian, crossed the Atlantic Ocean.

RIO GUAÍBA
The town is partly bounded by this river, whose waters are flecked with red at sunset. Before it was embanked, the river reached up as far as Rua dos Andradas, popularly known as Rua da Praia (Beach Street). To explore the river's islands take a trip in one of the boats tied up next to the Usina do Gasômetro, a disused thermoelectric plant dating from 1927 that is now used as an arts center.

The Portuguese crown founded the town of Porto Alegre for the purpose of stopping the invading Spanish from colonizing southern Brazil. The town's first inhabitants, sixty Portuguese couples brought from the Azores, arrived in 1752. Thanks to its diverse economy and the river port from which it derives its name, Porto Alegre has become a flourishing business center, also having the advantage of geographical proximity to the Mercosul countries ● *27*. The town also has its lively nightlife and is a dynamic center of culture.

PRAÇA 15 DE NOVEMBRO. A good place to start your exploration of Porto Alegre is the MERCADO PÚBLICO (Metro Mercado Modelo), a neoclassical building dating from 1869 where fresh fish, local produce such as *yerba maté* and utensils for preparing *chimarrão* ▲ *247* are on sale. Next to the market is the PAÇO MUNICIPAL (town hall), built in 1901 and adorned with fine sculptures. Opposite is the Talavera de la Reina fountain, covered with *azulejos* and ceramics.

PRAÇA DA ALFÂNDEGA. At the junction with Avenida Borges de Medeiros turn right into Rua da Praia, a pedestrianized street with stores and street vendors, and you will come to this square, where the Book Fair is held each October. In the square is the MUSEU DE ARTES DO RIO GRANDE DO SUL, an eclectic building of Germanic influence, built in 1913, mainly devoted to works by gaucho artists. Also of note here are the former Correios e Telégrafos (Post and Telegraph Office) in the German baroque style, the Banco Meridional, the Banco Safra, the Imperial cinema and the neoclassical Clube do Comércio.

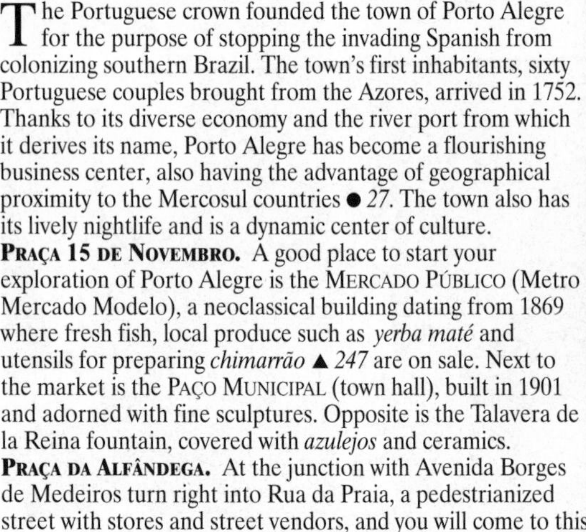

RUA GENERAL CÂMARA. From the corner of Praça da Alfândega this steep road, popularly known as Rua da Ladeira, leads to the BIBLIOTECA PÚBLICA, the public library (1871), then on to Praça Marechal Deodoro, where stands the imposing CATEDRAL METROPOLITANA (*left*), built in 1921, with a dome similar to that of St Peter's in Rome. Also in this square are the PALÁCIO PIRATINI (1909), in the French neoclassical style and containing magnificent frescos by the Italian artist Aldo Locatelli, and the TEATRO SÃO PEDRO (1858) with its combination of neoclassical and Portuguese baroque styles.

RUA DUQUE DE CAXIAS. At no. 968 on this street, next to the square, is the SOLAR DOS CÂMARA (1818). This former residence is now an arts center but the building's period furniture has been preserved. Nos. 1205 to 1231 house the MUSEU JÚLIO DE CASTILHOS.

RUA DOS ANDRADAS. Walk back down Rua General Câmara and turn left into this street. At no. 736 is the CASA DE CULTURA MÁRIO QUINTANA (1910–23). Once a hotel and the home of the gaucho poet Mário Quintana (1906–94), this eight-story building with elaborate eaves, balconies and arches and an elegant walkway linking the wings now accommodates a large arts center. The Café Concerto in the dome has a terrace with a splendid view of the town. Not far from here stands the IGREJA DAS DORES (1830–1906). This church combines both baroque and rococo styles.

MUSEU JÚLIO DE CASTILHOS
The museum is housed in a residence dating from 1887, that was the home of President Júlio de Castilhos, the most important gaucho political leader of the late 19th century. It contains documents and objects relating to the history of the state of Rio Grande do Sul, and most particularly that of the gauchos ▲ *246*, the Guaraní and the Jesuit missions ● *66* ▲ *248*.

ITAIMBEZINHO ★
This canyon stretches for nearly four miles and its sheer rockfaces descend to a depth of 2,320 feet. The enormous faults and crevices that score the undulating plain were created by the movement of tectonic plates, which occurred 130 million to 115 million years ago. As rivers feed the many waterfalls here, the canyon is continually being eroded and deepened. Both the canyon itself and the Parque Nacional dos Aparados da Serra, the national park in which it is located, can only be visited with a guide.

As you leave Porto Alegre on highway BR116 heading toward the Serra Gaúcha, you will notice that the landscape changes completely. Winding along the edge of precipices, the road leads up to the Região das Hortênsias (Hydrangea Region), which lies at an altitude of some 3,280 feet. It was first settled by Germans, in 1824. Along the way there are spectacular views of valleys and mountains and of the greenish-blue landscape of the Serra Atlantica.

GRAMADO. This tourist town, 83 miles from Porto Alegre, is the state's busiest mountain resort. It has several interesting sights: the CASCATA VÉU DE NOIVA, in the town center; the Lago Joaquina Bier, a lake bordered by araucarias; and the Parque Knorr. The BELVEDERE VALE DO QUILOMBO (2,800 feet high) provides a breathtaking view of the mountains and valleys. Besides the chocolate and hydrangea festivals, traditional events here include a film festival held in the Festival Palace in August, which attracts South American and European movie stars and directors.

CANELA. This town, five miles from Gramado on Highway RS235 (or Avenida das Hortênsias), is an excellent base for ecotourism. Two miles from the town center you will come to the PARQUE DO PINHEIRO GROSSO, founded to protect a 700-year-old araucaria ▲ *233*, which is almost 140 feet high and nine feet in diameter. The most famous natural site in the area is the CASCATA DO CARACOL, two miles from the park. This 430-foot-high waterfall, in the Parque Estadual do Caracol, attracts over 450,000 visitors per year. Four miles further on a dirt track leads to the PARQUE DA FERRADURA. The park, which offers stunning views, contains a horseshoe-shaped canyon, 1,300 feet deep and very popular with rock climbers.

PARQUE NACIONAL DOS APARADOS DA SERRA. This park, 87 miles from Canela via São Francisco de Paula, stretches across Rio Grande do Sul's coolest region, bordered by the towns of Cambará and Praia Grande. The park contains one of Brazil's natural wonders: the CÂNION DO ITAIMBEZINHO ★, the largest canyon in South America. The park, which must be visited with a guide, also has an extensive area of araucaria forest and a wide variety of animals, including maned wolves, cougars, squirrels, agoutis, king vultures and the azure jay.

COLONIAL BREAKFAST
This meal, brought to the region by German immigrants, is served in almost all the hotels, tearooms and restaurants in Gramado and Canela. It is so copious that you can easily skip lunch. It consists of many different kinds of food, including pastries, bread, cheese, cooked meats, *pastéis* (savory fritters), honey, butter and ham. This feast is served with an assortment of fruit juices, teas, coffee, milk and hot chocolate.

During the colonial period there were very few white men in what is the state of Rio Grande do Sul. While the population of white settlers was concentrated in villages on the coast and around Porto Alegre, the rest of the territory, a vast expanse of land, was inhabited by wild cattle. Portugal and Spain fought bitterly over this region and in the ensuing wars and skirmishes a distinctive group of men, the gauchos, won renown. The gauchos, who lived on the pampas, were of mixed Portuguese, Spanish and American Indian descent. They hunted down herds of livestock on horseback, then sold the hides. The *farroupilha* revolution changed the gauchos' way of life. With the arrival of landowners, cattle were penned in enclosures and the nomadic, intractable gauchos became cowherds on the large *fazendas*.

MOVIMENTO TRADICIONALISTA GAÚCHO

The Movimento Tradicionalista Gaúcho (MTG) was founded in 1947 in Porto Alegre to preserve the ways, customs and culture of the gauchos of Rio Grande do Sul. The organization is represented by over 1,500 Centros da Tradicão Gaúcho (CTG) both in Brazil and in Japan, Portugal and the United States. These centers help to preserve and disseminate the poetry, language, music and dances of the gauchos. Members wear traditional gaucho clothes: long dresses for women, and the *pilcha* for men. This is an outfit consisting of baggy trousers, a hat with a woven chinstrap, a linen shirt and a red scarf knotted around the neck. In winter both gaucho men and women wear a fringed poncho or *pala*. The best-known CTG is in Porto Alegre: CTG 35 at Avenida Ipiranga 5200. The center, which is open daily, serves *churrasco* 'in *rodízio*', meaning as much as you can eat. Performances of gaucho music and dance also take place there.

THE 'FARROUPILHA' REVOLUTION OR THE WAR OF THE FARRAPOS (1835–45)

The war of the *farrapos*, the 'ragged ones', as the radical liberals who dreamed of establishing a republic were known, was waged by the gauchos against the imperial government. The latter was accused of draining the profits made from the province's economic activities and of hindering its growth. For ten years many battles were fought in Rio Grande do Sul. A peace treaty signed in 1845 ensured that the state was accorded its rightful status within the empire ● 25.

'CHIMARRÃO'

This strong, bitter drink ▲ 232, which originated with the Guaraní American Indians, is made with the leaves of *Ilex paraguariensis*, or *yerba maté*. The leaves are roasted then pulverized. The powder is poured into a gourd (*far right*) and hot water is added. The *chimarrão* is drunk through a metal tube (*right*) with a wide base pierced with tiny holes that filter the infusion. The traditional way of drinking *chimarrão* is in a *roda de chimarrão* (*chimarrão* circle) where the gourd is passed round from hand to hand. This drink helps the gauchos to withstand the biting cold of winter on the pampas and also symbolizes fraternity and hospitality.

'CHURRASCO'

This is a barbecue of beef or mutton seasoned only with cooking salt. The meat is threaded onto long wooden-handled skewers and cooked over the embers of a fire. The most authentic way of preparing *churrasco* is by cooking it over a gaucho-style campfire on the ground. *Churrasco* is most commonly served with *arroz de carreteiro* (rice), with *charque* (dried, salted and jerked beef) and with well-seasoned *feijões tropeiros* (black beans mixed with cassava flour or corn flour and garnished with fried sausage and lardons).

RURAL TOURISM

Cattle farms supporting rural tourism (*left*) exist right across the state. These *fazendas* give visitors an insight into the lifestyle of the gauchos and allow them to watch the work involved in breeding livestock and breaking horses. You can also explore the valleys and pampas on horseback or go hiking. Many places offer this type of tourism, including the area around Lavras do Sul, about 200 miles from Porto Alegre (on highways BR290, BR392 then BR153). Lavras do Sul is the only gold-mining town in Rio Grande do Sul. The town is surrounded by extensive plains and stands on the edge of the pampas, which stretch away southward all the way to the border with Uruguay.

'CANGACEIROS'
The bandits of the *sertão* are often the heroes of tales in *literatura de cordel* ● *54*. Depictions of *canganceiros*, as wooden statues or in reliefs (*right*), are also an inspiration for the craftsmen of the *sertão*. *Canganceiros* live on in movies and *telenovelas* ● *60*.

The *sertão*, the dry region in the interior of the Nordeste, is the only semiarid zone in Brazil. It is also the birthplace of a unique, noble and tough culture. From among the mounted *vaqueiros* who worked for wealthy cattle ranchers and the poverty-stricken peasants who struggled to survive between periods of drought, came *cangaceiros*, honorable bandits whose exploits are glorified in Brazil's popular verse narratives, the *literatura de cordel*. Thanks to the construction of dams and widespread irrigation, this barren region has changed considerably, and metalled roads now provide easy access to the coast. However, the *sertão* is still Brazil's poorest region and its inhabitants continue to leave in search of illusory riches in the towns or in Amazonia.

THE SÃO FRANCISCO RIVER

The São Francisco river (*above*) is affectionately known to Brazilians as *Velho Chico* (Old Chico), Chico being a diminutive of Francisco. It flows through the arid region of the Nordeste. The river has long been an important channel of communication and navigation route between the Nordeste and Minas Gerais, so that it has been dubbed the 'river of national unity'. Great paddle steamers once plyed the river between the towns of Pirapora, in Minas Gerais, and Petrolina, in Pernambuco, on the border with the state of Bahia. Although the construction of a series of dams has threatened the future of these boats, the river now has other assets, the greatest of which is the irrigation that it provides. The water now held back by the dams is used to irrigate the land on either side of river. This has made it possible to cultivate grapes, which are now exported throughout Brazil. Most of the mangos grown in Brazil for export to other countries also come from this river valley.

A SEMIARID REGION

The only semiarid region in Brazil, the *sertão* supports plants and animals that are particularly well suited to these waterless conditions. Vegetation, in the form of *caatinga* ● *18*, includes many thorny bushes and cacti. This is why the region's *vaqueiros* need to protect themselves by wearing thick clothes and leather hats. Several of the animals of the *sertão* are emblematic of this region. They include the *tatu* (armadillo) and the *caracará*, a bird of prey that is swift, hardy and brave, just like the *sertão*'s human inhabitants. During times of relative plenty in this unusual habitat, the people of the *sertão* enjoy a balanced staple diet. But during periods of drought they must survive by seeking out more unusual sources of nourishment. Although a shower is all that is needed to make the *caatinga* burst into flower, the food-producing plants die. This is known as a 'green drought' because, despite the lush landscape, the peasants face famine unless they can find roots and herbs to eat, and even these are not very nutritious.

CANUDOS
The church of Canudos (*right*) was submerged when a dam was built. It reappears only when water levels are reduced by severe drought. Canudos, in the northern part of the state of Bahia, was the base of a great millennarian rebellion led by Antônio Macial, a prophet known as O Conselheiro (The Counselor). In the late 19th century he mobilized 20,000 to 30,000 people but the Brazilian republican government ● *25* sent several military expeditions to put a end to his activities.

'FEIRA' AND 'VAQUEIROS'
The *feiras* (fairs) of the *sertão* attract crowds of *vaqueiros*, the Brazilian (and Nordestino) equivalent of cowboys. Paid by wealthy cattle ranchers either in cash or in kind (at the rate of one calf in four), they come to town with their herds, keen to spend their well-earned though meager *reais* (*left*). These *feiras* led to the establishment of settlements that evolved into large towns, some retaining the word *feira* in their name. An example is Feira de Santana, in the state of Bahia.

The church of Nossa Senhora do Rosário dos Pretos *(right)*.

THE 'BENÇÃO'
Tuesday is traditionally the day when services are held in the church of São Francisco. In the morning the poor gather on the square fronting the church to receive clothes and food, which are given by members of the congregation. This honors a promise made to St Francis in thanks for a prayer answered. The Pelourinho district of Salvador has been renovated and the façades of the *sobrados* ● 74 repainted *(right)*, and now crowded bar terraces and bands of musicians enliven its squares *(bottom right)*, creating a festive mood on Tuesday evenings.

'PELOURINHO'
The literal meaning of the word *pelourinho* is 'pillory'. This was a whipping post to which slaves were tied and tortured in public. Until 1835 the post stood on Largo do Pelourinho, opposite the slave market building. It can now be seen in the Fundação Casa de Jorge Amado.

MUSEU AFRO-BRASILEIRO
On display here are photographs by Pierre Verger, *orixás* ● 43, African artefacts and a series of panels carved by the painter Carybé. This rich collection reveals the close cultural and religious ties between Bahia and the west coast of Africa.

On November 1, 1501, All Saints Day, the Italian navigator Amerigo Vespucci reached the east coast of Brazil, landing in a bay with a fine natural harbor. To give thanks to the saints and to Christ for a safe voyage that had so happily ended he named the bay São Salvador da Bahia de Todos os Santos. The town of Salvador, founded in 1549 by Tomé de Souza, was the capital of colonial Brazil ● *22* until 1763. It grew rapidly, not only because of the sugar trade but also because of trade in tobacco, cocoa and gold, and its wealth and importance were flaunted by the construction of churches, palaces and monasteries. Salvador was also renowned as the center of slavery in Brazil: hundreds of Africans were imported from the Gulf of Guinea and the coastal regions of Angola. This African heritage palpably lives on in the people, cuisine, music ▲ *273* and religion ● *42* of Salvador. The city is located at the tip of a peninsula, with the bay to the west and the Atlantic to the south. Salvador consists of a *cidade alta* (upper town), built on the cliffs overlooking the bay and Itaparica island, and a *cidade baixa* (lower town). The two towns are linked by the Elevador Lacerda, funicular railways (*planos inclinados*) and steep streets (*ladeiras*).

'Religious city, colonial city, Negro city of Bahia. Sumptuous churches bedecked with gold, wealthy houses decorated with *azulejos*, hovels, poverty-stricken slums, *ladeiras*, historic monuments, old fortresses…'

Jorge Amado

THE COLONIAL CITY

The limits of the Pelourinho district are marked by three squares: Terreiro de Jesus, Largo do Carmo and Largo do Pelourinho.

PRAÇA MUNICIPAL. The square, also known as Praça Tomé de Souza, is flanked by the modern city hall and the Palácio Rio Branco, the governor's palace, which dates from 1549. The square is a good point of departure for exploring the upper town. Take the Elevador Lacerda, then either continue up toward the historic districts of Pelourinho, Carmo and Santo Antônio, or make your way down toward the lower town as far as Barra.

PRAÇA DA SÉ. This new square, opened in 1999, is completely pedestrianized and is an attractive setting for the 17th-century baroque cathedral with a marble façade, wide nave and barrel vaulting. Originally the Jesuit collegiate church, it became a cathedral when the Jesuits were expelled in 1759 ● *28*. On the first Sunday of the month concerts are given in the cathedral by the Salvador baroque choir.

TERREIRO DE JESUS. A fountain of the Goddess of Plenty stands at its center of this esplanade next to Praça da Sé. On the left is the former medical school, founded in 1808 by the future Dom João VI ● *24*. The building houses the Museu de Etnologia e de Arquelogia and the MUSEU AFRO-BRASILEIRO. Just beyond the entrance to the museum stands the rococo church of SÃO PEDRO DOS CLÉRIGOS (1709). The Terreiro de Jesus is continued by Praça Anchieta, also known as Praça da Cruz de São Francisco, on one side of which stands the church and monastery of SÃO FRANCISCO, built in the early 18th century. The church, a masterpiece of baroque and neoclassical colonial architecture, is fronted by two tall bell towers and abundantly decorated with gold and jacaranda. The monastery has a large courtyard whose walls are covered with *azulejos* ● *71* depicting allegories of Virtue, Wealth and Death. Next to the church of São Francisco is the IGREJA DA ORDEM TERCEIRA DE SÃO FRANCISCO (1703), remarkable for its carved pediment of a shape, unique in Brazil, that recalls those on churches in Spanish-speaking Latin America. This church also contains a fine museum of religious art.

★ **THE HEART OF THE PELOURINHO DISTRICT.** Rua Inácio Accioli slopes down toward the colonial district of Pelourinho and Rua Gregório de Matos, where there are three museums: the MUSEU ABELARDO RODRIGUES, which contains an important collection of religious art dating from the 17th, 18th and 19th centuries; the Museu da Cidade, devoted to the history and culture of Salvador; and the Museu Tempostal, which has a collection of 30,000 postcards, many of them of old Salvador. Since the Pelo (as it is popularly known) was renovated, this district of cobbled streets and gaily colored houses has become the hub of Salvador's nightlife. As the sun goes

HISTORIC PELOURINHO ✪
Reached via Praça da Sé, this delightful colonial district with multicolored *sobrados* ● *74* is best explored on foot, either during the day or by night. The Pelourinho district, popularly known as the Pelo, was declared a Unesco World Heritage Site in 1985. Its streets, squares, churches and houses have been gradually renovated since 1992. The churches of São Francisco and of the Ordem Terceira de São Francisco ● *71* are of especial interest.

'ACARAJÉS'
Acarajés are fritters made from kidney bean flour. The Bahian *acarajé* sellers (*below*) prepare a smooth dough, stirring it with a wooden spoon. The fritters are steeped in red palm oil (*dendê* ▲ *252*) for several minutes. They are then cut in half and stuffed with *vatapá* (cream made with soft bread, cashew nuts and *dendê*), a tomato and onion salad, dried shrimps and *caruru*, made from *gombo* and also known as okra.

MONUMENTO DOIS DE JULHO
This monument commemorates Bahia's political independence, which was proclaimed on July 2, 1823. The column, unveiled in 1895, is over 67 feet tall and towers over Campo Grande, a large grassy square which is not only a popular place for a stroll but also the hub of Bahia's carnival festivities ▲ *273*. The column is crowned by a statue of an American Indian killing a serpent with a spear, symbolizing Brazil freeing itself from Portugal ● *24*.

down the district comes alive. Bars and terraces fill with customers, musicians tune up their instruments and *acarajé* sellers take up position at street corners. Rua Alfredo de Brito and Rua Gregório de Matos meet at LARGO DO PELOURINHO, opposite the Fundação Casa de Jorge Amado. Walking down the Largo do Pelourinho toward the Carmo district will bring you past the blue IGREJA DE NOSSA SENHORA DO ROSÁRIO DOS PRETOS, built in the 18th century for the use of slaves and freed slaves.

CARMO. The Ladeira do Carmo leads to the old working-class districts of Carmo, Cruz da Pascoal and Santo Antônio, all of which lie along the ridge of the cliff that separates the lower town from the upper town. On Largo do Carmo are the IGREJA E CONVENTO DE NOSSA SENHORA DO CARMO. The museum that now fills a wing of the convent is famous for a particular exhibit: a figure of Christ carved by Francisco Chagas, a slave.

CRUZ DA PASCOAL AND SANTO ANTÔNIO. Rua do Carmo continues toward Largo da Cruz do Pascoal, where there is a public oratory tiled with Portuguese ceramics. Several bar terraces also line the square. From Rua Direita de Santo Antônio you can take the Ladeira do Boqueirão, a steep street lined with *sobrados* ● *74* that are attractively faced with *azulejos* ● *71*. This walk ends at Praça de Santo Antônio Além do Carmo. The square offers a panoramic view of the bay and on either side of it are the fortress of SANTO ANTÔNIO (1703), currently under restoration and usually the home of certain *capoeira* schools ● *44*, and the yellow church of Santo Antônio, now without one of its bell towers, which collapsed after a storm.

FESTIVAL OF IEMANJÁ
This festival is held in honor of Iemanjá, a *candomblé* goddess ● *43* and the *Mãe e Rainha do Mar* (mother and goddess of the sea). It is held on February 2 in Rio Vermelho, around the house dedicated to Iemanjá, and near the beaches where fishing boats lie at low tide. Fishermen and devotees take to the boats to offer Iemanjá rafts made of flowers and coconuts, and perfume (*above*).

THE MODERN CITY

Most of the districts of the upper town date from the 19th and 20th centuries. Rua Chile leads down from Praça Municipal to Praça Castro Alves.

PRAÇA CASTRO ALVES. The statue of Castro Alves, author of the abolitionist *Navio Negreiro (Slave Ship)*, written in 1868, stands in this square overlooking the bay. This is where the *trios elétricos* ▲ *273* gather on Ash Wednesday in the famous *Encontro dos Trios* that marks the official end of the carnival.

MUSEU DE ARTE SACRA. Rua Carlos Gomes leads from the square to the Museum of Sacred Art, on Ladeira Santa Teresa. It occupies the former CONVENTO DE SANTA TERESA, built in the late 17th century and one of the most important examples of colonial religious architecture ● *70*. The museum contains over 1,400 pieces spanning the colonial and baroque periods. This wide-ranging collection comprises *azulejo* tilework panels, wooden and terracotta figurines and statuettes, and silverware and furniture.

AVENIDA 7 DE SETEMBRO. This avenue runs from Praça Castro Alves through a busy shopping district to Praça da Piedade. On the way you will pass the monastery of São Bento (on Praça de São Bento), built in 1581. It houses a

museum of religious art that includes sculptures by Frei Agostinho as well as objects and works of art dating from the 17th and 18th centuries.

Campo Grande. Rua Carlos Gomes and Avenida 7 de Setembro lead to Campo Grande, a huge grassy square with tall imperial palms that are almost as tall as the Monumento Dois de Julho (July 2 Monument) that also stands here. The Largo dos Aflitos and the Passeio Público, a little way from the center, afford a spectacluar view of the bay. On the other side of Campo Grande stands the Teatro Castro Alves. Opened in 1958 and renovated in 1993, this is Salvador's largest theater, and plays, ballets and performances by major names in *música popular brasileira* ● *52* are staged here.

Corredor da Vitória. After Campo Grande, Avenida 7 de Setembro becomes the Corredor da Vitória. This wide avenue is lined with mango trees and the skyscrapers and large houses here attest to the former wealth of the cocoa barons. At no. 2490 is a mansion containing the Museu Carlos Costa Pinto, which has a collection of paintings, silverware and Chinese porcelain. At no. 2195 is the Museu Geológico and at no. 2340 the Museu de Arte da Bahia, with a collection of paintings, sculptures and furniture dating from the 18th and 19th centuries.

Largo da Vitória and Graça district. The Corredor da Vitória leads to Largo da Vitória, a small square with a dazzlingly white church that is outlined by electric lights at night, and then to the Graça district, where one of the first churches founded in Salvador was built in the 17th century. The church contains the tomb of Catarina Paraguaçu, an American Indian woman. In the 16th century she married Diogo Álvarez Correio, who in 1535 established the first village to bring together Portuguese settlers and American Indians. This village stood in what are now the districts of Vitória and Graça.

Barra, the ocean and the Orla

Barra. Avenida 7 de Setembro then continues down through the Barra district and on toward the ocean. The fortresses of São Diogo (1596–1772) and Santa Maria (1625–96), built on two rocky promontories, flank the small beach of Porto da Barra. You will then come to the Farol da Barra, a lighthouse within the precinct of the fortress of Santo Antônio da Barra. Built in 1534, this stronghold is the oldest in Portuguese America. It now houses Bahia's Museu Hidrográfico and has a bar overlooking the ocean.

The Orla. This avenue skirts the coastline for about 20 miles. It leads first to Rio Vermelho, then to the modern districts of Amarelina and Pituba, and on to the beaches along the coastline as far as Itapoã, immortalized by the songs of Vinícius de Moraes ● *52* and Dorival Caymmi. Now part of the metropolis of Salvador, Itapoã is relatively quiet. Many reefs shelter its beaches from the Atlantic swell. Itapoã also has an ecoreserve that stretches as far as the Lagoa de Abaeté, a small freshwater lake nestling among white sand dunes.

The beach at Barra and the fortress of Santa Maria (*above*)

Dique do Tororó
This is a vast water reservoir on Avenida Vasco da Gama, beyond the central district of Lapa-Piedade and the Rodoviária (bus station). The lake was cleaned up in 1998 and its shore redeveloped. It is now popular with Bahians, who like to walk here, day or night. The Dique do Tororó is particularly worth a visit to see statues of *orixás* ● *43* carved by Tatti Moreno. They depict Oxalá, the creator-god in the *candomblé* pantheon, Ogum, Oxóssi, Oxum and Iemanjá.

Carnival in Barra
During Barra's carnival, the *trios elétricos* ▲ *273* and the crowd process down Avenida Oceânica, also known as the Orla. The meeting place is opposite the Farol da Barra (*below*). Processions form behind the trucks bristling with loudspeakers and musicians who are precariously perched. The procession goes on for several hours, which is the time it takes to reach the Ondina district.

FROM THE CIDADE BAIXA TO RIBEIRA

Most of the Cidade Baixa (lower town) was built on land reclaimed from the sea. Rua Gamboa de Cima leads down from Campo Grande to Avenida do Contorno, also known as Avenida Lafaiete Coutino, where the Solar do Unhão stands.

SOLAR DO UNHÃO. This old *engenho* ▲ *270*, where sugar cane was crushed and its juice distilled, is located on a cliff overlooking the sea. A fine example of 17th-century colonial architecture, it now houses the Museu de Arte Moderna, which displays works by Brazilian artists including Mário Cravo, Di Cavalcanti and Portinari ● *86*. There is also a sculpture park, a chapel and a restaurant.

IGREJA DE NOSSA SENHORA DA CONCEIÇÃO DA PRAIA. Avenida do Contorno leads to this beachside baroque church, built in the second half of the 18th century. The church is notable for its rococo façade and its wooden ceiling painted with religious scenes.

ELEVADOR LACERDA AND MERCADO MODELO. On the way to the Comércio district you will pass the entrance to the 236-foot high ELEVADOR LACERDA ★, an elevator linking the lower town to the upper town. Opposite the elevator, on the other side of the avenue, stands the Mercado Modelo, a large 19th-century building that was reconstructed in 1984 after being destroyed by fire. It is now filled with stalls selling handicrafts and souvenirs, where nothing changes hands without amicable haggling. *Rodas de capoeira* ● *44* are often held around the market.

COMÉRCIO. As you approach the business district, where the streets run at right angles to each other, the urban fabric becomes denser. Very crowded by day during the week, it is deserted after office hours and at weekends. There is a great deal of economic activity in this district, which is filled with banks, travel agencies, restaurants, *lanchonetes* (snack bars) and a wide variety of stores. The MUSEU DO CACAU, on Rua do Espanha, is devoted to cocoa farming, a major economic activity in southern Bahia ▲ *266*. Take Rua Miguel Calmon toward Bonfim, which brings you first to the jetty where you can catch a ferry to the Ilha de Itaparica ▲ *262*. Continue along the street and you will come to the MERCADO SÃO JOAQUIM, a fruit and vegetable market that also sells religious articles connected to the Catholic saints and the *orixás* ● *43* of the *candomblé* and the Umbanda sects.

SOLAR DO UNHÃO ✪
As the *solar*, on Avenida do Contorno 329, is difficult to reach, it is best to go there by taxi. The Museu de Arte Moderna there is open Tuesday through Friday 1–9pm, Saturday 3–9pm and Sunday 2–7pm. The restaurant, open 11am–midnight, hosts performances of folk music and dancing in the evenings.

FORTE SÃO MARCELO
This circular coastal fort was built between 1590 and 1728 to protect the bay from Dutch invasion ● *23*. Situated at the entrance to the port of Salvador, it is also known as the Forte do Mar. It will reopen to the public after restoration.

ELEVADOR LACERDA ✪
Salvador's division into an upper and lower town (Cidade Alta and Cidade Baixa) necessiated the installation of an elevator linking the two levels. The Elevador Lacerda, completed in 1873, stands opposite the rocky promontory between the levels. Each day tens of thousands of people crowd into its four cars to be whisked between Praça Cayru in Cidade Baixa and Praça Municipal in Cidade Alta.

The Solar do Unhão *(left)*.

Bonfim festival
The Lavagem do Bonfim, the ritual washing of the church steps ● *43*, is an important festival in the Bahian calendar. On the second Thursday in January thousands of people leave the Igreja da Conceição da Praia in a procession heading for the Igreja do Bonfim, six miles away. *Mães de santo* (*candomblé* priestesses ● *43*) take part in the ritual. The Bonfim (meaning 'happy ending') corresponds to the African Oxalá ▲ *259*.

Igreja de Nossa Senhora da Boa Viagem. Tall buildings gradually give way to the small houses of the districts around Bahia de Todos os Santos. The Igreja Nossa Senhora da Boa Viagem, with a marble cross and a façade tiled with *azulejos*, is a fine example of 18th-century colonial baroque architecture ● *70*. With the church of Nossa Senhora da Conceição da Praia, it is the focal point of the festivals held in honor of Nossa Senhor dos Navegantes, patron saint of sailors. On the morning of New Year's Day, a procession of boats ceremonially transports the statue of the saint from the Igreja Nossa Senhora da Conceição da Praia to the Igreja Nossa Senhora da Boa Viagem.

Forte de Monte Serrat. This fortress, situated on a promontory of the Itapagipe peninsula, offers a spectacular view of the bay and the Ilha Itaparica. Built in 1583, the fortress protected Salvador from attacks by the Dutch in the 17th century ● *23*. With its harmonious lines, it is a gem of Brazilian military architecture.

Pedra Furada. Beyond the district of Monte Serrat, on the way to the Bonfim district, you can stop in one of the small restaurants in the Pedra Furada district to sample *lambretas* (a type of clam), *caranguejos* (mangrove crabs), *caldo de sururu* (shellfish soup, renowned for its aphrodisiac properties), and many other seafood specialties.

Igreja do Nosso Senhor do Bonfim. This is probably the most famous church in Salvador. Built in 1754, it stands on a hill with a view of the city's hilly layout. The church's Sala dos Milagres (Miracle Room) contains votive offerings in the form of replicas of parts of bodies that were miraculously cured, left by members of the congregation in thanks for a cure or mercy granted. These offerings also take the form of notes detailing the promises made by believers. The square in front of the church is packed with sellers of *fitas,* colored ribbons (*above*). The *fitas* are fastened around the wrist with three knots, each corresponding to a wish that will be granted when the *fita* eventually falls off.

Ribeira. Steep *ladeiras* lead down from the hill, where stands the Igreja do Nosso Senhor do Bonfim, toward the port of Ribeira at the back of the bay. The road running alongside the beach is lined with restaurants with shady terraces where delicious fish and seafood, particularly *moqueca*, are served. You can finish your walk with a visit to the Sorveteria da Ribeira, which since 1932 has offered forty nine unusual flavors of ice-cream and sorbet, including *mangaba*, *cajá*, *açaí*, *acerola*, *cupuaçu* and *tapioca*.

'Moqueca'
This dish, one of Salvador's culinary specialties, is a blend of American Indian and African influences. The word comes from the Tupí *po-kêca,* referring to a method of cooking food wrapped in leaves. This dish is made of seafood or fish steamed in coconut milk and palm oil with tomatoes, onions, peppers and coriander (cilantro).

Ilha de Itaparica and the Recôncavo region

Mangrove swamps
The Recôncavo region's many *manguezais* (mangrove swamps) constitute a rich ecosystem that provides the local people with their staple diet of fish, shellfish and mollusks. Mangroves, trees with aerial roots, are the main type of vegetation in this environment of soft mud and silt where fresh water mingles with the salt water of the incoming tide.

Forte de São Lourenço
This fort stands at the edge of the town of Itaparica, on the northern tip of the Ilha de Itaparica. The fort was built by the Dutch ● *23* in the 17th century.

Irmandade da Boa Morte at Cachoeira
The Sisterhood of the Good Death is a religious sect that was founded by freed slaves, and it is a blend of Catholic and *candomblé* ● *43* beliefs. The festival

in honor of Nossa Senhora da Boa Morte (Our Lady of the Good Death) is held in the second week of August. You can watch rituals being performed and see the procession, led by members of the sisterhood, who are the descendants of slaves.

The Baía de Todos os Santos is the largest bay on the Brazilian coast. It covers 406 square miles and is dotted with fifty six islands, the largest of which is the Ilha de Itaparica. Crossing this island is the quickest way of getting from Salvador to the Recôncavo region, which follows the contours of the bay. From the 17th to the 19th centuries this fertile region was the hub of Salvador's economic development, with fortunes being made from the trade in precious woods, the sugar industry and tobacco farming. The lush landscapes of the Recôncavo region now consist of mangrove swamps, sugar cane and cassava plantations, bamboo groves and clusters of Atlantic forest ▲ *166*, *172* on a few of the region's steep hills.

Ilha de Itaparica

This large island, with a surface area of 92 square miles, lies at the mouth of the bay and is protected from the ocean by a barrier reef: Itaparica, its Tupí name, means 'hedge made of stone'. While car ferries sail from the Terminal São Joaquim ▲ *260* in Salvador to the town of Bom Despacho, boats carrying foot passengers depart from the Terminal da França, landing at Mar Grande. As well as beaches and restaurants, and Club Med, which draws thousands of tourists each year, the island has several fine buildings of historic interest.

Baiacu. The church of Nosso Senhor da Vera Cruz in Baiacu, a town on the west coast of the island, was built by the Jesuits in 1560. It is now in ruins and overgrown with enormous *gameleiras*, sacred trees in the *candomblé* religion ● *43*.

From Mar Grande to Cacha-Pregos. Mile upon mile of long beaches, such as Mar Grande, Penha, Conceição and Barra Grande, stretch away along the coastline in the direction of Salvador. The village of Cacha-Pregos, on the southwestern tip of Itaparica, is the point of departure for the mangrove swamps of the Pantanal Baiano ecoreserve.

Nazaré and Maragogipe

Nazaré. The west coast of Itaparica is linked to the mainland by the Ponte do Funil, a bridge leading on to Nazaré, 38 miles from Salvador. The town is renowned for its *sobradões* (large 19th-century mansions) and for the Feira dos Caxixas, an enormous annual market where ceramic figures are sold. The market is held on Praça José Bittencourt during Holy Week.

Maragogipe. This small town, 20 miles from Nazaré, stands in the midst of mangrove swamps on the banks of the Paraguaçú river. Once a tobacco-exporting port, Maragogipe was established on a hill. On Praça da Matriz, on the summit, stands the parish church, built in the late 17th century. From here narrow streets slope down to the banks of the Paraguaçú river, which is lined with mangrove forests. From the port, as well as from the beaches of Coqueiros and Pina, you can watch the occasional *saveiro* drift by. These heavy sailing boats are used for fishing and for transporting locally made goods and farm produce up and down the river.

CACHOEIRA ★
You will only need one day to visit this town on the banks of the Paraguaçú river, 72 miles from Salvador. Although it was declared a national monument in 1971, the municipal authorities lack the funds to restore the town's colonial houses and churches.

São Félix and Cachoeira ★

São Félix. This small town is 15 miles from Maragogipe. Visit the Centro Culturel Dannemann and take a riverside walk to admire the view across to Cachoeira. The town is linked to São Félix by the Ponte Dom Pedro II, a 1,200-foot-long bridge opened in 1885. Its ancient wooden planks, some of which are dangerously loose, clatter as vehicles, trains and pedestrians pass over them.

Cachoeira. This town, now with 32,000 inhabitants, grew in the 16th century as a result of the cultivation first of sugar cane then of tobacco. The wealth of those days gave the town its fine colonial architecture ● *74*, although many houses are now in ruins. Cachoeira is also known for its *terreiros*, places where *candomblé* rituals are held, and for its craftsmen. The town's restaurants and bars are concentrated on Praça de Freitas, overlooking the river. The square is continued by Praça da Aclamação, where the tourist office is located. Also on the square are a museum of Bahian independence, Cachoeira being the first town to recognize Dom Pedro I ● *24*, and the Igreja e Convento de Ordem Terceira do Carmo. This complex, built between 1691 and 1724 and renovated in 1981, houses a museum with paintings from Macao depicting the Passion of Christ, and there is also a *pousada* (inn) and conference center.

Convento de São Francisco de Paraguaçu. This Franciscan convent is located on the banks of the Paraguaçú river at Iguape, 27 miles from Cachoeira. It was built in 1686 and now houses a hospital and a novitiate but is under threat of demolition.

Centro Cultural Dannemann
This center on the quays at São Félix, in the buildings of the former Dannemann factory, exhibits works by local artists and illustrates old cigar-making techniques. In one room you can see cigars (*charutos*) being made and buy them as souvenirs.

Santo Amaro

The town of Santo Amaro, 43 miles from Salvador, was the birthplace of two famous singers, Caetano Veloso and his sister, Maria Bethânia ● *53*. The churches and the houses of *senhores de engenho* (sugar barons) here are vestiges of the wealth once enjoyed by this former sugar-producing town. Turn right beyond the bridge and walk along the Subaué river, passing a daily market, and you will come to the Convento de Nossa Senhora dos Humildes. Part of this late 18th-century convent now contains a museum, although the convent's right wing is still used by nuns belonging to a closed order. The museum has many painted statues as well as delicate opaline objects, chasubles and paintings by the nuns.

Museu Hansen de Cachoeira
This museum, on Rua 13 de Maio, was set up in 1978, shortly after the death of the German artist Karl Hansen, who came to Salvador in 1955. His woodcuts show his deep admiration for Salvador and Bahia. Exhibits at the museum include two of his major series: the *Drama do Calvário* depicting the horrors of World War Two, and illustrations for Castro Alves' *Navio Negreiro* (Slave Ship) ▲ *258*.

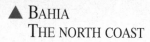

THE HIPPIE VILLAGE
In the 1960s around twenty people who wanted to escape the noise and pollution of Salvador set up home in a village north of Arembepe. The village has about thirty wooden houses roofed with palms, and the villagers live by selling handicrafts on the beaches. This village also has a gallery, Espaço 44, set up by the Bahian sculptor and artist Luís Cerqueira. There is a rustic *pousada* and restaurants serving organic food.

PRAIA DO FORTE ★
This coastal resort is located 53 miles from Salvador and two miles from the junction between the Rodovia do Côco and the Linha Verde. Cars are banned from the village at weekends, and must be left in one of the parking lots just outside it.

For a few days' respite from the big-city life of Salvador head out to Bahia's north coast, the scenic Litoral Norte, which is popular with *Soteropolitanos* (inhabitants of Salvador). The Litoral Norte, or Coconut Coast, has 120 miles of beaches, dunes, rivers, lagoons and Atlantic forest ▲ *166, 172,* and is one of the most beautiful stretches of coastline in Brazil. It extends from Salvador's international airport to Mangue Seco, on the border between the states of Bahia and Sergipe. It is reached via the Estrada do Côco (Coconut Road) then the Lina Verde (Green Line), highway BA099.

LAURO DE FREITAS AND VILAS DO ATLÂNTICO. Following highway BA099 the first beaches that you come to are lined with houses. The coastline and the coconut plantations here have been developed to make them suitable for such sports activities as cycling and jogging, and they have been attractively landscaped, with lawns and cactuses.

PRAIA DE JAUÁ. This one-mile beach, a little further on, is sheltered by a barrier reef. Bathers can enjoy the natural swimming pools at low tide and watch dramatic clouds of spray rise up into the air as the waves crash over the reef at high tide.

AREMBEPE. Some 12 miles further along the road becomes more sparsely lined with houses. These eventually give way to a low *restinga* forest growing on surprisingly white silica soil. At Km 24 on the Estrada do Côco turn off to Arembepe, an old fishing village on the border of the Parque Ecológico do Rio Capivara. This 2,700-acre park comprises the Rio Caipivara basin, a lagoon, a hippie village and a 544-acre campsite.

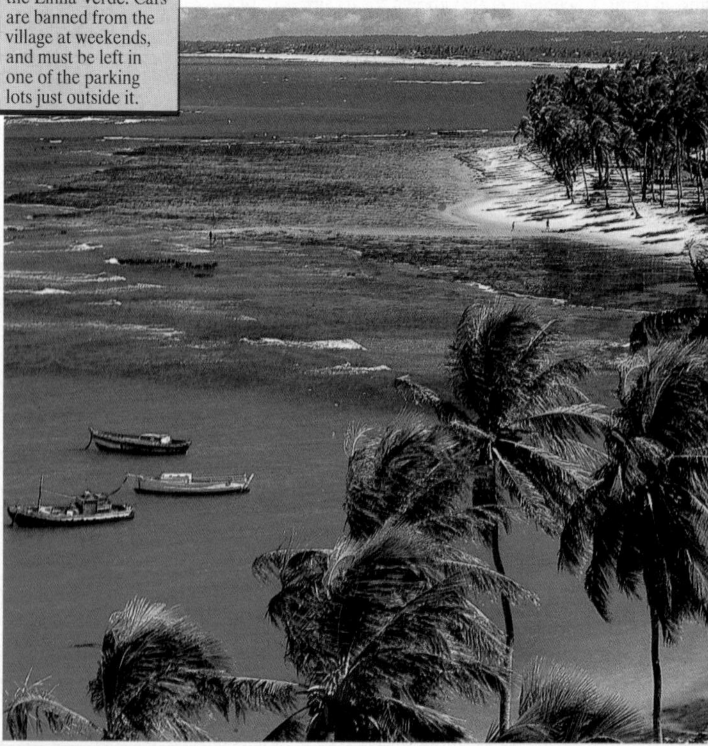

★ **Praia do Forte.** Continue along highway BA099 until you come to this fishing village at the heart of the Sapiranga reserve, where there are many hotels, *pousadas* (inns) and restaurants. The local people, who are keen to encourage ecotourism, will not allow the main road and the streets in the center of the village to be metalled. Praia do Forte is also the location of one of the sea turtle reserves along the coast. There are countless signs reminding visitors of the importance of protecting the region's natural heritage of plants and animals. Praia do Forte is not only popular for its beaches and beautiful scenery. This is also where one of the oldest Portuguese buildings in Brazil can be found. This is the Castelo Garcia d'Ávila, built on Morro Tatuapaçu in 1551–2. The Ávila family introduced coconut cultivation and stock-breeding to Brazil. Praia do Forte is two miles from the junction of the Estrada do Côco and the Linha Verde, which continues highway BA099 in the direction of the Sergipe region.

Imbassaí. After Praia do Forte, Imbassaí ('river path' in Tupí) is the first town that you will come to on the Linha Verde. Here several small rivers join a larger river that meanders through the dunes.

Linha verde. This road, opened in 1993, runs through the coast's *mata atlântica* ▲ *172* and fine eucalyptus forests. It is called the 'Green Line' because it is an ecologically planned road: the number of buildings and gas stations along it is restricted and large trucks are banned.

From Barra do Itariri to Seribinha. Numerous roads running at right angles off the Linha Verde lead to the villages that are dotted along the coast. Halfway between Praia do Forte and Mangue Seco, is the fishing village of Barra do Itariri. With basic facilities for tourists, it is an ideal starting point for exploring the coast as far as the village of Serinbinha. The track, which is impassable only in very wet weather, leads through the coastal coconut plantations to the fishing villages of Sítio, Poças and Seribinha. The town of Conde, which is equidistant from the four villages, offers the best hotel accommodation in the region.

★ **Mangue Seco.** This narrow sandy peninsula is separated from the state of Bahia by the Real, a wide river whose banks are lined with mangrove forest that aided by the tide is gradually widening the riverbed. The dunes at Mangue Seco are also shifting. Carried by the wind, the fine sand continuously threatens to engulf the roads, gardens and plantations in the locality. This small fishing village was the setting for *Tieta do Agreste*, a novel by Jorge Amado and the film adaptation of it, *Tieta do Brasil*. Because access to Mangue Seco is difficult, the town has remained protected from mass tourism. There are however five *pousadas* and a dozen bars and restaurants.

The Tamar project
Launched in 1980 by Ibama, the Brazilian environmental agency, the Tartarugas Marinhas project has been highly successful. The aim was to protect the five endangered species of sea turtles that lay their eggs on the Brazilian shore. The success appears to be the result of close cooperation between naturalists and fishermen. In 1999 the Tamar project celebrated the hatching of the three millionth sea turtle under its protection.

Mangue Seco ★
The only way to reach Mangue Seco is to take the Linha Verde heading out of the state of Bahia and follow this road for about six miles through the state of Sergipe to Pontal. Boats to Mangue Seco leave from Pontal.

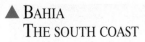

VALENÇA HARBOR
This busy harbor (*below*), filled with fishermen's *saveiros* (wooden sailing boats), is the town's focal point, with a market, old buildings, hotels and restaurants. It is also the departure point for expeditions to the Tinharé archipelago.

To the south of Salvador and the Recôncavo region lie the coasts of Dendê, Cacao, Descobrimento and Baleias. Southern Bahia has extensive areas of primary Atlantic forest. Mangrove swamps and coconut plantations fringe the coastline, which consists of a succession of long beaches that stretch out between high cliffs, and along which runs highway BA001.

THE DENDÊ COAST

VALENÇA. Built on the banks of the Una river, this small colonial town has a rich architectural heritage dating from the 18th and 19th centuries. The church of Nossa Senhora do Amparo, built in 1757 on a hill, the Alto da Colina, affords a spectacular vista, with Valença spread out below, the Tinharé archipelago beyond and the church of São Francisco de Assis in the village of Galeão on the horizon.

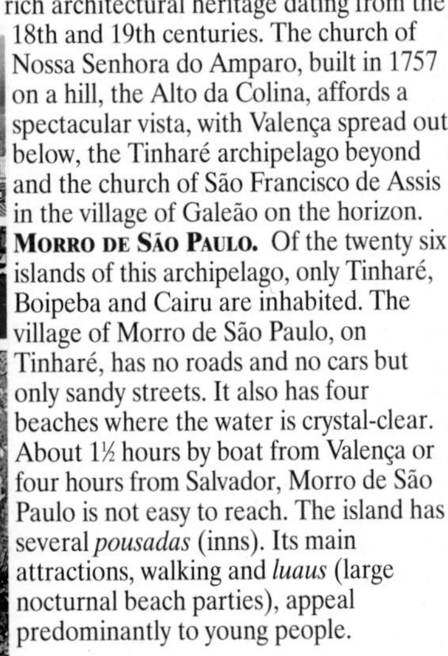

MORRO DE SÃO PAULO. Of the twenty six islands of this archipelago, only Tinharé, Boipeba and Cairu are inhabited. The village of Morro de São Paulo, on Tinharé, has no roads and no cars but only sandy streets. It also has four beaches where the water is crystal-clear. About 1½ hours by boat from Valença or four hours from Salvador, Morro de São Paulo is not easy to reach. The island has several *pousadas* (inns). Its main attractions, walking and *luaus* (large nocturnal beach parties), appeal predominantly to young people.

COCOA
The first cocoa tree was planted in 1749 in Canavieiras but it was not until the end of the 19th century that the cultivation of this Amazonian tree caused the rapid growth of Ilhéus and the rise of the cocoa society, consisting of poor planters and rich, powerful landowners, known as *coronels* (colonels). Jorge Amado, a native of the region, described this society in *Cocoa and Sweat*.

THE COCOA COAST

ITACARÉ. The road leading south out of Valença winds through vast expanses of Atlantic forest ▲ *172*. The village of Itacaré is located 40 miles north of Ilhéus. This is an unspoiled location with a strong appeal for nature lovers and surfing enthusiasts. Many rivers that have their source in the Chapada Diamantina ▲ *268* flow down on either side of Itacaré, forming freshwater pools and waterfalls on its easily accessible beaches (*opposite page*). Itacaré is linked to Ilhéus by a metalled road running parallel to the coast.

ILHÉUS. In the late 19th century this large town, now with 240,000 inhabitants, was the hub of cocoa cultivation and the trade in cocoa beans (*above*). The town center nestles between two hills, one with the chapel of Nossa Senhora de Lourdes, built in the 20th century, and the other with convent of Nossa Senhora da Piedade, built in the 19th century. The town stretches out between the 16th-century Igreja de São Jorge and the neoclassical Catedral de São Sebastião, dating from the 19th century. The hilltops offer a panorama of the town, the Cachoeira estuary and the Baía do Pontal. The Museu do Cacau in the town center traces the region's social and political history. The house where the writer Jorge Amado once lived is now a foundation devoted to his work.

CANAVIEIRAS. This town, 75 miles south of Ilhéus, is surrounded by beautiful beaches and is of interest for its colonial center, which, like the Pelourinho district in Salvador ▲ *256,* has been restored. It is also famous for its tasty cuisine and abundant shellfish from the sea, river and mangrove swamps. These include the clam-like shellfish known as *lambretas*, crabs (*caranguejos* and *siris*), shrimps and oysters.

THE DESCOBRIMENTO COAST

PORTO SEGURO. This historic town, whose name means 'safe port', was founded on a hill overlooking the ocean. It lies near the spot where Pedro Alvares Cabral landed in 1500 ● *22* and was declared a national monument in 1973. From Praça do Descobrimento, in the lower town, where restaurants, *pousadas* and bars are concentrated, climb the steps to the upper town. On the hilltop are the Igreja Nossa Senhora da Pena (built in 1555), the Igreja da Misericórdia (16th century) and the Igreja do Rosário dos Jesuitas (1551), the Casa de Câmara e Cadeia (1772) and the Marco do Descobrimento. This is a marble boundary stone brought from Portugal between 1503 and 1526, and symbolizing the appropriation of lands 'discovered' by the Portuguese crown ● *29*.

FROM ARRAIAL D'AJUDA TO CARAÍVA. Take the ferry across the Buranhém river, south of Porto Seguro, and follow the road running alongside several beaches backed by cliffs. This road passes the villages of Arraial d'Ajuda (28 miles from the landing pier), TRANCOSO (16 miles) and Caraíva (26 miles). The latter is the gateway to the Parque Nacional de Monte Pascoal, where Pataxó American Indians live.

THE BALEIAS COAST

CARAVELAS. Surrounded by mangroves in the extreme south of Bahia, this fishing village is a point of access to the Abrolhos archipelago, lying 36 nautical miles off the coast. Although visitors cannot land on the islands you can moor your vessel beside the *escunas* (motor schooners) of Caravelas overnight.

PARQUE NACIONAL MARINHO DE ABROLHOS. Created in 1983, this was the first marine park in Brazil. It consists of five islands, only one of which, Santa Bárbara, is inhabited. From June through October humpback whales come here to give birth in the warm, clear waters. Outside this period you can explore wrecks and underwater caves or watch the great variety of marine life. The park has nineteen species of coral, among which can be found barracudas, parrot fish, moray eels and seahorses. Sea turtles lay their eggs on the islands and frigate birds, black skimmers and *maçaricos* nest here.

BEACHES AND BOAT TRIPS ★
The coastline of southern Bahia has many beautiful beaches and is bathed in sunshine all year round, although rain may fall in July and August. From Porto Seguro you can take an *escuna* (motor schooner) to the Parque Marítimo de Recife de Fora and the sandbanks and coral reefs of Coroa Alta.

THE LION TAMARIN
The Ecoparque da Una, 31 miles from Ilhéus on the road to Canavieiras, has launched a project to save the *mico-leão-dourado,* or golden lion tamarin ▲ *176,* and its habitat, the Atlantic forest ▲ *172.* A biologist at the park takes groups of visitors on a trail through the forest to learn about the biodiversity of this threatened ecosystem.

MUSEU ABERTO DO DESCOBRIMENTO
This giant open-air museum stretches over 81 miles, from the town of Prado to Santa Cruz de Coroa, Coroa Vermelha, where the first mass to be said in Brazil was celebrated. The museum's 'displays' are natural habitats and its 'collections' comprise all Brazil's early settlement sites. The museum's purpose is to showcase the ecological, historical and cultural features of the Descobrimento coast, so named because it is here that the European discovery of Brazil began.

Brought to Brazil by the Portuguese in 1532, sugar cane was first cultivated around São Vicente, on the coast of São Paulo state. It soon became widespread as a crop in other coastal settlements. However, sugar cane proved better suited to the *masapé* (clayey humus) of the state of Pernambuco ▲ *274* and the Bahian Recôncavo ▲ *262*, areas where a flourishing economy and great wealth then developed. The sugar cane boom was also directly linked to transatlantic slave trafficking. From 1570 to 1670 Brazil held the monopoly for supplying all of Europe with sugar, and this led to the Dutch to occupy Pernambuco in 1630. Since the late 17th century the Brazilian sugar industry has been dogged by lack of competitiveness in the world and has constantly sought new markets. However sugar production is still the dominant industry in certain regions of the Nordeste.

Sugar cane (*below*).

A SUGAR PLANTATION'S MICROSOCIETY

The Jesuit Padre Antonil devoted the first part of his book *Cultura e Opulência do Brasil* (1711) to sugar and listed the people involved in running a sugar plantation, or *engenho de açucar*: 'Being the sugar mill owner [*senhor de engenho*] is a title to which many aspire, because of the privilege of being served, obeyed and respected... Just as commoners are answerable to gentlemen, farmer-planters are ruled by the sugar mill owners whose lands they work... The 'senhor' has an entire section of the productive population working for him: slaves who work in the plantations and the mill, the mulatto or Negro slaves in domestic service or who do other tasks, as well as sailors to man the boats..., potters, the cowherds, shepherds and fishermen. Any lord also inevitably has a head sugar producer, an overseer, a refiner, a bursar employed in the town, stewards in the sugar fields and subsistence gardens, a chief steward for the whole residence and a chaplain to take care of the spiritual side of things.' In the 19th century, the *engenhos* declined and were replaced by the more modern *usinas*, or factories.

LASTING INEQUALITY

In 1974 the oil crisis and the fall in world sugar prices caused Brazil's military government ● *27* to launch Proálcool (Brazilian National Alcohol Program) which subsidized ethanol-based fuel. Although these measures helped producers, they did nothing for the sugar cane cutters, the *boias frias* ('cold meals', *right*), who came to symbolize Brazil's struggling economy. Robert Linhart, a French journalist, described how hard it was for them to survive in *Le Sucre et la Faim. Enquête dans les régions sucrières du Nord-Est brésilien* (1980) (Sugar and Hunger. Inquiry into the sugar-producing regions of Brazil's Nordeste). 'Walk across the sugar cane fields. Here is a *feitor* (overseer): red shirt, portable scales in his belt, notebook in hand. He is supervising four or five laborers scattered among the cane, who are cutting and making bundles. We ask to see his notebook. He shows us: here are the names; there, on the opposite page, is the daily yield. The page from the day before: it generally varies from 500 to 1,500 kilos per day. "2,250 kilos on this line: why such a high figure?" "That's a bloke who comes to work with his little girl." "And here 150: why such a low figure?" "That's a six-year-old kid: that's what he does with his day." 150 kilos of cane; as wages are based on productivity that child earned 8 cruzeiros [about 10 pence] yesterday.'

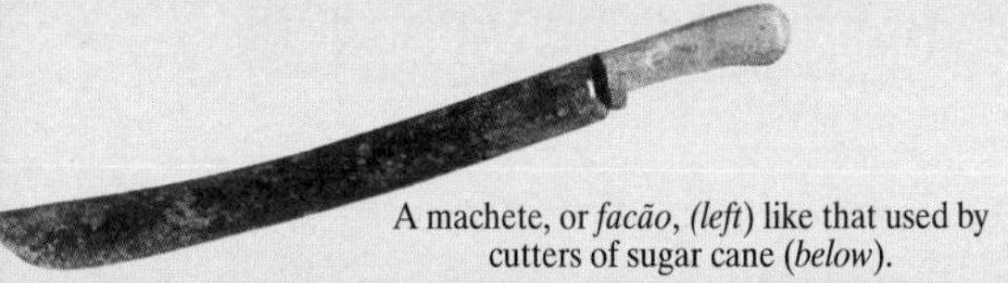

A machete, or *facão*, (*left*) like that used by cutters of sugar cane (*below*).

THE 'ENGENHO DE AÇÚCAR'

A sugar plantation, or *engenho de açucar*, consists of fields of sugar cane, often rented out to farmers, and of buildings, comprising a mill and a refining plant, where the cane is processed. The cane is crushed in a mill (*left*, portable sugar mill depicted by Debret ● *24, 84*). The juice is heated, purified to remove residue and then dried. Sugar production demands a large labor force and quantities of firewood. Sugar was largely responsible for the importation of slaves to Brazil ● *34* and for deforestation of the country.

FOOD FOR THOUGHT

According to the Brazilian sociologist Gilberto Freyre (1901–87), the key characteristics of Brazilian society and the country's first aristocracy were molded by this pro-slavery, patriarchal single-crop farming. Freyre also posits that the *casa grande* (the plantation-owner's house) was the melting pot for interbreeding between Portuguese and Africans. He developed this theory in his book *Masters and Slaves* (1933) and returned to it in *Nordeste* (1937). In similar vein is *Plantation Lad* (1932), by José Lins do Rego (1901–57). The first novel in his 'sugar cane cycle' it is imbued with a similar nostalgia for the lost world of the *engenhos.*

The *engenho* at Menjope in Pernambuco ▲ *279* (*left*).

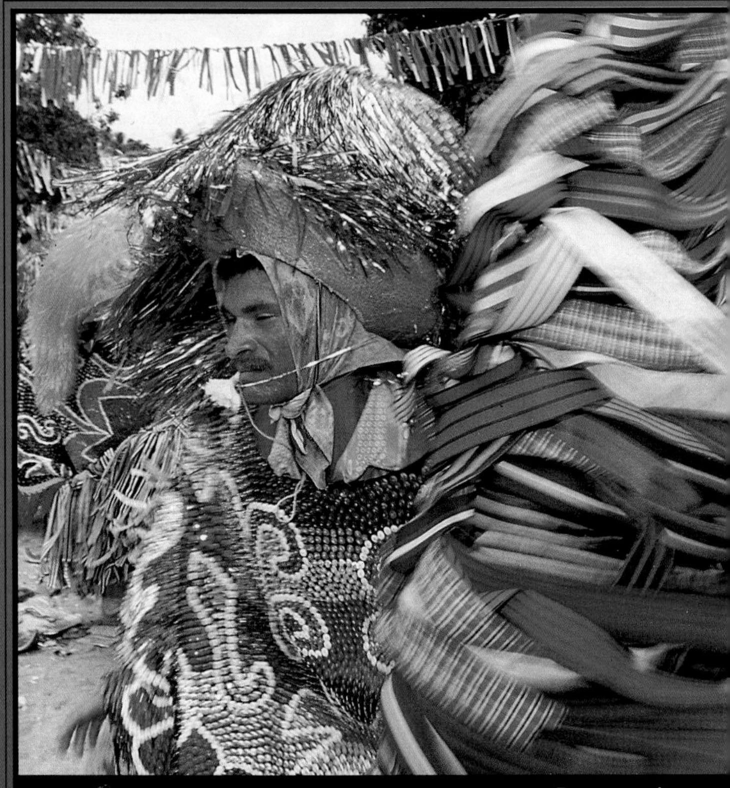

Some of Brazil's greatest musicians, such as Dorival Caymmi, with songs of the sea, and Luiz Gonzaga, with songs glorifying the Pernambucan *sertão*, have come from the Nordeste. The region is also the birthplace of certain popular styles of music, such as *embolada*, *baião*, *xote* and *xaxado*. Age-old musical traditions kept alive by *cantadores* and *repentistas* coexist with commercial trends such as *lambada* and *axé music* as well as avant-garde movements such as *mangue beat*. Carnivals in the Nordeste are more populist and informal than Rio's. During carnival Olinda throbs to the beat of *frevo*, and traditional *maracatu* and *caboclinho* parades take place in Recife. In Salvador *frevo* is performed on electrified instruments atop trucks called *trios elétricos*, while *afoxés* and Afro *blocos* flaunt black identity.

PERNAMBUCO'S 'MARACATUS' AND 'CABOCLINHOS'

Maracatus are black royal processions deriving from a colonial custom that involved crowning a slave king and queen for the Festival of the Rosary. Slaves in the royal retinue carry the standard and umbrella of the *nação* (nation) represented, while *batuqueiros* (percussionists) and Bahian choirs provide the musical accompaniment. On carnival Sunday the *maracatus* (*above*), in which anything from fifty to two hundred people take part, ceremoniously parade along a wide avenue in Recife ▲ *274*,

'Repentistas'

The Nordeste is the home of *cantadores* and *repentistas* (*below*). These sometimes illiterate troubadours improvise on a wide variety of topical themes and attempt to outdo each other in virtuosity during poetical and musical contests known as *desafios*. The most usual lyrical form is the *embolada*, which favors the old Portuguese seven-syllable form.

'Mangue beat'

In the 1990s, the musical scene in Recife was given a major new boost. While Antônio Nóbrega and Mestre Ambrósio found new audiences for the ancestral *rabeca* (popular violin), Chico Science (1966–97) founded *mangue beat* (a style of music originating in the mangrove swamps of the poor areas) with his band, Nação Zumbi. He recorded music with a sociopolitical message that revamped and updated traditional Pernambucan rhythms.

alternating with the *frevo* clubs and groups of *caboclinhos*. The latter, representing American Indians, are equipped with bows and arrows, which they use as percussion instruments. The *caboclinhos* mime warrior dances, skip and intone monotonous chants to the sound of a reed pipe, known as a *gaita* or *inúbia*. The *caboclinhos* are one of the most distinctive components of Recife's carnival processions.

'Frevo'

A product of late 19th-century military band music and fashionable society dances (such as the *matchiche*, quadrille, and polka), *frevo* is the hallmark of the Pernambucan carnival. Time-honored composers of *frevo* include Capiba (1904–97) and Nelson Ferreira (1902–76). The umbrella that they use helps the dancers (*passistas*) to keep their balance as they perform highly acrobatic movements, often virtually at ground level.

'Trio elétrico'

In 1950 the Vassourinhos *frevo* club from Recife stopped in Salvador on its way to Rio and wowed the Bahians with its style of music. Two musicians, Osmar and Dodô, began to play the *frevos* that they had heard on the electric guitars they played from the top of a truck. They were joined by a third musician and the *trio elétrico* was born. Trucks with sound systems now draw crowds of people, who dance to beats such as *lambada*, *fricote* and *axé music* ● *51*.

'Bloco Afro' and 'afoxé' in Salvador

Afro-Bahian *blocos* (individual processions in a carnival) such as Ilê-Aiyé, Araketu, Badauê, Muzenza and Malê-Debalê, appeared in the 1970s and 1980s as a spinoff of black militant movements. Based in the Salvador's central Pelourinho district ▲ *256*, Grupo Olodum and its followers, of which there are thousands and who are identifiable by the pan-African colors of their clothes (*left*), perform a mixture of samba and reggae with a percussion and brass base. The *afoxé* is a religious procession of Afro-Brazilian allegiance and closely linked to *candomblé* ● *43*. The *afoxé* was banned for many years but since the Filhos de Gandhi (Sons of Gandhi), the largest of these *afoxés*, was formed in 1949 it is now a key aspect of Bahian carnival.

▲ Parque Nacional Marinho de Fernando de Noronha

Marine fauna
Natural swimming pools allow you to observe at close range a wide variety of marine life, including many species of fish and mollusks, and several varieties of algae, sponges and coral.

The Fernando de Noronha archipelago lies in the Atlantic Ocean, 225 miles off the coast of Brazil. Covering a total area of ten square miles, it consists of the island of Fernando de Noronha, which has a surface area of seven square miles and is the archipelago's only inhabited island, and twenty other islands, islets and rocks. The archipelago's fourteen beaches, bays and coves are on the crest of an ancient volcanic cordillera, whose base is almost three miles below the surface of the ocean. Migratory birds use the archipelago, now an ecological reserve, as a resting place and marine animals come here to breed. Its geographical position gives the archipelago two very different aspects. The south side, which faces Africa, is known as the *mar de fora* (outer sea) and its jagged shoreline is buffeted by gusty wind and high waves. The north side, the *mar de dentro* (inner sea), has a more even shoreline and calm waters. The island's many footpaths allow visitors to see the flora and fauna of this natural paradise.

Flora
The archipelago's shallow soil and the strong winds that buffet it are not conducive to the growth of lush vegetation. While trees grow on its highest parts, the flatlands support shrubs. Trees on the archipelago include the impressive *gameleira* (*Ficus noronhae*) and *mulungu* (*Erythina auranthiaca*), which is covered in orange flowers in September. *Burra leiteira* (*Sapium sceleratum*), which produces a dangerous caustic latex, also grows here.

Getting to Fernando de Noronha ✪
The archipelago can be reached either by airplane or by boat. On your arrival you will be asked to pay an environmental protection tax of R$21.28 to Ibama (the Brazilian environment agency) and the Golfinho Rotador center that looks after Dolphin Bay. The best time to visit Fernando de Noronha is from August through January.

PONTA DA AIR FRANCE

In 1927 French officials working for the Compagnie Générale Aéropostale took up residence in the northern part of the island. The post office comprised three houses and served as a base for Air France hydroplanes. The surviving building houses the Association of Artists and Craftsmen.

SEA TURTLES

At the beginning of the mating season, in November, when males fight over the females, you can see groups of *aruana* (*Chelonia mydas*), or green turtles, near the surface of the water. From January through May the females leave the water to lay their eggs in nests, known locally as *panelas* (saucepans), that they excavate in the sand of Praia do Sancho and Praia do Leão Marinho. Some nests can hold more than 100 eggs. The incubation period is 50 days. When they hatch the young turtles are about 3 inches long and weigh just over half an ounce. By the time they reach adulthood they are almost 4 feet long and weigh over 660 lb. The *tartaruga-de-pente* (*Eretmochelys imbricata*), or hawksbill turtle, (*above*) also mates and lays its eggs on the Fernando de Noronha archipelago. This relatively large sea turtle is the second most endangered species of turtle as its beautiful shell is coveted as a material for making spectacle frames, combs and jewelry.

FEATHERED VISITORS

Many different species of migratory shorebirds stop to rest and feed on the archipelago during their journey across the Atlantic Ocean. Sheltered from the blustery ocean winds, the north side of the island, between Ponta da Sapata and the Baía dos Porcos, is the best place to watch these birds, including the sooty tern or *réis-das-rocas* (*Sterna fuscata*), black roddy or *viuvinhas* (*Anous minutus*) and the brown booby or *atobá* (*Sula leucogaster, left*).

BAÍA DOS GOLFINHOS

The huge natural aquarium in Dolphin Bay is home to a resident population of long-snouted spinner dolphins (*Stenella longirostris*), so called because of the high spinning leaps that they make as they propel themselves into the air (*left*). At sunrise the dolphins swim into the bay and spend most of the day there, resting or mating. In the late afternoon they head out to the deep waters where they spend the night and where they feed on small fish, squid and crustaceans. Although the bay is closed to visitors a 230-foot-high rock here provides a vantage point from which you can watch the dolphins and their young frolic in their natural habitat.

SEA LION BEACH

One of the most beautiful beaches on the rougher, south side of the island is named for an enormous block of stone projecting into the sea: it looks like a recumbent sea lion. The sand here is dazzlingly white and the coastline's natural swimming pools include that near the Pico Os Dois Irmãos (The Two Brothers, *above*). From January to June, when the turtles lay their eggs, the beach is closed from 6pm to 6am.

The Morro do Pico (*left*).

FORTALEZA'S CULINARY SPECIALTIES
Not surprisingly Fortaleza's cuisine gives pride of place to seafood, in the form of shrimps, crabs and various kinds of fish and most especially lobster, which is caught in large numbers in the region. Another recommended specialty, which comes from the interior of the Ceará, is *carne de sol*, meaning 'sunshine meat'. This flavorsome dish of salted and grilled beef is served with *baião-de-dois*, a mixture of rice and beans.

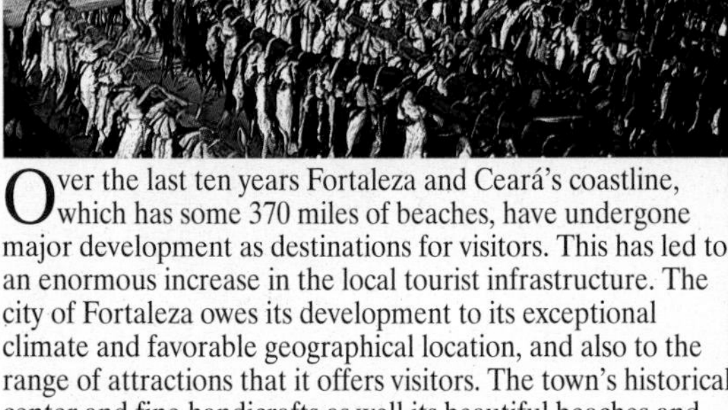

Over the last ten years Fortaleza and Ceará's coastline, which has some 370 miles of beaches, have undergone major development as destinations for visitors. This has led to an enormous increase in the local tourist infrastructure. The city of Fortaleza owes its development to its exceptional climate and favorable geographical location, and also to the range of attractions that it offers visitors. The town's historical center and fine handicrafts as well its beautiful beaches and the warm hospitality that it offers make it a popular vacation resort with visitors both from within Brazil and abroad.

FORTALEZA

The town's origins go back to 1649, when a fortress (*fortaleza*) was built by the Dutch. After several clashes with the Tabajara American Indians, the Dutch fought the Portuguese for control of the Nordeste ● *23* but were defeated by them in 1654. The village that then grew up around the fortress was named Nossa Senhora da Assunção but later came to be known as Fortaleza. However, it was not until 1808, when Brazilian ports were opened to international trade and cotton began to be exported to Britain, that Fortaleza's population began to grow markedly and its economy to expand. Fortaleza is now a town of over two million inhabitants. This bright, airy town consists of a grid of perpendicular streets punctuated by open spaces, squares and parks. The town center, built alongside the old historic district, is highly commercial and very typical of the Nordeste. During the day it is crowded with peddlers and sightseers, who also fill Praça José de Alencar, Praça do Ferreira, Praça dos Mártires and Praça dos Leões.

TEATRO JOSÉ DE ALENCAR. The theater is named for this famous writer, a native of Ceará and the author of *Iracema* and *O Guaraní*. The building dates from 1908–10 and shows the influence of the then-fashionable neoclassical and Art Nouveau styles (*left*).

PRAÇA DO FERREIRA. This square is a popular meeting place for the inhabitants of Fortaleza, who gather here to chat. Many political demonstrations have also taken place here, which is also regarded as a traditional platform for Cearense humor. During the early 20th century it was here, on April 1 every year, that the biggest liar in Fortaleza was elected. Also lining the square is the Cine São Luiz, the official venue of the Ceará's film festival. At Rua São Paulo 51 nearby is the

TEATRO JOSÉ DE ALENCAR
This theater stands on Praça José de Alencar, in the town center. It has a cast-iron framework, which contrasts with the building's brightly colored stained-glass windows and such wooden elements as the painted ceiling. The theater seats 800 and the program of ballets, plays and concerts regularly draws a full audience.

Museu do Ceará. This museum of local history documents the way of life of the region's American Indian tribes. There is also a section devoted to Padre Cícero, who is venerated throughout this region.

Fortaleza de Nossa Senhora da Assunção. This fortress, the nucleus around which the town developed, was built in 1649 and rebuilt in 1817. To look around it go to the entrance at Avenida Alberto Nepomuceno. Not far from the fortress is the Mercado Central, a market where the full range of handicrafts produced in the region of Ceará are offered for sale.

Centro Cultural Dragão do Mar. This arts and cultural center is located near Iracema beach in a colonial district of the town that is currently undergoing restoration. Opened in 1998, it is the largest arts complex in Fortaleza. It offers a wide range of attractions, including movies, theater, art exhibitions and concerts. There is also a planetarium, a bookstore, workshops and an art museum, and the Memorial to Cearense culture. The Dragão do Mar also houses restaurants and bars with excellent live music and it is a good place to go for a drink in the evening. The name Dragão do Mar (Sea Dragon) pays tribute to a 19th-century fisherman who, along with his companions, refused to continue transporting slaves.

THE BEACHES

With the exception of Praia do Futuro, Fortaleza's beaches are unfortunately quite polluted. Nevertheless they are very popular and have many restaurants, nightclubs and bars with live MPB (*música popular brasileira*) ● *51* and *forró* ● *51*.

Avenida Beira Mar. The 'avenue by the sea' borders a beach that stretches for almost three miles from the Ponte Metálica (or Ponte dos Ingleses) and Praia de Iracema, near the city center, to Mucuripe. The beach is lined with coconut palms and *barracas* (straw huts).

Mucuripe. Located just beyond the harbor, Mucuripe is Fortaleza's traditional fishing beach. Although the town has expanded at an ever-increasing pace, the beach has not been overtaken by the modern world. Early in the morning you can buy freshly caught fish here and watch *jangadas* ▲ *287*. Although swimming on this stretch of coastline is not recommended, the beach is still very crowded both during the day and in the evenings.

Praia do Futuro. Further away, beyond Mucuripe and the harbor area, is Praia do Futuro, a four-mile beach that is much cleaner than those nearer to the center of Fortaleza. It is a paradise for bathers and surfers, although the currents can be treacherous. It has *barracas* serving drinks and seafood. There is also live music, and welcome shade if you need a respite from the sun. On Thursday evenings you can dance to the beat of the *forró* bands that come to perform here.

Ceara handicrafts

The handicrafts of the Ceará show the influence both of the *sertão* ▲ *254*, in the interior, and of the coastal areas. From the *sertão*, a region of religious devotion and extensive cattle-ranching, come a variety of religious pieces such as Christmas crib figurines, sculptures and wood engravings. The *sertão* is also known for its ceramics, leatherwork and macramé, and for crafts with American Indian elements, such as braiding, basketwork, furniture-making and bags. Along the coast you will find crochet work and high-quality embroidery (*renda de bilro*), hammocks (*top*) and bottles skilfully filled with colored sand depicting landscapes (*above*). Pieces such as these can be found in the Mercado Central, at the Ceart at Avenida Santos Dumont 1589, and at the Feira do Artesanato on Avenida Beira Mar, opposite the Othon Palace.

GETTING TO THE PARK ★
Two buses a day, departing in the morning and in the evening, make the nine-hour journey from São Luís to Barreirinhas, the gateway to the park. Minibuses make the journey in eight hours and will collect passengers at their hotel. Contact the operators (Reis; tel 098 247 11 86) at least a day in advance. Another option, costing about 150 reais per person, is to charter a single-engined aircraft at the São Luís flying club. During the 40-minute flight you can look down on the park's stunning landscape, with its pattern of dunes and lakes spreading out over 116 square miles of sand.

LAKE BIRDS
Migratory birds frequently use the lakes as resting places. The most common species are *trinta-réis boreal*, *maçarico* (*Charadrius semipalmatus*) and *marrecas-de-asa-azul*, which come from the United States.

The Parque Nacional dos Lençóis Maranhenses (Maranhense Sheets National Park), about 220 miles from São Luís, is one of the most beautiful and most exotic parks in Brazil. Covering 370,000 acres of sand and dunes, the park takes in over 40 miles of beaches and stretches for 20 miles into the interior of the state. Maranhão's climate turns the park into a desert for six months of the year and a lush oasis the rest of the time. This is because the area has two very different seasons: in the summer, which runs from July through December, rainfall is very scarce and the heat is overwhelming; in the winter, which runs from January through July, the region receives almost 70 inches of rain. Troughs and valleys lying between the dunes of the Lençóis are then filled with water that forms lakes of a green or blue hue. The Parque Nacional dos Lençóis Maranhenses is named for this unusual phenomenon: when the lakes are full the local people think that the dunes look like sheets spread out to dry in the sun. The best time to visit the park is from May through July, at the end of the rainy period when the lakes are full. Getting to this paradisiacal location is difficult and some modes of transport are quicker than others.

BARREIRINHAS AND PONTA DO CABURÉ

BARREIRINHAS. The first stopping point is this pretty little town of some 30,000 inhabitants, founded on the banks of the Preguiça river, 170 miles from São Luís. The Preguiça river rises in the heart of the state, then flows alongside the Lençóis desert to the ocean. Barreirinhas is the main gateway to the park. Although it is relatively close to São Luís, the journey there is made quite difficult by a 90-mile stretch of unmetalled road. Barreirinhas not only has a river beach, but also some comfortable *pousadas* and several good restaurants. A boat ferries the local inhabitants to the riverside villages: daily departures are between 11am and noon depending on the tide, and the journey takes three hours. It is also possible to hire a *voadeira* (a small boat with an outboard motor) in the city; by this means the journey takes just 50 minutes. Hiring a *voadeira* is an excellent way of exploring the river and the villages along its course. The lush riverbanks are bordered with *buriti* and açaí palms and

stretches of mangrove swamp, and they are an unforgettable sight. From Barreirinhas you can take a boat to the Parque Nacional dos Lençóis Maranhenses, landing at the Ponta do Caburé peninsula.

Ponta do Caburé. This spit of sand between the Preguiça river and the sea is a stunningly beautiful natural site with basic facilities for visitors. It is a good base for visiting the small villages at the edge of the Lençóis dunes, such as Atins (half an hour's walk from the lakes) and Mandacaru (*opposite page*). The lighthouse in this village, opposite Caburé, offers a magnificent view of the river and the dunes. These villages are inhabited by communities of fishermen and mangrove crab gatherers. The small village bars serve fried shrimps and regional dishes.

The buriti palm
This palm is a very important tree to the inhabitants of the Lençóis, who use it as a building material, as a tool and as a source of food. Its leaves can be used as roofing for houses and can also be woven into straw mats and hats. The trunk is used to build houses and make dugout canoes. A very popular local sweet dish is made from its fruit.

Pequenos Lençóis and the Parnaíba delta

Pequenos Lençóis. The dunes to the west of Ponta do Caburé known as the Pequenos Lençóis (Little Sheets) are worth a detour. Covering a tenth of the park's total area, they are interspersed with lakes. There is also a deserted beach stretching for 20 miles to the sandbar of the Novo river, a stone's throw from Paulino Neves. This attractive little town, its streets lined with cashew and mango trees, is a pleasant and convenient place to stop because it is no more than 15 minutes' walk from the dunes and the lakes. In a four-wheel-drive vehicle, known as a *toyota* regardless of the make, it takes about 50 minutes to drive across the Pequenos Lençóis dunes from Ponta do Caburé to Paulino Neves.

Delta do Parnaíba. The Paranîba delta is the third-largest in the world. It consists of a labyrinth of rivers and mangrove swamps and more than 80 islands, and it straddles the border between the states of Maranhão and Piauí. About 65 percent of its land area lies within the Maranhão, and the remaining 35 percent within Piauí. Trips into the delta by four-wheel-drive leave from the small harbor town and beach resort of Tutóia, 50 minutes from Paulino Neves.

Delta do Parnaíba
The extensive mangrove swamp in this delta is still relatively unspoilt because economic development has not yet reached this area. Few regions in Brazil support such a wide variety of plants and animals.

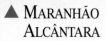

Alcântara ✪
The boat journey from São Luís to Alcântara takes about one hour. There are daily departures at 7am and 9.30am from the Terminal Hidroviário on Avenida Beira Mar, in Praia Grande. The timetable is subject to change, however, depending on the tide. Although you will need only a few hours to explore the town, it is worth spending a night in one of the simple *pousadas*. Lively dances are held at the Mangueira, the town's reggae club, at weekends.

Reggae
Boats from the Caribbean brought reggae to Maranhão in the 1970s. The beat won great popularity and the *radiolas* (groups of DJs who organize parties) took it to the four corners of the state. There are weekly reggae parties in São Luís and Alcântara.

'Doces de espécie'
This sweet is a Portuguese specialty made with coconut, cinnamon and cloves. It is sold in the streets and also from people's houses.

Centro de Lançamentos
This rocket-launching base four miles from the historic town is run by the Brazilian National Institute for Space Research (Instituto Nacional de Pesquisas Espaciais or INPE). It is the most modern rocket-launching center in Latin America.

Alcântara, a town of 19,800 inhabitants, lies opposite the island of São Luís on the other side of the Baía de São Marcos. Founded in the 17th century, it was one of the richest and most important towns in the state of Maranhão and the seat of the rural aristocracy. Until the second half of the 19th century Alcântara had a flourishing economy based on sugar ▲ *270*, salt production and the cultivation of rice and cotton. The long period of economic decline that ensued left Alcântara, like São Luís, frozen in time. Although São Luís has gradually been modernized, Alcântara is still virtually untouched, and it was listed as a historic town in 1948. It has an outstanding architectural heritage, with over three hundred colonial buildings as well as some interesting ruins, all of which are redolent of an illustrious past.

Praça Gomes de Castro. The most captivating sights in this beautiful colonial town are found here, a square, on which stands the Pelourinho, the whipping post where criminals and slaves were punished. Of the parish church, the Matriz de São Matias, built in 1648, only vestiges remain, and the Cadeia Pública, an 18th-century prison, is now the town hall (Prefeitura). Also of interest is the Museu Histórico, which contains religious artefacts and furniture dating from the 17th, 18th and 19th centuries, and festival costumes. Other interesting buildings here are the *sobrados* with *azulejos* ● *71* covering their façades.

Rua da Amargura. The ruins of the Pálacio Negro, a former slave market, and several small palaces that once belonged to the 'barons' ● *33* of Maranhão line this street.

Festa do Divino. The best time to visit Alcântara is at Whitsun, which comes in May or June. You will then have the opportunity to witness this colorful festival, which celebrates the Holy Spirit, albeit with a mixture of Catholic and African elements ● *42*. It lasts for twelve days and, accompanied by hymns and drumming, parades pass through the streets, where the houses are colorfully decorated for the occasion.

The North

'SERINGUEIRA'
The *seringueira* or rubber tree (*Hevea brasiliensis*) is indigenous to Amazonia. As its name suggests the latex extracted from its light, white wood is used to make rubber ▲ *312*. Rubber trees need warmth and plenty of moisture to sustain their growth. Their roots go down at least six feet below the ground and they have a spread of 65 feet. This means the soil must have a high water content. Although some rubber is still produced in Brazil, most now comes from extensive plantations in Southeast Asia.

MINING
In 1967 the largest deposits of iron ore in the world were discovered in the Serra dos Carajás, the mountainous territory of the Carajá American Indians, some 370 miles south of Belém. Since 1986 a huge open-cast mining operation (*below*) has scarred the landscape and some 50 million tons of ore are extracted each year. The discovery of a seam of gold at Serra Pelada (Bare Mountain) in 1980 attracted tens of thousands of gold panners. Today the mine's yield is markedly reduced.

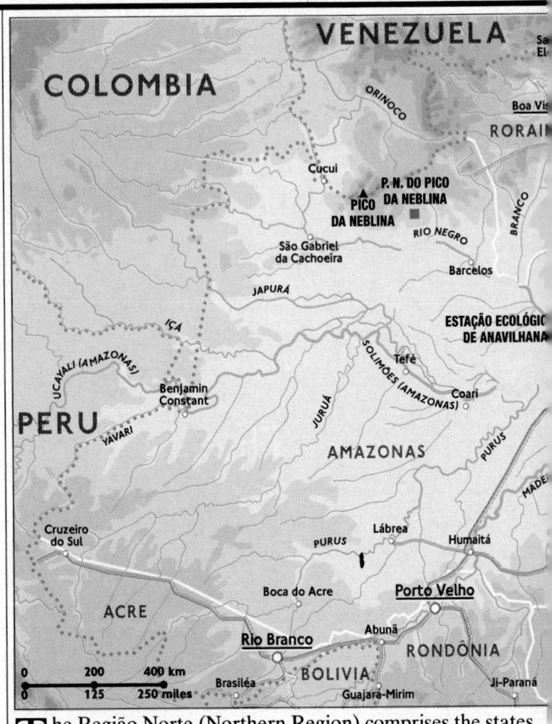

The Região Norte (Northern Region) comprises the states of Pará, Amazonas, Amapá, Roraima, Acre, Rindônia and Tocatins, and accounts for 45 percent of Brazilian territory. In 2002 the region's population was 11 million (or 7 percent of the population of Brazil), of which 200,000 were American Indians from 200 different ethnic groups ▲ *296*. The population, whose density averages 7.8 inhabitants per square mile, is irregularly distributed along the region's highways and rivers. With more than 160 species of tree per acre and the most diverse river wildlife in the world, the region's biodiversity is unparalleled. It is divided between three major ecosystems: unflooded forest (*terra firme*), flood plain (*varzéa*) and occasionally flooded forest (*igapós*) ▲ *306*.

HISTORY AND POPULATION

The Amazon and its many tributaries form the largest river network in the world. Until the 1970s these waterways were the only means of access into the great Amazonian basin. In the 17th century the Portuguese crown decided to assert its presence in Amazonia by establishing the city of Belém (in 1616) and building the fort of Barra (in 1669), around which Manaus was to grow. Mixed marriages and the settlement of American Indian in missions gave rise to *caboclos*, people of mixed European and American Indian descent who have long been in the majority in Amazonia. Until the 19th century the

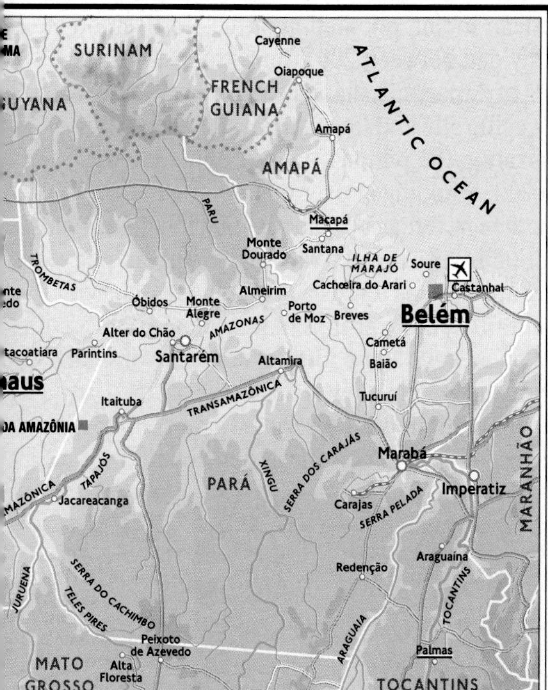

caboclos, who became nomadic, lived by hunting wild animals ▲ *307*, *308*, including jaguars, monkeys, caimans, tapirs, snakes and parrots, and collecting medicinal plants known collectively as *drogas do sertão*. In the second half of the 19th century the large-scale production of rubber led to the region's economic development. The Nordestinos who came in their thousands to work on the rubber 'plantations' also swelled its population ▲ *312*. This was the golden age of Manaus. The establishment of Brasília ▲ *200,* Brazil's new capital, led to the construction of highways that replaced the rivers as arteries of communication and turned the North into a region of roads bordered by agricultural land and pioneer towns. The main flow of migration came from the south and the roads enabled stock farmers to develop cattle farming on a huge scale. Pará, covering about 482,000 square miles, and Amazonas, covering about 600,000 square miles, are Brazil's largest states. Pará, whose capital is Belém ▲ *298*, occupies the eastern extremity of Amazonia and has been the focus of such major development projects as the Mineral Province of Carajás and the Barragem da Hidrelétrica de Tucuruí. Amazonas lies in the center of Amazonia, where ecosystems are still relatively intact, where most of the population lives along the rivers ● *56* and where overland communication is still difficult. Manaus ▲ *310*, the capital, lies at the confluence of the Solimões and Negro rivers. Like Belém, Manaus has a population of over one million but the inhabitants of Manaus live both on *terra firme* and in the *beiradões* (districts of houses built on piles) ● *82* that develop along the *igarapés* ▲ *304*. In 1967 the economy of Manaus was boosted by the creation of a Free Trade Zone for the electronics and mechanics industries and other activities.

The Amazon
Rising in the foothills of the Andes, the Ucayali and Marañón rivers merge to form the largest river in the world. The Amazon (known as the Amazonas in Peru and as the Solimões and then as the Amazonas in Brazil) flows west to east across the continent, covering more than 3,100 miles. Its 1,100 tributaries allied to torrential rainfall create a complex system of rivers whose waters are rich and muddy (in the case of the Solimões) and black and acidic (in the case of the Negro).

Endangered forest
Development, which began in the 1970s, has led to the degradation of environment and the destruction of the forest, which are particularly vulnerable in states such as Rondônia. Despite official initiatives and a heighted awareness among local populations, laws controlling the felling of trees are widely flouted. Slash-and-burn methods (*below*) are still used to extend pastureland and sustainable forestry management is still relatively unknown. Since 1975 15 percent of the Amazon forest (an area the size of France) has been destroyed.

▲ People of the Amazon Forest

In 1996 the American Indian population of the North stood at around 200,000, divided between 200 ethnic groups. Although the native peoples of Amazonia share a similar lifestyle, each of these groups is culturally and linguistically distinct. After Portuguese colonization the region's native population was dramatically reduced. Standing at over one million in the 16th century, it had been reduced to about 100,000 in the 1960s. Today the population is growing at a rate of 3.5 percent per year, although some groups have as few as a dozen members. While there are still about fifty ethnic groups that have no contact with the outside world, most have some form of contact, voluntary or enforced. Although Brazilian law is protective of the American Indian population, it is powerless to prevent the seizure of unmarked lands with no official demarcation.

Crafts and techniques

To whichever ethnic group they belong, all the American Indians of Amazonia are expert craftsmen. Their technical skill and knowledge of raw materials, which they obtain from plants and animals, allow them to produce beautiful handmade artefacts. The American Indians of Amazonia decorate pottery with the same patterns as they incorporate into their basketwork and weaving and use in body painting. They make pottery by mixing clay with organic or mineral substances. When the vessels have been shaped, they are made impermeable with an application of sap and are then vitrified by firing. Wild cotton is spun and woven into cloth that is used to make hammocks and loincloths. Palm leaves are woven to make baskets and hampers. They are also used for roofing houses.

Headdresses, feathers and ornaments

The peoples of many American Indian groups, for example the Kayapó, the Bororo, the Karajá (or Carajá) and the Caapor, appreciate the decorative value of feathers, the most colorful being those of parrots, macaws and toucans. They are skilled at making impressive and highly colorful headdresses, combining feathers with pearls and seeds or with any other kind of mineral or vegetable ornamentation. They also apply the down directly to their bodies. Feathers and other decorative elements such as tonsures, face and body paint, nasal piercing (sometimes with feather decoration), lip ornaments and pendant earrings are all used to decorate the body. Both men and women have a strong fondness for jewelry and both wear iridescent shells, necklaces and decorative belts.

American Indian protection

The SPI (Indian Protection Service) was set up in 1910 by Maréchal Rondôn, a military officer, explorer and defender of American Indian rights. His motto, 'Die if need be but never kill!', was unfortunately rarely put into practice. In 1967 the SPI was replaced by FUNAI, a public organization responsible for protecting American Indian culture and demarcating American Indian lands. Registering the ownership of land, which entails identification, demarcation and legalization, is a procedure that takes far too long. The American Indian lands that have been officially registered are barely 8 percent of their actual total and are inhabited by just 10 percent of the native population.

The shaman

In most American Indian villages the shaman represents the link between the visible and invisible worlds. He is a medicine man, a soothsayer and the guarantor of terrestrial and cosmic order. He plays a part in rituals when individuals or groups are threatened by chaos that may be brought by a birth, puberty, a death, illness or war. The shaman sometimes takes hallucinogenic drugs to help him fulfil his various responsibilities. Such drugs may also be taken by the rest of the group.

Ethnic groups and their languages

The 150 or so American Indian languages spoken in the North are divided into four main groups: Tupí (Parintintin and Mundurukú) and Gê (Kayapó, Bororo and Krenak), which have the highest number of speakers, and Carib and Arawak. Other, smaller linguistic families have a tighter geographical delimitation. This is the case of the Makú, Tucano and Yanomami languages. There are also about thirty languages that have no similarities with any other language of Amazonia. They are spoken by small numbers of people (in groups with as few as fourteen members to as many as 200). The only exception is the language spoken by the Tikuna, who with 20,000 members form the largest ethnic group.

▲ PARÁ ILHA DE MARAJÓ

BUFFALO
The buffalo, which feeds on aquatic plants and is quite at home in water, is perfectly adapted to the island's swamplands. According to local legend these animals swam ashore when a French ship carrying a cargo of buffalo from India to French Guiana went down off the Ilha de Marajó. Some buffalo have been domesticated and are ridden to school by children or by policemen as they go on their rounds.

CLIMATE AND SEASONS
Marajó has two clearly defined seasons. In winter (January–June) heavy rainfall floods one half of the island and turns the other half green. In summer (July–December) drought turns the landscape brown.

The Ilha de Marajó, which lies in the Amazon estuary just below the equator, is truly a world apart. Covering just over 19,000 square miles it is larger than the Netherlands or Belgium. It is in fact the largest delta island in the world. Its geographical location gave it the Guaraní name *Imbara-yo*, meaning 'barrier of the sea'. The Spanish explorer Vicente Yáñez Pinzón, who reached the island in 1500, is thought to be the first European to have set foot on it, before the fleet led by Pedro Álavrez Cabral 'discovered' Brazil ● *22* in the same year. The arrival of the Jesuit priest Antônio Vieira in 1658 marked the beginning of the European occupation of the island and the 'pacification' of its American Indian population. For the next hundred years the Ilha de Marajó was used as a base by Jesuit missionaries and its land was given over to extensive stock farming. Following the expulsion of the Jesuit order from Brazil ● *28* the island fell into decline but was later repopulated by Portuguese settlers and freed slaves. Today Marajó has not only some 250,000 inhabitants but also the largest buffalo herd in the country; the animals are reared mainly on the *fazendas* in the *região dos campos*, which cover almost 9,000 square miles in the eastern part of the island. The western part, the *região da mata*, which covers 10,000 square miles, consists predominantly of flooded forest. In this more typically Amazonian part of the island the main economic activity is the exploitation of the forest.

THE 'REGIÃO DOS CAMPOS'

The eastern part of the Ilha de Marajó is covered with wide swathes of pastureland. While some areas are flooded, others, where the topography reaches 65 feet above sea level, remain dry throughout the year. These arid areas are known locally as *tesos*. The eastern part of the island is given over to buffalo and zebu (a type of domesticated ox) ranching, Marajó's main economic activity, and it is not uncommon to come across herds of these cattle driven by herdsmen. The island's east coast is bordered by palm forests and dense mangrove forests.

Soure. With 18,000 inhabitants, Soure is the island's main town. The streets here are sandy and grassy, cars are a rarity and the bicycle and sometimes the buffalo are the principal forms of transport. Regular boat services from Belém and easy access to the region's most beautiful beaches as well as to its *fazendas* make Soure the best place on the island to stay. The beaches, vast expanses of sand reshaped from year to year by the tides, are the town's main attraction. The beach and bars of Praia do Pesqueiro are very popular at weekends. They are nine miles from Soure, and buses leave daily from the market place. Praia Araruna, by contrast, is within walking distance of the town. To reach it take the pathway that runs through cultivated fields and then cross the lagoon via the footbridge or by taking a ferry. These magnificent beaches also offer the opportunity to sample such local delicacies as *caranguejo* (crab) and *casquinha de caranguejo* (filled crab) in the shade of *barracas* (straw huts). Soure has a strong musical tradition and visitors can watch performances of *lundu* and *carimbó*, dances of African and American Indian origin that are typical of the state of Pará. In the 1970s, with the influence of such Caribbean rhythms as *zouk*, *salsa* and *merengue*, Pará became the birthplace of *lambada*, the pop version of *carimbó*.

'Fazendas'. Staying on a *fazenda* is one of the best ways to learn about life on the Ilha de Marajó. Many *fazendas*, which can be reached from Belém and Soure, are geared to receiving visitors. The more isolated ranches offer visitors the opportunity to observe the island's interesting wildlife. They also organize horse riding, night trips to watch *jacarés*, or caimans, and bird-watching trips to see the region's bird life, including *guarás* (graceful flamingos with long curved beaks).

Cachoeira do Arari. Founded around a *fazenda* established by Jesuits in the early 18th century, this is one of the oldest towns on the island. It is located on the banks of the Arari river, the main access route through this region. The town is the location of the island's sole museum, the Museu Marajoara, which contains a fine collection of *marajoara* pottery (*right*), made by American Indians from the first century BC. Cahoeira do Arari is 46 miles from Soure. The two towns are connected by an earth road that often becomes impassable during the rainy season.

Vila de Jenipapo. The boat journey from Cahoeira do Arari to Vila de Jenipapo takes five hours. The village is located on the shores of Lago Arari, which being 15 miles long and 3 miles wide is the island's largest lake. Because the region is flooded for most of the year, Vila de Jenipapo is built on piles and its sidewalks take the form of suspended footbridges.

Getting to the Ilha de Marajó ✪

The boat journey from Belém to Soure, on the east coast of the Ilha de Marajó, takes six hours. Riverboats operated by ENASA leave from the quay opposite the Mercado Ver-O-Peso in Belém. Boats leaving from the Cais da Escadinha, near the Mercado Ver-O-Peso, land at Camará, on the west coast of the island. It is advisable to check departure times and days in advance. The best time to visit the island is in summer, when it is easier to get around.

'Marajoara' pottery

Several important archeological sites on the Ilha de Marajó have yielded pottery made by the island's original inhabitants. Although the oldest pieces date from 980 BC, the art of potting on the island appears to have been at its height between AD 400 and 1300. Some very fine vases, funerary urns, dishes and other pieces can be seen in the Museu Paraense Emílio Goeldi in Belém ▲ *299* and in the Museu Marajoara in Cahoeira do Arari.

The Amazon basin is hot, humid and teeming with plant and animal life. Through it flows a majestic river that is the most powerful on the planet. As it rises and falls the water level constantly reshapes this vast and astonishingly complex fluvial landscape. The *varzéa*, or flood plain, and the *igapós*, the occasionally flooded forest, teem with fish and microorganisms. During the flood season *igarapés* appear. These navigable creeks can be used as shortcuts through the forest. A *furo* (hole) is a waterway linking two rivers or connecting a river and a lake.

QUEEN VICTORIA

Vitória régia, or Queen Victoria (*left*), is the giant water lily *Victoria amazonica* ▲ *143* named for the queen of England. Growing in stagnant water in the Amazon basin, it is the world's largest aquatic plant. Its huge platelike leaves can reach almost 7 feet in diameter. As the water level drops the plant dies off but its roots remain anchored in the mud. *Vitória régia* is one of the symbols of Amazonia.

TWO RIVERS AND THE GREAT ROAR
About six miles from Manaus ▲ *310* is the *encontro das águas*, the point at which the dark waters of the Negro and the greenish muddy waters of the Solimões meet, forming the Amazon. For three miles beyond their confluence the Negro and Solimões flow side by side without merging (*left*). Off the north coast of the Ilha de Marajó ▲ *300* you can watch a phenomenon known as the *pororoca* ('great roar' in Tupí-Guaraní). This great roaring wave, which can reach heights of 10 feet at high tide, runs for hundreds of miles up the Amazon. It is caused by the Amazon flowing into the Atlantic.

THE FLOODED FORESTS

In the *igapós*, or occasionally flooded forests, the water can reach depths of over 30 feet. The flowers, fruits and seeds of the forest's luxuriant vegetation then provide food for the fish and wildlife living in and around the river, who are attracted by its rich diversity. The Amazonian manatee (*opposite page, center*), which can weigh up to 1,100 lbs, feeds entirely on plants and is particularly fond of water hyacinths. The Amazon basin has some 3,000 species of fish and the abundance and variety of fish here have led to the development of fishing as a leisure acvitity.

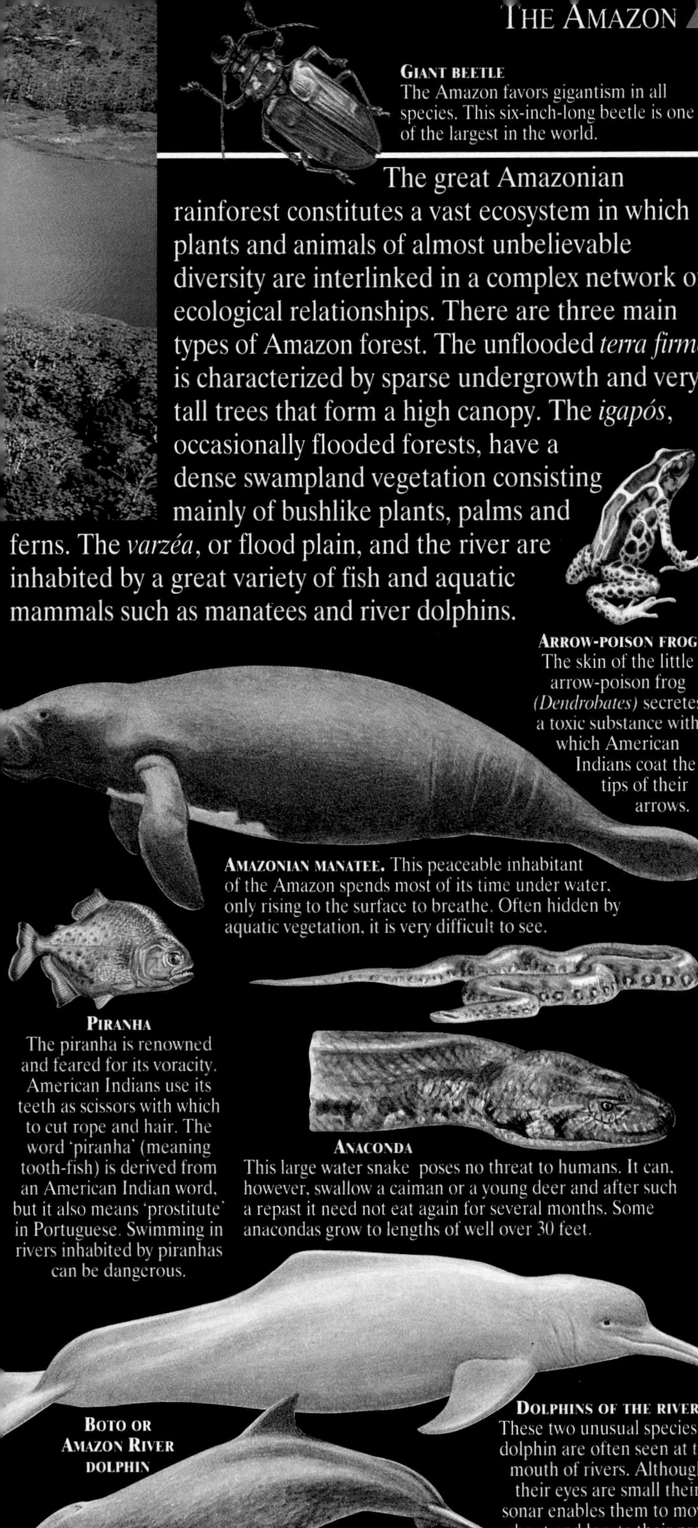

GIANT BEETLE
The Amazon favors gigantism in all species. This six-inch-long beetle is one of the largest in the world.

The great Amazonian rainforest constitutes a vast ecosystem in which plants and animals of almost unbelievable diversity are interlinked in a complex network of ecological relationships. There are three main types of Amazon forest. The unflooded *terra firme* is characterized by sparse undergrowth and very tall trees that form a high canopy. The *igapós*, occasionally flooded forests, have a dense swampland vegetation consisting mainly of bushlike plants, palms and ferns. The *varzéa*, or flood plain, and the river are inhabited by a great variety of fish and aquatic mammals such as manatees and river dolphins.

ARROW-POISON FROG
The skin of the little arrow-poison frog *(Dendrobates)* secretes a toxic substance with which American Indians coat the tips of their arrows.

AMAZONIAN MANATEE. This peaceable inhabitant of the Amazon spends most of its time under water, only rising to the surface to breathe. Often hidden by aquatic vegetation, it is very difficult to see.

PIRANHA
The piranha is renowned and feared for its voracity. American Indians use its teeth as scissors with which to cut rope and hair. The word 'piranha' (meaning tooth-fish) is derived from an American Indian word, but it also means 'prostitute' in Portuguese. Swimming in rivers inhabited by piranhas can be dangerous.

ANACONDA
This large water snake poses no threat to humans. It can, however, swallow a caiman or a young deer and after such a repast it need not eat again for several months. Some anacondas grow to lengths of well over 30 feet.

BOTO OR AMAZON RIVER DOLPHIN

TUCUXI OR ESTUARINE DOLPHIN

DOLPHINS OF THE RIVER
These two unusual species of dolphin are often seen at the mouth of rivers. Although their eyes are small their sonar enables them to move about and locate their prey in the turbulent waters in which they live.

YELLOW-RUMPED CACIQUE

THREE-TOED SLOTH
This tree-dwelling animal moves through the forest canopy with legendary slowness in search of the leaves on which it feeds.

The permanently warm, wet climate of the Amazon rainforest supports an infinite variety of plant and animal life. Here biological diversity is at its greatest. However, although the forest harbors a wealth of different species, most are rare and not easily seen.

HARPY-EAGLE

HOATZIN

CRIMSON TOPAZ HUMMINGBIRD

DARK-WINGED TRUMPETER

GREEN-WINGED MACAW

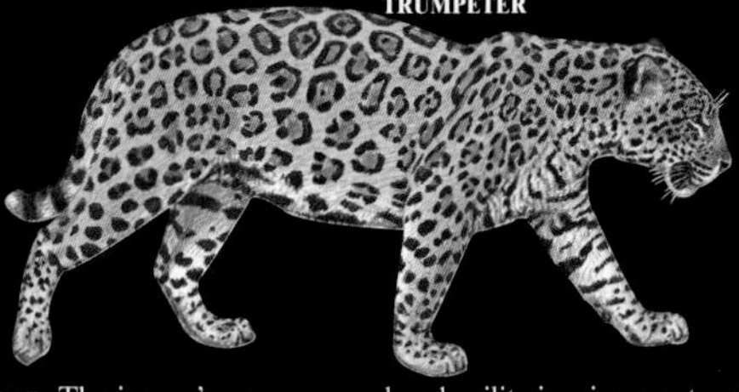

JAGUAR. The jaguar's power, speed and agility inspire great respect and the American Indians regard it as the undisputed king of the forest. It is rare and not usually a threat to humans, but its habit of using forest tracks cleared by the local inhabitants can lead to unexpected and rather alarming encounters.

SOUTH AMERICAN TAPIR
At around 550 lbs the tapir, a close relative of the horse and the rhinoceros, is the largest herbivorous mammal in Amazonia. It is an excellent swimmer and likes to stay near water, where it can take refuge to escape danger.

GREAT ANTEATER
Like the sloth the anteater belongs to the Edentata, an order of mammals native to South America. Its powerful claws enable it to break open ants' nests but are also a defense against predators.

Unparalleled biodiversity
The Amazon rainforest is a habitat that supports plant and animal life of unparalleled diversity. With patience and a little knowledge the interested and attentive observer will be able to see such wonders as orchids, chestnut-bellied herons and macaws, and may even glimpse a sloth. However, much of the biological wealth of the forest remains undiscovered and many species are still unknown and unrecorded. With almost every day that passes this unique ecosystem is increasingly severely threatened. Finding ways of preserving the 'great green hell' of myth and legend is an ever more urgent international challenge.

oati. The females and young live noisy bands that move through e forest by day. These lively and gile creatures are as much at home n the ground as in the trees.

EXCURSIONS FROM MANAUS ★
Because of its situation Manaus is an ideal base for excursions into the Amazonian forest. A boat ride from the city center lasting less than 30 minutes will take you to the heart of the forest, where you can experience its different environments (*igapós*, *igarapés* and *furos*) ▲ *304* at first hand. You can also take a ferry to Careiro and see the Negro and Solimões rivers merging majestically to form the Amazon ▲ *305*.

The city of Manaus, situated on the banks of the Rio Negro, is the capital of the state of Amazonas. It has a population of 1,200,000 and its principal economic activities are trade, industry and tourism. Manaus is a major staging post for tourists and its port is a starting point for trips into the Amazon forest ▲ *309*. The climate is hot and wet, with an average temperature of 79° F and torrential rains. Although the haphazard way in which it has developed has somewhat spoilt the city, Manaus still has a number of architectural treasures dating from its golden age as the country's rubber capital ▲ *312*.

HISTORY

The region was hardly exploited until the province of Amazonas and its capital, Manaus, were founded by the imperial government ● *25* in 1850, and when the Amazon was opened up to international shipping in 1866. The production of rubber production, latex being collected from the *seringueira* (*Hevea brasiliensis*) ▲ *294*, became increasingly important and was at its height from 1890 to 1910, when rubber was Brazil's second-largest export after coffee. This was Manaus' golden age and the foreign companies established in the city accelerated its development. From 1910 competition from Asian rubber plantations led to a decline in rubber production and the impoverishment of a city that had come to be known as the 'Paris of the tropics'. The economy did not recover until the Zona Franca de Manaus (Free Trade Zone) was created in 1967. It is, however, the tourist industry that promises to be the economic activity of the future. A walk through the center of Manaus allows a glimpse of its history.

TEATRO AMAZONAS. The Amazon Opera House, on Praça São Sebastião, was opened in 1896 and stands as a symbol of the prosperity brought by rubber when the industry was at its height. The materials used in the theate's construction include Italian and Portuguese marble, Venetian glass, steel from Glasgow, in Scotland, and tiles from Alsace, in France. The building's impressive cupola (*right*) can be seen from the Negro river. The theater, which has a seating capacity of 700, was classified as a historic monument and was completely restored in 1990, since when it has again been used as a concert hall and opera house.

PORTO FLUTUANTE. Manaus' floating harbor on Rua Marquês de Santa Cruz is filled with vessels of all kinds (*right*). The harbor is supported by floats in the form of huge metal cylinders that enable it to rise and fall with changes in the river level, which can fluctuate by as much as 50 feet. The floats also allow deep-drafted boats to moor here. The harbor was built by the British in 1902. It is now the only port of its kind in the world.

PALÁCIO RIO NEGRO. The palace, which was once the official residence of the governor of the state of Amazonas now houses a cultural center. It is located at Avenida 7 de Setembro 1540, an avenue that also has several buildings dating from the age of the rubber boom.

MUSEUMS IN MANAUS
The Museo do Índio, in a Salesian convent at Rua Duque de Caxias 356, contains weapons, woven artefacts, ritual objects and many pieces made by the American Indian tribes of the upper Negro river. The collections in the Museu do Homem do Norte at Avenida 7 de Setembro 1385 illustrate the lifestyle of the *caboclos* ● *56* of the Amazon.

THE NEGRO AND ARQUIPÉLAGO DE ANAVILHANAS

RIO NEGRO. You can hire a boat in the harbor at Manaus and make the three- to four-hour journey upriver to Anavilhanas, where you can swim off the Negro river's many white sand beaches. While the water near the riverbanks is warm, that of the midstream is cool and dark. The sandy riverbed purifies the waters, which are poor in nutrients, and rids them of mosquitoes.

ARQUIPÉLAGO DE ANAVILHANAS. The archipelago consists of some 400 islands scattered over an area about 60 miles long and 15 miles wide. During the rainy season many of the islands are completely submerged, while others have beautiful white sandy beaches all year round. The archipelago is an ecological reserve and you must therefore obtain prior authorization from the Ibama, the Brazilian organization for the protection of the environment.

MERCADO MUNICIPAL
The Mercado Municipal Adolfo Lisboa, on Rua dos Barás, is built in the Art Nouveau style and was opened in 1882. It consists of a central masonry structure flanked by two metal and glass pavilions. Situated on the bank of the Negro river, it is the main outlet for the fish caught in Amazonia as well as for other produce from the region.

▲ Rise and Fall of the Rubber Trade

In 1745, after exploring the Amazon, the French naturalist Charles de La Condamine returned home with a malleable substance produced by the tree *Hevea brasiliensis*. He called it *caoutchouc*, the French rendition of an American Indian word meaning 'weeping wood'. The vulcanization process developed by the American inventor Charles Goodyear in 1839 made rubber tougher, thus increasing the range of its potential applications. As industrialization took hold and the automobile was developed in the Unites States and in Europe, demand for this natural product rocketed. Rubber prices peaked in 1910 but subsequently collapsed when British and Dutch rubber plantations in Southeast Asia began to flood the world market.

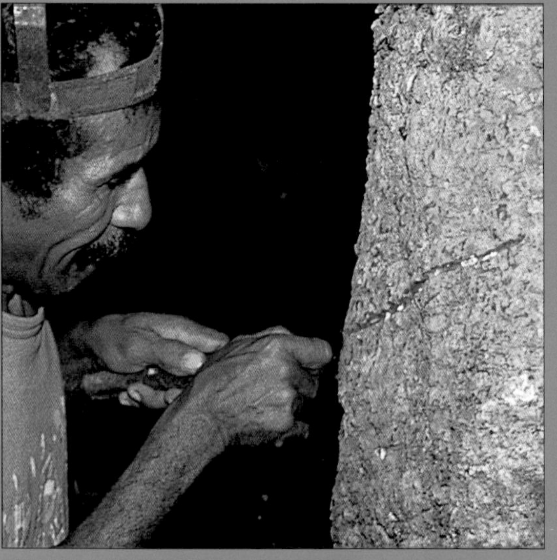

Collecting latex
Seringalistas are the owners of vast forest concessions. Every day *seringueiros* (tappers) cover huge distances within these concessions, following a very specific route as the rubber trees ▲ *294* are widely dispersed. They score (tap) the trees to collect the latex (*left*). It is then heated so that it coagulates, and is shaped into balls weighing over 65 lbs (*top*). The success of this system depended on the quality and number of rubber trees and the deployment of a ready workforce.

An endangered profession
Seringueiros still work in conditions barely unchanged since the 19th century. Today their livelihood is threatened because the forest is being destroyed to create pasture. The assassination of the *seringueiro* and union official Chico Mendes in 1988 focused world attention on the need to save the Amazonian forest.

Wealth and splendor
From 1880 to 1920 the population and prosperity of the Amazonian states increased dramatically. During this period rubber accounted for 25 percent of Brazil's exports and in volume was second only to its coffee exports ● *32*. The Amazon Opera House (1896) in Manaus stands as the symbol of Amazonia's golden age.

Practical information

◆ GETTING THERE

Websites, Climate, Useful addresses Currency, Telephones,

→ WEBSITES

■ **www.embratur.gov.br**
Brazil's official Ministry of Tourism web page containing comprehensive information about the country and its tourist industry.

■ **www.gringoes.com**
Informal and well-designed, a site written by gringos for gringos.

■ **www.maria-brazil.org**
Home of Brazilian culture on the web.

■ **www.brazil.com**
Special packages and flight deals.

■ **ww.braziltourism.org**
Slick, informative website.

■ **www.brazil.org.uk**
Information on all aspects of Brazil, including travel and tourism, culture and current affairs; plus an exhaustive list of websites on all things to do with Brazil.

CLIMATE

The seasons in Brazil are the reverse of those in the northern hemisphere. The country's proximity to the equator means that daylight hours are shorter. In Rio the sun sets at around 7.30 pm in summer, and in winter it's dark by 5.30 pm.

■ **December–March**
In December temperatures begin to rise, reaching 104° F in January.

■ **April–November**
Spring (Sep.–Nov.) and fall (March–May) are temperate seasons. The rainy season in the Nordeste lasts from April to July, later than in Rio state. In winter (June–Aug.) temperatures can fall to 59° F in Rio de Janeiro, 41° F in São Paulo and 64° F in Salvador.

Note:
You may need a few days to adjust to the high temperature and great humidity levels (especially in northern Brazil).

→ WHEN TO GO

If you want to catch the New Year celebrations and Carnival you need to buy your plane ticket and book your hotel several months in advance. If you go in June you'll be able to take part in the *festas juninas*, the June festivals held throughout the Nordeste on June 13, 24 and 29 in honor of saints Anthony, John and Peter. The best time to visit the Pantanal is from May through September, after the rainy season. In Amazonia the rainy season varies from region to region.

Note:
During the low season, March–May and Aug.–Nov., plane fares and the price of hotel rooms are reduced by as much as 50 percent.

USEFUL ADDRESSES

→ IN THE UK

■ **Brazilian Embassy**
32 Green St
London W1K 7AT
Tel. (020) 7399 9000
www.brazil.org.uk
(020) 7925 3979 (visa)
visa@cgbrasil.org.uk
(020) 7925 3977 (passport)
passaportes@cgbrasil.org.uk
7925 3982 (assistance to Brazilian citizens)
assistencia@cgbrasil.org.uk

■ **Tourist Office**
32 Green St
London W1K 7AT
Tel. (020) 7399 9000
tourism@brazil.org.uk

→ IN THE US

■ **Brazilian Embassy**
3006 Massachusetts Ave NW, Washington DC 20008 3634
Tel. (202) 238 2700
www.brasilemb.org

■ **Brazilian Consulate General**
1185 Avenue of the Americas, 21st Floor
New York, NY 10036
Tel. (917) 777 7777
www.brazilny.org
consulado@brazilny.org

■ **Brazilian Tourist Office**
3006 Massachusetts Ave NW, Washington DC 20008
Tel. 1 800 727 2945
www.braziltourism.org

Also see:
www.brazilsf.org
www.brazilhouston.org
www.brazilmiami.org

→ IN CANADA

■ **Brazilian Consulate General**
2000 Mansfield St
Suite 1700, Montreal, Quebec H3A 3A5
Tel. (514) 499 0968
consbras@total.net

■ **Brazilian Tourist Office**
Toronto Consulate
77 Bloor St West, Suite 1109, Toronto
Ontario M5S 1M2
Tel. (416) 922 2503
www.consbrastoronto.org

CURRENCY

Real; R$ (plural, reis)
R$10 = US$4.45/£2.50
US$1 = R$2.25
£1 = R$3.95 (at the time of writing). The best way of buying reis is through a bank. In Brazil the US dollar is the most highly valued foreign currency. Traveler's checks (in dollars) can easily be changed in banks and foreign exchange offices. Credit cards are accepted in most stores and restaurants.

Warning:
If you take a supply of dollars make sure you have plenty of small denominations for tips and small transactions. See also Money ◆ **321**.

TELEPHONES

→ CALLING BRAZIL

Dial the international code (00 from the UK, 011 from the US), followed by the country code (55), then the area code (for example 21 for Rio de Janeiro), followed by the number. See also Telephones ◆ **321**.

→ MOBILE PHONES

The main Brazilian operators are Telemar and TIM Brasil. US-style analog and digital networks also exist. The country's many network providers include TCO and Americel. GSM 1800 networks have recently been established.

FORMALITIES

→ PASSPORT

Your passport must be valid for six

months beyond the date of your intended return. You should also have a return ticket.
Warning:
To avoid unexpected fines, check with customs on your arrival in Brazil that the stamps and writing (even in pencil) on the immigration form and/or your passport and visas do in fact entitle you to stay in Brazil for the length of time you intend.

→ VISAS
UK passport-holders do not need a visa if they are staying in Brazil as tourists for up to 90 days. If you want to stay for longer (to a maximum of 180 days), contact the federal police on your arrival in Brazil. US and Canadian passport-holders need a visa and will be asked to show a return ticket. Contact your nearest Brazilian consulate or (if a US citizen) visit *www.braziltourism.org*

→ CUSTOMS
The luggage of travelers with nothing to declare is searched at random. It is forbidden to bring animal products into the country unless they are vacuum-packed. Any that are not packed in this way will be destroyed.
Note:
Gifts up to a value of $500 are exempt from customs duty.

→ AIRPORT TAX
Aiport tax is payable in cash, in US$ or R$, before boarding the plane: US$72/£38 for international flights and US$1.30–6.50 (£0.70–3.45) for internal flights. Call your airline for details of payment.

AIRLINE COMPANIES

The main points of entry into Brazil for visitors from Europe and North America are Rio de Janeiro and São Paulo. However flights also travel from Europe and North America to Fortaleza, Recife and Salvador.

→ FROM THE UK
Direct daily flights from London Heathrow to Rio de Janeiro and São Paulo are provided by British Airways, Varig and others. The flight time from London to Brazil is about 11 hours. Alternatively, Air France, Alitalia, KLM, Lufthansa, Swissair, TAP and Iberia operate connecting flights from London to Brazil, with a stop in a European capital. Round-trip flights from London are available for under £400.

■ Airlines
British Airways
Tel. 0870 850 9850
www.britishairways.com
Varig
Tel. (020) 8321 7170
Tel. 0845 603 7601
www.varig.co.uk
TAM
www.tam.com.br

→ FROM THE US
Regular flights from the US to Brazil are provided by Varig, TAM, Continental and United Airlines. To Rio de Janeiro or São Paulo the flight time from Los Angeles is 14 hours, from San Francisco 16 hours, from New York 10 hours, from Atlanta 11 hours and from Miami 9 hours. Round-trip flights from New York should cost under $700, and around $900 from California. Round-trip from Miami are around $500.
Note:
Flights from New York City no longer travel non-stop to Rio; most often a layover in Miami or São Paulo is required.

■ Airlines
British Airways
Tel. 1 800 AIRWAYS
www.ba.com
Continental
Tel. 1 800 525 0280
www.continental.com
United Airlines
Tel. 1 800 UNITED
www.united.com
Varig
Tel. 1800 468 2744
www.varigtravel.com

→ FROM CANADA
Delta, Continental and United Airlines offer connecting flights to Brazil with a stop in a major US city. Round-trip flights from Toronto or Montreal may begin at $1,500.

→ BRAZIL PASS
Brazilian companies offer airline vouchers for different areas (the South, the Nordeste and the whole of Brazil), valid for 21 days. These vouchers can be purchased in other countries with the presentation of a transatlantic ticket. See Airports ◆ 316
TAM
www.tam.com.br
Varig
www.varig.com

INSURANCE

As always it is best to arrange comprehensive travel and medical insurance before you go, through your insurance broker, credit card company or travel agent.

TIME DIFFERENCE

■ Main time zone
The main time zone runs north to south through the center and east of Brazil and includes the major state capitals: Belém, São Luiz, Rio de Janeiro, Recife, Salvador, Brasília, Belo Horizonte, São Paulo, Curitiba and Porto Alegre. The main time zone is 3 hours behind London (2 hours Nov.–March); it is 2 hours ahead of New York and 5 hours ahead of LA.
Warning:
The dates of time changes may vary according to the states and the year.

■ Ilha de Fernando de Noronda
The Ilha de Fernando lies to the east of Recife and is one hour ahead of the main time zone.

■ Pantanal and Amazonia
Western Brazil, from Amazonia to the Pantanal, is one hour behind the main time zone.

■ The far west
The far western part of Amazonia, up to the border with Peru, and the state of Acre are 2 hours behind the main time zone.

VACCINATIONS

■ Compulsory
If you are going to the Pantanal or Amazonia you must be vaccinated against yellow fever. If you enter Brazil from Bolivia or Peru you will be asked to show a vaccination certificate.

■ Recommended
Typhoid, tetanus, polio, hepatitis A and B, diphtheria and malaria.

■ Information
For the latest information on compulsory and recommended vaccinations consult the nearest Brazilian consulate.

AIRPORTS

→ INTERNATIONAL AIRPORTS

■ **Belém**
AEROPORTO INTERNACIONAL VAL-DE-CANS, 7 miles from the city center
Tel. (91) 210 60 00

■ **Belo Horizonte**
AEROPORTO TANCREDO NEVES, 25 miles from the city center
Tel. (31) 36 89 27 00

■ **Brasília**
AEROPORTO INTERNACIONAL, 7 miles from the city center
Tel. (61) 364 90 00

■ **Campo Grande**
AEROPORTO Avenida Duque de Caxias, 4½ miles from the city center
Tel. (67) 368 60 00

■ **Cuiabá**
AEROPORTO MARECHAL RONDON, 6 miles from the city center
Tel. (65) 614 25 00

■ **Curitiba**
AEROPORTO ALFONSO PENA, 10½ miles from the city center
Tel. (41) 381 15 15

■ **Florianópolis**
AEROPORTO HERCÍLIO LUZ, 7½ miles from the city center
Tel. (48) 331 40 00

■ **Fortaleza**
AEROPORTO PINTO MARTINS, 4 miles from the city center
Tel. (85) 34 77 12 00

■ **Fernando de Noronha Archipelago**
AEROPORTO, 2 miles from Vila dos Remédios
Tel. (81) 34 64 41 88

■ **Foz do Iguaçu**
AEROPORTO INTERNACIONAL 10 miles from the city center
Tel. (45) 521 42 00

■ **Manaus**
AEROPORTO INTERNACIONAL EDUARDO GOMES 9 miles from the city center
Tel. (92) 652 12 12

■ **Porto Alegre**
AEROPORTO SALGADO FILHO, 5 miles from the city center
Tel. (53) 33 58 20 00

■ **Recife**
AEROPORTO GUARAPES 7 miles from the city center
Tel. (81) 34 64 41 88

■ **Rio de Janeiro**
AEROPORTO GALEÃO ANTÔNIO CARLOS JOBIM, 13 miles from the city center
Tel. (21) 33 98 50 50

■ **Salvador**
AEROPORTO DOIS DE JULHO, 18 miles from the city center
Tel. (71) 204 10 10

■ **São Luís**
AEROPORTO INTERNACIONAL MARECHAL CUNHA MACHADO, 9½ miles from the city center
Tel. (98) 32 17 61 00

■ **São Paulo**
AEROPORTO GUARULHOS, 16 miles from the city center
Tel. (11) 64 45 29 45

→ INTERNAL AIRPORTS

■ **Belo Horizonte**
AEROPORTO TDE PAMPULHA, 6 miles from the city center
Tel. (31) 34 90 20 01

■ **São Paulo**
AEROPORTO CONGONHAS (PONTE AÉREA), 5 miles from the city center
Tel. (11) 50 90 90 00

→ INTERNAL AIRLINES

Varig, TAM, Gol and Vaspa are the largest internal carriers. Smaller airlines providing regional services include Nordeste in the Nordeste, Riosul in the Sud, and Taba in Amazonia. The monthly magazine *Panrotas* gives all timetables and fares for internal air travel.

→ BRAZIL AIRPASS

The airpass is available through Varig and can be purchased only outside of Brazil and only in conjunction with a Varig or British Airways international carrier ticket. One airpass may be purchased per person. The pass costs US$560 for up to five internal flights. Validity is for 21 days from first date of travel.

■ **Information**
Varig UK:
Tel. 0845 603 7601
www.varig.co.uk
Varig US:
Tel. 1 800 468 2744
www.varigtravel.com
It is also possible to buy equivalent airpasses with VASP, Transbrasil and TAM in conjunction with any international carrier.

BOATS

Brazil's 5,700 miles of coastline and its many rivers and islands can be reached by ferry or private boat. River and maritime transport is not as developed and competitive as road transport. Information on boat trips is available from tourist offices. Regular lines operate up and down the Amazon river between Manaus and Belém .

BUSES

→ URBAN BUSES

To travel by bus you need a good knowledge of local districts and bus routes. In large towns and cities bus networks are complicated and maps rare. Although the route is usually indicated on the front of the bus it's advisable to check before boarding. You board the bus at the back; the *cobrador* takes your fare and releases the turnstile that allows passengers through to the seats. Some routes are served by air-conditioned buses *(frescão)*, which are more expensive.
Warning: *Avoid taking valuables with you on the bus. It is also best to have your change ready before you board. To request the next stop pull the cord on the ceiling.*

→ MINIBUSES

Minibuses (known as *vans* in Rio and as *peruas* in São Paulo) are a common means of transport during rush hours. Traveling by minibus is cheaper than taking a cab and more comfortable than traveling by bus. Although minibuses are not regulated they are generally tolerated by the authorities.

BUS STATIONS

Coaches, a popular form of transport in Brazil, operate between major towns and cities. It's best to take a couchette *(leito)* or an air-conditioned coach *(com ar condicionado)*, especially for long journeys.

■ **Belém**
RODOVIÁRIA
Tel. (91) 266 26 25

■ **Belo Horizonte**
RODOVIÁRIA ISRAEL PINHEIRO
Tel. (31) 32 71 30 00

■ **Brasília**
RODOFERROVIÁRIA Eixo Monumental
Tel. (61) 363 22 81

■ **Curitiba**
RODOVIÁRIA CURIMBA
Tel. (41) 320 30 00

■ **Florianópolis**
RODOVIÁRIA In the city center
Tel. (48) 212 31 00

■ **Fortaleza**
RODOVIÁRIA
Tel. (85) 32 56 21 00

■ **Foz do Iguaçu**
RODOVIÁRIA INTERNACIONAL
Tel. (45) 522 25 90

■ **Manaus**
RODOVIÁRIA
Tel. (92) 642 55 22

■ **Porto Alegre**
RODOVIÁRIA
Two terminuses: one domestic, the other international
Tel. (51) 32 100 101
■ **Recife**
TERMINAL INTEGRADO DOS PASSAGEIROS
Tel. (81) 34 52 39 90
■ **Rio de Janeiro**
RODOVIÁRIA NOVO RIO
Avenida Francisco Bicalho 1, Santo Cristo
Tel. (21) 32 13 18 00
■ **Salvador**
RODOVIÁRIA
Tel. (71) 450 44 88
■ **São Luis**
RODOVIÁRIA
6 miles from the city center
Tel. (98) 32 49 24 88
■ **São Paulo**
TERMINAL DO TIETÊ
Coaches to Rio, the interior and neighboring countries
Tel. (11) 32 35 03 22
TERMINAL JABAQUARA
Coaches serving the coast
Tel. (11) 32 35 03 22

CAR RENTAL

You will find larger companies such as Hertz and Avis in all airports. Their Brazilian equivalents (Localiza and Unidas) may offer competitive rates. Read the rental contract carefully, checking that the insurance cover is comprehensive and that the excess is not too high.

Warning:
Some cars run on alcohol, so don't make a mistake at the gas station!

♦ AVIS
Tel. 0800 19 84 56
♦ HERTZ
Tel. 0800 701 73 00
♦ LOCALIZA
Tel. 0800 99 20 00
♦ UNIDAS (in São Paulo, Rio de Janeiro and Bahia)
Tel. 4001 22 22
♦ UNIDAS (elsewhere)
Tel. 0800 121 121

SUBWAY

■ **Brasília**
14 stations serving the city. Mon.–Sat. 6am–11pm.
■ **Porto Alegre**
15 stations serving the city, bus terminus and airport.
Daily 5am–11pm.
■ **Recife**
Linking the TIP (bus station) and the city center.
Daily 5am–11pm.
■ **Rio de Janeiro**
Reliable and air-conditioned, Rio's subway serves mainly the Centro and Zona Norte but also runs to Copacabana.
Mon.– Sat. 5am–midnight, Sun. 7am–11pm.
■ **São Paulo**
Limited for such a large city but fast and reliable. Daily 4.40am–midnight.

TRAFFIC

→ DRIVING
Brazilians drive on the right-hand side of the road.

→ ROAD SIGNS
Road signs are often inadequate. If you intend to travel around by car buy a *Quatro Rodas* road map of the relevant region (available at kiosks).

→ PARKING
Parking in towns and cities can be a problem. It is best to use supervized parking places. It is customary to tip (R$1–2) the person who has kept an eye on your vehicle.

Note:
Brazilian drivers can be unpredictable; many will pass on the right or use the hard shoulder in traffic jams.

When walking, always cross roads at pedestrian crossings and, although this may sound obvious, ensure that the traffic has stopped before crossing the road!

TAXIS

Cabs are a popular and affordable means of getting around. You can pick up an ordinary cab (yellow in Rio, white in São Paulo) virtually anywhere. The variously colored *rádio-táxis* are more comfortable and quite expensive but fares are preset.

→ FARES
A meter indicates the fare for the journey. The pick-up charge varies from city to city. Two rates usually apply.
■ **Rio de Janeiro**
The meter starts at R$3. Rate 2 is 8 percent higher.
♦ RATE 1 (BANDEIRA 1)
Mon.–Sat. 6am–9pm.
♦ RATE 2 (BANDEIRA 2)
Mon.–Fri. 9pm–6am, Sat.–Sun., public holidays, outside the city and on the hills. In Rio, Rate 2 also applies throughout December.

→ CAB COMPANIES
At bus stations and airports cab companies charge set rates according to zone. You pay at the time of booking. Fixed fares obviate the risk of nasty surprises when paying on arrival at your destination.

→ RADIO-TAXIS
■ **Brasília**
RÁDIO TÁXI
Tel. (61) 325 30 30
COOBRÁS
Tel. (61) 224 10 00
■ **Rio de Janeiro**
CENTRAL DE TÁXI
Tel. (21) 38 99 01 01
COOPERTRAMO
Tel. (21) 25 60 20 22
■ **Salvador**
ALÔTÁXI
Tel. (71) 388 44 11
TELETÁXI
Tel. (71) 341 99 88
■ **São Paulo**
CHAME TÁXI
Tel. (11) 37 35 10 58
COOPERTAX
Tel. (11) 69 41 25 55
APÓLO
Tel. (11) 69 14 82 44

TRAINS

The Brazilian rail network carries freight but virtually no passengers. There are, however, passenger services between some city centers and their outlying suburbs.

ACCOMMODATION

→ HOTELS

Most hotels are located in tourist areas: near historic sites, in city centers and on the seafront. Although the more modern hotels have a wider range of facilities and offer greater comfort, the quality of hotel accommodation still varies greatly.

■ **Hotel chains**

ACCOR
The Accor group has some 50 hotels and residential hotels throughout Brazil. Reservations: 0800 703 700
www.accor.com

OTHON
Most of the Othon chain's hotels are in São Paulo, Salvador, Belo Horizonte, Rio de Janeiro, Manaus, Maceio and Fortaleza. Reservations: 0800 701 00 98

■ **Prices**

Breakfast is almost always included in the price of a room but remember to take account of various taxes: a 10 percent service charge, sometimes 5 percent for local taxes and a 1 percent tourist tax. Often the prices that hotels actually charge are lower than those that they advertise, and you can always ask for a discount *(desconto)*, especially during the low season. Prices are higher at New Year and during Carnival. Book in advance.

→ RESIDENTIAL HOTELS

For longer stays it is generally more cost-effective to stay in a hotel apartment, which have their own kitchen. Daily rates tend to decrease the longer you stay.

→ 'POUSADAS'

The equivalent of family-run boarding houses, *pousadas* range from the basic to the luxurious (for example in a colonial residence). *Pousadas* are popular with Brazilians holidaying in small coastal resorts and in places aways from large towns and cities. Room service and breakfast are included in the price per night. The more modest *pousadas* don't have phones or air conditioning.

→ MOTELS

Brazilian motels are not the same as those in the US. They are more widely used for clandestine meetings, sometimes for just an hour or two, rather than as a lodging for tourists.

→ CAMPING

Camping is an attractive option for those wishing to explore the national parks. The *Quatro Rodas* camping guide (sold in kiosks) lists available camp sites.
www.campingclube.com.br

→ YOUTH HOSTELS

You will need an international YHA card. There are more than 90 youth hostels in Brazil.
www.hostel.org.br
An official directory can be consulted:

■ **In Brazil**
Tel. (21) 2531 2234

■ **In Rio de Janeiro**
Hosteling International
Rua General Dioníso, 63 – Botafogo
Tel. (21) 2286 0303

COMMUNICATIONS

→ MAIL

Stamps can be purchased at post offices. They're open Mon.–Sat. 8am–6pm (noon Sat).
Warning:
Do not leave stamped mail at the hotel reception desk.

→ INTERNET

Brazil's Internet network is well developed. You will find Internet cafés in most cities, tourist offices and hotels. Prices range from R$1 to R$3 for 10 minutes online.

→ TELEGRAMS AND FAXES

In hotels and at post offices.

→ TELEPHONE

The privatization of the Brazilian telephone network in 2001 led to extensive number changes. Many 7-digit numbers became 8-digit numbers, and intercity and international numbers required an additional 'operator' code. The best operator is Embratel, Brazil's largest telecommu-nications company. Its operator code (21) is not to be confused with the area code for Rio de Janeiro. Other operators include Intelig (code 23) or Telemar (code 31).

■ **Reduced rates**

Calls are cheaper in the evenings and at weekends. Precise times vary according to individual phone companies.

■ **Phone cards**

Cartões telefônicos are available from newspaper kiosks. They are sold without plastic

International calls
00 + (operator code) + (country code) + (local code, omitting the initial 0 if relevant) + the number

Intercity calls
0 + 21+ (operator code) + (area code) + the number

Local calls
Dial the number (7 or 8 digits)

International collect calls
0800 703 21 11 + speak to the operator

Intercity collect calls
90 + (operator code) + (area code) + the number

Local collect calls
90 + 90 + the number

AREA CODES OF THE MAIN STATE CAPITALS	
Belém (Pará)	91
Belo Horizonte (Minas Gerais)	31
Brasília (Distrito Federal)	61
Curitiba (Paraná)	41
Florianópolis (Santa Catarina)	48
Fortaleza (Ceará)	85
Manaus (Amazonas)	92
Porto Alegre (Rio Grande do Sul)	51
Recife (Pernambuco)	81
Rio de Janeiro (Rio de Janeiro)	21
Salvador (Bahia)	71
São Luis (Maranhão)	98
São Paulo (São Paulo)	11

USEFUL NUMBERS	
Ambulance	192
Overnight pharmacies	136
Police	190
Fire service	193
Information	102
International operator	0800 703 21 11

packaging and cost from R$2.50 to R$10.

■ International calls
International calls from Brazil are expensive: to the UK the rate is about US$3 per minute; to the US and Canada it is about US$2.50 per minute.

■ Mobile phones
You can rent mobile phones in Brazil: inquire at airports and in hotels. See Telephones ◆ **315.**

CRAFTS AND SOUVENIRS

→ CRAFTS

■ Soapstone
Soapstone is widely used by craftsmen in Minas Gerais to make all kinds of objects, including statuettes.

■ American Indian crafts
You will find these on sale in FUNAI (Fundação Nacional do Índio) stores and museum shops.

■ Lace
The very delicate *renda* (lace) *de bilro* is produced by lacemakers in Fortaleza and on the east coast of Ceará state.

■ Ceramic figurines
The specialty of craftsmen in the Nordeste, these figurines depict rural scenes typical of the daily life and traditions of the Nordeste, such as workers returning from the fields, a bride and groom, and immigrant families.

■ Hammocks
Hammocks made of rope, mesh, cotton or synthetic fabric are found in all Brazilian homes.

■ Wood carving
Although this is a craft practiced throughout Brazil, the carving of Minas Gerais is particularly intricate.

→ FITA DE NOSSO SENHOR DO BONFIM
A popular piece of folklore, this is a bracelet that is tied round the wrist with three knots. For each knot the wearer makes a wish that will be granted when the bracelet disintegrates naturally.

→ SEMIPRECIOUS STONES
Many semiprecious stones on sale in Brazil come from Minas Gerais. It is best to buy them from such reputable dealers as Amsterdam-Sauer.

DRINKS

■ Beer
Beer is served well chilled. It comes in small bottles *(lata)*, on draft *(chopp)* and in 600 ml bottles (about 1 US pint). The most popular brands are Antártica, Brahma, Skol and Bohemia.

■ Coffee
Bars usually serve black filter coffee (Americano), but espresso is becoming more and more popular.

■ Cocktails
The main ingredient of many cocktails is ***cachaça***, or Brazilian rum. The most popular cocktails are ***caipirinha*** (*cachaça*, lime, sugar, crushed ice), *caipirissima* (with rum instead of cachaça), *caipiroska* (with vodka); ***batida*** (*cachaça* and fruit, sometimes mixed with sweetened condensed milk); ***quentão*** (served hot, with cinnamon, ginger and cloves); ***capeta*** (with sweetened condensed milk and *guaraná*).

■ Water
Drinking tap water is not recommended. It is best to keep to mineral water, which is widely available.

■ Guaraná
Extracted from an Amazonian fruit, this powder is not only a mental and muscular stimulant but is also reputed to be an aphrodisiac. It comes as a fizzy or still drink.

■ Fruit juices
Graviola, *açaí*, *acerola*, *cajú*, *goiaba*, *manga* and *maracujá* are just a few of the fresh fruit juices sold on street corners. Tell the vendor if you don't want sugar or ice.

■ Wine
Brazilian wines are not yet on a par with those of Argentina and Chile.

DRUGS

The possession of drugs, even in small quantities, carries a heavy penalty.

EATING OUT

Brazilian food is a mixture of Portuguese, African and indigenous elements, with rice (*arroz*), black beans (*feijão*) and manioc flour (*farofa*) the staple ingredients. Rio, the city of immigrants par excellence, offers not only regional specialties but also dishes from Portugal, Lebanon, Italy etc.

→ EATING OUT ON A BUDGET

■ Appetizers
Some restaurants serve appetizers that you can nibble on before ordering your meal. They are often served as a matter of course but they will be added to the tab and can be refused.

■ Boteco, Botequim
A small local bar-café serving a range of good-quality hearty traditional dishes such as cod (*bacalhau*), squid (*lulas*), rice with broccoli. Portions can be shared between two people.

■ Comida a quilo
Self-service. A popular way of eating in business districts. You pay for your meal according to the weight of the food on your plate.

■ Comida caseira
Establishments advertising *comida caseira* serve simple family fare.

■ Lanchonete
Bar-sandwich store where you eat at the counter. It serves snacks and fresh fruit juice, with a great flair for combinations like pineapple-mint and carrot-beetroot-orange. Also, *açaí na tigela*: Amazonian fruit in the form of a sorbet.

→ SNACKING
Regional specialties, which may be savory, such as *acarajé* (deep fried pea balls) and *vatapá* (spicy shrimp puree) or sweet such as *quindim* (coconut pie) and *pé de moleque* (a dark spicy cake), are sold on street corners by *bainanas* in traditional white attire.

■ Petiscos
Bars, especially in Rio, often offer *petiscos*, snacks designed to accompany drinks, but that can easily make up a meal in their own right.
Frango à passarinho: pieces of fried chicken.
Pastel: fried or baked turnovers with filling.
Empada: small meat pasty.
Bolinho de bacalhau: cod fish ball.
Aipim frito: fried manioc.
Caldinho de feijão: black-bean broth, drunk hot.
Carne seca desfiada: strips of dried meat, with boiled onions,

farofa or fried manioc.

→ **SOME CULINARY TERMS**
Almoço executivo: dish of the day, served weekday lunchtime.
Feijoada: Brazil's national dish, invented by the slaves and served on Saturdays. Sausages, lard, smoked meat and black beans with cabbage, oranges, farofa and rice.
Prato feito: also called *prato comercial* is a full plate of fish or meat (whichever is the day's special) accompanied by the trio of *arroz, feijão* and *farofa*.

ELECTRICITY

Voltage in parts of the North and the Nordeste and in Brasília is 220 V. Elsewhere in Brazil it is 110 V/60 Htz. Most of the more recently built hotels have both voltages. Adaptors are sometimes available.

HEALTH

Although staffed by well-trained professionals, the public health infrastructure is not that reliable because there are shortages of equiment and medication. In the event of a serious medical problem, you'll have to choose between an expensive private clinic and repatriation. It is therefore advisable to take out a specific insurance policy for medical care before you leave. Consulates and hotels in Brazil have lists of doctors who speak English.

→ **PHARMACIES**
Basic medical care, such as dressings and injections, is provided by Brazil's many well-stocked pharmacies.

→ **FIRST AID KIT**
Your first aid kit should contain sunblock cream, insect repellent, band aids and dressings, antibiotics, painkillers, antidiarrhea medication, antiseptic and condoms, which are called *camisinhas*.

KNOW-HOW

→ **ABRAÇO**
The Brazilians are a demonstrative people who like to express their cordiality and friendship. This warmth of feeling is reflected in their body language. Greetings are soon accompanied by a warm embrace *(abraço)* and gentle pats on the back. Conversations are punctuated by gestures and physical contact between those involved. It's a way of expressing the joy of discussion and the pleasure of being with other people.

→ **THE BODY BEAUTIFUL**
Brazilians keep themselves in shape with workouts and bodybuilding sessions in the gym *(academia)*. This daily attention to the body, shown off to advantage by close-fitting clothes, seems to be the expression of the new Brazilian eroticism. The cult of the body beautiful is particularly noticeable on the coast. However, Brazilians are not self-conscious about their bodies and show them off proudly and quite naturally whatever their shape.

→ **FLIRTING**
Brazilian men and women are forward, without being overbearing. Flirting begins with sustained eye contact and is quickly followed by a verbal exchange. You may need to be firm to discourage unwanted attention.

→ **GRINGO**
Although the term *gringo* in Brazil refers mainly to a North American, it is broadly applied to anyone who isn't Brazilian. *Gringos* don't have to be blond with blue eyes: they are easily spotted by their clothes and the lack of rhythm in their walk.

→ **HYGIENE**
The tropical climate and the proximity of the ocean leads Brazilians to take great care of their physical appearance. Some Brazilians take up to four showers a day and pride themselves on using deodorants and wearing imported perfumes. In the Nordeste a *cheiro* is a sort of kiss that lets you breathe the scent of the other person.

→ **JEITINHO**
The term *jeitinho* describes the resourcefulness and cunning required to get yourself out of tricky situations. It is also a way of being, of bouncing back from the setbacks of everyday life.

→ **PUNCTUALITY**
Punctuality is rarely obligatory so don't be afraid to confirm appointments. According to a *carioca* saying 'yes' means 'perhaps' and 'perhaps' means 'no' – an outright 'no' is rare!

→ **SAUDADE**
This is a term used by Portuguese-speakers to express a feeling of nostalgia associated with absence or separation from a much-loved person or place. It is a feeling of melancholy rather than great sadness. *Saudade* is also mixed with the pleasure of memory and the desire to be reunited.

LOCAL TIMES

→ **STORES**
Open Mon–Fri 9am–6pm, Sat 9am–1pm.

→ **SHOPPING MALLS**
Open Mon.–Sat. until 10pm. On Sundays only the leisure facilities and restaurants are open.

MEDIA

→ **TELEVISION**
There are three national commercial channels (*TV Globo, SBT* and *Bandeirantes*); a public cultural channel *(TV Educativa)*; several regional channels and several pay-per-view and cable channels.

→ **PRESS**
■ **Daily newpapers**
The four leading dailies are *Folha de São Paulo* and *Estado de São Paulo* in São Paulo; *Jornal do Brasil* and *Globo* in Rio de Janeiro. Friday editions include a culture and entertainment supplement.
■ **Magazines**
There is a wide choice of weekly magazines, including *Veja, Exame* and *Isto é*.
■ **English-language newspapers**
The *Brazil Herald* and the *Rio Visitor*, which contain information for tourists, are both available in Rio de Janeiro. The *Brazil Post* carries

information on Brazilian current affairs.

■ **International press**
Sold in some city-center kiosks, at international airports and sometimes available in the larger hotels.

→ RADIO
The BBC World Service can be found on MHz 17.79, 15.19, 12.10 and 5.975. Voice of America can be found on MHz 13.79, 9.455, 6.130 and 5.995. There is a vast number of radio stations broadcasting in Portuguese, though none are particularly outstanding.

MONEY

The Brazilian unit of currency is the real (see also Currency ◆ 315). Inflation is generally less than 5 percent per annum.

→ CREDIT CARDS
Many stores and restaurants accept credit cards. However, outside large towns and cities it is best to carry a supply of cash as you cannot rely on finding ATMs and foreign exchange offices in smaller towns.

■ **ATMS**
Not all ATMs (automatic teller machines) accept foreign credit cards. Use ATMs of the Bradesco bank or Banco do Brasil for Visa cards, those of Banco 24 Horas for American Express, and those of the Itaú bank for Master Card and Diners Club. There are ATMs in all airports.

Note:
For security reasons ATMs in some towns are open only from 6am to 10pm.

■ **Lost or stolen cards**
DINERS CLUB
Tel. 4001 44 44 or 0800 784 480
MASTERCARD
Tel. 0800 891 3294
VISA
Tel. 0800 891 3680

→ FOREIGN EXCHANGE
All currencies can be exchanged in hotels and foreign exchange offices. However the latter tend to accept US dollars and euros more readily than other currencies.

■ **Banks**
Open Mon–Fri 10am–4pm. Closed Sat-Sun and public hols.

■ **Foreign exchange offices**
Foreign exchange offices are often incorporated into travel agencies and may offer more favorable rates than banks. The only real advantage in using the foreign exchange offices in hotels is their convenience and proximity to the hotel safe in your room.

→ TRAVELER'S CHECKS
These can be cashed in foreign exchange offices and banks in return for a small commission. The most widely accepted traveler's checks are those issued by American Express in US dollars.

PUBLIC HOLIDAYS

In addition to the following national holidays, each state has its own public holidays.

■ **January 1**
Ano novo
(New Year's Day)

■ **February/March**
Carnival: four days before Ash Wednesday. Mardi Gras (Shrove Tuesday) is a public holiday.

■ **April**
Paixão de Cristo
(Good Friday).

■ **April 21**
Anniversary of Tiradentes' execution.

■ **May 1**
Labor Day.

■ **May/June**
Corpus Christi.

■ **September 7**
National festival (Independence Day).

■ **October 12**
Festa de Nossa Senhora Aparecida
(patron saint of Brazil).

■ **November 2**
Finados

(All Souls' Day).
■ **November 15**
Proclamação da República (Proclamation of the Republic).
■ **December 25**
Natal (Christmas).

SECURITY

It is wise to take certain precautions, such as leaving your passport, jewelry and money in the hotel safe and taking only the basic necessities (and the minimum amount of cash) with you when you go out. In town a photocopy of your passport can be used in place of the original. In large towns and cities it is not advisable to walk on the beaches or in deserted streets at night.
Rio Tourist Police
Avenida Afranio de Melo Franco, Leblon
Tel. (21) 3399 7170

TIPPING

It is customary to leave a 10 percent tip in restaurants if the service has been satisfactory and if a service charge is not already indicated on the tab. In taxis round up the fare if the driver has been considerate or if your journey was only short.

TOURIST INFORMATION

Most airports and bus stations have tourist information points.

→ BELÉM
■ **Belemtur**
Avenida Governador José Malcher 592
Nazaré
Tel. (91) 242 09 00
■ **Paratur**
Praça Maestro Valdemar Henrique
Tel. (91) 212 05 75

→ BELO HORIZONTE
■ **Belotur**
Rua Pernambuco, 284
Bairro Funcionários
Tel. (31) 32 77 97 77
■ **Secretaria de Turismo**
Praça Rio Branco 56
Tel. (31) 32 72 85 85

→ BRASÍLIA
■ **Setur**
SNC Quadra 4
Bloco B,
Edifício Varig
Sala 502
Tel. (61) 429 76 00

→ CURITIBA
■ **Disque Turismo Municipal**
Rua da Glória 326
Tel. (41) 352 80 00
www.viaje.curitiba.pr.gov.br
■ **Paranatur**
Rua Deputado Marios de Barros 1290, 4th floor
Tel. (41) 254 69 33

→ FLORIANÓPOLIS
■ **Portal Turístico**
Avenida Engenheiro Max de Souza 236
Coqueiros
Tel. (48) 271 70 16
■ **Santur**
Rua Felipe Schmidt 249, ARS, 10th floor
Tel. (48) 212 63 00
www.santur.sc.gov.br

→ FORTALEZA
■ **Funset**
Rua Pereira Filgueiras 4
Tel. (85) 32 52 14 44
■ **Setur**
Avenida Senador Pompeu 350
Tel. (85) 34 88 74 11
www.turismo.ce.gov.br

→ MANAUS
■ **Amazonastur**
Tel. (92) 652 11 20
■ **Manaustur**
Avenida 7 de Setembro, 157
Tel. (92) 622 49 25

→ PORTO ALEGRE
■ **Central de Informações Turísticas**
Rua Vasco da Gama 253,
Bonfim
Tel. 0800 51 76 86
■ **Setur**
Avenida Borges de Medeiros 1501
11th floor
Tel. (51) 32 88 54 42
www.turismo.rs.gov.br

→ RECIFE
■ **Disque Turista**
Cais do Apolo 925, 8th floor
Bairro do Recife
Tel. (81) 34 25 84 09
■ **Empetur**
Tel. (81) 34 27 81 83
www.empetur.com.br

→ RIO DE JANEIRO
■ **Ponto de Informação Turística**
Avenida Princesa Isabel 183
Copacabana
Tel. 0800 707 1808
■ **Riotur**
Rua da Assembléia 10, 10th floor,
Centro
Tel. (21) 22 17 75 75
www.riodejaneiro-turismo.com.br

→ SALVADOR
■ **Informação Turistica Bahiatursa**
Agência
Mercado Modelo
Praça Cairú
Tel. (71) 321 21 33

→ SÃO LUIS
■ **Central de Serviços Turísticos**
Praça Benedito Leite
Tel. (98) 32 31 90 86
■ **Viva Cidadão**
Avenida Senador Vitorino Freire 2
Tel. (98) 32 31 20 00

→ SÃO PAULO
■ **Posto de Informação Estadual**
Rua Guaianazares, 1058, Campo Elíseos
Tel. (11) 33 31 00 33
■ **Central da Amhembi**
Avenida
O. Fontoura 1209
Tel. (11) 62 24 04 00

USEFUL ADDRESSES

→ UK CONTACTS
■ **British embassy**
Setor das Embaixadas Sul, Quadra 801,
Lote 8 Conjunto K
Brasília
Tel. (61) 225 27 10
www.reinounido.org.br
■ **British consulate**
Praia do Flamengo 284 (2nd floor),
Rio de Janeiro
Tel. (21) 2555 9600
(out of hours emergency tel. (21) 9646 6692)
www.reinounido.org.br
www.britishembassy.gov.uk
There are British consulates in São Paulo, Belém, Belo Horizonte, Curitiba, Fortaleza, Manaus, Porto Alegre, Recife, Rio Grande Salvador and Santos.

→ US CONTACTS
■ **US Embassy**
Avenida das Nações
Quadra 801, Lote 3
Brasília
Tel. (61) 321 70 00
www.embaixada-americana.org.br
■ **US Consulate**
Avenida Presidente Wilson 147, Centro,
Rio de Janeiro
Tel. (21) 22 92 71 17
There are US consulates in São Paulo and Recife.
www.consulado-americano-rio.org.br

→ CANADIAN CONTACTS
■ **Canadian embassy**
Avenida das Naçoes,
Quadra 803, Lote 16
Brasilia
Tel. (61) 321 21 71
www.dfait-maeci.gc.ca/brazil
■ **Canadian consulate**
Avenida Atlantica 1130, 4th Floor,
Copacabana
Rio de Janeiro
Tel. (21) 2543 3004
There are Canadian consulates in São Paulo and Belo Horizonte.

USEFUL EXPRESSIONS

Hello: bom dia (morning) boa tarde (afternoon) boa noite (evening)
Goodbye: até logo
See you tomorrow: até amanhã
Yes: sim
No: não
Thank you: obrigado (a)
Excuse me/sorry: me desculpe
I don't understand: não entendo
How much: quanto
When: quando
How: como
Be careful: cuidado
Attack: assalto
What's your phone number?: Qual é o seu número de telefone ?
Your address: o seu endereço

MONTHS & DAYS

January: janeiro
February: fevereiro
March: março
April: abril
May: maio
June: junho
July: julho
August: agosto
September: setembro
October: outubro
November: novembro
December: dezembro
Monday: segunda-feira
Tuesday: terça-feira
Wednesday: quarta-feira
Thursday: quinta-feira
Friday: sexta-feira
Saturday: sábado
Sunday: domingo
Weekend: fim de semana
Public holiday: feriado
Today: hoje
Yesterday: ontem
Tomorrow: amanhã

NUMBERS

Zero: zero
One: um/uma
Two: dois/duas
Three: três
Four: quatro
Five: cinco
Six: seis
Seven: sete
Eight: oito
Nine: nove
Ten: dez
Fifteen: quinze
Twenty: vinte
Twenty-five: vinte e cinco
Thirty: trinta
Forty: quarenta
Fifty: cinqüenta
Sixty: sessenta
One hundred: cem
Five hundred: quinhentos (as)
One thousand: mil

MONEY

To change money: cambiar dinheiro
What's the exchange rate for the real?: Qual é a taxa de câmbio do real ?
Traveler's checks: cheques de viagem
Credit card: cartão de crédito
Bank notes (bills): notas
Coins: moedas
To give change: dar o troco
To pay cash: pagar à vista
Wallet: carteira
ATM: caixa automático
Bank: agência bancária
Counter/window: guichê
Till/cash desk: caixa

AT THE HOTEL

Single/double room: quarto de solteiro/ de casal
Double bed: cama de casal
Bathroom with bath: banheiro com banheira
With shower: com chuveiro
Air conditioned: ar condicionado
Inclusive price: pacote

SHOPPING

To go shopping: fazer compras
Store: loja
Supermarket: supermercado
Market: feira
Baker's: padaria
Butcher's: açougue
How much is it: Quanto custa ?
Very expensive: muito caro
Very cheap: muito barato
Larger: maior
Smaller: menor
In another color: de outra cor
Crafts: artesanato
This one: este (a)
That one: esse (a), aquele (a)
Open: aberto
Closed: fechado

FOOD

Breakfast: café da manhã
Coffee with milk: café com leite
Black coffee: cafézinho
Tea: chá preto
Fruit juice: suco de frutas
Lunch: almoço
Dinner: jantar
Menu: cardápio
Set menu: prato do dia
Rice and black beans: arroz com feijão
Beef: carne de vaca
Barbecued meat: churrasco
Chicken: frango
Fish: peixe
Seafood: frutos do mar
Sparkling water: água com gás
Still water: água sem gás
Beer: cerveja
Red/white wine: vinho tinto/branco
Pineapple: abacaxi
Orange: laranja
Lime: limão verde
Papaya: mamão
Banana: banana
Bread: pão
Butter: manteiga
Olive oil: azeite
Salt: sal (**unsalted:** sem sal)
Sugar: açúcar (**without sugar:** sem açúcar)
Sweetener: adoçante
Cheese: queijo
Sweet desserts: doces
Dessert: sobremesa
Ice cream: sorvetes
To ask for the bill (tab): pedir a conta

ON THE ROAD

Car hire: locação de carro
Driving licence: carteira de motorista
Identity card: carteira de identidade
Passport: passaporte
To get into/out of (vehicle): entrar em/sair do
Road: estrada
Street: rua
Avenue: avenida
Square: praça, largo
Traffic: trânsito
Intersection: cruzamento
Red/green light: sinal aberto/fechado
To turn right/left: virar à direita/à esquerda
Straight on: em frente
No entry: contramão
One way: mão única
Dead end: sem saída
Parking: estacionamento
To go up: subir
To go down: descer
Petrol (gas) station: posto de gasolina
Oil: óleo
To fill the tank: encher o tanque
To check the brakes: verificar os freios
The car has broken down: o carro está enguiçado
Garage: oficina mecânica

TRANSPORT

Bus: ônibus
Where is the stop?: Onde é o ponto de ônibus ?
A bus ticket for...: uma passagem de ônibus para...
Bus station: estação rodoviária
Get on/off (bus etc.): apanhar/descer de
Subway: metrô
Airport: aeroporto
Plane ticket: passagem aérea
Taxi (cab): táxi
A taxi (cab) rank: um ponto de táxi
I would like to go to: quero ir para

HEALTH

Pharmacy: farmácia
Dressing: curativo
Ointment: pomada
Aspirin: aspirina
Antibiotic: antibiótico
Tablets: comprimidos
Condom: camisinha
To give an injection: aplicar uma injeção
Wound: ferida
Fracture: fratura
Doctor: médico
Hospital: hospital
Nurse (male): enfermeira (o)
Dentist: dentista
I have toothache: estou com dor de dente
I am ill: estou doente
I have a temperature: estou com febre

MAIL

Post office: Correio
To send a letter: mandar uma carta
Postcard: cartão postal
To register (a letter): registrar
Package: pacote
Stamps: selos
Fax: fax
E-mail: correio eletrônico

TELEPHONE

To make a call: ligar
Phone card: cartão telefônico
Phone booth: orelhã

◆ FESTIVALS AND EVENTS

See also *Public holidays* ◆ **321**

CULTURAL FESTIVALS		
JAN.	Olinda (PE)	**TORNEIO DE REPENTISTAS** (traditional song contest)
MARCH	Curitiba (PR)	**FESTIVAL DE TEATRO** (contemporary Brazilian theater)
JULY	Campos de Jordão (SP)	**FESTIVAL DE INVERNO** (classical music festival)
JULY	Ouro Preto (MG)	**FESTIVAL DE INVERNO DA UFMG** (theater, music and plastic arts festival)
MID-JULY	Joinville (SC)	**FESTIVAL INTERNACIONAL DE DANÇA**
AUGUST	Gramado (RS)	**FESTIVAL DE CINEMA** (Latin American, Portuguese and Spanish movie festival)
OCT.–DEC.	São Paulo (SP)	**BIENAL INTERNACIONAL** (the largest exhibition of plastic arts in Latin America; even-numbered years)

RELIGIOUS AND FOLK FESTIVALS		
JAN. 1	Angra Dos Reis (RJ)	**PROCISSÃO MARÍTIMA DE NOSSO SENHOR DOS NAVEGANTES**
	Salvador (BA)	**FESTA DE SÃO LÁZAR**
2ND THU. IN JAN.	Salvador (BA)	**LAVAGEM DO BONFIM**
JAN 22– FEB. 22	Santo Amaro (BA)	**FESTA DE NOSSA SENHORA DA PURIFICAÇÃO**
JAN 24 –FEB. 2	Nazaré (BA)	**FESTA DE NOSSA SENHORA DE NAZARÉ**
JAN. 24–FEB. 2	Salvador (BA)	**FESTA DE IEMANJÁ** (on the beach at Rio Vermelho)
HOLY WEEK	Ouro Preto (MG) Mariana (MG) Diamantina (MG)	**PROCISSÃO DA SEMANA SANTA**
WHITSUN (END MAY)	Parati (RJ) Alcântara (MA)	**FESTA DO DIVINO**
JUNE	Throughout Brazil, particularly Caruaru (PE)	**FESTAS JUNINAS** (festivals in honor of Saint Anthony, Saint John and Saint Peter)
JUN. 13–30	São Luis (MA) Olinda (PE) Recife (PE)	**BUMBA-MEU-BOI** (Nordeste folk festival in which the killing and resurrection of an ox is enacted through music, dance and drama)
JUN. 28–30	Parintins (AM)	**FESTIVAL FOLCLÓRICO** (major folk festival combining Native American dances and legends with charactersfrom *boi-bumba*)
JULY	Diamantina (MG)	**FESTA DO DIVINO**
AUGUST	São Paulo (SP)	**FESTA DE NOSSA SENHORA ACHIROPITA** (in the Italian district of Bixiga)
AUGUST	Cachoeira (BA)	**FESTA DE NOSSA SENHORA DA BOA MORTE**
AUGUST 15	Fortaleza	**FESTA DE IEMANJÁ**
MID-AUGUST	São Paulo (SP)	**TANABATA MATSURI** (festival of the stars in the Japanese district of Liberdade)
SEP. 7–14	Congonhas (MG)	**JUBILEU DO SENHOR BOM JESUS DO MATOSINHO**
SEP. 13–20	Porto Alegre	**SEMANA FARROUPILHA** (festival commemorating the Farrapos War)
SEP. 10–OCT.2	São Paulo (SP)	**FESTA DE SAN GENNARO** (in the Italian disticts of of São Paulo)
2ND SUN IN OCT.	Belém (PA)	**CÍRIO DE NAZARÉ** (procession in honor of Nossa Senhora de Nazaré)
DEC. 31	Rio de Janeiro (RJ)	**FESTA DE IEMANJÁ** (on Copacabana beach)
DEC. 31	Salvador (BA)	**PROCISSÃO MARÍTIMA DO SENHOR BOM JESUS DOS NAVEGANTES**

FAIRS		
HOLY WEEK,	Nazaré (BA)	**FEIRA DOS CAXIXIS** (ceramics market)
JUNE 15–JULY 15	Florianópolis (SC)	**FESTA DA TAÍNHA** (mule festival)
AUGUST	Parati (RJ)	**FESTIVAL DA PINGA** (*cachaça* festival)
2ND THU. IN OCT.	Blumenau (SC)	**OKTOBERFEST** (the Brazilian version of the Munich beer festival)

CARNIVALS		
SAT.–ASH WED.	Rio de Janeiro (RJ) Salvador (BA) Recife (PE) Olinda (PE)	Carnivals are held throughout Brazil, each having different characteristics according to the region. While the Sambódromo and local *blocos* are unique to Rio, *blocos de frevo* and *maracatu* are typical of Recife and Olinda, and *trios eléctricos* of Salvador. Ask at tourist offices for details of the Carnival program and events.

The hotels and restaurants given below are listed by states, which appear in the same order as in the Itineraries section of the guide. Following each state capital, towns and cities are listed alphabetically.
The ▲ symbol refers to the Itineraries sections and the ◆ to the Map section.

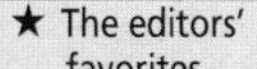
★ The editors' favorites
Credit cards accepted
not accepted
Swimming pool
Terrace
Park, garden
Quiet
In the town center
Beautiful view
Air conditioning
Disabled access
Live music

RIO DE JANEIRO CITY ▲ 114

→ ACCOMMODATION

★ Copacabana Palace
map **C** B2
Avenida Atlântica 1702, Copacabana
Tel. (21) 25 48 70 70
www.copacabanapalace.orient-express.com
Built in the early 1920s, the Copacabana Palace was one of the first buildings to grace the legendary beach. Famous past guests include Marlene Dietrich.
225 rooms (R$1,080)
Breakfast (R$50) not included.

Flórida
map **B** A2
Rua Ferreira Viana 81, Flamengo
Tel. (21) 25 55 60 00
www.windsorhoteis.com.br
Renovated in 1992, the Flórida offers high-class facilities and service at moderate prices. Spacious, well-decorated rooms and Internet access (extra charge).
Restaurant.
224 rooms (R$235)

★ Glória
map **B** A2
Rua do Russel 632 Glória
Tel. (21) 25 55 72 72
www.hotelgloriario.com.br
Opposite Sugar Loaf mountain, the Glória combines the appeal of an old-fashioned luxury hotel with excellent value for money.
Restaurant.
610 rooms (R$255)

★ Golden Tulip Ipanema Plaza
map **D** D4
Rua Farme de Amoeda 34, Ipanema
Tel. (21) 36 87 20 00
www.ipanemaplazahotel.com
You will not find a hotel in a better location than this one, one block from the beach in an area crowded with restaurants, bars, clubs, cafés and boutiques. The rooms, which are sunny and tastefully decorated, all offer views of either the sea or the Corcovado.
135 rooms (US$125)

Marina Palace
map **D** D2
Avenida Delfim Moreira 630, Leblon
Tel. (21) 25 40 52 12
www.hotelmarina.com.br
In a superb location overlooking Praia do Leblon.
Restaurant.
156 rooms (R$393)
Breakfast (R$22) not included.

Vermont
map **D** D3
Rua Visconde de Pirajá 254, Ipanema
Tel. (21) 25 22 00 57
www.ipanema.com/hotel/v.htm
Ideally located in the center of Ipanema, this is the most inexpensive hotel in the district. The rooms are small but clean and well equipped.
84 rooms (R$160–200)

→ RESTAURANTS

Alba Mar
map **A** B3
Praça Marechal Âncora 184, Centro
Tel. (21) 22 40 83 78
Daily 11.30am–6pm
The restaurant is in a tower that is the only surviving part of a historic metal-framed market hall, and therefore now a listed building. Enjoy the fish and seafood specialities while you take in a sweeping view of the bay and the Rio–Niterói bridge.
Average price of a dish: R$39

★ Antiquarius
Rua Aristides Espínola 19, Leblon
Tel. (21) 25 08 91 74
www.antiquarius.com.br
Open daily for lunch and dinner.
Consistently voted one of Rio's best restaurants, Antiquarius has won several awards for its outstanding and versatile menu that features classic Portuguese dishes with a Brazilian twist. Specialities include codfish moqueca, *a stew in coconut and tomato sauce, and* perna de carneiro *(leg of lamb).*
Dinner for two with a bottle of Chilean wine about US$100
(Diners Club only)

★ Aprazível
map **A** D1
Rua Aprazível, 62 Santa Tereza
Tel. (21) 25 08 91 74
Thu.–Sat. 8pm–midnight; Sun. and public hols 1–6pm
Aprazível, *meaning 'pleasant' or 'agreeable', certainly describes this restaurant located in Rio's bohemian area. The cuisine here has a strong Minas Gerais flavor and there is live* chorinho *on Thursday evenings. The restaurant is not easy to get to so it is best to go by car.*
Average price of a dish: R$50

Atrium
map **A** B3
Praça XV de Novembro 48 Centro
Tel. (21) 22 20 01 93 or (21) 22 20 32 82
Mon–Fri. 11.30am–3.30pm
This pleasant restaurant, located in the Paço Imperial, has a large clientele of people from the nearby offices of the legislative assembly. It is a good place to eat if you're visiting the city center during the week.
Average price of a dish: R$25.

Bar do Arnaudo
map **A** D2
Rua Almirante Alexandrino 316 Santa Teresa
Tel. (21) 22 52 72 46
Tue.–Fri.noon–11pm; Sat.–Sun. and public hols noon–8pm
This Nordestino restaurant is a traditional meeting place for Santa Teresa's bohemian set. The cuisine is unpretentious and the portions generous. The local trams run past the door.
Average price of a dish: R$35 (2 people)

Don Camillo Restaurante
map **C** C1
Av. Atlântica 3056
Tel. (21) 25 49 99 58
Daily noon–midnight
Enjoy pasta, fish and shellfish on one of the most delightful terraces

Prices given in the Hotels and Restaurants section are those that apply during the peak season. They are higher at New Year and during Carnival.

in Copacabana, overlooking the sea. Good service and excellent cuisine. Average price of a dish: R$40

Garota da Urca
map **B** C3
Avenida João Luis Alves 56B, Urca
Tel. (21) 25 41 50 40
Daily 11am–3pm
A restaurant with a pleasant atmosphere and a spectacular view. From the veranda you can see Praia da Urca and the boats on the beach, and in the distance the hills of Rio and the Cristo Redentor. Average price of a dish: R$46 (2 people)

Os Esquilos
map **F** C2
Estrada Barão de Escragnolle Alto da Boa Vista
Tel. (21) 24 92 21 97
Tue.–Sun. noon–6pm
Os Esquilos (The Squirrels) is located in the heart of the forest, 1,600 feet above sea level. The cuisine is plain but thoughtfully prepared. Meat and cheese fondues are served from May through October. Children's play area. Average price of a dish: R$21

Porcão Rio's
map **B** B3
Avenida Infante Dom Henrique Parque do Flamengo
Tel. (21) 34 61 90 20
Daily from 11.30am
The most pleasant restaurant in the Porcão chain, located opposite Sugar Loaf mountain and specializing in rodízio de carnes *(as many meat kebabs as you can eat). If you like meat, highly recommended.*

Average price of a dish: R$54

Sobrenatural
map **A** D2
Rua Almirante Alexandrino 432 Santa Teresa
Tel. (21) 22 24 10 03
Daily noon–midnight
*Excellent freshly caught fish, served grilled or en sauce (*moqueca*). Various* chorinho *groups perform here (dates to be checked).* Average price of a dish: R$50

★ Tia Palmira
OFF MAP
Caminho do Souza 18, Pedra de Guaratiba
Tel. (21) 24 10 81 69
Tue.–Fri. 11am–5pm, Sat.–Sun. 11am–6pm
The New York Times *wrote a rave review in July 2001 about this restaurant, in a fishing village near Rio, praising the fish and shellfish dishes. The set menu offers a range of dishes and desserts, and coffee. Reservation recommended.* Set menu: R$49

RIO DE JANEIRO STATE

ANGRA DOS REIS ▲162

→ ACCOMMODATION

Portogalo Suíte
Rodovia Rio–Santos, Highway BR101, Km 461, Fazenda Itapioacanga
Tel. 0800 282 43 43 or (24) 33 61 43 43
Fax (24) 33 61 43 61
Ideal for watersports enthusiasts, who need only walk out of the hotel to be on the beach. Spectacular view of Ilha Grande. Restaurant.
114 rooms: R$788 (2 people)

BÚZIOS ▲161

→ ACCOMMODATION

★ Le Relais la Borie
Rua Gravatás 1374, Praia de Geribá
Tel. (22) 26 20 85 04
www.laborie.com.br
A pousada with impeccable service and comfortable rooms. The setting is magnificent and facilities include a sauna, swimming pools overlooking the ocean and a terrace bar. Restaurant. R$600

→ RESTAURANT

Satyricon
Rua José Bento Ribeiro Dantas 500
Tel. (22) 26 23 15 95
Daily 4pm–1am (out of season 1pm–1am)
A restaurant specializing in fish and seafood, with a beautiful sea view. Average price of a dish: R$52

ILHA GRANDE ▲162

→ ACCOMMODATION

Hotel Fazenda Paraíso do Sol
Praia Saco das Palmas
Tel. (21) 22 62 12 26
For stays of two to six days in a beautiful natural setting. If you like seclusion you'll love the private beach, natural pool and waterfall and the steep paths leading to the unspoiled beach of Lopes Mendes. As there is no telephone in the hotel, reservations must be made in Rio. 32 chalets (full board for 3 nights: R$760, incl. boat link to the island)

PARATI ▲164

→ ACCOMMODATION

★ Pousada do Sandi
Largo do Rosário 1
Tel. (24) 33 71 21 00
Reservations: 0800 23 21 00
(55) 2433 71 2100
www.pousadadosandi.com.br
Outstandingly good and handsome two-story 18th-century colonial house in the historic center of Parati. The rooms are tastefully decorated with period furniture and works of art. The beautiful tropical garden is planted with bromeliads, wild papaya, orchids, ferns... Restaurant.
26 rooms: R$400 (2 people, breakfast included).

→ RESTAURANT

★ Eh-Laho
Ilha do Catimbau
Dec.–Feb, daily 11am–6pm (in low season, ask the local fishermen for opening times)
This charming restaurant is located on a rocky island covered with palm trees. From Parati it can be reached in about 15 minutes by motorboat or 50 minutes by fishing boat. The name comes from the English 'hello', heard in the days of whaling. Enjoy grilled fish and seafood in the shade of straw huts, looking out over a turquoise sea. You can swim in a natural pool hollowed out of rocks. Average price of a dish: R$25

PETRÓPOLIS ▲168

→ ACCOMMODATION

★ Pousada Capim Limão
Rodovia Philuvio Cerqueira Rodrigues, 1910
Tel. (24) 22 20 45 00
www.capimlimao.com.br

R$10 = US$4.45 or £2.50 at the time of writing

Located in 86 acres of parkland at an altitude of 2,460 feet, this pousada *is an ideal base for spectacular walks through the forest. The rooms have fireplaces and there is a gym and heated swimming pool.*
Restaurant.
24 rooms (R$360)

TERESÓPOLIS ▲ 170

→ ACCOMMODATION

★ Rosa dos Ventos
Highway RJ130 toward Nova Friburgo, Km 22.5
Campanha
Tel. (21) 26 44 99 15
www.rosadosventos.com.br
This upmarket hotel stands in an unspoiled natural setting. Guests may explore the surrounding 250 acres on foot or on horseback, following 6 miles of marked pathways, or go fishing or sailing on the lake. Children under 14 are housed in the annex with their parents.
Restaurant.
42 rooms (R$430)

→ RESTAURANT

★ Tutu–Terê
Rua Reinal do Viana 257, Inga
Tel. (21) 26 42 50 20
www.tocatere.com
Sat.–Sun. and public hols noon–5pm
Closed in December.
Excellent Minais Gerais cuisine served in terracotta dishes.
Average price of a dish: R$33 (adults); R$10 (children)

VALENÇA ▲ 175

→ ACCOMMODATION

Fazenda Ponte Alta Pousada
Avenida Silas Pereira da Mota–Parque Santana
Barra do Pirai
Tel. (24) 24 43 51 59
This beautiful early 19th-century fazenda, *with its original watermill and chapel, dates from the golden age of the coffee baron. The comfortable rooms are furnished in period style. Regional cuisine.*
9 rooms (full board: R$270)

VISCONDE DE MAUÁ ▲ 178

→ ACCOMMODATION

★ Fronteira
Estrada de Rio Preto, toward Mirantão, 3 miles
Tel. (24) 33 87 12 19
Fax (24) 33 87 13 66
A charming pousada *located at an altitude of 4,430 feet. All the rooms have heating, a fireplace and a conservatory. Guests may swim in the river in the Parque Nacional do Itatiaia nearby. No children under 16.*
Restaurant.
12 rooms (R$650)

MINAS GERAIS

BELO HORIZONTE ▲ 182

→ ACCOMMODATION

Hotel Floresta Mágica
Distrito Industrial Simão da Cunha
Santa Luzia
Tel (31) 36 91 15 15
www.florestamagica.com.br
A neo-Romanesque pousada *in a rural setting, 9 miles from the center of Belo Horizonte. All the rooms have a balcony, and facilities incude a sauna, swimming pool and gym. You can walk in the surrounding countryside.*
Restaurant.
30 rooms (R$160)

Liberty Palace
Rua Paraíba 1465
Tel. (31) 21 21 09 00
www.libertypalace.com.br
The most recently built luxury hotel in Belo Horizonte, located in Savassi, in the heart of the city's business and commercial district.
Restaurant.
94 rooms (R$168)

DIAMANTINA ▲ 196

→ ACCOMMODATION

Pousada do Garimpo
Avenida da Saudade 265, Diamantina
Tel. (38) 35 31 10 44
www.pousadadogarimpo.com.br
A basic but comfortable pousada *located about half a mile from the city center, with a fine view of the surrounding countryside. On Saturdays guests are treated to a traditional* seresta *(serenade).* Sauna and restaurant.
60 rooms (R$113)

OURO PRETO ▲ 184

→ ACCOMMODATION

Pousada do Mondego
Largo da Coimbra 38
Tel. (31) 35 51 20 40
www.roteirosdecharme.com.br
This beautiful colonial residence, built in 1747, is a remnant of Ouro Preto's golden age. The pousada is furnished in period style, and there is also an art gallery, a jeweler's and an antique shop. Guided tours of the town in a double-decker bus are arranged from here.
Restaurant.
24 rooms (R$200)

→ RESTAURANT

Le Coq d'Or
Hotel Solar Nossa Senhora do Rosário, Rua Getúlio Vargas 270
Tel. (31) 35 51 52 00
Daily 7–11pm (plus Sat. noon–3pm)
Excellent French cuisine prepared with regional produce. Try the lamb with gnocchi and leeks. Seasonal menu.
Average price of a dish: R$24

TIRADENTES ▲ 195

→ ACCOMMODATION

Solar da Ponte
Praça das Mercês
Tel. (32) 33 55 12 55
Fax (32) 33 55 12 01
An impressive colonial-style residence with attractively-decorated rooms. No children under 12.
Restaurant.
18 rooms (R$291; incl. breakfast and an elegant high tea)

DISTRITO FEDERAL

BRASÍLIA ▲ 200

→ ACCOMMODATION

Academia de Tênis Resort
Setor de Clubes Esportivos Sul
Trecho 4, Cj 5
Lote 1–B
Tel. (61) 316 61 61
www.academiaresort.com.br
This large tourist complex on the shores of Lago Paranoá offers a wide range of sport and leisure facilities, including heated swimming pools, tennis courts, a sauna and massage. Small, comfortable bungalows. Business centre with Internet access. Restaurant.
256 rooms (R$320)

★ The editors' favorites

MATO GROSSO DO SUL

PANTANAL ▲ 210

→ **ACCOMMODATION**

Pousada Aguapé
Highway BR262
Km 467.5
Tel. (67) 686 10 36
or (67) 241 28 89
www.aguape.com.br
Closed Christmas.
Located on the Fazenda de São José, 125 miles from Campo Grande and 37 miles from Aquidauana. It can be reached by car. Activities include horse riding and boat trips. In the dry season there are night trips by four-wheel-drive vehicles to watch the local wildlife.
14 rooms (full board: R$200 per person, including two activities)

Pousada Mangabal
Nhecolândia
Tel. (67) 326 14 13
www.pousada mangabal.com.br
Located 174 miles from Campo Grande. During the rainy season (Jan–May) it can be reached only by air (from Aquidauana or Campo Grande). Activities include photographic safaris, horse riding and seeing daily life on a cattle ranch. Parking available in the dry season only.
4 rooms (full board: R$180 per person, including activities)

SÃO PAULO STATE

SÃO PAULO ▲ 218

→ **ACCOMMODATION**

Eldorado Boulevard
Avenida
São Luís 234
Tel. (11) 32 14 18 33
Fax (11) 32 56 80 61
Ideally located next to the municipal theater and the República subway station, with easy access to the Memorial da América Latina and the city's main tourist sites.
Restaurant.
157 rooms (R$95)

L'Hôtel
Rua Alameda
Campinas, 266
Jardin Paulista
Tel. (11) 21 83 05 00
www.lhotel.com.br
Located near Avenida Paulista and offering all the services you would expect of a luxury hotel. On weekends, when there is no business clientele, the hotel offers attractive rates (Fri.–Sun. R$300, including breakfast).
Restaurant.
83 rooms (R$450)
Breakfast (R$28) not included.

→ **RESTAURANT**

★ Fasano
Rua Vittorio Fascino
88, Jardin Paulista
Tel. (11) 30 62 40 00
Mon.–Sat.
7.30pm–1am
Owned by the Fasano family for almost a century, this is the best Italian restaurant in São Paulo. The risotto and grilled partridge with polenta are excellent.
Average price of a dish R$58

SÃO SEBASTIÃO ▲ 228

→ **ACCOMMODATION**

Juquehy Praia
Rua Mãe
Bernarda 3221
Praia de Juqueí
Tel. (12) 38 91 10 00
www.juquehy.com.br
Overlooking Praia de Juqueî, one of the trendiest beaches on the coast of São Paulo state, this hotel is ideal for water-sports enthusiasts. Trips to the islands are also organized from here.
Restaurant.
55 rooms (R$440)

UBATUBA ▲ 230

→ **ACCOMMODATION**

Recanto das Toninhas
Highway SP55,
toward Caragua-tatuba Km 55
Praia das Toninhas
Tel. 0800 17 75 57
or (11) 32 88 20 22
www.toninhas.com.br
Faultless service and a range of leisure facilities including dry sauna, steam bath and gym. Rooms with balcony and a view of Praia das Toninhas, whose rollers attract surfers and windsurfers.
Restaurant.
54 rooms (R$380)

PARANÁ

CURITIBA ▲ 234

→ **ACCOMMODATION**

Inter Palace
Rua 15 de
Novembro 950
Tel. (41) 223 52 82
www.interpalace.com.br
This modern city-center hotel offers every comfort at reasonable prices.
Restaurant.
70 rooms (R$69)

FOZ DO IGUAÇU ▲ 238

→ **ACCOMMODATION**

★ Tropical das Cataratas
Parque Nacional
de Iguaçu
Tel. (45) 521 70 03
Fax (45) 574 16 88
A magnificent building in a fine natural setting. Rooms with a view of the Iguaçu falls.
Restaurant.
203 rooms (R$521)

ILHA DO MEL ▲ 237

→ **ACCOMMODATION**

Pousada Pôr do Sol
Praia do Limoeiro
Tel. (41) 426 80 09
www.pousada pordosol.com.br
A pousada near Nova Brasîlia, with a fine view of the ocean. Boat excursions possible.
Restaurant.
16 rooms (R$60 including dinner)

SANTA CATARINA

FLORIANÓPOLIS ▲ 240

→ **ACCOMMODATION**

Fazenda Engenho Velho
Estrada Geral de Rio
Vermelho, Km 10
Praia Grande
Tel. (48) 269 70 00
www.engenhovelho.com.br
The chalets, each sleeping up to five people, are located in extensive parkland, near a lake and only half a mile from the ocean. Activities include horse riding, fishing, sailing, tennis, swimming, cycling.
Restaurant.
45 chalets (R$190 including dinner)

★ Pousada Ilha do Papagaio
Praia da Pinheira
18 miles, then
5 minutes by
motorboat, Palhoça
Tel. (48) 286 12 42
www.papagaio.com.br
The Ilha do Papagaio is a natural paradise only 15 miles from Florianópolis. The pousada is also a fish farm that produces its own

R$10 = US$4.45 or £2.50 at the time of writing

seafood. Rooms have a sea view, balcony and hammock. Organized boat trips and walks on the island. In winter you can see right whales.
Restaurant.
20 chalets (R$556, dinner included)

LAGUNA ▲ 243

→ ACCOMMODATION

★ Pousada Quinta do Bucanero
Estrada Geral do Rosa, Praia do Rosa Imbituba
Tel. (48) 355 60 56
www.bucanero.com.br
An amazing pousada in an unspoiled natural setting overlooking a lake and just 20 yards from the beach. All rooms have a balcony and hammock. You can spot right whales during winter.
Restaurant.
10 rooms (R$391)
(Mastercard and Visa only)

SÃO FRANCISCO DO SUL ▲ 243

→ ACCOMMODATION

Pousada Zibamba
Rua Fernando Dias 27
Tel. (47) 444 20 20 or 444 00 77
This attractive colonial-style pousada is an ideal base from which to explore the historic town.
Restaurant.
36 rooms (R$140)

RIO GRANDE DO SUL

PORTO ALEGRE ▲ 244

→ ACCOMMODATION

Grande Hotel Master
Rua Riachuelo 1070
Tel. 0800 70 76 444 or (51) 32 87 44 11
www.masterhotel.com.br
Located in the heart of the town's cultural and commercial district. Good value for money.
Restaurant.
92 rooms (R$95)

CANELA ▲ 245

→ ACCOMMODATION

Grand Hotel Canela
Rua Getúlio Vargas, 300
Tel. (54) 282 12 85
The chalets, on the edge of a lake, each sleep up to seven people. Activities include fishing and tennis, and there is an indoor games room and heated swimming pool. All rooms have heating.
Restaurant.
64 rooms and chalets (R$100)
(Visa)

GRAMADO ▲ 245

→ ACCOMMODATION

★ Estalagem Saint Hubertus
Rua da Carriere, 974 Lago Negro
Tel. (54) 286 12 73
An attractive pousada in a natural setting beside Lago Negro. Heated swimming pool and heating in all rooms.
Restaurant.
26 rooms (R$245)

BAHIA

SALVADOR ▲ 256

→ ACCOMMODATION

Pestana Bahia
Rua Fonte do Boi 216, Rio Vermelho
Tel. (71) 453 8000 or 0800 26 63 32
www.pestanahotels.com.br
As well as all the facilities associated with a luxury hotel, the Pestana has a travel agency that organizes guided tours of Salvador and trips to more distant beaches. No charge for children under 12.
Restaurant.
473 rooms (R$220)

★ Pousada das Flores
Rua Direita do Santo Antônio 442
Tel. (71) 243 18 36
www.pflores.com.br
A fine colonial residence in the historic city center. Suites with four-poster beds, terrace and view of the bay. Generous breakfast.
Restaurant.
9 rooms (R$135)
(Visa)

→ RESTAURANTS

★ Sorriso de Dadá
Rua Frei Vicente 5 Pelourinho
Tel. (71) 321 96 42
Daily 11.30am–midnight
Nestling in the heart of the Pelourinho district, the Tempêro de Dadá serves light and innovative cuisine in a very pleasant setting
Average price of a dish: R$70 for two people.

Yemanjá
Avenida Otávio Mangabeira Jardim Armação
Tel. (71) 461 90 10
Daily 11.30am–midnight
The Yemanjá has set a standard for Bahian cuisine in Salvador, as have its sister restaurants in other Brazilian cities.
Average price of a dish: R$25.
(except Intercard)

CACHOEIRA ▲ 263

→ ACCOMMODATION

★ Pousada do Convento
Rua Inocência Boaventura
Tel. (75) 425 17 16
An impressive 17th-century former convent opening onto a courtyard. The wood-paneled cells have been converted into lovely rooms with period furniture.
Restaurant.
26 rooms (R$70)
(Visa & MasterCard)

ILHÉUS ▲ 266

→ ACCOMMODATION

Pousada Vitória
Highway BA001 toward Olivença Km 1, Sítio São Paulo
Tel. (73) 632 49 97
A pousada in a natural setting, 3 miles from the city center, overlooking the attractive Praia Sul, a beach popular with fishing and surfing enthusiasts.
Restaurant.
15 rooms (R$140)
(Visa)

LENÇOIS ▲ 268

→ ACCOMMODATION

Pousada Candombá
Vale do Campão Caete-açu Palmeiras
Tel. (75) 344 11 02
www.infochapada.com
This pousada makes an ideal base for walks to the impressive Fumaça and Rio Preto falls. You can swim in the river and take a sauna, heated with stones in the American Indian tradition.
Restaurant.
7 chalets (R$100)

★ Hotel de Lençois
Rua Altina Alves 747
Tel. (71) 369 50 00
www.hoteldelencois.com
The chalets are dotted over a large park. Breakfast by the pool is highly recommended.

Restaurant.
50 rooms (R$127)

MANGUE SECO
▲ 265

→ **ACCOMMODATION**

Mangue Seco Village
Praia do Mangue Seco
Tel. (75) 445 90 47 or (75) 00 82 55 53
Only 300 yards from the village, this is one of the few places to stay in Mangue Seco.
Restaurant.
20 rooms (R$80)
(MasterCard)

MORRO DE SÃO PAULO ▲ 266

→ **ACCOMMODATION**

★ Pousada o Casarão
Praça Aureliano Lima 190
Tel. (75) 483 10 22
The location of this pleasant pousada, *at at the top of a wooded hillside, sets it apart from the numerous other establishments on the island.*
Restaurant.
15 rooms (R$150)

PORTO SEGURO
▲ 267

→ **ACCOMMODATION**

Pau Brasil Praia
Praia de Taperapuã
Tel. (73) 288 76 00
www.paubrasil.net
Hotel on a fashionable beach about 4 miles from the town center.
Restaurant.
116 rooms (R$70)

PRAIA DO FORTE
▲ 265

→ **ACCOMMODATION**

Praia do Forte Eco-Resort
Avenida do Farol
Tel. (71) 67 64 000
www.praiadoforte.com
This luxury hotel overlooking the beach offers a wide range of sports activities including archery, windsurfing and volleyball. Swimming pool and sauna.
250 rooms (half board: R$1,002)

PERNAMBUCO

RECIFE ▲ 274

→ **ACCOMMODATION**

Marante Plaza
Avenida Boa Viagem, 1070 / Primero Jardin
Tel. (81) 34 65 10 70
www.marante.com.br
This is the city's newest hotel, offering top-quality service. The most expensive apartments have a view of the ocean.
Restaurant.
121 rooms (R$210)

FERNANDO DE NORONHA ▲ 282

→ **ACCOMMODATION**

Esmeralda do Atlântico
Alameda do Boldró
Tel. (81) 36 19 12 55
www.vistatur.com.br
This is the only hotel on the island with a star rating. Courtesy shuttle service to the airport. Booking essential.
Restaurant.
41 rooms (R$265)

ILHA DE ITAMARACÁ
▲ 279

→ **ACCOMMODATION**

Orange Praia
Estrada do Forte Orange, Praia do Forte Orange
Tel. (81) 35 44 11 94
Fax (81) 35 44 11 70
An ideal place for a family holiday, this hotel has a children's play area and a tennis court. It is very near Forte Orange, the peixe-boi conservation center and the ecological museum on Ilha Coroa do Avião (boats leave from the beach).
51 rooms (half board: R$176)

OLINDA ▲ 278

→ **ACCOMMODATION**

Hotel Akakoaras
Avenida Cláudio José Gueiros Leite 10 297
Praia Maria Farinha
Tel. (81) 34 36 17 54
Overlooking the clear, shallow waters of Praia Maria Farinha and only 9 miles from Olinda's historic center, the hotel is ideally located for visitors wanting a change of scenery and some culture. Basic but comfortable chalets.
Restaurant.
22 chalets (R$75)

Pousada dos Quatro Cantos
Rua Prudente de Morais 441
Tel. (81) 34 29 02 20
www.pousada4cantos.com.br
A small, basic and well-kept pousada *in the historic center of the town, conveniently located for visiting Olinda's main attractions.*
24 rooms (R$139)

CEARÁ

FORTALEZA ▲ 284

→ **ACCOMMODATION**

Cæsar Park Fortaleza
Av. Beira Mar, 3980
Praia do Mucuripe
Tel. (85) 40 06 50 00 or 0800 85 22 02
www.caesarpark-for.com.br
A luxury hotel at the western end of Praia do Meireles. The restaurant is renowned for its traditional Cearense cuisine and wide range of seafood.
230 rooms (R$220)

CANOA QUEBRADA
▲ 287

→ **ACCOMMODATION**

Porto Canoa Resort
Avenida Porto Canoa 500, Praia de Canoa Quebrada
Tel. (85) 32 16 89 02
www.portocanoa.com.br
This is the only large hotel in Canoa Quebrada. During vacations this small village is filled with tourists and visitors from all over the Ceará, and its many pousadas *are fully booked. There is a charge for the hotel parking.*
Restaurant.
136 rooms (R$110)
(Amex, MasterCard, Visa)

JERICOACOARA
▲ 286

→ **ACCOMMODATION**

Pousada Hippopotamus
Rua do Forró
Tel. (85) 32 42 91 91
This elegant and comfortable pousada *is located on a narrow street in the center of the village. Reservations recommended.*
Restaurant.
40 rooms (R$125)

MARANHÃO

SÃO LUÍS ▲ 288

→ **ACCOMMODATION**

★ Pousada do Frances
Rua 7 de Setembro 121, Centro

R$10 = US$4.45 or £2.50 at the time of writing

Tel. (98) 32 31 47 73
This charming hotel, in an 18th-century building in the historic center of the town, has the added advantage of being near the sea. Period furniture and plain but comfortable rooms.
Restaurant.
29 rooms (R$97)

Vila Rica
Praça
Dom Pedro II 299
Tel. (98) 32 32 35 35
www.hotelvilarica.com.br
Located between the Matriz da Sé and the ocean. The quality of the service and its proximity to the historic center of Vila Rica make up for the overly elaborate decor.
Restaurant.
213 rooms (R$106)

→ RESTAURANT

★ Restaurante Base de Lenoca
Avenida Dom Pedro II, Centro
Tel. (98) 32 31 05 99
Mon.–Sat. 11am–11pm;
Sun. 11am–5pm
Imaginative fish and seafood dishes and a magnificent view from the restaurant terrace.
Average price of a dish: R$25

PONTA DO CABURÉ ▲291

→ ACCOMMODATION

★ Pousada do Paulo
Tel. (98) 33 49 90 10
Basic but delightful small chalets set on the riverbank. Paulo, the proprietor, was among the first to see the potential of this rather isolated nature reserve.
19 rooms (R$70)

PARÁ

BELÉM ▲298

→ ACCOMMODATION

Parque dos Igarapés
Rodovia Augusto Montenegro toward Icoaraci, Km 7
Tel. (91) 248 17 18
Fax (91) 278 80 06
The chalets, built in natural materials, stand deep in the tropical forest. For non-residents there is a charge (R$10) for the use of the recreational facilities (pool, boat, football pitch and volleyball court)
Restaurant.
15 chalets (R$68)
(MasterCard and Diners Club)

ALTER DO CHÃO ▲303

→ ACCOMMODATION

Pousada Alter do Chão
Rua Lauro Sodré 74
Tel. (93) 527 12 15
This basic but comfortable pousada looks onto a beach on the Tapajós river and commands a superb view of Lago Verde. The owner has a collection of over 100 catalogued orchids indigenous to the region.
Restaurant.
9 rooms (R$50)

ILHA DE MARAJÓ ▲300

→ ACCOMMODATION

Ilha de Marajó
Traversa 2, 10 (between the 7th and 8th streets), Soure
Tel. (91) 241 32 18
Unusually for a small town, this hotel has some good facilities, including a swimming pool, tennis court and volleyball court.
36 rooms (R$120)

AMAZONAS

MANAUS ▲310

→ ACCOMMODATION

Tropical Manaus Resort
Avenida Coronel Teixeira, 1320
Ponta Negra
Tel. 0800 701 26 70
www.tropicalhotel.com.br
A hotel with a comprehensive infrastructure, private transport and a travel agency. Activities include performances of boi bumbá *and talks on Amazonian plants and animals.*
Restaurant.
588 rooms (R$423)

→ ACCOMMODATION IN THE JUNGLE
A specialty of tourism in Amazonia, 'jungle hotels' bring you into close contact with nature. Packages (payable in US dollars) are available for two days or more and include river transport, accommodation with full board and various activities.

Acajatuba Jungle Lodge
Lago Acajatuba
Iranduba
Tel. (92) 233 76 42
www.acajatuba.com.br
Four hours by boat from Manaus, bungalows in the jungle interconnected by wood and rope footbridges. Various day and night trips offer the opportunity to see the encontro das aguas *(the confluence of the Negro and the Solimões rivers), to observe the plants and animals of the Amazon and to visit the local peoples. A 90-foot-high viewing point offers a spectacular vista of the lake and the forest.*
30 rooms (R$410 per person for a two-day/one-night package)

Amazon Lodge
Lago do Juma
Autazes
Tel. (92) 656 33 57
www.naturesafaris.com
A floating pousada *built on* acaçu *trunks deep in the virgin forest, four hours by boat from Manaus. Three excursions depart each day, enabling you to fish for piranhas, observe the forest wildlife and meet with the local inhabitants.*
18 rooms (R$555 per person for a 4-day/3-night package)

PARINTINS ▲303

→ ACCOMMODATION

Avenida
Av. Amazonas 2416
Tel. (92) 533 11 58
During the folk festival held on June 28–30 the hotel is fully booked. So if you want to visit at this time, make your reservation as early as January. Credit cards are accepted only during the festival.
Restaurant.
26 rooms (package for June 27–July 1: R$450 for two people)
(Visa)

◆ PLACES TO VISIT

The places to visit given below are listed by state, which appear in the same order as in the Itineraries section of the guide. Following each state capital, towns and cities are listed alphabetically. The ▲ symbol refers to the Itineraries sections and the ◆ to the Map section.

RIO DE JANEIRO		
BIBLIOTECA NACIONAL Avenida Rio Branco 219	*Tel. (21) 22 20 94 84. Open Mon.-Fri. 9am–8pm, guided tours 11am, 1pm, 4pm.*	▲ 122 ◆ A C3
CAMPO DE SANTANA Praça da República	*Tel. (21) 25 54 80 31. Open daily 9am–5pm. Pleasant English-style park covering 30 acres.*	▲ 126 ◆ A B1
CASA DE RUI BARBOSA Rua São Clemente 134	*Tel. (21) 25 37 00 36. Open Tue.-Sun. 8am–5pm. Traces the life of Rui Barbosa (1849–1923).*	▲ 140 ◆ B D1
CASA FRANÇA-BRASIL Rua Visconde de Itaboraí 78	*Tel. (21) 22 53 53 66. Open Tue.-Sun. noon–8pm. Houses a Franco-Brazilian cultural center.*	▲ 119 ◆ A B3
CATEDRAL SÃO SEBASTIAO Av. Republica do Chile 245	*Tel. (21) 22 40 26 69. Open daily 7am–7pm. Museu das Artes Sagradas, open 10am–4pm.*	▲ 124 ◆ A C2
CENTRO CULTURAL BANCO DO BRASIL Rua Primeiro de Março 66	*Tel. (21) 38 08 2000/20 20. Open Tue.-Sun. noon–8pm. Restaurant facilities (tearoom & restaurant).*	▲ 119 ◆ A B3
CENTRO CULTURAL DA LIGHT Avenida Marechal Floriano 168	*Tel. (21) 22 11 29 21. Open Mon.-Fri. 11am–5pm.*	▲ 127 ◆ A B1
CENTRO CULTURAL LAURINDA SANTOS LOBO Rua Monte Alegre 306	*Tel. (21) 22 42 97 41. Open Tue.-Fri. 10am–6pm; Sat.-Sun. 2–6pm.*	▲ 133 ◆ A D1
CENTRO CULTURAL PARQUE DAS RUÍNAS Rua Murtinho Nobre 169	*Tel. (21) 22 52 10 39. Open Tue.-Sun. 10am–8pm. Magnificent view of Guanabara Bay.*	▲ 133 ◆ A D2
CENTRO DE ARTES HÉLIO OITICICA Rua Luis de Camões 68	*Tel. (21) 22 42 10 12. Open Tue.-Fri. 11am–7pm; Sat.-Sun. noon–6pm.*	▲ 121 ◆ A B2
CONFEITARIA COLOMBO Rua Gonçalves Dias 32	*Tel. (21) 22 32 23 00. Open Mon.-Fri. 8am–8pm; Sat. 8am–5pm. Edwardian tearoom (1894).*	▲ 121 ◆ A B2
CONVENTO DE SANTO ANTÔNIO Largo da Carioca 5	*Tel. (21) 22 62 01 29. Open Mon.-Fri. 2–6pm; Sat. 8–11.30am; Sun. 9.30–11am.*	▲ 120 ◆ A C2
CORCOVADO (ESTRADA DE FERRO) Rua Cosme Velho 513	*Tel. (21) 24 92 22 53. Open daily 8.30am–7pm. Trains leave the Estrada de Ferro every 40 min.*	▲ 151 ◆ F C3
ESPAÇO CULTURAL DA MARINHA Avenida Alfredo Agache	*Tel. (21) 38 70 60 25. Open Tue.-Sun. noon–5pm. Boat trips to the Ilha Fiscale opposite the center.*	▲ 118 ◆ A B3
ESTAÇÃO CENTRAL DO BRASIL Praça Cristiano Ottoni	*Tel. (21) 22 33 40 90. Aka the Estação Dom Pedro II*	▲ 127 ◆ A B1
ESTÁDIO SÃO JANUÁRIO Rua Gal Almério de Moura 131	*Tel. (21) 25 80 73 73. Open Mon-Fri 9am–5pm; Sat. 9am–noon. Stadium of the Vasco da Gama club.*	▲ 129 ◆ E A1
ESTUDANTINA Praça Tiradentes 79	*Tel. (21) 25 07 80 67. Traditional dance hall.*	▲ 121 ◆ A C2
FEIRA DE SÃO CRISTÓVÃO Campo de São Cristóvão	*Open Sat. 3pm; Sun. 4pm. Nordestino market. Hammocks, spices, dried meats. Forró groups (Nordestino music).*	▲ 129 ◆ E B2
FEIRA HIPPIE Praça General Osório	*Open Sun. 9am–6pm. Traditional crafts and souvenirs.*	▲ 145 ◆ D D4
FLAMENGO FUTEBOL CLUBE Av. Borges de Medeiros 997	*Tel. (21) 25 29 01 87. Open daily 9am–6pm. Guided tour available: 9–11am, 2–5pm.*	▲ 141 ◆ D C2
FLORESTA DA TIJUCA Praça Afonço Viseu	*Tel. (21) 24 92 22 53. Open daily 8am–6pm.*	▲ 150 ◆ F C1
FORTALEZA DE SÃO JOÃO Avenida João Luiz Alves	*Tel. (21) 25 43 33 23. Open Mon.-Thu. 9am–noon, 2–4pm; Fri. 7–11am.*	▲ 153 ◆ B C4
FORTE DE COPACABANA Avenida Âtlantica	*Tel. (21) 25 21 10 32. Open Tue.-Sun. 10am–4pm.*	▲ 153 ◆ C D2
BEIJA FLOR Pracinha Wallace Paes Leme 1025, Nilópolis	*Tel. (21) 27 91 28 66. It is advisable to go by car.*	◆ F B2

Place	Information	Ref.
G. R. ESCOLA DE SAMBA ESTAÇÃO PRIMEIRA DA MANGUEIRA Rua Visconde de Niterói 1072	*Tel. (21) 38 72 67 86. 'Rehearsal' dates are published in the local press. It is advisable to go by car.*	▲ 130 ◆ E C1
G. R. ESCOLA DE SAMBA UNIDOS DO SALGUEIRO Rua Silva Teles 104	*Tel. (21) 22 38 55 64. 'Rehearsal' dates are published in the local press. It is advisable to go by car.*	▲ 131 ◆ F B2
IGREJA DA ORDEM TERCEIRA DE N. S. DO MONTE DO CARMO Rua Primeiro de Março	*Tel. (21) 22 42 48 28. Open Mon.–Fri. 8am–3.30pm.*	▲ 118 ◆ A B3
IGREJA DE N. S. DA CANDELÁRIA Praça Pio X	*Tel. (21) 22 33 23 24. Open Mon.–Fri. 7.30am–4pm; Sat. 9am–noon; Sun. 9am–1.30pm.*	▲ 118 ◆ A B2
IGREJA DE N. S. DA GLÓRIA DO OUTEIRO Praça N. S. da Glória 135	*Tel. (21) 25 57 46 00. Open Mon.–Fri. 9am–noon, 1–5pm; Sat.–Sun. 9am–noon.*	▲ 134 ◆ B A2
IGREJA DE N. S. DA LAMPADOSA Avenida Passos 13	*Tel. (21) 22 21 03 51. Open Mon.–Fri. 7am–5pm; Sat. 7am–noon.*	▲ 121 ◆ A B2
IGREJA DE N. S. DA LAPA DOS MERCADORES Rua do Ouvidor 35	*Tel. (21) 25 09 23 39. Open Mon.–Fri. 8am–2pm. Mass: Mon. noon.*	▲ 118 ◆ A B3
IGREJA DE N. S. DE BONSUCESSO Largo da Misericórdia	*Tel. (21) 22 20 30 01. Open Mon.–Fri. 7am–3.30pm. The church is behind the Santa Casa da Misericórdia.*	▲ 116 ◆ A B3
IGREJA DE N. S. DO CARMO Rua Sete de Setembro 14	*Tel. (21) 22 42 08 30. Open Mon.–Fri. 8am–6pm. Mass: Mon., Tue., Thu. 8am; Wed. 8am, 9am; Fri. 8am, 12.20pm.*	▲ 117 ◆ A B3
IGREJA DE N. S. DO ROSÁRIO E S. BENEDITO Rua Uruguaiana 77	*Tel. (21) 22 42 44 92. Open Mon-Fri. 8.20am– 4.30pm. Mass: Mon.–Fri. 8am, 10am, noon; 1st Sun. in the month 11am.*	▲ 121 ◆ A B2
IGREJA DE SANTA LUZIA Rua de Santa Luzia 490	*Tel. (21) 22 20 43 67. Open Mon.–Fri. 8am–5pm; Sat.–Sun. 8–11am.*	▲ 117 ◆ A C3
IGREJA DE S. FRANCISCO DE PAULA Largo de São Fancisco de Paula	*Tel. (21) 25 09 00 67. Open Mon.–Fri. 9am–1pm.*	▲ 121 ◆ A B2
JARDIM BOTÂNICO Rua Jardim Botânico 920	*Tel. (21) 25 11 05 11. Open daily 8am–4pm.*	▲ 142 ◆ D B2
JARDIM ZOOLÓGICO Quinta da Boa Vista	*Tel. (21) 25 68 74 00. Open Tue.–Sun. 9am–4.30pm.*	▲ 128 ◆ E B-C1
MARACANÃ Rua Professor Eurico Rabelo	*Tel. (21) 25 68 99 62. Open Mon.–Fri. 9am–5pm; match days: 8–11am.*	▲ 131 ◆ E C1
MOSTEIRO DE SÃO BENTO Rua D. Gerardo 68	*Tel. (21) 22 91 71 22. Open daily 8–11am, 2.30pm–5.30pm. Only church open to the public.*	▲ 119 ◆ A A2
MUSEU CARMEN MIRANDA Avenida Rui Barbosa	*Tel. (21) 25 51 25 97. Open Tue.–Fri. 11am–5pm; Sat.–Sun. 1–5pm. The museum is located in the park.*	▲ 135 ◆ B C2
MUSEU CASA DO PONTAL Estrada do Pontal 3295	*Tel. (21) 24 90 40 13. Open Tue.–Sun. 9.30am–5pm. Museum of popular art.*	▲ 147 ◆ G D1
MUSEU CHÁCARA DO CÉU Rua Murtinho Nobre 93	*Tel. (21) 25 07 19 32. Open Wed.-Mon. noon–5pm. Private collections of R. de Castro Maya.*	▲ 133 ◆ A D2
MUSEU DA IMAGEM E DO SOM Praça Rui Barbosa	*Tel. (21) 22 62 03 09. Open Mon.-Fri. 11am–5pm*	▲ 116 ◆ A B3
MUSEU DA IMPERIAL IRMANDADE DE N. S. DA GLÓRIA DO OUTEIRO Praça N.S. da Glória 135	*Tel. (21) 25 57 46 00. Open Tue.-Fri. 9am–noon and 1–5pm; Sat.–Sun. 9am–noon. 19th-century objects bequeathed by the Brazilian aristocracy.*	▲ 134 ◆ B A2
MUSEU DA REPÚBLICA Rua do Catete 153	*Tel. (21) 25 58 63 50. Open Tue.-Fri. 9am–7pm; Sat-Sun. 1–6pm. Former presidential palace.*	▲ 139 ◆ B A2
MUSEU DE ARTE MODERNA Avenida Infante D. Henrique 85	*Tel. (21) 22 40 49 44. Open Tue.-Sun. noon–6pm. Collection of Gilberto Chateaubriand.*	▲ 125 ◆ A C3
MUSEU DO BONDE Rua Carlos Brant 14	*Tel. (21) 22 42 23 54. Open daily 9am–4.30pm. Santa Teresa tram museum.*	▲ 133 ◆ A D2

MUSEU DO FOLCLORE EDISON CARNEIRO Rua do Catete 181	*Tel (21) 22 85 04 41.* *Open Tue.–Fri. 11am–6pm; Sat.–Sun. 3–6pm.*	▲ 139 ◆ B A2
MUSEU DO ÍNDIO Rua das Palmeiras 55	*Tel. (21) 22 86 20 97.* *Open Tue.–Fri. 9am–5pm; Sat.–Sun. 1–5pm.*	▲ 140 ◆ B D1
MUSEU DO PRIMEIRO REINADO Avenida Pedro II 293	*Tel. (21) 25 89 96 27.* *Open Tue.–Fri. 11am–5.15pm.*	▲ 128 ◆ E B2
MUSEU DO TELEFONE Rua Dois de Dezembro 63	*Tel. (21) 31 31 14 33 . Open Tue.–Sun. 9am–7pm.*	▲ 135 ◆ B B2
MUSEU HISTÓRICO NACIONAL Praça Marechal Âncora	*Tel. (21) 25 50 92 24. Open Tue.–Fri. 10am–5.30pm; Sat.–Sun. 2–6pm.*	▲ 116 ◆ A B3
MUSEU INTERNACIONAL DE ARTE NAÏF Rua Cosme Velho 561	*Tel. (21) 22 05 86 12. Open Tue.–Fri. 10am–6pm; Sat.–Sun. noon–6pm.*	▲ 138 ◆ F C3
MUSEU NACIONAL Quinta da Boa Vista	*Tel. (21) 25 68 82 62. Open Tue.–Sun. 10am–4pm.*	▲ 128 ◆ E C2
MUSEU NACIONAL DE BELAS ARTES Avenida Rio Branco 199	*Tel. (21) 22 40 00 68 (ext. 29). Open Tue.–Fri. 10am–6pm; Sat.–Sun. 2–6pm.*	▲ 122 ◆ A C3
MUSEU NAVAL Rua Dom Manuel 15	*Tel. (21) 25 33 76 26. Open Tue.–Fri. 9am–5pm and 2nd weekend in the month: 9am–5pm.*	▲ 117 ◆ A B3
MUSEU VILLA-LOBOS Rua Sorocaba 200	*Tel (21) 22 66 38 45. Open Mon.–Fri. 10am–5.30pm. Exhibition of personal possessions, scores, etc.*	▲ 140 ◆ B D1
PAÇO IMPERIAL Praça XV de Novembro 48	*Tel. (21) 25 33 44 07. Open Tue.–Sun. noon–6pm. Houses a cultural center, bookstore and restaurant.*	▲ 118 ◆ A B3
PALÁCIO DUQUE DE CAXIAS Praça Duque de Caxias 25	*Tel. (21) 25 19 50 88. Open Mon.–Fri. 9am–5pm. Former war ministry.*	▲ 127 ◆ A B1
PALÁCIO GUSTAVO CAPANEMA Rua da Imprensa 16	*Tel. (21) 22 20 14 90. Guided tours Mon.–Fri. 9am–10am and 4–5pm. Access for administrative staff only.*	▲ 124 ◆ A C3
PALÁCIO ITAMARATY (MUSEU HISTÓRICO E DIPLOMÁTICO) Avenida Marechal Floriano 196	*Tel. (21) 22 53 76 91. Open Mon., Wed., Fri. 2–5pm. A rare example of 19th-century neoclassical architecture, furnishings, sculptures and paintings.*	▲ 127 ◆ A B1
PÃO DE AÇÚCAR (SUGAR LOAF MOUNTAIN) Avenida Pasteur 520	*Tel. (21) 25 46 84 00. Open daily 8am–10pm. Cable cars leave every 30 minutes.*	▲ 136 ◆ B D3
PARQUE DA CATACUMBA Avenida Epitácio Pessoa 3000	*Open daily 8am–7pm. Aka the Parque das Esculturas.*	▲ 141 ◆ D C4
PARQUE ECOLÓGICO CHICO MENDES Avenida das Américas, Km 17.5	*Tel. (21) 24 37 64 00. Open Tue.–Sun. 8am–5pm. Birds and caimans in a 100-acre park.*	▲ 147 ◆ G D1
PARQUE GAROTA DE IPANEMA Rua Francisco Otaviano	*Open daily 9am–6pm.*	▲ 145 ◆ D D4
PARQUE LAGE Rua Jardim Botânico 414	*Tel. (21) 25 38 18 79. Open daily 9am–5pm. The Escola de Artes Visuais stands in the park.*	▲ 140 ◆ D B3
PARQUE NACIONAL DA TIJUCA Serra da Carioca	*Tel. (21) 24 92 22 53. Open daily 8am–6pm. Beautiful viewing points. Access via Santa Teresa, Horto, São Conrado, Alto da Boa Vista.*	▲ 150 ◆ G C3
QUINTA DA BOA VISTA São Cristovão	*Open daily 7am–6pm. The Museu Nacional and Jardim Zoológico are in the park.*	▲ 128 ◆ E C2
REAL GABINETE PORTUGUÊS DE LEITURA Rua Luís Camões 30	*Tel. (21) 22 21 31 38 and (21) 22 21 29 60. Open Mon.–Fri. 9am–6pm. A beautiful library in Portuguese Manueline style.*	▲ 121 ◆ A B2
SAMBÓDROMO Rua Marquês de Sapucaí	*Tel. (21) 25 03 55 06. Prices vary according to day and sector (avoid the badly situated sectors 6 and 13). Book through hotels and travel agents.*	▲ 126 ◆ E C4
SÍTIO BURLE MARX Estrada da Barra de Guaratiba 2019	*Tel. (21) 24 10 14 12 (ext. 226). Visits by appt. Tue.–Sun. 9.30am–1.30pm. The gardens contain more than 2,000 species of plants.*	▲ 147
TEATRO CARLOS GOMES Rua D. Pedro II 22	*Tel. (21) 232 87 01. Open Mon.–Fri. 10am–6pm. Programs published in the press.*	▲ 121 ◆ A C2
TEATRO MUNICIPAL Praça Floriano	*Tel. (21) 22 32 87 01 (ext. 236). Open Mon.–Fri. 10am–6pm.*	▲ 123 ◆ A C2

STATE OF RIO DE JANEIRO

NITERÓI		
FORTALEZA DE SANTA CRUZ Estrada General Eurico Gaspar Dutra	*Tel. (21) 27 11 04 62 (ext. 27) and (21) 27 10 78 40. Open Tue.–Sun. 9am–4pm. Guided tours every hour.*	▲ 154
MUSEU DE ARTE CONTEMPORÂNEA Mirante da Boa Viagem	*Tel. (21) 26 20 24 00. Open Tue.–Sun. 11am–6pm. Building designed by Niemeyer.*	▲ 154
PAQUETÁ		
PARQUE DARKE DE MATOS At the end of the Praia José Bonifácio and the Rua Luiz de Andrade	*Open daily 8am–5pm. Magnificent view of Paquetá and the bay from the viewing point. Several footpaths allow visitors to explore the characteristic flora and birdlife of the mata atlântica.*	▲ 154
PARATI		
CENTRO DE ARTES E TRADIÇÕES POPULARES DE PARATI Morro da Vila Velha	*Open Wed.–Sun. 9am–noon, 2–5pm. Museum in the Forte Defensor Perpétuo, overlooking the Praia do Pontal. Regional crafts on sale.*	▲ 165
FAZENDA MURYCANA 3½ miles from Parati, toward Cunha	*Tel. (24) 33 71 39 30. Restaurant open daily 8am–6pm. Sugar-cane mill; horse riding.*	▲ 165
MUSEU DE ARTE SACRA Praça Santa Rita	*Tel. (24) 33 71 16 20. Open Wed.–Sun. 10am–noon, 2–5pm.*	▲ 164
PARQUE NACIONAL DE ITATIAIA		
MUSEU DA FLORA E DA FAUNA 112 miles from Rio, on the BR-116	*Tel. (24) 33 52 14 61 (ext. 29). Open Tue.–Sun. 8am–5pm. Follow the BR-485 highway, which runs through the park.*	▲ 177
PENEDO		
CLUBE FINLANDÊS Avenida das Mangueiras 2601	*Tel. (24) 33 51 13 74. Traditional Finnish dancing and music. 9pm–1am. Performance 10.30pm.*	▲ 178
MUSEU FINLANDÊS DE DONA EVA Avenida das Mangueiras 2601	*Tel. (24) 33 51 13 74. Open Wed.–Sat. 10am–5pm; Sun. 9am–3pm. Traces the history of Finnish settlers.*	▲ 178
PETRÓPOLIS		
CASA DE SANTOS-DUMONT Rua do Encanto 22	*Tel. (24) 22 47 31 58. Tue.–Sun. 9.30am–5pm. House of the famous pioneer of aviation.*	▲ 169
CASA DO BARÃO DE MAUÁ Praça da Confluença 3	*Tel. 0800 24 15 16. Tourist information office. Open Mon.–Sat. 9am–6.30pm; Sun. 9.30am–5pm.*	▲ 169
CATEDRAL DE SÃO PEDRO DE ALCÂNTARA Rua São Pedro de Alcântara 60	*Tel. (24) 22 42 43 00. Open Tue.–Sun. 8am–noon, 2–6pm.*	▲ 168
COLEGIO DO PADRE CORREIA Rua Álvares de Azevedo 24	*Tel. (24) 22 21 20 46. Sat.–Sun. visits by appt to the casa-grande and chapel. No charge. Formerly the Fazenda do Padre Correia.*	▲ 168
MUSEU IMPERIAL Rua da Imperatriz 220	*Tel. (24) 22 37 80 00. Open Tue.–Sun. 11am–5.30pm. Former imperial palace. Exhibits include the scepter and crown of Dom Pedro II, furniture, jewelry, documents and works of art that once belonged to the Portuguese royal family.*	▲ 168
PALÁCIO DE CRISTAL Rua Alfredo Pachá	*Tel. (24) 22 47 37 21. Open Tue.–Sun. 11am–5.30pm.*	▲ 169
PALÁCIO QUITANDINHA Avenida Estados Unidos 2	*Tel. (24) 22 37 10 12. Open Tue.–Fri. 9am–5pm; Sat.–Sun. 9am–6pm.*	▲ 169
PALÁCIO RIO NEGRO Avenida Köeller 255	*Tel. (24) 22 46 93 80. Wed.–Sun. 9.30am–5pm; Mon. noon–5pm. Former residence of the Barão de Rio Negro.*	▲ 169
TERESÓPOLIS		
MUSEU VON MARTIUS Estrada Rio-Teresópolis, Km 98	*Tel. (24) 33 52 22 65. Tue.–Sun. 10am–5pm. Botanical museum.*	▲ 171
SEDE DO PARQUE NACIONAL DA SERRA DOS ÓRGÃOS	*Tel. (24) 33 52 22 66. Open daily 8am–5pm. The park guides offer their services free of charge at*	▲ 171

Estrada Rio-Teresópolis, Km 111.5	*weekends. The Museu Von Martius (flora and fauna) stands in the park (closed Mon.).*	
VALENÇA		
FAZENDA CAMPO ALEGRE Access via the RJ-145, ½ mile	*Tel. (24) 98 13 96 31 or (24) 24 52 05 65 and (24) 24 53 18 88.*	▲ 175
FAZENDA PAU D'ALHO RJ-145 (Estrada Valença-Rio das Flores), Km 4	*Tel. (24) 24 53 30 33. Visits by appt. Guided tour by the owner who traces the family history. Tea served after the tour.*	▲ 175
FAZENDA PONTE ALTA RJ-145 Barra do Piraí Santanésia	*Tel. (24) 24 43 51 59. Senzala converted into a museum of slavery. Visits by appt.*	▲ 175
FAZENDA SANTA ROSA RJ-145, Km 88	*Tel. (24) 24 53 41 44. Visits by appt Mon.–Sat. Production of milk and cachaça. Fruit trees. Sugar-cane plantation.*	▲ 175
FAZENDA UNIÃO Estrada do Abarracamento, 2 miles Rio das Flores	*Tel. (24) 98 45 73 51 or (24) 24 58 41 02. Visits by appt. A beautiful coffee fazenda (1830) that has preserved its period furnishings. It offers an historical visit based on coffee cultivation. Accommodation available if you want to visit the other historic fazenda in the area.*	
VASSOURAS		
FAZENDA CACHOEIRA GRANDE Estrada Cachoeira Grande 1393	*Tel. (21) 33 22 50 40 or (24) 24 71 12 64. Daily visit (11/2 hours) followed by afternoon tea (regional produce). Collection of old cars.*	▲ 175
FAZENDA SÃO FERNANDO BR 393 (Rodovia Lúcio Meira), Km 218, Massambará	*Tel. (24) 24 88 91 00. Visits by appt.*	▲ 174
FAZENDA SECRETÁRIO RJ-115, 12½ miles, Ferreiros	*Tel. (21) 25 44 88 50. Visits by appt. Beautiful neoclassical-style architecture. The owner welcomes visitors from around 10am; afternoon tea.*	▲ 175
MUSEU CASA DA HERA Rua Doutor Fernandez Junior 160	*Tel. (24) 24 71 23 42. Open Wed.–Sun. 11am–5pm. Guided tours every 15 minutes.*	▲ 174
STATE OF MINAS GERAIS		
BELO HORIZONTE		
CASA DO BAILE Avenida Octacílio Negrão de Lima 751	*Tel. (31) 32 77 74 43. Open Tue.–Sun. 9am–6pm.*	▲ 182
IGREJA DE S. FRANCISCO DE ASSIS Avenida Otacílio Negrão de Lima	*Tel (31) 34 41 93 25. Open daily 8am–6pm.*	▲ 182
MUSEU DE ARTE DE PAMPULHA Avenida Otacílio Negrão de Lima 16.585	*Tel. (31) 34 43 45 33. Open Tue.–Sun. 9am–7pm. The museum of modern art is housed in the former casino.*	▲ 182
MUSEU DE MINERALOGIA Rua Bahia 1149	*Tel. (31) 32 71 34 15. Open Tue.–Sun. 9am–5pm. In the Centro de Cultura de Belo Horizonte.*	▲ 182
PARQUE MUNICIPAL Avenida Afonso Pena	*Tel. (31) 32 73 20 01. Open Tue.–Sun. 6am–6pm. The Palácio das Artes (cultural center) stands in the park.*	▲ 182
CONGONHAS		
BASÍLICA DO BOM JESUS DE MATOZINHOS Praça da Basílica	*Tel. (31) 37 31 15 90/15 91. Open Tue.–Sun. 6am–6pm. Mass: Mon.–Sat. 6.30am; Wed. 6.30am, 3pm, 7pm; Sun. 8am, 10am, 7pm. Classified as a World Heritage Site. A major work by sculptor Aleijadinho.*	▲ 192
CORDISBURGO		
GRUTA DO MAQUINÉ Via Alberto Ramos, Km 5	*Tel. (31) 37 15 10 78. Guided tours daily 8am–5pm.*	▲ 196
DIAMANTINA		
CASA DE CHICA DA SILVA Praça Lobo Mesquita 266	*Tel. (38) 35 31 24 91. Open Tue.–Sat. noon–5pm; Sun. 9am–noon.*	▲ 197
CATEDRAL Praça Correia Rabelo	*Tel. (38) 35 31 10 01/15 31. Open daily 7am–10pm. Mass: 7am, 6pm, 8pm.*	▲ 196

IGREJA DO CARMO Rua do Carmo	*Open Mon.–Sat. 9am–noon, 2–5pm; Sun. 9am–noon.*	▲ 197
MERCADO MUNICIPAL Praça Barão Guaicuí	*Open Sat. 8am–6pm. Market selling fresh produce and traditional crafts.*	▲ 197
MUSEU DO DIAMANTE Rua Direita 14	*Tel (38) 35 31 13 82. Open Tue.–Sat. noon–5.30pm; Sun. 9am–noon.*	▲ 196
MUSEU JUSCELINO KUBITSCHEK Rua São Francisco de Assis 241	*Tel. (38) 35 31 36 07. Open Tue.–Fri. 9am–5pm; Sat. 9am–6pm; Sun. 9am–2pm.*	▲ 197
MARIANA		
CATEDRAL BASÍLICA DA SÉ Praça Cláudio Manuel	*Tel. (31) 35 57 12 16. Open Tue.–Sun. 7am–6pm. Organ concert: Fri. 11am; Sun. 12.15pm. One of the richest churches in Brazil.*	▲ 191
IGREJA DE N. S. DO CARMO Praça Joaolinheiro	*No set opening times*	▲ 191
IGREJA DE N. S. DO ROSÁRIO DOS PRETOS Rua N. S. do Rosário dos Pretos	*Open Mon.–Fri. 10am–4pm.*	▲ 191
IGREJA DE S. FRANCISCO DE ASSIS Praça Minas Gerais	*Open Tue.–Sun. 9am–5pm.*	▲ 191
IGREJA DE S. PEDRO DOS CLÉRIGOS Rua D. Silvério	*The collection has been transferred to the Museu Arquidiocesano.*	▲ 191
MUSEU ARQUIDIOCESANO Rua Frei Durão 49	*Tel. (31) 35 57 25 16. Open Tue.–Sun. 9am–noon, 1.30–5pm.*	▲ 191
OURO PRETO		
CASA DE CÂMARA E CADEIA (MUSEU DA INCONFIDÊNCIA) Praça Tiradentes	*Tel (31) 35 51 11 21. Open Tue.–Sun. noon–6pm. The museum has taken the name of a famous rebellion in 1789. It exhibits works of art, objects and documents relating to this rebellion and colonial life in the 18th and 19th centuries.*	▲ 185
CASA DOS CONTOS Rua São José 12	*Tel. (31) 35 51 14 44. Open Mon.–Sat. 12.30–5.30pm; Sun. 9am–3pm. Former mint.*	▲ 185
IGREJA DE NOSSA SENHORA DO CARMO Rua Brigadeiro Mosqueira	*Tel. (31) 35 51 12 09. Open Tue.–Sat. noon–4.45pm; Sun. noon–4.45pm. Mass: Sun. 8.30–10am.*	▲ 185
IGREJA DE NOSSA SENHORA DO ROSÁRIO DOS PRETOS Largo do Rosário	*Tel. (31) 35 51 12 09. Open Tue.–Sat. noon–4.45pm. Mass: Sun. 3pm. NB: there are several 'do Rosário' churches in Ouro Preto!*	▲ 188
IGREJA DE SANTA EFIGÊNIA Ladeira Santa Efigênia	*Open Tue.–Sun. 8.30am–4.30pm. View of the city. Altar by Francisco Xavier de Brito. Aka Santa Efigênia do Rosário.*	▲ 189
IGREJA DE SÃO FRANCISCO DE ASSIS Largo do Coimbra	*Tel. (31) 35 51 32 82. Open Tue.–Sun. 8.30am–noon, 1.30–5pm.*	▲ 188
IGREJA DO PADRE FARIA Rua do Padre Faria	*Tel. (31) 35 51 50 47. Open Tue.–Sat. 8.30am–4.30pm; Sun. 9am–4.30pm. Rich interior decoration.*	▲ 189
MATRIZ DE NOSSA SENHORA DA CONCEIÇÃO Praça Antônio Dias 9	*Tel. (31) 35 51 32 82. Open Mon.–Sat. 8.30am–noon, 1.30–5pm; Sun. noon–5pm. Museu Aleijadinho in the sacristy.*	▲ 189
MATRIZ DE NOSSA SENHORA DO PILAR Praça Monsenhor Castilho Barbosa	*Tel. (31) 35 51 12 09 or (31) 35 51 47 35. Open Tue.–Sun. 9–10.45am, noon–4.45pm. The town's main church. Sculpted and gilt interior.*	▲ 185
MINA DE OURO DE PASSAGEM Rodovía Ouro Preto-Mariana, Km 4	*Tel. (31) 35 57 50 00. Open Mon.–Tue. 9am–5pm; Wed.–Sun. 9am–5.30pm. Former gold mine.*	▲ 190
MINA DO CHICO REI Rua Dom Silvério 108	*Tel. (31) 35 51 17 49. Open daily 9am–5.30pm. Former gold mine.*	▲ 189
MUSEU ALEIJADINHO Praça Antonio Dias 9	*Tel. (31) 35 51 46 61. Open Tue.–Sat. 8.30am–noon, 1.30–5pm; Sun. noon–5pm.*	▲ 189
MUSEU DE CIÊNCIA E TÉCNICA Praça Tiradentes	*Tel. (35) 35 59 15 97. Open Tue.–Sun. 9am–5pm. The museum occupies the Escola de Minas, in the governor's former palace. Collection of stones from all over the world.*	▲ 185

Place	Information	Page
MUSEU DO ORATORIOS Rua Brigadeiro Mosqueira	*Tel. (31) 35 51 53 69. Open daily 9.30–11.50am, 1.30–5.30pm. Collection of baroque shrines.*	▲ 185
TEATRO MUNICIPAL Rua Brigadeiro Mosqueira	*Tel. (31) 35 59 32 24. Open daily noon–5.30pm. Brazil's oldest theater.*	▲ 185
SABARÁ		
CAPELA DO Ó Largo do Ó	*Tel. (31) 36 71 17 24. Open Tue.–Sat. 9–11.30am, 1–5.30pm; Sun. 1–5.30pm.*	▲ 183
IGREJA NOSSA SENHORA DO CARMO Rua do Carmo	*Tel. (31) 36 71 24 17. Open Tue.–Sat. 9–11.30am, 1–5.30pm; Sun. 1–5.30pm.*	▲ 183
IGREJA NOSSA SENHORA DO ROSÁRIO Praça Melo Viana	*Open Tue.–Sun. 9am–noon, 1–5pm.*	▲ 183
MATRIZ DE N. S. DA CONCEIÇÃO Praça Getúlio Vargas	*Tel. (31) 36 71 17 24. Mon.–Fri. 9am–5pm; Sat.–Sun. 9am–noon, 2–5pm.*	▲ 183
MUSEU DO OURO Rua da Intendência	*Tel. (31) 36 71 18 48. Open Tue.–Sun. noon–5.30pm.*	▲ 183
TEATRO MUNICIPAL Rua D. Pedro II	*Tel. (31) 36 72 77 28. Open daily 8am–noon, 1–5pm. Brazil's second oldest working theater.*	▲ 183
SANTA BÁRBARA		
MATRIZ DE SANTO ANTÔNIO Praça Cleves de Faria	*Tel. (31) 38 32 12 64. Open daily 9–11.30am, 1.30–5pm.*	▲ 183
SÃO JOÃO DEL REI		
CATEDRAL DO PILAR Rua Getúlio Vargas	*Tel. (32) 33 71 25 68. Open Mon. 5–8pm; Tue.–Sun. 6–10.30am, 1–5pm, 5.30–8pm.*	▲ 194
IGREJA DE S. FRANCISCO DE ASSIS Praça Frei Orlando	*Tel. (32) 33 71 31 10 or (32) 33 71 21 49. Open daily 8am–5.30pm. Baroque mass: Sun. 9.15am.*	▲ 194
IGREJA DO CARMO Largo do Carmo	*Tel. (32) 33 71 79 96. Open Mon.–Fri. 6am–noon, 5–7pm; Sat.–Sun. 7–11am, 5–7pm.*	▲ 194
IGREJA DO ROSÁRIO Largo do Rosário	*Tel. (32) 33 71 47 89 or (32) 33 71 25 68. Open Tue.–Sat. 8–11am. Mass: Sun. 8.30am.*	▲ 194
MEMORIAL TANCREDO NEVES Rua Padre José Maria Xavier	*Tel. (32) 33 71 78 36. Open Fri.–Sun. 9am–5pm.*	▲ 194
MUSEU DE ARTE SACRA Largo do Rosário	*Tel. (31) 33 71 47 42.*	▲ 194
MUSEU FERROVIÁRIO Avenida Hemílio Alves 366	*Tel. (32) 33 71 84 85. Open Tue.–Sun. 9–11am, 1–5pm.*	▲ 194
MUSEU REGIONAL Rua Marechal Deodoro 12	*Tel. (32) 33 71 76 63. Open Tue.–Fri. noon–5.30pm; Sat.–Sun. 8am–1pm.*	▲ 194
TEATRO MUNICIPAL Avenida Hemílio Alves 170	*Tel. (32) 33 79 29 55. Interior not open to the public. See the local press for programs.*	▲ 194
SERRO		
CAPELA DE SANTA RITA Rua de Santa Rita	*Tourist information: Tel. (38) 35 41 13 68. Open Tue.–Sun. 1–4pm. Mass: Sat. 7pm.*	▲ 197
IGREJA DO CARMO Praça João Pinnheiro	*Tourist information: Tel. (38) 35 41 13 68. Open Tue.–Sun. 1–4pm. Mass: Wed. 7.30pm; Sat. 4pm.*	▲ 197
MATRIZ DA CONCEIÇÃO Praça Présidente Vargas	*Tourist information: Tel. (38) 35 41 13 68. Open Tue.–Sun. 1–4pm. Mass: Sun. 8am–7.30pm.*	▲ 197
PARQUE NACIONAL DA SERRA DO CIPÓ Km 96 on the BR-010	*Tel (31) 37 18 72 28/72 37. Open daily 8am–6pm, last admission 2pm. Bicycles and horses can be hired in the park.*	▲ 197
SETE LAGOAS		
GRUTA REI DO MATO BR-040, 3 miles from Sete Lagoas	*Tel. (31) 37 73 08 88. Open daily 8am–5pm, last admission 4.20pm. Rock paintings.*	▲ 196

TIRADENTES		
IGREJA DO ROSÁRIO DOS PRETOS Praça Padre Lourival	*Tel. (32) 33 55 12 38.* *Open daily 9am–1pm, 2–5pm.*	▲ 195
MATRIZ DE SANTO ANTÔNIO Rua da Câmara	*Tel. (32) 33 55 12 38. Open daily 9am–5pm.* *The most beautiful church in Minas.*	▲ 195
MUSEU DO PADRE TOLEDO Rua Padre Toledo	*Tel. (32) 33 55 15 49. Open Mon.– Fri. 9–11.30am, 1–5pm; Sat.–Sun. 9am–4.40pm.*	▲ 195
SOLAR DO RAMALHO Rua da Câmara 124	*Tel. (32) 355 13 15. Open Mon.–Fri. 9am–5pm.* *The oldest villa in Tiradentes. Art gallery.*	▲ 195
STATE OF THE DISTRITO FEDERAL		
BRASÍLIA		
CATEDRAL METROPOLITANA Eixo Monumental	*Tel. (61) 224 40 73. Open daily 8am–6pm.*	▲ 203
CONGRESSO NACIONAL Praça dos Três Poderes	*Chamber of deputies: Tel (61) 318 51 06. Guided tours: Mon.–Fri. 9.30am, 10.30am, 11.30am, 2.30pm, 3.30pm, 4.30pm; Sat.–Sun. 9am–1.30pm, every half hour. Senate: Tel (61) 311 21 49. Tours Mon.–Fri. 9.30am, 10.30am, 11.30am, 2.30pm, 3.30pm, 4.30pm; Sat.–Sun. 10am, 11am, noon, 1pm, 2pm.*	▲ 204
ESPAÇO LÚCIO COSTA Below the Praça dos Três Poderes	*Tel. (61) 321 98 43. Open Tue.–Sun. 9am–6pm.* *Model of Brasília.*	▲ 204
FUNDAÇÃO NIEMEYER Praça dos Três Poderes	*Tel. (61) 226 67 97.*	▲ 204
IGREJA DE N. S. DE FÁTIMA Entrequadra 307–308	*Tel. (61) 424 01 49. Open daily 6am–7pm.*	▲ 207
JARDIM BOTÂNICO QI 23, Sul	*Tel (61) 366 21 41. Opening times vary.*	▲ 209
MEMORIAL JUSCELINO KUBITSCHEK Praça do Cruzeiro	*Tel. (61) 225 94 51 or (61) 321 67 78.* *Open Tue.–Sun. 9am–6pm.*	▲ 206
MUSEU DA CIDADE Praça dos Três Poderes	*Tel. (61) 325 62 44. Open Tue.–Sun. 9am–6pm.*	▲ 204
MUSEU DE ARTE DE BRASÍLIA Setor de Hoteis e Turismo	*Open Tue.–Fri. 10am–5pm; Sat.–Sun. 1–5pm.* *Modern and contemporary art from 1950 to the present day.*	▲ 209
PALÁCIO DA ALVORADA On the Lago Paranoá	*Tel. (61) 411 23 17. Residence of the President of the Republic.*	▲ 208
PALÁCIO DA JUSTIÇA Praça dos Três Poderes	*Tel. (61) 429 33 95.* *Visits by appt Mon.–Fri. 9–11am, 3–5pm.*	▲ 204
PALÁCIO DO PLANALTO Praça dos Três Poderes	*Presidential palace. Tel. (61) 411 23 17. Guided tour: Sun. 9.30am–12.30pm (arrive as early as possible).*	▲ 205
PALÁCIO ITAMARATY Esplanada dos Ministeiros	*Tel. (61) 411 66 40. Open Mon.–Fri. 3–5pm; Sat.–Sun. 10am–2pm. Ministry of Foreign Affairs. Guided tours of the state rooms.*	▲ 204
PANTEÃO DA PÁTRIA TANCREDO NEVES Praça dos Três Poderes	*Tel. (61) 325 62 44. Open Tue.–Sun. 9am–6pm.*	▲ 205
PARQUE DA CIDADE Eixo Monumental	*Tel. (61) 225 24 51. 6 miles of walks.* *Wave pool.*	▲ 206
PARQUE NACIONAL DE BRASÍLIA Via EPIA BR-040 (setor Militar Urbano) Km 9	*Tel (61) 465 20 13. Natural pools hollowed out of the rock, fed by waterfalls.*	▲ 206
SANTUÁRIO DOM BOSCO W3 Sul, Quadra 702	*Tel. (61) 223 65 42. Open Mon.–Sat. 7am–7pm; Sun. 7am–noon, 3–8pm.*	▲ 207
SUPREMO TRIBUNAL FEDERAL Praça dos Três Poderes	*Tel. (61) 217 30 00. Sat.–Sun. 10am–3.30pm.*	▲ 205

Place	Information	Page
TEATRO NACIONAL CLAÚDIO SANTORO Setor Cultural Norte, Via N 2	*Tel. (61) 325 61 09. Guided tours dependent on the availability of staff, daily 3–6pm.*	▲ 202
TEMPLO DA BOA VONTADE W5 Sul, Quadra 915	*Temple open daily 10am–6.30pm. Pyramid open daily 24 hours.*	▲ 209
TORRE DA TELEVISÃO Eixo Monumental	*Open Mon. 2–8pm; Tue.–Sun. 8am–8pm.*	▲ 206
GAMA		
CATETINHO Km 0 on the BR-40 to BH	*Tel. (31) 338 86 94. Open 9am–5pm.*	▲ 209
NUCLEO BANDEIRANTE		
MUSEU VIVO DA MEMÓRIA CANDANGA EPIA Sul, Lt. D	*Tel. (61) 301 35 90 or (61) 301 30 22. Open Mon.–Fri. 9am–6pm. 9 miles from Brasília.*	▲ 209

STATE OF MATO GROSSO DO SUL

Place	Information	Page
PARQUE NATIONAL DA SERRA DA BODOQUENA: BONITO		
Access from Campo Grande: BR 060, Sidrolandia, Nioaque, Jardim, Guia Lopes da Laguna.	*Visitors must be accompanied by agency-approved guides. Tourist information: Tel. (67) 255 18 50.*	▲ 216

STATE OF SÃO PAULO

Place	Information	Page
SÃO PAULO		
BOSQUE DO MORUMBI PARQUE Alfredo Volpi Avenida 480	*Tel. (11) 30 31 70 52. Open daily 6am–6pm.*	
CASA DAS ROSAS Avenida Paulista 37	*Tel. (11) 288 94 47. Open Tue.–Sun. 1–8pm. Villa dating from the great era of coffee cultivation, converted into a cultural center.*	▲ 224
CATEDRAL METROPOLITANA DA SÉ Praça da Sé	*Tel. (11) 31 07 68 32. Open daily 8am–5pm.*	▲ 220
EDIFÍCIO BANESPA Rua João Brícola 24	*Tel. (11) 32 49 74 66. Open Mon.–Fri. 10am–5pm. Guided tours of the terrace by appointment.*	▲ 220
EDIFÍCIO ITÁLIA Avenida Ipiranga 344	*Tel. (11) 32 57 65 66. 42nd-floor restaurant with a panoramic view.*	▲ 221
ESTAÇÃO DA LUZ Praça da Luz	*Tel. 0800 55 01 21. The station (1901) is an historic monument.*	▲ 219
ESTÁDIO DE PACAEMBU Praça Charles Miller	*Tel. (11) 36 61 91 11 (ext. 108). Open Mon.–Fri. 9am–5pm, except match days.*	▲ 223
ESTÁDIO DO MORUMBI Praça Roberto Gomes Pedrosa	*Tel. (11) 37 49 80 65. Visits daily 9am–5pm, except match days and during ticket sales.*	▲ 225
FUNDAÇÃO MARIA LUÍSA E OSCAR AMERICANO Avenida Morumbi 3700	*Tel. (11) 37 42 00 77/41 62. Open Tue.–Fri. 11am–5pm; Sat.–Sun. 10am–5pm. Works by Lasar Segall, Portinari, Frans Post; documents and objects dating from the imperial age. Beautiful garden.*	▲ 225
IGREJA DE N. S. DO BRASIL Praça N.S. do Brasil	*Tel. (11) 30 82 97 86. Open daily 7–11.30am, 3.30–7pm.*	▲ 224
IGREJA DE SÃO JOSÉ Rua Dinamarca 32	*Tel. (11) 30 85 15 06. Open Tue.–Sat. 8.30–10.30am, 2.30–5.30pm.*	▲ 224
IGREJA DO PÁTIO DO COLÉGIO Pátio do Colégio	*Tel. (11) 31 05 68 99. Open Sun.–Fri. 8am–5pm. Museum open Tue.–Sun. 9am–5pm.*	▲ 220
INSTITUTO BUTANTÃ Avenida Doutor Vital Brasil 1500	*Tel. (11) 37 26 72 22. Open Mon.–Fri. 8am–5pm. Some of the 50,000 examples of the 1,000 species of snakes raised by the institute can be seen in the natural history museum.*	▲ 225

JARDIM DA LUZ Rua Ribeira de Lima 99	*Open Tue.–Sun. 6–9am, 10am–5.30pm. Get off at the Estação da Luz subway station.*	▲ 219
MEMORIAL DA AMÉRICA LATINA Avenida Auro Soares de Moura Andrade 664	*Tel. (11) 38 23 46 00. Open Tue.–Sun. 9am–6pm. Cultural center. In the Salão de Atos, frescos by Carybé and Poty.*	▲ 221
MERCADO MUNICIPAL Rua da Cantareira 306	*Tel. (11) 228 06 73. Open Mon.–Sat. 6am–6pm; Sun. 8am–1pm. Get off at the Tiradentes subway station.*	▲ 221
MOSTEIRO DE N. S. DA LUZ Avenida Tiradentes 676	*Only the chapel is open to the public: Tel. (11) 33 11 87 45. Open Mon., Fri. 6.30–11am, 2–4.45pm; Tue.–Thu., Sat.–Sun. 6.30am–4.45pm. Houses the comprehensive Museu de Arte Sacra: Tel. (11) 33 26 53 93. Tue.–Fri. 11am–6pm; Sat.–Sun. 10am–7pm.*	▲ 219
MOSTEIRO DE SÃO BENTO Largo de São Bento	*Tel. (11) 228 36 33. Only the church is open to the public. Open Fri.–Wed. 6am–noon, 2–6pm; Thu. 6–8am, 2–6pm. Gregorian chants: Mon.–Fri. 7am; Sat. 6am; Sun. 10am.*	▲ 220
MUSEU DA CASA BRASILEIRA Avenida Brigadeiro Faria Lima 2705	*Tel. (11) 30 32 25 64. Open Tue.–Sun. 1–6pm. Furniture from the 17th century to the present day.*	▲ 225
MUSEU DE ARTE CONTEMPORÂNEA Rua da Reitoria 160	*Tel. (11) 30 91 30 39. Open Mon.–Fri. 10am–7pm; Sat.–Sun. 10am–4pm. Rich collection of works by Picasso, Miró, Matisse, Cândido Portinari, Di Cavalcanti, Tarsila do Amaral, Anita Malfati.*	▲ 225
MUSEU DE ARTE DE SÃO PAULO (MASP) Avenida Paulista, 1578	*Tel. (11) 251 56 44. Open Tue.–Sun. 11am–6pm. Major collection of European (Velázquez, Goya, Van Gogh, Matisse) and Brazilian (Vitor Meirelles, Anita Malfatti, Portinari) artists.*	▲ 224
MUSEU DE ARTE MODERNA Parque do Ibirapuera – Portão 3	*Tel. (11) 55 49 96 88. Open Tue., Wed., Fri. noon–6pm; Thu. noon–10pm; Sat.–Sun. 10am–6pm. Major collection of Brazilian artists.*	▲ 224
MUSEU DO IPIRANGA Parque da Independência Ipiranga	*Tel. (11) 61 65 80 00. Open Tue.–Sun. 9am–4.45pm. Traces the history of Brazil from 1850 to the present day.*	▲ 219
MUSEU DO TEATRO MUNICIPAL Baixos do Viaduto do Chá	*Tel. (11) 32 41 38 15. Open Tue.–Sun. 9am–5pm.*	▲ 221
MUSEU HISTÓRICO DA IMIGRAÇÃO JAPONESA São Joaquin 381	*Tel. (11) 32 09 54 65. Open Tue.–Sun. 1.30–5.30pm.*	▲ 222
MUSEU PADRE ANCHIETA Pátio do Colégio 2	*Tel. (11) 31 05 68 99. Open Tue.–Sun. 9am–5pm. Museum dedicated to the Jesuit founder of the city.*	▲ 220
PALÁCIO DOS BANDEIRANTES Avenida Morumbi 4500	*Tel. (11) 37 45 32 63. Guided tours by appt. Mon.–Fri. 10am–3pm. Free admission.*	▲ 225
PARQUE BURLE MARX Avenida Dona Helena Pereira de Morais 200	*Tel. (11) 37 46 76 31. Open daily 7am–7pm.*	
PARQUE DO IBIRAPUERA Avenida Pedro Alvares Cabral	*Tel. (11) 55 74 51 77. Open daily 6am–midnight. Home of the Pavilhão da Bienal, Museu de Arte Moderna, Planetarium and Pavilhão Japonês.*	▲ 224
PINACOTECA DO ESTADO Avenida Tiradentes 141	*Tel. (11) 229 98 44. Open Tue.–Sun. 10am–6pm.*	▲ 219
TEATRO MUNICIPAL Praça Ramos de Azevedo	*19th- and 20th-century Brazilian paintings. Tel. (11) 222 86 98. Guided tours by appt Mon. 4–6pm; Wed. 10am–noon; Fri. noon–3pm.*	▲ 221
SÃO VICENTE		
MATRIZ DE SÃO VICENTE Praça do Mercado	*Tel. (13) 34 68 26 58.*	▲ 228

STATE OF PARANÁ

Place	Information	Page
CURITIBA		
CATEDRAL BASÍLICA MENOR Praça Tiradentes	*Tel. (41) 324 51 36. Open Mon.–Fri. 7am–7pm; Sat. 11am–7pm; Sun. 7–11am, 3–6pm.*	▲ 234
IGREJA DA ORDEM TERCEIRA DE SÃO FRANCISCO DAS CHAGAS Largo da Ordem	*Tel. (41) 223 75 45. Open Tue.–Sun. 8.30am–7.30pm. Houses the Museu de Arte Sacra: Tel. (41) 321 32. Open Tue.–Fri. 9am–noon, 2–6pm Sat.–Sun. 9am–2pm.*	▲ 234
MUSEU PARANAENSE Praça Generoso Marques	*Tel. (41) 322 20 16.*	▲ 234
CASTRO		
MUSEU DO TROPEIRO Praça Getúlio Vargas 11	*Tel. (42) 232 02 60. Open Tue.–Sun. 9–11.30am, 2–4.30pm.*	▲ 235
FOZ DO IGUAÇU		
PARQUE NACIONAL DE IGUAÇU Park entrance at the end of the Rodovia das Cataratas	*Tourist information: Tel. 0 800 45 15 16. Open Tue.–Sun. 8am–5pm; Mon. 1–5pm.*	▲ 239
GUARAQUEÇABA		
PARQUE NACIONAL DE SUPERAGÜI Access by boat from Guarequeçaba and Paranaguá	*Tourist information, Vila de Pescadores da Barra do Superagüi: Tel. (41) 455 15 64. Tourist information, Guaraqueçaba: Tel. (41) 482 12 62/80.*	▲ 237
ILHA DO MEL		
FORTALEZA DE N.S. DOS PRAZERES Praia da Fortaleza	*Allow an hour's walk. 18th- and 19th-century cannons. View of the Ilhas Superagüi and das Peças.*	▲ 237
PARANAGUÁ		
MUSEU DA ARQUEOLOGIA E ETNOLOGIA Rua 15 de Novembro 621	*Tel. (41) 422 12 44. Open Tue.–Sun. noon–5pm (former Jesuit college).*	▲ 237
PARQUE ESTADUAL DE VILA VELHA		
BR 376, Km 507.5 (for the water holes) or Km 511 (for the rock formations and park entrance)	*Tel. (42) 228 11 38. Usual opening times: 8am–6pm. Parking and snacks.*	▲ 235

STATE OF SANTA CATARINA

Place	Information	Page
FLORIANÓPOLIS		
CATEDRAL METROPOLITANA Praça XV de Novembro	*Tel. (48) 224 33 57. Open Mon.–Fri. 6.30am–6.30pm. Mass: Sat. 6.30am, 5pm; Sun. 6.30am–noon, 5pm.*	▲ 240
FORTALEZA DE SANTA CRUZ Ilha de Anhatomirim	*Tel. (48) 331 67 14. Open daily 9am–5pm. Boats leave from the Ponte Hercílio Luz and Canasvieiras.*	▲ 241
MERCADO PÚBLICO Avenida Paulo Fontes	*Fish, meat, vegetable and craft stalls. Open 7am–7pm, bars and restaurants until 11pm.*	▲ 240
PALÁCIO CRUZ E SOUZA (MUSEU HISTÓRICO DE SANTA CATARINA) Praça XV de Novembro 227	*Tel. (48) 221 35 04. Open Mon.–Fri. 10am–6pm; Sat.–Sun. 10am–4pm. Former seat of the government.*	▲ 241
LAGUNA		
CASA ANITA GARIBALDI Praça Vidal Ramos	*Tel. (48) 644 49 47. Open daily 8am–6pm.*	▲ 243
FAROL DE SANTA MARTA	*Boats leave from the village of Magalhães (10 min), then 101/2 miles along an unmetaled road.*	▲ 243
SAO FRANCISCO DO SUL		
MUSEU NACIONAL DO MAR Rua Manuel Lourenço de Andrade 133	*Tel. (47) 444 18 68. Open Mon. 11am–6pm; Tue.–Sun. 9am–6.30pm. Collection of boats used on the Brazilian coast, including the one that enabled Almir Klink to row across the Atlantic.*	▲ 243

STATE OF RIO GRANDE DO SUL

PORTO ALEGRE

Place	Information	Page
BIBLIOTECA PÚBLICA Rua Riachuelo 1190	*Tel. (51) 32 24 50 45. Open Mon.–Fri. 9am–7pm; Sat. 9am–1pm.*	▲ 244
CASA DE CULTURA MÁRIO QUINTANA Rua dos Andradas 736	*Tel. (51) 32 21 71 47. Open Tue.–Sun. 9am–9pm. The poet's former residence, now a cultural center (café, theater, movie theater).*	▲ 244
CATEDRAL METROPOLITANA Praça Marechal Deodoro	*Tel. (51) 32 28 60 01. Open Mon.–Fri. 7.30am–7pm; Sat.–Sun. 9am–7pm.*	▲ 244
IGREJA DAS DORES Rua Riachuelo 630	*Tel. (51) 32 28 73 76. Open Mon.–Fri. 8.30am–8pm; Sat.–Sun. 8.30am–noon, 1.30–8pm.*	▲ 244
MERCADO PÚBLICO Praça XV de Novembro	*Tel. (51) 32 89 17 56. Open Mon.–Sat. 7.30am–6pm; Sun. 7.30am–noon. Mercado Modelo subway station.*	▲ 244
MUSEU DE ARTES DO RIO GRANDE DO SUL Praça da Alfândega	*Tel. (51) 32 27 23 11. Open Tue.–Sun. 10am–7pm. Collection mainly devoted to gaucho artists.*	▲ 244
MUSEU JÚLIO DE CASTILHOS Rua Duque de Caixas 1205–1231	*Tel. (51) 32 21 39 59. Open Tue.–Fri. 10am–7pm; Sat.–Sun. 2–6pm. Collection of objects and documents tracing the state's history.*	▲ 244
PAÇO MUNICIPAL Praça Monte Vidéo 10	*Tel. (51) 32 86 10 65. Houses the town hall (prefetura).*	▲ 244
PALÁCIO PIRATINI Praça Marechal Deodoro	*Tel. (51) 32 10 41 00. Guided tours every half hour, Mon.– Fri. 9am–11am, 2–5pm. Seat of the government.*	▲ 244
SOLAR DOS CÂMARA Rua Duque de Caixas 968	*Tel. (51) 32 10 29 44. Open Mon.–Fri. 8.30am–6.30pm. Cultural center and library.*	▲ 244
TEATRO SÃO PEDRO Praça Marechal Deodoro	*Tel. (51) 32 27 51 00. Open Tue.–Fri. noon–6pm. Guided tours by appt.*	▲ 244
USINA DO GASÔMETRO Avenida Presidente João Goulart 551	*Tel. (51) 32 12 59 79. Open Tue.–Sun. 10am–10pm. Cultural center (movie theaters, exhibitions, café).*	

CANELA

Place	Information	Page
PARQUE DA FERRADURA Estrada do Parque do Caracol Km 16	*Tel. (54) 99 69 67 85. Open daily 9am–5.30pm. 1300-foot canyon.*	▲ 245
PARQUE DO PINHEIRO GROSSO Estrada do Parque do Caracol Km 3	*Tel. (54) 278 30 35. Open daily 8.30am–5.30pm. The park has a 700 year-old araucaria (Paraná pine).*	▲ 245
PARQUE ESTADUAL DO CARACOL Estrada do Parque do Caracol Km 9	*Tel. (54) 278 30 35. Opening times: daily 8.30am–6pm. Leave the park before nightfall. Forestry reserve. 430-foot waterfall.*	▲ 245

PARQUE NACIONAL DOS APARADOS DA SERRA

Place	Information	Page
11 miles along an unmetaled road from the exit of the RS-020 (via Cambará do Sul), or 12½ miles from the exit of the BR-101 (via Praia Grande)	*Tel. (54) 251 12 77. Open Wed.–Sun. 9am–5pm. The park has a limit of 1,000 visitors per day, so you need to book in advance.*	▲ 245

SANTO ÂNGELO ▲ 248

Place	Information	Page
CATEDRAL DE SANTO ÂNGELO Praça Pinheiro Machado	*Tel. (55) 33 13 58 55. Open 8.30am–5.30pm. Inspired by the church of São Miguel Arcanjo das Missões. It has a statue of Christ sculpted by the Guaraní Indians.*	
MUSEU DO DOUTOR JOSÉ OLAVO MACHADO Praça Pinheiro Machado	*Tel. (55) 33 12 01 75. Open Tue.–Sun. 9am–noon, 2–5pm; Sat.–Sun. 9am–5pm. Historical and archeological museum.*	▲ 248

SÃO MIGUEL DAS MISSÕES		
SÍTIO ARQUEOLÓGICO SÃO MIGUEL ARCANJO DAS MISSÂOS Take the São Miguel turn-off, Km 485 on the BR-285	*Tel. (55) 33 81 13 99. Open daily 9am–noon, 2–6pm (8pm in summer). The ruins of the mission, among the best preserved in the region, are classified as a World Heritage Site. Museu das Missões designed by Lúcio Costa. Son et lumière recounting the 'missionary saga': daily 7pm in winter, 8.30pm in summer. Tel (55) 33 81 12 94.*	▲ 250
STATE OF BAHIA		
SALVADOR		
CATEDRAL BASÍLICA DA SÉ Terreiro de Jesus	*Tel. (71) 321 45 73. Open Mon.–Sat. 8–11.30am, 1.30–5pm. Baroque organ concert: Sun. 11am.*	▲ 257
ELEVADOR LACERDA Praça Tomé de Sousa, Cidade Alta, Praça Visconte de Cairu Cidade Baixa	*Open daily 6am–1pm. Cars 1 and 2 date from the inauguration (1873) of the elevator, 3 and 4 date from 1930.*	▲ 260
FORTE DE MONTE SERRAT Rua Santa Durão, Ponta de Monte Serrat	*Tel. (71) 313 73 39. Open Tue.–Sun. 9am–12.30pm, 1.30–5pm.*	▲ 261
FORTE DE SANTO ANTÔNIO DA BARRA Farol da Barra	*Tel. (71) 274 32 96. Houses the Museu Nautico da Bahia. Fort and museum open Tue.–Sun. 9.30am–7.40pm.*	▲ 259
FORTE SÃO MARCELO On the bay	*Tel (71) 321 52 86 and (71) 91 22 87 76. Visits by appt.*	▲ 260
FUNDAÇÃO CASA DE JORGE AMADO Largo do Pelourinho 51	*Tel. (71) 321 01 22. Open Mon.–Sat. 9am–6pm.*	▲ 256
IGREJA DA GRAÇA Largo da Graça	*Tel (71) 247 46 70. Open Mon.–Fri. 8–11.30am, 2.30–5pm.*	▲ 258
IGREJA DA ORDEM TERCEIRA DE S. FRANCISCO Rua Inácio Accioly	*Tel. (71) 321 69 68. Open Mon.–Fri. 8am–5pm. Remarkable façade combining Spanish and Franciscan baroque styles. Museum of religious art.*	▲ 257
IGREJA DE N. S. DA BOA VIAGEM Largo da Boa Viagem	*Tel. (71) 314 18 00. Open Mon.–Fri. 6am–noon, 1–7pm.*	▲ 261
IGREJA DE N. S. DA CONCEIÇÃO DA PRAIA Largo da Conceição da Praia	*Tel. (71) 242 05 45. Open Mon. 7–11.30am; Tue.–Fri. 7–11.30am, 3–5pm; Sat.–Sun. 7.30–11am.*	▲ 260
IGREJA DE N. S. DO ROSÁRIO DOS PRETOS Largo do Pelourinho	*Tel. (71) 326 97 01. Open Mon.–Fri. 9am–6pm; Sat. 9am–5pm; Sun. 9am–1pm.*	▲ 258
IGREJA DE S. PEDRO DOS CLÉRIGOS Terreiro de Jesus	*Tel. (71) 321 09 66. Open Mon.–Wed., Fri. 2–6pm; Thu. 3.30–6pm.*	▲ 257
IGREJA DO NOSSO SENHOR DO BONFIM Largo do Bonfim	*Tel. (71) 316 21 96. Open Tue.–Sun. 7am–noon, 2–6pm. Ritual washing (lavagem) of the steps of the church, 2nd Thursday in January.*	▲ 261
IGREJA E CONVENTO DE N. S. DO CARMO Largo do Carmo	*Tel. (71) 242 01 82. Open Mon.–Fri. 8am–noon, 2–5pm.*	▲ 258
IGREJA E CONVENTO DE S. FRANCISCO Praça Padre Anchieta	*Tel. (71) 356 96 44. Open Mon.–Sat. 8am–5pm; Sun. 8am–4pm. Interior is richly decorated. Note the painting of the Madonna on the church's ceiling and the azulejos in the courtyard of the cloister.*	▲ 257
MERCADO MODELO Praça Cairú	*Tel. (71) 241 28 93. Open Mon.–Sat. 9am–7pm; Sun. 9am–2pm. Traditional craft items on sale.*	▲ 260

Place	Information	Page
MERCADO SÃO JOAQUIM Avenida Oscar Pontes, next to the ferry terminal	*Open Mon.–Fri. 6am–5pm; Sat.–Sun. 6am–noon. Salvador's largest market: vegetables, fruit, spices, meat, crafts. It is best to go in the morning.*	▲ 260
MOSTEIRO DE SÃO BENTO Largo de São Bento	*Tel. (71) 322 47 44. Church: open Sun.–Fri. 5.30am–noon, 4–7pm. Houses a museum of religious art with works by Frei Agostinho: open Mon.–Fri. 9am–noon, 1–4.30pm.*	▲ 258
MUSEU ABERLADO RODRIGUES Rua Gregório de Matos 45	*Tel. (71) 321 61 55 (ext. 231). Open Tue.–Fri. 9am–6.30pm; Sat.–Sun. 1–6pm.*	▲ 257
MUSEU AFRO-BRASILEIRO (MUSEU DA ETNOLOGIA E DA ARQUEOLOGIA) Praça Terreiro de Jesus	*Tel. (71) 321 20 13. Open Mon.–Fri. 9am–5pm.*	▲ 256
MUSEU CARLOS COSTA PINTO Avenida 7 de Setembro 2490	*Tel. (71) 336 60 81. Open Wed.–Mon. 2.30–7pm. 17th-century furniture, tapestries, jewelry, Chinese porcelain.*	▲ 259
MUSEU DA CIDADE Largo do Pelourinho 3	*Tel. (71) 321 19 67. Open Mon., Wed.–Fri. 9am–6pm; Sat. 1–5pm; Sun. 9am–1pm.*	▲ 257
MUSEU DE ARTE DA BAHIA Avenida 7 de Setembro 2340	*Tel. (71) 336 94 50. Open Tue.–Fri. 2–7pm; Sat.–Sun. 2.30–6.30pm. 18th-century paintings, furniture and religious art (biblical scenes).*	▲ 259
MUSEU DE ARTE MODERNA SOLAR DO UNHÃO Avenida do Contorno	*Tel. (71) 329 06 60. Open Tue.–Fri. 1–7pm; Sat.–Sun. 2–8pm. Exhibition of works by Di Cavalcanti, Mário Cravo Neto; restaurant and park.*	▲ 260
MUSEU DE ARTE SACRA Rua do Sodré 276	*Tel. (71) 243 63 10. Open Mon.–Fri. 11.30am–5.30pm.*	▲ 258
MUSEU DO CACAU Rua da Espanha	*Tel. (71) 242 12 29. Open Mon.–Fri. 9am–5pm.*	▲ 260
MUSEU GEOLÓGICO DO ESTADO Avenida 7 de Setembro 2195	*Tel. (71) 336 34 98/69 22. Open Tue.–Fri. 1.30–6pm; Sat.–Sun. 1–5pm. Rocks and precious stones.*	▲ 259
MUSEU TEMPOSTAL Rua Gregório de Matos 33	*Tel. (71) 322 59 36. Open Tue.–Fri. 9am–6pm; Sat.–Sun. 1–6pm.*	▲ 257
CACHOEIRA		
IGREJA E CONVENTO DA ORDEM TERCEIRA DO CARMO Praça da Aclamação	*Tel. (75) 425 17 16. Open Tue.–Fri. 2–4.30pm. Sculptures in polychrome Macao wood, baroque altar covered with gold and azulejo panels.*	▲ 263
MUSEU HANSEN DE CACHOEIRA Rua 13 de Maio	*Tel. (75) 425 14 53. Open Mon.–Fri. 9am–4pm; Sat. 9am–2pm; Sun. 9am–1pm. Exhibition of the artist's work.*	▲ 263
ILHÉUS		
ECOPARQUE DA UNA BA 001, Ilheus Canavieira, Km 45	*Tel. (73) 633 11 21 or (73) 634 21 79. Tourist information: Tel. (73) 634 35 10. Visits to the bio-reserve and research center: Tue.-Sun. 9am–2pm. Guided three-hour walk. Book in advance. Tea and mineral water included, take a swimsuit.*	▲ 267
PARQUE NACIONAL MARINHO DE ABROLHOS		
IBAMA Praia do Quitongo, Caravelas	*Tel. (73) 297 11 11. Open daily 8am–6pm. Only boats approved by the IBAMA (Brazilian Institute for the Protection of the Environment) can land on the island.*	▲ 267
PRAIA DO FORTE		
CASTELO GARCIA D'ÁVILA 1 mile from the Praia do Forte	*Tel. (71) 676 10 73. Open daily 8.30am–8pm.*	▲ 265

PROJETO TAMAR (CENTER FOR THE PROTECTION OF MARINE TURTLES) Avenida do Farol (on the beach)	*Tel. (71) 676 10 45. Open daily 9am–6.30pm. Open-air vivarium and aquarium. The turtles are born Nov.–March.*	▲ 265
SANTO AMARO		
CONVENTO DE N. S. DOS HUMILDES Praça Padre Inácio Teixeira	*Open Tue.–Sat. 9am–1pm. Houses a museum. Beautiful Portuguese azulejo panels.*	▲ 263
SÃO FELIX		
CENTRO CULTURAL DANNEMANN Avenida Salvador Pinto 29	*Tel (75) 425 22 08. Open Tue.–Sat. 8am–noon, 1–4pm. Houses a working cigar factory.*	▲ 263
STATE OF PERNAMBUCO		
RECIFE		
CAPELA DOURADA DA ORDEM TERCEIRA DE S. FRANCISCO Rua do Imperador 206	*Tel. (81) 32 24 05 30. Open Mon.–Fri. 8–11am, noon–5pm; Sat. 8–11am. Beautiful baroque interior. The church houses the Museu Franciscano de Arte Sacra.*	▲ 275
CASA DA CULTURA Rua Floriano Peixoto	*Tel. (81) 32 24 28 50. Open Mon.–Fri. 9am–7pm; Sat. 9am–6pm; Sun. 9am–2pm. Craft items on sale.*	▲ 275
CATEDRAL DE S. PEDRO DOS CLÉRIGOS Pátio de São Pedro	*Tel. (81) 32 24 29 54. Open Mon.–Fri. 8am–noon, 2–4pm.*	▲ 275
FORTE DAS CINCO PONTAS Largo das Cinco Pontas	*Tel. (81) 32 24 84 92. Open Mon.–Fri. 9am–6pm; Sat.–Sun. 1–5pm. Houses the Museu da Cidade.*	▲ 275
FORTE DO BRUM Praça Luso-Brasileira	*Tel. (81) 32 24 46 20. Open Tue.–Fri. 9am–4pm. Houses the Museu Militar.*	▲ 275
IGREJA DE MADRE DE DEUS Rua Madre de Deus	*Tel. (81) 32 24 55 87. Open Tue.–Fri. 8am–noon, 2–5pm; Sat.–Sun. 9am–noon. Splendid high altar.*	▲ 275
MERCADO DE SÃO JOSÉ Praça D. Vital	*Open Mon.–Sat. 6am–6pm; Sun. 6am–noon. Fruit and vegetables, fish, medicinal herbs, crafts.*	▲ 275
MUSEU ARQUEOLÓGICO E GEOGRÁFICO DE PERNAMBUCO Rua do Hospício 130	*Tel. (81) 32 22 49 52. Open Mon.–Fri. 1–5pm; Sat. 8am–noon. Collection of 17th-century furniture and objects, paintings and old maps.*	▲ 276
MUSEU DA IMAGEM E DO SOM Rua da Aurora 379	*Tel. (81) 32 31 27 16. Open Mon.–Fri. 8am–2pm.*	▲ 276
MUSEU DE ARTE MODERNA ALOÍSIO MAGALHÃES Rua da Aurora 265	*Tel. (81) 34 23 30 07. Open Tue.–Sun. noon–6pm. Works by Brazilian artists.*	▲ 276
MUSEU DO HOMEM DO NORDESTE Avenida 17 de Agosto 2187	*Tel. (81) 34 41 55 00 (ext. 626). Open Tue.–Wed., Fri. 11am–5pm; Thu. 8am–5pm; Sat.–Sun. 1–5pm. Collections of objects relating to sugar cultivation, traditional crafts, folklore, literatura de cordel, Afro-Brazilian cults and slavery.*	▲ 276
OFICINA CERÂMICA FRANCISCO BRENNAND Avenida Caxangá, 10 miles from the city center	*Tel. (81) 32 71 24 66. Open Mon.–Thu. 8am–5pm; Fri. 8am–4pm. Exhibition of the artist's work over an area of 17,940 sq yds.*	▲ 276
PARQUE CULTURAL SÍTIO DA TRINDADE Estrada do Arraial 5239	*Tel. (81) 32 68 51 07. Open daily 5am–10pm.*	▲ 276

CARUARU		
FEIRA DE ARTESANATO Parque 18 de Maio	*Open daily 9am–5pm. A market famous for its variety, size (5 acres) and Nordestino atmosphere. Clothes on Tuesdays and music on Saturdays.*	▲ 280
MUSEU DO BARRO E DA CERÂMICA Praça José de Vasconcellos 100	*Tel. (81) 37 21 16 33. Open Tue.–Sat. 9am–5pm; Sun. 9am–1pm. Visit also the Vila do Forró cultural center.*	▲ 280
FERNANDO DE NORONHA		
CENTRO DE VISITANTES Alameda do Boldró	*Tel. (81) 36 19 11 71. The park (an archipelago of 21 islands) is open daily 8am–6pm. Tourist activities: IBAMA, open daily 8am–10.30pm; daily talk 9–10pm on the archipelago, turtles, marine mammals, etc.*	▲ 282
IGARASSU		
CONVENTO DE SANTO ANTÔNIO Rua Barbosa Lima	*Tel. (81) 35 43 02 58. Guided tours, open Mon.–Fri. 8am–5pm; Sat.–Sun. 8am–4pm.*	▲ 279
IGREJA DE S. COSME E DAMIÃO Largo São Cosme e São Damião	*Open Tue.–Fri. 8am–1pm; Sat.–Sun. 9am–noon. Brazil's oldest church, dating from 1535. It houses the relics of saints.*	▲ 279
ITAMARACÁ		
FORTE ORANGE 3½ miles from Itamaracá, on the island	*Tel. (81) 35 44 16 66. Open Mon.–Sat. 9am–5pm; Sun. 8am–5pm. Houses an archeological museum and a craft store.*	▲ 279
OLINDA		
CONVENTO DE N. S. DA CONCEIÇÃO Largo da Misericórdia	*Tel. (81) 34 29 31 08. Beautiful view of the city.*	▲ 279
CONVENTO DE SÃO FRANCISCO Rua de São Francisco 280	*Tel. (81) 34 29 05 17. Open Mon.–Fri. 8am–noon, 2–5pm; Sat. 8am–noon. Includes the Igreja das Neves and the chapels of São Roque and Sant'Ana.*	▲ 278
IGREJA DA MISERICÓRDIA Rua Bispo Coutinho	*Tel. (81) 34 29 29 22. Open for mass only. Azulejo panels, gilt wood interior.*	▲ 279
IGREJA DA SÉ Alto da Sé	*Tel. (81) 91 37 40 87. Open daily 9am–noon, 2–5pm. Beautiful view of the city and sea from the parvis.*	▲ 278
IGREJA DE N. S. DO CARMO Praça do Carmo	*Tel. (81) 34 29 28 92. Open Mon.–Fri. 8am–5pm. On the Praça do Carmo, guides from the city hall offer free tours of the city.*	▲ 278
MOSTEIRO DE SÃO BENTO Rua de São Bento	*Tel. (81) 34 29 32 88. Open daily 8–11.20am, 2–5pm. Gregorian chants: Sun. 10am.*	▲ 279
MUSEU DE ARTE SACRA DE PERNAMBUCO Rua Bispo Coutinho 726	*Tel. (81) 34 29 00 32. Open Mon.–Fri. 9am–12.45pm. Exhibition of religious art and Latin-American paintings.*	▲ 278
STATE OF CEARÁ		
FORTALEZA		
BEACH PARK Praia do Porto das Dunas, Km 29	*Tel. (85) 361 30 00. Open Thu.–Mon. 11am–5pm. Restaurants and parking.*	▲ 286
CENTRO CULTURAL DRAGÃO DO MAR Rua Dragão do Mar 81	*Tel. (85) 488 86 00. Open Tue.–Thu. 9am–5.30pm; Fri.–Sun. 2–9.30pm. Bars and restaurants.*	▲ 284
FORTALEZA DE N. S. DA ASSUNÇÃO Avenida Alberto Nepomuceno	*Tel. (85) 255 16 00. Open daily. Info. from the warden at the entrance. Group visits by appt.*	▲ 285
MUSEU DO CEARÁ Rua São Paulo, 51	*Tel. (85) 251 15 02. Open Wed.–Fri. 8.30am– 5.30pm; Sat. 10am–4pm; Sun. 2–4pm.*	▲ 285

TEATRO JOSÉ DE ALENCAR Praça José de Alencar	*Tel. (85) 252 23 24. Guided tours Mon.–Fri. 8am–5pm. Programs in the local press.*	▲ 284
ARACATI		
MUSEU JAGUARIBANO Avenida Coronel Alexanzito 743	*Tel. (88) 421 33 96. Open Tue.–Sat. 7.30–11.30am, 1.30–5.30pm. Religious art and crafts. No shorts*	▲ 287
STATE OF MARANHÃO		
SÃO LUÍS		
CASA DAS TULHAS Rua da Estrela	*Market open Mon.–Sat. 6am–7pm. Regional produce on sale.*	▲ 289
MUSEU DO CENTRO DA CULTURA POPULAR Rua do Giz 221, 205	*Tel. (98) 231 15 57. Open Tue.–Sat. 9am–7pm. Guided tours available. Folkloric events, local and Indian crafts.*	▲ 289
TEATRO ARTUR AZEVEDO Rua do Sol	*Tel. (98) 232 02 99. Guided tours Mon.–Fri. 3pm.*	▲ 289
STATE OF PARÁ		
BELÉM		
BOSQUE RODRIGUES ALVES Avenida Almirante Barroso 2453	*Tel. (91) 276 23 08. Open Tue.–Sun. 8am–5pm. Mini-zoo, turtle vivarium, lake.*	▲ 299
CATEDRAL DA SÉ Praça Frei Caetano Brandão	*Tel. (91) 233 23 62. Open Mon. 3–7.30pm; Tue., Fri. 7am–noon, 2–7.30pm; Sat 5–8.30pm; Sun 6– 11.30am, 5–8.30pm. Organ dating from 1781.*	▲ 298
FORTE DO CASTELO Praça Frei Caetano Brandão 117	*Tel. (91) 219 11 34. Open Tue.–Fri. 10am–6pm; Sat.-Sun. 10am–8pm. Interior not open to the public.*	▲ 298
MERCADO DO VER-O-PESO Intersection of the avenidas Portugal and Castilhos França	*Open daily 7am–4pm. It's advisable to keep an eye on personal belongings.*	▲ 298
MUSEU DE ARTE SACRA DO PARÁ Praça Frei Caetano Brandão	*Tel. (91) 219 11 50. Open Tue.–Fri. 1–6pm; Sat.–Sun. 9am–1pm.*	▲ 298
MUSEU PARAENSE EMÍLIO GOELDI Avenida Magalhães Barata 376	*Tel. (91) 219 33 69. Open Tue.–Sun. 9am–5pm. The park has a zoo and aquarium.*	▲ 299
ALTER DO CHÃO		
CENTRO DE PRESERVAÇÃO DAS ARTES INDÍGENAS Rua D. Macedo Costa 500	*Tourist information, Santarem: Tel. (93) 523 24 34. 2,000 pieces of Indian art.*	▲ 303
STATE OF AMAZONAS		
MANAUS		
MERCADO MUNICIPAL Rua dos Barés 46	*Tel. (92) 663 35 32. Open Mon.–Sat. 5am–6pm; Sun. 5am-1pm. Fish, fruit, traditional crafts.*	▲ 311
MUSEU DO HOMEM DO NORTE Avenida 7 de Setembro 1385	*Tel. (92) 232 53 73. Open Mon.-Fri. 8am–noon, 1–5pm.*	▲ 311
MUSEU DO INDIO Rua Duque de Caxias 356	*Tel. (92) 635 19 22. Open Mon.-Fri. 8.30–11.30am, 2–4.30pm; Sat. 8.30–11.30am. Store.*	▲ 311
PALÁCIO RIO NEGRO Rua 7 de Setembro 1540	*Tel. (92) 232 44 50. Open Tue.-Sun. 10am–5pm; Sat.–Sun. 4–9pm. Houses a cultural center.*	▲ 311
TEATRO AMAZONAS Praça São Sebastião	*Tel. (92) 622 18 80. Open Mon.-Sat. 9am–4pm. Guided tours every 20 minutes. Guides in period costume Fri. 2pm; Sat. 10am, 11am.*	▲ 311

◆ BIBLIOGRAPHY

GENERAL

◆ Flemming (P.): *Brazilian Adventure*, Northwestern University Press, Illinois, 1999.
◆ Freye (G.): *New World in the Tropics: The Culture of Modern Brazil*, A.A. Knopf, New York, 1959.
◆ Levine (R.) and Crocitti (J.J.) (eds.): *The Brazil Reader: History, Culture, Politics*, Duke University Press, 1992.
◆ Page (J.A.): *The Brazilians*, Addison Wesley, 1995.
◆ Ribeiro (D.): *The Brazilian People: The Formation and Meaning of Brazil*, trans. Rabassa (G.) University Press of Florida, 2000.

AMERICAN INDIANS

◆ Abrea (J.C.D.): *Chapters of Brazil's Colonial History, 1500–1800*, Oxford University Press, 1997.
◆ Brookshaw (D.): *Paradise Betrayed : Brazilian Literature of the Indian*, CEDLA, 1988.
◆ Peters (J. F.): *Life Among the Yanomamí*, Broadview Press, 1998.

ARTS AND ARCHITECTURE

◆ Almeida (B.): *Capoeira: A Brazilian Art Form*, Berkely: North Atlantic, 1986.
◆ Dinneen (M.): *Brazilian Woodcut Prints*, Kegan Paul International, 2001.
◆ De Fiore (O.C): *Architecture and sculpture in Brazil*, University of New Mexico, 1985.
◆ Evenson (N.): *Two Brazilian Capitals: Architecture and Urbanism in Rio de Janeiro and Brasília*, Yale University Press, 1973.
◆ Holston (J.): *The Modernist City: An Anthropolitical Critique of Brasilia*, University of Chicago Press, 1989.
◆ Johnson (R.): *Cinema Novo x 5: Masters of Contemporary Brazilian Film*, University of Texas Press, 1984; *Brazilian Cinema*, Associated University Presses, 1981.
◆ Lemos (C.A.C), Leite (J.R.T) and Gismont (P.M): *The Art of Brazil*, trans. Jennifer Clay, Harper and Row, 1983.
◆ Nagib (L.) (ed.): *The New Brazilian Cinema*, London, 2003.
◆ Rodman (S.): *Genius in the Backlands: Popular Artists of Brazil*, Devin-Adair, 1977.
◆ Viera (J.L.) (ed.): *Cinema Novo and Beyond*, trans. Steve Hanley, Berlin Press, 1998.
◆ Weiermair (P.) (ed.): *In Search of Identity: New Brazilian Art*, Art Books Intl Ltd, 2002.

HISTORY

◆ Barman (R.): *Brazil, The Forging of a Nation, 1798–1852*, Stanford University Press, 1988.
◆ Burns (E.): *A History of Brazil*, Columbia University Press, 1993.
◆ Fausto (B.): *A Concise History of Brazil*, trans. Arthur Brakel, Cambridge University Press, 1999.

LITERATURE

◆ Amado (J.): *Dona Flor and her Two Husbands*, Serpent's Tale, 1999; *Gabriella, Clove and Cinnamon*, Bard Books, 1999; *The War and the Saints*, Bantam Books, 1995.
◆ Assis (J.M.M. De): *The Posthumous Memoirs of Bras Cubas*, Oxford University Press Inc., 1998.
◆ Coelho (P.): *The Fifth Mountain*, trans. Clifford Landers, HarperCollins, 1999;
◆ Coutinho (A.): *An Introduction to Literature in Brazil*, trans. Gregory Rabasso Columbia University Press, 1969.
◆ Cunha (E. da) *Rebellion in the Backlands*, Picador, 1985.
◆ Ellison (F.P.): *Brazil's New Novel: Four Northeastern Masters, Jose Lins do Rego, Jorge Amando, Graciliano Ramos, Rachel de Queiroz*, University of California Press, 1954.
◆ Graham (R.) (ed.) : *Machado de Assis: Reflections on a Brazilian Master Writer*, University of Texas Press, 1999.
◆ Hart (D.): *For Love or Honor Bound*, Xlibris Corporation, Philadelphia, 2001.
◆ Harmon (R.) Brazil: *A Working Bibliography in Literature, Linguistics , Humanities and the Social Sciences*, Arizona State University, 1975.
◆ Hulet (C.): *Brazilian Literature*, 3 vols, Georgetown University Press, Washington, 1974.
◆ Jesus (C.M.D.): *Bitita's Diary: The Childhood Memoirs of Carolina Maria de Jesus*, ed. Robert Levine, trans. Emanuelle Oliveira and Beth Joan Vinkler, M.E. Sharpe,1998.
◆ Lispector (C.): *The Foreign Legion: Stories and Chronicles*, New York, 1992; *The Hour of the Star*, Carcenet Press, W.W. Norton, 1992; *The Passion According to G.H.*, University of Minnesota Press, 1989; *The Stream of Life*, University of Minnesota Press, 1989.
◆ Llosa (M.V.): *The War of the End of the World*, Faber and Faber, 1997.
◆ Matthiessen (P.): *The Cloud Forest: A Cronicle of the South American Wilderness*, *The Harvill Press*, 1993.
◆ Queiroz (R.D.): *The Three Marias*, trans. Fred P. Ellison, Texas University Press, 1985.
◆ Ramos (G.): *Barren Lives*, Texas University Press, 1971.
◆ Slater (C.): *Stones on a string: The Brazilian Literatura de Cordel*, University of California Press, Berkeley, 1982.
◆ Smith (V.): *Encyclopedia of Latin American Literature*, Fitzroy Dearborn, 1997.
◆ Szoka (V.): *Fourteen Female Voices from Brazil*, Host Publications, 2003.
◆ Thomson (M.): *The Saddest Pleasure: A Journey on Two Rivers (A Greywolf Memoir)*, Greywolf Press, 1990.
◆ Updike (J.): Brazil, Penguin Books, 1995.

MUSIC AND SPORT

◆ Lever (J.): *Soccer Madness: Brazil's passion for the World's Most Popular Sport*, University of Chicago Press, 1995.
◆ McGowan (C.) and Pessanha (R.): *The Brazilian Sound : Samba, Bossa Nova and the Popular Music of Brazil*, Temple University Press, 1998.
◆ Schreiner (C.): *A History of Popular Music and the People of Brazil*, Marion Boyars Publishers, 1993.

POETRY

◆ Bishop (E.) (ed.): *An Anthology of Twentieth Century Brazilian Poetry*, Wesleyan University Press, 1972.
◆ Brasil (E.) and Smith (W.) (eds.): *Brazilian Poetry (1950–80)*, Wesleyan University Press. 1983.

RELIGION

◆ Brown (D.): *Umbanda: Religion and Politics in Urban Brazil*, Ann Arbour, UMI Research P, 1986.
◆ Bruneau (T.): *The Church in Brazil : Politics and Religion*, University of Texas Press, 1982.

SOCIETY AND ECONOMY

◆ Alves (M.H.M.) : *State and Opposition in Military Brazil*, University of Texas Press, 1985.
◆ Andrews (G.R.): *Blacks and Whites in Sao Paulo, Brazil, 1888–1988*, University of Wisconsin Press, 1991.
◆ Fontaine (P.M.) (ed.): *Race, Class and Power in Brazil*, UCLA, 1985.
◆ Hanchard (M.G.) (ed.): *Racial Politics in Contemporary Brazil*, Duke UP, Durham, 1999.
◆ Hewitt (W.E.): *Base Christian Communities and Social Change in Brazil*, University of Nebraska Press, Lincoln, 1991.
◆ Keck (M.E.): *The Workers' Party and the Democratization in Brazil*, Yale UP, New Haven, 1992.

CHORO

◆ *Classico do Choro,* Various Artisits, EMI Brazil, 1999.
◆ Jacob do Bandolim, *Original Classic Recordings, Vol. 1: Mandolin Master of Brazil*, Acoustic Disc, 1991.
◆ Paulo Moura, *Pixinguinha,* Light Year, 1998.

CLASSICAL

◆ Heitor Villa-Lobos, *Complete Guitar Works*, Azica, 2000.
◆ Nelson Freire et al., *Great Pianists of the 20th Century*, Polygram Records, 1999.

SAMBA

◆ Adoniran Barbosa, *Som Livre*, 2002.
◆ Antonio Candeia, *Samba Da Antiga,* Ouver, 2002.
◆ Ar Barroso, *O Mais Brasileiro dos Brasileiros*, Reviv, 1995.
◆ Beth Carvalho, *EPM Musique*, 1998.
◆ Bezerra Da Silva, *Presidente Cao Cao,* BMG, 1998.
◆ Carmen Miranda, *Cocktail Hour,* Columbia River Ent., 2000.
◆ *Casa de Samba,* Various Artists, Universal International, 2001.
◆ Charlie Byrd, Stan Getz, *Jazz Samba,* Polygram records, 1997.
◆ Clementia de Jesus, *Serie Raizes do Samba,* EMI, 1999.
◆ Elza Soares, *Do Coccix Ate O Pescoco,* Ybrazil, 2002.
◆ Elizeth Cardoso, *Cancao do Amor Demais*, Sony, 2002.
◆ Jackson do Pandeiro, *Comotem Ze Na Paraiba: O Melhor De,* Universal/Polygram, 1999.
◆ Jorge Berr, *Africa Brazil: Colcao Samba Soul*, Universal, 2001.
◆ Martinho Da Vila, *Canta Canta Minhagente*, BGM, 1999.
◆ Moreira da Silva, *Serie Raizes Do Samba,* EMI, 1999.
◆ Noel Rosa, *Fietio Da Vila*, Reviv, 1999.
◆ *Putumayo Presents: Samba Bossa Nova,* Various Artists, Putumayo World Music, 2002.
◆ *Samba Soul 70!*, Various Artists, Six Degrees, 2001.
◆ Vicente Ferreira Pastinha, *Brasil: Capoeira, Samba de Roda*, Maculel, Buda Musique, 1995.

PAGODE

◆ Almir Guineto, *Serie Gold*, Universal, 2002.
◆ Fundo de Quintal, *Nosso Grito*, Som Livre, 2000.
◆ Zeca Pagodinho, *Serie Sem Limite,* Universal International, 2001.

NORTHEAST AND BAHIA

◆ *Recife frevoé*, Various Artists, Sony, 1998.
◆ *Casa de Forró,* Various Artisits, Polygram International, 1999.
◆ Alceu Valença, *Forro de Todos Os Tempos,* Oasis (Stern's), 1998.
◆ Banda Eva, *Beleza Rara: O Melho Da,* Polygram International, 1998.
◆ Daniela Mercury, *Feijão com Arroz*, Sony International, 1997.
◆ Dominguinhos and Convidados, *Cantam Luiz Gonzaga, Vol. 1*, Velas Brazil, 1999.
◆ Dorival Caymmi, *Sem Limite,* Universal, 2001.
◆ Geraldo Azevedo, *Hoje E Amanha*, BMG, 2000.
◆ Luiz Gonzaga, *Sanfona Dourada,* Reviv, 1999.
◆ Margareth Menezes, *Afropopbrasileiros,* Universal, 2002.
◆ Olodum, *A Musica Do Olodum: 20 Anos,* Sony International, 2000.
◆ Timbalada, *Pense Minha Cor*, Musicrama, 1999.
◆ Tom Zé, *Jogos De Armar*, Trama, 2001.
◆ Zé Ramalho, *Zo Supersucessos*, Sony 1999.

BOSSA NOVA

◆ *Bossa Nova Sua História, Sua Gente*, Various Artists, Universal, Polygram, 1999.
◆ *The Best of Bossa Nova*, Various Artists, EMI, 1998
◆ Baden Powell, *Frankfurt Opera Concert, 1975*, Trop, 1998.
◆ Elis Regina, *Vento De Maio*, Blue Note Records, 1998*; Antonio Carlos Jobin, Elis and Tom*, Polygram Records, 1990.
◆ João Gilberto, *Amoroso/Brasil*, Warner Brothers, 1993.
◆ Nara Leao, *Garota De Ipanema*, Universal/Polygram, 1998.
◆ Rosa Passos, *The Best of Rosa Passos*, Velas, 2000.
◆ Stan Getz and João Gilberto, *Getz/ Gilberto*, Polygram Records, 1997
◆ Vinícius de Moraes and Toquinho, *O Melhor De Vol.1,* Universal, 2000.

MPB

◆ *Brazilectro 4,* Various Artists, Spv U.S., 2002.
◆ *Brazil Vibe Experience*, Various Artists, Iris Music, 2003.
◆ Caetano Veloso, *Noites Do Nortes,* Nonesuch, 2001.
◆ Celso Fonseca, *Natural*, Six Degrees, 2003.
◆ Chico Buarque *En Espanol*, Universal/ Polygram, 1998.
◆ Djavan, *Milagreiro,* Sony, 2002; *Seduzir,* Blue Note Records, 1990.
◆ Gal Costa, *Gal Canto Tom Jobim*, BMG, 1999; *GalTropical*, Polygram Records, 1990.
◆ Gilberto Gil, *Acoustic*, Atlantic, 1994; *Kaya N'Gan Daya*, WEA International, 2002.
◆ Gonzaguinha, *Serie Raizes Do Samba,* EMI, 1999.
◆ Hermeto Paschoal, *Musica Livre De Hermento Paschoal,* Polygram Special Import, 1995.
◆ João Bosco, *Afrocanto*, Trop, 1998; *Malabaristas Do Sinal Vermelho*, Sony International, 2003*; O Rongo Da Cuica*, Iris Music, 2000.
◆ Jorge Ben, *Samba Esquema Novo,* Universal, 2001.
◆ Leila Pinheiro, *Mais Coisas Do Brazil,* Universal International, 2002; *Coisas Do Breasil,* Universal/Polygram, 1996*; Isso E Bossa Nova*, EMI, 1999.
◆ Maria Bethânia, *Alibi*, Polygram Records, 1990*; Simplesmente,* Polygram Records, 1990; *A Interprete*, Universal Latino, 2001.
◆ Milton Nascimento, *Clube Da Esquina*, Blue Note Records, 1995; *Nascimento*, Warner Brothers, 1997
◆ Nana Caymmi, *Especial*, Ans Records, 2000*; Os Maiores Sucessos De Novelas,* EMI, 1999.
◆ Ney Matogrosso, *Batuque*, Universal, 2001*; Um Brasileiro,* Polygram Brazil, 1996.
◆ Roberto Carlos, *30 Grandes Canciones,* Sony International, 2000; *Un Gato En La Oscuridad*, Sony International, 1991.
◆ Suba, et al., *The Now Sound of Brasil*, Six Degrees, 2003.

ROCK, RAP, SOUL

◆ *Brésil Nouvelle Vague*, Various Artists, Declic, 1999.
◆ Arnaldo Antunes, *Um Som*, BMG, 2002; *Nome*, BMG, 1999; *Ninuem*, BMG, 1999.
◆ Cássia Eller, *Acusto*, Universal Latin, 2002.
◆ Carlinhos Brown, *Omelete Man*, Blue Note Records, 1999.
◆ Chico Science and Nacao Zumbi, *Da Lama Ao Caos*, Sony, 1999; *Grandes Sucessos*, Sony, 2002.
◆ Daúde, *Daúde*, Tinder, 1997.
◆ Ed Motta, *Manual Pratico Para Festas Bailes E Afin*, Universal, 1999*; Dwitza*, Universal, 2002.
◆ Fernanda Abreu, *Entidade Urbana*, EMI, 2002.
◆ Gabriel O Pensador, *Seja Voce Mesmo, Mas Nao Seja O Mesmo*, Sony, 2002; *Gabriel O Pensador*, Sony, 2002.
◆ Lenine, *O Dia Em Que Faremos Cantato,* BMG, 1998.
◆ Marisa Monte, *Memories, Chronicles and Declarations of Love*, Blue Note Records, 2000; *Rose and Charcoal (Verde Anil Amerelo Cor De Rosa e Carao)*, Blue Note Records, 1994.
◆ Paralamas do Sucesso, *Longo Caminho*, EMI International, 2003.
◆ Tim Maia, *O Melhor de*, Universal/ Polygram, 1998.
◆ Titãs, *Acustico MTV,* WEA, 1996*; Domingo*, WEA, 2002.
◆ Zeca Baleiro, *Pet Shop Mundo*, Abril, 2002; *Vo Imbola,* Universal/Polygram, 1999.

◆ LIST OF ILLUSTRATIONS

10–11 Guanabara Bay from the Corcovado, photo Augusto Malta, 1908, Museu da Imagem e do Som, Rio de Janeiro © Renata Mello/Tyba, Rio de Janeiro. **12–13** Fishermen in the port of Salvador, photo Pierre Fátúmbi Verger, 1946 © Revue Noire, Paris. **14** Construction of Brasília, 1958 © Fundação Oscar Niemeyer, Rio de Janeiro.**15** Toucan © Claus Meyer/Tyba. **16–17** Cross-section of the relief of Brazil, illustration Franck Stéphan/Gallimard. **16** Pico da Neblina © Roberto Linsker/Terra Virgem, São Paulo. Amazonia © R. Linsker/ Terra Virgem. **17** Map, ill. Patrick Mérienne/Gallimard. Iguaçu Falls © Ferrante Ferranti. Forest of Tijuca © Patrick Léger/ Gallimard. **18–19** Map, ill. P. Mérienne/Gallimard. **18** *Caatinga* © Hervé Théry. Amazonia © R. Linsker/ Terra Virgem. *Cerrado* © H. Théry. Pantanal © Rogério Reis/Tyba. **19** *Araucárias* © Zig Koch. Itaimbezinho canyon, Parque Nacional dos Aparados da Serra © Idem. **20** Maps, ill. P. Mérienne/Gallimard. **21** *History of the Voyages to the Indies*, detail, Ramusio, print, 1556, Biblioteca Marciana, Venice © Dagli Orti. **22–23** *Cabral landing at Porto Seguro*, Oscar Pereira da Silva, oil/canvas, Museu Histórico Nacional, Rio de Janeiro © Dagli Orti. *Battle of Guararapes*, February 18, 1649, details, ex-voto, oil/canvas, 1758, Museu Histórico Nacional, Rio de Janeiro © Dagli Orti. **24–25** *Portrait of Dom Pedro I in 1825*, Henrique J. da Silva, oil/canvas, Museu Histórico Nacional, Rio de Janeiro © Dagli Orti. Tiradentes' signature, Biblioteca Nacional, Rio de Janeiro. **24** *The Martyrdom of Tiradentes on April 21, 1792*, A. de Figueiredo, oil/canvas, Museu Histórico Nacional, Rio de Janeiro © Dagli Orti. **25** *Portrait of Dom Pedro II, Emperor of Brazil*, Castello di Miramare, Italy © Dagli Orti. **26** Arrival of the 'national integration' caravan in Brasília on February 2, 1960 © Arquivo Nacional, Rio de Janeiro. The Brazilian football team in 1958 © Keystone. **27** *Diretas Já* demonstration © The Bettmann Archive. **28–29** American Indians, hunters, wood cutters, in the 'Atlas Miller', Lopo Homem, 1519 © BNF, Paris. **28** Arrival of Tomé de Souza, governor general of Brazil, in Salvador, color print, 1549, RR. **29** *Indian Soldiers from the Province of Curitiba*, J.-B. Debret, watercolor, Museu Chácara do Céu, Rio de Janeiro. **30–31** Washing gold, photo Marc Ferrez, late 19th century © coll. Gilberto Ferrez/ Instituto Moreira Salles. **31** *Black slaves washing precious stones, supervised by the 'feitor'*, detail, Carlos Julião, watercolor, 1775, Biblioteca Nacional, Rio de Janeiro © Dagli Orti. *Mining diamonds in the mines of Brazil*, detail, Carlos Julião, watercolor, 1775, © Idem. *Collection for the upkeep of the Igreja do Rosário*, J.-B. Debret, watercolor, Museu Chácara do Céu, Rio de Janeiro. **32–33** Coffee *fazenda*, photo Marc Ferrez, late 19th century © coll. Gilberto Ferrez/ Instituto Moreira Salles. **32** Advertising poster, early 20th century © Selva. Brazilian stamp © Selva. **33** Loading coffee at Santos, postcard, early 20th century, coll. Monsenhor Jamil Nassif Abib © Rômulo Fialdini/ Gallimard. **34** Punishment of slaves, color print in *Voyage autour du monde* by Jacques Arago, 1840, Bibliothèque Municipale, Versailles © Jean Vigne. **35** The decree of May 13, 1888 (*lei áurea*) that finally abolished slavery in Brazil, Museu Histórico Nacional, Rio de Janeiro © Dagli Orti. *Negros carregadores de cangalhas* (negroes carrying a barrel), J.-B. Debret, color print, 1834, Biblioteca Nacional, Rio de Janeiro © Idem. Arrival of Japanese immigrants at Santos, 1930 © Museu da Imigração Japonesa, São Paulo. **36** Demonstration in support of Getúlio Vargas, Sep 2, 1942 © Arquivo Nacional, Rio de Janeiro. **37** Getúlio Vargas, 1939 © Fundação Getúlio Vargas-CPDOC, Rio de Janeiro. Getúlio Vargas with miners © Idem. **38** Farmácia Cícero © J.-P. Dutilleux. Fruit juices © Seymourina Cruse/ Gallimard. School in Santa Maria Velha, Rio Negro © R. Reis/Tyba. **39** Fruit stall in Amazonia © R. Linsker/ Terra Virgem. **40** Immigrant house, Rio Grande do Sul, postcard, early 20th century, coll. Mons. J. Nassif Abib © R. Fialdini/Gallimard. Indian chief © Carlos Freire. Young *Baiana* © Princiotta/Focus Team. Half-caste girl © R. Linsker/ Terra Virgem. Farmer from the state of Acre © Miguel Rio Branco/Magnum. **41** Elderly woman from Salvador © Daniel Bosler/ Fotogram-Stone Images. **42** Religious festival of Bonfim in Muritiba, Bahia © J.-C. Pinheira. **43** Pilgrimage (*romaria*) of Padre Cícero in Juazeiro do Norte © Abbas/ Magnum. Offering to Iemanjá © Carlos Humberto/ TDC-Pictor/Tyba. *Mãe de santo* from Salvador © Kadya Tall. **44–45** *Capoeira* dancers © Pascal Baudry/Côté Vues. **44** Musicians of the 'Meninos de Rua' *capoeira* band, Salvador, Bahia © Pascal Maitre/Cosmos. **45** *Capoeira* in Bahia © R. Reis/Tyba. *Capoeira* at the 'academy' of the master Tuxé © Christopher Pillitz/ Network/Rapho. *Capoeira* in Salvador © P. Baudry/ Côté Vues. **46–47** Carnival float at the Sambódromo © Catherine Alonso Krulik. **46** *Entrudo*, J.-B. Debret, watercolor, 1823, Museu Chácara do Céu, Rio de Janeiro. **47** Street carnival © Alex Larbac/Tyba. Making carnival decorations in the *barracão* of the Mangueira samba school © R. Reis/ Tyba. Carnival costume © F. Ancellet/ Rapho. **48** Member of the Unidos da Ilha samba school © C. Alonso Krulik. **49** The 'library' © C. Alonso Krulik. *Porta-bandeira* dancer © Idem. *Baianas* from the Viradouro samba school © Idem. Dancer from the Unidos da Ilha samba school © Idem. Percussion band from the Portela samba school © Idem. **50–51** Luiz Gonzaga © Vieira de Queiroz/Tyba.**50** *Pagode* player on a beach in Rio de Janeiro © John Maier. Caricature of Pixinguinha, RR. **51** The 'Trio Elétrico' in Salvador © T. Aramac/Tyba. Self-caricature of Noel Rosa, gouache, coll. João Baptista Figueiredo, RR. Nelson Sargento in Mangueira © J. Maier. **52–53** The creators of the *bossa nova* on Ipanema beach © El País. **53** Marisa Monte © R. Reis/Tyba. Milton Nascimento © Richard Romero/ Tyba. Chico Buarque © C. Alonso Krulik. Sleeve of the 'Tropicália' album, Philips, RR. **54–55** *Bumba-meu-boi* and the '*Eu acho é pouco*' band during the Olinda carnival © C. Alonso Krulik. **54** Dancers at the festival of São João de Campina Grande, Paraíba © R. Reis/Tyba. *Literatura de cordel* © J.-C. Pinheira. *Nordestino* family, terracotta © J.-C. Pinheira. **55** *Carranca*, painted wood totem © J.-C. Pinheira. **56–57** Village community in the state of Pará © H. Collart-Ordinetz/Sygma. **57** Gathering the fruits of the forest in Amazonia © R. Linsker/ Terra Virgem. Fishing for *pirarucu* © Loren McIntyre. *Caboclo* boat on the Trombetas, Pará © H. Collart-Ordinetz/ Sygma. **58** The footballer Ronaldo in the Brazil v. Netherlands match, July 1998, France © Gromik/ Tschaen/Sipa Press. Garrincha during the 1958 World Cup © Popperfoto. Pelé during the Brazil v. Mexico match in 1962 © Presse'E Sports. **59** Supporters at the Maracanã stadium, Rio de Janeiro © Daniel Layne/*L'Équipe*. Flamengo supporters, Rio de Janeiro © Bruno Veiga/Tyba. Street football in Rio de Janeiro © D. Layne/ *L'Équipe*. **60–61** Shots from *telenovelas* © Manchete. **62–63** Recipe for *feijoada* © Éric Guillemot/ Gallimard. **64** Fruit seller © R. Linsker/ Terra Virgem. Brazilian specialties © P. Léger/ Gallimard. **65** Detail of a *fazenda*, ill. Jean-Marie Guillou/ Gallimard. **66–67** Plan of the São João Batista mission, Rio Grande do Sul, 1756 © BNF. **66** *Ego Sum*, polychrome wood, 18th century, Museu das Missões, RS, ill. Philippe Candé/ Gallimard. Plan of the São Miguel mission © BNF. **67** Ill. P. Candé/ Gallimard. **68–69** *Fazendas*, ill. Christian Rivière/ Gallimard. **70–71** Religious baroque, ill. Jean Sylvain Roveri/ Gallimard. Computer graphics Claude Quiec/ Gallimard. Interior of São Bento, Rio de Janeiro © P. Léger/Gallimard. **72–73** Minas baroque, ill. J.-M. Guillou/ Gallimard. Computer graphics C. Quiec/ Gallimard. **74–75** Urban baroque, ill. P. Candé/ Gallimard. **76** Poster for the 'IV Congresso Pan-Americano de Architectos' in Rio de Janeiro, 1930, Hugo Segawa archives, RR. Teatro Municipal de Rio de Janeiro, ill. C. Quiec/Gallimard. Edifício Martinelli, São Paulo, ill. Bruno Lenormand/ Gallimard. **77** Plan of Belo Horizonte, computer graphics. C. Quiec/ Gallimard. The BANESPA bank in São Paulo, ill. B. Lenormand/ Gallimard. **78** Sketches of the *pilotis* of the Fundação Vargas, Rio de Janeiro © O. Niemeyer/ Fundação Oscar Niemeyer. Front elevation of the chevet of the Capela de São Francisco de Assis, Pampulha, MG, Oscar Niemeyer, ill. B. Lenormand/ Gallimard. Drawings of the principal cross sections of the Congresso Nacional de Brasília © O. Niemeyer/Fundação Oscar Niemeyer. Cross section of the Museu de Arte Moderna, Rio de Janeiro, ill. B. Lenormand/Gallimard. **79** Sketch for the Supremo

Arcanjo © F. Ferranti. Saint Stanislas Kostka, wood polychrome, 18th century, Museu das Missões , São Miguel das Missões © A. Azambuja. **251** Olinda © F. Ferranti. **253** *Caatinga* landscape © C. Meyer/ Tyba. *Jangada* © L. C. Marigo/Tyba. **254–255** Boat on the Rio São Francisco © R. Linsker/Terra Virgem. **255** *Cangaceiros*, sculpture on wood © J.-C. Pinheira. Ruins of Canudos © R. Linsker/Terra Virgem. Gathering of *vaqueiros* © T. Aramac/Tyba. **256** Nossa Senhora do Rosário dos Pretos in the Pelourinho district © R. Linsker/Terra Virgem. Painted façades in Pelourinho © Idem. Streets in Pelourinho © Idem. **257** *Baiana* in traditional costume © R. Reis/Tyba. **258** Decorated façade in Salvador © L. Guanaes. Festival of Iemanjá © J.-C. Pinheira. **259** Praia da Barra © J.-C. Pinheira. Farol da Barra © R. Mello/Tyba. **260** Elevador Lacerda © R. Linsker/Terra Virgem. **261** Solar do Unhão © Aílton Sampaio/RR. Religious artifacts © J.-C. Pinheira. *Berimbau* player © Idem. **262** Festival of the Irmandade da Boa Morte, Cachoeira © J.-C. Pinheira. **263** The town of Cachoeira © F. Ferranti. **264** Praia do Forte © P. Baudry/Côté Vues. **265** Gathering coconuts © L. C. Marigo/Tyba. The Tamar project © S. Kolumban/Tyba. **266** The town of Valença © R. Linsker/ Terra Virgem. Cocoa harvest © Mike Goldwater/Network/ Rapho. **267** Itacaré beach © R. Linsker/Terra Virgem. **268–269** Chapada Diamantina © R. Linsker/Terra Virgem.**268** Street in Lençóis © Paulo Miranda/Tyba.**269** Underground river in the Chapada Diamantina © R. Linsker/Terra Virgem.**270** Sugar cane plant, ill. Nicolas Wintz/ Gallimard.**271** Machete for cutting sugar cane © Musée de l'Homme, Paris. *Portable sugar mill*, J.-B. Debret, watercolor, 1834, Biblioteca Nacional, Rio de Janeiro © Dagli Orti. Field of sugar cane in the state of Alagoas, postcard, early 20th century, coll. Mons. J. Nassif Abib © R. Fialdini/Gallimard. Harvesting sugar cane © A. Larbac/Tyba. The old Monjope sugar factory in the state of Pernambuco © João Tavares/RR.**272–273** *Maracatu* dancer at the Olinda carnival © C. Alonso Krulik.**272** Drum © S. Kolumban/Tyba. **273** *Repentistas* on the beach © R. Reis/Tyba. Olodum band at the Salvador carnival © L. Guanaes. **274** Façades in Recife © R. Reis/Tyba. Aerial view of Recife and the Rio Capibaribe © Eduardo Queiroga/ Lumiar/Tyba. Ponte 6 de Março or Ponte Velha © Alexandre Belem/ Lumiar/ Tyba. **275** Shrimp seller at the Mercado de São José © R. Reis/Tyba. **276–277** Boa Viagem beach © R. Reis/Tyba. **276** Oficina cerâmica Francisco Brennand © R. Reis/ Tyba. **277** Fruit © J.-C. Pinheira. **278–279** Convento Nossa Senhora da Conceição, Olinda © P. Baudry/Côté Vues. **278** Carnival in Olinda © C. Alonso Krulik. **280** Market stall, Caruaru © Geyson Magno/Lumiar/Tyba. Hats on the market in Caruaru © C. Meyer/ Tyba. **281** *Cangaceiros*, traditional crafts © Ricardo Malta/ Tyba.Beach at Porto de Galinhas © O. Rodrigues/Tyba. **282–283** Beach and Morro do Pico © S. Kolumbam/ Tyba.**283** Turtle, ill. F. Desbordes/Gallimard. *Atobá* (brown booby) © R. Linsker/Terra Virgem.Dolphins © Idem. Os Dois Irmãos from the Praia do Leão © Flávio Vidigal /Tyba.**284** Drying fish © R. Linsker/Terra Virgem. Theatro José de Alencar, Fortaleza © R. Reis/Tyba. **285** Hammocks © T. Aramac/Tyba. Bottle pictures made from colored sand © R. Reis/Tyba. **286** Praia de Jericoacoara © R. Linsker/Terra Virgem. **287** Lacemakers in Canoa Quebrada © J.-C. Pinheira. Praia de Canoa Quebrada © R. Reis/Tyba. **288** Town of São Luís © J. R. Couto/Tyba. **289** Balcony of a house in São Luís © J.-C. Pinheira. Fonte do Ribeirão © Idem. *Bumba-meu-boi*, traditional crafts © Idem. **290** Lençóis Maranhenses © R. Linsker/Terra Virgem. **291** Lençóis Maranhenses © R. Linsker/Terra Virgem. *Buriti* palm © Idem.**292** Town of Alcântara © R. Linsker/Terra Virgem. Donkey and cart © J.-C. Pinheira. **293** *Caboclo* in a canoe © J.-C. Pinheira. **294** The iron mines of Carajás © J.-C. Pinheira. **295** Deforestation © J.-C. Pinheira. **296–297** Yanomamí Indian in the forest © Nicolas Tiphagne. **296** American Indian woman from the state of Roraima © R. Linsker/ Terra Virgem. Kayapó child © M. Rio Branco/Magnum. Girls from the Jurema tribe © J.-P. Dutilleux. **297** Yanomamí women and children in the *maloca* © H. Collart-Ordinetz/Sygma. **298** Mercado do Ver-O-Peso © J. R. Couto/Tyba. Façade in Belém © F. Ferranti. **299** Market seller, Ver-O-Peso © L. C. Marigo/Tyba. **300** Village of Jenipapo, Lago Acari © J.-C. Pinheira. Riding a water buffalo © L. C. Marigo/ Tyba. **301** Ceramic vase from Marajó © J.-C. Pinheira. **302–303** Boat on the Belém–Manaus line © J.-C. Pinheira. **303** Indian at the festival of Parintins © H. Collart-Ordinetz/ Sygma. *Boto* and pregnant girl © J.-C. Pinheira. **304–305** Arquipélago de Anavilhanas in the Rio Negro © C. Meyer/ Tyba. **304** *Victoria amazonica* water lilies © J.-C. Pinheira. **305** Confluence of the Rio Solimões and Rio Negro © R. Linsker/ Terra Virgem. **306–307** Rio Pirus © R. Linsker/ Terra Virgem. **306** Flooded forest © C. Meyer/Tyba. Amazonian vegetation © J.-C. Pinheira. Flooded forest © Idem. **307** Wildlife, ill. F. Desbordes/ Gallimard. **308–309** Wildlife, ill. F. Desbordes/ Gallimard. **308** Amazonian jaguar © C. Meyer/Tyba. **309** Forest around Manaus © J.-C. Pinheira. Equatorial vegetation © Idem. Equatorial vegetation © R. Linsker/Terra Virgem. **310** Port of Manaus © R. Reis/Tyba. **311** Teatro Amazonas © R. Linsker/Terra Virgem. Market in the port of Manaus © J.-C. Pinheira. **312** Heating latex, postcard, early 20th century, coll. Mons. J. Nassif Abib © R. Fialdini/ Gallimard. *Seringueiro* © R. Linsker/Terra Virgem. Rubber tree © H. Collart-Ordinetz/ Sygma. **314** Cristo Redentor © P. Léger/Gallimard. **317** Santa Teresa tram, Rio de Janeiro © P. Léger/Gallimard. Young fishermen from Manaus © J.-P. Dutilleux. **318** Traditional Indian crafts © J.-C. Pinheira. **319** Phone booth in Salvador, Bahia © R. Reis/Tyba. **320** Kiosk in Rio © P. Léger/Gallimard. Passenger boat in Amazonia © J.-C. Pinheira. **321** *Baiana* © L. Guanaes. Kiosk in Copacabana, Rio de Janeiro © P. Léger/ Gallimard. **322** Ouro Preto, Minas Gerais © C. Freire.

Front cover
Brazilian Forest Scene, 1864 by Martin Johnson Heade, Museum of Art, Rhode Island School of Design; gift of Mr. and Mrs. C. Richard Steedman. Photography by Cathy Carver.
Back cover
(Top photograph) © V.C.L./Getty Images.

We would like to thank the following publishers and copyright holder for permission to reproduce the following quotations of pages 92–106.

◆ Extract from *Brazil, Land of the Future* by Stefan Zweig. Reproduced by permission of Williams Verlag AG, Zurich © 1976.

◆ Extracts from Pedro Vaz de Caminha, Letter to King Manuel 1st May 1500 in the *Voyages of Pedro Alvares Cabral to Brazil and India from Contemporary Documents and Narratives*. Reproduced by permission of Hakluyt Society.

◆ Extract from *English and Irish Settlement on the River Amazon* by Joyce Lorimer. Reproduced by permission of Hakluyt Society.

◆ Extract from *Rebellion in the Backlands* by Euclides da Cunha. Reproduced by permission of University of Chicago Press.

◆ Extracts from *Brazilian Sketches* by Rudyard Kipling. Reproduced by permission of AP Watt Ltd on behalf of The National Trust for Places of Historical Interest or Natural Beauty.

We have not been able to trace the heirs or publishers of certain documents. An account is being held open for them in our offices.

N

O

P

Q, R

S

T

U, V, W, X, Z

Map section, Rio de Janeiro

GLOSSARY

Aqueduto: aqueduct
Avenida: avenue
Cabo: cape
Enseada: cove, small bay
Estação: station
Estrada: road
Ilha: island
Jardim: garden
Ladeira: slope, steep street
Lagoa: lagoon
Largo: small square, open public space
Morro: hill, hillock
Parque: park
Pedra: mount, mountain
Pico: peak
Pontal, ponta: point
Ponte: bridge
Praça: square
Praia: beach
Rodovia: freeway
Rua: street
Travessa: shortcut, road cutting across
Viaduto: viaduct

A

B

◆ STREET INDEX

Q

R

S

T

U

V

W

Z

◆ CENTRO

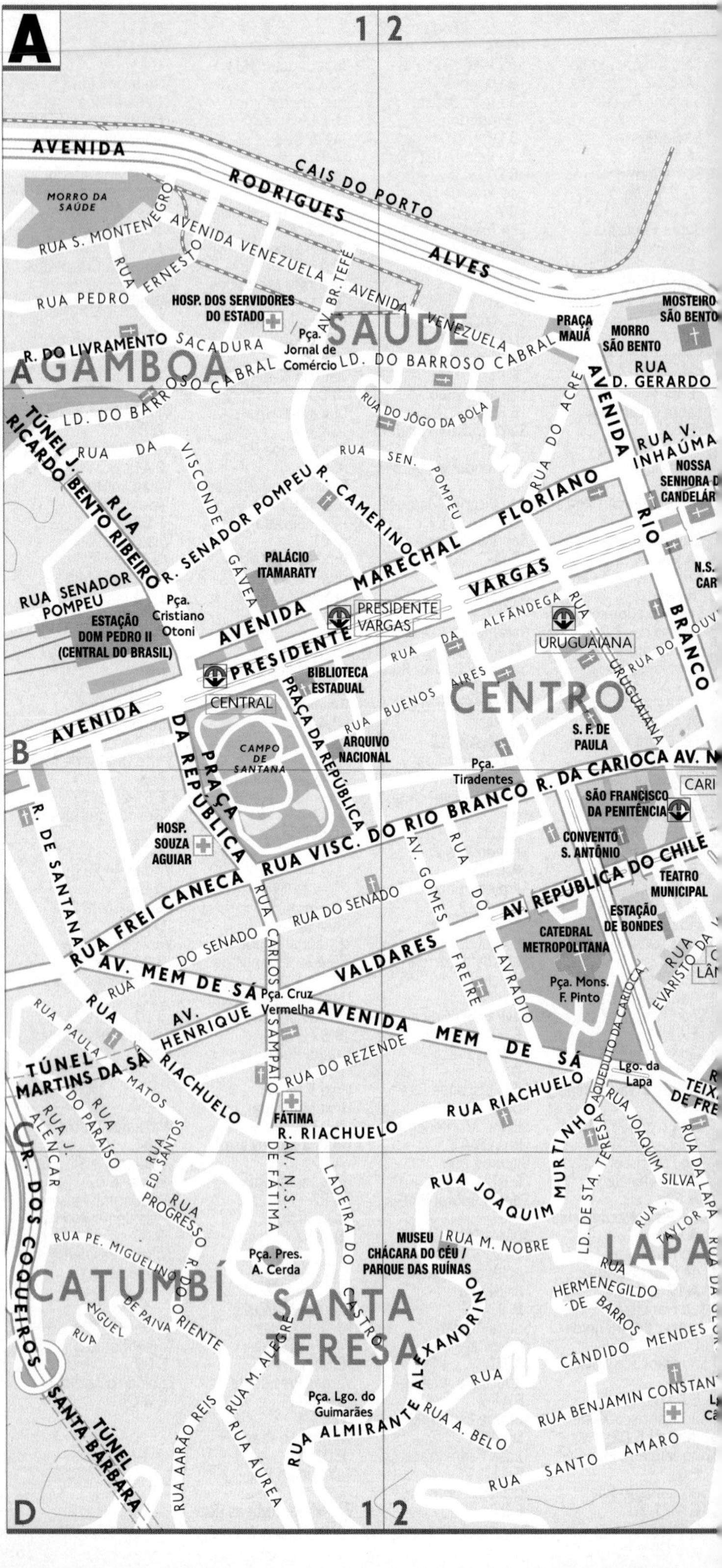

A
1 2
AVENIDA RODRIGUES ALVES
CAIS DO PORTO
MORRO DA SAÚDE
RUA S. MONTENEGRO
AVENIDA VENEZUELA
RUA ERNESTO
RUA PEDRO
HOSP. DOS SERVIDORES DO ESTADO
AV. BR. TEFÉ
SAÚDE
PRAÇA MAUÁ
MOSTEIRO SÃO BENTO
MORRO SÃO BENTO
R. DO LIVRAMENTO
SACADURA CABRAL
Pça. Jornal de Comércio
LD. DO BARROSO CABRAL
GAMBOA
RUA D. GERARDO
LD. DO BARROSO
RUA DO JÔGO DA BOLA
RUA DO ACRE
AVENIDA RIO BRANCO
TÚNEL J. RICARDO
RUA DA
VISCONDE GÁVEA
RUA SEN. POMPEU
RUA V. INHAÚMA
NOSSA SENHORA DA CANDELÁRIA
R. CAMERINO
AVENIDA MARECHAL FLORIANO
RUA BENTO RIBEIRO
R. SENADOR POMPEU
PALÁCIO ITAMARATY
RUA SENADOR POMPEU
Pça. Cristiano Otoni
ESTAÇÃO DOM PEDRO II (CENTRAL DO BRASIL)
AVENIDA PRESIDENTE VARGAS
PRESIDENTE VARGAS
RUA DA ALFÂNDEGA
URUGUAIANA
N.S. CAR
RUA DO OUV
CENTRAL
BIBLIOTECA ESTADUAL
RUA BUENOS AIRES
CENTRO
RUA URUGUAIANA
B
PRAÇA DA REPÚBLICA
CAMPO DE SANTANA
ARQUIVO NACIONAL
S. F. DE PAULA
Pça. Tiradentes
R. DA CARIOCA
AV. N
CARI
SÃO FRANCISCO DA PENITÊNCIA
R. DE SANTANA
HOSP. SOUZA AGUIAR
RUA VISC. DO RIO BRANCO
AV. GOMES FREIRE
RUA DO LAVRADIO
CONVENTO S. ANTÔNIO
AV. REPÚBLICA DO CHILE
TEATRO MUNICIPAL
RUA FREI CANECA
RUA CARLOS SAMPAIO
RUA DO SENADO
ESTAÇÃO DE BONDES
CATEDRAL METROPOLITANA
RUA EVARISTO DA
AV. MEM DE SÁ
VALDARES
Pça. Cruz Vermelha
Pça. Mons. F. Pinto
AQUEDUTO DA CARIOCA
RUA PAULA
AV. HENRIQUE
AVENIDA MEM DE SÁ
TÚNEL MARTINS DA SÁ
RUA RIACHUELO
RUA DO REZENDE
Lgo. da Lapa
R. TEIX. DE FRE
RUA MATOS
RUA DO PARAÍSO
RUA J. ALENCAR
FÁTIMA
R. RIACHUELO
RUA JOAQUIM SILVA
C
RUA ED. SANTOS
AV. N.S. DE FÁTIMA
LADEIRA DO CASTRO
RUA JOAQUIM MURTINHO
LD. DE STA. TERESA
RUA DA LAPA
RUA PROGRESSO
R. DOS COQUEIROS
RUA PE. MIGUELINO
R. DO ORIENTE
Pça. Pres. A. Cerda
MUSEU CHÁCARA DO CÉU / PARQUE DAS RUÍNAS
RUA M. NOBRE
LAPA
RUA TAYLOR
CATUMBÍ
SANTA TERESA
RUA HERMENEGILDO DE BARROS
RUA MIGUEL DE PAIVA
RUA M. ALEGRE
RUA ALEXANDRINO
RUA CÂNDIDO MENDES
Pça. Lgo. do Guimarães
RUA BENJAMIN CONSTANT
TÚNEL SANTA BÁRBARA
RUA AARÃO REIS
RUA ÁUREA
RUA ALMIRANTE
RUA A. BELO
RUA SANTO AMARO
D
1 2

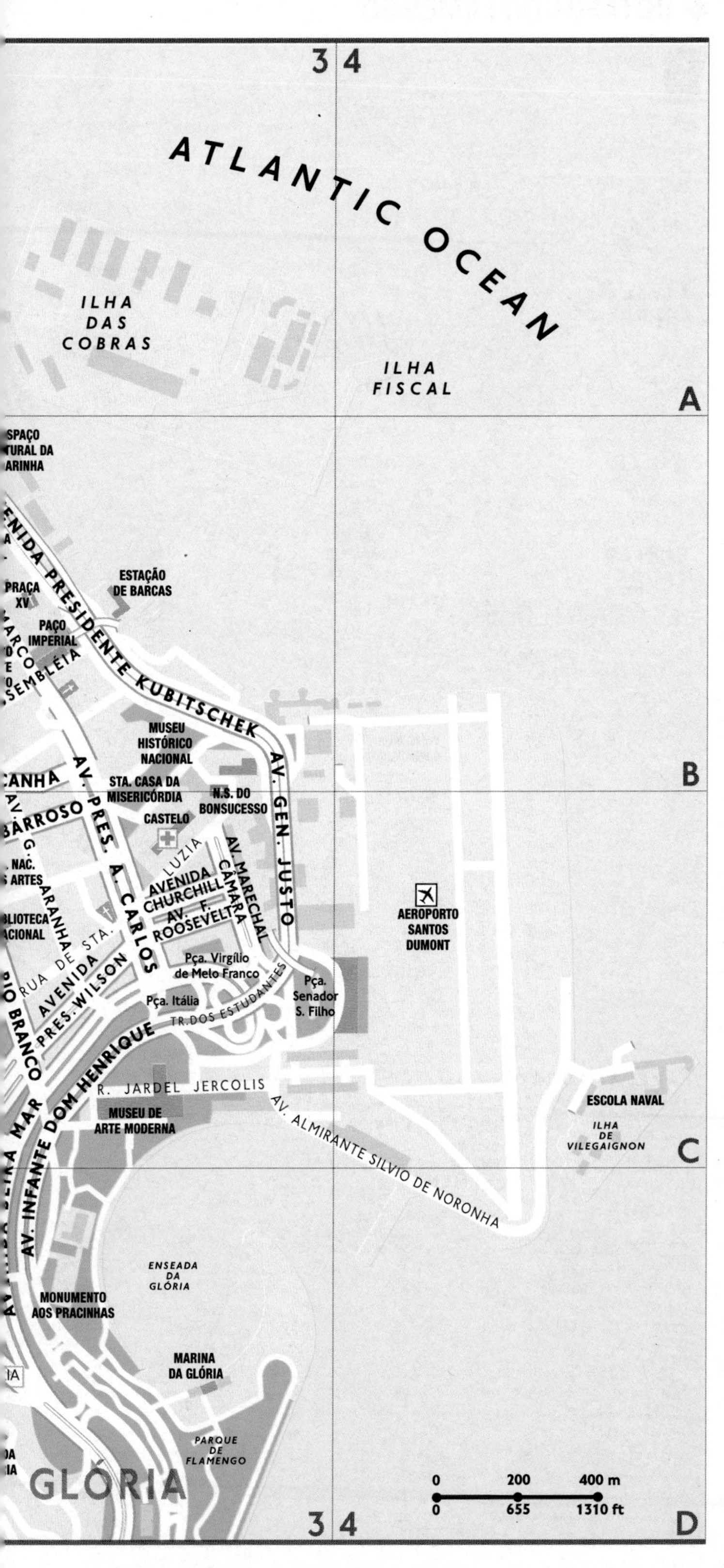
3
4
ATLANTIC OCEAN
ILHA DAS COBRAS
ILHA FISCAL
A
ESTAÇÃO DE BARCAS
PRAÇA XV
PAÇO IMPERIAL
AVENIDA PRESIDENTE KUBITSCHEK
MUSEU HISTÓRICO NACIONAL
B
STA. CASA DA MISERICÓRDIA
N.S. DO BONSUCESSO
CASTELO
AV. GEN. JUSTO
AV. PRES. A. CARLOS
AVENIDA CHURCHILL
AV. F. ROOSEVELT
AV. MARECHAL CÂMARA
LUZIA
AEROPORTO SANTOS DUMONT
Pça. Virgílio de Melo Franco
Pça. Senador S. Filho
Pça. Itália
TR. DOS ESTUDANTES
RUA DE STA.
AVENIDA PRES. WILSON
AV. INFANTE DOM HENRIQUE
R. JARDEL JERCOLIS
AV. ALMIRANTE SILVIO DE NORONHA
MUSEU DE ARTE MODERNA
ESCOLA NAVAL
ILHA DE VILEGAIGNON
C
ENSEADA DA GLÓRIA
MONUMENTO AOS PRACINHAS
MARINA DA GLÓRIA
PARQUE DE FLAMENGO
GLÓRIA
0 200 400 m
0 655 1310 ft
D

◆ BOTAFOGO/FLAMENGO

B

1 2

Pça. Paris
GLÓRIA
Pça. L. Camões
N.S. DA GLÓRIA
Lgo. P. Cândido
RUA C. MENDES
RUA BENJAMIN CONSTANT
RUA SANTO AMARO
LD. DO CASTRO
RUA ALMIRANTE ALEXANDRINO
RUA MONTE ALEGRE
Pça. Lgo. do Guimarães
RUA ÁUREA
R. AARÃO REIS
R. F. DE ANDRADE
TÚNEL SANTA BÁRBARA
FAVELA FALLET
R. ALMIRANTE ALEXANDRINO
MORRO DA NOVA CINTRA 876 ft
FAVELA TAVARES BASTOS
CATETE
GLÓRIA
RUA PEDRO AMÉRICO
RUA DO CATETE
RUA SILVEIRA MARTINS
PALÁCIO DO CATETE
MUSEU DO FOLCLORE
RUA FERREIRA VIANA
RUA BENTO LISBOA
RUA 2 DE DEZEMBRO
FLAMENGO
A
GEN. MARIANTE
RUA ERFURT
R. PAULO CESAR DE ANDRADE
PARQUE GUINLE
PALÁCIO LARANJEIRAS
RUA GAGO COUTINHO
LARGO DO MACHADO
RUA PEREIRA DA SILVA
FAVELA MALOCA
RUA DAS LARANJEIRAS
Pça. Del Prete
R. IPIRANGA
RUA CDE. BAEPENDI
R. BR. FLAMENGO
R. SEN. VERGUEIRO
LARANJEIRAS
FLAMENGO
VD. JARDEL FO.
AV. PRAIA DO FLAMENGO
AV. INFANTE
RUA ALICE
RUA SOARES CABRAL
RUA PAISSANDU
RUA PINHEIRO MACHADO
RUA PAULO VI
R. MARQUÊS DE ABRANTES
RUA SEN. VERGUEIRO
PALÁCIO DA GUANABARA
B
RUA DAS LARANJEIRAS
R. CARDOSO JÚNIOR
MORRO MUNDO NOVO 420 ft
FLAMENGO
AV. OSVALDO CRUZ
MORRO DA VIÚVA
RUA BELISÁRIO TAVORA
R. GEN. GLICÉRIO
R. PROF. LUIS CANTANHEDA
RUA MUNDO NOVO
RUA BARÃO DE ITAMBI
RUA DE BOTAFOGO
Pça. Nicaragua
AVENIDA
AV. INFANTE
R. M. OLINDA
RUA MUNIZ BARRETO
PRAIA DO BOTAFOGO
PRAIA DE BOTAFOGO
ENSEADA DE BOTAFOGO
RUA BAMBINA
FAVELA MORRO SANTA MARTA
BOTAFOGO
CASA RUI BARBOSA
C
RUA SÃO CLEMENTE
R. N. MANDELA
VD. PEDRO ALVARES CABRAL
Pça. Pimental Duarte
AVENIDA PASTEUR
BOTAFOGO
RUA 19 DE FEVEREIRO
MUSEU VILLA LOBOS
RUA DAS PALMEIRAS
MUSEU DO ÍNDIO
RUA VOLUNTÁRIOS DA PÁTRIA
R. PROF. ÁLVARO RODRIGUES
TÚNEL DO PASMADO
RUA B. PORTELA
UNIVERSIDADE FEDERAL DO RIO DE JANEIRO
RUA REAL GRANDEZA
R. SÃO JOÃO BATISTA
R. GEN. POLIDORO
R. DA PASSAGEM
R. GEN. SAVERIANO
AV. LAURO SODRÉ
Pça. Juliano Moreira
RUA LAURO MÜLLER
RUA MENA BARRETO
RUA ARNALDO QUINTELA
RUA GENERAL POLIDORO
RUA ÁLVARO RAMOS
STA. TEREZINHA DO MENINO JESUS
CEMITÉRIO SÃO JOÃO BATISTA
D

1 2

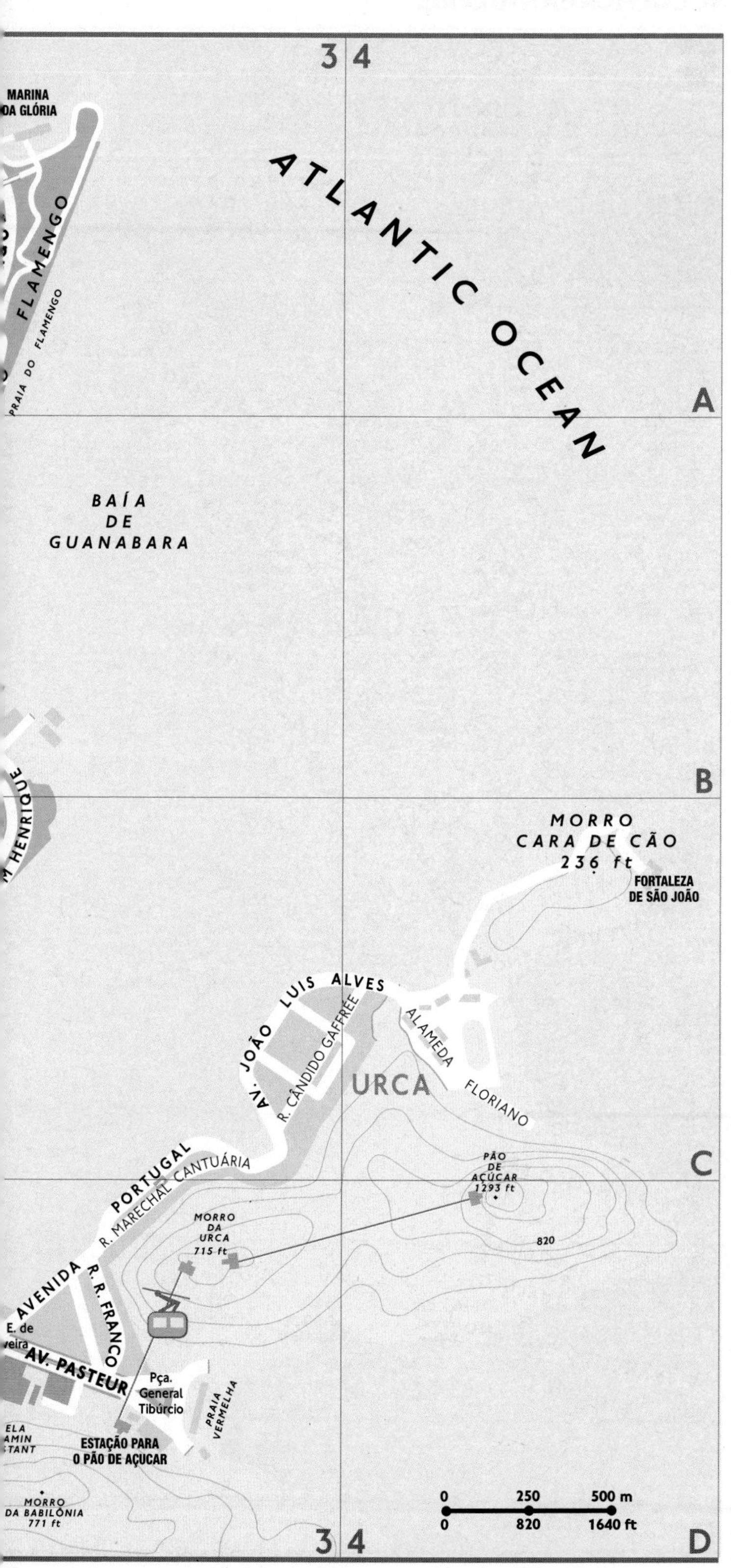

3 4
MARINA DA GLÓRIA
FLAMENGO
PRAIA DO FLAMENGO
ATLANTIC OCEAN
A
BAÍA DE GUANABARA
B
MORRO CARA DE CÃO 236 ft
FORTALEZA DE SÃO JOÃO
AV. JOÃO LUIS ALVES
R. CÂNDIDO GAFFRÉE
ALAMEDA FLORIANO
URCA
C
PORTUGAL
R. MARECHAL CANTUÁRIA
PÃO DE AÇÚCAR 1293 ft
MORRO DA URCA 715 ft
820
AVENIDA
R. R. FRANCO
AV. PASTEUR
Pça. General Tibúrcio
PRAIA VERMELHA
ESTAÇÃO PARA O PÃO DE AÇUCAR
MORRO DA BABILÔNIA 771 ft
0 250 500 m
0 820 1640 ft
3 4
D

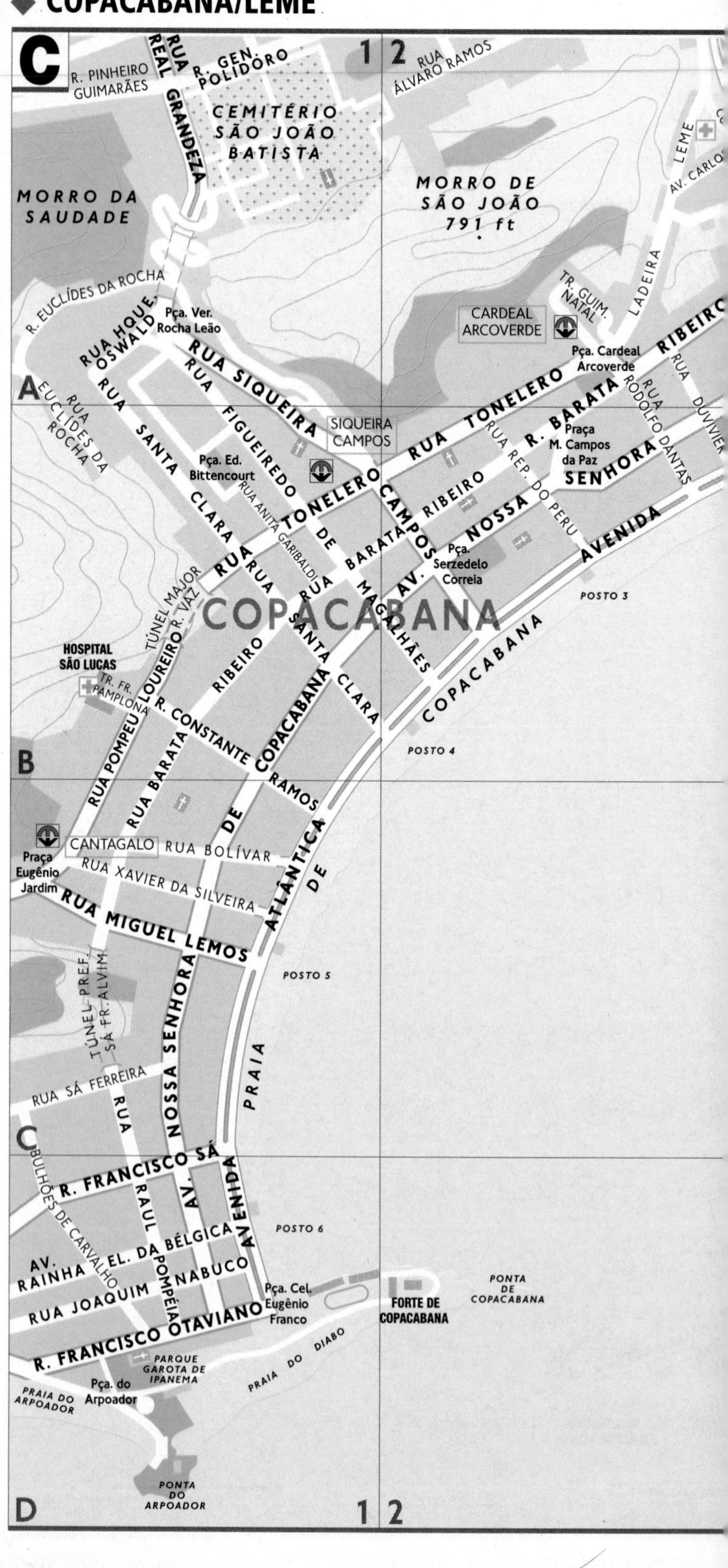
C
1 2
R. PINHEIRO GUIMARÃES
RUA REAL GRANDEZA
R. GEN. POLIDORO
CEMITÉRIO SÃO JOÃO BATISTA
RUA ÁLVARO RAMOS
MORRO DA SAUDADE
MORRO DE SÃO JOÃO 791 ft
LEME
AV. CARLOS
LADEIRA
TR. GUIM. NATAL
R. EUCLÍDES DA ROCHA
RUA HQUE. OSWALD
Pça. Ver. Rocha Leão
CARDEAL ARCOVERDE
Pça. Cardeal Arcoverde
RIBEIRO
RUA SIQUEIRA
RUA FIGUEIREDO
RUA TONELERO
RUA DUVIVIER
RUA RODOLFO DANTAS
A
RUA EUCLÍDES DA ROCHA
RUA SANTA CLARA
SIQUEIRA CAMPOS
R. BARATA
RUA REP. DO PERU
Praça M. Campos da Paz
SENHORA
Pça. Ed. Bittencourt
RUA ANITA GARIBALDI
TONELERO
CAMPOS
RIBEIRO
NOSSA
AVENIDA
DE
BARATA
Pça. Serzedelo Correia
RUA
RUA
RUA
AV.
POSTO 3
TÚNEL MAJOR R. VAZ
COPACABANA
SANTA
MAGALHÃES
HOSPITAL SÃO LUCAS
RIBEIRO
TR. FR. PAMPLONA
COPACABANA
CLARA
COPACABANA
R. CONSTANTE RAMOS
RUA POMPEU LOUREIRO
POSTO 4
B
RUA BARATA
DE
CANTAGALO
RUA BOLÍVAR
Praça Eugênio Jardim
RUA XAVIER DA SILVEIRA
ATLÂNTICA
DE
RUA MIGUEL LEMOS
POSTO 5
TÚNEL PREF. SÁ FR. ALVIM
NOSSA SENHORA
PRAIA
RUA SÁ FERREIRA
RUA
C
BULHÕES DE CARVALHO
R. FRANCISCO SÁ
RAUL
AV.
AVENIDA
POSTO 6
AV. RAINHA EL. DA BÉLGICA
RUA JOAQUIM NABUCO
POMPÉIA
Pça. Cel. Eugênio Franco
FORTE DE COPACABANA
PONTA DE COPACABANA
R. FRANCISCO OTAVIANO
PRAIA DO DIABO
PARQUE GAROTA DE IPANEMA
PRAIA DO ARPOADOR
Pça. do Arpoador
PONTA DO ARPOADOR
D
1 2

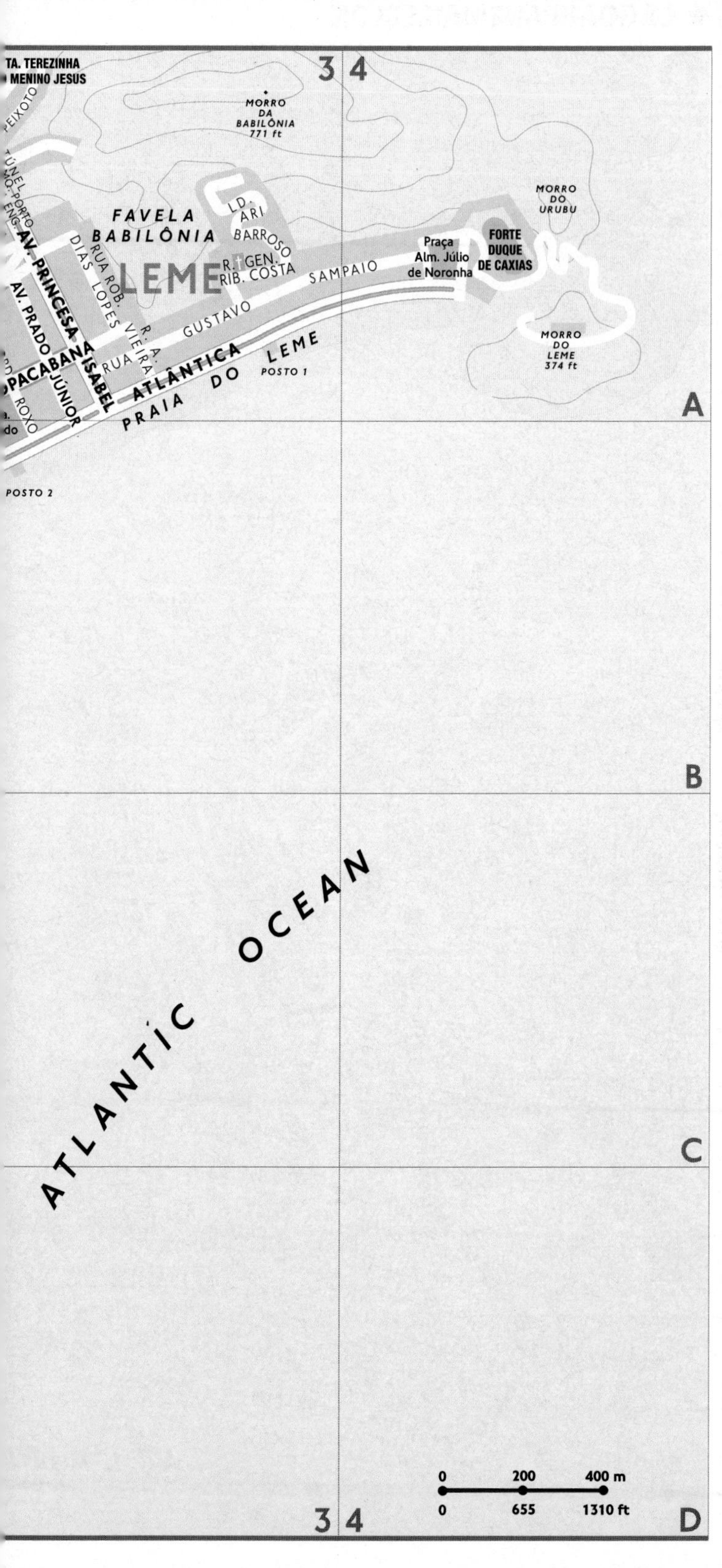

TA. TEREZINHA
MENINO JESUS
MORRO DA BABILÔNIA 771 ft
MORRO DO URUBU
FAVELA BABILÔNIA
LD. ARI BARROSO
LEME
R. GEN. RIB. COSTA
SAMPAIO
Praça Alm. Júlio de Noronha
FORTE DUQUE DE CAXIAS
MORRO DO LEME 374 ft
AV. PRINCESA ISABEL
RUA ROB. DIAS LOPES
R. A. VIEIRA
RUA GUSTAVO
AV. PRADO JÚNIOR
ATLÂNTICA
PRAIA DO LEME
POSTO 1
POSTO 2
ATLANTIC OCEAN
0 200 400 m
0 655 1310 ft

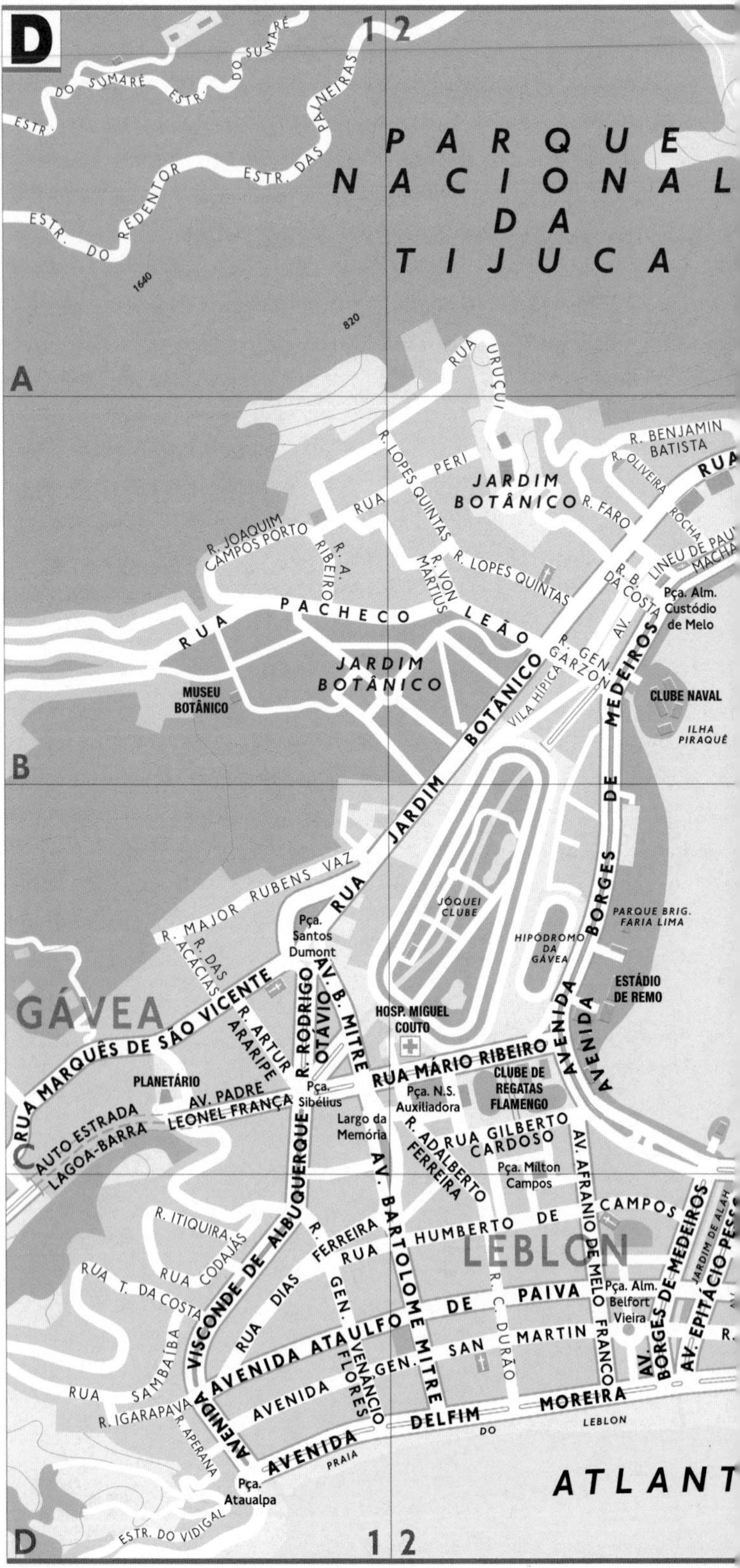

D

1 2

PARQUE NACIONAL DA TIJUCA
ESTR. DO SUMARÉ
ESTR. DAS PAINEIRAS
ESTR. DO REDENTOR
1640
820
RUA URUÇUÍ
R. BENJAMIN BATISTA
R. OLIVEIRA
RUA PERI
R. LOPES QUINTAS
JARDIM BOTÂNICO
R. FARO
RUA
ROCHA
LINEU DE PAULA MACHADO
R. JOAQUIM CAMPOS PORTO
R. A. RIBEIRO
R. VON MARTIUS
R. LOPES QUINTAS
R. B. DA COSTA
Pça. Alm. Custódio de Melo
RUA PACHECO LEÃO
R. GEN. GARZON
JARDIM BOTÂNICO
MUSEU BOTÂNICO
VILA HÍPICA
AV. BORGES DE MEDEIROS
CLUBE NAVAL
ILHA PIRAQUÊ
RUA JARDIM BOTÂNICO
R. MAJOR RUBENS VAZ
JÓQUEI CLUBE
PARQUE BRIG. FARIA LIMA
Pça. Santos Dumont
HIPÓDROMO DA GÁVEA
R. DAS ACÁCIAS
ESTÁDIO DE REMO
GÁVEA
RUA MARQUÊS DE SÃO VICENTE
R. ARTUR ARARIPE
R. RODRIGO OTÁVIO
AV. B. MITRE
HOSP. MIGUEL COUTO
AVENIDA
AVENIDA
PLANETÁRIO
RUA MÁRIO RIBEIRO
CLUBE DE REGATAS FLAMENGO
Pça. Sibélius
Pça. N.S. Auxiliadora
AV. PADRE LEONEL FRANÇA
AUTO ESTRADA LAGOA-BARRA
Largo da Memória
R. ADALBERTO FERREIRA
RUA GILBERTO CARDOSO
Pça. Mílton Campos
AV. AFRANIO DE MELO FRANCO
R. ITIQUIRA
VISCONDE DE ALBUQUERQUE
AV. BARTOLOMEU MITRE
R. DIAS FERREIRA
RUA HUMBERTO DE CAMPOS
LEBLON
RUA CODAJÁS
RUA T. DA COSTA
RUA DIAS FERREIRA
R. GEN. VENÂNCIO FLORES
R. C. DURÃO
AVENIDA ATAULFO DE PAIVA
Pça. Alm. Belfort Vieira
AV. BORGES DE MEDEIROS
AV. EPITÁCIO PESSOA
JARDIM DE ALAH
RUA SAMBAÍBA
GEN. SAN MARTIN
AVENIDA DELFIM MOREIRA
R. IGARAPAVA
R. APERANA
AVENIDA
PRAIA DO LEBLON
Pça. Ataualpa
ATLANT
ESTR. DO VIDIGAL

A
B
C
D

1 2

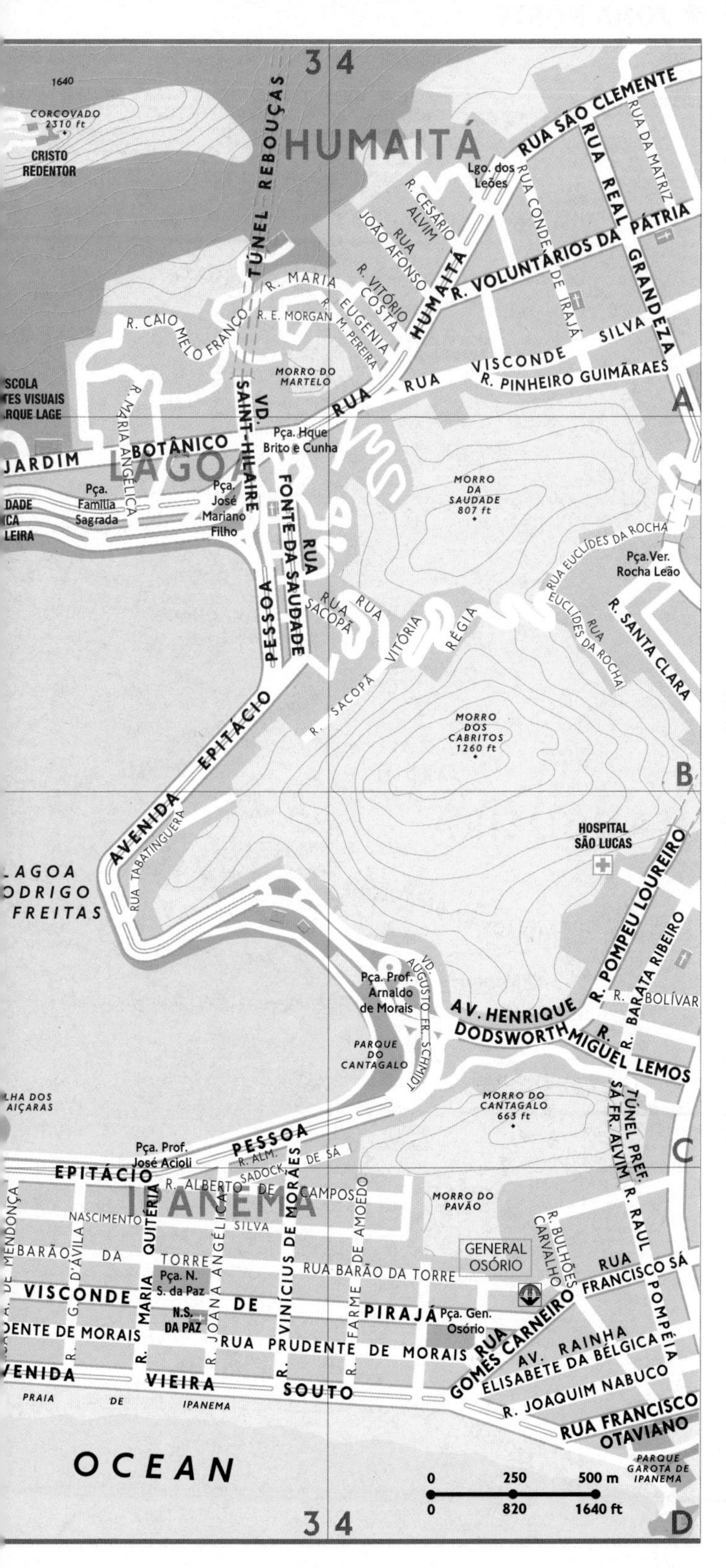

3 4
HUMAITÁ
CORCOVADO 2310 ft
1640
CRISTO REDENTOR
TÚNEL REBOUÇAS
RUA SÃO CLEMENTE
RUA REAL GRANDEZA
RUA DA MATRIZ
Lgo. dos Leões
RUA CONDE DE IRAJÁ
R. CESÁRIO ALVIM
RUA JOÃO AFONSO
R. VITÓRIO COSTA
HUMAITÁ
R. VOLUNTÁRIOS DA PÁTRIA
R. MARIA EUGENIA
R. M. PEREIRA
R. E. MORGAN
R. CAIO MELO FRANCO
VISCONDE SILVA
R. PINHEIRO GUIMARÃES
RUA
MORRO DO MARTELO
SCOLA
TES VISUAIS
RQUE LAGE
R. MARIA ANGÉLICA
VD. SAINT-HILAIRE
Pça. Hque Brito e Cunha
JARDIM BOTÂNICO
LAGOA
Pça. Familia Sagrada
Pça. José Mariano Filho
RUA FONTE DA SAUDADE
MORRO DA SAUDADE 807 ft
RUA EUCLÍDES DA ROCHA
Pça.Ver. Rocha Leão
PESSOA
RUA SACOPÃ
RUA VITÓRIA RÉGIA
R. SANTA CLARA
R. SACOPÃ
EPITÁCIO
MORRO DOS CABRITOS 1260 ft
B
AVENIDA
RUA TABATINGUERA
HOSPITAL SÃO LUCAS
LAGOA
ODRIGO
FREITAS
R. POMPEU LOUREIRO
R. BARATA RIBEIRO
R. BOLÍVAR
Pça. Prof. Arnaldo de Morais
VD. AUGUSTO FR. SCHMIDT
AV. HENRIQUE DODSWORTH
R. MIGUEL LEMOS
PARQUE DO CANTAGALO
LHA DOS
AIÇARAS
MORRO DO CANTAGALO 663 ft
TÚNEL PREF. SÁ FR. ALVIM
C
Pça. Prof. José Acioli
EPITÁCIO PESSOA
R. ALM. SADOCK DE SÁ
R. ALBERTO DE CAMPOS
IPANEMA
MORRO DO PAVÃO
NASCIMENTO SILVA
BARÃO DA TORRE
RUA BARÃO DA TORRE
R. MARIA QUITÉRIA
R. JOANA ANGÉLICA
R. VINÍCIUS DE MORAES
R. FARME DE AMOEDO
R. G. D'ÁVILA
A. DE MENDONÇA
GENERAL OSÓRIO
R. BULHÕES CARVALHO
R. RAUL POMPEIA
RUA FRANCISCO SÁ
VISCONDE DE PIRAJÁ
Pça. N. S. da Paz
N.S. DA PAZ
Pça. Gen. Osório
RUA GOMES CARNEIRO
PRUDENTE DE MORAIS
RUA PRUDENTE DE MORAIS
AV. RAINHA ELISABETE DA BÉLGICA
AVENIDA VIEIRA SOUTO
R. JOAQUIM NABUCO
RUA FRANCISCO OTAVIANO
PRAIA DE IPANEMA
PARQUE GAROTA DE IPANEMA
OCEAN
0 250 500 m
0 820 1640 ft
3 4
D

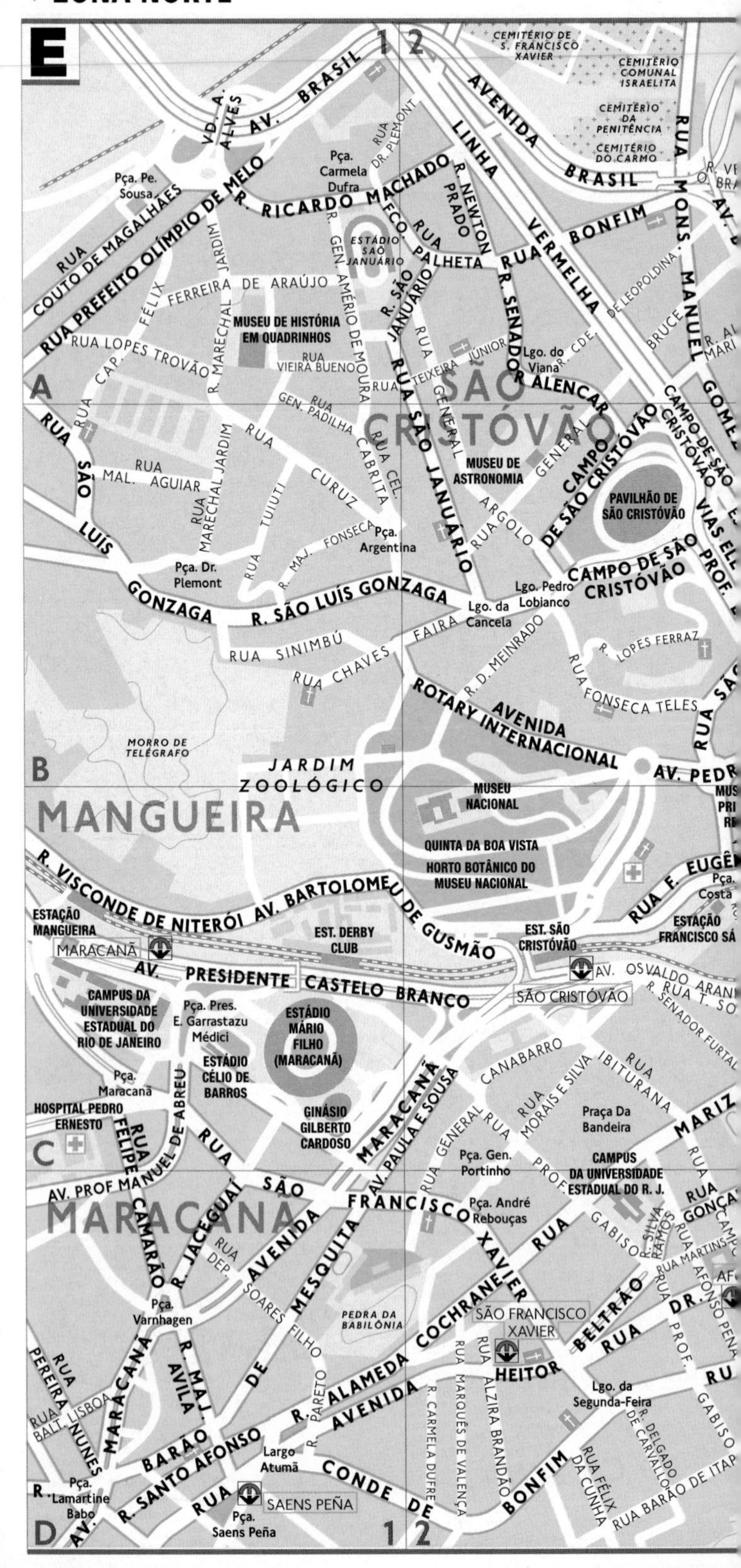
E
SÃO CRISTÓVÃO
MANGUEIRA
MARACANÃ
MUSEU DE HISTÓRIA EM QUADRINHOS
MUSEU DE ASTRONOMIA
PAVILHÃO DE SÃO CRISTÓVÃO
JARDIM ZOOLÓGICO
MORRO DE TELÉGRAFO
MUSEU NACIONAL
QUINTA DA BOA VISTA
HORTO BOTÂNICO DO MUSEU NACIONAL
ESTAÇÃO MANGUEIRA
EST. DERBY CLUB
EST. SÃO CRISTÓVÃO
ESTAÇÃO FRANCISCO SÁ
CAMPUS DA UNIVERSIDADE ESTADUAL DO RIO DE JANEIRO
ESTÁDIO MÁRIO FILHO (MARACANÃ)
ESTÁDIO CÉLIO DE BARROS
GINÁSIO GILBERTO CARDOSO
HOSPITAL PEDRO ERNESTO
CAMPUS DA UNIVERSIDADE ESTADUAL DO R. J.
PEDRA DA BABILÔNIA
ESTÁDIO SÃO JANUÁRIO
CEMITÉRIO DE S. FRANCISCO XAVIER
CEMITÉRIO COMUNAL ISRAELITA
CEMITÉRIO DA PENITÊNCIA
CEMITÉRIO DO CARMO
AV. BRASIL
AVENIDA BRASIL
LINHA VERMELHA
R. RICARDO MACHADO
RUA PREFEITO OLÍMPIO DE MELO
RUA COUTO DE MAGALHÃES
R. SÃO LUÍS GONZAGA
RUA SÃO JANUÁRIO
CAMPO DE SÃO CRISTÓVÃO
AVENIDA ROTARY INTERNACIONAL
R. VISCONDE DE NITERÓI
AV. BARTOLOMEU DE GUSMÃO
AV. PRESIDENTE CASTELO BRANCO
RUA SÃO FRANCISCO XAVIER
AVENIDA MARACANÃ
RUA CONDE DE BONFIM
R. SANTO AFONSO
RUA BARÃO DE MESQUITA
R. ALAMEDA COCHRANE
AVENIDA HEITOR BELTRÃO
Pça. Pe. Sousa
Pça. Carmela Dufra
Lgo. do Viana
Pça. Argentina
Pça. Dr. Plemont
Lgo. Pedro Lobianco
Lgo. da Cancela
Pça. Pres. E. Garrastazu Médici
Pça. Maracanã
Pça. Gen. Portinho
Pça. André Rebouças
Praça Da Bandeira
Pça. Varnhagen
Largo Atumã
Pça. Lamartine Babo
Pça. Saens Peña
Lgo. da Segunda-Feira
MARACANÃ
SÃO CRISTÓVÃO
SÃO FRANCISCO XAVIER
SAENS PEÑA

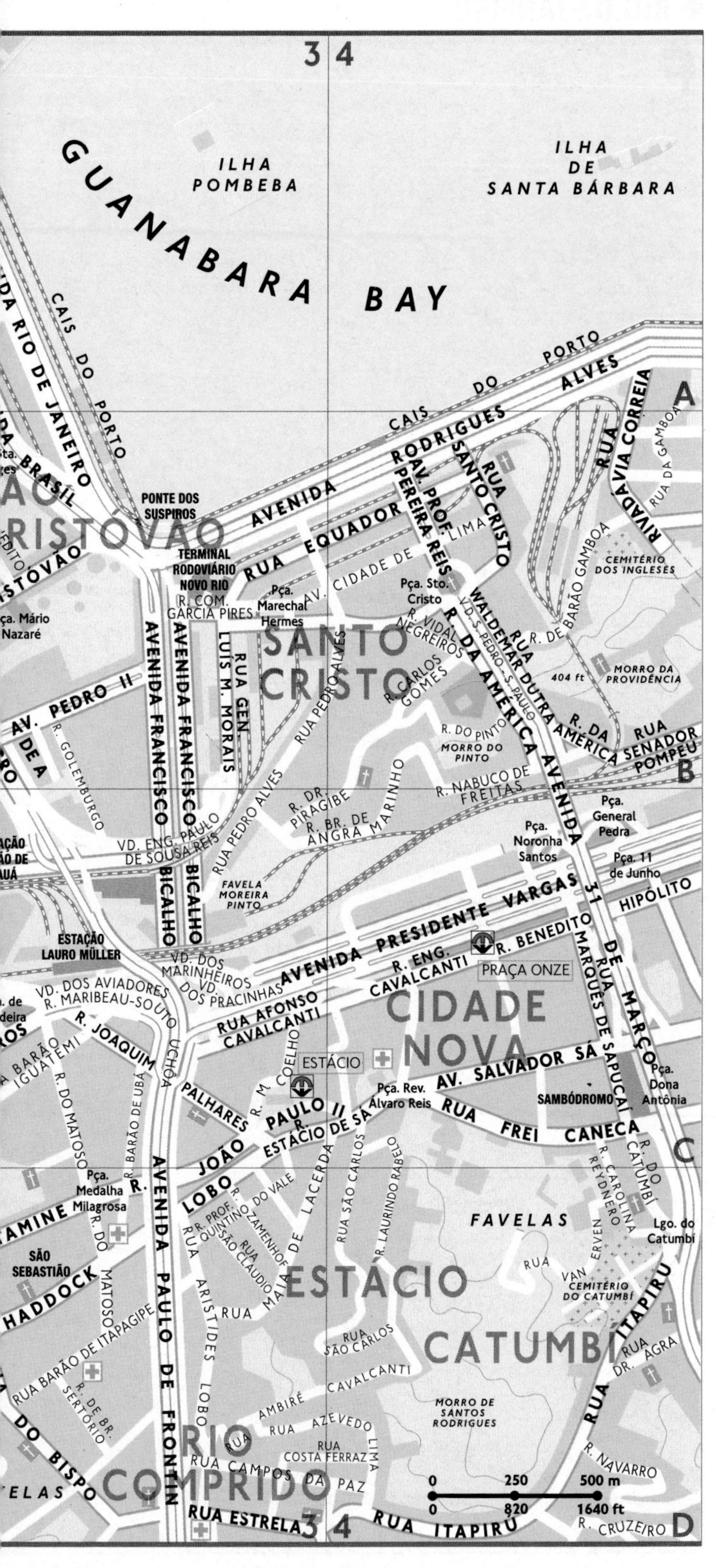

3 4
GUANABARA BAY
ILHA POMBEBA
ILHA DE SANTA BÁRBARA
CAIS DO PORTO
AVENIDA RODRIGUES ALVES
AVENIDA RIO DE JANEIRO
AVENIDA BRASIL
PONTE DOS SUSPIROS
SÃO CRISTÓVÃO
TERMINAL RODOVIÁRIO NOVO RIO
RUA EQUADOR
AV. PROF. PEREIRA REIS
RUA SANTO CRISTO
RUA RIVADAVIA CORREIA
RUA DA GAMBOA
AV. CIDADE DE LIMA
R. COM. GARCIA PIRES
Pça. Marechal Hermes
Pça. Sto. Cristo
CEMITÉRIO DOS INGLESES
R. DE BARÃO GAMBOA
Pça. Mário Nazaré
SANTO CRISTO
R. VIDAL NEGREIROS
VD. S. PEDRO - S. PAULO
RUA WALDEMAR DUTRA
R. DA AMÉRICA
MORRO DA PROVIDÊNCIA
404 ft
AV. PEDRO II
AVENIDA FRANCISCO BICALHO
RUA GEN. LUÍS M. MORAIS
RUA PEDRO ALVES
R. CARLOS GOMES
R. DO PINTO
MORRO DO PINTO
R. DA AMÉRICA
RUA SENADOR POMPEU
AVENIDA
R. GOLEMBURGO
R. NABUCO DE FREITAS
R. DR. PIRAGIBE
R. BR. DE ANGRA
MARINHO
Pça. General Pedra
Pça. Noronha Santos
Pça. 11 de Junho
VD. ENG. PAULO DE SOUSA REIS
FAVELA MOREIRA PINTO
AVENIDA PRESIDENTE VARGAS
HIPÓLITO
31 DE MARÇO
ESTAÇÃO LAURO MÜLLER
VD. DOS MARINHEIROS
VD. DOS PRACINHAS
R. BENEDITO
R. ENG. CAVALCANTI
PRAÇA ONZE
RUA MARQUES DE SAPUCAÍ
VD. DOS AVIADORES
R. MARIBEAU-SOUTO
RUA AFONSO CAVALCANTI
CIDADE NOVA
R. JOAQUIM PALHARES
UCHÔA
R. BARÃO IGUATEMI
ESTÁCIO
R. M. COELHO
AV. SALVADOR SÁ
Pça. Rev. Álvaro Reis
Pça. Dona Antônia
SAMBÓDROMO
RUA FREI CANECA
R. DO MATOSO
R. BARÃO DE UBÁ
AV. PAULO II
R. ESTÁCIO DE SÁ
R. JOÃO LOBO
RUA DE LACERDA
RUA SÃO CARLOS
RUA LAURINDO RABELO
R. DO CATUMBI
R. CAROLINA REYDNER
Pça. Medalha Milagrosa
R. AMINE
R. PROF. QUINTINO DO VALE
R. ZAMENHOF
RUA SÃO CLÁUDIO
RUA MAIA
FAVELAS
Lgo. do Catumbi
SÃO SEBASTIÃO
HADDOCK
R. DO MATOSO
RUA ARISTIDES LOBO
ESTÁCIO
RUA VAN ERVEN
CEMITÉRIO DO CATUMBI
RUA ITAPIRU
AVENIDA PAULO DE FRONTIN
RUA BARÃO DE ITAPAGIPE
RUA SÃO CARLOS
CATUMBI
RUA DR. AGRA
R. DE BR. SERTÓRIO
CAVALCANTI
MORRO DE SANTOS RODRIGUES
RUA AMBIRÉ
RUA AZEVEDO LIMA
RUA COSTA FERRAZ
R. DO BISPO
RIO COMPRIDO
RUA CAMPOS DA PAZ
R. NAVARRO
0 250 500 m
0 820 1640 ft
RUA ESTRELA
RUA ITAPIRU
R. CRUZEIRO
A
B
C
D

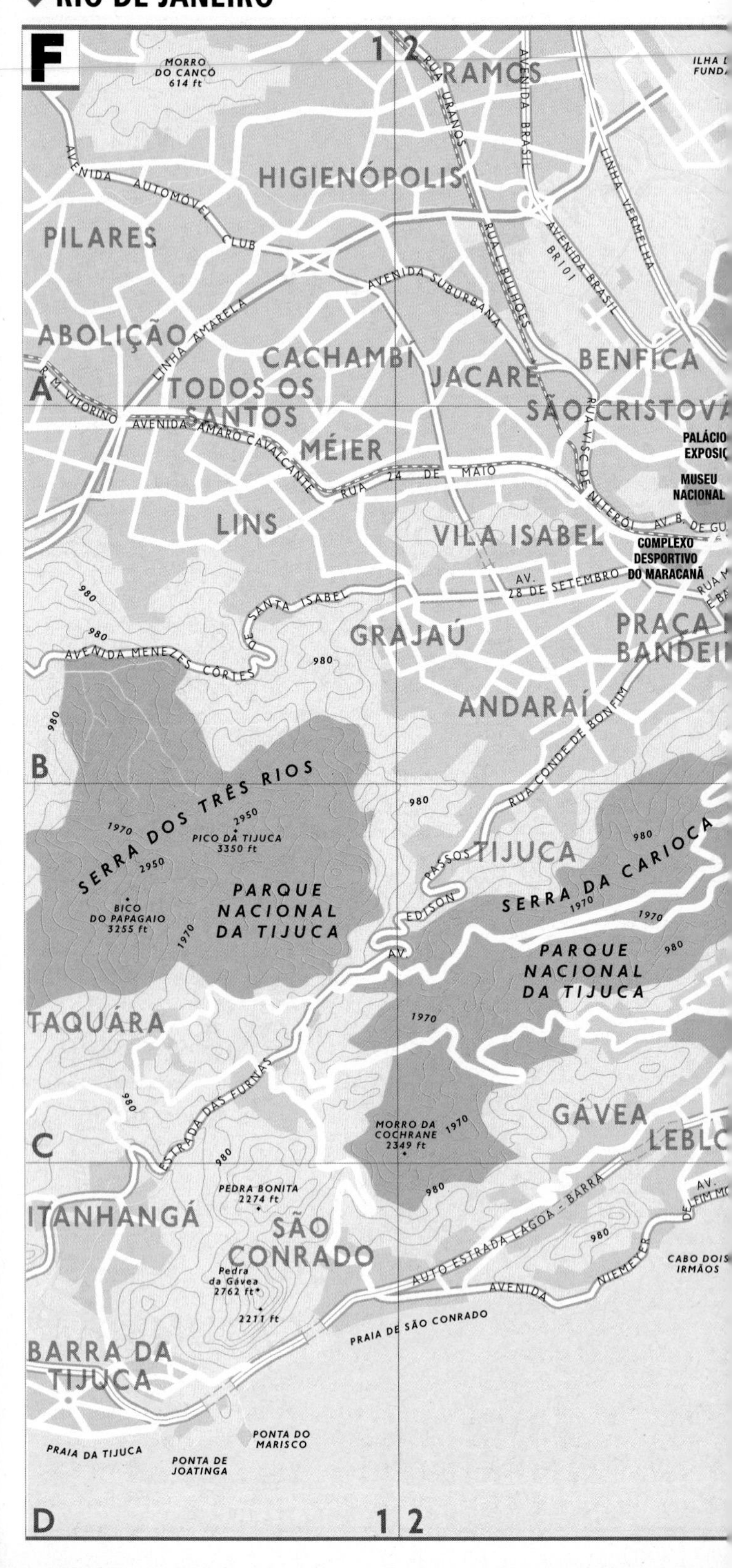
F
1 2
MORRO DO CANCÓ 614 ft
RAMOS
RUA URANOS
AVENIDA BRASIL
LINHA VERMELHA
HIGIENÓPOLIS
AVENIDA AUTOMÓVEL CLUB
PILARES
RUA L. BULHÕES
AVENIDA BRASIL BR101
AVENIDA SUBURBANA
ABOLIÇÃO
LINHA AMARELA
CACHAMBI
JACARÉ
BENFICA
R. M. VITORINO
TODOS OS SANTOS
SÃO CRISTOVÃ
RUA VISC. DE NITERÓI
AVENIDA AMARO CAVALCANTE
MÉIER
PALÁCIO EXPOSIÇ
RUA 24 DE MAIO
MUSEU NACIONAL
LINS
VILA ISABEL
AV. B. DE GU
COMPLEXO DESPORTIVO DO MARACANÃ
AV. 28 DE SETEMBRO
980
SANTA ISABEL
PRAÇA BANDEI
GRAJAÚ
AVENIDA MENEZES CÔRTES
ANDARAÍ
RUA CONDE DE BONFIM
B
SERRA DOS TRÊS RIOS
2950
PICO DA TIJUCA 3350 ft
1970
PASSOS
TIJUCA
SERRA DA CARIOCA
PARQUE NACIONAL DA TIJUCA
BICO DO PAPAGAIO 3255 ft
AV. EDISON
TAQUÁRA
ESTRADA DAS FURNAS
GÁVEA
MORRO DA COCHRANE 2349 ft
C
LEBLO
PEDRA BONITA 2274 ft
AUTO ESTRADA LAGOA - BARRA
ITANHANGÁ
SÃO CONRADO
Pedra da Gávea 2762 ft
2211 ft
AVENIDA NIEMEYER
CABO DOIS IRMÃOS
PRAIA DE SÃO CONRADO
BARRA DA TIJUCA
PONTA DO MARISCO
PRAIA DA TIJUCA
PONTA DE JOATINGA
D

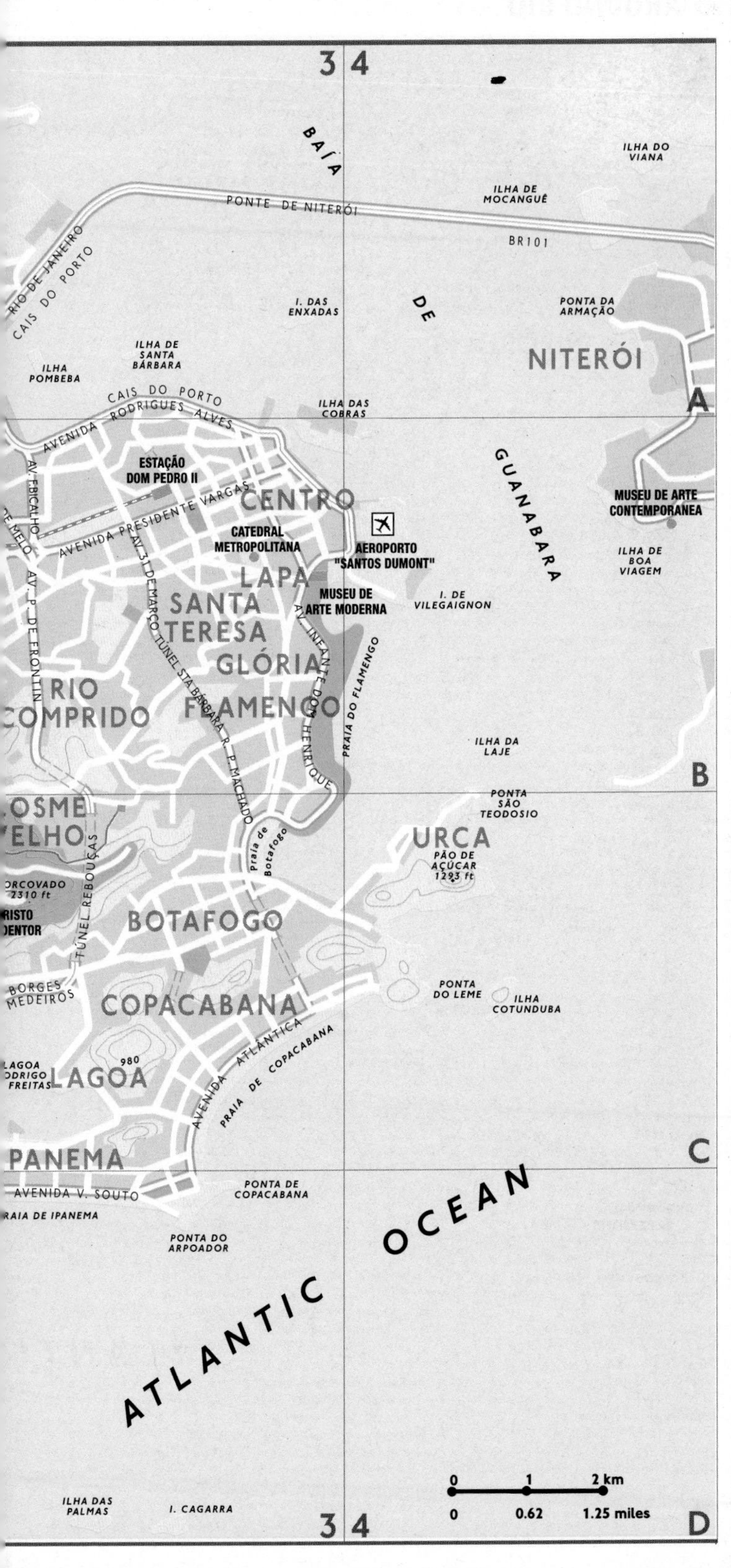

3 4
BAÍA
DE
GUANABARA
PONTE DE NITERÓI
BR101
ILHA DO VIANA
ILHA DE MOCANGUÊ
RIO DE JANEIRO
CAIS DO PORTO
I. DAS ENXADAS
PONTA DA ARMAÇÃO
NITERÓI
ILHA DE SANTA BÁRBARA
ILHA POMBEBA
CAIS DO PORTO
AVENIDA RODRIGUES ALVES
ILHA DAS COBRAS
A
ESTAÇÃO DOM PEDRO II
CENTRO
AV. F. BICALHO
AVENIDA PRESIDENTE VARGAS
MUSEU DE ARTE CONTEMPORANEA
CATEDRAL METROPOLITANA
AEROPORTO "SANTOS DUMONT"
ILHA DE BOA VIAGEM
LAPA
SANTA TERESA
MUSEU DE ARTE MODERNA
I. DE VILEGAIGNON
AV. 31 DE MARÇO
AV. P. DE FRONTIN
TÚNEL STA BÁRBARA
AV. INFANTE DOM HENRIQUE
PRAIA DO FLAMENGO
GLÓRIA
RIO COMPRIDO
FLAMENGO
R. P. MACHADO
ILHA DA LAJE
B
PONTA SÃO TEODOSIO
COSME VELHO
Praia de Botafogo
URCA
PÃO DE AÇÚCAR 1293 ft
CORCOVADO 2310 ft
CRISTO REDENTOR
TÚNEL REBOUÇAS
BOTAFOGO
BORGES MEDEIROS
PONTA DO LEME
ILHA COTUNDUBA
COPACABANA
AVENIDA ATLÂNTICA
PRAIA DE COPACABANA
980
LAGOA RODRIGO FREITAS
LAGOA
C
IPANEMA
AVENIDA V. SOUTO
PRAIA DE IPANEMA
PONTA DE COPACABANA
PONTA DO ARPOADOR
ATLANTIC OCEAN
0 1 2 km
0 0.62 1.25 miles
ILHA DAS PALMAS
I. CAGARRA
3 4
D

G
1 2
BELFORD ROXO
CANAL SARAPUI
DUQUE D
RODOVIA
NOVA IGUAÇU
SÃO JOÃO DE MERITI
PRESIDENTE
DUTRA
RIO SÃO JOÃO
CAN. DA PAVUNA
BR116
NILÓPOLIS
PAVUNA
ANCHIETA
RIO SARAPUI
IRAJÁ
RIO DA PAVUNA
BR101
AVENIDA
AUTOMÓVEL
AVENIDA BRASIL
MADUREIRA
BANGÚ
MORRO DA BANDEIRA 3130 ft
PEDRA BRANCA 3353 ft
SERRA DO QUILOMBO
2375 ft
PEDRA DO QUILOMBO 2487 ft
PICO DO SACARRÃO 2343 ft
JACAREPAGUÁ
RIO D
PARQU NACION DA TIJU
RIO DO AVRIL
RIO CENTRO
AUTÓDROMO DO RIO DE JANEIRO
AEROPORTO DE JACAREPAGUÁ
LAGOA DE JACARAPAGUÁ
AVENIDA SALVADOR ALLENDE
LAGOA DA TIJUCA
DAS AMÉRICAS
CANAL DO CORTADO
BARRA DA TIJU
AVENIDA
LAGOA DE MARAPENDI
LÚCIO COSTA
AVENIDA
PRAIA BARRA DA TIJUCA
RECREIOS DOS BANDEIRANTES
I. DA ALFAVACA
PONTAL DE SERNAMBETIBA
ILHA PONTUDA
ATLANTI
A
B
C
D
1 2

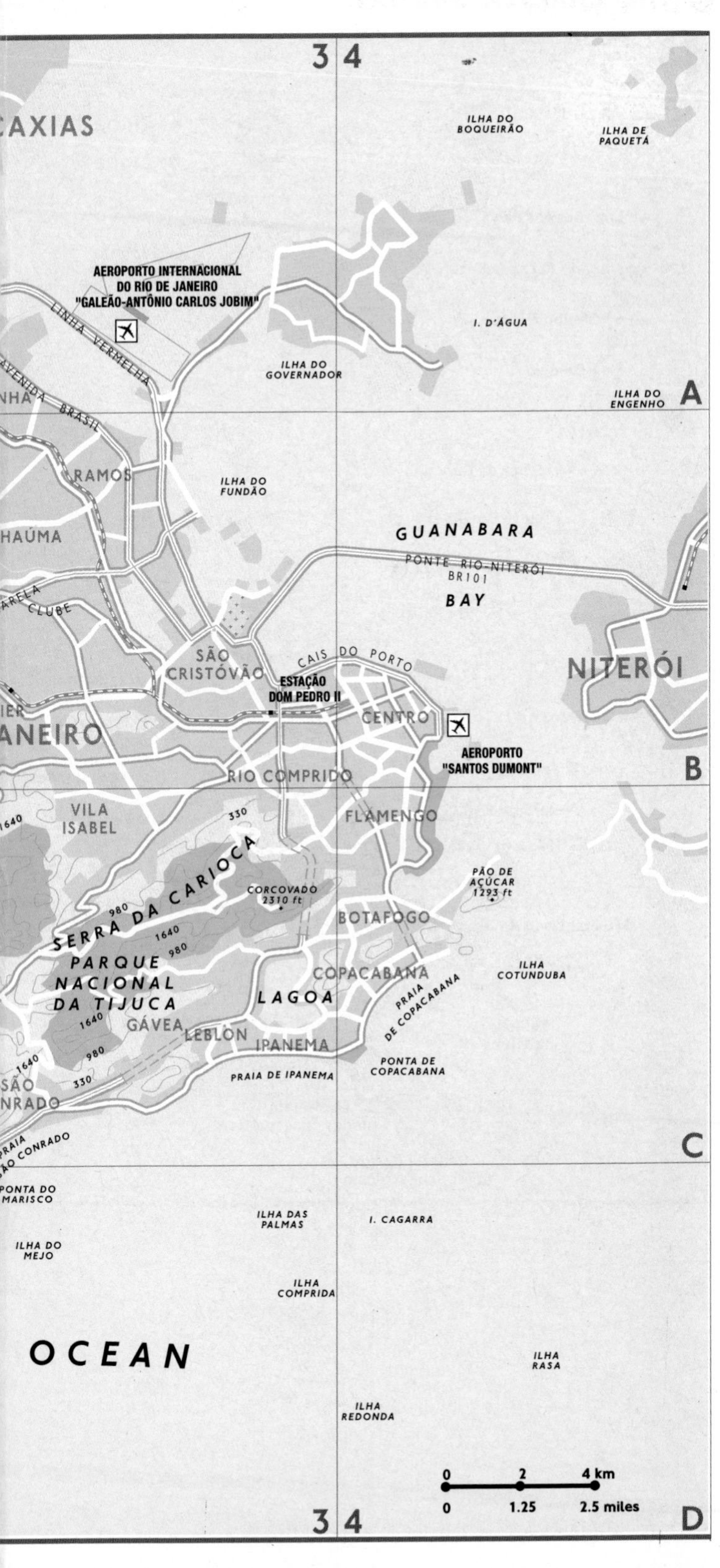

3 4
CAXIAS
ILHA DO BOQUEIRÃO
ILHA DE PAQUETÁ
AEROPORTO INTERNACIONAL DO RIO DE JANEIRO "GALEÃO-ANTÔNIO CARLOS JOBIM"
LINHA VERMELHA
AVENIDA BRASIL
I. D'ÁGUA
ILHA DO GOVERNADOR
ILHA DO ENGENHO
A
RAMOS
ILHA DO FUNDÃO
GUANABARA
PONTE RIO-NITERÓI BR101
BAY
CLUBE
SÃO CRISTÓVÃO
CAIS DO PORTO
ESTAÇÃO DOM PEDRO II
NITERÓI
CENTRO
AEROPORTO "SANTOS DUMONT"
B
RIO COMPRIDO
VILA ISABEL
1640
330
FLAMENGO
SERRA DA CARIOCA
CORCOVADO 2310 ft
PÃO DE AÇÚCAR 1293 ft
980
BOTAFOGO
PARQUE NACIONAL DA TIJUCA
COPACABANA
ILHA COTUNDUBA
LAGOA
PRAIA DE COPACABANA
GÁVEA
LEBLON
IPANEMA
PONTA DE COPACABANA
PRAIA DE IPANEMA
SÃO CONRADO
PRAIA SÃO CONRADO
C
PONTA DO MARISCO
ILHA DAS PALMAS
I. CAGARRA
ILHA DO MEJO
ILHA COMPRIDA
OCEAN
ILHA RASA
ILHA REDONDA
0 2 4 km
0 1.25 2.5 miles
D

◆ THE 'CARIOCA' SUBWAY

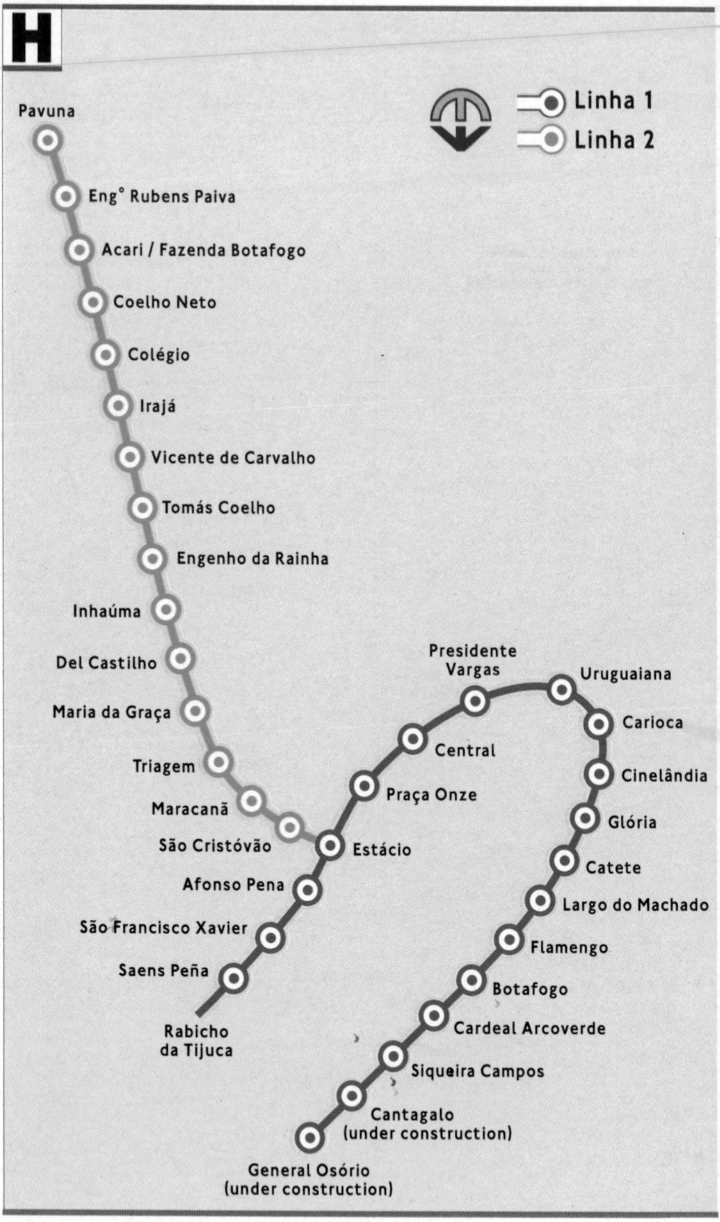

H

Linha 1
Linha 2

Pavuna
Eng° Rubens Paiva
Acari / Fazenda Botafogo
Coelho Neto
Colégio
Irajá
Vicente de Carvalho
Tomás Coelho
Engenho da Rainha
Inhaúma
Del Castilho
Maria da Graça
Triagem
Maracanã
São Cristóvão
Estácio
Afonso Pena
São Francisco Xavier
Saens Peña
Rabicho da Tijuca
Praça Onze
Central
Presidente Vargas
Uruguaiana
Carioca
Cinelândia
Glória
Catete
Largo do Machado
Flamengo
Botafogo
Cardeal Arcoverde
Siqueira Campos
Cantagalo (under construction)
General Osório (under construction)

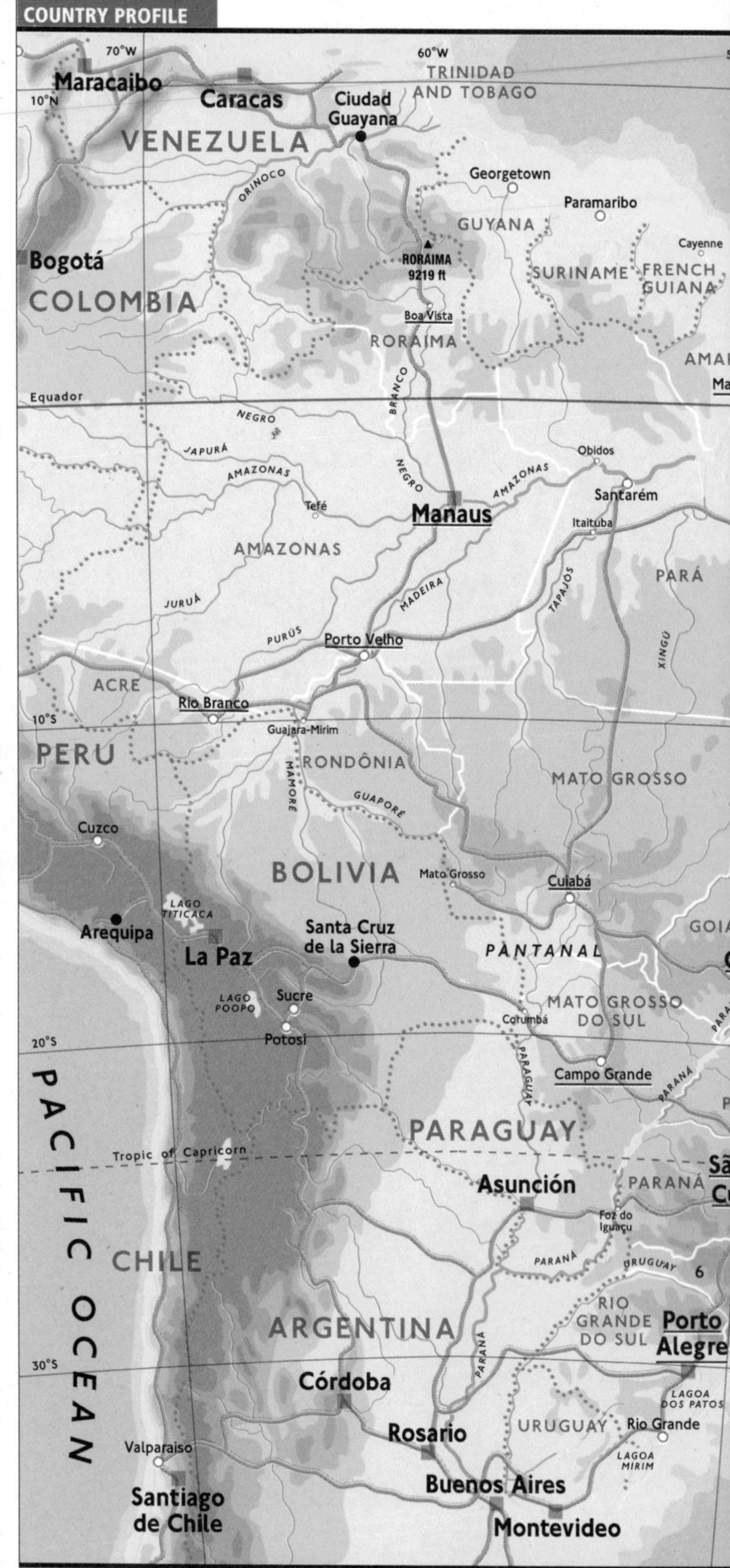

70°W
60°W
10°N
Maracaibo
Caracas
Ciudad Guayana
TRINIDAD AND TOBAGO
VENEZUELA
ORINOCO
Georgetown
Paramaribo
GUYANA
Cayenne
Bogotá
COLOMBIA
RORAIMA 9219 ft
SURINAME
FRENCH GUIANA
Boa Vista
RORAIMA
BRANCO
Equador
NEGRO
JAPURÁ
AMAZONAS
NEGRO
AMAZONAS
Obidos
Santarém
Tefé
Manaus
Itaituba
AMAZONAS
TAPAJÓS
PARÁ
MADEIRA
JURUÁ
XINGU
PURÚS
Porto Velho
ACRE
Rio Branco
10°S
Guajara-Mirim
PERU
RONDÔNIA
MAMORÉ
GUAPORÉ
MATO GROSSO
Cuzco
BOLIVIA
Mato Grosso
Cuiabá
LAGO TITICACA
Arequipa
Santa Cruz de la Sierra
La Paz
PANTANAL
LAGO POOPO
Sucre
Potosí
Corumbá
MATO GROSSO DO SUL
20°S
PARAGUAY
Campo Grande
PARANÁ
PACIFIC OCEAN
PARAGUAY
Tropic of Capricorn
Asunción
PARANÁ
Foz do Iguaçu
CHILE
PARANÁ
URUGUAY
6
RIO GRANDE DO SUL
Porto Alegre
ARGENTINA
PARANÁ
30°S
Córdoba
LAGOA DOS PATOS
URUGUAY
Rio Grande
Rosario
Valparaíso
LAGOA MIRIM
Buenos Aires
Santiago de Chile
Montevideo